ELEMENTS OF CRIMINAL JUSTICE

ELEMENTS OF CRIMINAL JUSTICE

Second Edition

James A. Inciardi

University of Delaware

New York   Oxford

OXFORD UNIVERSITY PRESS

Oxford University Press

Oxford   New York
Auckland   Bangkok   Buenos Aires   Cape Town
Chennai   Dar es Salaam   Delhi   Hong Kong   Istanbul   Karachi
Kolkata   Kuala Lumpur   Madrid   Melbourne   Mexico City   Mumbai   Nairobi
São Paulo   Shanghai   Singapore   Taipei   Tokyo   Toronto

and an associated company in Berlin

Published by Oxford University Press, Inc.
198 Madison Avenue, New York, New York 10016
http://www.oup-usa.org

Oxford is a registered trademark of Oxford University Press

ISBN: 0-19-515521-1
Library of Congress Catalog Card Number: 99-64581

Printing number: 9 8 7 6 5 4 3 2 1

Printed in the United States of America
on acid-free paper

Using *Elements of Criminal Justice* 2/e
A Guide to Learning from Your Textbook

CONCISE BUT AUTHORITATIVE COVERAGE, WITH REAL-WORLD ILLUSTRATIONS

Accessibility and Readability: Recognizing Student Priorities

The text is a comprehensive introduction to criminal justice, yet it is two-thirds the length of many other texts. The brief, paperback format ensures that reading assignments for the course will be manageable.

Clear presentation of the Most Current, Significant Research

The author is an internationally recognized researcher and scholar who also has extensive practical experience in the criminal justice system. No other text more successfully combines important research with the real-world interest of personal experience. This emphasis on currency is reflected in the new boxed exhibits on **Research on Crime and Justice,** and in the **expanded coverage of law enforcement,** including a new chapter on police misconduct, and expanded coverage of police issues and women in law enforcement.

Real-World Illustrations and Examples to Capture Student Interest

A hallmark of Inciardi's text is his use of gripping and relevant illustrations to enhance the text's discussion. Often disturbing, frequently provocative, and always committed to an unflinching look at reality, the illustrations in *Elements of Criminal Justice* complete the picture for the student.

NEW! Chapter-opening news stories from today's headlines provide a powerful demonstration of criminal justice concepts in action.

Elements of Criminal Justice

CHAPTER **1**

CRIME AND THE NATURE OF LAW

A rally protesting the presence of U.C. Berkeley campus sophomore David Cash who did nothing to prevent the assault and murder of seven-year-old Sherrice Iverson.

PRIMM, NEV. — On a May weekend in 1997, high school friends David Cash and Jeremy Strohmeyer joined Cash's father for a night of gambling and video games at a casino resort 40 miles outside of Las Vegas. At about 3:03 A.M., Strohmeyer lured 7-year-old Sherrice Iverson into a ladies' room while her father played the slots a floor above. Cash followed, and watched from an adjoining toilet stall as his friend threatened the little girl and placed his hand over her mouth to muffle her screams. Cash then left the ladies' room, and minutes later Strohmeyer sexually assaulted and murdered little Sherrice. He confessed his crime to Cash, who kept silent. Days later, after being identified from a video surveillance tape, Strohmeyer was arrested. He ultimately confessed to police, and on October 14, 1998, he was sentenced in a Nevada court to life without parole.[1] But what about David Cash? What ever happened to him? Had he committed a crime by not stopping Strohmeyer while observing him in the ladies' room with 7-year-old Sherrice Iverson? Was he guilty of "aiding and abetting," or "conspiracy," or some other crime? And this raises a series of even more important questions. What *is* crime? How is it that some behaviors become defined as "criminal" while others do not? What are the relationships between crime and law, and are there different kinds of law?

An **all** **NEW!** **art program** combines visual appeal with pedagogical usefulness.

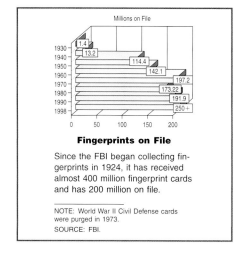

Millions on File

Year	Value
1930	1.4
1940	13.2
1950	114.4
1960	142.1
1970	197.2
1980	173.22
1990	191.9
1998	250+

0   50   100   150   200

Fingerprints on File

Since the FBI began collecting fingerprints in 1924, it has received almost 400 million fingerprint cards and has 200 million on file.

NOTE: World War II Civil Defense cards were purged in 1973.
SOURCE: FBI.

NEW! **Opinion-Editorial pieces** appear at the end of each chapter, recalling the chapter-opening news story in light of the concepts discussed in the chapter.

22   CHAPTER 1   *Crime and the Nature of Law*

directives, and awards; and the court opinions dealing with appeals from the decisions and with petitions by the agencies to the courts for the enforcement of their orders and directives. Much of the content of administrative law is not concerned directly with criminal behavior. Nevertheless, the rules of certain agencies bear directly on violations of behavior that would be dealt with by the criminal courts. The classification of heroin, PCP, and other drugs as "controlled substances" by the Drug Enforcement Administration, for example, is an administrative regulation that has been translated into criminal statutes in the federal as well as many state jurisdictions.

The case of Jeremy Strohmeyer and David Cash earned considerable media attention during the closing months of 1998, primarily because of Cash's actions. He had bragged to the *Los Angeles Times* that he was not going "to lose sleep over somebody else's problems" (Sherrice Iverson's suffering and death), and to a radio talk show he callously argued that he had done nothing wrong. But nevertheless, was he guilty of anything criminal?

It was concluded earlier in this chapter that Cash was not guilty of conspiracy or abetting, nor was he an accessory before the fact. Cash was not an accessory *after* the fact either, because he did nothing to cover up his friend's crime or prevent his apprehension. As for the misprision of felony statutes, did he have a duty to intervene? The answer is no, because under local laws he was not required to do so. As the Clark County, Nevada,

district attorney put it, Cash's inaction "may be a crime in the eyes of God, but not in the eyes of the Nevada legislature." In Nevada, and most other states, there is no "duty to aid" statute.

State legislatures have been reluctant to modify their "no duty to aid" rule. They argue that such a rule would be costly to enforce and would interfere with individual liberty. Only a few states — Vermont, Minnesota, Rhode Island, Colorado, Ohio, Massachusetts, Florida, and Washington — have enacted statutes requiring bystanders to aid someone in peril. Violation of such statutes is generally a petty misdemeanor. Cash's callousness, however, sparked a movement in both Nevada and California to enact a "Sherrice's law," which would require witnesses to intervene and report cases of sexual assault against children.

BOXED EXHIBITS TO ADD INTEREST, VISUAL APPEAL, AND UNIQUE PERSPECTIVES TO THE TEXT

NEW! **Historical Perspectives on Crime and Justice exhibits** highlight some of the historical roots of contemporary procedures, as well as help students to understand how modern notions of criminal justice have evolved over time. Examples include the origins of the "Mafia," police corruption in early New York, and national prohibition of alcohol.

Exhibit 12.1   **Historical Perspectives on Crime and Justice**
Alcatraz Island Penitentiary   WWW

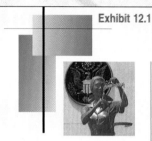

During the early years of the Great Depression, an unusual crime wave had spread across the American Midwest. Banks that had weathered the stock market crash of 1929 were being robbed at the rate of two a day. The outlaws operated with flair and skill. Armed with machine guns, they recreated a frontier pattern of rapid assault followed by elusive retreat. The millions of citizens caught in the drab round of idleness and poverty that characterized the times responded to the criminal exploits with acceptance and admiration. The bandits became folk heroes and such names as John Dillinger, Frank Nash, Charles "Pretty Boy" Floyd, Bonnie Parker, Clyde Barrow, and George "Baby Face" Nelson quickly found their way into American folklore. But to the Federal Bureau of Investiga-

Alcatraz Island Penitentiary might be the answer to the problem.

Originally named by eighteenth-century Spanish explorers *Isla de los Alcatraces* (Island of Pelicans) after the birds that then roosted there, Alcatraz has an area of 12 acres and rises steeply to 136 feet above San Francisco Bay. In 1859 a U.S. military prison was built on the island, and in March 1934 it was taken over by the Federal Bureau of Prisons.

Alcatraz became the most repressive maximum-security facility in the nation. Its six guard towers, equipped with .30-caliber carbines and high-powered rifles, could observe every square foot of the island. Barbed-wire barriers dotted the shorelines, and each entrance to the cell house had a three-door security system.

There were 600 one-man cells, built into three-tiered cell blocks. Measuring 8 feet by 4 feet, each cell contained a fold-up bunk hooked to the wall, fold-up table and chair, shelf, washbasin, toilet, and shaded ceiling light. Cell block D was the disciplinary barracks—solitary confinement for the more

and radio were denied in order to intensify the sense of isolation. One letter could be written each week and three could be received, but with severe restrictions: Correspondence could not be carried on with nonrelatives, and the content was restricted to family matters. One visit per month, from a family member or attorney, was permitted. Work was limited to cooking, cleaning, maintenance, and laundry. Security was rigid, with one guard for every three inmates.

With its policy of maximum security, combined with minimum privileges and total isolation for America's "public enemies," Alcatraz did have a number of underworld aristocrats and spectacular felons, including Arthur "Doc" Barker, last surviving son of Ma Barker's murderous brood; kidnapper George "Machine Gun" Kelly; Alvin Karpis, the most evasive bank robber of the 1930s; and bootlegger, murderer, and syndicate boss Al "Scarface" Capone. But for the most part, comparatively few big-time gangsters ever went to Alcatraz; many of the is-

---

NEW!

"Research in Crime and Justice" exhibits explore how historical, legal, and behavioral research impacts the field of criminal justice. Topics include crack cocaine in Miami, pickpockets at the Super Bowl, and interpretation of the right to bear arms as put forth in the Second Amendment. Many of the exhibits are from the author's own research.

Exhibit 2.2   **Research in Crime and Justice**
On the Grift at the Super Bowl

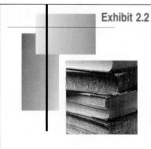

For centuries, pickpockets have congregated to work the crowds at sporting events. As early as the days of Shakespeare's youth, pickpocketing was a full-time profession common in London during the terms of court when thousands of citizens were drawn

Class cannon means experience, skill, connections and a sense for knowing when to steal. . . . It means that the *cannon* [picking pockets] is part of your life. . . . It means that you're not one of those amateurs who spend their time *grinding up nickels and dimes* [inept stealing for low stakes].

Field studies suggest that class cannons continued to operate in many American cities at least through the beginning of the 1980s. Research indicates that every December, when thousands

NEW! Legal Perspectives on Crime and Justice exhibits use a combination of current events and case law to shed light on the legal aspects of criminal justice. They highlight particular court decisions, criminal codes, and other legal and legislative matters related to the text material. The "Megan's Law" movement and sodomy laws in the U.S. are examples of issues discussed in these exhibits.

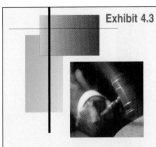

| Exhibit 4.3 | **Legal Perspectives on Crime and Justice**
The Megan's Law Movement |

Types of Notification

☐ **Passive:** Information is made public (via Internet, perhaps, or on CD-ROM at the police stations), but authorities do not reach out to warn neighborhoods.

■ **Active:** An offender is classified according to the threat he's thought to pose, and whom authorities inform of his presence depends on his classification: low, moderate, or high risk.

☐ **Combination:** Some states have laws with both passive and active elements.California, for instance, allows but does not require localities to notify neighbors about a sex offender, but also allows the public access to a sex offender registry on CD-ROM at county sheriffs' offices.

■ **Has no Megan's Law notification provision**

New Jersey was the scene of the crime that began the Megan's Law movement. The victim was 7-year-old Megan Kanka, raped and murdered in 1994 by a convicted sex offender who lived next door. Out of her death grew the notion that the government should notify citizens about sex offenders in their neighborhoods. New Jersey hastily enacted the first Megan's Law and required convicted sex offenders to register with local police. By 1999, with the exception of New Mexico, all states had a Megan's Law with some provision for notifying communities about the presence or general location of convicted sex criminals. As shown in the accompanying figure, they fell into three broad groups: passive systems, active systems, or a combination of the two.

Almost immediately after the New Jersey law was implemented, however, attorneys for sex offenders argued that the notification provisions were in violation of the Fifth Amendment's double jeopardy clause. As an issue of substantive due process,

they claimed that their clients were being punished twice for the same crime, since the notification and the public reaction it generated amounted to "punishment." In a petition to the U.S. Supreme Court, the New Jersey attorney general urged the justices to reject the sex offenders' appeal, on grounds that the features of Megan's Law had no hidden puni-

tive intent, and that the law was not a modern-day Scarlet Letter analogy. In 1997, in the case of *W. P. v. Verniero* (62 CrL 3163), the Supreme Court ruled in favor of the state of New Jersey, holding that the public notification provisions of Megan's Law did not impose punishment, and therefore did not constitute double jeopardy.

NEW! Careers in Criminal Justice exhibits

NEW! **Careers in Criminal Justice exhibits** describe the various professional roles available to students interested in criminal justice. They include descriptions of job requirements and duties for such positions as probation officer, FBI Special Agent, and crisis intervention counselor, just to name a few.

Exhibit 5.5   Careers in Justice
FBI Special Agent

The Federal Bureau of Investigation is the principal investigative arm of the U.S. Department of Justice and has investigatory jurisdiction over violations of more than 200 categories of federal crimes. In addition, the Bureau is authorized to investigate matters where no prosecution is contemplated.

History

The beginnings of the FBI can be traced to President Theodore Roosevelt's "trust-busting" and his war with the "malefactors of great wealth" and their kept men in Congress. Roosevelt was handicapped in these efforts against industrial combines and graft because, when the need to gather evidence arose, the Department of Justice's lack of an investigative arm forced the president to borrow detectives from other federal agencies. As a result of this problem, Roosevelt's attorney general, Charles J. Bonaparte (who was also the grand-

During its earliest years, the "Bureau of Investigation," as it was first named, occupied itself with small investigations—antitrust prosecutions, bankruptcy and fraud cases, crimes committed on government reservations, and interstate commerce violations. But with the passage of the Mann Act in 1910, sponsored by Congressman James Robert Mann, the Bureau of Investigation stepped into a more national posture.

It was a time when prostitution and commercialized vice had become big business, and there was growing worry over the number of women and young girls who were being imported into the United States "for immoral purposes."

International Perspectives on Crime and Justice exhibits give compelling examples of criminal justice concepts and procedures as they are applied in other nations and cultures. These provocative essays and photos invite students to think critically about our culture and its approach to justice. The exhibits include discussions of such topics as cocaine trafficking in Latin America, the prosecution of rape as a war crime, and code law in Bolivia.

Exhibit 5.4   International Perspectives on Crime and Justice
Women Police in the Republic of Fiji

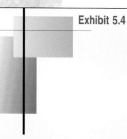

Once notorious as the "Cannibal Isles," Fiji is now the crossroads of the South Pacific, located some 3,200 miles southwest of Hawaii. Although the 322 islands that make up the Republic of Fiji reflect an interesting blend of Melanesian, Polynesian, Micronesian, Indian, Chinese, and European influences, only two ethnic groups—indigenous Fijians and

of the country's 1,913-member police force, and these 130 female officers were recruited only recently—an indication that policing in Fiji has traditionally been a male-dominated profession. In an effort to better understand the issues affecting women officers and to improve the problem of gender imbalance, a survey was recently commissioned by the Fiji Police Force. The results found gender bias to be widespread within the ranks of policing. For example, of the 115 police supervisors surveyed, only 35 percent felt that "policewomen" should perform the

same work as their male counterparts. More than half of the supervisors felt that women officers should spend their time doing office and administrative tasks, looking for lost children, caring for the victims of sexual assault, or participating in community policing activities. At the same time, 13.2 percent of the women officers complained that they had been sexually harassed or even assaulted by male officers while at work. These and other findings suggested that overall, most of the male officers either consciously or unconsciously believed that women did not deserve to be treated as their equals. Some even argued that it

Gender Perspectives on Crime and Justice exhibits discuss issues related to both women and men in various roles throughout the criminal justice system. Issues related to women in law enforcement, and men as victims of rape, are examples of this type of exhibit.

Exhibit 2.4   **Gender Perspectives on Crime and Justice**
Men as Victims of Rape

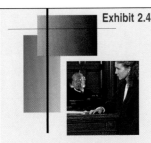

For most Americans, *rape* is a gender-specific term. That is, virtually every time the stand-alone word *rape* is used, it is automatically presumed that the victim is a female and the perpetrator is a male. This would appear to be logical, furthermore, because crime statistics indicate that as many as 90 percent of all rape victims are women and young girls. Moreover, until only recently rape laws defined women as the only possible victims and men as the only offenders. Even today, in 12 states—Alabama, Georgia, Idaho, Kansas, Maine, Maryland, Missouri, New York, North Carolina, Oregon, Utah, and Virginia—rape is defined as "the forced penetration of the vagina by the penis," or words to that effect. By contrast, like conversations about male nurses, female judges, and women's basketball, discussions of male-on-male rape result in gender-specific terminology; that is, "rape" becomes *male rape.* And furthermore, the rape of men by women is likely the least reported and most unaddressed violent crime.

Research suggests that between 5 percent and 10 percent of all reported rapes in any given year involve male victims. The rapes occur most often in all-male institutions, such as prisons, military barracks, college dormitories and fraternities, mental health institutions, nursing homes, boarding schools, and monasteries. The rapists are typically white, heterosexual men in their middle to late twenties, and their victims are generally the same age or younger. Men rape other men for the same reasons that they rape women—out of anger or an attempt to overpower, humiliate, and degrade their victims, rather than out of lust, passion, or sexual desire. Anal penetration is the most common form of assault, followed by oral penetration. Finally, men who rape tend to do so within their own social, cultural, or economic group, or rape those over whom they have power. For these reasons it is not surprising that the incidence of gay men raping heterosexual men is relatively low.

Little is known about female-on-male rape. In fact, in the once widely read textbook *Criminal Law for Policemen,* authors Neil C. Chamelin and Kenneth R. Evans suggested that a female cannot actually rape a male. This assumption, however, is both naive and incorrect. There are many women who can overpower men, and the biology of the male anatomy makes an erection through physical stimulation readily possible, even when sexual interest is totally absent. In fact, in some men and boys, states of pain, anxiety, panic, or fear have been known to cause a spontaneous erection and ejaculation. However, although it is unlikely that any man raped by a woman would bring the crime to the attention of the authorities for fear of ridicule, this does not mean it does not happen. Numerous such cases have indeed been documented.

Although there is no single, typical, emotional response that every man will exhibit after he has been raped, the range of responses is not unlike those seen among female victims of rape. Some may appear calm and rational, others may exhibit anger, depression, or hysteria. Still others may withdraw socially or sexually or appear nonresponsive. Rape trauma syndrome, a form of post-traumatic stress disorder, is also seen. In the majority of cases, furthermore, male rape victims experience stigma, shame, embarrassment, and self-blame as they begin to cope with what has happened to them. And as a final point, the range of symptoms is the same regardless of whether the perpetrator was another man, or a woman.

SOURCES: Michael Scarce, *Male on Male Rape: The Hidden Toll of Stigma and Shame* (New York: Plenum, 1997); Neil C. Chamelin and Kenneth R. Evans, *Criminal Law for Policemen* (Englewood Cliffs, N.J.: Prentice-Hall, 1976), p. 109; *Miami Herald,* September 17, 1982, p. 1B; *Psychology Today,* September 1983, pp. 74–75.

LEARNING AIDS TO HELP THE STUDENT UNDERSTAND, RETAIN, INTEGRATE, AND THINK CRITICALLY ABOUT THE INFORMATION PRESENTED

Media

SUMMARY

The concept of crime is only minimally understood by most people. It goes well beyond the rather imprecise boundaries of "street crime" or the limited issues of violence and theft that are focused on by mass media news and entertainment. In fact, crime includes thousands of offenses, the majority of which do not come to the public's attention.

Drawing on standards of what constitutes "sin" or immoral behavior, people have often defined crime as violations of natural law. However, this definition implies that all individuals have the same definition of right and wrong. Sociologists argue that people's ideas about appropriate and inappropriate behavior are culturally and historically specific. That is, they choose to focus on the

processes through which crime com
they suggest that crime is a social
changes over time and in different cont
argued that not all deviant behavior is
and that not all criminal behavior is
Rather, criminal and deviant behavior
culture.

The only precise definition of c
from a more legalistic posture. As su
tentional act or omission in violatio
(statutory and case law), committed
justification, and sanctioned by the s
misdemeanor.

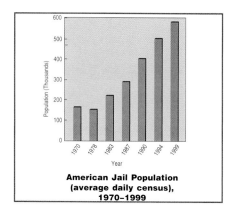

**American Jail Population
(average daily census),
1970–1999**

A **margin glossary** provides definitions of key terms for easy reference.

Brief **public opinion surveys** appear in the margin, highlighting timely and often controversial issues.

Chapter summaries help students to consolidate the information they learned in the chapter.

Page-referenced key terms appear at the end of the chapter, allowing students to easily review these terms.

Questions for Discussion at the end of each chapter provide ample opportunities for students to explore their own beliefs and perceptions about issues of crime and justice.

KEY TERMS

abettor **8**	crime **7**	*mens rea* **9**
accessory after the fact **8**	criminal law **11**	misdemeanor **18**
accessory before the fact **8**	defense **11**	misprision of fel
administrative law **20**	deviance **5**	M'Naghten Rule
case law **11**	Durham Rule **12**	natural law **4**
civil law **11**	entrapment **15**	*Robinson* v. *Cal*
common law **11**	felony **18**	statutory law **11**
conspiracy **8**	*Lambert* v. *California* **14**	vicarious liabilit
constitutional law **20**		

QUESTIONS FOR DISCUSSION

1. How do natural law conceptions of "sin," sociological considerations of deviance, and legalistic definitions of crime differ?
2. In the Leopold and Loeb case, when did the conspiracy actually begin? What elements were present?
3. Under what kinds of circumstances would the consent of the victim be an acceptable defense against crime? What are some examples?

4. What should be done about the in
5. Should the use of marijuana as "m
   be a defense against crime?

MEDIA RESOURCES

1. **Leopold and Loeb.** See Gilbert Geis and Leigh B. Bienen, *Crimes of the Century* (Boston: Northeastern University Press, 1998). This volume provides a detailed examination of what the authors consider the five most celebrated crimes of the twentieth century, including the Leopold and Loeb murder of Bobby Franks.
2. **Strohmeyer and Cash.** Numerous analyses of this case are on a variety of Web sites, including Time.com, Fortune Online, Court TV Online, and the *Las Vegas Review-Journal.* For best results, enter "strohmeyer AND cash" into your Internet search engine.

3. **The Hinckley Case.** There is a V this case provided by the Univer Kansas City, School of Law, which Hinckley trial, its aftermath, and the site address: http://www.law.umkc.e ftrials/hinckley/hb
4. **Crime Files.** *The Crime Files* is a V examination of unsolved crimes fro Web address: http://www.emerald crimefiles.htm

WWW.

NEW! The **Media Resources** section at the end of each chapter provides information about print and electronic resources, including complete postings of research papers prepared by the textbook author. **Web links** throughout the text identify additional material revelant to the topic posted on the companion Web site.

PREFACE

More than four decades ago, the noted scholar and columnist Max Lerner offered a rather curious description of criminal justice in the United States:

> The administration of American criminal justice has often been scored as inefficient, corrupt, and archaic, and all three charges are probably true, but again probably no truer than of past eras and other societies. The supervision of criminal justice is mainly in the hands of the local authorities; the Federal courts handle crimes under Federal jurisdiction but try to minimize the appeals from local and state jurisdictions. A lawbreaker is tracked down by local police, prosecuted by a local district attorney, defended by a local lawyer, tried in a local court house in a trial reported predominantly in the local press, convicted or cleared by a local jury, sentenced by a local judge, and shut up in a local or state prison. At every point there is a good deal of bungling, prejudice, poor judgment, or corruption. Yet on the whole there is a widespread feeling that the results are tolerably good and that the frailties of the whole process are a reflection of the frailties of the society in which it takes place.[1]

Interestingly, here at the beginning of the new millennium, the feelings about the criminal justice system are not that different from those expressed by Lerner in 1957. "Criminal justice," as described by Lerner and other observers, refers to the structure, function, and decision-making processes of agencies that deal with the management and control of crime and criminal offenders—police, courts, and correctional systems. Although this definition is relatively clear, criminal justice is often confused with the academic disciplines of criminology and police science. Criminology focuses on the role of crime in organized society, the nature and causes of crime and criminal behavior, and the relationships between crime and social behavior. Police science concentrates on the pragmatic aspects of law enforcement and peace-keeping operations—the prevention and detection of crime, the apprehension of offenders, the location and preservation of evidence, the questioning of suspects, the application of police resources, techniques of community policing, and the development of police-community relations.

As an independent academic activity, the study of criminal justice is comparatively new in the United States. The first degree-granting program appeared only half a century ago, and as recently as the 1950s, fewer than 5,000 college students were focusing on the study of crime and justice. During the past few decades, however, this situation has changed dramatically. The middle and late 1960s saw a rise in the interest of criminal justice education because of the "war on crime." The result: massive federal funding for the upgrading of criminal justice personnel, agencies, technology, and programming. Currently criminal justice courses enroll well over 200,000 students annually, and this trend is expected to continue.

Although criminal justice is a relatively new undergraduate major, the topics have been studied for centuries. It is indeed an interdisciplinary branch of knowledge. From the perspective of legal studies, it examines aspects of criminal law and procedure; from political science it takes elements of constitutional law and court practice; from the viewpoint of sociology it examines the structures of certain social institutions and how they affect the administration of justice. Criminal justice also uses research from psychology, history, public administration, anthropology, economics, and many other disciplines.

---

[1]Max Lerner, *America as a Civilization: Life and Thought in the United States Today* (New York: Simon & Schuster, 1957), p. 433.

As criminal justice education has evolved and expanded, so, too, has research on the various processes of justice. This growth has resulted in a dramatic proliferation in the criminal justice literature as scholars, researchers, and administrators seek to disseminate their work. So great has been the demand for classroom materials that during the past decade publishers have responded with thousands of new textbooks, supplementary readings, manuals, anthologies, monographs, and reports. Several dozen new introductory criminal justice textbooks and revised editions appear every year, and it is within this context of rapid change that this second edition of *Elements of Criminal Justice* has been published.

FEATURES OF THE BOOK

The second edition of *Elements of Criminal Justice* is designed to achieve a number of goals for introductory criminal justice courses. First, it offers basic information as to the nature of crime and the process of justice. Second, in theme and perspective, it provides an analysis of the administration of justice in its contemporary forms and historical roots. Third, the textbook is conceived and written to interest a wide range of students. Intended for those at both community colleges and four-year institutions, the data and subject matter have been drawn from the professional and popular media and the fields of law, sociology, political science, history, popular culture, anthropology, and oral tradition. To explain certain phenomena more effectively, a portion of the almost 200 photographs and cartoons—some comical, many serious, and all informative—emphasizes the fads and foibles that have historically characterized the administration of justice of the United States.

The features of the second edition of *Elements of Criminal Justice* include:

Accessibility and Readability Ensures Student Understanding

Because we know that accessibility and value are important to most students, *Elements of Criminal Justice* has been published in a brief, paperback format. The text is a comprehensive introduction to criminal justice, yet it is two-thirds the length of many other texts. This ensures that reading assignments for the course will be manageable.

The Most Current, Significant Research is Clearly Presented for Easy Understanding

Criminal justice is a rapidly changing field. Studying the most current research and empirical data is essential. As the most recently published text, this edition of *Elements of Criminal Justice* features data from the most current sources, including 1997, 1998, and 1999 statistics and cases. The author, James A. Inciardi, is an internationally recognized researcher and scholar who also has extensive practical experience in the criminal justice system. No text more successfully combines important research with the real-world interest of personal experience.

Real-World Illustrations and Examples Capture and Hold Student Interest

A hallmark of Inciardi's many books is his use of gripping and relevant illustrations to enhance the text's discussion. Each chapter opens with a news story from today's headlines that provide a powerful demonstration of criminal justice concepts in action. The chapter then closes with an Opinion/

Editorial piece, which references the opening news story and provides analysis and commentary. Throughout this new edition of *Elements of Criminal Justice* you will find photos and drawings that bring the worlds of crime and criminal justice into sharper focus. In addition, cartoons placed throughout the text illustrate principles with a lighter touch. Often disturbing, frequently provocative, and always committed to an unflinching look at reality, the illustrations in *Elements of Criminal Justice* complete the picture for the student.

The Applied Side of Criminal Justice is Clearly Presented to Illustrate How the Justice System Really Works

An important aspect of this edition of *Elements of Criminal Justice* is the idea of "applications." In addition to examinations of the structural aspects of criminal justice processing, real-world examples illustrate how the justice system really works.

Boxed Exhibits on Issues in Criminal Justice Focus on Historical and Current Events and Enduring Controversies

Throughout the text, you will notice boxes that focus on a wide range of issues and perspectives in criminal justice. These boxes present past and current events in the context of the chapter's theoretical and pragmatic concerns and illustrate how crime and justice enter our lives every day. In every chapter, there are three to six boxed exhibits in the following areas:

Gender Perspectives on Crime and Justice Exhibits focus on the special gender issues related to both women and men in various roles throughout the criminal justice system. The "PMS defense," men as victims of rape, and warrantless body searches are among the important discussions offered in this unique feature.

International Perspectives on Crime and Justice Exhibits offer comparative materials on the way criminal justice works in other nations and cultures. These provocative essays and photos illustrate diverse ways of thinking about crime and justice and invite students to think critically about our culture and its approach to justice. The boxes include discussions of cocaine trafficking in Latin America, the prosecution of rape as a war crime, crime in Colombia, and code law in Bolivia, among others.

Legal Perspectives on Crime and Justice Exhibits highlight particular court decisions, criminal codes, and other legal and legislative matters related to the text material. The "Megan's law" movement, sodomy laws in the U.S., and important Supreme Court decisions are among the many issues covered.

Historical Perspectives on Crime and Justice Exhibits draw upon interesting materials from the annals of criminal justice to highlight some of the historical roots of contemporary procedures as well as to reflect on how the system has changed over time. Just a few of the areas covered are the origins of the "Mafia," nineteenth-century homicide rates, police corruption in early New York, and national prohibition.

Research on Crime and Justice Exhibits briefly describe past and current research efforts to better understand how and why the system works as it does. In addition, these exhibits highlight experimental projects designed to upgrade particular activities in the management and control of criminal offenders. Topics include crack cocaine in Miami, pickpockets at the Super Bowl, cocaine-tainted cash, and the right to bear arms.

Careers in Justice Exhibits focus on particular employment opportunities in the criminal justice field, including brief descriptions of job requirements and duties. Some of the positions include police officer, probation officer, FBI Special Agent, and crisis intervention counselor.

Extensive Marginalia Help Organize Reading and Thinking

Marginal Topic Headings make studying, review, and reference easier.

Marginal Charts, Graphs, and Anecdotes present current data and issues in an easy-to-locate and easy-to-read format.

Marginal Glossary defines terms as they are used and locates them for easy review later.

Web Links identify additional material posted on the companion Web site.

Chapter End Materials Offer Opportunities for Study and Review

Chapter Summaries give students a quick review of the basic principles of the chapter and allow them to focus on understanding one point at a time.

Key Terms help with the study of vocabulary and concepts presented in the chapter. These terms are shown in **boldface** when they appear in the chapter.

Discussion Questions combine factual material with controversial issues to encourage students to think critically about the chapter. These questions will help them study for essay exams and confirm that they have a complete understanding of the chapter.

Media Resources include listings of Web sites, articles, and/or books where students can find additional information on the subject matter covered in the text.

ANCILLARIES

The second edition of *Elements of Criminal Justice* is accompanied by an integrated ancillary package designed to facilitate both learning and teaching.

The **Elements of Criminal Justice** *Web Site* is a cutting-edge criminal justice discipline site that enhances the student's learning experience. The place to begin is Criminal Justice Online at www.harbrace.com/crim. Criminal Justice Online contains links to the home pages of all fifty state governments. Case File links the student to international and national court cases. In addition, significant Supreme Court and Criminal Court of Appeals cases are summarized, and the impact on the criminal justice system is highlighted for the student's benefit. These resources provide valuable tools for learning Internet navigation skills. From this general criminal justice site, visitors can link to Inciardi's *Elements of Criminal Justice 2/e* Web site. It includes quizzes by chapter, downloadable Power Point slides, interactive Web activities, career resources, and Web links to sites listed in the book, including original research papers by Inciardi. These are just a few of the many features that combine to bring you one of the best interactive learning packages available in the educational arena.

The Criminal Justice Alive CD-ROM is an interactive study system that provides the perfect study companion to the Inciardi text. It is comprised of digital animation videos representing core concepts in criminal justice to enhance lectures and self-study. It offers self-directed quizzes, Web activities and readings, and further Web navigation in criminal justice topics.

The Student Study Guide was prepared by Laura B. Myers, Ph.D., of Sam Houston State University. It includes learning goals and objectives, contextual discussion of key concepts, suggested essay questions to help students prepare for essay exams, and self-quizzes.

The Instructor's Resource Guide presents a chapter summary, topic outline, and review of the major objectives and key terms. It also has extensive, useful lecture supplements, discussion topics, class projects, and transparency masters.

The Test Bank contains multiple-choice, true/false, and fill-in-the-blank questions. The test bank is available in printed and computerized formats.

The Computerized Test Bank is available in both Windows and Macintosh versions. *EXAMaster* software guides the instructor through the process of test creation by easy-to-follow screen prompts. *EXAMaster* has three test creation options: *EasyTest,* which allows the instructor to create a test from a single screen; *FullTest,* which gives the instructor a larger range of options including editing of items; and *RequesTest,* a test compilation service for the instructor who has no computer. For *RequesTest* services, call 1-800-210-7462. *EXAMaster* comes with EXAM-Record, a customized grade book software program. If questions arise, the Harcourt Software Support Hotline is available Monday through Friday 7 a.m.–6 p.m. (Central Time) at 800-447-9457.

The Harcourt Video Library provides a variety of updated video programs to enrich classroom presentations. Selections include "Lock-Up: The Prisoners of Rikers Island," "In Search of Law and Order," and "Date Rape: Behind Closed Doors," among others. The videos are selected from Films for the Humanities and Sciences and from the Public Broadcasting System's CPB Video Series.

ACKNOWLEDGEMENTS

Considerable help was received from a number of individuals during the preparation of this text. I would like to thank reviewers of the current edition: Carl E. Russell, Scottsdale Community College; C. Randall Eastep, Brevard Community College; Dante Pena, South Texas Community College; Dennis Lund, University of Nebraska-Kearney; Joan Luxenburg, University of Central Oklahoma; Kevin Thompson, North Dakota State University; Linda Clark, Wharton County Junior College; Louis Kontos, Long Island University; Patricia Zajac, California State University-Hayward; Ray Newman, Polk County Community College; Marsha Rogers, Daytona Beach Community College; Rebecca Nathanson, Housatonic Community College; and Donna Sherwood, Macomb Community College.

Special thanks must go to Binh Pok at the University of Miami School of Medicine, and Hilary Surratt, Christine Saum, Dana Rosenbaum, and Janice Atchley at the University of Delaware, who spent many weeks assisting me in selecting and editing material. Also, gratitude goes to the team at Harcourt College Publishers: Lin Marshall, acquisitions editor; Sarah Davis Packard, Web development editor; Caroline Robbins and Susan Holtz, picture and rights editors; Andrea Archer, production manager; Lisa Kelley, manufacturing manager; David A. Day, art director; and Claudia Gravier, project editor.

James A. Inciardi
October 1999

ABOUT THE AUTHOR

James A. Inciardi is the Director of the Center for Drug and Alcohol Studies at the University of Delaware; Professor in the Department of Sociology and Criminal Justice at the University of Delaware; Adjunct Professor in the Department of Epidemiology and Public Health at the University of Miami School of Medicine; and Guest Professor in the Department of Psychiatry at the Federal University of Rio Grande do Sul in Porto Alegre, Brazil.

Dr. Inciardi earned his Ph.D. in sociology at New York University and has research, clinical, field, and teaching experience in the areas of criminal justice, substance abuse, and HIV/AIDS. Before coming to Delaware, he was the Director of the National Center for the Study of Acute Drug Reactions at the University of Miami School of Medicine; Vice-President of the Resource Planning Corporation, based in Washington, D.C.; Associate Director of Research at the New York State Narcotic Addiction Control Commission; and a Parole Officer with the New York State Division of Parole.

Finally, Dr. Inciardi has done extensive research and consulting work both nationally and internationally and has published 50 books and 250 articles and chapters in the areas of substance abuse, criminology, criminal justice, history, folklore, social policy, AIDS, medicine, and law.

CONTENTS

PART 1 THE FOUNDATIONS OF CRIME AND JUSTICE

CHAPTER 1 CRIME AND THE NATURE OF LAW   2

Crime	**4**
Natural Law	4
Crime as a Social Construct	5
Crime as a Legal Definition	7
Criminal Law	**19**
Common Law	19
Other Sources of Criminal Law: Constitutional Law, Statutory Law, and Administrative Law	20
Op-Ed	**22**
Summary	**23**
Key Terms	**23**
Questions for Discussion	**23**
Media Resources	**23**
Notes	**24**

CHAPTER 2 THE LEGAL AND BEHAVIORAL ASPECTS OF CRIME   26

The Legal Aspects of Crime Categories	**28**
Criminal Homicide	30
Assault	31
Robbery	32
Arson	32
Burglary	33
Property Offenses	36
Sex Offenses	38
Drug Law Violations	41
Crimes Against Public Order and Safety	44
Behavior Systems in Crime	**45**
Major Criminal Behavior Systems	46
Domestic Violence	48
Hate Crime	49
Organized Crime	49
Op-Ed	**52**
Summary	**53**
Key Terms	**54**
Questions for Discussion	**54**
Media Resources	**54**
Notes	**54**

CHAPTER 3 CRIMINAL STATISTICS AND THE MEASUREMENT OF CRIME   56

The *Uniform Crime Reports*	**58**
Structure and Content	58
The Extent of Crime	62
Reliability of Estimates	64
The *UCR* in Retrospect	66
Victim Survey Research	**67**
The National Crime Survey	68
Victimization Survey Applications and Limitations	69
Self-Reported Criminal Behavior	**69**
Other Sources of Data on Crime and Justice	**71**
Op-Ed	**72**
Summary	**73**
Key Terms	**74**
Questions for Discussion	**74**
Media Resources	**74**
Notes	**74**

CHAPTER 4 CRIMINAL JUSTICE AND PROCEDURE: AN OVERVIEW   76

Systems of Justice	**78**
Criminal Due Process	**78**
The Bill of Rights	80
The Nationalization of the Bill of Rights	82
The Law of the Land	88
Substantive Due Process	88
Procedural Due Process	89
The Criminal Justice Process	**90**
Prearrest Investigation	90
Arrest	92
Booking	93
Initial Appearance	93
Preliminary Hearing	94
Determination of Formal Charges	95
Arraignment	96
The Trial Process	96
Sentencing	97
Appeals and Release	97
Criminal Justice as a "System"	**97**
Op-Ed	**100**
Summary	**101**
Key Terms	**101**
Questions for Discussion	**101**

Media Resources 101
Notes 102

PART 2 THE POLICE

CHAPTER 5 POLICE AND POLICING 104

The Functions of Police 106
  The Police Role 106
  The Right to Use Force 108
Police Systems in the United States 111
  Federal Law Enforcement Agencies 112
  State Police Agencies 113
  County and Municipal Policing 115
The Police Bureaucracy 115
  Division of Labor 116
  Chain and Units of Command 116
  Rules, Regulations, and Discipline 116
The Organization of Policing 118
  Patrol 118
  Detective Work 119
  Specialized Police Units 120
Police Discretion and Selective
  Law Enforcement 121
The Police Subculture 123
  The Police Personality 123
Women in Policing 127
  The Emergence of Women Police 127
  The Equal Opportunity Movement
    for Women in Policing 127
  The Current Status of Women
    in Policing 129
Community Policing 130
Op-Ed 134
Summary 135
Key Terms 136
Questions for Discussion 136
Media Resources 136
Notes 136

CHAPTER 6 POLICE AND THE
CONSTITUTION 138

Search Warrants 140
Probable Cause 142
Warrantless Search 142
  Search Incident to Arrest 142
  Stop and Frisk 144
  Automobile Searches 145
  Fresh Pursuit 147

  Consent Searches 148
  Other Warrantless Searches 149
  The "Plain View" Doctrine 151
The Exclusionary Rule 152
  Mapp v. *Ohio* 152
  The Impact of *Mapp* 153
  The Retreat From *Mapp* 154
Custodial Interrogation 155
  Twining v. *New Jersey* 155
  Brown v. *Mississippi* 155
  The Prompt Arraignment Rule 156
  Confessions and Counsel 157
  Miranda v. *Arizona* 158
  Show Ups and Lineups 159
  DNA and Other Nontestimonial
    Exemplars 161
Op-Ed 162
Summary 163
Key Terms 164
Questions for Discussion 164
Media Resources 164
Notes 165

CHAPTER 7 POLICE MISCONDUCT 166

Police Corruption 168
  Meals and Services 168
  Kickbacks 169
  Opportunistic Theft 169
  Planned Theft and Robbery 169
  Shakedowns 169
  Protection 169
  Case Fixing 171
  Private Security 171
  Patronage 171
Explanations of Police Corruption 172
  The Society-at-Large Explanation 172
  The Structural Explanation 172
  The Rotten-Apple Explanation 173
Police Violence 173
  Brutality 176
  Deadly Force 176
Controlling Police Misconduct 178
  Legislative Control 178
  Civilian Review Boards 180
  Police Control 180
Op-Ed 183
Summary 185
Key Terms 186
Questions for Discussion 186
Media Resources 186
Notes 187

PART 3 THE COURTS

CHAPTER 8 THE AMERICAN COURTS AND THE RIGHT TO COUNSEL 190

The State Courts **192**
Courts of Limited Jurisdiction 194
Major Trial Courts 198
Appellate Courts 198
Reform and Unification of State Courts 200
The Federal Judiciary **201**
U.S. Commissioner's and U.S. Magistrate's Courts 201
U.S. District Courts 202
U.S. Courts of Appeals 204
The U.S. Supreme Court 204
The Jurisdictional Scope of the Supreme Court 204
Affirming, Reversing, and Remanding 205
The Supreme Court's Mounting Problems 206
The Right to Counsel **208**
Powell v. *Alabama* 208
Extending the Sixth Amendment Right 209
Gideon v. *Wainwright* 210
Argersinger v. *Hamlin* 212
Op-Ed **214**
Summary **215**
Key Terms **215**
Questions for Discussion **216**
Media Resources **216**
Notes **216**

CHAPTER 9 THE COURT PROCESS FROM FIRST APPEARANCE THROUGH TRIAL 218

Bail and Pretrial Release **220**
The Right to Bail 220
Discretionary Bail Setting 221
The Bail Bond Business 222
Criticisms of the Bail System 223
Pretrial Detention 223
Prevention Detention 224
Release on Recognizance 225
The Grand Jury **226**
Operation of the Grand Jury 227
Grand Juries on Trial 227
The Plea **230**
Plea of Not Guilty 230
Guilty Plea 230
Nolo Contendere 230
Insanity Plea 231

Pleas of Statute of Limitations 231
Double Jeopardy 232
Plea Bargaining 232
Pretrial Motions **233**
Motion for Discovery 233
Motion for Change of Venue 233
Motion for Suppression 233
Motion for a Bill of Particulars 234
Motion for Severance of Charges or Defendants 234
Motion for Continuance 234
Motion for Dismissal 235
Speedy and Public Trial **236**
The Supreme Court and Speedy Trial 236
Speedy Trial and the States 237
The Right to a Public Trial 237
The Jury **240**
The Right to Trial by Jury 242
Jury Selection 243
The *Venire* 244
The *Voir Dire* 244
The Criminal Trial **247**
Opening Statements 248
Presentation of the State's Case 249
Motion for Directed Verdict 251
Presentation of the Defense's Case 251
Rebuttal and Surrebuttal 252
Closing Arguments 252
Charging the Jury 252
Jury Deliberations 253
Verdict and Judgment 253
Posttrial Motions 255
Op-Ed **254**
Summary **255**
Key Terms **256**
Questions for Discussion **256**
Media Resources **256**
Notes **257**

CHAPTER 10 SENTENCING, APPELLATE REVIEW, AND THE DEATH PENALTY 258

Sentencing **260**
Sentencing Objectives 260
Statutory Sentencing Structures 262
Sentencing Alternatives: Fines 264
Sentencing Alternatives: Imprisonment 265
Disparities in Sentencing 268
Sentencing Reform 269
Federal Sentencing Guidelines 270
Truth in Sentencing 271
The Sentencing Process 272

The Death Penalty in America   **273**
     Capital Punishment and
       Discrimination   274
     Cruel and Unusual Punishment   275
     Death and the Supreme Court   276
     The Return of Capital Punishment   279
     Methods of Execution   280
     The Death Penalty Debate   283
Appellate Review   **286**
     The Defendant's Right to Review   286
     The Prosecutor's Right to Review   287
     Appellate Review of Sentences   288
     The Appeal Process   289
Op-Ed   **289**
Summary   **290**
Key Terms   **290**
Questions for Discussion   **290**
Media Resources   **290**
Notes   **291**

PART 4   CORRECTIONS

CHAPTER 11   THE AMERICAN PRISON EXPERIENCE   294

American Prisons in Perspective   **296**
     The Walnut Street Jail   297
     The Separate System   298
     The Silent System   300
     Prison Industries   300
     The Reformatory Era   301
     The Twentieth-Century Industrial
       Prison   304
The Federal Prison System   **305**
Jails and Detention Centers   **307**
     Gaols, Hulks, and the Origins of
       American Jails   307
     Contemporary Jail Systems   308
     The Jail Population   309
     Jail Conditions   309
Op-Ed   **313**
Summary   **313**
Key Terms   **314**
Questions for Discussion   **314**
Media Resources   **314**
Notes   **315**

CHAPTER 12   BEHIND THE WALLS: A LOOK INSIDE THE AMERICAN PENITENTIARY   316

Types of Prisons   **318**
     Maximum-Security Prisons   318
     Medium-Security Prisons   320

     Minimum-Security Prisons   320
     Open Institutions   320
     Women's Institutions   321
Correctional Organization and Administration   **322**
     Prison Administration   322
     Prison Personnel   322
Institutional Routines   **323**
     Prison Facilities   324
     Classification   324
     Prison Programs   326
     Drug Abuse Treatment   330
Prison Discipline   **331**
Sex in Prison   **334**
     Same-Gender Sex   334
     Conjugal Visitation   335
     Coeducational Prisons   336
The Inmate Social System   **337**
     Prisonization   337
     The Inmate Code   339
     The Social Order of Women's
       Prisons   340
The Effectiveness of Correctional Treatment   **340**
     The Martinson Report   341
     New Approaches to Correctional
       Treatment   343
     Obstacles to Effective Correctional
       Treatment   343
Op-Ed   **344**
Summary   **345**
Key Terms   **345**
Questions for Discussion   **345**
Media Resources   **346**
Notes   **346**

CHAPTER 13   THE CONDITIONS OF INCARCERATION AND THE CONSTITUTIONAL RIGHTS OF PRISONERS   348

Attica, 1971   **350**
     The Uprising and Revolt   351
     The Negotiations and Assault   352
In Pursuit of Prisoners' Rights   **353**
     The Writ of *Habeas Corpus*   355
     Civil Rights and Prisoners' Rights   355
Legal Services in Prison   **357**
     Johnson v. *Avery*   357
     Jailhouse Lawyers   358
Constitutional Rights and Civil Disabilities   **358**
     Religion   359
     Prison Mail   360
     Rehabilitative Services   361

Medical Services 362
Prisoner Labor Unions 362
Prison Discipline and Constitutional Rights **363**
The Arkansas Prison Scandal 363
Solitary Confinement 364
The Lash 366
Prison Disciplinary Proceedings 367
The Conditions of Incarceration **369**
The Texas Prison Suit 370
The New Mexico Inmate Massacre 371
From Texas and New Mexico to Attica and Beyond 372
Reform Versus Law and Order **373**
Op-Ed **375**
Summary **376**
Key Terms **377**
Questions for Discussion **377**
Media Resources **377**
Notes **377**

CHAPTER 14 COMMUNITY-BASED CORRECTION **380**

Criminal Justice Diversion **382**
The Development of Diversion 382
Patterns of Diversion 383
The Impact of Diversion 384
Probation **385**
The Probation Philosophy 385
Suspended Sentences and Conditional Release 387
The Presentence or Probation Investigation 387
Conditions of Probation 388
Restitution Programs 389
Probation Services 389
Shock Probation 390
Intensive Probation Supervision 391
Probation Violation and Revocation 392
The Effectiveness of Probation 394
Parole **395**
The Origins of Parole 395
Parole Administration 396
Eligibility for Parole 396
Parole Supervision and Services 399
Parole Violation and Revocation 399
Parole Discharge 400
Trends in Community-Based Correction **400**
Furlough and Temporary Release 401
Op-Ed **405**
Summary **405**
Key Terms **406**
Questions for Discussion **406**

Media Resources 406
Notes 407

PART 5 JUVENILE JUSTICE

CHAPTER 15 THE JUVENILE JUSTICE SYSTEM **410**

The Nature of Juvenile Justice **412**
The Emergence of Juvenile Justice 414
Parens Patriae 414
Modern Juvenile Courts 415
Processing Juvenile Offenders **417**
Youths and the Police 417
Petition and Intake 417
Detention and Bail 420
Adjudication and Disposition 421
Juveniles and the Constitution **422**
Due Process and Juvenile Proceedings 422
Police Encounters and Juvenile Rights 423
Critical Issues in Juvenile Justice **425**
Status Offenders 425
Juveniles in the Adult Courts 427
Juvenile Detention 429
Juvenile Corrections 430
Op-Ed **433**
Summary **434**
Key Terms **435**
Questions for Discussion **435**
Media Resources **435**
Notes **435**

GLOSSARY **437**

CREDITS **445**

INDEX **449**

EXHIBITS

Historical Perspectives on Crime and Justice

The Emergence of National Prohibition 6
The Origins of *la Mafia* ("the Mafia") 50
Late-Nineteenth Century Homicide Rates in the US 59
Ashford v. *Thornton* 80

The Thief-Takers of Seventeenth Century
  England   109
Weeks v. *United States*   152
"Clubber" Williams   174
Judge Roy Bean and the Law West of
  the Pecos   196
The Scopes "Monkey" Trial   238
A Consequence of Sentencing Disparity?   270
Punishment in the American Colonies   296
Alcatraz Island Penitentiary   319
Old Red Hannah   366
The Roots of Probation   386
The House of Refuge   416

Legal Perspectives on Crime and Justice

Robinson v. *California*   12
Sodomy Laws in the United States   40
The Megan's Law Movement   89
Delaware v. *Prouse*   147
Human Rights Abuses and the
  "Blue Wall of Silence"   182
Faretta v. *California* and the Right *Not*
  to Have Counsel   212
Grand Jury Procedure and the Supreme
  Court   228
Witherspoon v. *Ilinois* and the "Death-
  Qualified" Jury   278
Controlling the Spread of HIV/AIDS in
  Prisons   327
Excerpts from the Court Opinion in
Holt v. *Sarver*   365
Morrissey v. *Brewer*   393
New Jersey v. *T.L.O.*   426

Research on Crime and Justice

Attitudes on the Hinckley Verdict   13
On the Grift at the Superbowl   34
Crack-Cocaine and Crime in Miami   71
The Second Amendment's "Right to
  Bear Arms"   82
Police Use of Force   110
Cocaine-Tainted Cash   150
Satisfaction with Local Police in
  12 American Cities   179
The Effectiveness of Drug Courts   200
The Use of the "Three Strikes" and
  "Two Strikes" Law   267
A Model Prison Therapeutic Community   332
The Rand Study of Probation Effectiveness   394
The Geography of Juvenile Homicide   418

Careers in Justice

Majoring in Criminal Justice   21
Crisis Intervention Counseling   53
Document Examiners and Fingerprint
  Analysts   73
United States Marshals Service   99
FBI Special Agent   132
Police Officers   163
Court Officers and Justices of the Peace   214
Legal Assistants   253
Advocacy for the Abolition of the Death
  Penalty   288
Federal Bureau of Prisons   312
The Corrections Connection   343
Jailhouse Lawyers and the Prison Law
  Project   375
Parole Officer   404
Juvenile Probation Officer   434

Gender Perspectives on Crime and Justice

The "PMS" Defense   17
Men as Victims of Rape   43
Men and Women as Victims of Violence   67
The Tragic Outcome of a Milwaukee
  911 Call   124
Warrantless Vaginal Cavity Searches   146
J.E.B. v. *Alabama ex rel. T.B.*   246
Women on Death Row   281
Differences Between Male and Female
  Inmates   305
Sexual Assault in Prison   335
Female "Boot Camps"   432

International Perspectives on Crime and Justice

The Prosecution of Rape as a War Crime   10
The Abduction of Women and Young Girls
  in China   29
Crime in Colombia   64
Constitution and Code Law in Bolivia   91
Women Police in the Republic of Fiji   131
Cocaine Trafficking and Police Corruption
  in Latin America   170
Judicial Corruption in Peru   199
Law and Disorder in the Italian Courts   242
Punishment Under Taliban Islamic Rule   284
Jails and Prisons in Brazil   310
Prisoners, HIV/AIDS, and Harm Reduction
  Around the World   325
Food and Drink in Hong Kong Prisons   360
Parole in Canada   401

Part 1

FOUNDATIONS OF CRIME AND JUSTICE

Chapter 1
Crime and the Nature of Law

Chapter 2
The Legal and Behavioral Aspects of Crime

Chapter 3
Criminal Statistics and the Measurement of Crime

Chapter 4
Criminal Justice and Procedure: An Overview

CHAPTER 1
CRIME AND THE NATURE OF LAW

Elements of Criminal Justice

Primm, Nev. — On a May weekend in 1997, high school friends David Cash and Jeremy Strohmeyer joined Cash's father for a night of gambling and video games at a casino resort 40 miles outside of Las Vegas. At about 3:03 A.M., Strohmeyer lured 7-year-old Sherrice Iverson into a ladies' room while her father played the slots a floor above. Cash followed, and watched from an adjoining toilet stall as his friend threatened the little girl and placed his hand over her mouth to muffle her screams. Cash then left the ladies' room, and minutes later Strohmeyer sexually assaulted and murdered little Sherrice. He confessed his crime to Cash, who kept silent. Days later, after being identified from a video surveillance tape, Strohmeyer was arrested. He ultimately confessed to police, and on October 14, 1998, he was sentenced in a Nevada court to life without parole.[1] But what about David Cash? What ever happened to him? Had he committed a crime by not stopping Strohmeyer while observing him in the ladies' room with 7-year-old Sherrice Iverson? Was he guilty of "aiding and abetting," or "conspiracy," or some other crime? And this raises a series of even more important questions. What *is* crime? How is it that some behaviors become defined as "criminal" while others do not? What are the relationships between crime and law, and are there different kinds of law?

The story of Jeremy Strohmeyer and David Cash is recalled here not only because of its horrific nature, but also because the media attention it received vividly illustrates the American fascination with crime. Stories of brutal violence and clever theft are continually offered to the public imagination, and the virtues and vices of such personages as Charles Manson, Al Capone, John Gotti, and John Wayne Gacy, to name only a few, have become well known. Murderers, rapists, and sinister sneak thieves are given prominent attention by the news media; violent crime is traditionally the major pursuit of the villains and scoundrels who appear in popular mystery and detective literature; and homicide, robbery, and assault are the common themes in both television and Hollywood portrayals of crime. In consequence, many Americans have developed rather distorted and one-sided conceptions of crime. Moreover, crime goes well beyond the limited catalog of violence and thefts that are discussed in the popular media. It includes a wide range of violent and nonviolent offenses, many of which rarely come to the attention of most observers.

The study of criminal justice begins with a discussion of the nature and meaning of *crime.* However, because "crime" is a term that is subject to both variable and uncritical usage, the task of this first chapter is to develop a fuller understanding of its meaning, and to do so through an analysis of crime and its relation to law.

CRIME

Crime as drama

Crime as sin

Crime is an aspect of human experience that brings to mind images of evil and lawbreaking, and that has been subject to a variety of definitions and interpretations. For the classical and literary scholar, crime can be drama, a pre-sentation of conflict between elements of the good and the profane as typified so eloquently in the Greek tragedies, Shakespeare's *Macbeth,* and Dostoyevsky's *Crime and Punishment.* To the moralist and reformer, crime is a manifestation of spiritual depravity; it is that festering evil and disease of the soul that must be eradicated both fully and immediately by the powers of restraint and virtue. Crime has also been equated with sin — with violations of a natural law, the Ten Commandments, or the proscriptions embodied in the Bible, the Talmud, and the Koran. For others, crime has different meanings: to the reporter it is news, to the detective it means work, to the thief it is business, and to the victim it suggests fear and loss. But to most individuals, crime is the violation of a generally accepted set of rules that are backed by the power and authority of the state. Yet, while these and many other conceptions of crime may be important to a particular perspective, they are of little help in arriving at an explicit definition of crime. Nevertheless, the notion of crime as "sin" suggests a starting point, for the evolution of criminal definitions is intricately linked to historical images of right and wrong and the concepts of *natural law.*

Natural Law

Natural law: General principles that determine what is right and wrong according to some higher power.

Natural law, a concept that has run through human affairs for more than 20 centuries, focuses on perhaps the earliest understanding of crime. It refers to a body of principles and rules, imposed upon individuals by some power higher than man-made law, that are considered to be uniquely fitting for and binding on any community of rational beings. As such, natural law is synonymous with "higher law" and is believed binding even in the absence of man-made law. This would suggest the existence of natural crimes — "thou shalt not kill" and "thou shalt not steal" — acts considered criminal by rational persons everywhere. However, research has failed to yield examples of activities that have been universally prohibited. Moreover, there are differing conceptions of natural law. These difficulties discredit its importance in the understanding and definition of crime, which has led legal scholars and social scientists to other areas in their search for the meaning and parameters of crime.

Crime as a Social Construct

The ideas of natural law and natural crime assume the existence of universal standards as to what constitutes sin or immoral behavior, but a definition of crime framed in these terms lacks both clarity and precision. Furthermore, conceptions of crime as amoral behavior become even more confused when one considers that there is no moral code to which all persons, even in a single society or community, subscribe. A number of social scientists, therefore, have examined crime as a human construction. They suggest that the definition of behavior as "deviant" or "criminal" comes from individuals and social groups, and involves a complex social and political process that extends over a period of time. As such, they suggest, persons and social groups create crime by making rules whose infraction constitutes crime.

This more sociological view of crime rejects the notion that the rightness or wrongness of actions is of divine origin, and begins with an examination of how behaviors become deviant and criminal within societies. Known as the "sociology of deviance" or the "labeling perspective," this point of view focuses specifically on **deviance** — a concept considerably broader than that of crime. This position rests on the idea that rules that might be violated are not created spontaneously but, rather, come about only in response to behavior perceived to be harmful to a group. More specifically, and in contrast to the natural law concept,

> *deviance* is not a quality of an act the person commits, but rather a consequence of the application by others of rules and sanctions to an "offender." The deviant is one to whom that label has successfully been applied; deviant behavior is behavior that people so label.[2]

Deviance: Conduct that the people of a group consider so dangerous, embarrassing, or irritating that they bring special sanctions to bear against the persons who exhibit it.

Vandalism of abandoned automobiles.

An illustration of the labeling of behavior as "deviant" and "criminal" was the antiliquor crusades that resulted in the ratification in 1919 of the Eighteenth Amendment to the U.S. Constitution, which prohibited the manufacture, sale, and distribution of intoxicating liquors (see Exhibit 1.1).

Exhibit 1.1

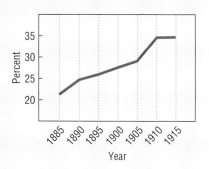

Historical Perspectives on Crime and Justice
The Emergence of National Prohibition

The prohibition "movement," in great part, was the assertion of a rural Protestant ethic against that of an urban culture that was emerging at the close of the nineteenth century. And this rural –urban cleft had its roots in the earliest chapters of American history. The first colonial settlers designated country and village life as good, and deemed only farmers and their agrarian way of life to be pure and wholesome; life in the city was seen as wicked. Farmers were viewed as the "stock of the earth," the backbones of American democracy. Living in communion with nature, they had an integrity that could never be attained by those surrounded with the evil and depravity of the city.

This agrarian myth so permeated the ideals and thinking of the frontier peoples and their descendants that it tended to shape their perceptions of reality and overt behaviors. Furthermore, their anti-city bias extended to drinking and the liquor trade, which they saw as symbols of urban morality — or immorality — and of urbanism in general. They viewed urbanism as undisputedly opposed to the rural creeds of the Methodists, Baptists, Presbyterians, and Congregationalists, with their emphasis on individual human toil and a profound faith in the Bible. And to them, the commercialism of the cities was destroying the self-sufficiency of the farm and village, creating a

situation of unwanted dependence. Urbanism, therefore, was the *real* sin in society, and the reform movement was simply an organization of rural interests striving against the "wicked city" and its impending dominance.

In general, the crusading reformers included many members of the middle and upper classes who felt that prohibition would bring salvation to the cities and to the less-privileged members of society. The best-known of the reformers was Carry Nation, the uncrowned queen of the temperance movement, who often referred to liquor sellers as "booze-sodden, soul-killing, filth-smeared spawn of the Devil," or words to that effect.

The prohibition movement culminated in the passage of the Vol-

stead Act in 1919, which prohibited the manufacture, sale, and advertising of alcoholic beverages, as well as their consumption in public places.

Alcoholic Beverage Consumption, per Capita of Drinking Age (15+) Population (in gallons) in Years Prior to National Prohibition

Disposing of alcohol during National Prohibition.

SOURCES: Edward Behr, *Prohibition: Thirteen Years That Changed America* (New York: Arcade, 1996); J. C. Furnas, *The Life and Times of the Late Demon Rum* (New York: Capricorn, 1973); W. J. Rorabaugh, *The Alcoholic Republic* (New York: Oxford, 1979).

Although the deviance perspective can suggest how some deviance and crime can come into being, it fails to account for all definitions of crime. That is, some crimes may come into being by moral enterprise, and some behavior may become criminal when that label is applied to acts previously regarded as noncriminal; but this does not explain how or why many long-standing definitions regarding crimes against person and property came into being. Murder, for example, appears as a proscription in both the Old and New Testaments, and its designation as a capital offense appears in an early chapter of the Book of Genesis.

Furthermore, not all deviant behavior is criminal behavior, and conversely, not all criminal behavior is deviant behavior. Numerous kinds of activities receive social disapproval and may even be deemed blatantly antisocial, but they are not necessarily crimes. While picking one's nose in public, espousing the doctrines of communism or nazism, or being an alcoholic are considered deviant by most Americans, the activities themselves are not criminal and they are not treated as such. Social disapproval might even be strong, with the deviants being subject to severe ostracism by their peers, but criminal sanctions would not be brought to bear against them.

Is all crime deviant behavior, and is all deviant behavior crime?

By contrast, numerous other behaviors are indeed criminal, but the participants are not even called deviant. The Saturday night poker game for modest stakes may be a violation of the criminal law in some jurisdictions, yet to the society at large the occasional poker player is hardly a deviant. Similarly, many of the intimate sexual practices that occur between adults in contemporary society may violate state and local criminal laws, but within the context of a consenting adult relationship the activities are considered normal.

And finally, although the labeling perspective fails to offer a basis for a working definition of crime, it does point out how some crime comes into being and, in that sense, how crime can be a social construction. More importantly, however, it provides a useful perspective for understanding how persons come to be labeled deviant or criminal, how society may react to them, and how the process of labeling them as outsiders can affect their behavior. Society may react to disapproved behavior in a variety of ways — with disgust, anger, hate, gossip, isolation, physical punishment, incarceration, or even execution. Moreover, differences in definitions of what constitutes appropriate conduct, or deviance, or crime can be especially pronounced in the cross-cultural dimension.

Crime as a Legal Definition

If definitions of crime as violations of natural law or as antisocial behavior or deviance lack precision and are ambiguous, then we may need to look directly at law for a formal definition of crime.

The word *crime* has its roots in the Latin *crimen,* meaning "judgment, accusation, or offense," and its origins are clearly legalistic. Numerous social scientists and legal scholars have offered definitions of crime within this legal perspective. The late Edwin H. Sutherland, perhaps the most renowned American criminologist of the mid-twentieth century, suggested that "the essential characteristic of crime is that it is behavior which is prohibited by the State and against which the State may react."[3] *Black's Law Dictionary* defines **crime** as "a positive or negative act in violation of the penal law; an offense against the state."[4] In the field of criminal justice it is defined simply as "a violation of the criminal law."[5] Yet these definitions, while correct in focusing on the law to delineate the limits of crime, fail to offer the kind of precision necessary for a full understanding of the term. We cannot simply call crime a violation of the law, for there are numerous circumstances under which identical behaviors would not be classified as criminal. However, lawyer and sociologist Paul W. Tappan has offered a definition of crime that does mark its major boundaries:

Crime: An intentional act or omission in violation of criminal law, committed without defense or justification, and sanctioned by the state as a felony or misdemeanor.

Crime is an intentional act or omission in violation of criminal law (statutory and case law), committed without defense or justification, and sanctioned by the state as a felony or misdemeanor.[6]

Tappan's definition will be accepted as the meaning of the term *crime* throughout this text. The following subtopics analyze the definition in detail.

Act or Omission Central to the American system of law is the philosophy that a person cannot be punished for his or her thoughts. Thus, for there to be a crime, an act or the omission of an act that is legally required must be present. A person may wish to commit a crime, or think of committing a crime, but the crime does not occur until the action takes place. If one were to consider murdering a relative, there would be no crime until the killing, or its attempt, had actually occurred. Furthermore, one could conceivably plan for a long while to commit a crime, but again, the crime would not necessarily come into being until the action took place.

Referring back to the case of Jeremy Strohmeyer and David Cash, and the killing of Sherrice Iverson, Strohmeyer's actions certainly constituted a crime; he had sexually assaulted the 7-year-old, and then took her life. But what about David Cash's *inaction?* Did his failure to intervene constitute a crime? Could he have been guilty of "conspiracy" to commit crime, or was he a "party" to crime?

Perhaps the best-known case of conspiracy was related to the Leopold and Loeb killing of 14-year-old Robert Franks in 1924. Nathan F. Leopold, Jr., was a graduate of the University of Chicago and the son of a multimillionaire shipping magnate; Richard A. Loeb was a University of Michigan graduate and the son of Albert A. Loeb, vice president of Sears, Roebuck and Company. Leopold and Loeb had structured what they felt would be the perfect crime — the kidnapping, ransoming, and killing of an innocent youth. Their planning extended over many weeks and involved renting a car; opening a bank account for the ransom money; riding trains to the tentative ransom site; purchasing rope, a chisel, and hydrochloric acid with which they would garrote, stab, and mutilate their victim; gathering rags with which they would bind and gag the victim; selecting wading boots to be worn in the swamp where they would leave the victim's body; preparing a ransom note; and discussing potential victims. At this point, Leopold and Loeb were already guilty of **conspiracy** to commit crime. Their very agreement to murder, combined with their extensive preparations, constituted a crime. When Leopold and Loeb selected Robert Franks as their victim, and then abducted and murdered him, their crimes advanced from the conspiracy stage to include kidnapping and homicide.[7]

Clearly, because David Cash had only followed his friend Strohmeyer into the ladies' room and observed him with the little girl, he was not guilty of conspiracy; there was no "concert in criminal purpose." But did his inaction make him a party to crime? People become *parties to crime* when they assist, aid and abet, incite, or otherwise encourage others to commit crimes. Cash neither assisted, incited, nor encouraged Strohmeyer in the assault and killing, nor was he an **abettor** — one who, with the requisite criminal intent, encourages, promotes, instigates, or stands ready to assist the perpetrator of a crime. Furthermore, Cash was not an **accessory before the fact** — one who abets a crime but is not present when the crime is committed. However, being an **accessory after the fact** — one who, knowing that a felony has been committed, receives, relieves, comforts, or assists the felon to hinder apprehension or conviction — is a crime in virtually all jurisdictions. Do the facts of the case suggest that Cash was an accessory?

Failure to act in a particular case *can* be a crime if there is some legal duty to do so. Consider, for example, the case of *People* v. *Beardsley,*[8] which involved a man who spent a weekend with his mistress. After a serious argument,

Conspiracy: Concert in criminal purpose. Legislatures have made conspiracy a separate offense because they perceive collective criminal activity to be a greater risk than individual actions.

People become *parties to crime* when they assist, aid and abet, incite, or otherwise encourage others to commit crimes.

Abettor: A person who, with the requisite criminal intent, encourages, promotes, instigates, or stands ready to assist the perpetrator of a crime.

Accessory before the fact: A person who abets a crime but is not present when the crime is committed.

Accessory after the fact: A person who, knowing that a felony has been committed, receives, relieves, comforts, or assists the felon to hinder apprehension or conviction.

the woman took an overdose of morphine tablets and the man made no attempt to obtain medical help to save her life. His failure to assist her did not constitute a crime. Although he may have had a moral obligation to help her, he had no legal duty to do so. There was no contractual relationship as might exist between parents and a day care center or between a patient and a hospital; there was no status relationship that imposed a legal duty such as that between husband and wife; and there was no legal statute imposing a legal duty on the man.

In contrast to *Beardsley,* in 1988 the California Supreme Court upheld manslaughter and felony child endangerment convictions of a woman who used prayer in lieu of medical attention in treating her 4-year-old's fatal attack of meningitis.[9] The defendant argued that the use of medicine violated her religious beliefs. The court countered that parents may not martyr their children to their own religious beliefs.

Less complex instances of failures to act that constitute crime can be found under the **misprision of felony** statutes. Misprision of felony refers to the offense of concealing a felony committed by another, even if the party to the concealment had not been part of the planning or execution of the felony.[10] Thus, if two individuals should overhear a group discussing their participation in a recent bank robbery, that couple would be guilty of misprision of felony if they failed to report the conversation to the authorities. Even though David Cash was not prosecuted, was he guilty of misprision of felony? And on the matter of cases that clearly are crimes but are not prosecuted, see Exhibit 1.2.

Misprision of felony: The concealment of a felony committed by another.

Criminal Intent
For an act or omission to be a crime, the law further requires criminal intent, or ***mens rea*** — from the Latin meaning "guilty mind." The concept of *mens rea* is based on the assumption that people have the capacity to control their behavior and to choose between alternative courses of conduct. Thus, the notion of criminal intent suggests an awareness of what is right and wrong under the law with an intention to violate the law, as contrasted with the retarded, the insane, or the young, who may not have their full use of reason.

***Mens rea* (criminal intent):** A person's awareness of what is right and wrong under the law, with an intention to violate the law.

Most legal commentaries divide *mens rea* into two basic types of intent: specific and general. *Specific intent* is present when one can gather from the circumstances of the crime that the offender must have consciously and subjectively desired the prohibited result. The crime of burglary reflects the notion of specific intent. Burglary involves two broad elements: entry into the dwelling of another and the intention to commit a crime (usually a theft) therein. The burglar manifests specific intent because he or she consciously desires the prohibited result — theft.

Specific intent

By contrast, consider the case of a man outraged by his neighbor's barking dog. He expresses his disfavor by warning that if the dog is not quieted, he will shoot the animal. When the threat is ignored and the dog continues to bark, the angered man fires three shots through his neighbor's window intending to kill the dog. Instead, one of the bullets kills his neighbor. Although specific intent is not present in this case, general intent is. As such, *general intent* refers to a matter of conscious wrongdoing from which a prohibited result follows, without a subjective desire for the accomplishment of that result. Or more specifically, general criminal intent involves the conscious and intentional commission of a crime when the specific result of that crime was not necessarily intended.

General intent

Although criminal intent, whether specific or general, is necessary for an act to be a crime, there are some exceptions to this rule of law. Under the doctrine of **vicarious liability,** referred to in some jurisdictions as the doctrine of *respondeat superior,* liability can be imposed on an employer for certain illegal acts of his employees committed during the course and scope of their employment. This doctrine is generally directed at the protection of the public,

Vicarious liability: The doctrine under which liability is imposed upon an employer for the acts of employees that are committed in the course and scope of their employment.

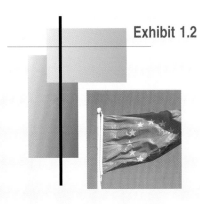

Exhibit 1.2

International Perspectives on Crime and Justice
The Prosecution of Rape as a War Crime

International criminal law has always included crimes of sexual violence. Rape can be a violation of the 1949 Geneva conventions, the 1948 Genocide convention, and the 1984 Torture convention. After World War II, furthermore, the International Military Tribunal at Nuremberg established rape as a crime against humanity. Yet despite these legal precedents, rape has long been mischaracterized and dismissed by military and political leaders as a private crime — the ignoble act of the occasional soldier. Worse still, it has been ignored because it has tended to be commonplace, and because long-standing discriminatory attitudes have viewed sexual crimes against women as incidental or less serious than others. Since 1990, however, some progress has been made, particularly after the outbreak of genocidal strife in Rwanda in 1994.

Rwanda is a small nation in central Africa with a population of almost 8 million, composed primar-

ily of two groups: the Hutu and the Tutsi. Formerly a Belgian colony, Rwanda has a long history of internal strife, which resulted in civil war between the Hutu and the Tutsi during the early 1990s. In the Rwandan genocide, thousands of Tutsi women were targeted by Hutu militia and soldiers of the former government armed forces of Rwanda. Tutsi women were individually raped, gang-raped, raped with objects such as sharp sticks or gun barrels, held in sexual slavery, or sexually mutilated.

In 1995, the U.N. Security Council established the International Criminal Tribunal for Rwanda for the prosecution of those responsible for the genocide

and other violations of international humanitarian law. One of these was Jean-Paul Akayesu, a former Rwandan official, who was accused of allowing police and others under his authority to rape and torture mostly Tutsi women who had sought his protection. On September 2, 1998, history was made when Akayesu was found guilty of nine counts of genocide, crimes against humanity, and war crimes. This was the first conviction for genocide by an international court; the first time an international court punished sexual violence in a civil war; and the first time that rape was found to be an act of genocide to destroy a group.

Rwandan detainees accused of genocide.

SOURCES: *International Criminal Tribunal for Rwanda,* United Nations Security Council, Resolution 955, November 8, 1994; "Human Rights Watch Applauds Rwanda Rape Verdict," Human Rights Watch press release, September 2, 1998.

as indicated in the following example. The defendant owned a tavern and his bartender had served minors in violation of the Pennsylvania Liquor Code. The tavern owner was neither aware that minors were served alcoholic beverages, nor was he present when the event occurred. Nevertheless, under the doctrine of vicarious liability, he was convicted. On appeal, the Pennsylvania Supreme Court upheld the conviction with the following statement:

> While an employer in almost all cases is not criminally responsible for the unlawful acts of his employees, unless he consents to, approves, or participates in such acts … the intent of the legislature in enacting this Code was not only to eliminate the common law requirement of a *mens rea,* but also to place a very high degree of responsibility upon the holder of a liquor license to make certain

that neither he nor anyone in his employ commit any of the prohibited acts upon the licensed premises.[11]

As a final point here, when vicarious liability is imposed, only minor penalties are typically levied. In the Pennsylvania case noted above, the defendant was a second-time offender. As such, he faced a mandatory penalty of a $500 fine and 3 months in jail. However, only the fine was ordered, for as the court explained it, "A man's liberty cannot rest on so frail a reed as whether his employee will commit a mistake in judgment."

Violation of Criminal Law   For an act or its omission to be a crime, not only must there be criminal intent, but the behavior must be in violation of the criminal law. **Criminal law,** as opposed to noncriminal law or civil law, is the branch of jurisprudence that deals with offenses committed against the safety and order of the state. As such, criminal law relates to actions that are considered so dangerous, or potentially so, that they threaten the welfare of the society as a whole. And it is for this reason that in criminal cases the government brings the action against the accused. **Civil law,** by contrast, is the body of principles that determines private rights and liabilities. In these cases, one individual brings an action against another individual — a *plaintiff* versus a *defendant* — as opposed to the state versus an accused, as in criminal cases. More specifically, civil law is structured to regulate the rights between individuals or organizations; it involves such areas as divorce, child support, contracts, and property rights. Civil law also includes torts, civil wrongs for which the law gives redress.

Criminal law includes a variety of types: statutory law, case law, and common law. **Statutory law** is law passed from the legislatures, which create it by statute. Each state has a statutory criminal code, as does the federal government. The laws that define the boundaries of such commonly known offenses as homicide, rape, burglary, robbery, and larceny are generally of a statutory nature. By contrast, **case law** is law that results from court interpretations of statutory law or from court decisions where rules have not been fully codified or have been found to be vague or in error. A classic example of case law is the Supreme Court decision involving ***Robinson* v. *California***[12] (see Exhibit 1.3).

Common law refers to the customs, traditions, judicial decisions, and other materials that guide courts in decision-making but that have not been enacted by the legislatures into statutes or embodied in the Constitution. Among the better-known aspects of common law are the rights set forth in the Declaration of Independence and other doctrines protecting life, liberty, and property.

Defense or Justification   For an act (or the omission thereof) to be a crime, it must not only be intentional and in violation of the criminal law, but it must also be committed without defense or justification. **Defense** is a broad term that can refer to any number of causes and rights of action that would serve to mitigate or excuse an individual's guilt in a criminal offense. Defenses most commonly raised include insanity, mistake of fact, mistake of law, duress and consent, consent of the victim, entrapment, and justification.

Insanity is any unsoundness of mind, madness, mental alienation, or want of reason, memory, and intelligence that prevents an individual from comprehending the nature and consequences of his or her acts or from distinguishing between right and wrong conduct. Insanity is a legal concept rather than a medical one. Furthermore, it is a complex legal issue. A few jurisdictions recognize that some defendants can be partially insane in respect to the circumstances surrounding the commission of a crime, but sane as to other matters. The cornerstone of the insanity defense emerged from the case of

Criminal law: The branch of jurisprudence that deals with offenses committed against the safety and order of the state.

Civil law: The body of principles that determines private rights and liabilities.

Statutory law: Law created by statute, handed down by legislatures.

Case law: Law that results from court interpretations of statutory law or from court decisions where rules have not been fully codified or have been found to be vague or in error.

***Robinson* v. *California*:**   The 1962 Supreme Court ruling that sickness may not be made a crime, nor may sick people be punished for being sick. The Court viewed narcotic addiction to be a "sickness" and held that a state cannot make it a punishable offense any more than it could put a person in jail "for the 'crime' of having a common cold."

Common law: Customs, traditions, judicial decisions, and other materials that guide courts in decision-making but have not been enacted by the legislatures into statutes or embodied in the Constitution.

Defense: Any number of causes and rights of action that serve to excuse or mitigate guilt in a criminal offense.

Insanity

Exhibit 1.3

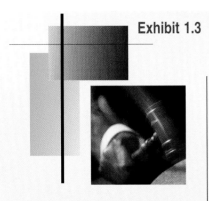

In *Robinson* v. *California,* the appellant had been convicted of being a narcotics addict under a section of the California Health and Safety Code, which read:

No person shall use, or be under the influence, or be addicted to the use of narcotics, excepting when administered by or under the direction of a person licensed by the State to prescribe and administer narcotics. It shall be the burden of the defense to show that it

Legal Perspectives on Crime and Justice
Robinson v. *California*

comes within the exception. Any person convicted of violating any provision of this section is guilty of a misdemeanor and shall be sentenced to serve a term of not less than 90 days nor more than one year in the county jail.

Mr. Robinson had been convicted after a jury trial in the Municipal Court of Los Angeles. In terms of evidence, the arresting officer testified that he had observed scar tissue, discoloration, and what appeared to be needle marks on the inside of the defendant's left arm, and that the defendant had admitted to the occasional use of narcotics. Under the California law, the use of narcotics was considered a status or condition — not an act; it was a continuing offense that could sub-

ject the offender to arrest at any time before he or she "reformed." Mr. Robinson was convicted of the offense charged. He then took his case to the Appellate Department of the Los Angeles County Superior Court, where the original judgment of conviction was ruled to be valid. Upon appeal to the U.S. Supreme Court, the decision was reversed on the grounds that status offenses such as "being addicted to the use of narcotics" were unconstitutional, and that imprisonment for such an offense was cruel and unusual punishment in violation of the Eighth Amendment to the Constitution. Thus, the *Robinson* case, after the lower courts' decisions were reversed, represented case law in that it defined narcotic addiction as a status that was no longer punishable under the law.

SOURCE: *Robinson v. California,* 370 U.S. 660 (1962).

M'Naghten Rule: The "right-or-wrong" test of criminal responsibility.

Durham Rule: Legal standard by which an accused is not held criminally responsible if he or she suffers from a diseased or defective mental condition at the time the unlawful act is committed.

Daniel M'Naghten in 1843. M'Naghten killed the secretary to England's Sir Robert Peel. At his trial he claimed that at the time he committed the act he had not been of a sound state of mind. From this came the **M'Naghten Rule** — the "right-or-wrong" test of criminal responsibility — which states:

If the accused was possessed of sufficient understanding when he committed the criminal act to know what he was doing and to know that it was wrong, he is responsible therefore, but if he did not know the nature and quality of the act or did know what he was doing but did not know that it was wrong, he is not responsible.[13]

The M'Naghten test has been severely criticized on the grounds that it is arbitrary and applies to only a small percentage of people who are actually mentally ill. In 1954 the U.S. Court of Appeals for the District of Columbia broadened the M'Naghten test in favor of what has become known as the **Durham Rule.** In *Durham* v. *United States,*[14] it was held that an accused is not criminally responsible if he or she suffers from a diseased or defective mental condition at the time the unlawful act is committed. This rule has also been criticized, but on opposite grounds from M'Naghten. Critics claim that it is far too broad and places too much power in the hands of psychiatrists and juries for determining the legal issue of insanity.

In retrospect, the defense of "not guilty by reason of insanity" has been debated for generations. Critics argue that defendants acquitted on insanity pleas spend less time in mental institutions than those sent to prison for similar crimes. Supporters of the insanity defense claim that it would be morally unjust to convict and punish an individual who acted under the condition of an unsound mind. Or as Harvard University law professor Alan M. Dershowitz once put it, "Would anyone seriously think of convicting someone for murder who thought he was shooting a robot or squeezing a melon?"[15]

John W. Hinckley, Jr., was tried in the shooting of President Ronald Reagan in 1981. His acquittal on insanity grounds the following year fully rekindled the controversy over the insanity defense. Confidence was lost in the criminal justice system because in this case it was unable to punish a man who admitted trying to assassinate the president of the United States. There were calls for reform, even abolition of the insanity defense entirely[16] (see Exhibit 1.4).

In the aftermath of the Hinckley verdict, Montana, Utah, and Idaho barred the insanity defense except in extreme cases. Several other states adopted a procedure that permits juries to find defendants "guilty but mentally ill." The aim of such a finding is to guarantee psychiatric treatment to an offender while ensuring that he or she will serve as much prison time as another convicted person.[17] Moreover, the 1983 U.S. Supreme Court's decision in *Jones* v. *United States*[18] held that persons found not guilty of crimes by reason of insanity may be confined to mental hospitals for a longer time than they would have spent in prison if convicted — a ruling that applied to John W. Hinckley, Jr.

The problem with the insanity defense is that insanity is a legal, not a medical term. Furthermore, there is little agreement on the actual meaning of the word. On the other hand, and in contrast to conventional wisdom, few serious offenders use the insanity plea to avoid incarceration. Studies demonstrate that

Percentage of felony defendants the public thinks use the insanity plea: 37%

Percentage of felony defendants who actually do use the insanity plea: 1%

Exhibit 1.4

Research in Crime and Justice
Attitudes on the Hinckley Verdict

Shortly after the 1982 trial of John Hinckley, Jr., researchers at the University of Delaware conducted a scientific survey of a representative sample of 434 adults to determine their opinions about the insanity plea in general, and the Hinckley verdict of *not guilty by reason of insanity* (NGRI) in particular. Respondents were asked a series of questions about the fairness of the verdict, how they would have judged Hinckley had they been on the jury, whether Hinckley was insane, whether the insanity defense was a loophole, and what should be done

with Hinckley. The general findings of the research were as follows:

Fairness of Hinckley verdict:
Unfair	53.7%
Somewhat or slightly fair	37.8
Very fair	8.5

Respondent's verdict:
Guilty	73.3%
NGRI	14.7
Don't know	12.0

Is Hinckley insane?
No	65.7%
Yes	24.4
Don't know	10.0

Is the insanity defense a loophole?
Yes	87.1%
No	6.8
Don't know	6.1

What should happen to Hinckley?
Punishment	26.4%
Treatment	14.1
Punishment and treatment	59.5

In addition to these findings, it was clear that the respondents were not well informed about the insanity defense, with the majority believing that Hinckley would be confined for only a short period of time. That was almost two decades ago, and at the end of the 1990s Hinckley was still in custody. However, in 1999 a federal appeals court authorized Hinckley to have authorized day trips at the discretion of his physicians.

SOURCES: Valerie P. Hans and Dan Slater, "John Hinckley, Jr., and the Insanity Defense: The Public's Verdict," *Public Opinion Quarterly* 47 (1983): 206; *Miami Herald*, January 16, 1999, p. A4.

Mistake of fact

Mistake of law

Lambert v. California: Ruling whereby the Supreme Court held that due process requires that ignorance of a duty must be allowed as a defense when circumstances that inform a person as to the required duty are completely lacking.

Duress and consent

the plea is used in less than 1 percent of serious criminal cases, is rarely successful, and when it is, defendants generally spend more time in mental institutions than they would have spent in prison had they been convicted.

Mistake of fact is any erroneous conviction of fact or circumstance resulting in some act that would not otherwise have been undertaken. Mistake of fact becomes a defense when an individual commits a prohibited act in good faith and with a reasonable belief that certain acts are correct, which, if they were indeed accurate, would have made the act innocent. Further, the mistake must be an honest one and not the result of negligence or poor deliberation.

For example, if James Smith walks away with Hilary Jones's suitcase thinking that it is his own, Smith's defense would be that he was operating under a mistake of fact since both parties had identical luggage. Such a mistake precludes Smith from having criminal intent and, as a result, he has a defense against a conviction for larceny. Mistake of fact has been used as a defense in cases of statutory rape. Statutory rape refers to sexual intercourse with a person under a certain age (usually 16 or 18) despite his or her consent. Although a defendant may claim that the underage partner looked older than his or her actual age, or even misrepresented his or her age, the courts are decidedly mixed in their acceptance of the defense. In 1984, for example, the Utah Supreme Court accepted the defense of reasonable mistake of age on the grounds that "a person cannot be found guilty of a criminal offense unless he harbors a requisite criminal state of mind."[19] During the same year, however, the Michigan Supreme Court refused to recognize the defense, holding that the statutory rape laws impose criminal liability without requiring proof of specific criminal intent.[20]

Mistake of law is any want of knowledge or acquaintance with the laws of the land insofar as they apply to the act, relation, duty, or matter under consideration. There is a well-worn cliche that "ignorance of the law is no excuse," which suggests that the notion of mistake of law offers no release from prosecution of such a crime. Indeed, simple ignorance of forbidden behavior is not usually an acceptable defense against crime; all persons are assumed to have knowledge of the law. This is true for both citizens and noncitizens alike. If a resident of England, for example, were to take a motor tour of the United States and unwittingly drive on the left side of the road, as is the law in Great Britain, his or her ignorance would be no defense against a U.S. traffic violation. Similarly, in many jurisdictions it is a crime to fail to come to the aid of a police officer when so ordered and if the request is not hazardous to the citizen. This law is not well known to most citizens. Nevertheless, should an individual fail to comply with such an order on the basis of ignorance, his or her lack of knowledge of the law would not be an adequate defense against the crime. In contrast, however, as the Supreme Court ruled in *Lambert* v. *California*,[21] ignorance of the law may be a defense against crime if the law has not been made reasonably well known.

Duress and consent refers to any unlawful constraints exercised on an individual forcing him or her to consent to committing some act that would not have been done otherwise. Duress implies that one is not acting of his or her own free will, and the American system of law emphasizes both criminal intent and responsibility. A typical example of duress and consent has been seen often in television and movie themes. The local bank official is forced to aid the holdup team in a bank robbery while his wife and children are held captive by a second group of bandits. If the banker fails to cooperate, his family will be harmed. In this case duress and consent is a legal defense against crime, since there is no criminal intent and since the rule includes injuries, threats, and restraints exercised not only against the individual, but on his or her parent, child, or spouse as well. However, such threats or restraints must be against a person (as opposed to property), and they must be immediate (not future). Had the bank official been threatened with the slaying of his family at some future date, there would be no immediate and imposing threat. Similarly, if the threat was to destroy his house, again the notion of duress would be a poor defense.

Consent of the victim is any voluntary yielding of the will of the victim, accompanied by his or her deliberation, agreeing to the act of the offending party. The victim's consent to a crime can be a defense recognized by the law, but there are several elements to a defense of consent. First, the victim must be capable of giving consent, and this rule excludes any consent offered by the insane, the retarded, or those below the age of reason. Second, the offense must be a "consentable" crime. Murder is considered to be a nonconsentable crime, as is statutory rape. Furthermore, there are offenses such as disorderly conduct for which no consent can generally be given. Third, the consent cannot be obtained by fraud. For example, should an auto mechanic suggest to a customer that the transmission must be fully replaced when indeed only a small bolt requires tightening, the victim's consent to have it replaced is not a legal defense. Fourth, the person giving consent must have the authority to do so. Although one party may have the right to give consent to have his or her property taken, such authority cannot be given to the property of another party.

Entrapment is the inducement of an individual to commit a crime not contemplated by him or her, undertaken for the sole purpose of instituting a criminal prosecution against the offender. Cases of entrapment occur when law enforcement officers, or civilians acting at their behest, induce a person to commit a crime that he or she would not have otherwise undertaken. *Inducement* is the key word in the entrapment defense and refers to the fact that the accused had no intention of committing the crime until persuaded to do so by the law officer. Should a police officer approach a group of youths and convince them to carjack an auto, and then place them under arrest after the carjacking was committed, the defense of police entrapment would be available. Similarly, in some jurisdictions, if a vice squad officer in plain clothes approaches a prostitute and offers her a sum of money for sexual favors, and then arrests her after their encounter, entrapment might be an available defense. Even though the accused is by profession a prostitute, the case could nevertheless be one of entrapment since the particular offense for which she was arrested had occurred only because of police inducement.

In recent years, the strength of the entrapment defense has been weakened by court decisions that have considered the offender's "predisposition" to committing a crime. In the 1976 case of *Hampton* v. *United States,*[22] the Supreme Court ruled that it was not entrapment for an undercover agent to supply illicit drugs to a suspected dealer and then for another agent to act as a buyer, when there was reason to believe that the suspect was inclined, or "predisposed," to commit the crime anyway. What makes this case different from that of the prostitute is the legality of the primary behavior in question. Sexual intercourse, whether the female partner is or is not a prostitute, is generally legal behavior. What constituted the crime was her acceptance of money for the sexual act, and what constituted entrapment was the plainclothes officer's inducement of money. In contrast, Hampton's dealing in illicit drugs was illegal behavior, and it was not the undercover agent's inducement that made the primary act illegal.

Justification is any just cause or excuse for the commission of an act that would otherwise be a crime. The notion of justification as a defense against crime typically involves the use of force or violence in the protection of one's person or property, the lives and property of others, the prevention of crime, and the apprehension of offenders. *Justifiable homicide* includes those instances of death that result from legal demands — the execution of a duly condemned prisoner, the killing of a fleeing inmate by a correctional officer, or the shooting of an armed robber by a police officer. *Excusable homicide* includes death from accidents or misfortunes that may occur during some

Consent of the victim

Entrapment: The inducement of an individual to commit a crime not contemplated by him or her.

POLICE ENTRAPMENT

If a cop comes up to a prostitute and engages in vague generalities or responses to her leads, this is not entrapment. The scenario might go something like this:

HE: Hi.
SHE: Hi, wanna party?
HE: Sure. What's the tariff, and what do you do?
SHE: Fifty dollars for a blow job.

This is a perfectly legitimate vignette for a legal arrest. The twist on this exchange would be:

HE: Hi.
SHE: Hi.
HE: I'm willing to give you $50 for a blow job, how about it?
SHE: Sure.

Because the officer initiated the action … the arrest, if made, would be illegal.

SOURCE: Former Minneapolis Police Chief Anthony V. Bouza.

Justification

Justifiable homicide includes instances of death that result from legal demands, whereas *excusable homicide* includes deaths from misfortunes that occur during some lawful act.

lawful act. Self-defense or the defense of some other individual can be viewed as either a justifiable or excusable act depending on the circumstances surrounding the particular case.

Beyond these general areas, some jurisdictions have particular statutes that may extend the boundaries of justifiable cause or excuse. Until 1974, for example, a Texas law defined as justifiable homicide a husband's shooting and killing his wife's lover if he found them in the very midst of the act of adultery. The law specified, however, that the actual shooting had to occur before the couple separated and that the husband must not have been a party to, or approved of, the adulterous connection. (Interestingly, this Texas statute did not extend to women who found their husbands engaging in adultery.)

There are many issues raised as defenses or justifications of crime that in most instances are not allowed by the courts. Although the First Amendment to the Constitution guarantees religious freedom, *religious practice* that violates criminal law can generally not be used to justify or excuse criminal conduct. Similarly, if it is *custom* that a given law is typically not enforced, such a tradition does not justify the violation of that law. Many have attempted to use *intoxication* as a defense against crime, claiming that while under the influence of alcohol or drugs they were not in control of their behavior and therefore not criminally responsible. However, most jurisdictions make a distinction between voluntary and involuntary intoxication. Voluntary intoxication is not a defense under most circumstances. In cases of involuntary intoxication, however, where liquor or drugs are forced upon an individual, a reasonable defense can be mounted depending on the defendant's "degree of intoxication" at the time of the criminal act. One of the more novel defenses in recent years was used by a Colorado woman who had been charged with hitting her husband in the head with an ax — not once, but 23 times. She argued that she had "snapped." The snapping defense was also used by heavyweight boxer Mike Tyson, in 1997, when he chewed on the ear of his opponent, Evander Holyfield. Tyson explained that his breach of ring etiquette was because he had just "snapped."

On the other hand, there have been a number of unusual defenses that the courts have accepted. Courts periodically accept *medical necessity* as a legitimate defense for individuals charged with possession of marijuana. In these cases, the defendants are typically cancer patients who smoke marijuana to relieve chronic pain or alleviate the side effects of chemotherapy.[23] A *PMS defense* (premenstrual syndrome), as well, has been accepted by the courts in a few instances (see Exhibit 1.5).

Law Sanctioned by the State   Under the American system of law, the maxim *nullum crimen sine poena* ("no crime without punishment") dictates that a law must be written, that persons cannot be tried for acts that are not crimes in law, and that persons cannot be punished for acts for which the state provides no penalty. In the absence of such doctrines a social order would quickly fall into a state of *anomie*. If a legal system had no written law, *any* act could potentially be construed as a crime at the pleasure of the court or state, resulting in a situation of ironbound tyranny. Furthermore, if certain types of behavior were defined as crimes but no penalties were embodied in

Anomie is a condition within a society or group in which there exists a weakened respect or lack of adherence to some or most of the norms.

Exhibit 1.5   **Gender Perspectives on Crime and Justice**
The "PMS" Defense

Premenstrual syndrome, or PMS, is a complex of symptoms including nervous tension, irritability, weight gain, retention of fluids, headache, breast tenderness, depression, and lack of coordination. PMS typically occurs during the last few days of the menstrual cycle before the onset of menstruation. One or more of the symptoms occur in most women, to a greater or lesser degree. Several theories have attempted to explain the syndrome — including nutritional deficiency, stress, hormonal imbalance, and various emotional disorders. Regardless of the cause, in some women PMS can be quite severe, with a week or more spent in extreme discomfort and distress.

In 1980 and 1981, two British women escaped murder convic-

tions by arguing that their legal responsibility had been diminished by premenstrual syndrome. In other words, they were invoking a "PMS defense," and in both cases the women were convicted only of manslaughter due to "PMS-diminished responsibility."

Encouraged by these legal precedents, the attorney for Shirley Santos, a New York woman charged with assault in 1981 for having badly beaten her 4-year-old daughter, used the PMS defense to argue that the defendant was not conscious of her actions. It would appear that both the prosecutor and the judge found merit in the argument; they accepted a guilty plea to harassment, a misdemeanor.

As the first American case involving a successful PMS defense, the Santos decision generated considerable controversy. Members of the medical profession and women suffering from severe premenstrual symptoms applauded the decision because it had given long overdue attention to a crippling disorder. At the same time,

law review articles defended the use of PMS as a defense against crime. By contrast, however, many women's advocates found it appalling that a concept of "raging hormones" was being used to deny women the status of responsible adults. In fact, Elizabeth Holtzman, a Brooklyn district attorney, argued:

> Allowing women to plead some special kind of insanity because of physical reactions to their menstrual cycle is not only medically unjustified, but dangerous to the legal rights of all women.

The problem with the PMS defense is that, among other things, it is gender-specific, suggesting that it can only apply to women. A result is that it makes PMS — a normal biological process — a value-laden concept that can encourage a diminution of nonbiological aspects of many women's lives. Nevertheless, the defense continues to be used, although infrequently.

SOURCES: Christopher Boorse, "Premenstrual Syndrome and Criminal Responsibility," in *Premenstrual Syndrome,* ed. Benson E. Ginsburg and Bonnie Frank Carter (New York: Plenum, 1987), pp. 81 – 124; DeNeen L. Brown, "PMS Defense Successful in Virginia Drunken Driving Case," *Washington Post,* Section A, June 7, 1991.

Prostitution — mala in se, or a consequence of the legislation of morality?

Mala in se

Mala prohibita

Felony: A crime punishable by death or imprisonment in a federal or state penitentiary.

Misdemeanor: A crime punishable by no more than a $1,000 fine and/or 1 year of imprisonment, typically in a local institution.

the law for their commission, then again a hopeless level of confusion and disregard for law would likely ensue. In contrast, American law consists of written codes describing the various prohibited forms of behavior and the range of punishments that would occur for their commission.

The law must be specific, however, for there are many acts that, depending on the attendant circumstances, may or may not be crimes. The physical act of sexual intercourse, for example, describes any number of situations, including adultery, fornication, forcible and statutory rape, seduction, and incest. And, in addition to these six different crimes, it is also a normal, lawful act between mates. However, as a lawful act even between married couples, the act might be called obscenity, pornography, indecent exposure, or disorderly conduct, depending on the place it occurs. Thus, the law must be specific as to what sex acts are prohibited and among whom and where and under what circumstances they may and may not occur.

Also significant in American criminal law is the doctrine that only the offender can be punished. This posture has its roots in the Old Testament, that "every man shall be put to death for his own sin," and has endured in current legal doctrine. However, there are a variety of situations in which this may not necessarily be the case. Recall, for example, the doctrine of vicarious liability, which says an employer can be held responsible for certain crimes of his or her employees.

Felonies and Misdemeanors Crimes have been classified in many ways, among which are *mala in se* and *mala prohibita* offenses. Acts are considered to be *mala in se* when they are inherently and essentially evil — immoral in their nature and injurious in their consequences — such as murder, rape, and theft. *Mala prohibita* crimes are those that may not necessarily be wrong in themselves, but that are wrong simply because they have been prohibited by statute. Moral turpitude — that is, depravity or baseness of conduct — is the basis of distinction between these two types of crime, but since attitudes regarding moral turpitude tend to vary from one jurisdiction to the next, the distinction that is almost universally used instead is that between felonies and misdemeanors.

Historically, under common law felonies were crimes punishable by death or forfeiture of property and included such offenses as murder, rape, theft, arson, and robbery. Misdemeanors were considered lesser offenses that lacked the moral reprehensibility of felonies. The current distinction between the two is similar. In most jurisdictions, **felonies** are serious crimes punishable by death or by imprisonment (usually for 1 year or longer) in a federal or state penitentiary. **Misdemeanors** are minor offenses generally punishable by no more than a $1,000 fine and/or 1 year of imprisonment, typically in a local institution. The felony-misdemeanor classification goes beyond the *mala in se – mala prohibita* distinction, since a number of felonies fail to reflect moral turpitude. For example, the crimes of prison escape, wiretapping, carrying a concealed deadly weapon, or possession of forgery instruments are felonies in some jurisdictions in spite of the perpetrator's lack of moral turpitude.

In the legal codes of most jurisdictions, felonies and misdemeanors encompass the boundaries of what is defined as crime. In a few states, however, there is a third generic category. This category has resulted from the redefinition of certain offenses as less serious than misdemeanors; such offenses are generally referred to as *violations*. In the New York Penal Law, for example:

> "Violation" means an offense for which a sentence to a term of imprisonment in excess of fifteen days cannot be imposed.[24]

Included in this category of violations are such minor offenses as disorderly conduct, loitering, public intoxication, and patronizing a prostitute.

CRIMINAL LAW

Legal scholars Sir Frederick Pollock and F. W. Maitland have commented that "law may be taken for every purpose, save that of strictly philosophical inquiry, to be the sum of the rules administered by the courts of justice."[25] To legal scholar Sir James Fitzjames Stephen, law is "a system of commands addressed by the sovereign of the state of his subjects, imposing duties and enforced by punishments."[26] There have been numerous attempts to frame more philosophical definitions of law, but few have been widely accepted. Even more numerous have been definitions that are more pragmatic. These have all generally signified that law is a body of rules of human conduct that the courts recognize and enforce.

The origins of law are buried in antiquity, for they likely date before the beginning of recorded history. It would be safe to assume, however, that even the crudest forms of primitive social organization needed some regulation, and law quickly evolved to fill that need.

Since the beginnings of civilization a number of distinct legal systems have emerged, including the Egyptian, Mesopotamian, Chinese, Hindu, Hebrew, Greek, Roman, Celtic, Germanic, Catholic church (canon), Japanese, Islamic, Slavic, Romanesque, and Anglican.[27] The earliest of these was the Egyptian, dating to perhaps 4000 B.C., followed by the Mesopotamian in 3500 B.C., and the Chinese in 3000 B.C. U.S. law is comparatively recent; it draws from Greek, Roman, and Catholic church law but has its major roots in the Anglican or English common law. Other sources of U.S. law include the state and federal constitutions, statutory law, and the regulations of administrative agencies.

Common Law

The history of common law can be traced to eleventh-century England, when the existing collection of rules, customs, and traditions was declared the law of the land by King Edward the Confessor. Common law was judge-made law, and much of it was unwritten.

As time passed, a process emerged whereby this largely unwritten customary law of the land was translated into specific rules. As judges reached their decisions in judicial proceedings, a body of maxims and principles

SELECTED CAPITAL OFFENSES FROM THE *ORIGINAL CRIMINAL CODE OF 1676*

If any person within this Government shall deny the true God and His attributes, he shall be put to death.

If any person shall commit any willful and premeditated murder he shall be put to death.

If any person slayeth another with a sword or dagger who hath no weapon to defend himself, he shall be put to death.

If any man bear false witness maliciously and on purpose to take away a man's life, he shall be put to death.

If any child or children, above sixteen years of age, and of sufficient understanding, shall smite their natural father or mother, unless thereunto provoked and forced for their self-protection from death or maiming, at the complaint of said father and mother, and not otherwise, there being sufficient witness thereof, that child or those children so offending shall be put to death.

Constitutional law: The legal rules and principles that define the nature and limits of governmental power, and the duties and rights of individuals in relation to the state.

Administrative law: A branch of public law that deals with the powers and duties of government agencies.

developed that was derived, in theory, from customs. The result was a set of legal rules in the form of judicial decisions, rather than legislative statutes, that provided precedents for the resolution of future disputes. This body of decisions became what is referred to as common law. Thus, common law was case law as opposed to law created by statute. Much of common law, furthermore, reflected natural law ideas of right and wrong, as well as direct statements from the Holy Scriptures.

The early criminal laws of the American colonies developed within the tradition and structure of English common law and the English charters for the founding of settlements in the New World. As the colonies became more mature, they developed their own legal systems, but in substance these varied little from English common law. The *Original Criminal Code of 1676*, for example, handed down by the Duke of York and applied to the residents of the Pennsylvania colony, was among the early bodies of law in the New World. Much of it was based on common law, combined with a series of rules structured for maintaining British dominance over colonial interests. The influence of biblical proscriptions was also apparent in this code, with many capital offenses drawn virtually from the Ten Commandments.[28]

Other Sources of Criminal Law: Constitutional Law, Statutory Law, and Administrative Law

Although English common law rests at the foundation of American criminal law, contemporary criminal codes also reflect the content of constitutional law, administrative law, and federal and state statutory laws. At the apex of the American legal system is **constitutional law** — law set forth in the Constitution of the United States and in the constitutions of the various states. Constitutional law is the supreme law of the land. As such, it presents the legal rules and principles that define the nature and limits of governmental power as well as the rights and duties of individuals in relation to the state and its governing organs, and that are interpreted and extended by courts exercising the power of judicial review.

The U.S. Constitution, which embodies the fundamental principles by which the affairs of the United States are conducted, was drawn up at the federal Constitutional Convention in Philadelphia in 1787. It is brief and concise, and it includes a preamble, seven articles, and 27 amendments. Although not all of the Constitution relates to criminal law, Supreme Court and lower court interpretations of its articles and amendments have had a direct impact on criminal law and criminal procedure, as will be seen throughout this text.

Next in order of authority to constitutional law are the federal statutes, enacted by Congress, and state statutes, ordained by state legislatures. Federal statutes must conform to the prescriptions and proscriptions of the Constitution, and state statutes must conform to the U.S. Constitution as well as to the constitution of the jurisdiction in which they are enacted.

With 50 separate state legislatures creating laws, and an even greater number of separate court systems interpreting them, the application of statutory laws becomes exceedingly complex. Furthermore, statutory laws are far from uniform. For this reason criminal laws established by statute tend to vary from one jurisdiction to another, and what may be a violation of the criminal law in one state may not necessarily be so in another.

Finally, criminal law can descend from **administrative law**, a branch of public law that deals with the powers and duties of government agencies. More specifically, administrative law refers to the rules and regulations of administrative agencies; the thousands of decisions made by them; their orders,

Exhibit 1.6

Careers in Justice
Majoring in Criminal Justice

Criminal justice — the study of the agencies and procedures set up to manage both crime and the persons accused of violating the criminal law — has become one of the most popular undergraduate majors in the United States. In some colleges and universities it is by far the largest major; in others it ranks second or third, outpaced only by psychology and/or business. Why is there so much interest in obtaining a degree in criminal justice? Could it be that all of these students are interested in working in the criminal justice field?

At the University of Delaware, I have been teaching courses in criminal justice for more years than I'd like to admit, and in fact, since 1976 I have had the satisfaction of teaching the introductory course in CJ to more than 10,000 students. Because of my curiosity as to why my students select this course, I always ask: "Why are you here?" I have kept a tally of the answers over the years, and they turn out to be quite interesting.

First of all, a little over a third of the students have been non-majors or undeclared. They had chosen the course as an elective because they heard it was interesting and had a number of "real-world applications," as they put it. The remaining students were criminal justice majors, with the following career goals:

Law enforcement (local, state, or federal)   15%

Legal profession (paralegal or attorney)   13

Administration (courts or justice organizations)   7

Corrections (probation, parole, or correctional officer)   10

"Other" positions in criminal justice   6

Well, these responses account for only about half of the criminal justice majors. What about the rest? Why did they choose the major? Interestingly, almost all had yet to make any career decisions and felt that criminal justice was a "good," "safe," and "practical" choice. The following statement from a recent undergraduate sums up the sentiments of most of these students:

To be honest, I don't know yet what I want to do. I guess you could say I don't know what I want to be when I grow up. I knew when I came to college that I needed a liberal arts degree, and criminal justice sounded far more interesting than sociology, economics, or fifteenth-century English literature. Besides, I knew it would be good for pre-law if I decided to go in that direction, and also, I knew that I could learn things of use in the real world — about how justice works, and about my legal rights.

For fifteen of my years at the University of Delaware, I was director of its undergraduate criminal justice program, and on more than one occasion I conducted follow-up studies of criminal justice graduates. The findings were quite fascinating. Most of those who had specific career plans at the outset of their undergraduate studies ultimately secured those positions. Many of these had begun to move up the ranks in their chosen occupations, or had shifted into other aspects of criminal justice work.

One of the things that the former students repeatedly emphasized was that after they had begun at entry-level positions in policing, the courts, or corrections, they began to hear about the many less-visible occupations in the criminal justice field. Scores of graduates shifted into these areas. In fact, in addition to the traditional roles in police, courts, and corrections, former majors were employed in well over a hundred different types of CJ positions, including such jobs as crime lab technician, polygraph operator, police photographer, youth gang street worker, school safety officer, and witness protection agent.

Of the undergraduates who had no specific career plans when they entered college, about a third were working in the myriad of criminal justice positions mentioned above. Of the balance, they seemed to be everywhere — in business, social work and counseling, advertising, media and journalism, hotel management, teaching, and sales. In addition, one was a judge, another was an attorney for the U.S. Senate Judiciary Committee, a third was a professor (you guessed it: English literature), a fourth was a stockbroker, and still another was an editor with a major publishing company. And on the negative side of the picture, there were several who were among the chronically unemployed, and two were prison inmates.

In each of the remaining chapters of this text, a particular position in the criminal justice field will be described at length, with sources for obtaining further information.

SOURCE: James A. Inciardi.

directives, and awards; and the court opinions dealing with appeals from the decisions and with petitions by the agencies to the courts for the enforcement of their orders and directives. Much of the content of administrative law is not concerned directly with criminal behavior. Nevertheless, the rules of certain agencies bear directly on violations of behavior that would be dealt with by the criminal courts. The classification of heroin, PCP, and other drugs as "controlled substances" by the Drug Enforcement Administration, for example, is an administrative regulation that has been translated into criminal statutes in the federal as well as many state jurisdictions.

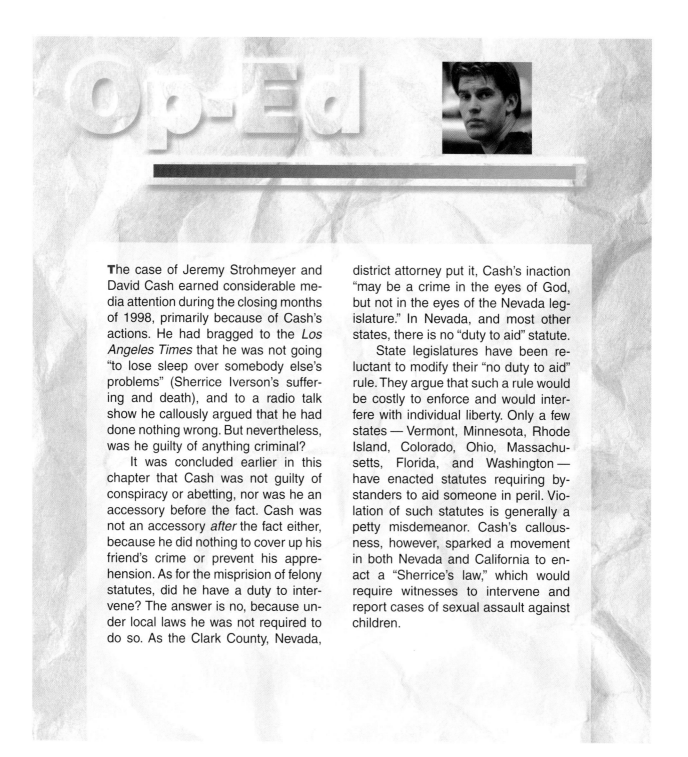

The case of Jeremy Strohmeyer and David Cash earned considerable media attention during the closing months of 1998, primarily because of Cash's actions. He had bragged to the *Los Angeles Times* that he was not going "to lose sleep over somebody else's problems" (Sherrice Iverson's suffering and death), and to a radio talk show he callously argued that he had done nothing wrong. But nevertheless, was he guilty of anything criminal?

It was concluded earlier in this chapter that Cash was not guilty of conspiracy or abetting, nor was he an accessory before the fact. Cash was not an accessory *after* the fact either, because he did nothing to cover up his friend's crime or prevent his apprehension. As for the misprision of felony statutes, did he have a duty to intervene? The answer is no, because under local laws he was not required to do so. As the Clark County, Nevada,

district attorney put it, Cash's inaction "may be a crime in the eyes of God, but not in the eyes of the Nevada legislature." In Nevada, and most other states, there is no "duty to aid" statute.

State legislatures have been reluctant to modify their "no duty to aid" rule. They argue that such a rule would be costly to enforce and would interfere with individual liberty. Only a few states — Vermont, Minnesota, Rhode Island, Colorado, Ohio, Massachusetts, Florida, and Washington — have enacted statutes requiring bystanders to aid someone in peril. Violation of such statutes is generally a petty misdemeanor. Cash's callousness, however, sparked a movement in both Nevada and California to enact a "Sherrice's law," which would require witnesses to intervene and report cases of sexual assault against children.

SUMMARY

The concept of crime is only minimally understood by most people. It goes well beyond the rather imprecise boundaries of "street crime" or the limited issues of violence and theft that are focused on by mass media news and entertainment. In fact, crime includes thousands of offenses, the majority of which do not come to the public's attention.

Drawing on standards of what constitutes "sin" or immoral behavior, people have often defined crime as violations of natural law. However, this definition implies that all individuals have the same definition of right and wrong. Sociologists argue that people's ideas about appropriate and inappropriate behavior are culturally and historically specific. That is, they choose to focus on the processes through which crime comes into being, and they suggest that crime is a social construction that changes over time and in different contexts. Scholars have argued that not all deviant behavior is criminal behavior and that not all criminal behavior is deviant behavior. Rather, criminal and deviant behavior are defined by the culture.

The only precise definition of crime, then, comes from a more legalistic posture. As such, crime is an intentional act or omission in violation of criminal law (statutory and case law), committed without defense or justification, and sanctioned by the state as a felony or misdemeanor.

KEY TERMS

abettor **8**	crime **7**	*mens rea* **9**
accessory after the fact **8**	criminal law **11**	misdemeanor **18**
accessory before the fact **8**	defense **11**	misprision of felony **9**
administrative law **20**	deviance **5**	M'Naghten Rule **12**
case law **11**	Durham Rule **12**	natural law **4**
civil law **11**	entrapment **15**	*Robinson* v. *California* **11**
common law **11**	felony **18**	statutory law **11**
conspiracy **8**	*Lambert* v. *California* **14**	vicarious liability **9**
constitutional law **20**		

QUESTIONS FOR DISCUSSION

1. How do natural law conceptions of "sin," sociological considerations of deviance, and legalistic definitions of crime differ?
2. In the Leopold and Loeb case, when did the conspiracy actually begin? What elements were present?
3. Under what kinds of circumstances would the consent of the victim be an acceptable defense against crime? What are some examples?
4. What should be done about the insanity plea? Why?
5. Should the use of marijuana as "medically necessary" be a defense against crime?

MEDIA RESOURCES

1. **Leopold and Loeb.** See Gilbert Geis and Leigh B. Bienen, *Crimes of the Century* (Boston: Northeastern University Press, 1998). This volume provides a detailed examination of what the authors consider the five most celebrated crimes of the twentieth century, including the Leopold and Loeb murder of Bobby Franks.
2. **Strohmeyer and Cash.** Numerous analyses of this case are on a variety of Web sites, including Time.com, Fortune Online, Court TV Online, and the *Las Vegas Review-Journal.* For best results, enter "strohmeyer AND cash" into your Internet search engine.
3. **The Hinckley Case.** There is a Web home page for this case provided by the University of Missouri – Kansas City, School of Law, which has material on the Hinckley trial, its aftermath, and the insanity plea. Web site address: http://www.law.umkc.edu/faculty/projects/ftrials/hinckley/hb
4. **Crime Files.** *The Crime Files* is a Web site offering an examination of unsolved crimes from around the world. Web address: http://www.emeraldcity.com.crimefiles/crimefiles.htm

NOTES

1. Benjamin, Caren, "Strohmeyer Faces Nevada Charges," *Las Vegas Review-Journal,* July 10, 1997, p. 1; Tim Dahlberg, "Guilty Plea a Surprise in Casino-Slaying Trial," *Seattle Times,* September 8, 1998, p. 1.

2. Howard S. Becker, *Outsiders: Studies in the Sociology of Deviance* (New York: Free Press, 1963), p. 9.

3. Edwin H. Sutherland, *White Collar Crime* (New York: Dryden, 1949), p. 31.

4. Henry Campbell Black, *Black's Law Dictionary,* 4th ed. (St. Paul, Minn.: West, 1968), p. 444.

5. George B. Rush, *Dictionary of Criminal Justice* (Boston: Holbrook, 1977), p. 92.

6. Paul W. Tappan, *Crime, Justice, and Correction* (New York: McGraw-Hill, 1960), p. 10.

7. For the story of the Leopold and Loeb case, see Nathan F. Leopold, *Life Plus Ninety-Nine Years* (New York: Doubleday, 1958).

8. *People* v. *Beardsley,* 113 N.W. 1128 (1907).

9. *Walker* v. *Superior Court,* 44 CrL 2193 (1988).

10. *United States* v. *Perlstein,* C.C.A.N.J. 126 F.2d 789, 798 (1946).

11. *Commonwealth* v. *Koczwara,* 155 A.2d 825 (1959, Penna.).

12. *Robinson* v. *California,* 370 U.S. 660 (1962).

13. Black, *Black's Law Dictionary,* p. 1101.

14. *Durham* v. *United States,* C.A.D.C. 214 F.2d 862 (1954).

15. *National Law Journal,* May 3, 1982, pp. 1, 11 – 13.

16. Valerie P. Hans and Dan Slater, "John Hinckley, Jr., and the Insanity Defense: The Public's Verdict," *Public Opinion Quarterly* 47 (1983): 202 – 212.

17. Lincoln Caplan, *The Insanity Defense and the Trial of John W. Hinckley, Jr.* (Boston: Godine, 1984).

18. *Jones* v. *United States,* 33 CrL 3233 (1983).

19. *State* v. *Elton,* Utah SupCt 35 CrL 2071 (1984).

20. *People* v. *Cash,* Mich SupCt 35 CrL 2345 (1984).

21. *Lambert* v. *California,* 355 U.S. 225 (1957).

22. *Hampton* v. *United States,* 425 U.S. 484 (1976).

23. *Sowell* v. *Florida,* Fl CtApp, 1st Dist., No. 96 – 1317 (2/19/98).

24. State of New York, *Penal Law,* 10.00 (3).

25. Sir Frederick Pollock and F. W. Maitland, *The History of English Law Before the Time of Edward I* (Cambridge: University Press, 1911), p. xxv.

26. Sir James Fitzjames Stephen, *History of the Criminal Law of England,* Vol. 2 (New York: Macmillan, 1883,), p. 75.

27. John H. Wigmore, *A Panorama of the World's Legal Systems* (Washington, D.C.: Washington Law Book Co., 1936), p. 4.

28. Harry Elmer Barnes, *The Repression of Crime: Studies in Historical Penology* (New York: Doran, 1926), pp. 44 – 45.

Elements of
Criminal
Justice

Swastika graffiti on the doors of a church.

L ARAMIE, WYO. — On October 8, 1998, a passing bicyclist spotted what he thought was a scarecrow lashed to the fence of a local ranch. A closer look found that it was the burned, battered, and nearly lifeless body of 22-year-old Matthew Shepard, who had been tied to the fence in near freezing temperatures 18 hours earlier.

An openly gay student at the University of Wyoming, Shepard was allegedly the victim of a hate crime, and the incident quickly awakened much of the nation. When he died 5 days later, the outrage became even greater — spawning vigils, demonstrations, and even calls from President Clinton for passage of federal hate crime legislation. In addition, Shepard's death fueled debates over hate crime laws in a number of jurisdictions, including Wyoming, one of only a few states that still resisted them.[1] But why were there so many debates over hate crime legislation? Shepard's attackers, after all, were arrested on kidnapping, robbery, and murder charges that could bring them the death penalty. And furthermore, what *is* "hate crime" anyway?

The acceptance of homosexuality is the last step in the decline of Gentile civilization.
— *Pat Robertson of the Christian Broadcasting Network, who also warned that hurricanes could hit Orlando, Florida, because of gay events there*

Treason is the only crime specifically mentioned in the Constitution of the United States.

The 1998 killing of Matthew Shepard is referenced here because it illustrates some of the complex issues surrounding the nature and meaning of crime. Although crime may be any conduct that is prohibited by criminal law, it has many designations in legal statutes. Moreover, its dynamics go well beyond the sterile descriptions, classifications, provisions, and subsections that appear in state and federal criminal codes. Crime includes patterns and systems of behavior that occur at one or several points in time. It can involve varying sets of circumstances, social and political environments, and victim-offender relationships. And too, crime can be an isolated event that occurs at only one point in the offender's lifetime; it can reflect the best developed aspects of a well-established career in illicit enterprise; or it can be the product of an organization structured for the pursuit of illegal behavior. In any study of crime it is important to understand not only the content of criminal codes, but the behavior systems that surround the prohibited acts as well—for all of these factors influence the images of crime, societal reactions to crime, and the criminal justice management of crime and criminals.

Studies of behavior systems in crime are generally the subject matter of courses in criminology and are only rarely discussed in basic texts on criminal justice. Yet such designations as "domestic violence," "organized crime," and "hate crime" reflect criminal acts that are undertaken within the context of specific behavior systems. As such, this chapter first discusses the legal aspects of various crimes as they are described in criminal codes and then briefly analyzes a few of the behavior systems within which they often occur.

THE LEGAL ASPECTS OF CRIME CATEGORIES

As noted in Chapter 1, there are literally thousands of acts that are prohibited by law and that are designated as felonies, misdemeanors, violations, and other infractions in federal, state, and local criminal codes. There is also the area of administrative law, which sets forth an alternative list of criminal violations. All these laws result in a potential catalog of behaviors defined as crime that is so long that even their numbers would be difficult to count. Of course, due to space limitations only a few categories of crime can be discussed here, and those chosen for study are the ones that appear most often in our local criminal courts and the ones that receive the most attention from state-level criminal justice agencies. The crime categories to be covered here include the following:

- Criminal homicide
- Assault (except sexual assault)
- Robbery
- Arson
- Burglary
- Other property offenses
- Sex offenses
- Drug law violations
- Crimes against public order and safety

This list, although brief, encompasses more than 90 percent of the criminal law violations handled by state and local criminal justice agencies. This is not to say that other crimes are not serious or important, of course. Treason, for example, the only crime specifically mentioned in the Constitution of the United States, is clearly an act that can threaten the society as a whole. Yet treason is relatively infrequent, and only rarely does it come to the attention

---

How do you feel about homosexual relationships?

	1998	1978
Acceptable for others, but not self	52%	35%

Are homosexual relationships between consenting adults morally wrong, or not a moral issue?

	1998	1978
Yes, morally wrong	48%	53%
Not a moral issue	45%	38%

Do you favor or oppose permitting people who are openly gay or lesbian to serve in the military?

Favor 52%   Oppose 39%

Do you favor or oppose permitting people who are openly gay or lesbian to teach in schools in your community?

Favor 51%   Oppose 42%

SOURCE: Adapted from *Time*/CNN Poll, October 1998.

of a local criminal justice system. By contrast, *kidnapping*—the forcible taking or detaining of a person against his or her will and without lawful authority—is a serious offense that receives little attention in the media but occurs quite frequently, especially in other parts of the world (see Exhibit 2.1).

Kidnapping is the forcible taking or detaining of a person against his or her will and without lawful authority.

Exhibit 2.1 | **International Perspectives on Crime and Justice**
The Abduction of Women and Young Girls in China

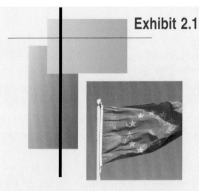

The great majority of kidnapping cases in the United States involve abductions of children by parents who have lost custody through separation or divorce, infants by individuals unable to have children of their own, and both children and adults for sexual exploitation. In addition, but uncommonly, there are instances of kidnapping for ransom. Quite rare in the United States, however, but relatively common in China are abductions of young women and girls for subsequent sale in rural communities to men desperate for wives. In fact, throughout the 1990s no fewer than 10,000 females were abducted each year and sold by traffickers who specialize in this type of kidnapping.

The demand for abducted women is high in China because of a significant shortage of potential wives. The Chinese Academy of Social Sciences estimates that nationwide, there are only 100 females for every 120 males. In rural areas this ratio jumps to 100 women for every 130 men. The reasons for both the gender imbalance and the trafficking are deeply rooted in Chinese culture.

There is the long-standing preference for sons, resulting in selec-tive abortion, infanticide, neglect, and abandonment of baby girls. The imbalance is aggravated, furthermore, by China's strict population policy, which limits parents to one child: Among peasant families in rural areas, it is more practical to have a boy who can do heavy labor in the field. At the same time, in a country where the average wage is only US$60 per

Chang Nan-ping, a dancer and woman activist, wearing a wedding gown as a sign of purity, sits on a chair tied by ropes to a road overpass during her protest against child prostitution in Taiwan.

month, it is less expensive for a man to purchase a wife from a trafficker for 2,000 to 4,000 yuan (about $240 to $480) than to pay a traditional dowry that could run upwards of 10,000 yuan or $1,200. Complicating matters further was the emergence of a market economy in China during the 1980s. Millions of villagers migrated to the cities in search of a better life. Women, especially, left home to marry in wealthier communities while the men stayed behind, tied to the land that they owned.

Currently, as young peasant women arrive by train in China's major cities, they are approached by men speaking their hometown dialects offering work in factories, shops, and households. But instead they are kidnapped and carried off to remote areas, held in captivity, and then sold—sometimes into prostitution but most often into marriage.

Wife-selling has been against the law in China since 1949, and the government has taken a strong stand against the practice. In addition, provincial police departments and the China Women's Federation have organized special task forces devoted to rescuing kidnapped women, and schools have begun to teach their students about the legal rights of women and children. Nevertheless, the practice of kidnapping and wife-selling continues unabated. Moreover, the abducted women remain in the rural villages out of fear of being beaten if they try to leave, or out of a sense of duty if they have borne children to their captors.

SOURCES: Bay Fang, "China's Stolen Wives," *U.S. News and World Report,* October 12, 1998, pp. 35–38; "Stolen Children: A Mother's Story," *Columbia Missouri Tribune Online,* April 19, 1998.

Criminal Homicide

Homicide: The killing of one human being by another.

Homicide is the killing of one human being by another. If it is not excusable or justifiable (see Chapter 1), it is called criminal homicide. Criminal homicide is usually divided by statute into murder and manslaughter, each of which is typically subdivided into many degrees.

Murder: The felonious killing of another human being with malice aforethought.

Murder   Under common law, **murder** was defined as the felonious killing of another human being with malice aforethought. That last phrase implies a definite malicious intent to kill. Common law did not differentiate between murder in the first or second degree, however, and difficulties in proving cases often emerged due to varying interpretations of malice, aforethought, and the two terms taken together as a phrase. In modern criminal codes the law is more specific, and the concepts of malice aforethought, deliberation, and premeditation are all crucially different.

Also, today, murder is generally divided into two degrees: first and second. In most jurisdictions, *first-degree murder* includes the notions of malice aforethought, deliberation, and premeditation. **Malice aforethought** refers to the intent to cause death or serious harm, or to commit any felony whatsoever. **Deliberation** refers to a full and conscious knowledge of the purpose to kill, suggesting that the offender has considered the motives for the act and its consequences. **Premeditation** refers to a design or plan to do something before it is actually done; it is a conscious predecision to commit the offense even though such a decision may occur only moments before the final act.

Malice aforethought: The intent to cause death or serious harm, or to commit any felony whatsoever.

Deliberation: The full and conscious knowledge of the purpose to kill.

Premeditation: A design or conscious decision to do something before it is actually done.

In a number of jurisdictions, statutes also designate murder to be in the first degree depending on the specific circumstances involved. In many states, for example, murder by poisoning automatically carries a first-degree charge, and in some areas the "murder-one" charge is also mandatory if the homicide involved torture, ambush, the use of destructive devices, the killing of a law enforcement officer, or a murder for hire.

Murder in the second degree refers to instances of criminal homicide committed with malice aforethought but without deliberation and premeditation. Murders of this type are often the impulse killings that occur among members of a family, or lovers, often as the outgrowth of an argument or difference of opinion. It is that spur-of-the-moment episode that occurs without planning or full consideration.

Felony-murder doctrine: Principle maintaining that if a death occurs during commission of a felony, the person committing the primary offense can also be charged with murder in the first degree.

The Felony-Murder Doctrine   The common law conception of the felony-murder doctrine maintained that any death resulting from the commission of, or attempt to commit, the crimes of arson, burglary, larceny, rape, or robbery was murder. In many contemporary legal statutes, the **felony-murder doctrine** provides that if a death occurs during the commission of a felony, the person committing the primary offense can also be charged with murder in the first degree.[2] Thus, should an individual commit the felonious crime of arson by setting fire to his place of business, and should one of his employees be killed in that fire, the arsonist would be charged with first-degree murder.

A great deal of confusion surrounds this doctrine. First, the statute is unusual in that although under the law first-degree murder requires malice aforethought, deliberation, and premeditation, with the felony-murder rule these three essential elements are treated as being implied. The offender is seen to act in a deliberate manner and is thus responsible for any natural and probable consequences. A second difficult issue in the doctrine is whether the felon must be the agent of the killing. Thus, if a case of arson results in the death of a firefighter who is attempting to control the blaze, can the arsonist be charged with first-degree murder under the felony-murder doctrine? Many courts say yes. Beyond this hypothetical example, however, the Matthew Shepard case illustrates how the felony-murder rule is applied in most jurisdictions. As noted earlier, both of Shepard's attackers were charged with robbery, kidnapping, and murder. They had admitted that their intent was robbery—that they had pistol-whipped and beaten Shepard, but that their plan had never been to kill him. Using the felony-murder rule, however, the defendants were charged with first-degree murder.

Manslaughter   Manslaughter is an alternative category of criminal homicide, typically charged when a killing occurs under circumstances not severe enough to constitute murder but nevertheless beyond the defenses of justifiable or excusable homicide. **Manslaughter** is distinguished from murder in that the latter implies malice while manslaughter does not. Furthermore, some jurisdictions divide manslaughter into as many as four degrees, although most differentiate only between voluntary and involuntary manslaughter.

Voluntary manslaughter refers to intentional killings committed in the absence of malice and premeditated design. Its essential elements include a legally adequate provocation resulting in a killing done during the heat of passion. Thus, if two persons become involved in a quarrel and one kills the other, the offender can be charged with voluntary manslaughter. In contrast, *involuntary manslaughter* exists when a death results unintentionally as the consequence of some unlawful act or through negligence.

To cite an example, if a motorist is driving while intoxicated and loses control of the vehicle, killing a pedestrian, involuntary manslaughter could be charged. In this case, the killing would be unintentional, yet the motorist's intoxicated condition while driving is a violation of the law. (In some jurisdictions, however, more serious charges might be applied.) In 1998, for example, a Durham, North Carolina, man was convicted of first-degree murder and sentenced to life imprisonment without parole for a drunk-driving related killing.[3] A recent case in DeKalb County, Georgia, furthermore, demonstrates how broadly the involuntary manslaughter statutes can be interpreted. A dog owner was convicted of involuntary manslaughter and sentenced to 5 years in prison after three of his pit bull terriers killed a 4-year-old boy.[4] His prosecution was based on the *doctrine of implied malice,* in which a person can be convicted of criminal homicide if "wanton disregard for human life" can be proved.

As a final note here, since voluntary manslaughter can refer to deaths resulting from unlawful acts, it must be differentiated from the felony-murder doctrine. In jurisdictions where all homicides occurring during the commission of a felony are classified as murder, then involuntary manslaughter can apply only to misdemeanor cases. Also, in many cases the differences that separate second-degree murder from voluntary manslaughter are not always immediately clear. Both offenses, for example, can relate to crimes of passion, and what differentiates one from another is often a reflection of the degree of passion involved, the court's interpretation of the circumstances of the killing, and the particular legal codes that define the boundaries of the two offenses in a given jurisdiction.

Assault

Contrary to popular notions, **assault** does not refer to the infliction of an injury on another person. Rather, in legal terms, it is simply an intentional attempt or threat to physically injure another. Battery is the nonlethal culmination of an assault. Thus, **assault and battery** is an assault carried into effect by doing some violence to the victim. Aggravated assault refers to an assault made with the intent to commit murder, rape, robbery, or to inflict serious bodily harm; simple assault is one in which the intended harm fails or where no serious harm was ever intended.

Manslaughter: The unlawful killing of another, without malice.

Voluntary manslaughter refers to intentional killing in the absence of malice and premeditated design, whereas *involuntary* manslaughter exists when a death results unintentionally as the consequence of some unlawful act or through negligence.

The doctrine of implied malice holds that a person can be convicted of criminal homicide if "wanton disregard for human life" can be proven.

Assault: An intentional attempt or threat to physically injure another.

Assault and battery: An assault carried into effect by doing some violence to the victim.

Menacing

Mayhem

Jostling

Although aggravated assaults are usually felonies and simple assaults are misdemeanors, many jurisdictions separate the two according to degree of assault rather than name. Furthermore, some states have defined specific kinds of assault as distinct offenses. For example, while assault in the third degree can generally be construed as simple assault and a misdemeanor, other categories of nonfelonious assault might include *menacing* (touching a person with an instrument or part of the body, causing offense or alarm to that person).[5] Similarly, although *mayhem* (willfully maiming or crippling a person) can be considered a serious and aggravated assault, in some states it is classified as a separate felony.

Perhaps the most peculiar of the categories of assault are to be found in the jostling statutes. *Jostling* refers to the pushing or crowding of an individual, and it is generally believed that pickpockets jostle their victims (bump into and throw them off balance) while stealing their money. In New York the jostling statute enables police officers to arrest pickpockets even though they are not caught stealing.[6] In fact, this statute is so widely used in some areas that many career pickpockets have numerous arrests for jostling and few for actually stealing (see Exhibit 2.2). It might be added, however, that expert pickpockets rarely jostle their victims. As one "class cannon" commented on the subject:

> No, you never throw them the jostle. . . . All that does is wake up the mark and tell him that something's happening. . . . If a cop knows you and thinks you're going to score, he'll grab you and call it jostling, even though you did nothing.[7]

Robbery

Robbery: The felonious taking of the money or goods of another, from his person or in his presence and against his will, through the use or threat of force and violence.

Robbery is the felonious taking of the money or goods of another, from his person or in his presence and against his will, through the use or threat of force and violence. As such, robbery is an offense involving aspects of both theft and assault, and because the use or threat of violence is present it is generally classified as a crime against the person. The specific elements necessary for a robbery to take place are clear in its definition: (1) the felonious taking (with the intent to steal) (2) of the money or goods of another (3) from his person or in his presence (or in his custody, care, or control) (4) against his will (5) through the use or threat of force and violence. If one or more of these elements were missing there would be no robbery, but rather, some other crime or no crime at all. If the use or threat of force were absent, for example, the crime would be one of theft.

Some jurisdictions divide robbery into degrees. Robbery in the first degree is charged when the offender is armed with a deadly weapon or dangerous instrument. Others have specific statutes that recognize unarmed robbery, armed robbery, train robbery, safe and vault robbery, and most recently, carjacking.

Arson

Arson: The willful or malicious burning or attempt to burn, with or without intent to defraud, any dwelling, other building, vehicle, or personal property.

Common law conceptions of **arson** referred to the malicious burning of the dwelling of another, but modern statutes have extended the parameters of arson in a variety of ways. First, while arson originally carried the ideas of fire and burning, most jurisdictions now include the use of explosives. Second, contemporary statutes include not only dwellings, but also other types of buildings, as well as the property of the arsonist if there is an attempt to defraud an insurer or if the building is occupied. Thus, a person is guilty of arson when he or she intentionally damages a building by starting a fire or causing an explosion.[8]

Arson is a felony in all jurisdictions, and most often is divided into at least two degrees and sometimes three. In general, if the premises set afire are occupied, the charge will be first-degree arson. If they are unoccupied, the case will be one of second-degree arson. A person is guilty of arson in the third degree if the premises burned are his or her own, if they are unoccupied, and if the purpose is to defraud the insurer.

From a legalistic perspective, the major problem in arson cases is the element of criminal agency, or *intent.* A conviction depends on the state's proving that an accused had both the intent and opportunity to commit arson, which is difficult in many cases. Studies have shown that the reasons for arson are both numerous and obscure, and sometimes hard to detect. There are "revenge firesetters," for example, whose crimes result from anger, hatred, or jealousy in personal relationships; there are "excitement firesetters," who simply enjoy watching fires and the operations of fire equipment; there are "insurance-claim firesetters," who incinerate business property for its insurance value; there are "vandalism firesetters," who set buildings ablaze as part of adolescent peer-group activities; there are "criminal vindication firesetters," who use arson for hiding the evidence of other crimes.[9] To these might be added the "professional torches" who incinerate buildings for a fee, the firebombers of activist and political terrorist organizations, the large number of skid row vagrants who seem to be overrepresented among those arrested for arson, and the many other types for whom intent and motivation are not altogether clear.

Burglary

At one time, burglary was viewed as a crime against the habitation—that is, an invasion of the home—and referred only to the breaking and entering of a dwelling, at night, with the intent to commit a felony therein. The term comes directly from English common law and has its roots in the Saxon words *burgh* ("house") and *laron* ("theft"). The offense has been materially broadened in current statutes: It includes structures other than a dwelling; it is applicable whether the illegal entry occurs during the night or day; and it can involve an intended felony or misdemeanor.

The term **breaking and entering** is often used synonymously with burglary, but this can be misleading since both breaking and entry need not be formally present for a burglary to occur. "Breaking" suggests forcible entry,

Breaking and entering: The forcible entry into a building or structure, with the intent to commit a crime therein.

© 1999 Harley Schwadron

Exhibit 2.2

Research in Crime and Justice
On the Grift at the Super Bowl

For centuries, pickpockets have congregated to work the crowds at sporting events. As early as the days of Shakespeare's youth, pickpocketing was a full-time profession common in London during the terms of court when thousands of citizens were drawn to the city for business and pleasure. The thieves frequented bowling alleys, dicing houses, and the resorts, assemblies, plays, and fairs where unsuspecting visitors were easy prey. The pickpockets worked in mobs of two, three, or four members, each playing a specific role in the total operation: There was the selection of the *mark* (victim), the locating of the money or valuables on his or her person (*fanning*), maneuvering the mark into position, the act of theft, and the passing of the stolen property. In more recent times, the same phenomenon has been apparent in New York, Chicago, Philadelphia, and other major American cities, and the pattern of theft has been identical.

Although the literature over the years has referenced various types of pickpockets, ranging from the rank amateur to the seasoned expert, both history and folklore have described the pickpocket as a professional thief and "class cannon." As one professional described the term:

Class cannon means experience, skill, connections and a sense for knowing when to steal. . . . It means that the *cannon* [picking pockets] is part of your life. . . . It means that you're not one of those amateurs who spend their time *grinding up nickels and dimes* [inept stealing for low stakes].

Field studies suggest that class cannons continued to operate in many American cities at least through the beginning of the 1980s. Research indicates that every December, when thousands of tourists filled their wallets and traveled to South Florida for a winter vacation, along with them came a small flock of professional pickpockets who considered the Miami area a pickpocket mecca. My entree to the Miami pickpocket community occurred in 1972, and for a decade I followed them on a sporadic basis—watching them operate and becoming familiar with their lifestyle. One of their specialties was traveling to the Super Bowl each year to steal from those attending the games.

According to the pickpocket informants, stealing at football games was nothing new. The annual journey of Miami's class cannons to Super Bowl city, however, at least for most of those interviewed, did not begin until 1977. According to one:

Sure, we know that there are *dips* [pickpockets] everywhere, and we know that from the day of the first football playoff game —wherever and whenever it was—the local amateurs and pros hit the stadiums. But for

but the mere opening of a closed door is sufficient to constitute a breaking. Furthermore, simply remaining in a building until after it has closed, for some criminal purpose, can also constitute a burglary, even though there is no actual breaking aspect. "Entry" is the more essential element; it can be limited to the insertion of any part of the body or any instrument or weapon and still be sufficient to constitute a burglary.

Pittsburgh Steelers' Lynn Swann dives as he catches a pass from quarterback Terry Bradshaw during Super Bowl X action held at the Orange Bowl in Miami, Florida, on January 18, 1976, against the Dallas Cowboys. As fans stood up to watch the play, pickpockets stole their wallets.

most of us here, the idea of jacking across the country for one game didn't come up till a few years ago. Here we were down in the South hitting every Dolphins game at the Orange Bowl. The day's work was pretty good—$200–$400 a game. Then when the year's biggest sporting event came to town, we noticed a difference that day . . . a different kind of fan . . . richer, preoccupied, crazier, and a lot of pandemonium for 2–3 days.

This individual went on to describe how, over the Super Bowl week-

end, the total thefts of his mob of three pickpockets amounted to over $3,000.

Despite the presence of the class cannons at the Super Bowl each year and their winter congregations in Miami, evidence has suggested that these expert pickpockets have all but disappeared. It was once estimated that in 1945 there were some 5,000 to 6,000 class cannons operating in the United States, with a reduction to about 1,000 by 1955. By 1965, according to one expert cannon from New York City's Times Square area, the total number suffered

even further reductions. In 1976, a 62-year-old cannon operating in downtown Miami stated:

> Each year you'll see about fifty of us pass through Miami; . . . it's a tradition. You go up to New York and Philly in the summer, and to Chicago in the fall, and you see the same guys most of the time. . . . I'd say if you put all of us together you couldn't fill an old-time nickelodeon . . . maybe three hundred, maybe four.

And in 1982, another commented:

> There's just a handful of the experts left. Most of what you see now are bums, amateurs and Colombians. . . . The Colombian dips are what you see most . . . but they have no class.

The decline of the class cannon was the result of many factors, but primarily because the profession had become unprofitable. Better communication systems among law enforcement agencies, habitual offender laws, and the bureaucratization of the criminal justice system combined to increase the arrest, conviction, and incarceration rates of pickpockets. The result was that there were few new recruits to the profession. The subculture began to decay, leaving behind only the seasoned old-timers who had no other profession to turn to, yet had enough accumulated experience to survive. Given this process, it is likely that the cannon will continue to atrophy until its more unique qualities become only brief references within the history of crime.

SOURCE: Adapted from James A. Inciardi, "On the Grift at the Super Bowl: Pickpockets and the NFL," in *Career Criminals,* ed. Gordon P. Waldo (Beverly Hills: Sage, 1983), pp. 31–41.

Burglary is another offense that appears in any number of degrees and varieties. A person is typically guilty of burglary in the third degree when he or she knowingly enters or remains unlawfully in a building with the intent to commit a crime therein. The burglary becomes an offense in the second degree if the building happens to be a dwelling, or if the offender is armed, or if there is physical injury to any person who is not a participant in the crime.

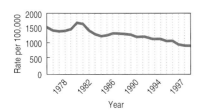

**Burglary in the U.S.,
1978 – 1997**

SOURCE: *Uniform Crime Reports.*

MIAMI'S BURGLARS, JEWEL THIEVES, AND FOLK HEROES

Miami has always had a problem with burglars, particularly those who target the diamonds, rubies, and sapphires of the city's many wealthy residents. But curiously, many of the jewel thieves have also become local folk heroes. The first was Jack (Murph the Surf) Murphy, the surfing champion who stole the 563-carat Star of India sapphire in 1964. Then there was John Henry (The Lizard) Coulthurst in the 1970s, who pulled up to waterfront mansions in his skiff, then scaled their balconies with a padded hook and a boat ladder. Most recently there was Derrick (Spiderman) James, a former Army paratrooper suspected of stealing more than $6 million in cash and jewelry in more than 130 high-rise burglaries. In 1998, however, Spiderman's career came to an end when a video surveillance camera taped his exit from one of his burglary sites.

SOURCE: Adapted from *New York Times,* December 8, 1998, p. A21.

Theft: The unlawful taking, possession, or use of another's property, without the use or threat of force, and with the intent to deprive permanently.

"I said no to drugs, but I couldn't say no to drug money."

Burglary in the first degree involves unlawful entry or remaining in a dwelling at night, combined with the offender being armed or causing physical injury.

Since there is a criminal intent aspect to burglary — that is, unlawful entry for some criminal purpose — two additional points must be stressed. First, even if the purpose of the entry involves only a minor crime, such as petty theft or some other misdemeanor, the burglary has been consummated and a felony has been committed. Further, the offender can be charged not only with burglary, but with the other offense as well. Second, the criminal intent aspect has resulted in a number of jurisdictions structuring their laws so that attempted burglary is included in the definition of burglary.[10]

Property Offenses

Attempting to approach the full range of property offenses in some systematic way is difficult, for most jurisdictions use alternative ways of defining and categorizing them. In Louisiana, for example, the technical dimensions of the theft statute are quite broad and cover a multitude of property crimes, including what other states may separately define as larceny, embezzlement, and fraud. Further, while many states may have a broad *larceny* statute, which refers to the taking and carrying away of the personal property of another with intent to deprive permanently, other states, such as Delaware, define shoplifting — a clear instance of larceny — as a separate offense.[11] In Ohio and several other jurisdictions, theft statutes include the unlawful use of a person's service.[12] In general, however, **theft** seems to be the broadest of terms relating to property offenses and can be loosely defined as the unlawful taking, possession, or use of another's property, without the use or threat of force, and with the intent to deprive permanently. Within the boundaries of this definition, theft would include the following:

Larceny: The taking and carrying away of the personal property of another with the intent to deprive permanently.

Shoplifting: The theft of goods, wares, or merchandise from a store or shop.

Pickpocketing: The theft of money or articles directly from the garments of the victim.

Embezzlement: The fraudulent appropriation or conversion of money or property by an employee, trustee, or other agent to whom the possession of such money or property was entrusted.

Fraud: Theft by false pretenses; the appropriation of money or property by trick or misrepresentation, or by creating or reinforcing a false impression as to some present or past fact that would adversely affect the victim's judgment of a transaction.

Forgery: The making or altering of any document or instrument with the intent to defraud.

Counterfeiting: The making of imitation money and obligations of the government or corporate body.

Confidence games: The obtaining of money or property by means of deception through the confidence a victim places in the offender.

Blackmail: The taking of money or property through threats of accusation or exposure.

Plagiarism: The copying or adopting of the literary, musical, or artistic work of another and publishing or producing it as one's own original work.

Removal of landmarks: The relocation of monuments or other markings that designate property lines or boundaries for the purpose of fraudulently reducing the owner's interest or holdings in lands and estates.

Criminal bankruptcy: The fraudulent declaration of a person's excessive indebtedness or insolvency in an effort to avoid partial or full payment of one's debts.

Usury: The taking of or contracting to take interest on a loan at a rate that exceeds the level established by law.

Ransom: The demanding of money for the redemption of captured persons or property.

Buying, receiving, or possessing stolen goods: The purchase, receipt, or possession of any property or goods known to be stolen.

This list may be longer or shorter depending on how an offense is interpreted in a particular jurisdiction. Furthermore, list entries are by no means mutually exclusive. What has been defined as counterfeiting may appear under forgery statutes; confidence games are clearly special varieties of fraud; and shoplifting and pickpocketing are forms of larceny. The most attention is devoted here to **larceny,** since this classification includes many types of theft, and because, at least in terms of official criminal statistics, larceny is the most common of all major crimes.

Given the legal definition provided in the previous list, the crime of larceny includes five essential elements: (1) the taking (2) and carrying away (3) of the personal property (4) of another (5) with the intent to deprive

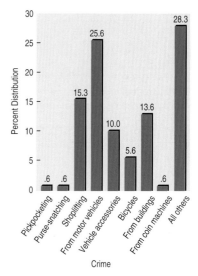

U.S. Larceny-Theft in 1997

SOURCE: *Uniform Crime Reports.*

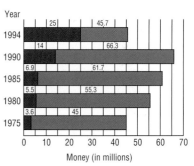

Counterfeit Money in the United States (in millions)

SOURCE: U.S. Secret Service.

Larceny: The taking and carrying away of the personal property of another, with the intent to deprive permanently.

Carrier's Case: The 1473 legal ruling whereby a person in possession of another's packaged goods, who opens the package and misappropriates its contents, is guilty of larceny.

Pear's Case: The 1779 legal ruling whereby a person who has legal control of another's property, and converts that property so as to deprive the owner of his possessory rights, is guilty of larceny.

permanently. The element of taking suggests that the offender has no legal right to possession of the property in question. In this sense, *taking* involves a trespass in that the possession of property has been wrongfully obtained. And this point highlights the difficult distinctions among *possession, custody,* and *control* as they relate to the parameters of larceny. The renowned **Carrier's Case** of 1473 provided an initial interpretation of this distinction when a mover, entrusted with the task of transporting bales of wool dye and thus having legal custody of them, broke into several bales and took part of the contents. From this case came the time-honored doctrine of "breaking bulk," which maintained that although the mover or carrier had legal custody of the property, his breaking into the bales was a trespass against the possessory interests of the owner, and as such was larceny.[13] In 1779, the famous **Pear's Case** approached an alternative situation in which the accused hired a horse from a livery stable, gave the owner a false address, and then took the animal to a local market and sold it as his own. The legal issue was that the stableman had willingly delivered the animal and that Pear had not used force or stealth to obtain its custody. The court ruled that it was larceny "by trick." The horse had been hired for a purpose that the accused never intended to execute, and as such, his taking of the horse with the intention of selling it was a trespass against the stableman's right of possession.[14] The point, then, is that a taking can occur even when a person has authorized custody or control of an object if his or her conversion of that object ultimately deprives someone else of their possessory rights.

The *carrying away* aspect of larceny, also known as "asportation," involves the removal of the property from the place it formerly occupied. The distance of movement, however, need not be significant. The removal of a wallet from a pocket, for example, represents complete asportation.

Personal property, as the third element of larceny, refers to anything that is capable of ownership except land or things permanently affixed to it. The property must also be that of *another,* since larceny is a crime against possession and therefore cannot occur with what one already possesses.

The final element of larceny involves *intent*—intent to permanently deprive. If the intent is to deprive only temporarily, then there is no larceny, although many states have structured their criminal codes to cover these latter situations with such lesser offenses as unauthorized use of a vehicle and misappropriation of property. Whether the intent is to deprive permanently or only temporarily, however, is a question of fact on which the court must rule, and the distinction between permanent and temporary can be a matter of interpretation.

The distinction between larceny as a felony or misdemeanor, or "grand larceny" versus "petty larceny," is of a statutory nature. The dividing point ranges from as little as $50 in Oklahoma, to as much as $2,500 in Arkansas.[15] At a value below these amounts the larceny is a misdemeanor, while anything valued at or above the statutory figure is a felony.

Sex Offenses

The scope of illegal sexual activity is quite broad in American society. This is due in part to the legacy of the early Puritan codes and the Holy Scriptures; to attempts to maintain standards of public decency through the legislation of morality; to requirements of community consensus as to an individual's right to sexual self-determination; and to an effort to protect those who are too young or otherwise unable to make decisions as to their own sexual conduct. Although in recent years the codes regulating many sexual activities, such as contraception and *miscegenation* (marriage or cohabitation between white and nonwhite persons), have been eliminated or severely limited, the list is still long and includes the following:

Forcible rape: Having sexual intercourse with a female against her will and through the use or threat of force or fear.

Statutory rape: Having sexual intercourse with a female under a stated age (usually 16 or 18, but sometimes 14), with or without her consent.

Seduction: The act of enticing or luring a woman of chaste character to engage in sexual intercourse by fraudulently promising to marry her or by some other false promise.

Fornication: Sexual intercourse between unmarried persons.

Adultery: Sexual intercourse between a man and woman, at least one of whom is married to someone else.

Incest: Sexual intercourse between parent and child, between any sibling pair, or between close blood relatives.

Sodomy: Certain acts of sexual relationship including fellatio (oral intercourse with the male sex organ), cunnilingus (oral intercourse with the female sex organ), buggery (penetration of the anus), homosexuality (sexual relations between members of the same sex), bestiality (sexual intercourse with an animal), pederasty (unnatural intercourse between a man and boy), and necrophilia (sexual intercourse with a corpse).

Indecent exposure (exhibitionism): Exposure of the sexual organs in a public place.

Lewdness: Degenerate conduct in sexual behavior that is so well known that it may result in the corruption of public decency.

Obscenity: That which is offensive to morality or chastity and is calculated to corrupt the mind and morals of those exposed to it.

Pornography: Literature, art, film, pictures, or other articles of a sexual nature that are considered obscene by a community's moral standards.

Bigamy: The act of marrying while a former marriage is still legally in force.

In 1938, singer Frank Sinatra was arrested in Hackensack, N.J., for the crime of seduction. Although the case was ultimately dismissed, his initial charge stated that: "On the second and ninth days of November 1938, under the promise of marriage, Mr. Sinatra did then and there have sexual intercourse with the said complainant, who was then and there a single female of good repute."

Polygamy: The practice of having several spouses.

Prostitution: The offering of sexual relations for monetary or other gain.

Child molesting: The handling, fondling, or other contact of a sexual nature with a child.

Sexual assault: Any sexual contact with another person (other than a spouse) that occurs without the consent of the victim or is offensive to the victim.

Voyeurism (peeping): The surreptitious observance of an exposed body or sexual act.

Although the offenses of forcible rape, incest, and child molesting appear in all jurisdictions throughout the United States in one form or another, not all of the sexual behaviors listed here are universally prohibited. Fornication, seduction, and pornography are disappearing from the penal codes of many state and local areas; indecent exposure, in the form of topless dancing or bathing and live sex shows, has been decriminalized in several jurisdictions; and prostitution is legal in several parts of Nevada. However, American sodomy statutes, although neither uniform nor universal, persist in modern criminal codes. The great majority of sodomy arrests that occur in the United States involve men who have sex with men caught in the act of fellatio in public restrooms, parks, and other public places. Other sodomous acts, however, can be and are prosecuted. Even acts of fellatio and cunnilingus between husband and wife have resulted in criminal processing. Furthermore, violation of the sodomy statutes is a felony in a few jurisdictions (see Exhibit 2.3). Similarly, adultery statutes remain in force in most states, and in Alabama, Wisconsin, Michigan, and Oklahoma, adultery continues to be a felony.[16]

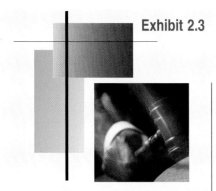

Exhibit 2.3

Legal Perspectives on Crime and Justice
Sodomy Laws in the United States

When Michael Hardwick looked up from the privacy of his Atlanta apartment one day in 1982, he was stunned to see a police officer standing in his doorway. "What are you doing in my bedroom?" he asked the officer. Mr. Hardwick, a gay man, was then arrested and later convicted for sodomy, even though the act had taken place in the privacy of his own home. The Georgia law, which dated from 1833, defined sodomy as "any sexual act involving the sex organs of one person and the mouth or anus of another." When the case when to the U.S. Supreme Court in 1986, Georgia Attorney General Michael Bowers attacked "homosexual sodomy" as "anathema to the basic units of our society— marriage and the family." The critical constitutional question raised by the attorney for Mr. Hardwick, on the other hand, "was not what Michael Hardwick was doing in his bedroom, but rather what the state of Georgia was doing there." By a 5-to-4 majority, however, the Supreme Court upheld Georgia's sodomy law, which applied equally to both gays and heterosexuals.

In 1998, some 12 years after the Supreme Court decision in *Bowers* v. *Hardwick,* Georgia's own supreme court invalidated the state's sodomy law by ruling that private consensual sodomy between adults is protected under the privacy rights of the Georgia constitution. Despite this ruling, 19 states still have antisodomy laws of some kind. Fourteen prohibit both homosexual and heterosexual sodomy, while five ban only same-sex sodomy. And interestingly, during the same week as the decision by the Georgia Supreme Court, two Texas men were convicted of violating that state's 119-year-old, and rarely enforced, sodomy law.

SOURCES: *Bowers* v. *Hardwick,* 30 CrL 3261 (1986); *Powell* v. *State,* Ga SupCt, No. S98A0755 (11/23/93); *New York Times,* November 21, 1998, p. A16.

Forcible rape is the one sex offense about which there is the most concern, and it is a crime whose statutes are often quite peculiar. For more than a century in the United States, rape was defined as "the unlawful carnal knowledge (sexual penetration) of a female without her consent and against her will." As such, the law of rape defined men as the only possible offenders and women as the only possible victims. Although this definition persists in at least a dozen jurisdictions, most states have adopted more gender-neutral language, defining **rape** as sexual penetration without consent. However, because women are the most common victims of rape, few discussions of the crime focus on male victims. Yet there is extensive evidence that the raping of men is not uncommon (see Exhibit 2.4).

Rape: Sexual penetration without consent.

Rape is considered the most serious of the sex offenses, but prostitution seems to be the most visibly common. Prostitution is sex for hire, implying some gain, typically money. It includes not only sexual intercourse, but also any other form of sexual conduct with another person for a fee. Where prostitution is illegal, it is typically a misdemeanor or some lesser offense.

Related to prostitution is *procuring,* also referred to as pandering or "pimping." Procuring involves promoting prostitution through the operation of a house of prostitution or managing the activities and contacts of one or more prostitutes for a percentage of their earnings. Procuring is most often a felony at the state level, and in some circumstances can be prosecuted under federal law.

Procuring

Drug Law Violations

The federal and state statutes that regulate the nonmedical use of drugs as well as control the manufacture, sale, and distribution of "dangerous" drugs are relatively recent, having evolved only during the twentieth century. Although a few local ordinances focused on certain types of drug use and sale during the late 1800s, the *Pure Food and Drug Act of 1906* was the first piece of federal legislation that targeted the distribution of what were considered dangerous drugs. The purpose of the law was to limit the uncontrolled manufacture of patent medicines and over-the-counter drugs containing cocaine, opium, morphine, and other narcotics. The *Harrison Act of 1914,* initially a revenue measure designed to make narcotics transferrals a matter of record, evolved into a sweeping law that defined as criminal any manufacture, prescription, transfer, or possession of narcotics by persons who were not authorized to pay a tax on them.[17] In 1937, the *Marijuana Tax Act* resulted in a total prohibition of marijuana, and during the 1950s a series of federal statutes were passed to increase the penalties associated with the sale and use of narcotics, marijuana, and cocaine.[18]

The *Comprehensive Drug Abuse and Control Act of 1970,* in effect since May 1, 1971, brought together under one law most of the drug controls that had been created since the Harrison Act of 1914. Title II of the new law, known separately as the *Controlled Substances Act,* categorized certain substances into five "schedules" and defined the offenses and penalties associated with the illegal manufacture, distribution, and dispensing of any drug in each schedule.

Prior to the enactment of the Controlled Substances Act in 1970, federal and state drug laws often varied greatly from one another, and the penalties for many drug violations varied considerably from one jurisdiction to another. Many state marijuana laws, for example, specified that the penalties for marijuana should be the same as those for heroin, and in at least 19 jurisdictions there was no distinction in the law between the penalties for the mere possession of one marijuana cigarette and those for the sale of large quantities of heroin. By 1972, however, the majority of the states adopted the provisions

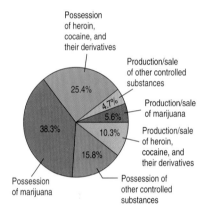

Drug Law Arrests, 1997

SOURCE: *Uniform Crime Reports.*

The Controlled Substances Act

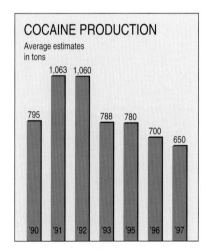

Cocaine Production

SOURCE: Bureau for International Narcotics and Law Enforcement Affairs.

Exchanging drugs for money.

Exhibit 2.4 **Gender Perspectives on Crime and Justice**
Men as Victims of Rape

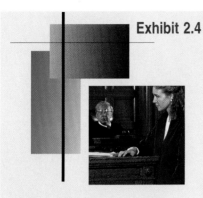

For most Americans, *rape* is a gender-specific term. That is, virtually every time the stand-alone word *rape* is used, it is automatically presumed that the victim is a female and the perpetrator is a male. This would appear to be logical, furthermore, because crime statistics indicate that as many as 90 percent of all rape victims are women and young girls. Moreover, until only recently rape laws defined women as the only possible victims and men as the only offenders. Even today, in 12 states—Alabama, Georgia, Idaho, Kansas, Maine, Maryland, Missouri, New York, North Carolina, Oregon, Utah, and Virginia—rape is defined as "the forced penetration of the vagina by the penis," or words to that effect. By contrast, like conversations about male nurses, female judges, and women's basketball, discussions of male-on-male rape result in gender-specific terminology; that is, "rape" becomes *male rape.* And furthermore, the rape of men by women is likely the least reported and most unaddressed violent crime.

Research suggests that between 5 percent and 10 percent of all reported rapes in any given year involve male victims. The rapes occur most often in all-male institutions, such as prisons, military barracks, college dormitories and fraternities, mental health institutions, nursing homes, boarding schools, and monasteries. The rapists are typically white, heterosexual men in their middle to late twenties, and their victims are generally the same age or younger. Men rape other men for the same reasons that they rape women—out of anger or an attempt to overpower, humiliate, and degrade their victims, rather than out of lust, passion, or sexual desire. Anal penetration is the most common form of assault, followed by oral penetration. Finally, men who rape tend to do so within their own social, cultural, or economic group, or rape those over whom they have power. For these reasons it is not surprising that the incidence of gay men raping heterosexual men is relatively low.

Little is known about female-on-male rape. In fact, in the once widely read textbook *Criminal Law for Policemen,* authors Neil C. Chamelin and Kenneth R. Evans suggested that a female cannot actually rape a male. This assumption, however, is both naive and incorrect. There are many women who can overpower men,

and the biology of the male anatomy makes an erection through physical stimulation readily possible, even when sexual interest is totally absent. In fact, in some men and boys, states of pain, anxiety, panic, or fear have been known to cause a spontaneous erection and ejaculation. However, although it is unlikely that any man raped by a woman would bring the crime to the attention of the authorities for fear of ridicule, this does not mean it does not happen. Numerous such cases have indeed been documented.

Although there is no single, typical, emotional response that every man will exhibit after he has been raped, the range of responses is not unlike those seen among female victims of rape. Some may appear calm and rational, others may exhibit anger, depression, or hysteria. Still others may withdraw socially or sexually or appear nonresponsive. Rape trauma syndrome, a form of post-traumatic stress disorder, is also seen. In the majority of cases, furthermore, male rape victims experience stigma, shame, embarrassment, and self-blame as they begin to cope with what has happened to them. And as a final point, the range of symptoms is the same regardless of whether the perpetrator was another man, or a woman.

SOURCES: Michael Scarce, *Male on Male Rape: The Hidden Toll of Stigma and Shame* (New York: Plenum, 1997); Neil C. Chamelin and Kenneth R. Evans, *Criminal Law for Policemen* (Englewood Cliffs, N.J.: Prentice-Hall, 1976), p. 109; *Miami Herald,* September 17, 1982, p. 1B; *Psychology Today,* September 1983, pp. 74–75.

of the Controlled Substances Act, thus helping standardize drug laws in most parts of the nation.

In contrast, the laws in jurisdictions that have not adopted the full text of the federal model vary considerably. While the federal penalties for the possession of even small quantities of marijuana specify probation or a sentence of up to 1 year imprisonment and/or fines up to $5,000, penalties in some jurisdictions range from as little as a citation without arrest (Oregon), to imprisonment up to 10 years in Georgia, Texas, and Louisiana.[19]

This series of photos shows a drug sale in Detroit. The buyer indicates how much he wants and places his money in a cup attached to a long piece of twine, which is raised by the drug dealer. The dealer then throws the crack to the buyer standing below.

Crimes Against Public Order and Safety

The final category—crimes against public order and safety, or public order crimes—tends to be a rather sweeping collection of offenses, mostly misdemeanors, that nevertheless account for a considerable portion of criminal justice activity. The criminal codes that have been structured for the maintenance of public order and safety tend to vary considerably from place to place, but the following crimes all seem to appear in one form or another in most jurisdictions:

Disorderly conduct: Any act that tends to disturb the public peace, scandalize the community, or shock the public sense of morality.

Disturbing the peace: Any interruption of the peace, quiet, and good order of a neighborhood or community.

Breach of the peace: The breaking of the public peace by any riotous, forcible, or unlawful proceeding.

Harassment: Any act that serves to annoy or alarm another person.

Drunkenness: The condition of being under the influence of alcohol to the extent that it renders one helpless.

Public intoxication: The condition of being severely under the influence of alcohol or drugs in a public place to the degree that one may endanger persons or property.

Loitering: Idling or lounging upon a street or other public way in a manner that serves to interfere with or annoy passersby.

Criminal nuisance: Any conduct that is unreasonable and that endangers the health and safety of others.

Vagrancy: The condition of being idle and having no visible means of support.

Desecration: The defacing, damaging, or mistreatment of a public structure, monument, or place of worship or burial.

Driving while intoxicated (DWI) or driving under the influence (DUI): The operation of a motor vehicle while under the influence of alcohol or illegal drugs.

Gambling: The playing or operation of any game of chance that involves money or property of any value that is prohibited by the criminal code.

Violation of privacy: Any unlawful trespass, interception, observation, eavesdropping, or other surveillance that serves to infringe on the private rights of another.

In recent years, the constitutionality of many criminal codes designed for the preservation of public order and safety has been challenged. Numerous cases of disorderly conduct, breach of the peace, and vagrancy have come before the Supreme Court on the grounds that they violate First Amendment protections of free speech and assembly or because they are too vague. Furthermore, the use of such statutes as mechanisms for penalizing those who are viewed in some communities as political and social undesirables has been questioned as a violation of rights of due process. Nevertheless, these statutes remain in force in the criminal codes of most American jurisdictions, and arrests for vagrancy and disorderly conduct alone approach 1 million annually.

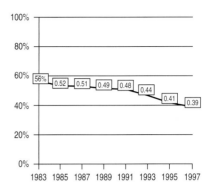

Drunk Driving Deaths in the U.S., 1983–1997

Almost 40% of the 41,967 traffic fatalities in the U.S. in 1997 were alcohol related. While this percentage is a cause for concern, it has not changed dramatically over the past 15 years.

SOURCE: National Highway Traffic Safety Administrator, 1998.

BEHAVIOR SYSTEMS IN CRIME

The preceding discussion provides a basis for understanding the legal definitions and boundaries of the major categories of crime. However, in their descriptions of prohibited acts and their delineations of penalties, what the criminal codes cannot do is offer some insight and explanation of the social and behavioral contexts in which certain crimes tend to occur, the lifestyles associated with particular offenses, and the relationship of certain criminal acts to the wider social order. Further, the criminal law tells us nothing of the differences in styles and patterns of crime, of the various types of offenders, of victim-offender relationships, of varying techniques for committing crimes, and of how all of these affect the criminal justice management of crime. In short, each variety of crime has two important aspects—its legal description as stated in the law, and the behavior system that brings it into being. Consider, for example, the crime of shoplifting, which penal codes define as the theft of money, goods, or other merchandise from a store or shop. As such, the law is quite clear as to what may constitute shoplifting. But the law cannot help us understand the numerous behavior patterns associated with shoplifting. For example, there are many pensioners, students, and others for whom an instance of shoplifting may be a first or only offense, committed perhaps out of desperation or for the sake of excitement. There are also numerous department store employees who pilfer merchandise in an attempt to supplement their legal incomes in a potentially safe manner. There are street hustlers in the central cities for whom shoplifting is but one of many petty crimes undertaken on a sporadic basis for the sake of economic gain. And finally, there are professional *boosters* or "class cannons," described earlier in Exhibit 2.2, a small fraternity of skilled thieves who have elevated their techniques to an art form and carry them out regularly as a full-time business and vocation. The skills and techniques of the four types vary considerably, as do the frequency of their thefts and their methods for the disposal of the stolen goods. Furthermore, the first two varieties of shoplifters rarely view themselves as criminals, while the others are often proud of the labels of "class cannon" and "professional thief."

Major Criminal Behavior Systems

The fields of criminology and criminal justice recognize at least six major criminal behavior systems, including the following:

1. Violent personal crime
2. Occasional property crime
3. Organized robbery and gang theft
4. White-collar and corporate crime
5. Organized crime
6. Professional theft

Violent personal crime describes criminal acts resulting from conflicts in personal relations in which death or physical injury is inflicted. Thus, violent personal crime is a reflection of individual and personal violence and includes specific forms of criminal homicide, assault, forcible rape, child abuse, and other forms of domestic violence.[20]

Occasional property crime includes types and instances of burglary, larceny, forgery, and other thefts undertaken infrequently or irregularly, and often quite crudely. Offenders include amateur thieves for whom crime is incidental to their way of life, as well as the rank and file of urban street criminals or youthful groups who partake in sprees of burglaries, auto thefts, shoplifting, and vandalism as part of peer-group activities or for economic gain.[21]

Organized robbery and gang theft refers to highly skilled criminal activities using or threatening to use force, violence, coercion, and property damage, and accomplished by planning, surprise, and speed in order to diminish the risks of apprehension. Criminals of this type pursue crime as a career for financial gain; they generally work in teams and are heavily armed; their planning is careful and their timing precise; and their pursuits include armed robbery, hijacking, kidnapping, and large-scale industrial theft.[22]

White-collar and corporate crime describes offenses committed by persons acting in their legitimate occupational roles. The offenders include businesspeople, members of the professions and government, and other varieties of workers who, in the course of their everyday occupational activities, violate the basic trust placed in them or act in unethical ways. Crime is neither the way of life nor the chosen career of white-collar or corporate offenders, but rather something that occurs in conjunction with their more legitimate work activities.[23]

White-collar and corporate crime covers a multitude of areas, as shown in these examples:

- In the business sector—financial manipulations, unfair labor practices, rebates, misrepresentation of goods and consumer deception by false labeling, fencing of stolen goods, shortchanging, overcharging, black-marketeering
- In the labor sector—misuse of union funds, failing to enforce laws affecting unions, entering into collusion with employers to the disadvantage of union members, illegal mechanisms for controlling members
- In the corporate sector—restraint of trade, infringement of patents, monopolistic practices, environmental contamination, misuse of trademarks, manufacture of unsafe goods, false advertising, disposal of toxic wastes
- In the financial sector—embezzlement, violation of currency control measures, stock manipulation
- In the medical sector—illegal prescription practices, fee-splitting, illegal abortions, fraudulent reports to insurance companies
- In the legal sector—misappropriation of funds in trusts and receiverships, securing prejudiced testimony, bribery, instituting fraudulent damage claims

$100,000—$999,999
$1 million or more
23.0%
40.0%
6.0% under $5,000
13.0%
19.0%
$5,000—$24,999
$25,000—$99,999

Business Losses to Fraud

SOURCE: Department of Justice.

"Kickbacks, embezzlement, price fixing, bribery ... this is an extrmely high-crime area."

- In the criminal justice sector—accepting bribes, illegal arrest and detention practices, illegal correctional practices
- In the civil sector—illegal commissions, issuance of fraudulent licenses and certificates, illegal tax evaluations, misuse of campaign funds, illegal campaign practices

Organized crime refers to business activities directed toward economic gain through unlawful means. Organized crime provides illegal goods and services through activities that include gambling, loan-sharking, commercialized vice, bootlegging, trafficking in narcotics and other drugs, disposing of stolen merchandise, and infiltrating legitimate businesses.[24]

Professional theft includes nonviolent forms of criminal occupation pursued with a high degree of skill to maximize financial gain and minimize the risks of apprehension. The more typical forms of professional theft include pickpocketing, shoplifting, safe and house burglary, forgery, counterfeiting, sneak-thieving, and confidence swindling.[25]

Before going further, a number of points need to be raised. First, this list of six behavior systems includes a wide variety of criminal activities and offense categories, yet it clearly does not include all prohibited acts. Second, any given criminal offense can fall within one or more behavior systems. For example, and as noted earlier, shoplifting can be carried out in different ways, under different circumstances, with different levels of skill, and with different relationships to the offender's social, economic, and criminal careers. And third, there are several patterns of criminal behavior—such as "domestic violence" and "hate crime"—that include elements of several behavior systems. As such, a fully comprehensive classification would be difficult to achieve. Nevertheless, the six types outlined above cover most of the major categories of serious crime.

Since behavior systems in crime, as noted earlier in this chapter, are typically addressed at length in courses in criminology, only a few will be analyzed

Domestic violence: Activities of a physically aggressive nature occurring among members of the family, current or former spouses or lovers, live-ins, and others in close relationships, resulting from conflicts in personal relations.

Acquaintances 27.7%
Other family 2.0%
Sibling 0.92%
Child 3.2%
Parent 2.0%
Spouse 5.0%
Unknown relationship 38.4%
Stranger 13.5%
Neighbor 1.0%
Girlfriend 2.8%
Boyfriend 1.0%
Friend 2.8%

Murder Circumstances by Relationship, 1997

SOURCE: *Uniform Crime Reports.*

In 1998, 49-year-old James Byrd, Jr., of Jasper County, Texas, was the victim of the most gruesome hate crime in recent memory. On the way home from a family reunion, Byrd had apparently hitched a ride with three white men. They drove him to a wooded area, where he was beaten, chained by his ankles to a pickup truck, and dragged down the road for at least 2 miles. His body fell to pieces, and among the remnants was found a cigarette lighter with the Ku Klux Klan insignia.

here. Because domestic violence and hate crime seem to be in the public and media spotlight at this time, and because organized crime not only persists but continually re-creates itself, the focus is limited to these three patterns of criminality.

Domestic Violence

Domestic violence is a form of violent personal crime, and is best defined as activities of a physically aggressive nature occurring among members of the family, current or former spouses or lovers, live-ins, and others in close relationships, resulting from conflicts in personal relations. Domestic violence typically occurs in the home, but it can also take place at another family member's or neighbor's house, the victim's place of employment, a commercial establishment, or even in public. The victims and offenders are most often members of the opposite gender, although it occurs as well among members of the same sex.

The scope of domestic violence is quite broad and includes a wide range of behavioral patterns and offense categories. There is *battering* by spouses and lovers, involving a consistent pattern of behavior that seeks to establish dominance and control over another through the use or threat of force or violence. There is *abuse,* which may be nonphysical but more psychological or economic in nature, involving ridicule, threats, and harassment.

Other forms of domestic violence include marital and date rape, elderly abuse, and child neglect and abuse. These, however, are broad categories reflecting domestic violence behavioral categories. The actual criminal statutes involved include murder and manslaughter, assault, rape, incest, harassment, and stalking, to name but a few.

The origins of domestic violence are likely buried in antiquity. For centuries, however, in many cultures men were legally and socially permitted to chastise their wives and children for their disobedience or disloyalty. Moreover, much of what is now referred to as domestic violence was once considered a legitimate means by which men could maintain control over the family.[26]

An important aspect of domestic violence is the victim-offender relationship, a factor that suggests a large portion of such behavior is well beyond the control of law enforcement. In the case of murder, for example, the majority of offenses occur among persons who know one another. In 1997, of all the murders reported during that year, 5 percent of the victims were spouses, 8.1 percent involved other family members, and 35.3 percent included neighbors or other close acquaintances. In the remaining cases, the homicide was of the stranger-to-stranger type, or the relationship could not be established. In terms of domestic violence, the majority of these killings involved romantic triangles, quarrels over money or property, or other arguments.

Although official statistics on assaults are not as complete as those on criminal homicide, similar reflections of domestic violence are apparent. Street muggings do indeed occur, but it is also relatively clear that nearly two-thirds of all known aggravated assaults result from domestic quarrels, altercations, jealousies, and arguments over money and property. Further, victim-offender relationships are typically intimate, close, and frequent, primarily involving family members and close acquaintances.

Child abuse, which is a particular variety of domestic violence directed against children, is a form of personal violence that has received attention only during recent years. Known in medical terminology as the "battered child syndrome," studies suggest that the offenders are typically parents or guardians, and that the abuse is an enduring pattern provoked by the kinds of aggravation that can be typical of children—persistent crying, failure to use the toilet, aggression toward siblings, breaking toys or household items, or disobedience.[27]

An alternative pattern is child molestation, which is most frequently manifested as parent-child incest, the sexual fondling of a child, or the persuasion or coercion to engage in other sexual acts with a parent, sibling, or guardian.

As a final point here, and contrary to many popular beliefs, women are not the only victims of domestic violence and men are not the only offenders. Although men indeed are the more typical predators in domestic violence situations, studies document that men are at risk as well, that there is indeed a "battered husband syndrome."[28]

Hate Crime

Hate crime can be defined as offenses motivated by hatred against a victim because of his or her race, ethnicity, religion, sexual orientation, handicap, or national origin. Also referred to as "bias-motivated crimes," hate crimes are often difficult to identify, primarily because criminal acts motivated by bias can easily be confused with forms of expression which are protected by the U.S. Constitution.

From the Romans' persecution of the Christians almost two millennia ago and the Nazis' "final solution" for the Jews during World War II, to the "ethnic cleansing" in Bosnia and Kosovo and genocide in Rwanda during the 1990s, hate crimes have shaped and sometimes defined world history. In the United States, it has been racial and religious biases that have inspired most hate crimes. During the early days of the American republic, first it was Native Americans who became the targets of bias-motivated intimidation and violence, then it was lynchings of African Americans, followed by hate crimes directed against Chinese laborers. The more current examples of hate crimes include cross burnings to drive black families from predominantly white neighborhoods, assaults on gays, and the painting of swastikas on Jewish synagogues.[29]

The number of hate crimes that occur in the United States is difficult to calculate and would appear to be quite small in official statistics. According to Justice Department estimates, less than one out of every 2,000 homicides and one of every 8,000 reported rapes are bias motivated.[30] But by contrast, many hate crimes likely go unreported.

The victims of hate crimes in the United States are most often African Americans, followed by Jews, gays, Muslims, and, increasingly, Asian Americans. Although the Ku Klux Klan and the myriad of Nazi skinhead groups tend to be the most visible perpetrators of hate crimes, the majority of offenders are individuals rather than groups. During 1997, for example, there were 10,255 victims of hate crimes reported to the FBI, and 8,474 offenders. In addition, 63 percent of the suspected offenders were white, 19 percent were black, and the remaining 18 percent were Native American, Asian/Pacific Islander, multiracial, or of unknown race or ethnicity.[31]

Organized Crime

Organized crime designates business activities directed toward economic gain through unlawful means. At the heart of what is often meant by organized crime are such activities as gambling, loan-sharking, commercialized vice, bootlegging, trafficking in narcotics and other drugs, and disposing of stolen merchandise — enterprises that provide illegal goods and services to members of both the underworld and upperworld. Such activities, however, are not always highly organized. Instead, they range on a continuum from freelance prostitutes and neighborhood bookmakers to regionally organized gambling or drug syndicates. Some forms of organized crime, furthermore, are both national and international in scope.

As a behavior system, organized crime is typically pursued as an occupational career. In its most organized aspects, there is a hierarchical structure that

Hate crime: Offenses motivated by hatred against a victim because of his or her race, ethnicity, religion, sexual orientation, handicap, or national origin.

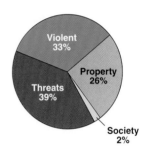

Hate Crimes by Type, 1997

SOURCE: *Uniform Crime Reports.*

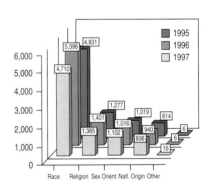

Hate Crimes by Motivating Factor, 1995–1997

SOURCE: *Uniform Crime Reports.*

Organized crime: Business activities directed toward economic gain through unlawful means.

Exhibit 2.5

Historical Perspectives on Crime and Justice
The Origins of *la Mafia* ("the Mafia")

Sicilians have always had a kind of primitive chivalry that stresses cohesion among friends in their united offense against common enemies. This prevailing moral code fosters a distrust for formal law and authority, defends the individual's dignity, and requires the strictest silence in secret matters. These cultural traits have existed for the past millennium and their strictures are demanded unconditionally regardless of cost. Such an ideological climate was both initiated and encouraged by the endless foreign conquests of Sicilian soil; each successive invasion was marked by rapacious governments and marauding bands of native *malviventi*. Within this setting of oppression and resentment, *la Mafia* ("the Mafia") developed and prospered. The Mafia appeared in 1282 during the great revolt known as the Sicilian Vespers. Defense and revolution against French tyranny generated a *compagnie d'armi*, a Sicilian peasant band that emphasized primitive justice. The *compagnie d'armi* defended the weak, punished the thief and transgressor, and fought to right the inhumanity of alien law. Yet,

over time, its members degenerated into outlawry and brutality through multilevel extortion systems directed against both landowners and laborers.

Descriptions of the Mafia have been numerous and dogmatic, with striking disagreement about its specific root in Sicilian history. Writer Ed Reid, for example, suggested that the first use of the term *mafia* was at the outbreak of the Sicilian Vespers on March 30, 1282, tracing it to the motto of the insurrection: *"Morte Alla Francia Italia Anela!"* ("Death to the French Is Italy's Cry!"). Author Andrew Varna preferred a different theory: that the term *mafia* was created in 1860 by Joseph Mazzini, a Sicilian gang leader. Mazzini allegedly contracted the initials of his slogan, which (translated into English) was "Mazzini authorizes theft, arson, and poisoning." And the contemporary popular historian Gay Talese goes back to Easter Monday in 1282, and relates the rape of a maiden on her wedding day and the anguished cries of her mother: *"Ma fia, ma fia"* ("My daughter, my daughter").

An analysis of the Italian language during these periods, combined with an examination of Sicilian history, suggests that such derivations represent little more than pure fiction. More laudable explanations of *mafia* come from Sicilian historical and literary works that link its root and mean-

includes leaders (or "godfathers" and "dons," as the media and popular culture would insist) at the uppermost levels, followed by a middle echelon of gangsters and "lieutenants" who carry out the orders of their "bosses" and the *capo di tutti capi* ("the boss of all bosses"). And at the bottom of the structure are those only marginally associated with the organization—prostitutes, enforcers, drug sellers, bookmakers—who may sometimes operate independently of the power structure and who typically deal directly with the public.

People who pursue organized crime as an occupational career most often focus on this type of criminality as a mechanism of upward mobility and are

ing to elements prevailing within Sicilian culture. *Mafia* is seemingly Sicilian-Arabic, descending from the early linguistic form *hafa* ("to preserve, protect, and act as guardian"), which derived from *mo'hafi* ("friend or companion"), from *mo'hafah* ("to defend"), and from *mo'hafiat* ("preservation, safety, power, integrity, strength, and a state that designates the remedy of damage and ill"). That the Arabic *mo'hafiat* became *mafiat* by elision (the omission of a vowel in pronunciation) and then became *mafia* by apocope (the cutting off of the last sound of a word) can be drawn from works of Guiseppe Pitre, the Italian historian and folklorist who described *mafia* as a dialect term common in pre-1860 Palermo. It expressed "beauty and excellence," united with notions of "superiority" and "bravery"; in reference to *man,* it also meant "the consciousness of being a man," "assurance of the mind," "boldness but never defiance," and "arrogance but never haughtiness." Thus, both Arabic-Sicilian references and common usage in Palermo—Sicily's capital city—contributed to *mafia*'s many meanings: protection against the arrogance of the powerful, remedy to any damage, sturdiness of body, strength and serenity of spirit, and the best and most exquisite part of life.

Mafia's first use in a criminal context can be attributed to Guiseppe Rizzoto's dialect play *I Mafuisi della Vicaria,* which was dedicated to "the handsome and

daring men" of Palermo's local jail. Following its initial performance in 1863, *I Mafuisi* was an immediate success and remained popular for a number of years. The term *mafiosi* was rapidly seized upon and has been commonly used by non-*mafia* members ever since. Actual *mafiosi* (mafia members) have never used it. They prefer to call one another *amici* ("friends" or "friends of friends") and refer to their organization as *Societa onorata* ("the honored society" or "the society of friends").

The spirit and structure of the Sicilian *Societa onorata* has changed little over the past century. The first nucleus is the family; unions of more powerful fami-

lies are known as *cosche.* Numerous *cosche* pursuing similar activities often form an alliance called *consorteria*—and all of the *consorteria* in Sicily form the *Societa onorata* or *Mafia.* Numerous *mafie* exist in Sicily, each specializing in exacting tribute from a variety of occupations—citrus groves, wholesale fruit, irrigation, and others. They establish order, provide protection, fix prices, and arrange contracts, each in a specific territory. Immunity from prosecution is supported by *l'omerta,* the Sicilian code of silence, and is reinforced by fear of death consignments extended for noncompliance with *Societa* demands.

"Godfathers," young and old.

SOURCE: Adapted from James A. Inciardi, *Careers in Crime* (Chicago: Rand McNally, 1975).

recruited on the basis of kinship, friendship, or contacts within lower-class environments, where such activities are sought out as means for economic respectability. Whether individual criminals are within a highly structured "syndicate" or are low-level independent prostitutes or drug dealers, their commitment to the career is long-term and their entire social organization and lifestyle revolve around crime.

Historically, discussions of organized crime have focused almost exclusively on such activities as prostitution and gambling, such groups as the Mafia (see Exhibit 2.5) and *La Cosa Nostra,* and such individuals as Al Capone,

Forty states and the federal government have laws that single out crimes based on race, color, religion, or national origin, but only 21 states have statutes that single out crimes based on the victim's sexual orientation. This is why the killing of Matthew Shepard rekindled interest in proposals to extend federal hate crime laws to include sexual orientation. What hate crime laws accomplish is to enhance the penalties given to the perpetrators of hate crime. But are hate crime laws really necessary, or fair?

The idea behind hate crime laws is to provide special protection for minorities who are frequently attacked simply because of who they are. Supporters of these laws argue that hate crime does double damage—first to the immediate victim, and then to members of his or her minority group in the form of terror and intimidation. They also emphasize that the enhanced penalties have a deterrent effect.

Those opposed to the laws claim that this tenet of special protections violates the principle of equality under the law. Why, they ask, should someone who utters a racial slur while assaulting a black man receive a more severe sentence than another person who says nothing while committing a similar assault? Why should gays get special protections? Why should there be legislation that endorses homosexuality and gay rights in this manner? Opponents also claim that deterrence doesn't work, and that in many instances it is not necessary: The killers of Matthew Shepard, whose case was described at the beginning of this chapter, and the

killers of James Byrd, Jr., the East Texas black man dragged by his ankles from the rear of a pickup truck, will likely receive the death penalty anyway.

In response to all of these arguments, consider this. Although established criminal law will likely suffice in the murders of Shepard and Byrd, in other cases justice is not as easily defined. Spray-painting swastika graffiti on a synagogue wall is far more than just petty vandalism, and the law should acknowledge that. Furthermore, hate crime laws are a separate issue from gay rights legislation. A hate crime law would simply identify sexual orientation as an "aggravating factor" in an existing criminal act and would have no connection to any imaginary homosexual, religious, feminist, or racial "agenda."

■ Laws include crimes based on sexual orientation.   ■ Laws do not include crimes based on sexual orientation.   □ No hate crime laws or none based on specific categories

Hate Crime Legislation in the U.S.

Note: Maryland and Utah require data collection for crimes based on sexual orientation, but do not specify such crimes in penalty laws.

SOURCE: *National Gay and Lesbian Task Force.*

Meyer Lansky, Benjamin "Bugsy" Siegal, Vito Genovese, and more recently John Gotti and Sam "the Bull" Gravano. Current analyses, however, have extended their interest to other criminal groups—not just Italians, but also Asians, Jamaicans, Latin Americans, and Russians, to name but a few. In fact, already well known to observers of organized crime are the Jamaican "posses," Mexico's "Gulf Cartel," Colombia's "Cali Cartel," the Chinese "triads," and the Japanese *Yakuza,* as well as a myriad of African American, Dominican, Korean, Cuban, and Sicilian criminal organizations, many of whom are already working together in a complex mosaic of illicit enterprise.[32]

The same people who tell us that the death penalty has no deterrent effect at all find themselves having to argue that a few extra months in jail deters racial attacks.
— *John Leo, of* U.S. News and World Report

Exhibit 2.6   **Careers in Justice**
Crisis Intervention Counseling

Because of the more than 1 million violent crimes that occur in the United States each year, many police departments, schools, hospitals, and numerous other public and private agencies have crisis intervention counselors to help victims deal with emotional trauma. Crisis intervention is just one specialization in the broader area of counseling, which provides

employment for more than a million people in the United States. In addition to crisis work, counseling in the criminal justice field includes work in correctional institutions, drug and alcohol programs, and halfway houses and group homes for both adult and juvenile offenders.

The majority of counselors have undergraduate degrees in either criminal justice, psychology, or one of the other social or behavioral sciences, and many have graduate degrees in counselor education. Counseling certification programs are also offered in almost every state. Counseling li-

censure requirements vary from state to state, as do employment opportunities and salaries. In 1998, however, the majority of counselors earned between $25,000 and $50,000 a year, with the top 10 percent earning in excess of $60,000 annually.

For more information on counseling as a career, contact the American Counseling Association in Alexandria, Virginia. Information on national certification requirements for counselors is available on the Internet from the National Board for Certified Counselors (Web site address: http://www.nbcc.org/).

SUMMARY

Thousands of acts are prohibited by law and designated as felonies or misdemeanors in federal, state, and local criminal codes across the United States. Such crimes as homicide, assault, robbery, arson, burglary, sex offenses, drug law violations, and offenses against the public order and safety are by no means all that appear in criminal statutes and codes, but they account for some 90 percent of the criminal law violations that are processed by U.S. courts.

However, although crime may be conduct prohibited by the criminal law, its dynamics include certain patterns and systems of behavior. Furthermore, definitions of crime are culturally and historically specific. Some be-

haviors are tolerated on a wider scale than others, and some have been accepted at different points in history. For example, such sexual activities as sodomy and fornication are prohibited by law in many jurisdictions but are engaged in by otherwise law-abiding citizens on a regular basis and are less likely to be prosecuted. By contrast, the laws against rape are vigorously enforced.

It is important for students of crime and criminal justice to understand not only the content of criminal codes, but the behavior systems that surround the prohibited acts as well. It is valuable to observe the lifestyles associated with particular offenses and the relationship of the criminal act to the wider social order.

KEY TERMS

arson **32**
assault **31**
assault and battery **31**
breaking and entering **33**
Carrier's Case **38**
deliberation **30**
domestic violence **48**

felony-murder doctrine **30**
hate crime **49**
homicide **30**
larceny **37**
malice aforethought **30**
manslaughter **31**
murder **30**

organized crime **49**
Pear's Case **38**
premeditation **30**
rape **41**
robbery **32**
theft **36**

QUESTIONS FOR DISCUSSION

1. In cases in which the felony-murder doctrine has been invoked, the intent to commit murder has often been absent. In such circumstances, is conviction of murder in the first degree a just disposition? Why or why not?
2. Which sex offenses, if any, should be abolished from contemporary criminal codes? Why?

3. Why do you think there are so many sex offenses?
4. Are there are types of property offenses other than those listed in this chapter?
5. Should "hate crime" be a separate offense?

MEDIA RESOURCES

1. **Matthew Shepard and Hate Crime.** Numerous resources and information links on hate crime can be located on the Internet through the Missouri Victim Assistance Network. Web site address: http://mova.missouri.org/hatecrms.htm
2. **Pickpockets.** James Inciardi's research on pickpockets at the Super Bowl is briefly discussed in Exhibit 2.2. A complete paper on the topic, "On the Grift at the Super Bowl: Pickpockets and the NFL," is on the textbook Web site and can be downloaded.

3. **Domestic Violence.** The National Domestic Violence Hot Line (1-800-799-7233) has a Web site with links to related sites, including the National Organization for Women, Women Leaders Online, and the Center for the Prevention of Sexual and Domestic Violence. Web site address: www.ndvh.org
4. **Violence Against Women.** A comprehensive overview of current knowledge on this topic can be found in Nancy A. Crowell and Ann W. Burgess, eds., *Understanding Violence Against Women* (Washington, D.C.: National Academy Press, 1996).

NOTES

1. *New York Times,* October 10, 1998, p. A9; *New York Times,* October 13, 1998, p. A1.
2. Jerome Hall, "Analytic Philosophy and Jurisprudence," *Ethics* 77 (October 1966): 14–28.
3. *New York Times,* April 19, 1998, p. 21.
4. *Miami Herald,* March 23, 1989, p. 3B.
5. *Delaware Code,* Title 11, Section 601.
6. David M. Maurer, *Whiz Mob* (New Haven, Conn.: College and University Press, 1964), p. 68.
7. This comment was made to the author by a Miami Beach pickpocket. Additional comments on this topic can be found in James A. Inciardi, "The Pickpocket and His Victim," *Victimology: An International Journal* 1 (Fall 1976): 446–453.
8. John F. Boudreau, Quon Y. Kwan, William E. Faragher, and Genevieve C. Denault, *Arson and Arson Investigation: Survey and Assessment* (Washington, D.C.: U.S. Government Printing Office, 1977), p. 1.

9. James A. Inciardi, "The Adult Firesetter: A Typology," *Criminology* 8 (August 1970): 145–155; James A. Inciardi, *Reflections on Crime* (New York: Holt, Rinehart and Winston, 1978), pp. 127–128.
10. See, for example, *Delaware Code,* Title 11, Sections 824, 825, 826.
11. *Delaware Code,* Title 11, Section 840.
12. *Ohio Code,* 2913.02.
13. *Carrier's Case,* Yearbook, 13 Edward IV, 9, pl. 5 (1473).
14. *Pear's Case,* 1 Leach 212, 168 Eng. Rep. 208 (1779).
15. Wayne Logan, Lindsay S. Stellwagen, and Patrick A. Langan, *Felony Laws of the 50 States and the District of Columbia* (Washington, D.C.: Bureau of Justice Statistics, 1987).
16. *National Law Journal,* April 20, 1987, p. 14; *New York Times,* May 9, 1990, p. A26.

17. See David F. Musto, *The American Disease: Origins of Narcotic Control* (New Haven, Conn.: Yale University Press, 1973).

18. For a brief history of drug use in the United States, see James A. Inciardi, *The War on Drugs II* (Mountain View, Calif.: Mayfield, 1992), chapters 1 and 2.

19. *A Guide to State-Controlled Substances Acts* (Washington, D.C.: Bureau of Justice Assistance, and the National Criminal Justice Association, 1988).

20. See Marvin Wolfgang, *Patterns in Criminal Homicide* (Philadelphia: University of Pennsylvania Press, 1958); David J. Pittman and William Handy, "Patterns in Criminal Aggravated Assault," *Journal of Criminal Law, Criminology and Police Science* 55 (December 1964): 462–470; Marshall B. Clinard, Richard Quinney, and John Wildeman, *Criminal Behavior Systems: A Typology* (Cincinnati: Anderson, 1994). Also see Duncan Chappell, Robley Geis, and Gilbert Geis, eds., *Forcible Rape: The Crime, the Victim, and the Offender* (New York: Columbia University Press, 1977); D. J. West, C. Roy, and F. L. Nichols, *Understanding Sexual Attacks* (London: Heinemann, 1978).

21. Edwin M. Lemert, "An Isolation and Closure Theory of Naive Check Forgery," *Journal of Criminal Law, Criminology, and Police Science* 44 (1953): 296–307; Mary Owen Cameron, *The Booster and the Snitch* (New York: Free Press of Glencoe, 1964); Loren E. Edwards, *Shoplifting and Shrinkage Protection for Stores* (Springfield, Ill.: Thomas, 1958).

22. Werner J. Einstadter, "The Social Organization of Armed Robbery," *Social Problems* 17 (Summer 1969): 64–83.

23. See Gilbert Reis, "From Deuteronomy to Deniability: A Historical Perlustration of White Collar Crime," *Justice Quarterly* 5 (March 1988): 7–32.

24. For a discussion of organized crime, see Joseph L. Albini, *The American Mafia: Genesis of a Legend* (New York: Appleton-Century-Crofts, 1971); Daniel Bell, *The End of Ideology: On the Exhaustion of Political Ideas in the Fifties* (New York: Free Press, 1962), pp. 127–150; Norval Morris and Gordon Hawkins, *The Honest Politician's Guide to Crime Control* (Chicago: University of Chicago Press, 1970), pp. 202–235; James A. Inciardi, *Careers in Crime* (Chicago: Rand McNally, 1975), pp. 109–121.

25. Inciardi, *Careers in Crime,* pp. 5–82.

26. See Cliff Mariani, *Domestic Violence Survival Guide* (Flushing, N.Y.: Looseleaf, 1996).

27. See Eve S. Buzawa and Carl G. Buzawa, *Domestic Violence: The Criminal Justice Response* (Thousand Oaks, Calif.: Sage, 1996; M. P. Mendel, *The Male Survivor: The Impact of Sexual Abuse* (Thousand Oaks, Calif.: Sage, 1995).

28. See Coramae Richey Mann, *Women Who Kill* (Albany: SUNY Press, 1996); Murray A. Straus, "Physical Assaults by Wives: A Major Social Problem," in *Current Controversies in Family Violence,* ed. Richard J. Gelles and Donileen R. Loseke (Newbury Park, Calif.: Sage, 1993).

29. James B. Jacobs and Kimberly Potter, *Hate Crimes: Criminal Law and Identity Politics* (New York: Oxford University Press, 1998); Bureau of Justice Assistance, *A Policymaker's Guide to Hate Crimes* (Washington, D.C.: Office of Justice Programs, 1997).

30. Bureau of Justice Assistance, *Policymaker's Guide,* p. x.

31. Federal Bureau of Investigation, *Crime in the United States—1997* (Washington, D.C.: U.S. Department of Justice, 1998), p. 62.

32. William Kleinknecht, *The New Ethnic Mobs: The Changing Face of Organized Crime in America* (New York: Free Press, 1996).

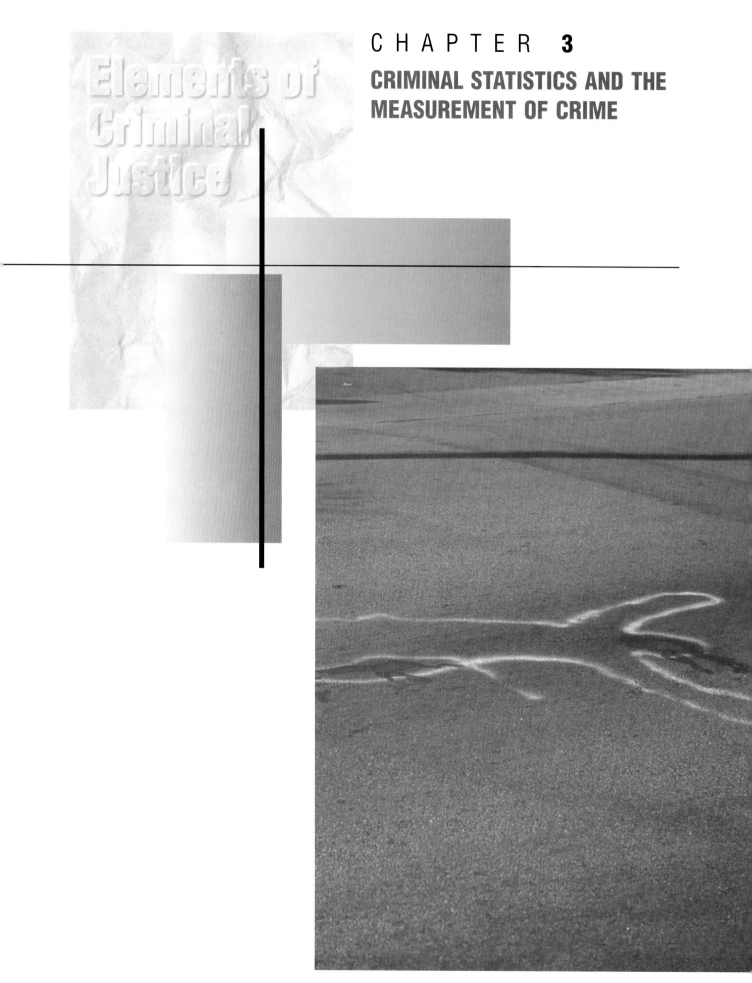

Elements of
Criminal
Justice

Washington, D.C.:—The Federal Bureau of Investigation announced that serious crime in the United States had declined in 1997—the sixth consecutive annual reduction! The FBI also reported that the rate of violent crime was the lowest since 1987, and that the nation's murder rate had dropped to a 30-year low.[1] Some of the greatest decreases in crime occurred in the country's largest cities, such as New York and Los Angeles, but to the surprise of many observers, violent crime *increased* dramatically during the 1990s in many mid-size cities. In Louisville and Nashville, for example, the number of murders increased by more than 50 percent during the decade, and in Cincinnati, murders went up almost 75 percent in just 1 year.

Given these crime statistics, what explains why crime is going down in most parts of the country but up in others? And there are even more important questions: What are the sources of information about the nature and extent of crime in the United States? How are crime data collected and are the statistics accurate? What is a crime rate and how does one really know if crime is declining or increasing?

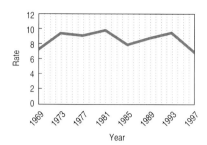

Murder Rates in the U.S., 1969–1997

SOURCE: *Uniform Crime Reports.*

PERCENT INCREASE OR DECREASE IN MURDERS, 1990–1997	
In America's historic murder capitals:	
Boston	−70%
New York	−66%
Los Angeles	−41%
Washington, D.C.	−36%
Atlanta	−35%
Miami	−20%
In America's newest murder capitals:	
Indianapolis	+60%
Albuquerque	+44%
Durham, N.C.	+43%
Jackson, Miss.	+39%
Portland, Ore.	+39%
Phoenix	+37%

SOURCE: *Uniform Crime Reports.*

Uniform Crime Reports (UCR): The annual publication of the FBI presenting official statistics on the rates and trends in crime in the United States.

Aggregate crime rates, such as those depicted in the *UCR* "crime clocks," should not be used to assess one's personal risk of crime victimization. One's individual risk varies enormously by age, gender, lifestyle, geographic location, and a whole range of other variables.

Within the context of the foregoing questions, this chapter describes the major sources of information on the magnitude and trends of crime. It explains how the information is compiled, what it includes, how it might be best interpreted, and how it has been misused. The shortcomings and the usefulness of official crime statistics are also discussed. The chapter's final section looks at alternate and supplementary sources of crime data.

THE *UNIFORM CRIME REPORTS*

The uniform collection of crime statistics on a national basis in this country began some three-quarters of a century ago. Prior to that time, little was known about the actual extent of crime in the United States (see Exhibit 3.1). At the 1927 annual meeting of the International Association of Chiefs of Police, the Committee on Uniform Crime Reports was appointed to respond to a demand for national crime data. It was commissioned to prepare a manual on standardized crime reporting for use by local police agencies. Based on the efforts of this committee, on June 11, 1930, Congress authorized the Federal Bureau of Investigation (FBI) to collect and compile nationwide data on crime. Pursuant to the congressional order, the FBI assumed responsibility for directing the voluntary recording of data by police departments on standard forms provided by the FBI and for compiling and publishing the data received. Known as the **Uniform Crime Reports (UCR),** they were issued monthly at first, quarterly until 1941, semiannually through 1957, and annually since 1958.

The main publication of the *UCR* is an annual booklet, *Crime in the United States,* which has helped establish the FBI's image as the nation's leading authority on crime trends. This annual periodical is the only source of information on the magnitude and trends of crime in the United States. It is relied on heavily by administrators, politicians, policy and opinion makers, the press, criminal justice agencies, and the public at large. Yet the FBI reports have their problems. They are incomplete and structurally biased, resulting in the creation and persistence of many myths about crime in the United States. Furthermore, they have been misused and misinterpreted. In consequence, inaccurate and distorted representations of crime are continually being offered to both professional and lay audiences, and public pronouncements about "the crime problem" often have only limited basis in fact. The following commentary includes an explanation of official criminal statistics, an examination of their reliability, and a discussion of how these and other sources of information can be used to understand the nature and extent of crime in America.

Structure and Content

The FBI's *Uniform Crime Reports* presents us with a nationwide view of crime based on statistics submitted by city, county, and state law enforcement agencies throughout the country. As of 1997, more than 17,000 law enforcement agencies were contributing crime data to this reporting program, representing coverage for more than 98 percent of the national population.

The *UCR* begins with a rather alarming *crime clock.* The one in Figure 3.1 suggests that in 1997 there was one murder every 29 minutes, one forcible rape every 5 minutes, one robbery every minute, a property crime every 3 seconds, as well as other crimes in similarly frequent intervals. The reader is quickly cautioned in the FBI report that the crime clock display should not be interpreted to imply some regularity in the commission of crimes; it simply represents the annual ratio of crime to fixed time intervals. Unfortunately this cautionary comment is easily overlooked, and invariably, mass-media

Exhibit 3.1

Historical Perspectives on Crime and Justice
Late-Nineteenth-Century Homicide Rates in the United States

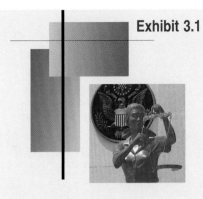

Year	Total Homicides	Rate per 100,000 Population
1890	4,290	6.9
1891	5,906	9.2
1892	6,791	10.4
1893	6,615	10.0
1894	9,800	14.5
1895	10,500	15.2
1896	10,652	15.1
1897	9,520	13.3
1898	7,840	10.7
1899	6,225	8.4

John Billington was among the 102 Pilgrims aboard the *Mayflower* to arrive at Plymouth in 1620. He was described as a rather violent individual, prone to fight and feud with his neighbors. In 1630, only 10 years after the establishment of the Puritan settlement, Billington shot one of his adversaries at close range, was hanged for the killing, and earned the distinction of becoming the country's first known murderer. Since that time, homicide has been a highly visible aspect of American social history.

From the beginning of the 1960s through the closing years of the 1990s, homicide rates in the United States have been quite high, reaching a peak of 9.8 per 100,000 population in 1991. But as indicated in the accompanying table, homicide rates for most of the 1890s were well above those of the 1990s.

Why homicide rates were so high during the 1890s would be difficult to unravel. However, it was a period of transition in the United States brought on by the closing of the western frontier, the rapid growth of cities, and social conflicts associated with the high rates of immigration from Europe. One thing that is certain, however, is that homicide rates during this period were likely higher than those shown in the table. At the time, there was no uniform method for the collection of crime statistics on a national basis, and as such, the underreporting of murders was likely significant.

19th-century police officers examining a homicide scene.

SOURCES: James A. Inciardi, *Reflections on Crime* (New York: Holt, Rinehart and Winston, 1978); Arthur Train, *Courts and Criminals* (New York: Scribner's, 1925).

commentary on crime in the United States makes frequent reference to the literal meaning of the crime clock.

The *UCR* places its compilations into two categories: *crimes known to the police* and *arrests.* "Crimes known to the police" include all events either reported to or observed by the police in those categories of crime that the FBI designates as **Part I offenses,** which are serious crimes including criminal homicide, forcible rape, robbery, aggravated assault, burglary/breaking and entering, larceny-theft (except motor vehicle theft), motor vehicle theft, and arson. "Arrests" include compilations of arrest reports for all the Part I offenses

Part I offenses: Crimes designated by the FBI as the *most serious* and compiled in terms of the number of reports made to law enforcement agencies and the number of arrests made.

Figure 3.1 Crime Clock, 1997

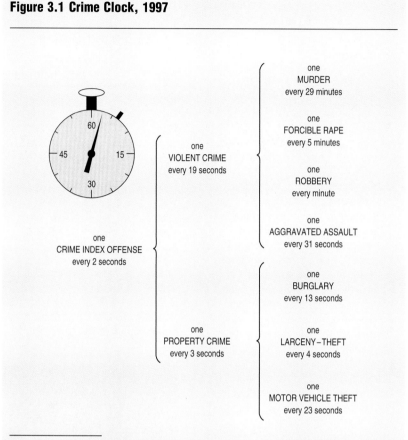

one
VIOLENT CRIME
every 19 seconds

one
CRIME INDEX OFFENSE
every 2 seconds

one
PROPERTY CRIME
every 3 seconds

one
MURDER
every 29 minutes

one
FORCIBLE RAPE
every 5 minutes

one
ROBBERY
every minute

one
AGGRAVATED ASSAULT
every 31 seconds

one
BURGLARY
every 13 seconds

one
LARCENY–THEFT
every 4 seconds

one
MOTOR VEHICLE THEFT
every 23 seconds

NOTE: The crime clock should be viewed with care. Being the most aggregate representation of *UCR* data, it is designed to convey the annual reported crime experience by showing the relative frequency of occurrence of the Index offenses. This mode of display should not be taken to imply a regularity in the commission of the Part I offenses; rather, it represents the annual ratio of crime to fixed time intervals.

Part II offenses: Crimes designated by the FBI as *less serious* than the Part I offenses and compiled in terms of the number of arrests made.

Crime Index: The sum of Part I offenses reported in a given place for a given period of time.

combined with those of 21 additional categories that the FBI designates as **Part II offenses,** less serious crimes including other assaults, forgery and counterfeiting, fraud, embezzlement, stolen property (buying, receiving, possessing), vandalism, weapons (carrying, possessing), prostitution and commercialized vice, sex offenses (except forcible rape, prostitution, and commercialized vice), drug abuse violations, gambling, offenses against the family and children (nonsupport, neglect, desertion), driving under the influence (of alcohol or drugs), liquor law violations, drunkenness, disorderly conduct, vagrancy, violations of curfew and loitering laws, suspicion, runaways, and "all other."

Information on Part I offenses, which are the most widely quoted and often misinterpreted, are grouped by city, metropolitan area, state, region, and the nation as a whole to reflect an "Index of Crime" for the given year, and it is these **Crime Index** data that are relied on for estimating the magnitude and rates of crime. A sample of the *UCR* data appears in Figure 3.2, which contains 10 classifications of crime, their absolute numbers, rates, and percent changes between 1988 and 1997. Some of the terms and variables are important for reading and interpreting any crime statistics:

Total Crime Index: The sum of all Part I property offenses reported to or observed by the police (that is, "crimes known to the police") during a given period of time in a particular place (in this example, during 1997 for the total United States).

Violent crime: The sum of all Part I violent offenses (homicide, forcible rape, robbery, and aggravated assault).

Property crime: The sum of all Part I property offenses (burglary, larceny-theft, motor vehicle theft, and arson).

Rate per 100,000 inhabitants: The **crime rate,** or the number of Part I offenses that occurred in a given area for every 100,000 persons living in that area, calculated as follows:

Crime rate: The number of Part I offenses that occur in a given area per 100,000 inhabitants living in that area.

$$\frac{\text{Total Crime Index}}{\text{Population}} \times 100,000 = \text{Rate}$$

Figure 3.2 Index of Crime for the United States, 1988–1997

	Total U.S. Population	Total Crime Index*	Violent Crime	Property Crime	Murder
1988	245,807,000	13,923,086	1,566,221	12,356,865	20,675
Rate per 100,000 inhabitants	—	5,664.2	637.2	5,027.1	8.4
1997	267,637,000	13,175,070	1,634,773	11,540,297	18,209
Rate per 100,000 inhabitants	—	4,922.7	610.8	4,311.9	6.8
Percent change, 1988–1997					
by crimes	—	−5.4	+4.4	−6.6	−11.9
by rate	—	−13.1	−4.1	−14.2	−19.0

Forcible Rape	Robbery	Aggravated Assault	Burglary	Larceny-Theft	Motor Vehicle Theft
92,490	542,970	910,090	3,218,100	7,705,900	1,432,900
37.6	220.9	370.2	1,309.2	3,134.9	582.9
96,120	497,950	1,022,490	2,461,100	7,725,500	1,353,700
35.9	186.1	382.0	919.6	2,886.5	525.8
+3.9	−8.3	+12.4	−23.5	+0.3	−9.5
−4.5	−15.8	+3.2	−29.8	−7.9	−13.2

*Arson is not included due to incomplete reporting.

SOURCE: *Uniform Crime Reports.*

OCCUPATIONAL HOMICIDES AMONG U.S. WOMEN

According to the Centers for Disease Control and Prevention, homicide is the leading cause of job-related death among women. Of an estimated 7,000 fatal work-related injuries each year, 13 percent result from homicide. Among women, who represent 47 percent of the workforce, homicide accounts for 42 percent of deaths—the most common case being a robbery-related shooting. Although the majority of on-the-job deaths involve men, who dominate the more dangerous occupations, homicides for this group represent only 12 percent of the deaths.

SOURCE: Centers for Disease Control and Prevention.

In Figure 3.2, the crime rate in the United States for 1997 was 4,922.7 per 100,000 inhabitants. That is, 4,922.7 Part I offenses were "known to the police" for every 100,000 persons in the nation. As such:

$$\frac{\text{1997 Total Crime Index}}{\text{1997 Population}} \times 100,000 = \text{Rate}$$

$$\frac{13,175,070}{267,637,000} \times 100,000 = 4,922.7$$

Percent change: The percentage of increase or decrease ($+$ or $-$) in the Crime Index or crime rate over some prior year, calculated as follows:

$$\frac{\text{Current Total Crime Index} - \text{Previous Total Crime Index}}{\text{Previous Total Crime Index}} = \frac{\text{Percent}}{\text{change}}$$

The Total Crime Index was 13,923,086 in 1988. The Total Crime Index decreased by 5.4 percent from 1988 to 1997. This percentage is calculated according to the following equation:

$$\frac{\text{1997 Total Crime Index} - \text{1988 Total Crime Index}}{\text{1988 Total Crime Index}} = \text{Percent change}$$

$$\frac{13,175,070 - 13,923,086}{13,923,086} = \text{Percent change}$$

$$\frac{-748,016}{13,923,086} = -0.054 = -5.4 \text{ percent}$$

While most *UCR* data present Part I offense information for thousands of cities and towns, other material also appears. For example, arrest data are broken down for each offense by the age, sex, and race/ethnicity of those arrested, and by population area, for both Part I and Part II offenses. In addition, the *UCR* provides totals of the number of law enforcement personnel in the communities that contribute to the reporting system, as well as extensive information on the number of law enforcement officers assaulted or killed during the given year.

The Extent of Crime

The data presented in Figure 3.2 provide some preliminary indicators of the extent of crime in the United States, at least in terms of those Index crimes

Investigating a drive-by shooting scene in Washington, D.C.

that become known to the police. There were about 13.2 million Part I crimes reported during 1997, including 18,209 murders, 96,120 rapes, 497,950 robberies, 1,022,490 serious assaults, 2,461,100 burglaries, 7,725,500 larcenies, and 1,353,700 motor vehicle thefts.

It was noted earlier that Part II offenses are reported in the *UCR* only in terms of arrests. Therefore, there is no measure of even the relative incidence of these crimes throughout the nation. As indicated in Figure 3.3, however, there were approximately 9,886,024 arrests during 1997, of which more than 8 million involved Part II–type crimes. (For a glimpse into crime in another country, see Exhibit 3.2.)

Figure 3.3 Total Estimated Arrests for the United States, 1997

Crime	Number of Arrests
Total	9,886,024
Murder and nonnegligent manslaughter	12,226
Forcible rape	20,654
Robbery	90,146
Aggravated assault	349,818
Burglary	230,960
Larceny-theft	970,552
Motor vehicle theft	111,288
Arson	12,993
Violent crime[a]	472,844
Property crime[b]	1,325,793
Crime Index Total[c]	1,798,637
Other assaults	905,536
Forgery and counterfeiting	77,773
Fraud	248,370
Embezzlement	11,763
Stolen property; buying, receiving, possessing	102,229
Vandalism	206,418
Weapons; carrying, possessing, etc.	145,105
Prostitution and commercialized vice	70,559
Sex offenses (except forcible rape and prostitution)	65,655
Drug abuse violations	1,046,246
Gambling	10,793
Offenses against family and children	94,216
Driving under the influence	924,754
Liquor laws	397,835
Drunkenness	481,090
Disorderly conduct	518,080
Vagrancy	18,936
All other offenses	2,510,843
Suspicion (not included in totals)	3,882
Curfew and loitering law violations	121,419
Runaways	129,947

NOTE: Arrest totals are based on all reporting agencies and estimates for unreported areas. Because of rounding, items may not add to totals.

[a]Violent crimes are offenses of murder, forcible rape, robbery, and aggravated assault.
[b]Property crimes are offenses of burglary, larceny-theft, motor vehicle theft, and arson.
[c]Includes arson.

SOURCE: *Uniform Crime Reports.*

Exhibit 3.2

International Perspectives on Crime and Justice
Crime in Colombia

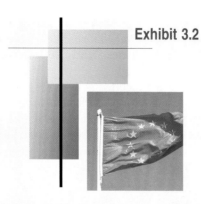

From reading the newspaper and listening to television commentators, it is easy to get the impression that the streets of America are dangerous places—at least in terms of murder, robbery, and other street crimes. The international press tends to reflect similar images. Overall, however, the United States is a relatively safe place in which to live and travel. In parts of Latin America, for example, there are continuous problems with violence by narco-traffickers, insurgent guerrillas, paramilitary groups, and other criminal elements. The Republic of Colombia, situated at the north-western end of South America, is particularly hazardous in these respects, so much so that the U.S. Department of State emphasizes the following to travelers:

> Colombia is one of the most dangerous countries in the world. Based on Colombian government statistics,

Colombia's per capita murder rate of 77.5 murders per 100,000 inhabitants is more than ten times higher than that of the United States. While narcotics and guerrilla-related violence account for part of this, common criminals are responsible for an estimated 75 percent of the reported murders.

Minor crime is prevalent in cities, especially in the vicinity of hotels and airports. Theft of hand luggage and travel documents at airports is common, particularly at El Dorado Airport in Bogotá. Taking illegal taxis, which are sometimes characterized by a driver and a companion and irregular markings, is dangerous. Getting into a taxi that already has one or more passengers is not advisable. Travel by bus is risky. Attempts at extortion and kidnappings on rural buses are not unusual. Violence occurs frequently in bars and nightclubs.

Visitors are urged to exercise caution as they would in any large city in the U.S. Criminals sometimes use the drug "scopolamine" to incapacitate tourists in order to rob them. The drug is administered in drinks (in bars), through ciga-

MURDER CITY

What city was the murder capital of the world during the second half of the 1990s? New York? Chicago? Miami? Bogotá? Rio de Janeiro? Lima? Moscow? Hong Kong? Washington, D.C.?

During part of the 1990s, murders increased dramatically in a number of U.S. cities, particularly in New Orleans and Indianapolis. But *murder city* was neither of these, nor was it Miami or New York City as urban folklore would suggest. It was Bogotá, Colombia, where more than 3,000 killings occurred annually as the result of drug trafficking, gang warfare, and street crime in general. Not too far behind Bogotá were Caracas (Venezuela), Lima (Peru), and Rio de Janeiro (Brazil).

For those who said New York City, it should be noted that murder has been on a dramatic decline there throughout the 1990s. By contrast, Chicago reported more killings than any other American city during 1998. This is especially remarkable considering that Chicago has only a third of the population of New York City.

Reliability of Estimates

It must be emphasized at the outset that with the exception of the data on homicide, *UCR* estimates of the volume and rates of crime are considerably lower than the actual frequency of such occurrences. Homicide figures tend to be nearly complete, since most deaths and missing persons are investigated in one way or another. Furthermore, comparisons of homicide rates compiled by the FBI and by the Office of Vital Statistics reflect similar figures.[2] But in all other crime categories, *UCR* estimates are severely deficient.

Crime, by its very nature, is not easily measurable. It is subject to both concealment and nonreporting—concealment by victims and offenders, and nonreporting by authorities—with the result that official crime statistics fall significantly short of the full volume and range of offenses. There are, for example, wide areas of criminal behavior that rarely find their way into official compilations. When sex, family, and other human relationships are involved, criminal codes are often in sharp conflict with emotions and social norms,

The body of one of 16 young men massacred in a Medellin suburb. Masked gunmen fired indiscriminately on people at a bus stop and a pool hill, killing 16 and wounding 4. The attack was one of the worst in Medellin, a city where militias, common criminals, and other armed bands control zones in poor neighborhoods.

disoriented and can cause prolonged unconsciousness and serious medical problems.

Another common scam is an approach to an obvious tourist by an alleged "policeman," who says he wants to "check" the foreigner's money for counterfeit U.S. dollars. The person gives the criminal his/her money, receives a receipt, and the "policeman" disappears.

Kidnapping for ransom occurs throughout Colombia. Since 1980, the U.S. Embassy in Bogotá has learned of 95 U.S. citizens kidnapped in Colombia and adjacent border areas; of these, 11 were murdered, one died from malnutrition during captivity, and the whereabouts of several others remain unknown. U.S. citizens of all age groups and occupations have been kidnapped, and kidnappings have occurred in all major regions of Colombia. Because of widespread guerrilla activity and U.S. policy that opposes concessions to terrorists, including payment of ransom in kidnapping cases, the U.S. government can provide only limited assistance in these cases.

rettes and gum (in taxis), and in powder form (tourists are approached by someone asking directions, with the drug concealed in a piece of paper). The drug renders the person

SOURCE: U.S. Department of State, *Colombia—Consular Information Sheet,* November 20, 1998.

resulting in the concealment of statutory rape, adultery, sodomy, illegal abortion, desertion, and nonsupport. In the legal and health professions, there are unreported white-collar crimes by both practitioners and clients, primarily in the areas of illegal child adoption practices, fee-splitting, illegal prescription and drug dispensing practices, falsification of claims, perjury, bribery, and conflicts of interest. Within the business sector are instances of consumer fraud, purchase and sale of stolen merchandise, short-changing, price-fixing, and concealment of income. Within the public sector there is untold bribery and corruption, and to these offenses can be added "victimless crimes" and syndicate rackets involving prostitution, procuring, commercialized vice, drugs, gambling, and liquor violations, which involve another group of nonreporting clientele. Finally, to these might be added the perhaps millions of victims of Part I and Part II offenses who fail to report crimes to the police out of fear of publicity and reprisal, a lack of confidence in law enforcement or other criminal justice authorities, or a desire not to get involved with crime reporting and control.[3]

At the same time, crime statistics are also subject to concealment, non-reporting, overreporting, and other manipulations by criminal justice authorities, often for political and public relations purposes. For example, as crime rates were falling in many parts of the United States during the 1990s, police officials in a number of cities were under pressure to show decreasing crime statistics. This occurred during 1997 in Boca Raton, Florida, and police officials systematically downgraded many burglaries to vandalism, trespassing, and missing property. The result was an almost 11 percent decrease in the city's felony crime rate for the year. In Philadelphia, furthermore, the city was forced to withdraw its crime figures from the *UCR* for 1996, 1997, and for at least the first half of 1998 because of underreporting and downgrading of crimes to less serious incidents.[4]

In addition to these problems of concealment and nonreporting, which occur at the victim and agency levels, there are other contaminations of the statistics that result from the *UCR* process itself. The FBI's *Uniform Crime Reporting Handbook* provides specific definitions of the 29 crime categories in the *UCR;* the FBI also provides standard reporting forms to police agencies across the country for compiling their data. However, not all law enforcement bureaucracies follow directions and instructions to the letter, resulting in many contaminated categories.

The *UCR* in Retrospect

How useful, then, are the *Uniform Crime Reports?* Are they reliable enough to provide the researcher, administrator, and observer with baseline data on the phenomenon of crime? As has been pointed out, the *UCR* data do have limitations, including incompleteness and bias, and they fall considerably short in reporting the full extent of crime in the United States.

By examining *UCR* figures within the perspective of rates and proportions, however, as opposed to absolute numbers, a degree of bias is eliminated. Such analyses can help determine the overall growth, decline, or persistence of particular offense behavior; they can be a mechanism for determining the extent to which the phenomenon is or is not being brought under control; they can suggest the parameters of the population cohort or cohorts most responsible for a particular form of criminality; and they can indicate the changing social and economic severity of a given offense.

Second, the most effective use of rate and proportion analysis occurs at the local level. Combining existing *UCR* data with statistical compilations available from local, county, and state criminal justice agencies provides planners, administrators, and observers with the specific information necessary for isolating community crime trends.

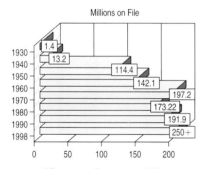

Millions on File

1930	1.4
1940	13.2
1950	114.4
1960	142.1
1970	197.2
1980	173.22
1990	191.9
1998	250+

0   50   100   150   200

Fingerprints on File

Since the FBI began collecting fingerprints in 1924, it has received almost 400 million fingerprint cards and has 200 million on file.

NOTE: World War II Civil Defense cards were purged in 1973.
SOURCE: FBI.

Is the man lying on this park bench in Philadelphia's Franklin Square homeless and sleeping, or a victim of crime? Passersby are typically unwilling to find out.

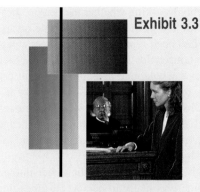

Exhibit 3.3 **Gender Perspectives on Crime and Justice**
Men and Women as Victims of Violence

Although every American is a potential victim of crime, for certain crimes of violence your likelihood of victimization is greater or lesser according to who you are—your gender, race/ethnic group, age, and occupation.

Data from the *Uniform Crime Reports* combined with the findings of specific research studies indicate that homicide victims are disproportionately male, African American or Latino, and between the ages of 20 and 34. The typical victims are unmarried and employed, and the most dangerous occupations for homicide victimizations are taxi drivers and chauffeurs, police and other law enforcement officials, hotel clerks, and garage and service station employees. Also at high risk are drug users/dealers, gang members, and street people. The typical victims of robbery and assault are not unlike those of homicide: young African American and Latino men living in inner-city neighborhoods. By contrast, the least likely victims of homicide, robbery, and assault are white, non-Latina women under age 65.

According to *Uniform Crime Reports* definitions, rape is gender-specific, in that only women can be victims. Yet despite this anachronism, police reports and national victimization surveys indicate that rape victims are typically women, young, unmarried, and economically disadvantaged. Only 5 percent to 10 percent of rape victims are males, but more than half of all rape victims are under age 18.

SOURCES: Terance D. Miethe and Richard C. McCorkle, *Crime Profiles: The Anatomy of Dangerous Persons, Places, and Situations* (Los Angeles: Roxbury, 1998); *Uniform Crime Reports—1997.*

In 1987, the Department of Justice began a redesign of the *UCR* program with the testing and implementation of a new *National Incident-Based Reporting System* (NIBRS). When the NIBRS program is fully set in motion, data will be collected and reported in 22 crime categories made up of 46 specific crimes with regard to the following factors:[5]

- *Incident*—date and time
- *Offense*—whether completed or attempted, type(s) of criminal activity, weapons or force involved, premises involved and method of entry (if applicable), location, whether computer equipment was used, whether the offender used alcohol or drugs during or before the crime
- *Property*—type of property loss, value, recovery date, type and quantity of drugs involved (if appropriate)
- *Victim*—type (person or business), characteristics (age, sex, race, ethnicity), circumstances if homicides/assaults (such as lovers' quarrel, killed in line of duty, etc.), victim-offender relationship (see Exhibit 3.3)
- *Offender*—characteristics (age, sex, race), date of arrest, arrest offense

Because conversion to the NIBRS program will require computerization, training, technical assistance, and support at each reporting, full implementation on a nationwide basis is not expected before the year 2000.[6]

VICTIM SURVEY RESEARCH

In 1965, in an effort to determine the parameters of crime that did not appear in official criminal statistics, the President's Commission on Law Enforcement and Administration of Justice initiated the first national survey of crime victimization ever conducted. During the year, the National Opinion Research

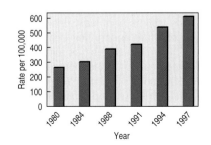

**Drug-Related Arrests,
1980–1997**

SOURCE: *Uniform Crime Reports.*

CRIME RATE COMPARISONS BETWEEN THE FIRST NORC SURVEY AND THE *UCR*

Crime	NORC	*UCR*
Homicide	3.0	5.1
Forcible rape	42.5	11.6
Robbery	94.0	61.4
Aggravated assault	218.3	106.6
Burglary	949.1	605.3
Larceny	606.5	393.3
Motor vehicle theft	206.2	251.0
Total violent crimes	357.8	184.7
Total property crimes	1,761.8	1,249.6

SOURCE: President's Commission on Law Enforcement and Administration of Justice, 1967.

Victimization surveys: Surveys of the victims of crime based on interviews with representative samples of the household population.

WOMEN AS VICTIMS OF VIOLENCE

- Every hour 16 women are confronted by rapists, and one woman is raped an average of every 5 minutes.
- Three to four million are battered each year by their husbands, ex-husbands, or boyfriends, and a woman is beaten an average of every 18 seconds.
- Three out of four women will be the victims of at least one violent crime during their lifetime.
- The United States has a rape rate nearly 4 times higher than Germany's, 13 times higher than Britain's, and more than 20 times higher than Japan's.
- One in seven women in college have been raped.

SOURCE: Senator Joseph R. Biden, "Battling Violence in America" (Speech, University of Delaware, 1994).

Center (NORC) surveyed 10,000 households, asking whether the person questioned, or any member of the household, had been a victim of crime during the preceding year; whether the crime had been reported to the police; and if not, the reasons for not reporting.[7] The households were selected so that they would be representative of the nation as a whole, and as is the case with political polling and election forecasting, the results were considered to be accurate within a small degree of error. More detailed surveys were undertaken in medium- and high-crime areas in Washington, D.C., Boston, and Chicago by the Bureau of Social Science and Research, located in Washington, and the Survey Research Center of the University of Michigan.

These **victimization surveys** quickly demonstrated that the actual amount of crime in the United States at that time was likely to be several times that reported in the *UCR*. The NORC survey suggested that during 1965, forcible rapes were almost four times the reported rape, larcenies were almost double, and burglaries and robberies were 50 percent greater than the reported rate. Vehicle theft was lower, but by a smaller amount than the differences between other categories of crime, and the homicide figure from the NORC survey was considered too small for an accurate statistical projection. As high as the NORC rates were for violent and property crimes, they were still considered to have understated the actual amounts of crime to some degree, since the victimization rates for every member of each surveyed household were based on the responses of only one family member interviewed.

The National Crime Survey

The interest and knowledge generated by the initial victim survey research stimulated the Law Enforcement Assistance Administration (LEAA) to continue the effort with surveys of its own. Its first survey, conducted by the U.S. Bureau of the Census in 1972, further documented the disparities between unreported crime and "crimes known to the police." In some cities the ratio of the two was greater than 5 to 1.[8]

Since that 1972 effort, victimization research has continued under the title of the National Crime Survey (NCS). NCS data reflect the nature and extent of criminal victimization, the characteristics of the victim, victim-offender relationships, the times and places of the crimes, the degree of weapon use, extent of personal injury, extent of victim self-protection, amount of economic and worktime loss due to victimization, the degree to which crimes are reported to police, and the reasons for nonreporting. Although NCS and *UCR* data are not fully comparable (this is discussed below), the number of crimes projected by the NCS goes well beyond what appear in *UCR* data each year.

The major reason for these discrepancies is that significant numbers of these crimes are not reported to the police by victims. Based on NCS estimates, it would appear that the reporting rate for violent crimes is a little over half; for larcenies, less than a third. The major reason for this high level of nonreporting is the victims' beliefs that there is nothing the police can do about the crimes or their beliefs that victimizations are simply not important enough to report. Less frequently mentioned are such reasons as fear of reprisal, reporting is too inconvenient or time-consuming, the police do not want to be bothered, or the crime is a private and personal matter.

Although *UCR* and NCS data have been often compared, the two are still not fully comparable. First, the *UCR* bases its crime rates on the total U.S. population, while the NCS victimization data relate only to those persons who are age 12 and older. Second, the NCS measures crime by the victimization rather than by the incident, and for crimes against persons the number of victimizations is normally greater than the number of incidents, because more than one person can be involved in any given incident. Third, NCS and *UCR* crime classifications are not always uniform. While purse-snatching is included with robbery according to *UCR* definitions, it appears as theft in NCS data. Fourth, NCS data on homicide are considered to be unreliable because violence of that type is relatively rare, and the few unreported instances that do emerge during a survey of a population cross section are too small in numbers to project accurately for the nation as a whole.

Comparisons between NCS and *UCR* crime figures and rates must be viewed with caution. Neither reporting mechanism alone can offer a fully accurate picture of the extent of specific crimes. Nevertheless, comparisons do indicate some general weaknesses of the *Uniform Crime Reports* and suggest the relative amounts of crime that go unreported to the police.

Victimization Survey Applications and Limitations

The rediscovery of the victim as a more complete source of information on instances of criminal activity has been the chief contribution of victim survey research. The material derived from crime victim surveys helps determine to a great degree the extent and distribution of crime in a community. In addition, the surveys target not only victimizations but also public conceptions of the fear of crime, characteristics of the victim and offender, conceptions of police effectiveness, as well as other data. Therefore victim-focused studies such as these can also be used to do the following:

1. Describe the characteristics of victims and high-crime areas
2. Evaluate the effectiveness of specific police programs
3. Develop better insights into certain violent crimes through the analysis of victim-offender relationships
4. Structure programs for increased victim reporting of crimes to the police
5. Sensitize the criminal justice system to the needs of the victim
6. Develop training programs that stress police-victim and police-community relations
7. Structure and implement meaningful public information and crime prevention programs

The uses of victimization surveys

Nevertheless, victimization studies do have limitations. A number of weaknesses affect their accuracy. The people who conduct these surveys find that those interviewed tend to incorrectly remember exactly when a crime occurred; in property offenses, they forget how much the losses were. But by far the major problem associated with the victimization survey technique is its cost. The greatest advantages come from surveys at the local level that focus on what can be done to improve neighborhood crime prevention and police effectiveness programs. However, the cost of conducting victimization surveys on an annual basis in most communities would be staggering, and most communities simply cannot afford them.

The limitations of victimization data

SELF-REPORTED CRIMINAL BEHAVIOR

Since the 1930s, when the FBI began publishing the *Uniform Crime Reports,* criminological research has produced studies confirming the limitations of official crime statistics. Among the earliest of these research efforts was a rudimentary victimization survey in 1933, which found that of 5,314 instances of shoplifting that occurred in three Philadelphia department stores, less than 5 percent were ever reported to the police.[9]

Self-reported crime: Crime statistics
compiled on the basis of self-reports by
offenders.

*The uses and advantages of self-report
studies*

The limitations of self-reports
Validity

Reliability

Another primary mechanism for determining the nature and extent of this
"dark figure," or *unknown crime,* has been the study of **self-reported crime.**
The first major study of self-reported crime came in 1947, when two researchers obtained completed questionnaires from 1,020 men and 678 women
of diverse ages and with a wide range of conventional occupations regarding
their involvement in 49 different offenses. Ninety-nine percent of the respondents admitted committing one or more of the offenses listed. The percentages of both men and women who had engaged in many types of crime were
significant.[10]

This pioneer effort demonstrated that criminal activity was considerably
more widespread than police files even began to suggest. Since then, studies
of self-reported criminal involvement have become more common. In addition to their use as a check on the limitations of standard crime-reporting mechanisms, they can also be used to determine the following information:

1. The extent of crime commission within the "normal" (typically noncriminal) population
2. What kinds of crime typically remain unknown
3. How the official system of crime control selects its cases
4. Whether certain categories of offenders are over- or under-selected by
   official control mechanisms
5. Whether explanations and theories of crime developed for officially
   known offenders apply to nonregistered offenders as well[11]

Studies of self-reported crime have provided numerous insights into these
issues, but such research has not been without limitations and problems. First,
there are methodological questions of validity and reliability. *Validity* refers
to how good an answer the study yields. When the respondents admit to criminal behavior, are their answers true? Do they underreport or exaggerate their
offense behavior? Are the respondents' estimates of the frequency of their
crimes accurate? *Reliability* refers to the precision or accuracy of the instruments used to record and measure self-reported behavior. In other words, does
the interview measure what it is intended to measure? Does the respondent
interpret the meaning of words such as *burglary, robbery,* or some other
offense the same way the researcher does? Besides these potential methodological problems there are other possible sources of error, such as the
following:

- Those who agree to answer questions may be markedly different from those
  who refuse, which leaves in doubt the representativeness of any sample of
  persons interviewed.
- Those who respond to such inquiries may be truthful in their answers but
  may elect to conceal large segments of their criminal backgrounds.
- Most studies have focused on groups of students and other juveniles, stressing the incidence of unrecorded *delinquency,* while few efforts have targeted populations of adult offenders.

One of the more recent studies that did examine the extent of unknown crime
within an adult population involved the collection of extensive self-reported
data on drug use and criminality in Miami (see Exhibit 3.4).

In general, despite sample biases and other methodological limitations,
the studies of self-reported crime that have been made over the past four
decades are important to criminological research. First, there are the advantages mentioned earlier. Second, studies that focus on particular populations
(such as drug users) can tell us more about the patterns and styles of criminal careers than any other form of data.

Exhibit 3.4   **Research in Crime and Justice**
Crack-Cocaine and Crime in Miami

For more than two decades I have been doing street-based research with delinquents, street criminals, drug users, and prostitutes in Miami, Florida. One of the more recent studies in this regard included 699 crack and cocaine users, the majority of whom were actively using drugs and committing crimes in the community at the time that they were contacted. All subjects were interviewed at length about the number of their crimes and arrests during the previous 90 days. The findings of the study found that the incidence of crime was strikingly high, while the rate of arrest was almost insignificant. There were a total of 1,766,630 offenses, but fewer than

1 percent resulted in arrest. Although most of these offenses were the so-called "victimless" crimes of procuring, drug sales, prostitution, and gambling, the

number of Index crimes was significant—almost 5,000 robberies and assaults and more than 20,000 larcenies of one type or another.

Smoking crack in the back alleys of Miami Beach.

SOURCE: James A. Inciardi and Anne E. Pottieger, "Drug Use and Street Crime in Miami: An (Almost) Twenty-Year Retrospective," *Substance Use and Misuse* 33 (1998): 1839–1870.

OTHER SOURCES OF DATA ON CRIME AND JUSTICE

Throughout the history of crime statistics in the United States, writers in this field have recognized the gaps and abuses in crime data and have stressed the need for a comprehensive statistics program that would give an accurate picture of crime in the United States. One of the earliest suggestions for achieving this appeared in Louis Newton Robinson's *History and Organization of Criminal Statistics in the United States* in 1911. Robinson proposed to use a model designed by the Bureau of the Census for collecting mortality statistics, with the responsibility for compilation resting with individual states and cities.[12] In 1931, the National Commission on Law Observance and Enforcement (the Wickersham Commission) recommended the development of a comprehensive plan for a complete body of statistics covering crime, criminals, criminal justice, and correctional treatment at federal, state, and local levels, with the responsibility of the program entrusted to a single federal agency.[13] More than 30 years later, in 1967, the President's Commission on Law Enforcement and Administration of Justice again called for a national crime

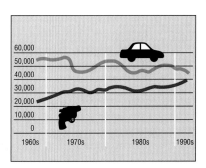

Converging Causes of Death

SOURCE: National Center for Health Statistics.

statistics program.[14] In 1973, the same plea was made by the National Advisory Commission on Criminal Justice Standards and Goals.[15] As recently as 1984, the Justice Department made a similar recommendation.[16]

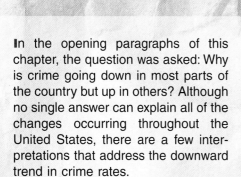

To date, the long-awaited national statistics program has yet to emerge. The *Uniform Crime Reports* still continues as the primary data source on crime, supplemented to some extent by victimization surveys, and to a lesser degree by a smattering of self-report studies. However, these are not the only sources of data on crime, criminals, and criminal justice processing. Many state and federal agencies compile data on their own particular areas of interest, which are available to students and researchers in crime and justice. These appear in the *Sourcebook of Criminal Justice Statistics,* published annually by the U.S. Department of Justice.

Op-Ed

In the opening paragraphs of this chapter, the question was asked: Why is crime going down in most parts of the country but up in others? Although no single answer can explain all of the changes occurring throughout the United States, there are a few interpretations that address the downward trend in crime rates.

First, there is the economy. Because of greater prosperity and reduced unemployment, youths in particular have more hope of finding legal jobs, and view crime as a less desirable option. Second, there is prevention. The 1990s witnessed an increased number of early intervention programs for high-risk youths, and after-school programs during the 3 P.M. to 8 P.M. peak hours for juvenile violent crime. Third, there are the higher rates of incarceration. Between 1979 and 1991, the number of offenders sent to prison for violent crimes doubled, and as the noted political scientist James Q. Wilson observed: "Putting people in prison is the single most important thing we've done."[17] Fourth, there is better policing in a number of jurisdictions. Not only are there more police on the streets, but there is an increased use of "community policing" techniques (see Chapter 5). Fifth, there has been a dramatic reduction in the number of street-corner crack markets. The withering of these markets lessens the violence associated with rivalries in the crack distribution system, the large number of drug transactions among highly agitated buyers and sellers, and the number of handguns that users and dealers carry to protect themselves from robberies. And finally, the increased rates of violent crime in many mid-sized cities was the result of crack markets arriving there late.[18] As criminologist Alfred Blumstein of Carnegie Mellon University recently put it:

> Smaller cities are going through what bigger cities went through five years ago. There is a lag effect in the smaller cities, caused not necessarily by the saturation of drugs in the big cities but the propagation of markets. There may be entrepreneurs from the big cities looking to expand or new entrepreneurs in small cities looking to get involved.[19]

Exhibit 3.5 **Careers in Justice**
Document Examiners and Fingerprint Analysts

Two positions that operate behind the scenes in the criminal justice field are document examiners and fingerprint analysts. Document examiners establish the genuineness of letters, papers, contracts, and other documents as part of police investigations, as expert witnesses in court, or as consultants to law enforcement agencies. They scrutinize such things as handwriting, watermarks, inks, paper fibers,

typeface, and erasures, and conduct other forms of technical analysis. Minimum qualifications include a community college degree in criminal justice or related field, 3 years of experience in law enforcement or other investigative work, and/or 2 years of technical work in examining handwriting. Annual salaries range from $36,000 to $70,000 depending on qualifications, experience, and geographical location.

A related area of expertise is fingerprint analysis. Although the FBI is moving toward computerized fingerprint examinations, the need for human analysts will remain both for the verification of computer results and for routine

fingerprint examinations in agencies and jurisdictions where computer technology is unavailable or impractical. Fingerprint analysts compare latent prints to known inked prints, brief court and other criminal justice personnel on findings of fingerprint analyses, construct courtroom exhibits illustrating fingerprint evidence, and maintain latent fingerprint files. Minimum qualifications include a community college degree in criminal justice or related field, and completion of the FBI basic fingerprint identification course. Salaries range from $25,000 to $45,000 annually in state and local agencies, and higher at the federal level.

SUMMARY

Most of the data on the nature, extent, and trends of crime in the United States come from official crime statistics. Official statistics are collected and compiled by the FBI and published annually as the *Uniform Crime Reports (UCR)*. The *UCR* includes crimes known to the police and arrests. Data are broken down into Part I and Part II offenses, and arrests are subdivided by age, race/ethnicity, and sex. The *UCR* also includes rates of crime, percent changes from year to year, and breakdowns by region, state, and metropolitan area.

Although official statistics are the primary source of crime data, they have numerous shortcomings. Most criminal acts are not reported to the police, and statistical data are subject to concealment, overreporting, nonreporting, and other manipulations. On the other hand, despite these difficulties, *UCR* data are useful for gaining insight into the relative amount of crime and for analyzing crime and arrest trends.

In an effort to determine the parameters of crime that did not appear in official statistics, in 1965 the President's Commission initiated the first national survey of crime victimization ever conducted. Similar surveys have been undertaken since then. These surveys demonstrate that

the actual amount of crime is probably several times greater than that estimated in the *UCR*. Victimization and *UCR* data, however, are not fully comparable. The bases of their rates are different, the yardsticks of measurement are different, and crime classifications are not uniform.

Victimization data have numerous useful applications for understanding the characteristics of victims, evaluating the effectiveness of police programs, developing insights into victim-offender relationships, sensitizing the criminal justice system to the needs of the victim, and structuring more focused crime prevention programs. On the other hand, victimization surveys have their shortcomings. They are expensive and they raise a number of basic methodological issues.

Self-reported data on offenses represent a third source of information on crime. These data reflect the so-called "dark figure" or unknown crime. The findings of these studies suggest the extent of crime in "normal" populations, what kinds of crimes are committed that typically remain unknown, and how the official system of crime control may select its cases. Self-report studies, however, have problems of validity and reliability.

KEY TERMS

Crime Index **60**	Part II offenses **60**	*Uniform Crime Reports (UCR)* **58**
crime rate **61**	self-reported crime **70**	victimization surveys **68**
Part I offenses **59**		

QUESTIONS FOR DISCUSSION

1. What issues of validity and reliability are most apparent with regard to official criminal statistics?
2. Can the *UCR* be improved? How?
3. How might official statistics, victimization data, and self-reported crime data be collected and combined to provide a more accurate picture of crime in the United States?

4. Why is it difficult to use official statistics to make universal claims about crime trends and patterns?
5. What do self-respect studies tell us?

MEDIA RESOURCES

1. ***Uniform Crime Reports.*** The entire *Uniform Crime Reports* can be found on the Internet and can be either downloaded or printed out. Web site address: http://www.fbi.gov
2. **Crime Trends.** The March 1998 issue of *U.S. News and World Report* contains a number of articles on the changing rates of crime in the United States.
3. **Self-Reported Crime.** See James A. Inciardi and Anne E. Pottieger, "Drug Use and Street Crime in Miami: An (Almost) Twenty-Year Retrospective," *Substance Use & Misuse* 33 (1998): 1839–1870. The article has also been reproduced on the textbook Web site.

4. **NIBRS and Elderly Victimization.** See Kimberly A. McCabe and Sharon S. Gregory, "Elderly Victimization: An Examination Beyond the FBI's Index Crimes," *Research on Aging* 20 (May 1998): 363–373. This article uses NIBRS data from South Carolina to demonstrate both the use of NIBRS and how the elderly are at higher risk for criminal victimization.
5. **National Crime Victimization Survey.** The most recent surveys and numerous supplementary analyses are available on the Internet. Web site address: http://www.ojp.usdoj.gov/bjs/pub

NOTES

1. Federal Bureau of Investigation, *Crime in the United States—1994* (Washington, D.C.: U.S. Government Printing Office, 1998). Throughout this text, these FBI crime reports are referenced simply as *Uniform Crime Reports* or *UCR*.
2. Daniel Glaser, "National Goals and Indicators for the Reduction of Crime and Delinquency," *Annals* 371 (May 1967): 104–126.
3. See Harry Manuel Shulman, "The Measurement of Crime in the United States," *Journal of Criminal Law, Criminology and Police Science* 57 (1966): 483–492.
4. *New York Times,* August 3, 1998, pp. A1, A16.
5. *Structure and Implementation Plan for the Enhanced UCR Program* (Washington, D.C.: Federal Bureau of Investigation, 1989).
6. Federal Bureau of Investigation, *UCR Handbook, NIBRS Edition* (Washington, D.C.: U.S. Department of Justice, 1998).

7. President's Commission on Law Enforcement and Administration of Justice, *Crime and Its Impact: An Assessment* (Washington, D.C.: U.S. Government Printing Office, 1967), p. 17.
8. Law Enforcement Assistance Administration, *Criminal Victimization in the United States—1977* (Washington, D.C.: U.S. Government Printing Office, 1979).
9. Thorsten Sellin, *Research Memorandum on Crime in the Depression* (New York: Social Science Research Council, 1937).
10. James S. Wallerstein and Clement J. Wyle, "Our Law-Abiding Law-Breakers," *Probation* 35 (April 1947): 107–118.
11. J. Andenaes, N. Christie, and S. Skirbekk, "A Study in Self-Reported Crime," *Scandinavian Studies in Criminology,* Scandinavian Research Council on Criminology (Oslo: Universitelsforloget, 1965), pp. 87–88.

12. Louis Newton Robinson, *History and Organization of Criminal Statistics in the United States.* (New York: Hart, Schaffner & Marx, 1911).

13. U.S. National Commission on Law Observance and Enforcement, *Report on Criminal Statistics* (Washington, D.C.: U.S. Government Printing Office, 1931).

14. President's Commission on Law Enforcement and Administration of Justice, *The Challenge of Crime in a Free Society* (Washington, D.C.: U.S. Government Printing Office, 1967), pp. 123–137.

15. National Advisory Commission on Criminal Justice Standards and Goals, *A National Strategy to Reduce Crime* (Washington, D.C.: U.S. Government Printing Office, 1973).

16. *New York Times,* November 19, 1984, p. B11.

17. Cited in Gordon Witkin, "The Crime Bust," *U.S. News and World Report,* May 25, 1998, pp. 28–37.

18. *Louisville Courier-Journal,* December 28, 1998, p. A1; *New York Times,* December 28, 1998, p. A16.

19. Cited in *New York Times,* January 15, 1998, p. A16.

C H A P T E R **4**

CRIMINAL JUSTICE AND PROCEDURE: AN OVERVIEW

President Clinton and Monica Lewinsky.

Washington, D.C.: —On December 19, 1998, the U.S. House of Representatives impeached William Jefferson Clinton, the forty-second president of the United States. The impeachment stemmed from the president's attempt to conceal a sexual relationship with a young White House intern, and the process had begun with the delivery of a massive document from Independent Counsel Kenneth Starr to the members of the House. Known as *The Starr Report,* it urged the impeachment of the president. Many observers found the document to be biased, unfair, and unbalanced, and held that the president's actions did not meet the constitutional standard for impeachment—that is, "high Crimes and Misdemeanors."

During the preceding weeks, sentiments in Congress about impeachment were split along party lines—Republicans supported it, while Democrats opposed it. Most Americans, however, felt that the president should not be impeached. Nevertheless, because of the Republican majority in the House of Representatives, Clinton became only the second president in U.S. history to be impeached. Then there was the trial in the Senate, with much of the proceedings and decisions based on partisan politics.

What happened in Washington raises a number of questions. What are "high Crimes and Misdemeanors," and was the president really guilty of them? At the same time, is this the way that the justice system in the United States really operates? Is it fair? Did the president receive what is referred to in the Bill of Rights as "due process"?

Given these crucial questions, the following discussion examines the concept of due process of law and how it emerged in American jurisprudence. In addition, the various stages of the criminal justice process are introduced. A more complete analysis of the process is presented in later chapters.

SYSTEMS OF JUSTICE

Down through the ages, processes of justice have emerged in many forms. During the early centuries of Christianity, for example, when a thief was caught in the act of stealing, no trial was considered necessary. If he was a poor man who could not pay even the smallest of fines, he was simply put to death with little formality. But in the more doubtful cases, some degree of innocence or guilt had to be determined. Typical in such instances was the *ordeal by water,* adopted by the Catholic church and carried out by a priest.

Before the *trial by ordeal* actually began, a cauldron of boiling water was placed in the center of the church. Spectators, who were required to be fasting and "abstinent from their wives during the previous night," assembled into a row on each side of the church and were blessed by the priest. While they prayed that God would "make clear the whole truth," the priest bandaged the arm of the accused. Into the bottom of the vat of boiling water the priest dropped a small stone.

If the accused were to undergo only the single ordeal, he had simply to place his hand into the water up to his wrist; but if the more serious triple ordeal had been prescribed, he then had to plunge his entire forearm to the bottom of the cauldron and pluck out the stone. After 3 days, the bandages were removed, and evidence of scalding was deemed proof of guilt.[1]

Trials by ordeal, or perhaps by battle, were the cornerstone of the **inquisitorial system** of justice. The assumption of guilt was the guiding factor, and the accused was considered guilty until he could prove himself innocent. Inquisitorial justice became manifest when some form of divine intervention spared the accused from pain, suffering, or death, or when the accused would readily admit his or her guilt, usually elicited through torture or other forms of corporal punishment. This system—which now might more properly be called the **inquiry system** so as to remove from it the aura of terror associated with the word *inquisition*—still exists in a modified form in most countries of the world that did not evolve from English or American colonial rule. In the modern inquiry court, all persons—judge, prosecutor, defense attorney, defendant, and witnesses—are obliged to cooperate with the court in its inquiry into the crime. Out of this inquiry it is believed that the truth will emerge.

By contrast, American judicial process reflects the **adversary system,** in which the innocence of the accused is presumed, and the burden of proof is placed on the court. In the adversary court, the judge is an impartial arbiter or referee between battling adversaries—the prosecution and defense. Within strict rules of procedure, the opposing sides fight to win, and it is believed that the side with truth will be victorious. Adversary proceedings are grounded in the right of the defendant to refrain from hurting himself or herself (as opposed to the lack of such a right in an inquiry court) and in the notion of **due process of law,** a concept that asserts fundamental principles of justice and implies the administration of laws that do not violate the sacredness of private rights.

CRIMINAL DUE PROCESS

During the age of chivalry, when the championing of the weak was emphasized as the ideal and when valor, courtesy, generosity, and dexterity in arms were the summit of any man's attainment, inquisitorial justice was dominant.

PUBLIC OPINION ON THE PRESIDENTIAL CRISIS (OCTOBER 1998)

Do you think Congress should impeach Bill Clinton?

Yes	27%
No	67%
No opinion	6%

Do you think Bill Clinton should resign from office?

Yes	36%
No	61%
No opinion	3%

SOURCE: Gallup Poll, October 29, 1998.

Trial by ordeal

Inquisitorial system: A system of justice in which the accused is considered guilty until he or she is proven innocent.

Inquiry system: A system of justice in which all participants in a proceeding are obliged to cooperate with the court in its inquiry into the crime.

Adversary system: A system of justice in which the innocence of the accused is presumed and the burden of proof is placed on the court.

Due process of law: A concept that asserts fundamental principles of justice and implies the administration of laws that do not violate the sacredness of private rights.

In the Middle Ages "due process" meant nothing more than adhering to the *law of the land,* and torture was the common method of ascertaining guilt. Periods of active torture were usually preceded by imprisonment in some foul dungeon or small cell. Defendants were ill-fed and left in an uncomfortable and half-starved condition to contemplate the infinitely worse treatment that awaited them.

Medieval torture and "due process"

Eventually, the defendant was brought to a torture room to face his or her accusers and those in charge of the gruesome ceremonies. If confessions could not be forced by the many exercises in horror that were introduced, the final stage of torture, which typically led to death, was initiated. This, during the Middle Ages, was viewed as "due process," since the use of torture for eliciting confessions was sanctioned by existing law (see Exhibit 4.1).

No person shall be deprived of life, liberty, or property, without due process of law.
—From the Fifth Amendment

Nor shall any State deprive any person of life, liberty, or property, without due process of law.
—From the Fourteenth Amendment

Even during the early years of the American republic, the concept of due process was vague at best. The framers of the Constitution had stated in the Fifth Amendment that persons shall not be deprived of life, liberty, or property "without due process of law." The due process guarantee was repeated when the Fourteenth Amendment was added to the Constitution in 1868. But what was intended by these words?

The Bill of Rights

Constitution: The institutions, practices, and principles that define and structure a system of government, and the written document that establishes or articulates such a system.

During the 1st Congress, in June 1789, 2 years after the signing of the **Constitution,** James Madison of Virginia, who was later to become the fourth president of the United States, proposed a dozen constitutional amendments. Congress approved 10 of the amendments in September 1791, and they took effect on December 15 of that year, after ratification by the requisite number of

---

Exhibit 4.1

Historical Perspectives on Crime and Justice
Ashford v. *Thornton*

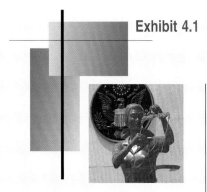

The English case of *Ashford* v. *Thornton,* less gruesome than the use of torture to elicit confessions, reflects an equally curious example of early conceptions of due process. Ashford appeared before the king's justices charging Thornton with murder. He swore that Thornton had raped and drowned Mary Ashford, the accuser's young sister. Based on Ashford's accusa-

tion, the sheriff found Thornton, brought him to the court, and the justices ordered him to make his plea. "Not guilty," he declared, "and I am ready to defend the same with my body." Thornton then drew off his glove and threw it to the floor of the court, a signal that he was demanding a trial by battle. It would be his life against Ashford's, and if Thornton won, he would be judged innocent. Ashford argued that the circumstances were so exceptional that Thornton should be denied the right to defend himself in battle, but the judges were not persuaded. They ruled that the established procedure for cases of this kind must be followed—that

is, trial by battle. Ashford refused to fight, and "due process" followed its course: The judgment was that Thornton should go free.

Interestingly, the case of *Ashford* v. *Thornton* did not occur during the era of the Norman Conquest of 1066 or even the age of the Plantagenet kings a few generations later. Rather, it was less than two centuries ago. The year was 1818, almost 30 years after both the U.S. Constitution and its Bill of Rights, which were the basis of the emerging system of modern rational jurisprudence, had been written.

SOURCE: Charles Rembar, *The Law of the Land: The Evolution of Our Legal System* (New York: Simon & Schuster, 1980), pp. 18–23.

states. These first 10 amendments to the Constitution have become known as the **Bill of Rights.**

The significance of the Bill of Rights is that it restricts government, rather than individuals and private groups. It was added to the Constitution at the insistence of those who feared a strong central government.

Within the Bill of Rights, the *First Amendment* prohibits laws and practices that have the effect of establishing an official religion, and it protects the freedoms of speech, the press, religion, assembly, and the right to petition the government for redress of grievances; the *Second* ensures the right to keep and bear arms as part of a well-regulated militia (see Exhibit 4.2); the *Third* forbids the government to quarter soldiers in people's homes; and the *Fourth* protects a person's right to be secure in his or her person, house, papers, and effects against unreasonable searches and seizures. The *Fifth Amendment* requires indictments for proceedings in serious criminal offenses; it forbids compelling an individual to incriminate himself or herself and forbids trying a person twice for the same offense ("double jeopardy"); it also contains the initial constitutional statement on "due process of law." The *Sixth Amendment* sets out certain requirements for criminal trials, including the defendant's right to counsel, notification of the charges, a speedy and public trial before an impartial jury in the jurisdiction in which the crime was allegedly committed, and the related rights to confront hostile witnesses and to have compulsory processes for obtaining defense witnesses. The *Seventh* preserves the right to a jury trial in common law civil suits involving $20 or more; and the *Eighth* forbids excessive bail, excessive fines, and cruel and unusual punishments. The *Ninth Amendment* has never been cited as the sole basis of a U.S. Supreme Court decision, and there has long been a debate over what the Founding Fathers intended it to mean.[2] On its face, it states that the enumeration of specific rights elsewhere in the Constitution should not be taken to deny or disparage unenumerated rights retained by the people. The *Tenth Amendment* clearly was designed to protect states' rights and guard against the accumulation of excessive federal power; but it, too, is subject to a variety of interpretations by judges and legal scholars.

Since no rights are absolute, and since they are subject to reasonable regulation through law, *the original intent of due process was not self-evident.*

Bill of Rights: The first 10 amendments to the Constitution of the United States, which restrict government actions.

Exhibit 4.2 | **Research in Crime and Justice**
The Second Amendment's "Right to Bear Arms"

A well regulated Militia being necessary to the security of a free State, the right of the people to keep and bear Arms shall not be infringed.

Otherwise known as the Second Amendment, these may be the most argued and misunderstood 27 words in the U.S. Constitution. But what do these words really mean? Is there a constitutional right, or isn't there? Opinions differ. Pro-gun advocates interpret the amendment phrase by phrase, and quite literally, too, concluding that the right to bear arms is self-evident. Gun control advocates argue the reverse: that the amendment is distorted when split into phrases; that taken as a whole, it restricts the right to activities that the state determines necessary to maintain a militia.

Both historical and legal research, however, suggest some-

thing that is quite clear. It would appear that the Second Amendment was spurred by the early colonists' fear that military forces composed of professional soldiers—such as those used by King George III—were not to be trusted. Federalist James Madison drafted the Bill of Rights for presentation at the 1st Congress, but his writing of the Second Amendment was ultimately restructured into its present form in order to place greater emphasis on the militia purpose in dealing with the right to keep and bear arms and to diminish the broad individual powers of Madison's original version.

The federal courts, in interpreting the Second Amendment, have created a principle of law that says the right to bear arms was not extended to each and every individual, but rather was expressly limited to maintaining effective state militia. During the past half-century, the courts have ruled repeatedly on Second Amendment cases, brought primarily by gun advocates seeking greater ownership rights. In an explicit comment on the amendment, a federal district court ruled in the

Madison, the father of these amendments, expected the federal courts to play the major role in implementing their guarantees, and he clearly emphasized this point to his fellow members of Congress:

> Independent tribunals of justice will consider themselves in a peculiar manner the guardians of those rights; they will be an impenetrable bulwark against every assumption of power in the Legislative or Executive; they will naturally be led to resist every encroachment upon rights expressly stipulated for in the Constitution by the declaration of rights.[3]

The Nationalization of the Bill of Rights

Barron v. Baltimore The Supreme Court ruling that the Bill of Rights was added to the Constitution to protect citizens only against the action of the federal, not state or local, government.

In 1833, the Supreme Court made it quite clear that the Bill of Rights provided no protection against state or local action, but only against that of federal authority. In **Barron v. Baltimore,**[4] the owner of a wharf challenged a local action that seriously impaired the value of his wharf by creating shoals and shallows

Charlton Heston, president of the National Rifle Association.

1971 case of *Stevens* v. *United States* as follows:

> Since the Second Amendment applies only to the right of the State to maintain a militia and not to the individual's right to bear arms, there can be no serious claim to any express constitutional right of an individual to possess a firearm.

More recently, the Supreme Court refused to hear a challenge to a 1984 Illinois Supreme Court ruling that upheld the right of an Illinois town to ban the sale and possession of handguns.

At the same time, other federal courts consistently have ruled that the Second Amendment is not an entitlement to gun ownership. In 1976, the 6th Circuit Court of Appeals stated in *United States* v. *Warin* that the supposition that the Second Amendment is concerned with the rights of individuals rather than those of states were erroneous.

In support of federal court rulings, most Americans support gun control—even gun owners. In a recent nationwide Harris Poll, 69 percent of all adults and 57 percent of gun owners were in favor of stricter gun laws.

SOURCE: Earl R. Kruschke, *The Right to Keep and Bear Arms: A Continuing American Dilemma* (Springfield, Ill.: Thomas, 1985); The Harris Poll, May 27, 1998.

around it. Barron maintained that this represented a "taking" of his property without just compensation, in violation of the Fifth Amendment. Chief Justice John Marshall ruled, however, that the Bill of Rights had been adopted to secure individual rights only against the encroachments of the federal government.

Barron v. *Baltimore* seemingly had closed the judicial door on the argument that the provisions of the Bill of Rights should provide protection against abuses of individual rights by state and local governments. However, with the ratification of the Fourteenth Amendment to the Constitution in 1868, it once again became possible to argue that the Bill of Rights should be understood to restrict the powers of the state and local governments as well as the federal government. This is because of the following language in Section 1 of the amendment:

> No State shall make or enforce any law which shall abridge the privileges or immunities of the citizens of the United States; nor shall any State deprive any person of life, liberty, or property, without due process of law; nor deny to any person within its jurisdiction the equal protection of the laws.

The Fourteenth Amendment

"Incorporating" the Bill of Rights

Gitlow v. New York: The Supreme Court ruling that the First Amendment prohibition against government abridgment of the freedom of speech applies to state and local governments as well as to the federal government.

IDENTIFYING THE BILL OF RIGHTS

In 1991, to coincide with the 200th anniversary of the ratification of the Bill of Rights, the American Bar Association commissioned a nationwide poll to determine what proportion of adults could identify the content and purpose of this historic document. Multiple-choice questions were provided, and the answers were as follows:

1. What is the Bill of Rights?
   a. The Preamble to the U.S. Constitution 28%
   b. The Constitution's first 10 amendments 33%
   c. Any rights bill passed by Congress 22%
   d. A message of rebellion from the Founding Fathers to the British monarchy 7%
   e. Don't know 10%
2. What was the Bill's original purpose?
   a. To limit abuses by the federal government 9%
   b. To limit abuses by states 1%
   c. To ensure equality for all citizens 33%
   d. All of the above 55%
   e. Don't know 2%

The proportions of correct answers (1.b. and 2.a.) suggest that most Americans don't know much about their Constitution.

Fiske v. Kansas

Near v. Minnesota

Legal historians disagree on the question of whether Congress intended these words to make all of the provisions of the Bill of Rights binding on the states.[5] In its first decisions after the ratification of the Fourteenth Amendment, the Supreme Court rejected the notion that the due process clause of that amendment ("nor shall any State deprive any person of life, liberty, or property, without due process of law") had "incorporated" the Bill of Rights, thus making each of the provisions of the Bill of Rights applicable to state and local governments.

Gitlow v. New York   The first step toward incorporating most of the provisions of the Bill of Rights came in 1925 in the famous case of *Gitlow* v. *New York*.[6] Benjamin Gitlow, a member of the Socialist party, had been convicted of violating a New York sedition law because he had printed and distributed some 16,000 copies of the "Left Wing Manifesto." This tract called for the overthrow of the U. S. government by "class action of the proletariat in any form" and urged the proletariat to "organize its own state for the coercion and suppression of the bourgeoisie."

Gitlow appealed his conviction to the Supreme Court, his primary contention being that the New York statute unconstitutionally deprived him of his First Amendment right to freedom of speech. The High Court ultimately sustained Gitlow's conviction, holding that free speech was not an absolute right and that Gitlow's manifesto fell within the category of speech that could properly be prohibited by law. Over the dissenting votes of Justices Louis Brandeis and Oliver Wendell Holmes, both of whom argued that political speech should be proscribed only when it created a "clear and present danger" to the security of the nation, the majority of the justices reasoned that Gitlow's tract could properly be suppressed even if it merely contained language that tended to have the effect of inciting violent attempts to overthrow the government (the so-called bad tendency test).

Although Benjamin Gitlow lost his effort to overturn his conviction, he won one of his other arguments—a victory that would come to have enormous influence on the evolution of the American criminal justice system. To convince the justices to hear his appeal, Gitlow had asserted that the First Amendment rights of free speech and free press were enforceable against the states. If the High Court did not accept this proposition, it would lack any legal basis for accepting the case for review and considering the merits of Gitlow's First Amendment arguments. But in a seemingly casual passage in his majority opinion, Justice Edward T. Sanford made judicial history by formally accepting the principle of incorporation of the free speech and free press provisions of the Bill of Rights:

> For present purposes we may and do assume that freedom of speech and of the press—which are protected by the First Amendment from abridgement by Congress—are among the fundamental personal rights and "liberties" protected by the due process clause of the Fourteenth Amendment from impairment by the States.

It soon became apparent that *Gitlow*'s incorporation decision was no aberration, but rather the first step in a case-by-case process that would significantly expand the Supreme Court's authority to protect individual rights against the unconstitutional acts of state and local government officials. In 1927, a unanimous Supreme Court confirmed the incorporation of freedom of speech in the case of *Fiske* v. *Kansas*.[7] Four years later, in *Near* v. *Minnesota*,[8] the Court again declared that freedom of the press was enforceable against state infringement when it struck down the so-called Minnesota Gag Law as an infringement of the liberty of the press that is guaranteed by the Fourteenth Amendment.

In 1932, the Court overturned the convictions of seven indigent, illiterate African American youths who had been convicted of the rapes of two white women in a 1-day trial in a raucous Alabama courtroom without the opportunity to consult with a defense attorney. The case was *Powell* v. *Alabama*,[9] the first of the notorious Scottsboro Boys cases, and the Court's 7-to-2 holding made it obligatory for the states to provide defense counsel in capital cases in which indigent defendants faced such disadvantages as illiteracy, ignorance, and extreme community hostility. Although the *Powell* ruling affected only certain types of capital trials, it represented at least the partial incorporation of the Sixth Amendment's right-to-counsel clause.

Powell **v.** *Alabama*

Palko v. Connecticut

Palko v. Connecticut The next provisions of the Bill of Rights to be nationalized were the First Amendment's guarantees of freedom of religion,[10] freedom of assembly, and freedom to petition the government for a redress of grievances.[11] By 1937, the process of incorporation was well under way. But many questions remained unanswered. Should all of the commands of the Bill of Rights be made binding upon the states? Were only certain provisions worthy of nationalization? If so, what guiding principles should the Court apply in deciding which provisions to incorporate? What was needed was an opportunity to elaborate more fully the legal and philosophical issues involved in nationalizing the Bill of Rights.

That opportunity came in the historic 1937 case of *Palko* v. *Connecticut*.[12] The state of Connecticut had charged Frank Palko with first-degree murder for the shooting deaths of two police officers. However, the jury chose to convict Palko of second-degree murder—a decision that resulted in a sentence of life imprisonment but spared Palko from the death penalty that surely would have followed a conviction for murder in the first degree. Undaunted, the prosecutor, citing a Connecticut statute that permitted prosecutorial appeals based on an "error of law to the prejudice of the state," sought and won a retrial on the original first-degree charges. At the second trial, the unfortunate Palko was promptly convicted and sentenced to die in Connecticut's electric chair. After losing all of his appeals in the courts of the state, he and his attorneys appealed

Two of the "Scottsboro Boys," still incarcerated, six years after the decision in Powell v. Alabama.

to the U.S. Supreme Court on the grounds that his second trial constituted a violation of the Fifth Amendment protection against double jeopardy and that the Fifth Amendment was binding upon the states as a result of the Fourteenth Amendment's due process clause.

There was—and is—no question that Frank Palko's retrial and conviction had violated the double jeopardy clause. In a majority opinion authored by Justice Benjamin Cardozo, however, the Supreme Court ruled against his claims, and Palko was subsequently electrocuted. But, ironically, it would be reasonable to say that Frank Palko did not die in vain. For Justice Cardozo's majority opinion laid the foundation—a series of guidelines and principles—that would eventually lead to the incorporation of not only the double jeopardy clause, but also nearly all of the other key provisions of the Bill of Rights.

At the heart of Justice Cardozo's *Palko* opinion was his rejection of the notion of total incorporation and an effort to establish what has been called the "Honor Roll of Superior Rights." Cardozo wrote eloquently of "those fundamental principles of liberty and justice which lie at the base of all our civil and political institutions." He cited freedom of speech as the cardinal example of a "fundamental right," stressing that the right to speak freely "is the matrix, the indispensable condition, of nearly every other form of freedom." Justice Cardozo also cited freedom of the press and the Fifth Amendment's prohibition against governmental takings of private property without just compensation (the so-called eminent domain clause) as examples of fundamental rights in a democratic society.

On the other end of the continuum of rights, however, were "formal" rights that were admirable and worthy of respect, but without which "justice would not perish." As examples, Cardozo cited the Sixth Amendment right to trial by jury and the Fifth Amendment right to be indicted by a grand jury when charged with "a capital or otherwise infamous crime." As he explained:

> [Such rights] are not of the essence of a scheme of ordered liberty. To abolish them is not to violate a principle of justice so rooted in the traditions and conscience of our people as to be ranked as fundamental.

Justice Cardozo next turned to the Fifth Amendment protection against compulsory self-incrimination. This too was not a "fundamental" right, he asserted, because "justice would not perish if the accused were subject to a duty to respond to orderly inquiry." Having articulated the standards to be applied, Cardozo finally posed the question that would determine the fate of Frank Palko: Did Connecticut's denial of Palko's Fifth Amendment protection against double jeopardy violate those "fundamental principles of liberty and justice which lie at the base of all our civil and political institutions"?

The answer "surely must be 'no,'" wrote Justice Cardozo. The state of Connecticut wasn't trying to harass and wear down Mr. Palko by repeatedly charging him with the same crime; the Connecticut authorities merely were asking that "the case against him…go on until there shall be a trial free from the corrosion of substantial legal error." This, asserted Cardozo, was no great affront to fundamental principles of justice. Indeed, "the edifice of justice stands, in its symmetry, to many, greater than before." And thus the double jeopardy clause failed to make the Honor Roll of Superior Rights, thereby leaving the states free to pass laws in violation of the Fifth Amendment's command that no person shall "be subject for the same offense to be twice put in jeopardy of life or limb."

Justice Cardozo's distinctions between "fundamental" rights, on the one hand, and "formal" rights, on the other hand, are still in effect. The criteria articulated in *Palko* are firmly in place and unlikely ever to be modified or transformed by the Supreme Court. And, in fact, Justice Cardozo's Honor Roll itself was changed only twice between 1937 and 1961. In 1947, the Court added the First Amendment's requirement of "separation of church and state" to the list of rights that applied to the states as an element of the Fourteenth Amendment's due process clause.[13] One year later, the Sixth Amendment's guarantee of the right to a "public trial" was incorporated, thus prohibiting the states from conducting trials and sentencings in secret.[14]

The Criminal Law "Revolution"   By the early 1960s, the composition of the Supreme Court had changed and so, arguably, had the beliefs and values of the American people. Under Chief Justice Earl Warren, who had been appointed by President Eisenhower in 1953, the Supreme Court had made it clear that constitutional rights were not static concepts, frozen in eighteenth-century notions of justice and fairness. The protections of the Bill of Rights, in Chief Justice Warren's memorable phrase from *Trop* v. *Dulles,*[15] "must draw [their] meaning from evolving standards of decency that mark the progress of a maturing society."

The year 1961 marks the beginning of what many legal scholars call "the criminal law revolution." Throughout the 1960s, the Supreme Court, applying the very same guiding principles articulated by Justice Cardozo in *Palko,* expanded the Honor Roll of Superior Rights considerably. By 1969, almost all of the criminal law–related provisions of the Bill of Rights had been made binding upon the states as elements of Fourteenth Amendment due process.

In the historic 1961 case of *Mapp* v. *Ohio,*[16] the High Court declared that both the Fourth Amendment's proscription of "unreasonable searches and seizures" and the exclusionary rule (prohibiting the use of illegally seized evidence in a criminal trial) were applicable to the states. The Eighth Amendment's ban on cruel and unusual punishments was incorporated in 1962,[17] and the Sixth Amendment's right to counsel was imposed on the states 1 year later in the famous case of *Gideon* v. *Wainwright.*[18] In 1964, the Fifth Amendment's protection against self-incrimination was incorporated,[19] and in 1965, the Sixth Amendment right to confront hostile witnesses was given the same status.[20] In 1966, *Parker* v. *Gladden* incorporated the Sixth Amendment right to an impartial jury.[21] The year 1967 saw two Sixth Amendment protections added to the Honor Roll: the guarantee of a speedy trial[22] and the right to compulsory processes for obtaining defense witnesses.[23]

The process of nationalizing the Bill of Rights reached its climax in two decisions announced shortly before the end of the Warren Court era. In 1968, the Court declared that the Sixth Amendment's guarantee of trial by jury applies to state criminal trials involving serious offenses.[24] And in the 1969 case of *Benton* v. *Maryland,*[25] the justices finally ruled that the time had come to make the Fifth Amendment ban on double jeopardy binding upon the states. The Court's determination in *Benton* that the provision against double jeopardy was indeed a "fundamental right that was implicit in the concept of ordered liberty" overruled *Palko* v. *Connecticut* (32 years too late for Frank Palko) and completed—for now—the process of nationalizing the Bill of Rights.

Since *Benton,* the Supreme Court has not incorporated any more of the specific provisions of the Bill of Rights. However, it is worth mentioning that in 1965, the Court in **Griswold** v. **Connecticut**[26] incorporated the right to "privacy"—a right not specifically cited in the Bill of Rights (or anywhere else in the U.S. Constitution). The Court overturned a Connecticut law that made it a crime for any person, married or single, to use any kind of contraceptive. Speaking through a majority opinion written by Justice William Douglas, the Court reasoned that a right to privacy was implicit in the Constitution as a result of "zones of privacy" created by the "liberty" safeguards in the due process clauses of the Fifth and Fourteenth Amendments and by the "penumbras" surrounding the First, Third, Fourth, Fifth, and Ninth Amendments.

Mapp v. Ohio

Gideon v. Wainwright

Benton v. Maryland

Griswold v. Connecticut: The Supreme Court ruling that a right of personal privacy is implicit in the Constitution.

The Law of the Land

Currently, nearly all of the specific provisions of the Bill of Rights and the *Griswold*-created right of privacy are binding upon the states as elements of the Fourteenth Amendment due process clause. The easiest way to remember what is and is not incorporated is to list the rights that have not been made obligatory upon the states. Of the first eight amendments (the amendments that refer to the specific rights of individuals), these are the only provisions that have not been incorporated:

1. The Second Amendment right to bear arms as part of a well-regulated militia
2. The Third Amendment protection against the involuntary quartering of soldiers in our houses
3. The Fifth Amendment protection against being prosecuted for "a capital, or otherwise infamous crime, unless on a presentment or indictment of a grand jury"
4. The Seventh Amendment right to a jury trial in cases involving more than $20
5. The Eighth Amendment protection against excessive bail
6. The Eighth Amendment protection against excessive fines

This textbook traces the case-by-case process by which incorporation has occurred in greater detail in such areas as self-incrimination and search and seizure, the right to counsel, and protection against cruel and unusual punishments. It is important to understand that although the Supreme Court has not achieved total incorporation of the Bill of Rights, it has accomplished what legal scholars call *selective incorporation*. This means simply that most, but not all, of the provisions of the Bill of Rights are binding upon the states. This accomplishment—the nationalization of the Bill of Rights—has radically altered the American system of criminal justice as practiced by state and local governments. None of the major Court-imposed changes in criminal procedure to be discussed in this text (such as the exclusionary rule, the *Miranda* rule, and changes in death penalty laws) could have occurred in the absence of selective incorporation.

Selective incorporation

The process of selective incorporation also added greater specificity to the meaning of the words *due process of law*. But the concept of due process is anything but precise. Whether a particular police practice or court rule is held to violate due process will always depend on the totality of facts and circumstances in a particular case and upon a court's effort to apply those facts and circumstances in the context of one or more principles of law. Thus, due process should be understood as asserting a fundamental principle of justice rather than a specific rule of law. It implies and comprehends the administration of laws that do not violate the very foundations of civil liberties; it requires in each case an evaluation based on a disinterested inquiry, on a balanced order of facts exactly and fairly stated, on the detached consideration of conflicting claims, and on a judgment mindful of reconciling the needs of continuity and change in complex society. Or as statesman Daniel Webster maintained, due process suggested "the law which hears before it condemns; which proceeds upon inquiry, and renders judgment only after trial."[27] Yet even these comments fail to explain fully the due process clause. A better understanding might be achieved by considering due process in its two aspects: *substantive* and *procedural*.

Due process in American law

Substantive Due Process

Substantive due process: Due process protection against unreasonable, arbitrary, or capricious laws or acts.

Substantive due process refers to the content or subject matter of a law. It protects persons against unreasonable, arbitrary, or capricious laws or acts by all branches of government. In the criminal justice process, one illustration of substantive due process is the **void-for-vagueness doctrine.** Under its precepts, due process requires that a criminal law must be clear in its meaning and application.[28] The Supreme Court has struck down criminal statutes and local ordinances that, for example, made it unlawful to wander the streets late at night "without lawful business,"[29] to "treat contemptuously the American flag,"[30] and to willfully "obstruct public passages."[31] In all of these cases, the issue of substantive due process and the void-for-vagueness doctrine came into play because the statutes were neither definite nor certain as to the category of persons they referred to or the conduct that was forbidden (see Exhibit 4.3).

Void-for-vagueness doctrine: The rule that criminal laws that are unclear or uncertain as to *what* or to *whom* they apply violate due process.

Procedural Due Process

Procedural due process is concerned with the notice, hearing, and other procedures that are required before the life, liberty, or property of a person may

Procedural due process: The procedures that are required before the life, liberty, or property of a person may be taken by the government.

Exhibit 4.3

Legal Perspectives on Crime and Justice
The Megan's Law Movement

Types of Notification

☐ **Passive:** Information is made public (via Internet, perhaps, or on CD-ROM at the police stations), but authorities do not reach out to warn neighborhoods.

■ **Has no Megan's Law notification provision**

■ **Active:** An offender is classified according to the threat he's thought to pose, and whom authorities inform of his presence depends on his classification: low, moderate, or high risk.

☐ **Combination:** Some states have laws with both passive and active elements.California, for instance, allows but does not require localities to notify neighbors about a sex offender, but also allows the public access to a sex offender registry on CD-ROM at county sheriffs' offices.

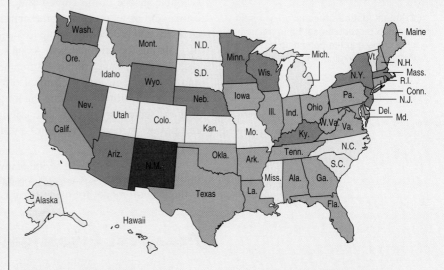

New Jersey was the scene of the crime that began the Megan's Law movement. The victim was 7-year-old Megan Kanka, raped and murdered in 1994 by a convicted sex offender who lived next door. Out of her death grew the notion that the government should notify citizens about sex offenders in their neighborhoods. New Jersey hastily enacted the first Megan's Law and required convicted sex offenders to register with local police. By 1999, with the exception of New Mexico, all states had a Megan's Law with some provision for notifying communities about the presence or general location of convicted sex criminals. As shown in the accompanying figure, they fell into three broad groups: passive systems, active systems, or a combination of the two.

Almost immediately after the New Jersey law was implemented, however, attorneys for sex offenders argued that the notification provisions were in violation of the Fifth Amendment's double jeopardy clause. As an issue of substantive due process,

they claimed that their clients were being punished twice for the same crime, since the notification and the public reaction it generated amounted to "punishment." In a petition to the U.S. Supreme Court, the New Jersey attorney general urged the justices to reject the sex offenders' appeal, on grounds that the features of Megan's Law had no hidden puni-

tive intent, and that the law was not a modern-day Scarlet Letter analogy. In 1997, in the case of *W. P.* v. *Verniero* (62 CrL 3163), the Supreme Court ruled in favor of the state of New Jersey, holding that the public notification provisions of Megan's Law did not impose punishment, and therefore did not constitute double jeopardy.

The major distinction between substantive due process and procedural due process is that the former focuses on *what* the government is doing and the latter on *how* the government does it.

be taken by the government. In general, procedural due process requires the following:

1. Notice of the proceedings
2. A hearing
3. Opportunity to present a defense
4. An impartial tribunal
5. An atmosphere of fairness

Since the criminal law revolution of the 1960s, when questions concerning the procedural rights of criminal defendants came under closer and more frequent scrutiny by the U.S. Supreme Court, the due process clauses of the Fifth and Fourteenth Amendments have been clarified and extended. The decisions handed down by the High Court have significantly affected the processing of defendants and offenders through all phases of the criminal justice process—from arrest to trial and from sentencing through corrections. In the remainder of this chapter, these phases of the criminal justice process are outlined and described. The influence of the Supreme Court's decisions involving questions of due process and other constitutional rights in arrest, trial, and sentencing practices are examined in later sections of this textbook.

In retrospect, the High Court's interpretations of the content of the Constitution, the incorporation of the provisions in the Bill of Rights, and the continuous clarifications of what the Framers meant by "due process of law" all suggest that the U.S. Constitution has endured well and will continue to do so. As indicated in Exhibit 4.4, however, not all constitutions fare as well.

THE CRIMINAL JUSTICE PROCESS

Criminal justice process: The agencies and procedures set up to manage both crime and the persons accused of violating the criminal law.

Criminal justice in the United States exists for the control and prevention of crime, and as a "process"—the **criminal justice process**—it involves those agencies and procedures set up to manage both crime and the persons accused of violating the criminal law. As an organizational complex, criminal justice includes the agencies of law enforcement charged with the prevention of crime and the apprehension of criminal offenders; it includes the court bureaucracies charged with determining the innocence or guilt of accused offenders and with the sentencing of convicted criminals; and it includes the network of corrections charged with the control, custody, supervision, and treatment of those convicted of crime.

There are many steps in the criminal justice process. Figure 4.1 broadly outlines the phases of case processing at the federal level. The federal system is the general model followed by most state and local courts.

Prearrest Investigation

Although the first phase of the criminal justice process would seem logically to be arrest, this is usually the case only when a crime is directly observed by police. In other situations, the process begins with some level of investigation. Prearrest investigation can be initiated when police receive a complaint from a victim or witness, an inside tip from informers, or through surveillance. Typically, investigative activities include an examination of the scene of the crime, a search for physical evidence, interviews with victims and witnesses, and the quest for the perpetrator. Data from informers or general surveillance can suggest that some "suspicious" activity is occurring—perhaps gambling, drug sales, prostitution, or disorderly behavior—at which point an officer's or a detective's "go-out-and-look" investigations take place.

Exhibit 4.4

International Perspectives on Crime and Justice
Constitution and Code Law in Bolivia

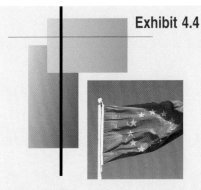

The term *constitution* refers to the institutions, practices, and principles that define and structure a system of government, as well as to the written document that establishes or articulates such a system. Every nation has a constitution in the first sense, and since World War II virtually every country—Britain, New Zealand, and Israel are among the few exceptions—has a written constitution as well.

Some constitutions are quite durable. The U.S. Constitution, for example, has lasted for more than two centuries, with additions (the amendments) rather than major changes. At the other end of the spectrum is Bolivia.

Straddling the Andes, Bolivia is a land of gaunt mountains, cold desolate plains, and semitropical lowlands. Its 424,165 square miles occupy an area about the size of Texas and California combined. It is a big country, but with a population of only 6.7 million. About 14 percent are of European heritage; the balance are Aymara (25 percent) and Quechua Indians (30 percent), and *mestizos* (mixed Indian and European ancestry). Since gaining its independence from Spain in 1825 under the leadership of Simón Bolívar, three main features have dominated Bolivian history: the importance of mining to the economy; the loss of territory through disputes and wars with neighboring countries;

and chronic political instability. Of the three, it would appear that the last has had the most disruptive impact.

During the past 175 years, Bolivia has had more than 60 revolutions, 72 presidents, and 16 constitutions. The government has changed hands at least 250 times—189 times by coup. From 1978 through the end of the 1990s, there have been 16 presidents, with a few having rather colorful politics. In 1980, for example, the presidential election yielded no clear winner. Before the Bolivian congress could meet to decide between the main contenders, a military junta led by army commander General Luis Garcia Meza staged a coup. Interestingly, Garcia Meza was a major cocaine trafficker, who proceeded to establish alliances between the government and civilian drug en-

General Garcia Meza of Bolivia — former president and cocaine trafficker.

terprises. A year later Garcia Meza was ultimately forced to resign, not because of his involvement with the cocaine trades, but for his fiscal mismanagement. Three years later, Bolivian President Hernan Siles Zuazo, the fourth person to hold that office since Garcia Meza's resignation, announced a war on cocaine. In 1984 Zuazo was kidnapped from the presidential palace by a group of cocaine traffickers. Although he was released unharmed and the attempted coup was aborted, the political system was left in a shambles. Following Zuazo, another president was elected, but he quickly resigned out of frustration with his government's seemingly unsolvable problems.

Currently, Bolivia is a republic, based on a 1967 constitution (which was interrupted by several coups). The government is headed by a president, who is elected to a 4-year term. There is a two-house legislature consisting of a 130-seat chamber of deputies and a 27-seat senate. The judicial branch is headed by a supreme court, whose justices are appointed to 10-year terms. Bolivia's legal system is based on Spanish code law, as is common throughout Spanish Latin America. There are two principal differences between *code law* and common law: First, legal decisions are based strictly on the written code—that is, on statutory rather than case law; and second, in the criminal courts, innocence, rather than guilt, must be proven. Bolivia's current president was elected in 1997, but how long his government and constitution will endure is difficult to predict.

SOURCES: U.S. Department of State, *Bolivia—Country Profile,* October 1997; Herbert S. Klein, *Bolivia: The Evolution of a Multi-Ethnic Society* (New York: Oxford, 1992); Department of State, Bureau of International Narcotics Matters, *International Narcotics Control Strategy Report* (Washington, D.C.: U.S. Department of State, 1985).

Figure 4.1 An Overview of the Criminal Justice Process

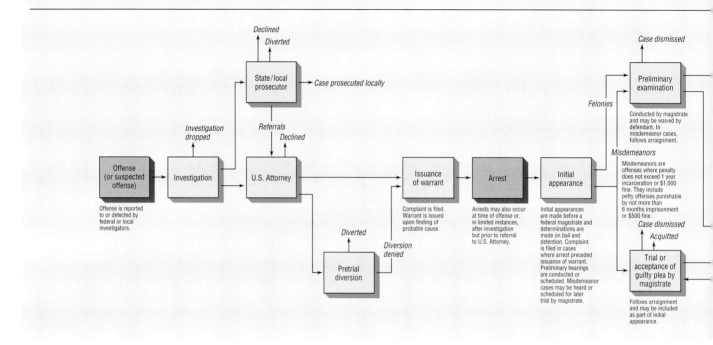

Prearrest investigations can also occur in another manner, sometimes even before a crime has actually been committed. Law enforcement agencies at the local, state, and federal levels become involved in long-term investigations when crime is not necessarily known but is strongly suspected or believed about to occur. This type of investigation is most typical of federal enforcement agencies, such as the Federal Bureau of Investigation, the Internal Revenue Service, the Customs Service, and the Postal Inspection Service.

Arrest

Arrest: The action of taking a person into custody for the purpose of charging with a crime.

When an investigation suggests that a crime has been committed, or when a crime has been directly observed by a law enforcement officer, an **arrest** is made. Although the legal definition of *arrest* tends to vary from one jurisdiction to another, it is simply the action of taking a person into custody for the purpose of charging him or her with a crime. In most jurisdictions, an arrest *warrant* is necessary in misdemeanor cases, unless the crime has been observed by a police officer. The warrant is a written order giving authorization to arrest and is issued by a magistrate or someone of equal authority. Felony arrests can be made without a warrant if the officer has reasonable certainty that the person being arrested is indeed the offender. *Reasonable certainty* (or probable cause) refers to the arresting officer's "rational grounds of suspicion, supported by circumstances sufficiently strong in themselves to warrant a cautious man in believing the accused to be guilty."[32]

The statutes of most jurisdictions governing arrest are quite specific. Criminal codes designate who can make arrests, the circumstances under which arrests can be made, and the conditions under which an arrest warrant is and is not mandatory. There are exceptions, however, that can place law enforcement agencies, private citizens, and other individuals in criminal justice proceedings in a tenuous position with regard to the constitutionality of how they make an arrest (see Chapter 6).

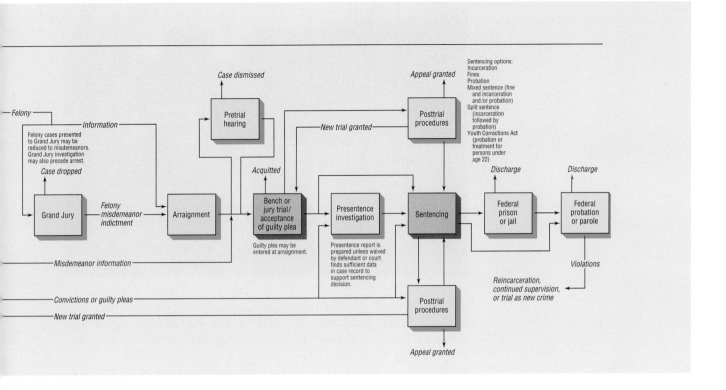

Booking

For some lesser offenses—as in New York state, for example, where prostitution is a minor offense punishable in some circumstances by no more than a fine[33]—the police may be permitted to issue a *citation,* which is an order to appear before a judge at some future date. In all other circumstances, however, a physical arrest occurs when the suspect is present, and the process continues to the booking phase.

　Booking refers to the administrative steps and procedures carried out by the police in order to record an arrest properly and officially. At the time of booking, the accused's name and address, the time and place of arrest, and the arrest charge are entered into the police log. Booking can also include fingerprinting and photographing of the suspect.

Booking: The police administrative procedures for officially recording an arrest.

　The booking phase is the first point at which the accused can drop out of the criminal justice process with no further criminal proceedings. Charges may be dropped if the suspect has been arrested for a minor misdemeanor, or if there was a procedural error by the police, such as a lack of probable cause for arrest or illegal search and seizure. In the case of a procedural error, the decision to drop the charges can be made by an assistant prosecutor or by someone of high rank in the police system. Booking is also the first point at which some defendants can be released on bail.

　Bail, taken from the French term *baillier* meaning "to deliver or give," is the most common form of temporary release. It involves the posting of financial security by the accused (or by someone on his or her behalf), guaranteeing an appearance at trial.

Initial Appearance

Due process requirements mandate that within a reasonable (not extreme or arbitrary) time after arrest, the accused must be brought before a magistrate

and given formal notice of the charge. Such notice occurs at the initial appearance. At this same time, the accused is also notified of his or her legal rights, and bail is determined for those who did not receive such temporary release during the booking phase. *Release on recognizance* (ROR), a substitute for bail, can also occur, typically at the recommendation of the magistrate when there seems to be no substantial risk that the accused will fail to appear for trial.

For some kinds of minor offenses, such as being drunk and disorderly, or in other cases where a simple citation has been issued, summary trials and sentencing are conducted at this initial appearance, with no further court processing. In other situations, the magistrate presiding at the initial appearance may determine that the evidence available is not sufficient to warrant further criminal processing and consequently may dismiss the case.

Preliminary Hearing

Due to the complexity of criminal processing and the delays generated by overloaded court calendars, in many jurisdictions defendants have the option to bypass the initial appearance and instead proceed directly to the preliminary hearing.

The major purpose of the preliminary hearing is to protect defendants from unwarranted prosecutions. Thus, the presiding magistrate seeks to do the following:

- Determine whether a crime has been committed
- Determine whether the evidence establishes probable cause to believe that the defendant committed it
- Determine the existence of a probable cause for which the warrant was issued for the defendant's arrest
- Inquire into the reasonableness of the arrest and search and the compliance of the executing officer with the requirements of the warrant
- Fix the appropriate bail or temporary release, if this was not already done

Preliminary hearings are rarely held. In some jurisdictions, the defense may waive this hearing in order to keep damaging testimony temporarily out of the official records in the hope that by the time the trial does occur witnesses may have forgotten some things, become confused, or disappeared.[34] However, other defense attorneys insist on this hearing as a tactic for gaining insight into the strengths and weaknesses of the state's case.

Determination of Formal Charges

Whether the initial court processing does or does not include an initial appearance or preliminary hearing, the next step in the criminal justice process is the formalization of charges. One mechanism is *indictment* by a grand jury. The indictment is a formal charging document based on the grand jury's determination that there is sufficient cause for a trial. The decision must be a majority decision, and when it is reached, a *true bill* is signed, containing the following information:

Indictment

True bill

- The type and nature of the offense
- The specific statute alleged to have been violated
- The nature and elements of the offense charged
- The time and place of the occurrence of the crime
- The name and address of the accused or, if not known, a description sufficient to identify the accused with reasonable certainty
- The signature of the foreman of the grand jury to verify that it has been returned as a true bill
- The names of all codefendants in the offense charged, as well as the number of criminal charges against them

Because the grand jury does not weigh the evidence presented, its finding is by no means equivalent to a conviction; it simply binds the accused over for trial. If this tribunal returns a *no bill*—that is, if it fails to achieve the required majority vote and thus refuses the indictment—the accused is released.

No bill

Grand juries are available in about half of the states and in the federal system, but in only a limited number of jurisdictions are they the exclusive mechanism for sending a defendant to trial. The most common method for bringing formal charges is the *information,* a charging document drafted by a prosecutor and tested before a magistrate. Typically, this testing occurs at the

Information

preliminary hearing. The prosecutor presents some, or all, of the evidence in open court—usually just enough to convince the judge that the defendant should be bound over for trial. As indicated earlier, however, the preliminary hearing is sometimes waived, and in those circumstances the information document is not tested before a magistrate.

Arraignment

After the formal determination of charges through the indictment or information, the actual trial process begins. The first phase in this segment of the criminal justice process is the arraignment, at which the accused is taken before a judge, the formal charges are read, and the defendant is asked to enter a plea. There are four primary pleas in most jurisdictions:

1. *Not guilty:* If the not-guilty plea is entered, the defendant is notified of his or her rights, a determination is made of competence to stand trial, counsel is appointed if indigency is apparent, and in some jurisdictions the defendant can elect to have a trial by judge or a trial by jury.
2. *Guilty:* If a plea of guilty is entered, the judge must determine if the plea was made voluntarily and if the defendant has an understanding of the full consequences of such a plea. If the judge is satisfied, the defendant is scheduled for sentencing; if not, the judge can refuse the guilty plea and enter "not guilty" into the record.
3. *Nolo contendere:* This plea, not available in all jurisdictions, means "no contest" or "I will not contest it." It has the same legal effect as the guilty plea but is of different legal significance in that an admission of guilt is not present and cannot be introduced in later trials.
4. *Standing mute:* Remaining mute results in the entry of a not-guilty plea. Its advantage is that the accused does not waive his or her right to protest any irregularities that may have occurred in earlier phases of the criminal justice proceedings.

The Trial Process

Pretrial motions

The complete trial process can be long and complex (see Chapter 8). It may begin with a hearing on *pretrial motions* entered by the defense to suppress evidence, relocate the place of the trial, discover the nature of the state's evidence, or postpone the trial itself. After the pretrial motions (if there are any), the jury is selected and the trial proceeds as follows:

1. *Opening statements by prosecution:* The prosecutor outlines the state's case and how the state will introduce witnesses and physical evidence to prove the guilt of the accused.
2. *Opening statements by the defense:* The defense, if it elects to do so, explains how it plans to introduce witnesses and evidence in its own behalf.
3. *Presentation of the state's case:* The state calls its witnesses to establish the elements of the crime and to introduce physical evidence; the prosecutor accomplishes this through direct examination of the witnesses followed by their cross-examination by the defense.
4. *Presentation of the defense's case:* The defense may open with a motion for dismissal on the grounds that the state failed to prove the defendant guilty "beyond a reasonable doubt." If the judge concurs, the case is dismissed and the accused is released; if the judge rejects the motion, the defense's case proceeds in the same manner as the state's presentation.
5. *Prosecutor's rebuttal:* The prosecutor may elect to present new witnesses and evidence, following the format of the state's original presentation.

6. *Defense's surrebuttal:* The defense may again make a motion for dismissal; if denied, it too can introduce new evidence and witnesses.

7. *Closing statements:* First the defense attorney and then the prosecutor make closing arguments, which sum up their cases and the deductions that can be made from the evidence and testimony.

8. *Charging the jury:* In jury trials, the judge instructs the jurors as to possible verdicts and charges them to retire to the jury room to consider the facts of the case, to deliberate on the testimony, and to return a just verdict.

9. *Return of the verdict:* Once the jurors have reached a decision, they return to the courtroom with a verdict, which is read aloud by a member of the court. The jury may be *polled,* at the request of either the defense or the prosecution; that is, each member is asked individually whether the verdict announced is his or her individual verdict.

In the case of a trial by judge, the steps involving the jury are eliminated and the judge makes the determination of innocence or guilt.

Posttrial motions can also occur if the defendant is found guilty, and the defense is given the opportunity to seek a new trial or have the verdict of the jury *set aside* (revoked).

Posttrial motions

Sentencing

After conviction or the entry of a guilty plea, the defendant is brought before the judge for the imposition of the sentence. The sentencing process may begin with a presentence investigation, which summarizes the offender's family, social, employment, and criminal history, and which serves as a guide for the presiding judge in determining the type of sentence to be imposed. Depending on the nature of the offense and the sentencing guidelines established by statute, a simple fine or adjudication to probation in the community might be imposed. Sentences can also include other forms of community-based corrections, imprisonment, or even death.

Appeals and Release

Subsequent to conviction and sentencing, defendants found guilty may appeal their cases to a higher court. Appeals are based on claims that due process was not followed, that new evidence has become available, or that the sentence imposed was "cruel and unusual," in violation of constitutional rights.

Release from imprisonment occurs after the time specified in the sentence has been served or if the offender is released on *parole*—a conditional release that occurs after only a portion of the sentence has been served. Release from prison, or any type of sentence, can also occur through *pardon*—a "forgiveness" for the crime committed that bars any further criminal justice processing. Other factors that can affect a sentence are the *reprieve,* which delays the execution of a sentence, and the *commutation,* which reduces a sentence to a less severe one.

Parole

Pardon

Reprieve
Commutation

CRIMINAL JUSTICE AS A "SYSTEM"

The preceding summary of the various stages in the criminal justice process might suggest that the administration of justice is a *criminal justice "system"*—some orderly flow of managerial decision-making that begins with the investigation of a criminal offense and ends with a correctional placement.

The criminal justice "system"

And this indeed was the ideal fostered by the President's Commission on Law Enforcement and Administration of Justice some years ago in its commentary on criminal justice in America:

> The criminal justice system has three separately organized parts—the police, the courts, and corrections—and each has distinct tasks. However, these parts are by no means independent of each other. What each one does and how it does it has a direct effect on the work of the others. The courts must deal, and can only deal, with those whom the police arrest; the business of corrections is with those delivered to it by the courts. How successfully corrections reforms convicts determines whether they will once again become police business and influences the sentences the judges pass; police activities are subject to court scrutiny and are often determined by court decisions. And so reforming or reorganizing any part or procedure of the system changes other parts or procedures. Furthermore, the criminal process, the method by which the system deals with individual cases, is not a hodgepodge of random actions. It is rather a continuum—an orderly progression of events—some of which, like arrest and trial, are highly visible and some of which, though of great importance, occur out of public view. A study of the system must begin by examining it as a whole.[35]

The criminal justice "nonsystem"

However, the notion of criminal justice operating as an orderly system was and remains a myth. The justice process is composed of a series of bureaucracies operating along alternative and often conflicting paths; also, one

A simplified guide to the criminal justice system

segment of the system often serves as a dumping ground for each of the others. In addition, questions of definition and interpretation can confound the complexities of criminal procedure even further:

> Law enforcement agents interpret the definition of a situation to determine if a law has been indeed violated. Prosecutors and defense attorneys interpret the law and the social situation of the alleged offense to determine which laws were violated and to assess the culpability of the accused. Juries interpret the information provided by the police and courts to determine the innocence or the extent of guilt of the defendant. Judges interpret the evidence presented and the character of the offender to determine the nature and type of sentence and to insure that "due process" has been achieved. And finally, correctional personnel interpret their knowledge of the law, social science, correctional administration, and human behavior to determine the appropriate custodial, correctional, rehabilitative, and punitive treatment for each convicted criminal.[36]

Not only is there a lack of unity of purpose and organized interrelationships among police, courts, and corrections, but also, individual interpretations of crime, law, evidence, and culpability at every phase of the process create further inefficiency. Criminal justice in the United States, therefore, is hardly a "system." However, this is to be expected from a process of justice in a democratic society in which checks and balances have been built in at every level so that the fairness of due process can be achieved.

Exhibit 4.5 **Careers in Justice**
United States Marshals Service

There are numerous career opportunities in the Marshals Service. To qualify as a U.S. Deputy Marshal, an applicant must be a U.S. citizen, in excellent physical condition, between the ages of 21 and 37; have a bachelor's degree; pass a written test and an oral interview; and permit a background investigation.

Since 1789, the missions of the U.S. Marshals Service have changed to meet the needs of the nation. At first, it conducted the census and protected the president. Today, the Marshals Service is responsible for providing protection for the federal judiciary, transporting federal prisoners, protecting endangered federal witnesses, and managing assets seized from criminal enterprises. In addition, the men and women of the Marshals Service pursue and arrest 55 percent of all federal fugitives—more than all other federal agencies combined.

Op-Ed

A number of questions were raised early in the chapter about "high Crimes and Misdemeanors," the fairness of the process that resulted in the impeachment of President Clinton, and whether the congressional procedures were a reflection of the American system of criminal justice.

When considering the meaning of "high Crimes and Misdemeanors" and if the president was guilty of them, one must look at the entire phrase in the Constitution that referred to impeachable offenses. The constitutional language was "Treason, Bribery, or other high Crimes and Misdemeanors." The first thing to remember is that impeachment was intended by the framers of the Constitution to be reserved for serious offenses against the state, such as treason and bribery. There is no other way to read the law. Secondly, the term *high misdemeanor* came from eighteenth-century England, where it referred to a serious offense against the state. Within this context, was President Clinton's

attempted cover-up of a sexual affair a "high crime"? Most constitutional scholars said no.

As for the process, it was nothing like the American system of justice, and "due process" was a charade. Both Republicans and Democrats turned the impeachment hearings and the Senate trial into something resembling warfare. Democrats were convinced that Clinton had done nothing to deserve removal from office, while many Republicans saw it as their last chance to get him out of the White House. Republican diehards detested Clinton for his ideology (which sometimes mimicked theirs), the misdeeds he was charged with, and as a person. The president's supporters, in turn, detested his detractors. Trial managers, drawn from the House of Representatives, were pictured as sanctimonious hypocrites whose own misdeeds were exposed by the publisher of *Hustler* magazine and whose impeachment charges, in the words of one Democratic senator, amounted to nothing more than "a pile of dung." Overall, the process was a destructive and embarrassing one. But interestingly, outside of the United States it was referred to as America's "Republican problem."

PUBLIC OPINION ON THE PRESIDENTIAL CRISIS (JANUARY 1999)

Do you think the Senate should convict Bill Clinton?

Yes	32%
No	63%
No opinion	5%

Do you approve of the way that Bill Clinton is doing his job?

Yes	69%
No	29%
No opinion	2%

SOURCES: Gallup Poll, January 8, 1999; CNN/*USA Today*/Gallup Poll, January 19, 1999.

© Chris Britt/Copley News Service

SUMMARY

Interpretations of the meaning of *due process* have varied throughout history. In the Middle Ages, due process merely meant adhering to the *law of the land.* Currently, due process of law—as guaranteed by the Fifth and Fourteenth Amendments—implies and comprehends the administration of laws that do not violate the very foundations of civil liberties. It requires in each case an evaluation based on disinterested inquiry, a balanced order of facts exactly and fairly stated, the detached consideration of conflicting claims, and a judgment mindful of reconciling the needs of continuity and change in a complex society. The concept of due process is anything but precise. It should be understood as asserting a fundamental principle of justice rather than a specific rule of law. This process can be better understood by considering it in its two aspects: *substantive* and *procedural.* Substantive due process refers to the content or subject matter of a law, and protects individuals against unreasonable, arbitrary, or capricious acts by the government. Procedural due process, on the other hand, is concerned with the notice,

hearing, and other procedures that are required before the life, liberty, or property of a person may be taken by the government. The major distinction between substantive due process and procedural due process is that the former focuses on *what* the government is doing and the latter on *how* the government does it.

The criminal justice process, from investigation and arrest through trial and sentencing, is structured to guarantee due process of law at each of its many stages. Moreover, it is designed to be a system, an orderly flow of managerial decision-making that begins with the investigation of a criminal offense and ends with a correctional placement. It can be argued, however, that the criminal justice process is anything but a system, that it lacks unity of purpose and organized interrelationships among its various components. The conflicting paths within the system and the disparate goals among the various players (lawyers, judges, police officers, defendants, and so on) all contribute to a "nonsystem" of criminal justice.

KEY TERMS

adversary system **78**	constitution **80**	inquiry system **78**
arrest **92**	criminal justice process **90**	inquisitorial system **78**
Barron v. *Baltimore* **82**	due process of law **78**	procedural due process **89**
Bill of Rights **81**	*Gitlow* v. *New York* **84**	substantive due process **88**
booking **93**	*Griswold* v. *Connecticut* **87**	void-for-vagueness doctrine **89**

QUESTIONS FOR DISCUSSION

1. What do you think the framers of the Constitution meant by due process of law?
2. How does due process of law differ from the law of the land?
3. What other rights and liberties do you think should have been incorporated into the Bill of Rights?
4. How do you interpret the Second Amendment?
5. What are "high Crimes and Misdemeanors"?

MEDIA RESOURCES

1. **Second Amendment.** There are several good books and more than 1,000 Web sites on this topic. Some recommendations include Earl R. Kruschke, *The Right to Keep and Bear Arms: A Continuing American Dilemma* (Springfield, Ill.: Thomas, 1985); and David T. Hardy, *Origins and Development of the Second Amendment* (Southport, Conn.: Blacksmith, 1986). There is also a comprehensive Web site on gun control and Second Amendment issues: http://www.guncite.com/

2. **Megan's Law.** The Web has thousands of entries. A good place to start is the Web site of the St. Clair County (Illinois) Sheriff's Department, which has background information on the law and notification procedures as well as listings of registered sex offenders. Web site address: http://www.sheriff.co.stclair.il.us/sexofd.htm

3. **U.S. Marshals Service.** The Marshals Service has its own Web site, which contains historical and contemporary materials as well as contacts for employment inquiries. Web site address: http://www.usdoj.gov/marshals/
4. **The Constitution.** "High Crimes and Misdemeanors" is but one of many terms in the U.S. Constitution that have been a topic of scholarly debate. For an analysis of the original text of the Constitution, see Leonard W. Levy, *Original Intent and the Framers' Constitution* (New York: Macmillan, 1988).
5. **The Bill of Rights.** One of the better recent works on the Bill of Rights is Akhil Reed Amar, *The Bill of Rights: Creation and Reconstruction* (New Haven: Yale University Press, 1998).

NOTES

1. Luke Owen Pike, *A History of Crime in England,* Vol. 1 (London: Smith, Elder, 1873–1876), pp. 52–55; Christopher Hibbert, *The Roots of Evil* (Boston: Little, Brown, 1963), pp. 5–8.
2. See Randy E. Barnett, ed., *The Rights Retained by the People: The History and Meaning of the Ninth Amendment* (Fairfax, Va.: George Mason University Press, 1989).
3. Cited in Irving Brant, *The Bill of Rights* (Indianapolis: Bobbs-Merrill, 1965), pp. 49–50.
4. *Barron* v. *Baltimore,* 7 Pet. 243 (1833).
5. See Richard C. Cortner, *The Supreme Court and the Second Bill of Rights* (Madison: University of Wisconsin Press, 1981), pp. 3–11; Henry J. Abraham, *Freedom and the Court: Civil Rights and Liberties in the United States,* 4th ed. (New York: Oxford University Press, 1982), pp. 30–48.
6. *Gitlow* v. *New York,* 268 U.S. 652 (1925).
7. *Fiske* v. *Kansas,* 274 U.S. 380 (1927).
8. *Near* v. *Minnesota,* 283 U.S. 697 (1931).
9. *Powell* v. *Alabama,* 287 U.S. 45 (1932).
10. *Hamilton* v. *Regents of the University of California,* 293 U.S. 245 (1934). Some legal scholars argue that the Court did not make it entirely clear that it intended to incorporate the freedom of religion clause until *Cantwell* v. *Connecticut,* 310 U.S. 296 (1940).
11. These latter two First Amendment rights were incorporated in *DeJonge* v. *Oregon,* 299 U.S. 353 (1937).
12. *Palko* v. *Connecticut,* 302 U.S. 319 (1937).
13. *Everson* v. *Board of Education,* 330 U.S. 1 (1947).
14. *In re Oliver,* 333 U.S. 257 (1948).
15. *Trop* v. *Dulles,* 356 U.S. 86 (1958).
16. *Mapp* v. *Ohio,* 367 U.S. 643 (1961).
17. *Robinson* v. *California,* 370 U.S. 660 (1962).
18. *Gideon* v. *Wainwright,* 392 U.S. 335 (1963).
19. *Malloy* v. *Hogan,* 378 U.S. 1 (1964).
20. *Pointer* v. *Texas,* 380 U.S. 400 (1965).
21. *Parker* v. *Gladden,* 385 U.S. 363 (1966).
22. *Klopfer* v. *North Carolina,* 386 U.S. 213 (1967).
23. *Washington* v. *Texas,* 388 U.S. 14 (1967).
24. *Duncan* v. *Louisiana,* 391 U.S. 145 (1968).
25. *Benton* v. *Maryland,* 395 U.S. 784 (1969).
26. *Griswold* v. *Connecticut,* 381 U.S. 479 (1965).
27. *Dartmouth College* v. *Woodward,* 4 Wheat 519 (1819).
28. Peter W. Lewis and Kenneth D. Peoples, *The Supreme Court and the Criminal Process—Cases and Comments* (Philadelphia: Saunders, 1978), p. 92.
29. *Coates* v. *City of Cincinnati,* 402 U.S. 611 (1971).
30. *Smith* v. *Goguen,* 415 U.S. 566 (1974).
31. *Cox* v. *Louisiana,* 379 U.S. 536 (1965).
32. *Brinegar* v. *United States,* 338 U.S. 161 (1949).
33. State of New York, Penal Code, 40, 80.
34. Herbert Jacob, *Justice in America: Courts, Lawyers, and the Judicial Process* (Boston: Little, Brown, 1978), p. 173.
35. President's Commission on Law Enforcement and Administration of Justice, *The Challenge of Crime in a Free Society* (Washington, D.C.: U.S. Government Printing Office, 1967), p. 7.
36. James A. Inciardi, *Reflections on Crime* (New York: Holt, Rinehart and Winston, 1978), p. 160.

Part 2

THE POLICE

Chapter 5
Police and Policing

Chapter 6
Police and the Constitution

Chapter 7
Police Misconduct

CHAPTER 5
POLICE AND POLICING

Beverly Hills, Calif.—"The X-Files," one of America's more popular television series, deals with the adventures of two FBI agents, Fox Mulder and Dana Scully, who work in the Bureau's Violent Crimes section. They work with the " X-files"—cases that have unexplainable elements and often involve the paranormal. Weekly episodes have focused on alien abductions, extraterrestrial visitations, mysterious impregnations, puzzling viruses, government conspiracies, extrasensory perception, and other unusual topics.

But is working on cases of paranormal events really what the FBI is all about? If not, what does the FBI do? Is the work of an FBI agent like that of other law enforcement officers? What do most police do, and what, in general, is "police work"? Is what we see on such television series as "NYPD Blue" and "Law & Order" a good portrayal of what police officers and detectives do?

Within this context, this chapter examines the character and structure of police work and offers some perspectives on the complexities and frustrations of attempting to enforce the law and maintain order in a democratic society. The chapter material seeks to answer such questions as: What do police do? What do citizens ask them to do? What do they decide to do upon their own initiative? What influences their decisions to do what they do?

THE FUNCTIONS OF POLICE

Police work suggests conflicts between law officers and lawbreakers, dusting for fingerprints and the search for elusive clues, the investigation and chase, and the ultimate apprehension and arrest of the suspected offender. It might also suggest that the functions of police are only the control of crime and the protection of society. But police work goes well beyond these tasks.

The Police Role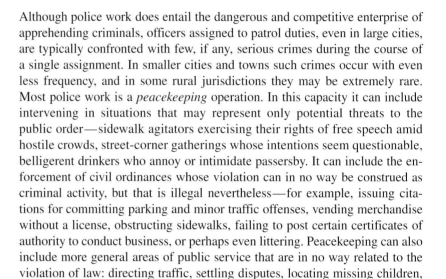

Although police work does entail the dangerous and competitive enterprise of apprehending criminals, officers assigned to patrol duties, even in large cities, are typically confronted with few, if any, serious crimes during the course of a single assignment. In smaller cities and towns such crimes occur with even less frequency, and in some rural jurisdictions they may be extremely rare. Most police work is a *peacekeeping* operation. In this capacity it can include intervening in situations that may represent only potential threats to the public order—sidewalk agitators exercising their rights of free speech amid hostile crowds, street-corner gatherings whose intentions seem questionable, belligerent drinkers who annoy or intimidate passersby. It can include the enforcement of civil ordinances whose violation can in no way be construed as criminal activity, but that is illegal nevertheless—for example, issuing citations for committing parking and minor traffic offenses, vending merchandise without a license, obstructing sidewalks, failing to post certain certificates of authority to conduct business, or perhaps even littering. Peacekeeping can also include more general areas of public service that are in no way related to the violation of law: directing traffic, settling disputes, locating missing children, returning lost pets, offering counsel to runaways, providing directions to confused pedestrians, and delivering babies.

Police work encompasses preventive and protective roles as well, for peacekeeping also includes *patrol,* which lessens opportunities to commit crimes. In addition, prevention and protection can involve initiating programs to reduce racial tensions, promote safe driving, reduce opportunities for crime victimization, and educate the public about home security measures.

Finally, police work involves many tasks that occur well beyond public notice and that are often time-consuming, overly routine, and excessively burdensome. Such activities include maintaining extended surveillances, transporting suspects, protecting witnesses, writing arrest and other reports, and testifying in court.[1] In short, peacekeeping operations generally do not involve criminal activities and often are not even in the area of law enforcement.[2]

Even in the law enforcement aspects of police work, a significant proportion of activity does not involve "dangerous crime." One perspective on this issue emerges through an examination of police *arrest activity.* Of the millions of arrests each year in the United States, only about 20 percent involve the more serious Index crimes of homicide, forcible rape, robbery, aggravated assault, burglary, larceny, vehicle theft, and arson. In contrast, just a third of arrests are for such lesser crimes as gambling, driving while intoxicated, liquor law violations, disorderly conduct, prostitution, vagrancy, and drunkenness.

POLICE AND PUBLIC SERVICE

When a sample of Lansing, Michigan, residents were asked to choose the most important public service–oriented activities that police should engage in, the following were indicated by the majority of respondents:

Assisting stranded motorists	85%
Checking/welfare of senior citizens	79
Investigating vehicle accidents	77
Home security checks for vacationers	56
Teaching pedestrian safety to children	54
Teaching rape prevention programs	52

SOURCE: National Neighborhood Foot Patrol Center, Michigan State University.

Police patrol

In some instances, police work can be unusual. In this case, Detroit police are responding to a home-owner's report of roaring coming from a neighbor's house.

Data from studies of the police testify to the fact that police work involves keeping the peace more so than enforcing the law. And the value of police peacekeeping activities should not be underestimated. A large proportion of the annual homicide and assault rates is an outgrowth of various kinds of disputes, and responding to such disputes takes up a considerable amount of police time. If police no longer intervened in these disputes, we could expect a considerable increase in assaults. For a seventeenth-century perspective on policing, see Exhibit 5.1.

The Right to Use Force

Peacekeeping role: The legitimate right of police to use force in situations in which urgency requires it.

The **peacekeeping role** is what mainly separates the functions of police from those of private citizens. This role involves the legitimate right to use force in situations whose urgency requires it. One police observer described it this way:

Exhibit 5.1 **Historical Perspectives on Crime and Justice**
The Thief-Takers of Seventeenth-Century England

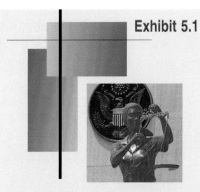

One of the more colorful chapters in the history of policing is that of the "thief-takers" of seventeenth-century England. The thief-takers were private detectives of a sort who were paid by the Crown on a piecework basis. They had no official status as police and no more authority than private citizens, and anyone could be a thief-taker. Like the bounty hunters of the American West, thief-takers received a reward in return for the apprehension of a criminal.

Thief-takers emerged in England in response to the troublesome nature of highway robbery, which had been flourishing since the early years of such legendary outlaws as Robin Hood and Little John. By the seventeenth century, although romanticized in literature, highway robbery in the grand manner of Jack Sheppard, Dick Turpin, Claude Duval, and Captain

Lightfoot made traveling through the English countryside so perilous that no coach or traveler was safe. As a result, in 1693 an act of Parliament established a reward of £40 for the capture of any highwayman or road agent. The reward was payable upon conviction, and to the thief-taker also went the highwayman's horse, arms, money, and property, unless these were proven to have been stolen.

This system was extended during the reigns of Anne and George I to cover offenses other than highway robbery, and soon a sliding scale of parliamentary rewards came into existence. Burglars, housebreakers, and footpads (street robbers), for example, were worth the same as a highwayman, but the sheep stealer brought only £10, and the army deserter only £1. In some communities, homeowners joined together and offered supplementary rewards, typically £20, for the apprehension of any highwayman or footpad within their districts. When there were especially serious crime waves, Parliament provided special rewards of £100 for particular felons.

As the system expanded, a class of professional thief-takers sprang up. Not unexpectedly, many thief-takers were themselves criminals, since the offer of a pardon was an additional incentive. But thief-taking also had its drawbacks. Arresting desperate criminals was dangerous, rewards were not paid if the criminal was acquitted, and thief-takers always had to fear the private revenge of their victims' friends and associates. The result was that thief-takers often became "thief-makers." Many would seduce youngsters into committing crimes, then have another thief-taker arrest the youth in the midst of the offense. Others framed innocent parties by planting stolen goods on their persons or in their homes. Although some real criminals were apprehended by the professional thief-takers, the system generally created more crime than it suppressed. As a result, it was not too long before thief-takers passed into obscurity and the necessity of organized police forces was taken more seriously by English officials.

SOURCES: Arthur L. Hayward, *Lives of the Most Remarkable Criminals* (New York: Dodd, Mead, 1927); Patrick Pringle, *The Thief-Takers* (London: Museum Press, 1958).

I share a property line with my neighbor. About one foot to my side of the property line there stands my horticultural pride and joy: a 25-foot apple tree. (Needless to say, a small portion of this gorgeous tree graces my neighbor's yard.) Though the tree is mine and I am willing to share its bounty with my neighbor, he does not like apples. He likes still less the fact that my apples fall off, rot, and litter his yard. One day he gets fed up with my stinking apples and yells to me that he is going to cut down my tree unless I do. "No way," I say. He revs up his chain saw.

Modern democratic society offers me two options in such a situation. First, I can drive to court and file a civil suit against my neighbor and, years hence, recover damages from him. The problem with this remedy is that I love my apple tree and don't want it cut down even if at some time in the future I am rewarded handsomely for its loss. Hence, modern democratic society offers me another option: call the cops and get them to stop my chain saw–wielding neighbor before his chain bites the bark. What police have that suits them to this task is a right to use coercive force. That is, they can tell my neighbor to stop and if he doesn't, they can use whatever force is necessary to stop him.

I guess what our job really boils down to is not letting the assholes take over the city. Now I'm not talking about your regular crooks . . . they're bound to wind up in the joint anyway. What I'm talking about are those shitheads out to prove that they can push everybody around. Those are the ones we gotta deal with and take care of on patrol. They're the ones that make it tough on the decent people out there. You take the majority of what we do and it's nothing more than asshole control.
—*A veteran police officer*

Exhibit 5.2 **Research in Crime and Justice**
Police Use of Force

During 1996, the U.S. Bureau of the Census interviewed a representative sample of persons age 12 and older to determine the nature and extent of police encounters with civilians. Projected to the national population, the findings were as follows:

Prevalence of citizen contact with police

- An estimated 44.6 million persons (21 percent of the population age 12 or older) had face-to-face contact with a police officer during 1996.
- Men, whites, and persons in their twenties were the most likely to have face-to-face contact.
- Hispanics and blacks were about 70 percent as likely as whites to have contacts with the police.

- Nearly 3 in 10 persons with a contact in 1996 reported multiple contacts with police during the year.

Reasons for citizen contact with police

- An estimated 33 percent of residents age 12 or older who had contact with police had asked or provided the police with some type of assistance.
- An estimated 32 percent of those who had contact with police had reported a crime, either as a victim or a witness.
- Receiving traffic tickets and being involved in traffic accidents were also common reasons for police contacts.
- For just under a third of those with contacts, the police initiated the contact. For most—nearly half of those with contacts—the citizen had initiated the contact. (The remainder were unclear from the data.)
- Teenagers were the most likely to have a police-initiated contact, and persons age 60 and older were the least likely.

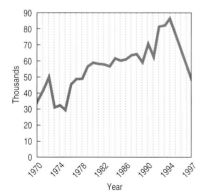

**Police Officers
Assaulted, 1970–1997**

SOURCE: *Uniform Crime Reports.*

This is not true of me, of course. I do not have a general right to use coercive force. Modern democratic society would look very dimly on me if I appeared on the scene with a gun and threatened to blast my neighbor and his revving chain saw into the great orchard in the sky.[3]

The point is simply that modern democratic society severely restricts the right of private citizens to use force and urges them to use legal channels to work out their disputes. This restriction extends to virtually all cases except self-defense; and even there one must show that all reasonable means of retreat were exhausted. The law does recognize, however, that there are occasions in which something has to be done immediately—occasions in which resort to the courts or other mechanisms of dispute settlement would simply take too long and the damage would already be done. It is for handling such occasions that there are police—an idea based on the notion that it is better to have a small group of people (police) with a monopoly on the legitimate right to use force than to allow everyone with a club, gun, knife, or chain saw to use force in such immediately demanding situations. That right to use force

- Persons age 60 or older were the most likely to have a citizen-initiated contact with the police, and teenagers were the least likely.
- Hispanics had a higher level of police-initiated contacts and a lower level of self-initiated contacts.

Police actions during contacts with citizens

- An estimated 1.2 million persons were handcuffed during 1996, or about 0.6 percent of the population age 12 or older.
- Men, minorities, and persons under the age of 30 represented a relatively large percentage of those handcuffed, compared to their representation among persons with contact with police.
- An estimated 500,000 persons (0.2 percent of the population age 12 or older) were hit, held, pushed, choked, threatened with a flashlight, restrained by a police dog, threatened or actually sprayed with chemical or pepper spray, threatened with a gun, or experienced some other form of police force. Of the 500,000, about 400,000 were also handcuffed.

Los Angeles police officers move in at the Bank of America in the North Hollywood section of Los Angeles, Friday, February 28, 1997. Wearing commando garb, several heavily armed, masked robbers bungled a bank heist, then fired hundreds of shots in a gun battle getaway try that left two dead, at least 11 hurt, and a broad trail of damage.

SOURCE: Bureau of Justice Statistics, *Police Use of Force* (Washington, D.C.: U.S. Department of Justice, 1998).

in situations that demand it is held by the police in modern democratic society and justifies their role in crime control, peacekeeping, traffic, and everything else they do. In short, this is the essence of the peacekeeping role of the police. For some indication as to the extent of the use of force by police, see Exhibit 5.2.

POLICE SYSTEMS IN THE UNITED STATES

With a population of approximately 270 million people, all of whom are under the authority of competing political jurisdictions at federal, state, county, and local levels, law enforcement in the United States today reflects a structure more complex than in any other country. There are 20,000 to 25,000 professional police agencies in the public sector alone—each representing the enforcement arm of a specific judicial body. To these can be added numerous others in the private sphere. The duties and authority of each are generally quite clear, but in many respects they can also be rather vague and overlapping. Although enforcing the law and keeping the peace may be the responsibilities of a municipal police agency within a small suburban village, for example, also active in that same community may be officers from the county sheriff's department, the state police bureaucracy, and numerous federal enforcement bodies. This level of complexity can be further complicated by possible jurisdictional disputes, agency rivalries, lack of coordination and communication, and failure to share intelligence and other resources.

Jurisdictional complexities in modern policing

Consider, for instance, the jurisdictional and administrative complexities that exist in Dade County, Florida. Located at the southeastern tip of the state of Florida, Dade County has a population of almost 2 million and occupies some 2,109 square miles—a land area larger than the entire state of Delaware. In addition to the cities of Miami and Miami Beach, the county includes 26 other incorporated municipalities. Each of these is an independent political jurisdiction with its own municipal police force. Also included in this essentially urban-suburban county is the Dade County Public Safety Department—whose jurisdiction is countywide—as well as the Florida State Police and the Florida Marine Patrol. At the federal level, numerous agencies also have jurisdiction, including the Federal Bureau of Investigation, the Immigration and Naturalization Service, the Drug Enforcement Administration, the Internal Revenue Service, the Customs Service, and the United States Coast Guard. In the private sphere, detective agencies control all security operations at Miami International Airport and other locations; the railroad industry has its own police force; and hundreds of other businesses and industries use private police agencies.

New York City reflects another complex situation. First, there is the well-known N.Y.P.D. (New York City Police Department), a force of some 39,000 officers whose jurisdiction covers the five boroughs that make up the city as a whole. There are also the state police, private police, federal enforcement bodies, and an interstate agency—the New York/New Jersey Port Authority Police—whose jurisdiction and authority cross both county and state lines.

Multiagency policing is evident not only in large urban areas, but also in smaller cities, suburban communities, and towns and villages across the nation. Because of these complexities, jurisdictional issues in law enforcement are often ignored in studies of police. As such, the balance of this section attempts to differentiate among the three major levels of police authority—federal, state, and local.

Federal Law Enforcement Agencies

Federal law enforcement agencies have two features that make them unique within the spectrum of police activity. *First,* since they were structured to enforce specific statutes—those contained in the U.S. Criminal Code—their units are highly specialized, often with distinctive resources and training. *Second,* because of this linkage to federal codes—all of which were created at one time or another by the U.S. Congress—their jurisdictional boundaries, at least in theory, have been limited by congressional authority. The major agencies include the **Federal Bureau of Investigation** (FBI); the Drug Enforcement Administration (DEA); the Immigration and Naturalization Service (INS); the U.S. Marshals Service; the Intelligence Division of the Internal Revenue Service (IRS); the Secret Service; the Bureau of Alcohol, Tobacco, and Firearms (ATF); the Customs Service; the Postal Inspection Service; the U.S. Coast Guard; and the National Parks Service. In addition to these, there are a variety of other federal agencies with enforcement functions. For example, the departments of Labor, Agriculture, Defense, Interior, and others have developed enforcement or quasi-enforcement units to deal with operations of

Federal Bureau of Investigation: The chief investigative body of the Justice Department, with jurisdiction extending to all federal crimes that are not the specific responsibility of some other federal enforcement agency.

a criminal or regulatory nature. Independent regulatory bodies such as the Interstate Commerce Commission (ICC), the Securities and Exchange Commission (SEC), and the Federal Trade Commission (FTC) require enforcement powers to ensure compliance. During peacetime, the Department of Transportation has administrative authority over the Coast Guard, whose enforcement powers overlap with those of the Customs Service, FBI, DEA, and INS. Special investigative and enforcement bodies appear from time to time, descending directly from the executive, judicial, or legislative branches of government.[4]

Interpol and the U.S. intelligence community also play a role in the federal law enforcement bureaucracy. Founded in 1923, **Interpol** (International Criminal Police Organization) is the largest crime-fighting organization in the world. With its current headquarters in Lyon, France, it is an organization of 177 member countries that serves as a clearinghouse and depository of intelligence information on wanted criminals. For example, it keeps data on criminal identification and circulates wanted notices. Although it is neither an investigative nor an enforcement agency, it plays active roles in crime prevention, extradition, and forensic science.[5] The Treasury Department is the U.S. representative to this international group, and its American liaison office is staffed by federal law enforcement personnel.

State Police Agencies

The **Texas Rangers,** well known to both history and legend, represent the earliest form of a state police body to appear on American soil. Equipped in 1823 by Stephen Austin to protect settlers from raiding parties of Native Americans whose lands were being encroached upon, the Rangers were organized into a corps of irregular fighters at the outbreak of the Texas revolution against Mexico in 1835.

After 1870, the Rangers developed into an effective law enforcement agency.[6] In other locales, state police forces emerged through a slow process of evolution. In 1865, for example, the governor of Massachusetts appointed

Interpol: An international police organization of 177 member countries that serves as a depository of intelligence information on wanted criminals.

Federal Criminal Caseload, by Category, 1947 and 1997

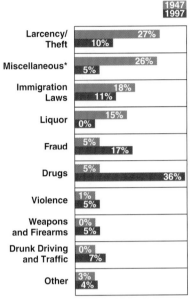

■ 1947
■ 1997

Category	1947	1997
Larcency/Theft	10%	27%
Miscellaneous*	5%	26%
Immigration Laws	11%	18%
Liquor	0%	15%
Fraud	5%	17%
Drugs	5%	36%
Violence	1%	5%
Weapons and Firearms	0%	5%
Drunk Driving and Traffic	0%	7%
Other	3%	4%

*Includes crimes involving agricultural, antitrust, and civil rights issues, food and drug law, postal law, and other criminal acts committed by or against federal employees.

SOURCE: Administrative Office of U.S. Courts.

Texas Rangers: Founded by Stephen Austin in 1823, the first state police agency in the United States.

The Lone Ranger.

a small force of "state constables," primarily for the suppression of commercialized vice. In 1879, the group was reorganized into the Massachusetts District Police and was granted more general police powers.[7] In 1920 it was absorbed into a new department of public safety and designated as the Massachusetts State Police.

During the late 1800s and early 1900s, other states began experimenting with similar forces, all because of the basic deficiencies in existing rural police administration and practices. In the decades that followed the Civil War and Reconstruction, population growth and demographic shifts, changing economic conditions, and the numerous complexities characteristic of any pluralistic society resulted in numerous increases in crime. The office of the sheriff, the only form of law enforcement that existed in many communities, manifested a variety of weaknesses that limited its effectiveness in the prevention and control of crime. Most sheriffs were elected by popular vote for terms of only 2 years, a practice that inhibited freedom from political and local influence and limited the possibility of securing sheriffs with professional qualifications and experience. Statutes in many states prohibited incumbents from succeeding themselves, and in many instances deputies could not even succeed their sheriffs. Furthermore, sheriffs were responsible for the execution of civil processes, for the administration of the county jail, and in some cases for the collection of taxes as well. Also, the fee system under which they received compensation made civil duties more attractive—resulting in an unwillingness to exercise their law enforcement powers. These difficulties also existed in communities where civil and police duties were in the hands of local constables.

Weaknesses of the sheriff system

If the unwillingness and inability of sheriffs and constables to combat rural crime were not enough, there was an additional problem that affected both rural and urban areas. At the turn of the twentieth century, crime had become more global in nature and was less often localized in a particular community. Improvements in transportation and communication had opened new vistas for criminals, providing them with convenient access to numerous geographical areas and ready means of escape to others. Yet there was no effective communication or cooperation between the police of one municipality and those of other cities and towns. The emergence of state police agencies was in direct response to these issues. The agencies were a mechanism of law enforcement that was geographically unconfined, with organization, administration, resources, training, and means of communication adaptable to an entire state.

The beginning of modern police administration

The beginning of modern state police administration dates to 1905, with the creation of the Pennsylvania State Constabulary. It was the first professional statewide force whose superintendent had extensive administrative powers and was responsible only to the governor. From the beginning it operated as a uniformed force, used a system of troop headquarters and widely distributed substations as bases of operations, and patrolled the entire state, including the most remote rural areas.[8] In the years that followed, other states established state police departments based on the Pennsylvania model, and by 1925 formal state police departments existed throughout most of the nation.

Currently, each state has its own police apparatus, and although the structures and functions of these 50 state organizations vary somewhat, they all generally fulfill some of the regulatory and investigative roles of the federal enforcement groups as well as some of the uniformed patrol duties of local police. In general, they are organized into one of two models. Some, like the Michigan State Police and the state forces in New York, Pennsylvania, Delaware, Vermont, and Arkansas, have general police powers and enforce state laws. In addition to performing routine patrol and traffic regulation, they have a full range of support services including specialized units that investigate major crimes, intelligence units that investigate organized criminal activities, and drug trafficking, juvenile units, crime laboratories, and statewide computer facilities for identification and intelligence information. Other state police agencies direct most of their attention to enforcing the laws that govern the operation of motor vehicles on public roads and highways. These state highway patrols, as in California, Ohio, Georgia, Florida, and the Carolinas, are not limited to the enforcement of traffic laws, however. In some cases they also have the responsibility to investigate crimes that occur in specific locations or under particular circumstances such as on state highways or state property, or crimes that involve the use of public carriers. State police operations can also include investigative functions relating to alcoholic beverage control, racetrack operations, and environmental pollution.

County and Municipal Policing

Despite the existence of the large federal enforcement bureaucracies and the state police agencies, most law enforcement and peacekeeping in rural, urban, and unincorporated areas is provided by county and municipal authorities.

The office of sheriff has been established by either a state constitution or statutory law in virtually all state jurisdictions. The sheriff serves as the chief law enforcement officer in his or her county and has countywide jurisdiction. In most counties the sheriff is elected. In years past, this practice brought into question the qualifications of sheriffs as professional police agents as well as the effectiveness of county police organizations in enforcing the law. This issue continues today, because as is the case with most if not all political positions, the ability to get elected is not necessarily related to one's ability to do the job.

Currently, the sheriff's office has three primary responsibilities in most communities. *First,* it provides law enforcement services to the county. *Second,* it maintains the county jail and receives prisoners who are in various stages of the criminal justice process or who are awaiting transportation to a state institution. *Third,* as an officer of the county courts, the sheriff provides personnel to serve as court bailiffs, to transport defendants and prisoners to and from the courts or to various institutions, and to act in civil matters such as in delivering divorce papers or subpoenas and enforcing court-ordered liens, eviction notices, forfeitures of property, and the administration and sale of foreclosed property.

Modern sheriff's officers

With the establishment of city, town, and other municipal police agencies during the twentieth century, a number of jurisdictional disputes emerged between county and municipal police. Currently, many states have given cities and towns statutory authority to provide for their own police protection, thus limiting the sovereignty and jurisdiction of the county police or sheriff's office to rural and unincorporated areas. In other instances, agreements have been reached between county and town police departments whereby sheriffs will not enforce the criminal laws in particular municipalities, except in instances of civil strife, police corruption, or when called on to do so.

THE POLICE BUREAUCRACY

Virtually every police organization throughout the Western world is structured around a military model. Furthermore, combined with their paramilitary character and with modifications related to size, police departments are bureaucratically structured. Thus, there are clearly defined roles and responsibilities. Activities are guided by rules and regulations, and there is both a chain of command and an administrative staff charged with maintaining and increasing

**Police Officers Slain
on Duty, 1970–1997**

SOURCE: *Uniform Crime Reports.*

organizational efficiency. Both the military and bureaucratic characteristics of police organizations are best illustrated by a description of the division of labor, the chain and units of command, and organizational rules, regulations, and discipline.

Division of Labor

All large police organizations and many smaller ones have a relatively fixed and clearly defined division of labor. Each separate responsibility falls within a specific unit, and the designated tasks of one division are precluded from being carried out by others (see Figure 5.1).

Chain and Units of Command

In theory at least, individual orders, requests, or any other types of information should flow up or down through each level of the organizational hierarchy, and no level of supervision or command should be bypassed.

Within this structure, each employee of a policy agency has but one immediate superior to whom he or she must answer. In addition, the bureaucratic principle of delegation of responsibility is quite refined. Supervisors in the chain of command have complete and full authority over their subordinates, and the subordinates, in turn, are fully responsible to their immediate superiors.

Although no uniform terminology has been adopted in American police service for ranks, grades of authority, functional units, territorial units, and time units, those most commonly used are military-style designations. Ranks and titles include *officers, commanders, sergeants, lieutenants, captains, majors, chiefs,* and sometimes even *colonels.* Functional units include *bureaus,* which are composed of *divisions,* and these, in turn, can include *sections, forces,* or *squads.* Territorial units may be called *posts* (fixed locations to which officers are assigned for duty), *routes* or *beats* (small areas assigned for patrol purposes), *sectors* (areas containing two or more posts, routes, or beats), and *districts* and *areas* (large geographic subdivisions). Finally, time units include *watches* and *shifts,* and those assigned to a particular watch or shift are members of a *platoon* or *company.*[9]

Rules, Regulations, and Discipline

Most police organizations have a complex system of rules and regulations designed to control and guide the actions of officers. Operations manuals and handbooks are generally lengthy, containing regulations and procedures to guide conduct in most situations. Officers are instructed as to when they can legitimately fire weapons (clear and present danger of injury to an officer or citizen, no warning shots, and never from a moving car). If any shots are indeed fired, there are detailed rules and procedures for "sweeping the street" (locating spent bullets and determining whether any injury or property damage occurred at the base of the trajectory of a bullet that missed its target). Written reports of such matters must follow certain guidelines, and their preparation must be done in a specific manner (in black ink with no erasures). Elaborate regulations also exist dealing with such varied phases of a police agency's internal operations as the receipt of complaints from citizens, the keeping of records, the transportation of nonpolice personnel in official vehicles, and the care and replacement of uniforms, ammunition, and other equipment. And there are policies and rules to guide the manner in which an officer makes an arrest, deals with medical emergencies, inspects the residence of a vacationing

Figure 5.1 Organization of the Cincinnati Police

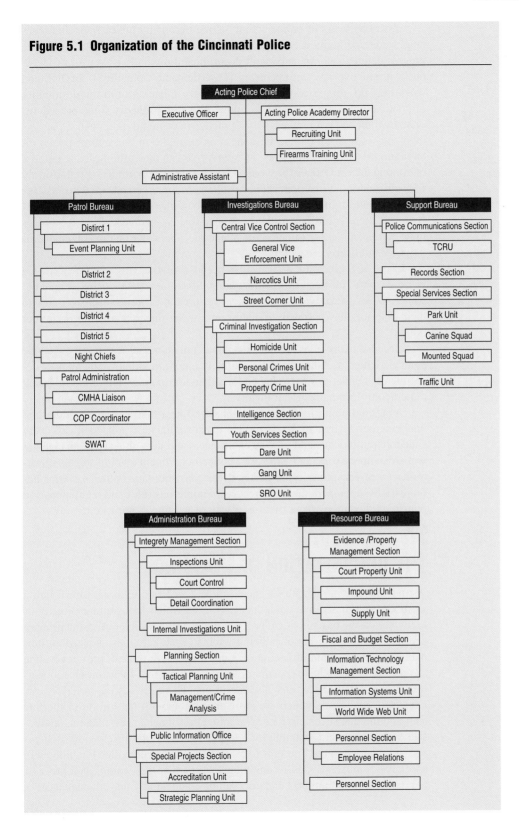

citizen, or takes a stray dog into custody. There are even rules governing procedures for mundane activities.

> Even going to the toilet . . . the rules dictate the formula by which . . . [an officer] . . . must request permission from a superior officer to leave post for "personal necessity."[10]

SUICIDE BY COP

It is estimated that of the roughly 600 fatal police shootings that occur each year, as many as 10 percent are provoked by people seeking to die. "Suicide by cop," as it is typically referred to, is usually not a capricious act of mania or rage, but a calculated attempt to force the police to act as executioners. The effects of such suicides on police officers are often dramatic,
typically resulting in premature retirement from policing.

SOURCE: *New York Times,* June 21, 1998.

Most observers of police activity agree that many police rules and regulations are essentially useless and for the most part unenforceable. The police process demands compliance with departmental regulations as well as vigorously productive law enforcement. These demands sometimes conflict, and when they do, proper conduct must often take a back seat to the desirability of good "collars" (arrests). Furthermore, although in theory some procedures seem explicit and comprehensive, in practice they are no more than vague sermonizing as to what should be done. For example, in the area of police intervention in domestic disputes, no single rule can cover the possible number of contingencies. Officers are told to deal politely, impartially, and uniformly with citizens—but in a domestic quarrel one or more persons may express aggression, fear, or anger. One might be ill, the other might be drunk and abusive, and there could be children or other parties involved. What the officer must do depends more often on the nuances of the situation than on any regulation or published procedure.

There are other areas as well—because of the very nature of police work—where rules can be unenforceable. Since most officers are assigned to some type of patrol work on the street or in cars, they are unsupervised and their superiors have no way of determining what they actually are or are not doing.[11]

Because many rules are unenforceable, police management must practice strategic leniency. Administrators routinely ignore the minor violations of departmental regulations in exchange for adherence to a few important rules and a modicum of organizational loyalty.

As a final point, it should be emphasized here that it is not the titles and uniforms per se that make the police quasi-military. If police officers were suddenly put in jeans and crew neck sweaters and their titles were changed to workers, supervisors, and enforcers, police departments would remain quasi-military organizations. What makes them quasi-military is their *punitive* administrative approach: the specification of numerous rules and regulations and punishing deviations from them as a way of gaining compliance.

THE ORGANIZATION OF POLICING

Line services

Administrative services

Auxiliary services

As bureaucratic organizations, most police agencies are broken down into a variety of administrative components—all of which focus either directly or indirectly on the basic police mission. *Line services,* which reflect the primary and most visible aspects of policing, include such activities as patrol, criminal investigation, and traffic control. Depending on the size of the agency, line services might also have specific divisions or units that focus on vice, organized crime, intelligence, and juvenile crime. There are also a variety of *administrative services,* which are structured to back up the efforts of the line staff and include such activities as training, personnel issues, planning and research, legal matters, community relations, and internal investigation. *Auxiliary services* assist the line staff in carrying out the basic police function, with specialized units assigned to communications, record keeping, data processing, temporary detention, laboratory studies, and supply and maintenance.

Patrol

Patrol: A means of deploying police officers that gives them responsibility for policing activity in a defined area and that usually requires them to make regular circuits of that area.

For generations, the "cop on the beat" has been considered the mainstay of policing. In fact, to most people, the omnipresent force of officers dispersed throughout a community, in uniform, armed, and on call 24 hours a day, is policing. Whether officers are on foot or in cars, **patrol** remains basic to police work in both concept and technique.

Policing city streets entails a variety of tasks. Some of these are mundane, others are somewhat routine and boring, and a few can be dangerous. Patrol work includes such a wide spectrum of activities that it defies any specific description. It could involve catching dogs, administering first aid, breaking up family fights, pursuing a fleeing felon, directing traffic, investigating a crime scene, calming a lost child, or writing a parking ticket. Whatever the tasks might include, the patrol force is the foundation of the police department and its largest operating unit. In both cities and towns, along highways and in rural areas, uniformed patrol personnel directly perform all the major functions of modern law enforcement.

More specifically, police patrols have five distinct functions: to protect public safety, to enforce the law, to control traffic, to conduct criminal investigations, and to interpret the law.[12] In their role as *protectors,* patrols promote and preserve the public order, resolve conflicts, and respond to requests for defensive service. Patrol *enforcement* duties include both the preservation of constitutional guarantees and the enforcement of legal statutes. The *traffic control* functions of patrol involve enforcing the motor vehicle and traffic laws and handling accidents and disasters. As *investigators,* police officers on patrol conduct preliminary examinations of complaints of criminal acts, gather physical evidence, and interview witnesses. During such investigations they may also uncover evidence, identify and apprehend suspects, and recover stolen property. Finally, patrol officers have *quasi-judicial functions,* making the first interpretation of whether a law has been violated. It is here that the discretionary aspects of policing begin to surface. In such circumstances police may choose to take no action or to arrest, or they may only advise, instruct, or warn.

The functions of police patrol

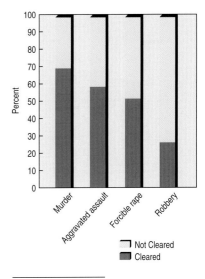

Violent Crimes Cleared by Arrest, 1997

SOURCE: *Uniform Crime Reports.*

Detective Work

Although patrol units conduct preliminary investigations of criminal acts, most sustained investigations are assigned to a police department's detective force, which specializes in the apprehension of offenders. Detective-level policing, specifically *detective work,* includes a variety of responsibilities, all of which fall into the area of criminal investigation: (1) the identification, location, and apprehension of criminal offenders; (2) the collection and preservation of physical evidence; (3) the location and interviewing of witnesses; and (4) the recovery and return of stolen property. In addition, detective duties may involve some of the law enforcement functions of patrol units, such as responding to the dispatch of a "burglary in progress," but these would generally be exceptions rather than general practice.

In reality, detectives are responsible for proportionately few arrests. However, they are evaluated, in part, on a variety of criteria, including their success with major cases, their ability to keep up with paperwork, their skill at handling special types of cases, their capacity to reflect a positive and professional image, and importantly, the number of felony arrests they make during the course of a year, and the "clearance rate" for specific crimes. A crime is "cleared" when the offender has been taken into custody, and the **clearance rate** refers to the proportion of crimes that result in arrest. Thus, detectives generally choose to investigate seriously and intensively only those crimes that are most likely to be cleared.

Since detective bureaus are under organizational, administrative, and political pressure to solve crimes, they also use a variety of mechanisms, sometimes illegitimate, to increase local clearance rates. Through the *multiple-clearance method,* one single arrest may ultimately clear numerous unsolved crimes. Unfounding and reclassification are also reliable, although sometimes illegitimate, methods of increasing clearance rates and getting the

The duties and responsibilities of detectives

Clearance rate: The proportion of crimes that result in arrest.

Property Crimes Cleared by Arrest, 1997

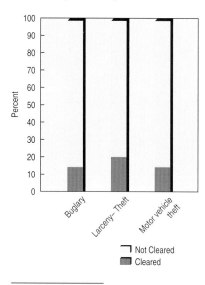

SOURCE: *Uniform Crime Reports.*

crime rate down.[13] *Unfounding* is a formal declaration that certain crimes previously thought to have occurred never actually happened. *Reclassification* is the reduction of certain crimes from felonies to misdemeanors. There are also "exceptional clearances," when some element beyond police control precludes taking the offender into custody, such as the death of a known but unapprehended criminal, a deathbed confession, or the refusal of a victim to prosecute after the perpetrator is identified.

All of this should not suggest that clearance rates are always or regularly manipulated. However, it is clear that different police agencies have different policies and practices in claiming and calculating clearance rates—so much so, in fact, that clearance rates are very poor indicators of the effectiveness of a detective bureau.

Specialized Police Units

In addition to the patrol and investigative aspects of police work, there are numerous specialized approaches to crime control that occur within the context of highly focused bureaus and squads. For example, many large urban police departments have juvenile or *youth bureaus,* which employ proactive strategies to prevent and deter delinquent behavior. These large departments also have specialized units for enforcing vice laws or gathering intelligence concerning organized crime.

Of a less conventional nature is the use of police decoys and "blending"— essentially, two related types of undercover work. In *decoy* operations, nonuniformed officers pose as potential high-risk victims—drunks, tourists, young women, the elderly, and the disabled—in high-crime areas in order to attract and apprehend street criminals. *Blending* involves the use of police officers posing as ordinary citizens, who are strategically placed in high-risk locations to observe and intervene should a crime occur.

The most controversial of the special approaches to crime control are the elite police teams that use aggressive military procedures in exceptionally dangerous or potentially explosive situations. The forerunner of these groups was perhaps New York City's Tactical Patrol Force (TPF), a fast-moving battalion of shock troops trained in mob control and culled from the very best of police academy recruits. Even more visible and controversial are the commando-style police units known under such names as SWAT (Special Weapons and

An FBI SWAT team, deployed during the 1994 World Cup.

Tactics), ERT (Emergency Response Team), TNT (Tactical Neutralization Team), or PPU (Police Paramilitary Unit). SWAT teams or PPUs, which are carefully chosen and trained in the use of weapons and strategic invasion tactics, are typically used in situations involving hostages, airplane hijackings, and prison riots.[14]

The controversy over PPUs comes from the fact that a significant number of these specialized tactical forces are regularly engaged in everyday police work. For example, a recent study of the nation's police departments by the Criminal Justice Research and Training Center found that 36 percent of the agencies surveyed used tactical units for routine patrol activities on a frequent basis.[15]

In addition to the specialized police units already discussed, *sting operations* have also become a part of urban law enforcement in recent years. The typical sting involves using various undercover methods to control large-scale theft. Police officers pose as purchasers of stolen goods ("fences"), setting up contact points and storefronts wired for sound and videotape. And finally, almost every urban locale has one or more specialized *drug enforcement units,* organized to disrupt street-level drug dealing and/or cooperate with state and federal drug enforcement groups in the investigation and apprehension of upper-level trafficking organizations.

POLICE DISCRETION AND SELECTIVE LAW ENFORCEMENT

Among the major roles of police peacekeeping operations is the enforcement of laws that protect people and property. In carrying out this directive, police have the power to make arrests—official accusations of law violation. Thus, police officers stand on the front lines of the criminal justice process and must serve as chief interpreters of the law. Based on their knowledge of criminal codes, they must make immediate judgments as to whether a law has been violated, whether to invoke the powers of arrest, and whether to exercise the use of force when invoking that power. This situation tends to be exceedingly complex, especially since laws are not and cannot be written to take into account the specific circumstances surrounding every police confrontation. Moreover, all laws cannot be fully enforced, and most police officers, having only minimal if any legal training, are not equipped to deal with the intricacies of law. Therefore, police must exercise a great deal of discretion in deciding what constitutes a violation of the law, which laws to enforce, and how and when to enforce them.

To define **police discretion** in a single phrase or sentence would be difficult, for the term has come to mean different things to different people. In the broadest sense, discretion exists whenever a police officer or agency is free to choose among various alternatives—to enforce the law and to do so selectively, to use force, to deal with some citizens differently from others, to provide or not provide certain services, to train recruits in certain ways, to discipline officers differently, and to organize and deploy resources in a variety of forms and levels. Most discussions of police discretion seem to focus on a narrower area, examining decisions regarding only when and how to enforce the law, and hence, invoke the criminal justice process.

Studies of actual police practices demonstrate that discretion is not only widespread, but also that it occurs in many different kinds of situations. Based on extensive field observations of police practices, sociologist Wayne R. LaFave identified many of the reasons for this exercise of discretion. According to LaFave, police use of discretion most frequently originates from three specific types of circumstances: (1) situations in which the conduct in question

YOU BETTER WATCH OUT!

In 1998, the Covington (Kentucky) Police Department came up with a sting operation to see if local Christmas shoppers were naughty or nice. Shopping bags filled with gift-wrapped packages and a Nintendo game box were left in the back seats of "bait cars." The vehicles were placed in shopping center parking lots. Car doors were left unlocked. The police staked out nearby to arrest any thieves who took the gifts, and camera crews from local TV stations were on hand, hoping to catch a crime in progress for nightly news broadcasts. Guess what? From the week after Thanksgiving to just before Christmas, no one took the bait. Although the sting was a bust, it spoke well for Covington shoppers.

SOURCE: *Wall Street Journal,* December 23, 1998, p. 1B.

Police discretion: The freedom to choose among a variety of alternatives in conducting police operations.

is clearly illegal, but police have reason to believe that legislators never intended full enforcement; (2) situations in which the act of enforcing the law would place unreasonable constraints on a police agency's time, personnel, and/or financial resources; and (3) circumstances in which an arrest is technically prescribed but is inhibited by situational determinants.[16]

In the first instance, the conduct in question is undoubtedly illegal, but there is some speculation about the intentions of legislators regarding its enforcement. This can occur when the laws are ambiguous or vague, as is often the case with statutes aimed at nuisance behavior like vagrancy and loitering. In some cases, criminal statutes are directed at a wide range of activities in order to reduce any "loophole" opportunities for criminal entrepreneurs (for example, laws that prohibit not only large-scale organized gambling, but friendly poker games as well). Police may also use discretion when the law appears to be intended as an expression of a moral standard (for example, the sodomy statutes that prohibit certain sexual acts among consenting adults) and/or when the law appears to be antiquated (as in the case of "blue laws" regulating work and commerce on Sunday).

In the second case, full enforcement of the law would become problematic because it would drain personnel, time, and financial resources. This can occur when the offense is trivial, such as smoking in an elevator, or when the proscribed activity is an acceptable behavior among a particular group, such as the use of peyote in religious ceremonies among some Native American groups. Discretion might also become evident when the victim of the offense refuses to bring a complaint, or when the victim is party to the offense—the client of a massage parlor, for instance, who complains of being *rolled* (robbed) by a prostitute.

The third instance involves those circumstances in which an arrest would have been technically correct but situational determinants create the potential for the use of discretion. In some situations arrests are inappropriate or ineffective (such as arrests of skid row drunks) or may cause a loss of public support for the police (for example, crackdowns on gambling). In addition, some arrests would ultimately serve to subvert long-range enforcement goals, as in the case of an officer who arrests an informant. Finally, some arrests may cause undue harm to the offender. Police often use discretion, for example, in handling young, first-time, minor offenders who have good reputations in the community.

The issue of police discretionary power is a problematic one, for the need for selective law enforcement is inescapable. **Full enforcement** of the law would involve an investigation of every disturbing event and every complaint, and the tenacious enforcement of each and every statute on the books—from homicide, robbery, and assault to spitting on the sidewalk or littering the street. Full enforcement would mean arresting the little old lady down the street for gambling at an illegal bingo game, arresting your neighbor for not having his or her dog licensed, or perhaps even arresting your spouse for initiating oral sexual contacts in the privacy of your own bedroom.

Full enforcement, of course, is impossible and undesirable. It establishes mandates that exceed the capabilities and resources of police agencies and the criminal justice system as a whole. It places demands on police officers that exceed their conceptions of justice and fairness. And it transcends the public's conception of the judicious use of police power. Thus, police departments and officers are forced to select the options of underenforcement of some laws and nonenforcement of others, according to the dictates of any given situation. However, there are few clear-cut policies describing when to invoke powers of arrest, and therein lies the problem. The very nature of police discretion creates situations in which good judgment suggests that enforcement should be initiated, *but it is not,* and others in which police power ought not be invoked, *but it is.*

Full enforcement: The tenacious enforcement of every statute in the criminal codes.

Selective law enforcement is inescapable, for full enforcement of the law is both impossible and impractical.

Studies of police discretionary power have demonstrated that the most significant factor in the decision to arrest is the seriousness of the offense committed. This is supplemented by other information such as the offender's current mental state, past criminal record (when known to the arresting officer), whether weapons were involved, the availability of the complainant, and the relative danger to the officer involved.[17] In addition to these seemingly objective criteria, other factors come into play as well. What many police view as "safe" arrests often involve individuals without the power, resources, or social position to cause trouble for the officer. The social position of the complainant is also a matter of concern. In addition, a variety of studies have documented that police use their discretionary power of arrest more often when disrespect is shown them.[18]

A different level of police discretion involves decisions made by police command staff regarding departmental objectives, enforcement policies, the deployment of personnel and resources, budget expenditures, and the organizational structure of police units. Known as *command discretion,* it is implicit in the very structure of a police force. It tends to be less problematic than other types of discretion since it provides at least some uniform guidelines for street-level decision-making.[19] Examples of command discretion might involve orders to "clear the streets of all prostitutes," or conversely, to "look the other way" when observing the smoking of marijuana at rock concerts. Police discretion has other problematic aspects as well, such as when sexual attitudes come into play, as illustrated in Exhibit 5.3.

THE POLICE SUBCULTURE

A *subculture* is the normative system of a particular group that is smaller than and essentially different from the dominant culture. It includes learned behavior common to the group and characterizes ways of acting and thinking that, together, constitute a relatively cohesive cultural system. The police are members of a subculture. Their system of shared norms, values, goals, career patterns, style of life, and occupational structure, and thus their social organization, is essentially different from those of the wider society within which they function and are charged to protect. Entry into the **police subculture** begins with a process of socialization whereby police recruits learn the values and behavior patterns characteristic of experienced officers. Ultimately, many develop an occupational or working personality, as a response to the danger of their work and their obligation to exercise authority.

Police subculture: The values and behavior patterns characteristic of experienced police officers.

The Police Personality

For generations, the notion that policing attracts persons predisposed toward authoritarianism and cynicism has been shared by many. There is even a body of research that supports this point of view.[20] Yet, the overwhelming majority of studies over the past three decades have consistently indicated that policing does not attract a distinctive personality type, but rather, that the nature of police socialization practices creates a working personality among many patrol officers.[21]

Perhaps the most definitive statement on the development of the police personality comes from Jerome H. Skolnick, who summarized the process as follows:

> The policeman's role contains two principal variables, danger and authority, which should be interpreted in the light of a "constant" pressure to appear efficient. The element of danger seems to make the policeman especially attentive to signs indicating a potential for violence and lawbreaking. As a result, the policeman is

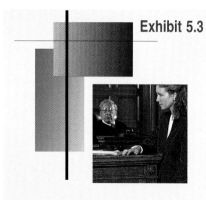

Exhibit 5.3

Gender Perspectives on Crime and Justice
The Tragic Outcome of a Milwaukee 911 Call

On May 27, 1991, the following conversations occurred between two unidentified callers and members of the Milwaukee Police Department, the Fire Department, and the 911 emergency service:

911 OPERATOR: Operator 71.

CALLER: Hi, I'm on 25th and State, and there is this young man. He is butt naked. He has been beaten up. He is very bruised up. He can't stand up. He has no clothes on. He is really hurt. I got no coat on. I just seen him. He needs some help.

OPERATOR: Where, where is he at?

CALLER: 25th and State. At the corner of 25th and State.

OPERATOR: He's just on the corner of the street?

CALLER: Yeah, he's in the middle of the street. He fell out. We're trying to help him. Some people are trying to help him.

OPERATOR: O.K. And he's unconscious right now?

CALLER: They're getting him. He's bruised up. Somebody must have jumped on him and stripped him or whatever.

OPERATOR: O.K. Let me put the Fire Department on the line. They'll send an ambulance. Just stay on the phone, O.K.?

CALLER: O.K.

(The phone rings and a man answers, "Fire Department.")

CALLER: Can you send an ambulance to the corner of 25th and State?

FIRE OPERATOR: What's the problem?

CALLER: This butt naked young boy, or man, or whatever. He's butt naked. He's been beaten up real bad and he's fell out and people are trying to help him stand up. He can't stand up. He's butt naked. He has no clothes on. He is very hurt.

FIRE OPERATOR: Is he awake?

CALLER: He ain't awake. They're trying to get him to walk. But he can't walk straight. He can't even see straight. Every time he stands up, he falls out.

FIRE OPERATOR: 25th and State?

CALLER: Yeah, a one way.

FIRE OPERATOR: O.K.

CALLER: O.K. Bye.

generally a "suspicious" person. Furthermore, the character of the policeman's work makes him less desirable as a friend, since norms of friendship implicate others in his work. Accordingly, the element of danger isolates the policeman socially from that segment of the citizenry which he regards as symbolically dangerous and also from the conventional citizenry with whom he identifies.[22]

(The police were then dispatched.)

OFFICER: The intoxicated Asian naked male was returned to his sober boyfriend.

(In the background, there was some laughter, although it is unclear whether the laughter occurred in the police car or with the police dispatcher. Shortly afterward the police received another call.)

CALLER: A moment ago, 10 minutes, my daughter and my niece flagged down a policeman when they walked upon a young child being molested by a male guy. And no information or anything was being taken, but they were taken downtown. I was wondering . . . I mean I'm sure further information must be needed. The boy was naked and bleeding.

OFFICER: O.K.

(The caller was transferred by the dispatcher to another police officer, where the woman caller went through her story again.)

CALLER: I wondered if this situation was being handled. This was a male child being raped and molested by an adult.

POLICE: Where did this happen?

(She was transferred to another officer.)

OFFICER: Hello, this is the Milwaukee police.

CALLER: Yes, there was a Squad Car No. 68 that was flagged down earlier this evening, about fifteen minutes ago.

OFFICER: That was me.

CALLER: Yeah, uh, what happened? I mean my daughter and niece witnessed what was going on. Was there anything done about the situation? Do you need their names, or information or anything from them?

OFFICER: No, not at all.

CALLER: You don't?

OFFICER: It was a young intoxicated boyfriend of another boyfriend.

CALLER: Well, how old was this child?

OFFICER: He was more than a child. He was an adult.

CALLER: Are you sure?

OFFICER: Yup.

The subject of these conversations was Konerak Sinthasomphone, an abducted 14-year-old Laotian boy who had apparently escaped from his kidnapper. The police, however, had considered the incident a domestic dispute between two gay men and returned the boy to his captor. Would the police have acted in the same manner had the "butt naked" youth in the street been a female?

The boy's captor, by the way, was a Milwaukee candy factory worker who was arrested 2 months later and charged with multiple murders. His name was Jeffrey Dahmer. During the investigation subsequent to his arrest, police found rotting body parts stuffed in boxes and plastic bags, barrels filled with acid and bones, a refrigerator holding human skulls and genitals, and photographs of nude, mutilated bodies. Konerak Sinthasomphone's remains were among the carnage found in Dahmer's home.

Serial killer Jeffrey Dahmer.

SOURCE: *New York Times*, August 2, 1991, p. A10.

Skolnick further suggests that the element of authority reinforces the element of danger in isolating the policeman. That is, police are required to enforce laws that are unpopular, some of which are more morally conservative and others that are more morally liberal than the values of the communities in which they work. Police are also charged with enforcing the traffic laws and other codes that regulate the flow of public activity. In these situations, in which police direct the citizenry and enforce unpopular laws that come from some idealized middle-class morality, they become viewed as adversaries. The public denies any recognition of police authority, while stressing the police obligation to respond to danger.

Skolnick and others have elaborated on other elements that contribute to the development and crystallization of the police **working personality.** All officers, for example, enter the police profession through the same mechanism: academy training followed by the constabulary role of the "cop on the beat." Because of this, officers share early experiences in a paramilitary organization that places a high value on similarity, routine, and predictability. Furthermore, as functionaries charged with enforcing the law and keeping the peace, police are required to respond to all assaults against persons and property. Thus, in an occupation characterized by an ever-present potential for vio-lence, many police develop a perceptual shorthand to identify certain kinds of people as "symbolic assailants."[23] As a consequence, police develop conceptions that are shaped by persistent suspicion. In fact, police are specifically *trained* to be suspicious.

Working personality: A personality characterized by authoritarianism, cynicism, and suspicion developed in response to danger and the obligation to exercise authority.

Another integral part of the police personality is cynicism—the notion that all people are motivated by evil and selfishness. **Police cynicism** develops among many officers through their contact with the police subculture and by the very nature of police work. Police officers are set apart from the rest of society because they have the power to regulate the lives of others, a role symbolized by their distinctive uniform and weapons. Moreover, their constant dealing with crime and the more troublesome aspects of social life serve to diminish their faith in humanity.

Police cynicism: The notion that all people are motivated by evil and selfishness.

Furthermore, although Skolnick's conceptualization of the police personality was based on his studies of male officers, because of the very nature of all police work a number of the same characteristics are also apparent among female officers. In addition, recent research on the personality of women in policing found them to be independent, self-confident, and idealistic about their role. Moreover, personality tests found women police to score lower than average in terms of anxiety, conformity, social participation, and tolerance— all of which suggests that, like male officers, female police officers have personality characteristics far different from those of the general population.[24]

In sum, the police personality emerges as a result of the very nature of police work and of the kindred socialization processes in which most police officers seem to partake. To combat the social isolation that descends from the authoritarian role of the police, they develop resources within their own world—other police officers—to combat social rejection. In the end, most police become part of a closely knit subculture that is protective and supportive of its members and that shares similar attitudes, values, understandings, and views of the world.

The Pompano Beach, Florida, "jet ski" police.

WOMEN IN POLICING

In the majority of jurisdictions in the United States, legislation has mandated that male and female police officers have the same professional opportunities. State and local codes require that the hiring of police recruits be based on physi-cal standards and competitive examinations that are designed to be nondiscriminatory; that all recruits receive the same training and that all officers have the same legal authority; that promotions are awarded on merit as decided by competitive procedures to determine professional knowledge and decision-making abilities; and that equal positions rate equal pay regardless of the officer's gender. However, this was not always the case, and even now at the beginning of a new millennium, gender bias in policing remains a problem.

The Emergence of Women Police

At the beginning of the twentieth century, many women could be found in the ranks of policing. However, they were *not* "police officers." Rather, they were employed in police departments as welfare and social workers, clerks and secretaries, or "police sisters" who helped officers and detectives with their paperwork and other mundane activities. Also common were "police matrons," who had limited authority with duties restricted to such tasks as searching female prisoners and inspecting nightclubs for delinquent girls.[25]

In 1910, a Los Angeles woman by the name of Alice Stebbins Wells became the first female in the United States to hold the rank of "police officer." She worked as a plainclothes officer with the Los Angeles Police Department, and, like her male counterparts, she had arrest powers.[26] But despite this breakthrough by Officer Wells, the movement of women in policing was slow. By the end of the 1920s there were less than 500 women police officers throughout the country. Furthermore, well into the second half of the twentieth century women officers were biased by separate criteria for selection and limited opportunities for advancement. In addition, most were given either menial or gender-biased tasks.

Early 20th-century "police matrons."

The Equal Opportunity Movement for Women in Policing

Opportunities for women in policing began to expand with the passage of the Civil Rights Act of 1964 and the Equal Employment Opportunity Act of 1972. Title VII of the Civil Rights Act "prohibits discrimination on the basis of race, religion, creed, color, sex, or national origin with regard to hiring, compensation, terms, conditions, and privileges of employment." Title VII also holds that gender *may* be used as an excuse not to hire if an employer can prove that it is a "bona fide occupational qualification" for the position (such as body cavity searches of male prisoners only by male correctional officers). However, the wording of Title VII does not mean that an employer can refuse to hire a woman because of assumptions about the comparative employment characteristics of women in general (for example, that they are not as strong as men) or because of gender stereotypes (for example, that women are less capable of aggressive tactics than men).

Pursuant to the intent of Title VII, state and federal court decisions helped considerably in the movement for equal employment opportunities, not only for women in general but for women police officers in particular. A leading case in this regard was *Griggs* v. *Duke Power Company,*[27] decided by the U.S. Supreme Court in 1971. In *Griggs,* the Court held that if job qualifications disproportionately excluded a group or class, the burden falls on the employer to prove that the requirements are "bona fide occupational qualifications" and that no other selection mechanisms can be substituted. As such, a plaintiff was not required to prove that the employer intended to discriminate.

In the wake of *Griggs,* numerous other court decisions during the 1970s and 1980s significantly altered the role of women in policing in five crucial areas: (1) sex-segregated jobs; (2) minimum height and weight requirements; (3) strength or physical fitness tests and requirements; (4) oral interviews and written examinations; and (5) blatant gender discrimination. Perhaps the most important case in this regard was *Blake* v. *Los Angeles,*[28] decided by the United States Court of Appeals in 1979. At the time that Officer Fanchon Blake and several other women officers had filed their class action lawsuit in 1973 against the Los Angeles Police Department, women and men had separate designations—"policewoman" and "policeman"—and policewomen could neither be

assigned to patrol work or promoted beyond the rank of sergeant. The Court of Appeals held that the "Los Angeles Police Department's use of a dual-classification system barring women from police patrol work and from promotions above the rank of sergeant (1) neither complied with the requirements of Title VII of the Civil Rights Act nor could be justified on grounds of business necessity and (2) was not substantially related to the achievement of an important governmental objective." Along with the impermissible sex-segregation that existed in the L.A.P.D., the minimum height requirement of the department was also held to be improper because it could not offer proof that such a requirement was "significantly correlated with minimal use of force so as to justify height as a business necessity."

Griggs, Blake, and numerous other cases brought by women against police departments in the United States resulted in the implementation of affirmative action policies in many police agencies.[29] As a result, by the 1980s, the number of women in policing finally began to expand.

The Current Status of Women in Policing

Studies of women officers have examined their academy performance, capabilities for patrol work, physical training, responses in hazardous situations, and handling of violent confrontations. Virtually all of this research has concluded that women do indeed have such capabilities.[30] Nevertheless, it would appear that women entering police work continue to encounter numerous difficulties, primarily as a result of the negative attitudes of male officers and supervisory staff. Specifically, male officers expect that women will fail; they doubt that women can equal men in most job skills; they do not consider women as doing "real" police work; and they perpetuate myths about women's emotional fitness for the job.

As such, although women represent a significant number of the police officers in the United States, few have been fully accepted into the police subculture. A 1998 survey of 800 police departments conducted by the International Association of Chiefs of Police (IACP) found that overall, only 12 percent of the nation's more than 600,000 officers were women, and that this proportion had not changed significantly in nearly a decade. In addition, the IACP survey found the following to be true:

- Almost 20 percent of the departments surveyed had no women officers at all.
- Some 91 percent of the departments reported having no women in policy-making positions.
- Of the nation's 17,000 police departments, only 123 have women chiefs.
- Almost 10 percent of departments list "gender bias" among the reasons why women are not promoted.
- Although top law enforcement officials want more female officers, more than 25 percent of the departments surveyed expressed concerns about the ability of women officers to handle physical conflicts.
- Sexual harassment of women officers was widespread, to an extent that more than one-third of bias and harassment suits were won by the women involved.[31]

The IACP findings parallel those of a survey of the largest U.S. police departments conducted by the National Center for Women and Policing (NCWP) in 1997.[32] In addition to high levels of harassment, intimidation, bias, and discrimination, the NCWP study documented that women's representation in policing has increased so slowly over the years that it may never reach the level of men. The reasons cited for this discrepancy include recruitment

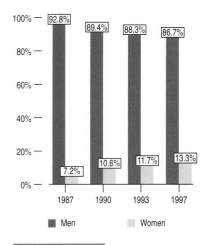

Women as Percentage of Sworn Law Enforcement Officers at Largest Agencies, 1987–1997

SOURCE: Bureau of Justice Statistics.

policies that favor men, the support for outdated models of policing that reward aggressive behavior, and the large numbers of women officers who are driven from their jobs as the result of unrelenting abuse.

Gender bias in policing, finally, is not a problem that is limited to departments in the United States. As illustrated in Exhibit 5.4, for example, the difficulty exists even in some of the most remote parts of the world.

COMMUNITY POLICING

Community policing: A collaborative effort between the police and the community to identify the problems of crime and disorder and to develop solutions from within the community.

In recent years, American policing has seen the emergence of a new vocabulary, and to some extent a new approach to policing. Generally referred to as **community policing,** it is more of a philosophy than a set of tactics and is best defined as a collaborative effort between the police and the community to identify the problems of crime and disorder and to develop solutions from within the community.

Community policing seems to be sweeping the country, and at its heart is the idea that police departments should be more responsive and connected to the communities they serve, that policing is a broad problem-solving enterprise that includes much more than reactive law enforcement, and that individual line officers on the street and in the community should have a major role in community crime prevention.[33]

Under community policing, officers are assigned to small areas—neighborhoods. Some are encouraged to own a home within their city or neighborhood and work out of a substation in order to have a personal stake in the quality of life of their area. The officers patrol their areas, often on foot, "walking the beat," listening to the concerns of residents. By building trust between police and citizens, community policing makes people feel safer. It also makes it more likely that officers will receive information from residents that will allow them to more effectively enforce the law and keep the peace.

An important aspect of community policing is the recognition that much crime control is already accomplished informally by the people of a

The U.S. Fish and Wildlife Service has a small team of "caviar cops," so to speak, who use DNA testing to determine the origin of caviar imported into the United States. Their work is the result of new international regulations established to stop the flow of illegally harvested eggs from the dwindling supplies of sturgeon around the world.

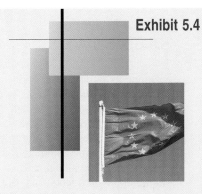

Exhibit 5.4

International Perspectives on Crime and Justice
Women Police in the Republic of Fiji

Once notorious as the "Cannibal Isles," Fiji is now the crossroads of the South Pacific, located some 3,200 miles southwest of Hawaii. Although the 322 islands that make up the Republic of Fiji reflect an interesting blend of Melanesian, Polynesian, Micronesian, Indian, Chinese, and European influences, only two ethnic groups—indigenous Fijians and the descendants of indentured Indian laborers brought from Bengal and Bihar during the nineteenth century—account for most of Fiji's 803,000 inhabitants.

Historically, Fijian women were confined to the home, while men dealt with most matters outside the immediate family. The clear-cut roles of the women as homemakers and men as defenders and decision makers were believed to have given stability to village life. In recent years, however, Western education and influences have caused many Fijian women to question their subordinate positions, and changing lifestyles have resulted in the movement of many women into the labor market. Yet despite considerable progress, cultural barriers continue to hinder Fijian women's access to education, employment, and occupational mobility.

Although women represent 50 percent of the Fijian population, they account for less than 7 percent of the country's 1,913-member police force, and these 130 female officers were recruited only recently—an indication that policing in Fiji has traditionally been a male-dominated profession. In an effort to better understand the issues affecting women officers and to improve the problem of gender imbalance, a survey was recently commissioned by the Fiji Police Force. The results found gender bias to be widespread within the ranks of policing. For example, of the 115 police supervisors surveyed, only 35 percent felt that "policewomen" should perform the

Fiji police officers.

same work as their male counterparts. More than half of the supervisors felt that women officers should spend their time doing office and administrative tasks, looking for lost children, caring for the victims of sexual assault, or participating in community policing activities. At the same time, 13.2 percent of the women officers complained that they had been sexually harassed or even assaulted by male officers while at work. These and other findings suggested that overall, most of the male officers either consciously or unconsciously believed that women did not deserve to be treated as their equals. Some even argued that it went against their "culture" for women to play the same roles as men.

Some recommendations of the research that the commissioner of the Fiji Police Force is attempting to implement include the following:

- Improving the gender balance to better reflect the demographics of the community
- Including gender issues and the role of women in society as core courses in police training
- Appointing an equal employment opportunity officer to facilitate complaints made by woman police officers
- Increasing the number of women in the supervisory ranks and including women from outside the Fiji Police Force in the recruitment and promotion process

SOURCES: David Stanley, *Fiji Handbook* (Chico, Calif.: Moon Publications, 1999); Fiji Police Force, *What Is X? An Organisational Training Analysis of the Fiji Police Force* (Suva: Fiji Police Training Project, 1996); U.S. Department of State, Fiji Report on Human Rights Practices, 1997; FijiLive online (Web site address: http://www.FijiLive.com/infofiji).

Exhibit 5.5   **Careers in Justice**
FBI Special Agent

The Federal Bureau of Investigation is the principal investigative arm of the U.S. Department of Justice and has investigatory jurisdiction over violations of more than 200 categories of federal crimes. In addition, the Bureau is authorized to investigate matters where no prosecution is contemplated.

History

The beginnings of the FBI can be traced to President Theodore Roosevelt's "trust-busting" and his war with the "malefactors of great wealth" and their kept men in Congress. Roosevelt was handicapped in these efforts against industrial combines and graft because, when the need to gather evidence arose, the Department of Justice's lack of an investigative arm forced the president to borrow detectives from other federal agencies. As a result of this problem, Roosevelt's attorney general, Charles J. Bonaparte (who was also the grandnephew of Emperor Napoleon I), appealed to Congress in 1907 and 1908 to create a permanent detective force in Justice.

During its earliest years, the "Bureau of Investigation," as it was first named, occupied itself with small investigations—antitrust prosecutions, bankruptcy and fraud cases, crimes committed on government reservations, and interstate commerce violations. But with the passage of the Mann Act in 1910, sponsored by Congressman James Robert Mann, the Bureau of Investigation stepped into a more national posture.

It was a time when prostitution and commercialized vice had become big business, and there was growing worry over the number of women and young girls who were being imported into the United States "for immoral purposes."

Jodie Foster, as Special Agent Clarice Starling in "Silence of the Lambs."

UP WITH THE COPS

Most Americans believe that cops are doing their best to fight the drug war, though a full third disagree. Sixty-one percent of those polled would pay extra taxes to support larger police staffs.

Do you think the police in your community are working as hard as they can to combat drugs?

55%   Yes   36%   No

If more money is spent to fight crime, what should it go for?

44%   More drug treatment programs and social services
28%   More police
17%   More prisons
 4%   More judges

Would you be willing to pay extra taxes for a larger police force in your community?

61%   Yes   35%   No

Note: "Don't Know" answers omitted.
SOURCE: The Gallup Organization.

neighborhood. When residents report suspicious activity to the police, leave their lights on to deter intruders, watch the houses of the neighbors who are away, and make sure that the local park has enough lighting, they are helping to prevent crime. Most street criminals avoid neighborhoods where residents look out for one another and take care of their surroundings. As such, an important aspect of community policing is the fostering of cooperation between citizen-initiated crime prevention activities and those that the police can do. Or as noted in the report of the National Criminal Justice Commission in 1996:

Under community policing, residents must learn to identify and report not only crime but the precursors to crime. If they spot suspicious activity, they should

Proponents of Victorian morality led an outcry for stern law enforcement action. Under the Mann Act, officially known as the White Slave Traffic Act, it was forbidden to transport women for immoral purposes in interstate or foreign commerce, to assist in procuring transportation for immoral purposes, or to persuade or induce any female to cross state lines for such purposes.

On May 10, 1924, J. Edgar Hoover became director of the Bureau and set out to build a new image for his national police force. By 1935, when its name had been changed to the Federal Bureau of Investigation, Hoover had established a vast fingerprint file, a crime laboratory, the Uniform Crime Reporting system, and a training academy. During the same decade, he mounted a campaign to offset the glamorous publicity that was being given John Dillinger, Alvin Karpis, Bonnie Parker and Clyde Barrow, and other criminals. For a time his "G-men" were included among the top heroes of American culture. The Bureau's lists of "ten most wanted criminals" and "public enemies" provided a continuing scoreboard of Hoover's successes against bank robbers, kidnappers, gangsters, and other lawbreakers. The entire agency reveled in its image of fearless law enforcement—an image that endured for many

decades. By 1960, Hoover's FBI was considered to be the finest law enforcement agency in the world.

During the 1960s, however, disclosures revealed that the FBI had engaged in illegal wiretapping, a mail-opening program aimed at American citizens, the discrediting of its political enemies by attempting to destroy their jobs and credit ratings, accepting kickbacks and bribes, systematically stealing government property, and inciting radicals to commit illegal acts. Amid the turmoil surrounding his years as director, J. Edgar Hoover died on March 2, 1972, at the age of 77. In the years since, there has been a succession of directors, and the agency has taken on a new image. Agents are chasing fewer bank robbers and car thieves and are focusing more on organized and white-collar crime, public corruption, espionage, terrorism, and drug trafficking.

Careers

The FBI currently has almost 12,000 "special agents," more than 16,000 support personnel, and an annual budget of almost $3 billion.

The general requirements for training as an FBI special agent include (1) U.S. citizenship; (2) being at least 23 and not more than 36 years of age and having the ability to pass standard vision tests; (3) availability for assignment anywhere in the FBI's juris-

diction; (4) having a valid driver's license and a degree from a four-year resident program at an accredited college or university.

The FBI has four entry programs: Law, Accounting, Language, and Diversified.

- *Law:* To qualify under the Law Program, the candidate must have a J.D. degree from an accredited law school.
- *Accounting:* To qualify under the Accounting Program, the candidate must have a B.S. degree with a major in accounting or a related discipline, and be eligible to take the CPA examination. Candidates who have not passed the CPA exam will also be required to pass the FBI's accounting test.
- *Language:* To qualify under the Language Program, the candidate must have a B.S. or B.A. degree in any discipline, including criminal justice, and be proficient in a language that meets the needs of the FBI. Candidates will be expected to pass a language proficiency test.
- *Diversified:* To qualify under the Diversified Program, the candidate must have a B.S. or B.A. degree in any discipline, including criminal justice, plus 3 years of full-time work experience, or an advanced degree accompanied by 2 years of full-time work experience.

SOURCES: Fred J. Cook, *The FBI Nobody Knows* (New York: Macmillan, 1964); Sanford J. Unger, *FBI* (Boston: Little, Brown, 1976); Nancy Gibbs, "Under the Microscope," *Time,* April 28, 1997, pp. 28–35; Bruce Porter, "Running the FBI," *New York Times Magazine,* November 2, 1997, pp. 40–45, 56–57, 72, 77–78. (For further information, see the FBI Web site: http://www.fbi.gov)

notify the police. If they see vandalism, they should make sure it is repaired as soon as possible. In turn, the police department must relinquish some of its control over crime prevention to the community. Officers must become community advocates and serve as a link between residents and law enforcement agencies.[34]

Going further, there is a problem-solving dimension to community policing that requires police to analyze problems and develop solutions. When crime occurs, rather than merely disposing of each case, police try to find out *why* the crime happened and what can be done to avoid it in the future. And central to problem-oriented policing is what political scientist James Q. Wilson referred to as the theory of "broken windows."[35] Wilson argued that if the first broken window in a building is not repaired, then people who like breaking windows will assume that nobody cares about the building and break more windows. Soon, the building will have no windows at all. The sense of decay in the neighborhood will increase and social disorder will flourish, and law-abiding citizens will experience fear and hide indoors. Thus, the task is to fix the windows as quickly as possible. It has a ripple effect that influences the quality of life throughout the neighborhood.

Community policing efforts are under way in many jurisdictions, but there are many obstacles to its full implementation. Not all police officers and administrators are ready to accept this new style of policing, feeling that if it involves working with citizens, it is doomed to failure. Others feel that police already have far too many responsibilities, and that adding the community policing dimension will make their tasks even more difficult. And still others feel that the police subculture is so committed to the traditional police roles of fighting crime and keeping the peace that a community policing perspective will render officers ineffective in their basic tasks.[36]

As you likely suspected already, the "X-Files" television series is not based on true events or real FBI cases. The episodes are fiction, and the plots are loosely based on news reports of unexplained events around the world and other unusual phenomena. Although the first episode of the show opened with a note saying that the events were based on an actual real-life story, that was not meant to imply that there are "real" X-files in the FBI archives.

Unlike the fictional agents Mulder and Scully, the FBI is not in the business of chasing down paranormal phenomena. Rather, the organization is the chief investigative body of the Justice Department, with legal jurisdiction extending to all federal crimes that are not the specific responsibility of some other federal enforcement agency. The more significant crimes that fall into FBI jurisdiction are kidnapping, crimes against banks, aircraft piracy, violations of the Civil Rights Act, interstate gambling, organized crime, and interstate flight to avoid prosecution, custody, or confinement. (What it takes to become an FBI agent is described in Exhibit 5.5.)

Television series like "NYPD Blue," "Law & Order," and "Homicide: Life in the City" are somewhat closer to the real world of policing. However, these stories focus more on detective work and arrest situations than the day-to-day activities of most police officers. As illustrated throughout this chapter, contemporary policing is primarily a peacekeeping operation, and at times it can be quite routine, mundane, and uneventful.

SUMMARY

Police have many functions. In a democratic society like the United States they serve as enforcers, investigators, and traffic controllers. In addition to these roles, police also serve a quasi-judicial function in that officers must determine if a crime has actually been committed, and if so, which response is the most appropriate for the situation. In spite of conventional beliefs, the chief function of the police is not to enforce the law, but to keep the peace.

The peacekeeping role of the police is the key factor that differentiates them from private citizens. Peacekeeping involves the legitimate right to use force in situations where urgency requires it.

Federal law enforcement agencies enforce specific statutes as contained in the U.S. Criminal Code, and their units are highly specialized. State police agencies generally fulfill a number of the regulatory and investigative roles of the federal enforcement groups as well as a portion of the uniformed patrol duties of the local police. The majority of modern policing is provided by county and municipal authority.

Police departments are bureaucratically structured on a military model. All large police organizations and many smaller ones have a fixed division of labor, chains and units of command, and rules, regulations, and discipline.

Patrol is the most basic concept and technique of police work. It is through patrol that police protect public safety, enforce the law, control traffic, conduct criminal investigations, and interpret the law. In years past, foot patrols were considered the mainstay of policing. Currently, they have been replaced almost universally by motor patrols, although several researchers and law enforcement professionals have expressed growing interest in "putting the cop back on the beat."

A police department's detective force specializes in the apprehension of offenders. Detective work includes the identification and arrest of criminal offenders, the collection and preservation of physical evidence, the locating and interviewing of witnesses, and the recovery and return of stolen property.

Police officers, whether detectives or those in uniform, are called on to immediately judge whether a law has been violated, whether to invoke the powers of arrest, and whether to use force in invoking that power. Considerable discretion must be used in making these judgments because departmental rules and guidelines are frequently ambiguous. An outgrowth of this discretionary power is selective law enforcement.

There is the police subculture—a system of shared norms, values, goals, and style of life that is essentially different from that of the wider society within which officers function and which they are charged to protect.

In the majority of jurisdictions in the United States, legislation has mandated that male and female police officers have the same professional opportunities. State and local codes require that the hiring of police recruits be based on physical standards and competitive examinations that are designed to be nondiscriminatory; that all recruits receive the same training and that all officers have the same legal authority; that promotions are awarded on merit as decided by competitive procedures to determine professional knowledge and decision-making abilities; and that equal positions rate equal pay regardless of the officer's gender. However, this was not always the case, and even now at the beginning of a new millennium gender bias in policing remains a problem.

Finally, in recent years there has been an emphasis on community policing, which involves a variety of linkages between police officers and the communities they patrol.

KEY TERMS

clearance rate **119**
community policing **130**
Federal Bureau of Investigation **112**
full enforcement **122**

Interpol **113**
patrol **118**
peacekeeping role **108**
police cynicism **126**

police discretion **121**
police subculture **123**
Texas Rangers **113**
working personality **126**

QUESTIONS FOR DISCUSSION

1. What is the relative importance of patrol units, detective forces, and specialized squads to big-city policing?
2. Do the advantages of police discretion outweigh the disadvantages?

3. How should the problem of gender bias in policing be solved?
4. In what ways can community policing best be used in both large and small cities?

MEDIA RESOURCES

1. **The X-Files.** Curiously, there are almost 20,000 Web sites dealing with X-files phenomena. The most comprehensive is that provided by the producers of the television show. Web site address: http://www.thex-files.com/

2. **Federal Bureau of Investigation.** As America's most elite law enforcement agency, the FBI also has a comprehensive Web site outlining its history and activities. It also has extensive information on careers. Web site address: http://www.fbi.gov/

3. **Police Paramilitary Units (PPUs).** Type SWAT into your internet search engine, and about 14,000 different Web sites will pop up. Most common are descriptions of individual PPUs, or complaints about SWAT activities. Two excellent journal articles are Peter B. Kraska and Victor E. Kappeler, "Militarizing American Police: The Rise and Normalization of Paramilitary Units," *Social Problems* 44 (1997): 1–18; David B. Kopel and Paul M. Blackman, "Can Soldiers Be Peace Officers? The Waco Disaster and the Militarization of American Law Enforcement," *Akron Law Review* 30 (1997): 619–659.

4. **Police Use of Force.** The material in Exhibit 5.2 was drawn from Bureau of Justice Statistics, *Police Use of Force* (Washington, D.C.: U.S. Department of Justice, 1998). The entire report appears on the Web. Web address: http://www.ojp.usdoj.gov/bjs/pubalp2.htm

5. **The Status of Women in Policing.** See International Association of Chiefs of Police, *The Future of Women in Policing: Mandates for Action* (Alexandria, Va.: IACP, 1998). In addition, the report of the National Center for Women and Policing referred to in the discussion of women in policing can be found on the Web site of the Feminist Majority Foundation. Web address: http://www.feminist.org/police/status.html

6. **Community Policing.** There are two excellent works on community policing that are readily available: William Bratton, *Turnaround: How America's Top Cop Reversed the Crime Epidemic* (New York: Random House, 1998); George L. Kelling and Catherine M. Ross, *Fixing Broken Windows* (New York: Free Press, 1996).

NOTES

1. For a more detailed discussion of police tasks, see Egon Bittner, *The Functions of Police in Modern Society* (New York: Aronson, 1975); Jonathan Rubinstein, *City Police* (New York: Farrar, Straus & Giroux, 1973); Herman Goldstein, *Policing a Free Society* (Cambridge, Mass.: Ballinger, 1977).

2. James Q. Wilson, *Varieties of Police Behavior: The Management of Law and Order in Eight Communities* (Cambridge, Mass.: Harvard University Press, 1968); Albert J. Reiss, Jr., *The Police and the Public* (New Haven, Conn.: Yale University Press, 1971); Richard J. Lundman, "Police Patrol Work: A Comparative Perspective," in *Police Behavior: A Socio-*

logical Perspective, ed. Richard J. Lundman (New York: Oxford University Press, 1980), pp. 52–65.

3. Carl B. Klockars, *The Ideal of Police* (Beverly Hills, Calif.: Sage, 1985), pp. 15–16.

4. United States General Accounting Office, *Federal Law Enforcement: Investigative Authority and Personnel at 32 Organizations* (Washington, D.C.: U.S. Government Printing Office, 1997). Also see the GAO Web site (Web address: http://www.gao.gov).

5. Raymond Kendall, "Interpol Expands Services in Global War on Crime," *CJ Europe Online* (Web address: http://www.acsp.uic.edu/OICJ/PUBS/CJE/060409_2.htm).

6. Walter Prescott Webb, *The Texas Rangers: A Century of Frontier Defense* (Boston: Houghton Mifflin, 1935).

7. Bruce Smith, *The State Police: Organization and Administration* (New York: Columbia University Institute of Public Administration, 1925), pp. 1–40.

8. Advisory Commission on Intergovernmental Relations, *State-Local Relations in the Criminal Justice System* (Washington, D.C.: U.S. Government Printing Office, 1971).

9. O. W. Wilson and Ray C. McLaren, *Police Organization* (New York: McGraw-Hill, 1977), pp. 70–73.

10. Arthur Niederhoffer, *Behind the Shield* (Garden City, N.Y.: Doubleday, 1967), pp. 41–42.

11. Richard J. Lundman, *Police and Policing* (New York: Holt, Rinehart and Winston, 1980), p. 53; Bittner, *Functions of Police in Modern Society,* p. 56; President's Commission on Law Enforcement and Administration of Justice, *Task Force Report: The Police* (Washington, D.C.: U.S. Government Printing Office, 1967), p. 17.

12. National Advisory Commission on Criminal Justice Standards and Goals, *Police* (Washington, D.C.: U.S. Government Printing Office, 1973), p. 192.

13. Lundman, "Police Patrol Work," pp. 64–65.

14. See William L. Tafoya, "Special Weapons and Tactics," *Police Chief,* July 1975, pp. 70–74; "The SWAT Squads," *Newsweek,* June 23, 1975, p. 95; C. Gordon Jenkins, "Countdown to Teamwork," *Security Management,* March 1989, pp. 46–49; *Washington Post,* April 1, 1991, p. A8.

15. *The Nation,* November 1, 1993, pp. 483–484; *FBI Law Enforcement Bulletin,* April 1993, p. 14; *FBI Law Enforcement Bulletin,* March 1989, pp. 3–9. See also Peter B. Kraska and Victor E. Kappeler, "Militarizing American Police: The Rise and Normalization of Paramilitary Units," *Social Problems* 44 (1997): 1–18.

16. Wayne R. LaFave, *Arrest: The Decision to Take a Person Into Custody* (Boston: Little, Brown, 1965).

17. Larry J. Siegel, Dennis Sullivan, and Jack R. Greene, "Decision Games Applied to Police Decision Making," *Journal of Criminal Justice,* Summer 1974, pp. 131–142; Kenneth Culp Davis, *Police Discretion* (St. Paul, Minn.: West, 1975).

18. Irving Piliavin and Scott Briar, "Police Encounters With Juveniles," *American Journal of Sociology* 70 (September 1964): 206–214.

19. Paul M. Whisenand and R. Fred Ferguson, *The Managing of Police Organizations* (Englewood Cliffs, N.J.: Prentice-Hall, 1973), pp. 199–201.

20. For example, see Richard Bennett and Theodore Greenstein, "The Police Personality: A Test of the Predispositional Model," *Journal of Police Science and Administration* 3 (1975): 439–445.

21. The most significant studies of this viewpoint include Niederhoffer, *Behind the Shield;* Jerome H. Skolnick, *Justice Without Trial: Law Enforcement in Democratic Society* (New York: Wiley, 1966).

22. Skolnick, *Justice Without Trial,* p. 44.

23. Skolnick, *Justice Without Trial,* p. 45–46.

24. Laura L. Manuel, Paul Retzlaff, and Eugene Sheehan, "Policewomen Personality," *Journal of Social Behavior and Personality* 8 (1993): 149–153.

25. Dorothy Moses Schultz, "Invisible No More: A Social History of Women in United States Policing," in *The Criminal Justice System and Women: Offenders, Victims, and Workers,* ed. B. R. Price and N. J. Sokoloff (New York: McGraw-Hill, 1995), pp. 372–382.

26. Dorothy Moses Schultz, "From Policewoman to Police Officer: An Unfinished Revolution," *Police Studies* 16 (1993): 90–99.

27. *Griggs* v. *Duke Power Company,* 401 U.S. 424 (1971).

28. *Blake* v. *Los Angeles,* 595 F.2d 1367 (1979).

29. *Jordan* v. *Wright* (1976) 417 F. Supp. 42 U.S. District; *Harless* v. *Duck* (1979) 619 F.2d 611; *Curl* v. *Reavis* (1984) 608 F. Supp. 1265 U.S. District; *Vanguard Justice Society* v. *Hughes* (1979) 471 F. Supp. 670; *Officers for Justice* v. *Civil Service Commission* (1975) 395 F. Supp. 378; *Burney* v. *Pawtucket* (1983) 563 F. Supp. 1088; *Thomas* v. *City of Evanston* (1985) 610 F. Supp. 422; *Griffin* v. *Omaha* (1986) 785 F.2d 620; *Williams* v. *San Francisco* (1979) 483 F. Supp. 335; *Howard* v. *Ward County* (1976) 418 F. Supp. 494; *Henson* v. *Dundee* (1982) 682 F.2d 897; *Webb* v. *City of Chester, Illinois* (1987) 813 F.2d 824; *Thorne* v. *El Segundo* (1983) 726 F.2d 459.

30. Barbara Raffel Price, "Female Police Officers in the United States," National Criminal Justice Reference Service, 1996 (Web site address: http://www.ncjrs.org/unojust/index.html).

31. International Association of Chiefs of Police, *The Future of Women in Policing: Mandates for Action* (Alexandria, Va.: IACP, 1998).

32. National Center for Women and Policing, *Equality Denied: The Status of Women in Policing* (Arlington, Va.: Feminist Majority Foundation, 1997).

33. Ralph A. Weisheit, L. Edward Wells, and David N. Falcone, "Community Policing in Small Town and Rural America," *Crime and Delinquency* 4 (October 1994): 549–567.

34. Steven R. Donziger, ed., *The Real War on Crime: The Report of the National Criminal Justice Commission* (New York: HarperPerennial, 1996), p. 171.

35. James Q. Wilson and George Kelling, "The Police and Neighborhood Safety," *Atlantic Monthly,* March 1982, pp. 29–38.

36. See Malcolm K. Sparrow, Mark H. Moore, and David M. Kennedy, *Beyond 911: A New Era for Policing* (New York: Basic Books, 1990).

Elements of Criminal Justice

CHAPTER **6**

POLICE AND THE CONSTITUTION

Albany, N.Y.—In his State of the State message on January 5, 1999, laden with numerous anticrime proposals, New York Governor George E. Pataki called for the collection of DNA fingerprints from all felony offenders and the logging of the DNA prints into state computers. Governor Pataki stressed that "DNA is going to be the fingerprinting of the 21st century."[1] This was the second call for DNA fingerprinting in New York State in so many weeks. Less than a month earlier, New York City Police Commissioner Howard Safir recommended that everyone arrested for a crime—never mind whether convicted—be required to submit a DNA sample to police. Civil rights advocates condemned the idea, arguing that police already have too much power, that once a DNA database is compiled it is unlikely to ever be disassembled, and that it would only be a matter of time before the data would grow to include not just wrongdoers but law-abiding citizens as well.

Given these proposals and arguments, what is DNA and should police be permitted to collect it? And even more importantly, what kinds of powers do police already have and how broad are they? What do the U.S. Constitution and the U.S. Supreme Court have to say about police powers?

The right of the people to be secure in their persons, houses, papers, and effects, against unreasonable searches and seizures, shall not be violated, and no warrants shall issue, but upon probable cause, supported by oath or affirmation, and particularly describing the place to be searched, and the persons or things to be seized.

—Fourth Amendment, Constitution of
the United States

Within the context of the foregoing questions, police powers are numerous and can be broadly divided into two general areas: investigative powers and arrest powers. Police *investigative powers* include but are not necessarily limited to the following:

- The power to stop
- The power to frisk
- The power to order someone out of a car
- The power to question
- The power to detain

Police *arrest powers* include:

- The power to use force
- The power to search
- The power to exercise seizure and restraint

Because the Constitution of the United States was designed to protect each citizen's rights, it placed certain restrictions on the exercise of these powers. This chapter discusses the legal constraints on police powers and traces their evolution through Supreme Court decisions, focusing on the Court's impact on law enforcement practice.

SEARCH WARRANTS

The law enforcement functions of the police are accomplished through the investigation of crimes and the apprehension of offenders. Each of these functions becomes manifest by means of a complex and interrelated series of specific activities. The first objective of investigation is to determine if a crime has been committed (although not all crimes require investigation) and, if so, what type of crime it was. Police generally analyze the available information to learn if the elements are present that constitute violation of criminal codes. The next objective is to identify the offender through further gathering of intelligence. When the investigation has been fruitful, an arrest is made; that is, a suspect is taken into custody. Beyond the investigation and apprehension aspects of law enforcement, police also have responsibility for gathering additional evidence if necessary and for preserving it so that the prosecution phase of the criminal justice process can be effective. Yet each and every action in police investigation and apprehension is circumscribed by procedural issues that are governed by law and constitutional rights, and it is when these procedures and issues are called into question that law enforcement practice becomes a matter for judicial review.

At the onset, evidence gathering typically depends on *search*—the examination or inspection of premises or person with a view to discovering stolen or illicit property or evidence of guilt to be used in the prosecution of a criminal action. Associated with search is *seizure*—the taking of a person or property into the custody of the law in consequence of a violation of public law. **Search and seizure,** then, involves means for the detection and accusation of crime: the search for and taking of persons and property as evidence of crime.

The language of the Fourth Amendment, however, prohibits "unreasonable searches and seizures." Unreasonableness, in the constitutional sense, is an elastic term with an ambiguous definition that may vary depending on the particular considerations and circumstances of a given situation. In general, however, it refers to that which is extreme, arbitrary, and capricious and which is not justified by the apparent facts and circumstances.

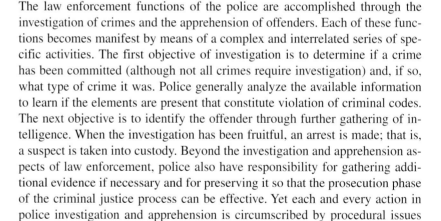

**Actions Police Chiefs
Believe Will Have the
Greatest Impact on
Reducing Violent Crime**

SOURCE: Death Penalty Information Center, Washington, D.C.

Search and seizure: The search for and taking of persons and property as evidence of a crime.

"You have the right to remain silent . . ."

Search warrant: A written order, issued by a magistrate and directed to a law enforcement officer, commanding a search of a specified premises.

Search warrants obviate much of the problematic nature of search and seizure, for they reflect the formal authority of the law in their sanctioning of the use of police search powers. A **search warrant** is a written order, issued by a magistrate and directed to a police officer, commanding search of a specified premise for stolen or unlawful goods, or for suspects or fugitives, and the bringing of these, if found, before the magistrate.

PROBABLE CAUSE

Probable cause: Facts or apparent facts that are reliable and generate a reasonable belief that a crime has been committed.

Warrants authorizing a search must pass the constitutional test of reasonableness. In the language of the Fourth Amendment, "no warrants shall issue, but upon probable cause." **Probable cause,** in the constitutional sense, refers to facts or apparent facts that are reliable and generate a reasonable belief that a crime has been committed. In the absence of such "facts," the probable cause element has not been met, and the validity of the warrant can be questioned. And while probable cause "means less than evidence which would justify condemnation,"[2] it does require "belief that the law was being violated on the premises to be searched; and the facts are such that a reasonably discreet and prudent man would be led to believe that there was a commission of the offense charged."[3]

Establishing probable cause for the issuance of a search warrant is a matter that the Supreme Court has addressed at length. As a result of *Aguilar* v. *Texas* in 1964 and *Spinelli* v. *United States* in 1969,[4] the general rule for many years was that probable cause for search could not be based solely on hearsay information received by the police. Rather, a valid warrant had to contain a statement that there was a reasonable cause to believe that property of a certain kind might be found "in or upon a designated or described place, vehicle, or person," combined with "allegations of fact" supporting such a statement. The High Court's ruling in **Illinois v. Gates** in 1983,[5] however, eliminated the Aguilar-Spinelli test, replacing it with a "totality of circumstances analysis." *Gates* required magistrates to simply make a practical, commonsense decision whether, given all the circumstances set forth in an affidavit, there was a fair probability that contraband would be found in a particular place.

Illinois v. *Gates*: The Supreme Court ruling that magistrates, in establishing probable cause for the issuance of a search warrant, may make a common-sense decision, given all the circumstances set forth in an affidavit, whether there is a fair probability that contraband can be found in a particular place.

WARRANTLESS SEARCH

Although the general rule regarding the application of the Fourth Amendment is that any search or seizure undertaken without a valid search warrant is unlawful, there are exceptions, provided that the arrest, search, and seizure are not unreasonable. The major exceptions include the following situations or circumstances:

- A search incident to a lawful arrest
- Stop and frisk procedures
- Probable cause and inventory searches of automobiles
- Fresh pursuit
- Consent searches

Search Incident to Arrest

Traditionally, a search without a warrant is allowable if it is made incident to a lawful arrest. The Supreme Court explained why in 1973:

> It is the fact of the lawful arrest which establishes the authority to search, and we hold that in the case of a lawful custodial arrest a full search of the person is not

only an exception to the warrant requirement of the Fourth Amendment, but is also a "reasonable" search under that Amendment.[6]

But given the language expressed by the Court, what would constitute a lawful arrest?

Until recently, it was generally assumed that the Fourth Amendment did not require the issuance of a warrant for an arrest to be lawful. Moreover, in 1976 the Supreme Court ruled that a police officer could make an arrest in a public place without a warrant even if he had enough time to obtain one.[7] However, in 1980 the Court ruled that in the absence of exigent circumstances the home of an accused could not be entered to make an arrest without a warrant.[8]

The foregoing at least suggests that arrests made *with* warrants are lawful, assuming, of course, that the arrest warrants themselves are procedurally correct. Furthermore, as indicated in the language of *Gates*, the provisions that determine the validity and legality of search warrants also apply to arrest warrants.

In the absence of a warrant, the legality of an arrest can be somewhat more problematic. As a general rule of common law, an arrest could not be made without a warrant, but if the felony or breach of the peace that was threatened or committed occurred within the view of an officer who was authorized to make an arrest, it was that officer's duty to arrest without warrant. If a felony had been committed and there was probable cause to believe that the particular person was the offender, then he or she could be arrested without a warrant. This common law rule of arrest, which is not at odds with constitutional guarantees, tends nevertheless to be vague, leaving much to the interpretation of the individual police officer.

Although a warrantless search incident to a lawful arrest is permissible, the Supreme Court has placed limitations on the scope of such a search. The key case in this regard was **Chimel v. California,**[9] decided in 1969.

By way of introduction to this important case, it can be safely suggested that Ted Steven Chimel was not a particularly astute thief. Prior to the burglary of the coin store for which he was arrested and convicted, Chimel had engaged in a variety of incriminating blunders. He approached the owner of the store, told him that he was planning a big robbery, and questioned him about his alarm system, insurance coverage, and the location of the most valuable coins. Chimel also carefully cased the store. Following the burglary, he called the owner of the shop and accused him of robbing himself. When the victim suggested to Chimel that the crime had been sloppy, Chimel argued that it had been "real professional." And on the night of the burglary itself, Chimel declined an invitation for a bicycle ride, commenting that he "was going to knock over a place" and that "a coin shop was all set."

According to the facts in *Chimel*, on the afternoon of September 13, 1965, three police officers arrived at Ted Chimel's home in Santa Ana, California, with a warrant authorizing his arrest for the burglary of the coin shop. The officers knocked at the door, identified themselves to Chimel's wife, who admitted them inside, where they waited until Chimel returned from work. Upon his arrival, the officers handed him the arrest warrant and asked permission to "look around." He objected, but was advised that although no search warrant had been issued a search could nevertheless be conducted on the basis of the lawful arrest.

Accompanied by Chimel's wife, the police officers searched the entire three-bedroom house, during which time they requested that she open drawers in the master bedroom and sewing room and physically move contents of the drawers from side to side so that they might view any items that would have come from the burglary. When the full search was completed, the officers seized a variety of items, including a number of coins.

Chimel v. *California:* The Supreme Court ruling that a search incident to a lawful arrest in a home must be limited to the area into which an arrestee might reach in order to grab a weapon or other evidentiary items.

At Chimel's trial on two counts of burglary, the coins were admitted into evidence against him in spite of his objections that they had been illegally seized. Chimel was convicted, and the judgment was later affirmed by the California Supreme Court. On appeal to the U.S. Supreme Court, however, Chimel's conviction was reversed, and the majority opinion of the Court analyzed the constitutional principle underlying search incident to arrest:

> When an arrest is made, it is reasonable for the arresting officer to search the person arrested in order to remove any weapons that the latter might seek to use in order to resist arrest or effect his escape. Otherwise, the officer's safety might well be endangered, and the arrest itself frustrated. In addition, it is entirely reasonable for the arresting officer to search for and seize any evidence on the arrestee's person in order to prevent its concealment or destruction. And the area into which an arrestee might reach in order to grab a weapon or evidentiary items must, of course, be governed by a like rule. A gun on a table or in the drawer in front of one who is arrested can be as dangerous to the arresting officer as one concealed in the clothing of the person arrested. There is ample justification, therefore, for a search of the arrestee's person and the area "within his immediate control"—construing that phrase to mean the area from within which he might gain possession of a weapon or destructible evidence. There is no comparable justification, however, for routinely searching rooms other than that in which an arrest occurs—or, for that matter, for searching through all the desk drawers or other closed or concealed areas in that room itself. Such searches, in the absence of well-recognized exceptions, may be made only under the authority of a search warrant.

There can be several consequences of "unlawful" or "false" arrest. First, evidence seized as an outgrowth of an unlawful arrest is inadmissible. Similarly, any conviction resulting from an illegal arrest may be overturned. Typically, however, if it is clear in the early stages of the criminal justice process that the arrest in question was indeed unlawful, it is likely that the charges against the suspect will be dropped before adversary proceedings follow their full course. Second, in most jurisdictions a citizen wrongly taken into custody can institute a civil suit against the officer and the police department that initiated or authorized the arrest (although these suits are seldom won).

Finally, virtually all states place no liability for wrongful arrest on police officers if the arrest was made on the basis of a valid warrant or on probable cause, but a verdict of not guilty was returned. Thus, an acquittal is *not* tantamount to a finding of no reasonable grounds for arrest. However, in 1986 the Supreme Court ruled that a police officer could be held liable for damages if an arrest was made without probable cause—even if he or she had obtained an arrest warrant.[10]

Stop and Frisk

Field interrogation or *stop and frisk* procedures can be a useful mechanism for police officers in areas where crime rates are high or where the potential risk for crime seems visibly present. In fact, it is not uncommon for police to stop on the street persons whose behavior seems suspicious, to detain them briefly by questioning for identification purposes, and to frisk (conduct a limited search by running the hands over the outer clothing) those whose answers or conduct suggest criminal involvement or threaten police safety.

Before the Supreme Court finally clarified the legal status of stop and frisk procedures in *Terry v. Ohio*,[11] the authority for stop and frisk came from individual department directives, state judicial policy, police discretionary practices, and legislative statutes. In *Terry*, decided in 1968, the Supreme Court held that a police officer is not entitled to seize and search every person he

Terry v. Ohio: The Supreme Court ruling that when a police officer observes unusual conduct and suspects a crime is about to be committed, he may "frisk" a suspect's outer clothing for dangerous weapons.

sees on the streets and of whom he makes inquiries. Before placing a hand on the person of a citizen in search of anything, the officer must have constitutionally adequate, reasonable grounds for doing so.

Any evidence found during the course of a frisk that is contrary to the *Terry* decision falls under the long-standing **fruit of the poisonous tree** doctrine. Under this rule, evidence seized illegally is considered "tainted" and cannot be used against a suspect. Furthermore, subsequent evidence derived from the initially tainted evidence must also be suppressed.

In 1993, the U.S. Supreme Court significantly expanded the power of police to seize property from a suspect who is undergoing a *Terry*-type frisk. The original purpose of *Terry* was to allow police to conduct "pat-down" searches for weapons when confronting suspicious persons. In **Minnesota v. Dickerson,**[12] however, the officer conducting the frisk admitted that he did not feel anything like a weapon, but he did feel a "small lump" in the suspect's jacket pocket. He immediately reached into the pocket and pulled out a small packet of cocaine. The Minnesota Supreme Court suppressed the cocaine, holding that although the stop and frisk were permissible under *Terry*, the seizure of the cocaine went beyond the search for a weapon and thus violated the Fourth Amendment. The U.S. Supreme Court agreed that the cocaine must be suppressed, but disagreed with the narrow scope of the Minnesota court's decision. The High Court created what is now known as the "plain feel" doctrine; that is, when police officers conduct *Terry*-type searches for weapons, they are free to seize items detected through their sense of touch, as long as the "plain feel" makes it "immediately apparent" that the item is contraband. Interestingly, however, since the officer in the *Dickerson* case conceded that he did not instantly recognize the lump as drugs, the "plain feel" did not apply and the cocaine was inadmissible in Dickerson's trial.

Automobile Searches

As early as 1925, the Supreme Court established that due to the extreme mobility of motor vehicles, there were situations under which their warrantless search could be justified. In *Carroll* v. *United States,*[13] petitioner George Carroll was convicted of transporting liquor for sale in violation of the federal prohibition law and the Eighteenth Amendment. The contraband liquor used as evidence against him had been taken from his car by government agents acting without a search warrant. But the Supreme Court sustained Carroll's conviction against his contention that the seizure violated his Fourth Amendment rights. The Court determined that there had been probable cause for search. Chief Justice William Howard Taft explained the decision:

> The guaranty of freedom from unreasonable searches and seizures by the Fourth Amendment has been construed practically since the beginning of the government, as recognizing a necessary difference between a search of a store, dwelling house, or other structure in respect of which a proper official warrant readily may be obtained and a search of a ship, motor boat, wagon, or automobile for contraband goods, where it is not practicable to secure a warrant, because the vehicle can be quickly moved out of the locality or jurisdiction in which the warrant must be sought.

Known as the **Carroll doctrine,** the High Court's decision maintained that an automobile or other vehicle may, upon probable cause, be searched without a warrant even though in a given situation there might be time to obtain one. Subsequent rulings made clear the breadth of the Carroll doctrine. In 1931, the Court upheld the search of a parked car as reasonable, since the police could not know when the suspect might move it.[14] The Carroll doctrine

Fruit of the poisonous tree: The doctrine that evidence seized illegally is considered "tainted" and cannot be used against a suspect.

Minnesota v. Dickerson: The Supreme Court ruling that established the "plain feel" doctrine; that is, an object a police officer detects on a suspect's person during the course of a valid protective frisk under *Terry* v. *Ohio* may be seized without a warrant if the officer's sense of touch makes it immediately apparent to the officer that the object, though not threatening in nature, is contraband.

"Plain feel" doctrine

Carroll doctrine: The ruling, from the Supreme Court's decision in *Carroll* v. *United States*, that warrantless searches of vehicles are permissible where reasonable suspicion of illegal actions exists.

was reaffirmed in 1970 when the Supreme Court held that a warrantless search of an automobile that resulted in the seizure of weapons and other evidence, but conducted at a police station many hours after the arrests of the suspects, was lawful.[15] (For a discussion of the search of a passenger, see Exhibit 6.1.)

Police spot checks

Related to automobile searches are the random stopping of cars and the searches and arrests that may follow. Known as *spot checks*, the random stopping of automobiles for the purpose of checking driver's licenses and vehicle registrations has often been used as a form of proactive police patrol. One New York City police officer reflected on this practice:

> You try to stop the cars and drivers that look suspicious, but other times you go the pot luck route to break the monotony and start with every 20th car. Some nights we'll stop just blue cars, and other times it'll be big cars or old cars or whatever. Other times we'll pull over just blacks, or white guys with beards.[16]

Spot checks can aid in the apprehension of criminals, as a Miami Beach police officer related:

> Depending on the time of night and where you are, maybe you'll pick up something. A few weeks back I see this guy stop at a light and I just don't like the looks of him . . . so I pull him over. . . . It ends up that the car is stolen and he's wanted in two other states on forgery charges.[17]

Delaware v. *Prouse:* The Supreme Court ruling that police may not randomly stop motorists, without any probable cause to suspect crime or illegal activity, to check their driver's licenses and auto registrations.

The reflections of these police officers point to the dangers of spot checks, for although they can result in the apprehension of some offenders, they also lend themselves to discriminatory enforcement procedures. The Supreme Court, however, has taken a strong stand against random spot checks, as was indicated in *Delaware* v. *Prouse*[18] (see Exhibit 6.2).

Exhibit 6.1

Gender Perspectives on Crime and Justice
Warrantless Vaginal Cavity Searches

As Virginia police were pursuing a suspect who was carrying marked drug money in his vehicle, they saw a brown object come from the passenger-side window, presumably the paper in which the cash had been wrapped. When they stopped the car, they found a passenger, Denise Gilmore, riding with the suspect. They also discovered marijuana—but were unable to locate the marked money. Gilmore was taken into custody and strip-searched, but the police

found nothing. A female deputy then inserted the tips of her fingers into Gilmore's vagina, and discovered the marked bills. Prior to trial, Gilmore moved to suppress the evidence, arguing that the search violated her Fourth Amendment rights.

When the decision by the trial court supported Gilmore's argument, the case was appealed by the prosecution, and the Court of Appeals of Virginia agreed that a lawful arrest of a suspect authorizes the police to conduct a "full search" of the arrestee's person. The court asserted, however, that such a search "is only skin deep," citing the U.S. Supreme Court's decision in *Schmerber* v. *California*, which ruled that "a search of a body cavity is considered an intru-

sion into the body that falls outside the permissible scope of a search incident to arrest." The Virginia appellate court held as follows:

> A warrantless search involving a bodily intrusion, even conducted incident to a lawful arrest, violates the Fourth Amendment unless (1) the police have a "clear indication" that evidence is located within a suspect's body and (2) the police face exigent circumstances.

Here, the Virginia court emphasized, the police had no "clear indication" that the money would be found in Denise Gilmore's vaginal cavity, and exigent circumstances did not exist.

SOURCE: *Commonwealth of Virginia* v. *Gilmore*, No. 2700-97-2, May 6, 1998.

Exhibit 6.2   **Legal Perspectives on Crime and Justice**
Delaware v. *Prouse*

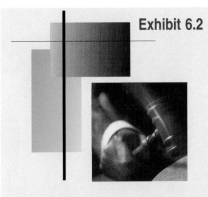

A police roadblock inspection.

On November 30, 1976, at about 7:30 P.M., a New Castle County, Delaware, police officer stopped the automobile in which William J. Prouse was riding. The car belonged to Prouse, but he was not the driver. As the officer approached the vehicle, he smelled marijuana smoke, and when he came abreast of the window he observed marijuana on the floor of the automobile. Prouse was arrested and later indicted for illegal possession of the drug.

At a hearing on Prouse's motion to suppress the marijuana seized as a result of the stop, the New Castle County police officer characterized the stopping of the car as "routine," explaining that "I saw the car in the area and was not answering any complaints so I decided to pull them off." He further indicated that before stopping the vehicle he had not observed any traffic or equipment violations, nor was he acting in accordance with directives relating to spot checks of automobiles.

The trial court ruled that the stop and detention had been wholly capricious and therefore violative of Prouse's Fourth Amendment rights. When the prosecution appealed, the Delaware Supreme Court ruled in favor of Prouse, and the case went on to the U.S. Supreme Court. The High Court granted *certiorari* in an effort to resolve the conflict between the Delaware Supreme Court decision (and similar decisions in five other jurisdictions) against random spot checks, and the opposite decision (rendered in six other jurisdictions) that the Fourth Amendment does *not* prohibit the kind of automobile stop that occurred.

Ultimately, the Supreme Court ruled that random spot checks were a violation of constitutional rights. In so doing, however, the Court did not preclude states from devising methods for making spot checks of drivers' credentials that do not involve the unconstrained exercise of police discretion, such as roadblock inspections in which *all* motorists are stopped. Since *Prouse*, a number of states have established roadblock-type stops, primarily for combating drunk-driving.

SOURCE: *Delaware* v. *Prouse*, 24 CrL 3079 (1979).

Fresh Pursuit

Warrantless arrest and search is permissible in the circumstance of fresh, or "hot," pursuit, which involves chasing an escaping criminal or suspect into a house—and consequently searching that house—or into an adjoining jurisdiction. In common law, fresh pursuit referred to the immediate pursuit of a person for the purpose of arrest—pursuit that continued without substantial delay from the time of the commission or the discovery of an offense. Thus,

The tragic consequence of a U.S. Border Patrol "fresh pursuit" auto chase. The fleeing car hit another, splitting it in two and killing four Temecula, California, high school students.

fresh pursuit is the following of a fleeing suspect who is endeavoring to avoid immediate capture.

Although there is statutory authority for hot pursuit, the practice of high-speed automobile chases has raised considerable controversy in recent years. The National Highway Safety Administration has estimated that more than 250 people are killed and another 20,000 injured each year because of high-speed police pursuits.[19] Many of these deaths and injuries involve bystanders. Police departments have responded with new regulations and training initiatives. Similarly, the courts are also examining the matter.[20] Ultimately, the issue is a matter of police discretion, with individual officers having to balance the demands of law enforcement duty with the risks to public safety.

Consent Searches

Warrantless searches may be undertaken by law enforcement officers when the person in control of the area or object consents to the search. But consent searches can often precipitate complex and problematic legal issues, since a consent to search waives a person's right to the Fourth Amendment protection against unreasonable search and seizure. Thus, in a consent search, neither probable cause nor a search warrant is required, but when using evidence obtained through such a search the burden of proving consent becomes the responsibility of the prosecution. The issues involved are (1) *who* can give consent to search what, (2) *what* constitutes free and voluntary consent, and (3) is there a principle of *limited* consent?

Ordinarily, courts are unwilling to accept blindly the simple waiver of a defendant's Fourth Amendment right and require the state to prove that the consent was voluntarily given. In *Wren v. United States*,[21] the United States

Court of Appeals ruled that a consent was indeed "voluntary" when the search was expressly agreed on or invented by the person whose right was involved. *United States* v. *Matlock* expanded the range of voluntary consent to third parties who possessed common authority with the defendant over the property or premises to be searched.[22] In *Bumper* v. *North Caroline*,[23] the issue of coercion by law enforcement officers was addressed. In *Bumper*, the police had obtained the consent of the defendant's grandmother to search her house in connection with a crime he was suspected of committing. But the police had incorrectly informed the woman that they had a lawful search warrant, and it was on that premise that she had consented to the search. The Court ruled that it was not a constitutionally valid consent. Finally, in *Schneckloth* v. *Bustamonte*,[24] the Supreme Court ruled that police officers are not required to advise the persons whose consent they are seeking that they are not obliged to give consent.

Although *Wren*, *Matlock*, and *Schneckloth* offer police wide latitude and discretion in the area of consent searches, the Supreme Court has also ruled that voluntary consents are also, to some degree, limited consents. The Court has ruled that a search based on voluntary consent must be limited to those items connected to the crime that triggered the desire to search and to other items clearly connected to that crime.[25] Yet by contrast, in 1991 the Supreme Court ruled in two cases that expanded the scope of consent. In *Florida* v. *Jimeno*,[26] for example, the Court held that a consent to search an automobile automatically includes a consent to search any closed containers found therein.

Going further on the issue of consent searches, in ***Florida v. Bostick***[27] the Supreme Court cleared away all constitutional doubts about the drug interdiction technique known as "working the buses." When Broward County, Florida, police officers boarded a Miami-to-Atlanta bus during a stopover in Fort Lauderdale during 1985, without any particular suspicion they conversed with passenger Terrance Bostick. After telling him that he could refuse, they requested his consent to search his luggage. He agreed, and the officers found cocaine in his bag. Bostick was arrested and charged with drug trafficking, but he argued that the seizure of the cocaine was in violation of the Fourth Amendment. After the case moved through the Florida courts, the Supreme Court ultimately ruled against Bostick, holding that "bus sweeps" for drugs do not inevitably result in "seizures" requiring reasonable suspicion. The Court explained that it was only applying the same constitutional rules it had developed for police encounters on the streets and in other public places to sweeps on buses, trains, and commercial aircraft. The ruling "follows logically," the Court argued, from prior decisions permitting police to approach individuals for questioning even when the officers have no "reasonable suspicion" that crime was afoot. The Court did emphasize, however, that in such cases (1) consent prior to search is required; (2) officers may not convey a message that passenger compliance with their request is required; and (3) police may not use intimidating gestures or actions to coerce a consent to a search. (For a related case from the front lines of the "war on drugs," see Exhibit 6.3.)

***Florida* v. *Bostick*:** The Supreme Court ruling that police officers' conduct in boarding stopped passenger buses and approaching seated passengers to ask them questions and to request consent to search their luggage does not constitute a Fourth Amendment "seizure" in every instance, but instead must be evaluated in each case.

Other Warrantless Searches

In addition to lawful arrest, stop and frisk, automobile searches, fresh pursuit, and consent, there are numerous other instances in which the search warrant requirement has been waived. State and federal courts have struggled with the scope of border searches, inventory searches, electronic eavesdropping, searches of abandoned property, searches where there is no expectation of privacy, and searches in open fields.

Exhibit 6.3

Research in Crime and Justice
Cocaine-Tainted Cash

For years, there was the widely held belief that a positive "alert" to cash by a drug-sniffing dog meant that the money was connected to illegal drug activity. The logic was that if the cash had traces of cocaine on it, it must have been touched by drug traffickers, suppliers, dealers, money launderers, or someone else who was regularly in contact with cocaine. Prosecutors in drug trafficking and money laundering cases successfully used this assumption to connect suspects to the cocaine trades and to confiscate the tainted cash.

All this began to change, however, when studies began to demonstrate that the *majority* of U.S. paper bills in circulation were contaminated with microscopic traces of cocaine residue. The research suggested that the contamination was so widespread that it was unlikely that all tainted bills had been touched by a cocaine dealer or someone else involved in a cocaine transaction. The more probable scenario was that the contamination was "innocent," in that it had resulted from money-counting machines and bills already contaminated by cocaine, spreading traces of the drug to clean bills they came in contact with. Armed with these research findings, defense attorneys pushed the theory that a positive alert to cash by a drug-sniffing dog meant nothing, since so

much currency appeared to be contaminated.

Many courts agreed. In 1994, for example, the Ninth U.S. Circuit Court of Appeals ruled that the police could not confiscate cash from a Los Angeles man because there was little evidence that the money was "drug-connected" other than the fact that a drug-sniffing dog had alerted to it. Noting that 75 percent of the bills in Los Angeles were tainted, the court stated that drug-sniffing drugs would likely alert whenever they were confronted with large sums of cash.

But many drug enforcement groups were baffled by the research findings, because they knew that the drug dogs did not alert every time they encountered

A "special agent" of the United States Customs Service, sniffing through packages for illegal drugs.

cash. In fact, since 1989, Metro-Dade County (Miami) Florida police had documented 70 nonalerts to currency, ranging from several thousand dollars to as much as $50,000. So what was happening?

In 1997, research by Dr. Kenneth Furton, a chemist at Florida International University, found that drug-sniffing dogs do not react to cocaine itself, but to *methyl benzoate*, a cocaine by-product. His tests of numerous drug-sniffing dogs found that it takes at least 1 microgram (a millionth of a gram) of methyl benzoate to prompt a drug alert, and that roughly a gram of street-grade cocaine generates that much methyl benzoate. Most importantly, Furton found that although micro traces of cocaine will remain on bills for long periods of time, the methyl benzoate dissipates in just a few hours if the cash is frequently handled or left out in the open air. By contrast, cash sealed in bags or briefcases, or stacked in piles, retained the methyl benzoate much longer. Thus, Furton reported as follows:

> My conclusion is that when a drug-sniffing dog alerts it indicates that the money was either recently, or just before packaging, in close or actual proximity to a significant amount of cocaine, and not the result of innocent environmental contamination.

Federal prosecutors in Miami recently used Furton's research findings to successfully prosecute a case involving $500,000 in cash that was seized after a positive dog alert.

SOURCES: *Miami Herald*, February 19, 1985, pp. 1C–2C; Jonathan Oyler, William D. Darwin, and Edward J. Cone, "Cocaine Contamination of United States Paper Currency," *Journal of Analytical Toxicology* 20 (1996): 213–216; *Drug Enforcement Report*, November 10, 1998, pp. 1, 6–7; K. G. Furton, Y.-L. Hsu, T. Luo, N. Alvarez, and P. Lagos, "Novel Sample Preparation Methods and Field Testing Procedures Used to Determine the Chemical Basis of Cocaine Detection by Canines," in *Forensic Evidence Analysis and Crime Scene Investigation*, ed. John Hicks, Peter De Forest, and Vivian M. Baylor, Proc. SPIE Vol. 2941 (1997), pp. 56–62.

The "Plain View" Doctrine

Pertinent to this discussion of warrantless search and seizure is the **"plain view" doctrine,** examined by the Supreme Court in *Harris* v. *United States* in 1968.[28] In *Harris*, the Court ruled that anything a police officer sees in plain view, when that officer has a right to be where he or she is, is not the product of a search and is therefore admissible as evidence. In the *Harris* case, James E. Harris's automobile had been observed leaving the scene of a robbery in Washington, D.C. The vehicle was traced, and Harris was later arrested near his home as he was getting into his car. The arresting officer made a quick inspection of the car and then took his suspect to the police station.

After some discussion, a decision was made to impound the car as evidence. Harris's vehicle was towed to the station house about 90 minutes after the arrest, arriving there with its doors unlocked and its windows open. Then it began to rain.

According to police procedures in the District of Columbia, the arresting officer in instances such as these is required to thoroughly search the impounded vehicle, remove any valuables, prepare a written inventory, and submit a report detailing the impounding. The officer undertook his search, and tied a property tag to the steering wheel. After this was done, he began to close up and lock the auto. When he opened the front door on the passenger side for the purpose of rolling up the window, the officer for the first time observed a registration card, which lay face up on the metal stripping over which the door closes. The card, which was in "plain view," belonged to the victim of the robbery.

Harris moved to suppress the registration card on the grounds that its seizure was not contemporaneous with his arrest. In the Supreme Court's opinion, however, the observation of the card was not the outcome of a search, but rather, came about from a measure to protect the vehicle while in police custody. As such, the seizure was lawful.

Although the Court made the nature of "plain view" relatively clear in this case, a few police officers have apparently perjured themselves in using the doctrine as a mechanism for justifying illegal searches. If one were to sit in a courtroom in a large urban area where drug dealing is common, he or she would very quickly get the impression that many drug users suffer from "dropsy." Miami attorney Steven M. Greenberg explained the phenomenon:

> Dropsy is claimed by the police in situations where they have searched a suspect without probable cause or consent and found contraband. To insure the admission of the illegally seized evidence the police will "improvise" a story similar to the following: As I drove past [a certain] School, I noticed two or three suspicious-looking suspects standing in the schoolyard, who glanced apprehensively at me as I passed. I drove on down the street, parked my vehicle, and walked toward them. As I approached, one of the suspects reached into his pocket and dropped a clear plastic bag at his feet. I bent down to pick it up and noticed that it contained a substance which resembled marijuana.[29]

Under the **protective sweep doctrine,** examined in numerous court cases during recent years, the scope of plain view has been considerably expanded. The protective sweep doctrine, as it is currently understood, suggests that when law enforcement officers execute an arrest on or outside private premises, they may, despite the absence of a search warrant, examine the entire premises for other persons whose presence would pose a threat, either to their safety or to evidence capable of being removed or destroyed. Furthermore, these protective sweep procedures may be initiated even if there is only a suspicion that other such persons are present on the premises, and any evidence falling in plain view during the search, or sweep, may be lawfully seized.[30]

"Plain view" doctrine: The rule, from the Supreme Court decision in *Harris* v. *United States*, that anything a police officer sees in plain view, when that officer has a right to be where he or she is, is not the product of a search and is therefore admissible as evidence.

Protective sweep doctrine: The rule that when police officers execute an arrest on or outside private premises, they may conduct a warrantless examination of the entire premises for other persons whose presence would pose a threat, either to their safety or to evidence capable of being removed or destroyed.

THE EXCLUSIONARY RULE

In 1914, the U.S. Supreme Court announced its well-known and highly controversial **exclusionary rule,** which prohibited the use in federal courts of evidence seized by federal agents in violation of the Fourth Amendment prohibition against unreasonable search and seizure. The rule was an outgrowth of **Weeks v. United States,**[31] and during the eight and a half decades since *Weeks*, it has been hotly debated whether the decision has been an effective remedy or an expensive constitutional right (see Exhibit 6.4).

Mapp v. Ohio

It was not until almost a half century after the Supreme Court first announced the exclusionary rule in *Weeks* that it fully extended the principle to the states. The precipitating case was **Mapp v. Ohio,**[32] decided in 1961.

Exhibit 6.4

Historical Perspectives on Crime and Justice
Weeks v. United States

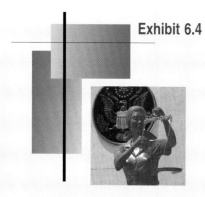

In common law proceedings, the admissibility of evidence in criminal cases was unrelated to any illegal actions the police may have engaged in when securing such evidence. An attorney might argue that a certain piece of evidence was immaterial, inappropriate, irrelevant, or even incompetent, but if it passed these tests it was clearly admissible. The courts, even at the appellate and supreme levels, had no concern with the legality of the methods used to obtain it. If the evidence had been stolen, common law provided for the prosecution of the thief, or a civil action for trespass and return of the property, but the illegally obtained evidence was nevertheless allowable in court proceedings.

Yet it had long been argued that any evidence illegally obtained should not be admissible, and that such a refusal would provide the only effective deterrent to illegal search and seizure.

In *Weeks*, the defendant was arrested at his place of business. The police officer then searched Weeks's house and turned over the articles and papers found there to a United States marshal. Thereupon, the marshal, accompanied by police officers, repeated the search of Weeks's room and confiscated other documents and letters. No warrants had been obtained for the arrest or the search. Before his trial, Weeks petitioned the federal district court for the confiscated articles and papers, but the court refused and allowed the materials to be used against him at trial, resulting in his conviction.

On appeal, the U.S. Supreme Court ruled in Weeks's favor, thus initiating the exclusionary rule. Speaking for the Court, Justice William R. Day explained:

If letters and private documents can thus be seized and held and used in evidence against a citizen accused of an offense, the protection of the Fourth Amendment, declaring his right to be secure against such searches and seizures, is of no value, and, so far as those thus placed are concerned, might as well be stricken from the Constitution. The efforts of the

courts and their officials to bring the guilty to punishment, praiseworthy as they are, are not to be aided by the sacrifice of these great principles established by years of endeavor and suffering which have resulted in their embodiment in the fundamental law of the land.

The decision in *Weeks* quickly became the subject of much legal controversy. By denying prosecutors the use of certain evidence, the rule sometimes caused the collapse of the government's case and the freeing of a defendant against whom there was strong evidence of guilt.

But *Weeks* was only a partial victory for the Fourth Amendment. The exclusionary rule applied only to material obtained in an unconstitutional search and seizure by a federal agent in a federal case, and did not pertain to state actions. In addition, *Weeks* made possible the *"silver platter"* doctrine, permitting federal prosecutors to use evidence obtained by state agents through unreasonable search and seizure—provided that the evidence was obtained without federal participation and was turned over to federal officials.

SOURCE: *Weeks v. United States*, 232 U.S. 383 (1914).

The *Mapp* case began on May 23, 1957, when three Cleveland police officers arrived at the residence of Dollree ("Dolly") Mapp. The visit was pursuant to information that a suspect, wanted for questioning in a recent bombing, was hiding out in her home, and also that a large amount of gambling paraphernalia was being concealed at the residence. Mapp and her daughter lived on the top floor of the two-family dwelling. Upon arriving, the police knocked at the door and demanded entry. Mapp, after telephoning her attorney, refused to admit them without a search warrant. The officers then advised their headquarters of the situation and undertook a surveillance of the house.

The police again sought entrance some 3 hours later when at least four additional officers arrived on the scene. When Mapp did not come to the door immediately, the police forced their way into the dwelling. Meanwhile, Mapp's attorney arrived, but the police prohibited him from either seeing his client or entering the house. From the testimony, Mapp was apparently about halfway down the stairs from the second floor when the police broke into the lower hall. She demanded to see the search warrant. Thereupon one of the officers held up a paper, which he claimed to be a warrant.

Mapp grabbed the alleged warrant and stuffed it into her bra. A struggle ensued during which the officers removed the paper and at the same time handcuffed her because she had reportedly been "belligerent" in resisting their official rescue of the warrant paper from her person. Running roughshod over Mapp, the officers then took her forcibly, in handcuffs, to her bedroom, where the officers searched a dresser, a chest of drawers, a closet, and some suitcases. They also looked through a photo album and some of Mapp's personal papers.

The search then spread to the remainder of the second floor, including the child's bedroom, the living room, the kitchen, and the dining area. The basement of the building and a trunk found there were also searched. Neither the bombing suspect nor the gambling paraphernalia were found, but the search did turn up an unspecified amount of pornographic literature.

Following the search, Mapp was arrested on a charge of possessing "lewd and lascivious books, pictures, and photographs," and was subsequently convicted in an Ohio court on possession of obscene materials. At the trial, no search warrant was produced by the prosecution, nor was the failure to produce one ever explained or accounted for.

The issue in *Mapp*, of course, was the legality of the arrest, search, and seizure. There was no search warrant and no consent to search, but one could argue, as the prosecution heatedly did, that at the time the police applied force and searched her apartment, Dolly Mapp was indeed under arrest—hence, it was a search incident to arrest. Yet, as the defense pointed out, and the facts of the case substantiated, there was no "probable cause" for arrest. The only background the police had was "information that a fugitive was hiding in her home."

It was on the basis of these facts, or rather lack of them, that the Supreme Court reversed the decision of the Ohio court and extended the exclusionary rule to all 50 states. The Supreme Court indicated that the Fourth Amendment is incorporated, by inference, in the due process clause of the Fourteenth— and from the day of its decision, June 19, 1961, any evidence that was illegally obtained by the police would be inadmissible in any and every courtroom in the country!

The Impact of *Mapp*

In 1965, the Court held in *Linkletter* v. *Walker* that the *Mapp* decision would not be retroactively applied to overturn state criminal convictions that occurred prior to the expansion on the exclusionary rule in 1961.[33] The Court stated that the purpose of *Mapp* was to deter future unlawful police conduct and thereby carry out the guarantee of the Fourth Amendment against unreasonable searches and seizures. The purpose was to deter, not to redress the injury to the privacy of a former search victim, and no deterrent function could be served by making the rule retroactive. But despite *Linkletter*, to the 26 state jurisdictions that had rejected the exclusionary rule in toto prior to *Mapp*, the *Mapp* decision was an explosive one. Not only were police search and seizure procedures required to change suddenly, but the rule also immediately applied to all cases that were currently under court review.

The Retreat from *Mapp*

Throughout the 1960s and into the following decade, dissatisfaction with the *Mapp* suppression rule continued. Considerable agitation for the rule's abridgment, if not outright abolition, was manifest not only in Congress but also on the bench of the Supreme Court and among the public at large, who were fearful of the increased levels of street crime.

The justices who wished to modify *Mapp* thought it had developed into a series of confusing and complicated requirements that puzzled the police more than it restrained them. The Fourth Amendment prohibited "unreasonable" searches, but *unreasonable* was a term that had never been fully defined by either the Constitution or the Court. Furthermore, the Fourth Amendment also required that police obtain a warrant, and that it be issued only when "probable cause" was shown. Yet the Court, over the years, had allowed numerous exceptions to this warrant requirement.

Chief Justice Burger, even prior to his appointment to the Supreme Court, had been an articulate advocate of a change in the exclusionary rule. He argued, both on and off the bench, that society had paid a monstrous price for the rule, that evidence should be suppressed only when there was genuine police misconduct, that it was absurd to free a thief or murderer because a police officer had made a minor error in an application for a search warrant, that the rule had little deterrent effect on police misconduct, and that in place of the rule there should be a remedy such as disciplinary action against police officers who abused constitutional rights. Yet while some justices opposed *Mapp*, others were its strong supporters.

The retreat from *Mapp* finally began in 1974 with a series of decisions that limited its scope.[34] A significant setback for the exclusionary rule came in 1984 with the Supreme Court's long anticipated enunciation of the *"good faith" exception*. The announcement came in **United States v. Leon** and *Massachusetts* v. *Sheppard*,[35] two cases involving defective search warrants. In *Leon*, the leading case, probable cause to support the warrant was lacking, yet this defect had not been ascertained by the prosecutors who reviewed the application, the magistrate who approved the warrant, or the officers who executed the search in accordance with its authorization. In *Sheppard*, an inappropriate warrant form had been used. Moreover, it had been improperly filled out. Trial courts had held that these defects required the suppression of evidence seized under the Fourth Amendment's exclusionary rule. Disagreeing with this result, the Supreme Court adopted a good faith exception to the rule in *Leon* and then applied the exception in *Sheppard*, thus allowing the evidence as a result of the warrants to be admissible.

As a final note to this discussion, it should be emphasized that police powers, and the mechanisms for controlling these powers, are issues not confined to the United States and other Western nations.

United States v. Leon: The Supreme Court ruling that the Fourth Amendment exclusionary rule does not bar the use of evidence obtained by police officers acting in objectively reasonable reliance on a search warrant issued by a magistrate but ultimately found to be unsupported by probable cause.

The "good faith" exception to the exclusionary rule

CUSTODIAL INTERROGATION

Confessions, the Supreme Court stated more than a century ago, are "among the most effectual proofs of the law,"[36] but by constitutional implication they are admissible as evidence only when given voluntarily. This has long been the rule in the federal courts where the Fifth Amendment clearly applies. A confession, whether written or oral (but now usually recorded), is simply a statement by a person admitting to the violation of a law. The Court stressed that for a confession to be valid it had to be voluntary, defining as involuntary or coerced any confession that "appears to have been made, either in consequence of inducements of a temporal nature . . . or because of a threat or promise . . . which, operating upon the fears or hopes of the accused . . . deprive him of that freedom of will or self-control essential to make his confession voluntary within the meaning of the law." In 1896 the Court restated this position, ruling that the circumstances surrounding the confession had to be considered in order to determine if it had been voluntarily made.[37]

Twining v. New Jersey

The inadmissibility of involuntary confessions, however, did not apply to the states. The 1908 decision in *Twining* v. *New Jersey* specifically emphasized this.[38] In the *Twining* case, defendants Albert C. Twining and David C. Cornell, executives of the Monmouth Safe and Trust Company, were indicted by a New Jersey grand jury for having knowingly displayed a false paper to a bank examiner "with full intent to deceive him" as to the actual condition of their firm. At trial, Twining and Cornell refused to take the stand, and presiding judge Webber A. Heisley commented both extensively and adversely on this point. To the jury Heisley stated:

> Because a man does not go upon the stand you are not necessarily justified in drawing an inference of guilt. But you have a right to consider the fact that he does not go upon the stand where a direct accusation is made against him.

The jury returned a verdict of guilty, at which point Twining and Cornell appealed to the U.S. Supreme Court. They contended that the exemption from self-incrimination was one of the privileges and immunities that the Fourteenth Amendment forbade the states to abridge, and that the alleged compulsory self-incrimination constituted a denial of due process. In an 8-to-1 decision, the Court ruled against Twining and Cornell, stating that the privilege against self-incrimination was "not fundamental in due process of law, not an essential part of it."

Twining was not a case of forced confession in the strictest sense of the term, for no confession had actually occurred. But as an issue in self-incrimination, the notion of a potentially involuntary confession was inferred, and the resulting decision in 1908 was that state defendants did not enjoy the Fifth Amendment privilege against compelled self-incrimination.

Brown v. Mississippi

Although more than half a century would pass before the Supreme Court would specifically apply the Fifth Amendment privilege against state action, the Court, through its unanimous decision in *Brown* v. *Mississippi*,[39] forbade states in 1936 to use coerced confessions to convict persons of crimes.

No person . . . shall be compelled in any criminal case to be a witness against himself.
—From the Fifth Amendment

In all criminal prosecutions the accused shall enjoy the right . . . to have the assistance of counsel for his defense.
—From the Sixth Amendment

In *Twining* v. *New Jersey*, decided in 1908, the Supreme Court inferred that *state* defendants did not enjoy the Fifth Amendment privilege against compelled self-incrimination.

In *Brown* v. *Mississippi*, decided in 1936, the Supreme Court held that physically coerced confessions could not serve as the basis for a conviction in a state prosecution. Just as these confessions could not be introduced in federal criminal trials under the *Fifth* Amendment, neither could they be allowed in state courts under the *Fourteenth* Amendment's due process clause.

In *Brown*, three black men were arrested for the murder of a white man. At trial, they were convicted solely on the basis of their confessions, and were sentenced to death. But the confessions had been coerced. The defendants had been tied to a tree, whipped, twice hanged by a rope from a tree, and told that the process would continue until they confessed. And although the use of torture to elicit the confessions was undisputed, the convictions were affirmed by the Mississippi Supreme Court.

On appeal to the U.S. Supreme Court, Mississippi defended its use of the confessions extracted through beatings and torture by citing the earlier *Twining* decision—that state defendants did not enjoy the Fifth Amendment privilege. The Court agreed with *Twining*, but rejected the Mississippi defense maintaining that the state's right to withdraw the privilege of self-incrimination was not the issue. In speaking for the Court, Chief Justice Charles Evans Hughes saw a distinction between "compulsion" as forbidden by the Fifth Amendment, and "compulsion" as forbidden by the Fourteenth Amendment's due process clause:

> The compulsion to which the Fifth Amendment refers is that of the processes of justice by which the accused may be called as a witness and required to testify. Compulsion by torture to extort a confession is a different matter. . . .
>
> Because a state may dispense with a jury trial, it does not follow that it may substitute trial by ordeal. The rack and torture chamber may not be substituted for the witness stand. . . . It would be difficult to conceive of methods more revolting to the sense of justice than those taken to procure the confessions of these petitioners, and the use of the confessions thus obtained as the basis for conviction and sentence was a clear denial of due process.

In the years that followed, the Supreme Court reversed numerous decisions in which confessions had been compelled, examining in every instance the totality of circumstances surrounding the arrest and the interrogation procedures. And further, the Court's philosophy made it clear that coercion could be psychological as well as physical.[40]

The Prompt Arraignment Rule

Just before the turn of the twentieth century, the Supreme Court had implied that delay in charging a suspect with a crime might be one of the factors in determining whether a confession had been voluntary or not.[41] A number of federal statutes served to clarify the Court's intent. Their purpose was to prevent federal law enforcement agents from using postarrest detention as a way of exacting confessions through interrogation and from justifying illegal arrests through confessions subsequently obtained by means of prolonged questioning.

Prompt arraignment

But the rules had no compelling force until 1943, when the Supreme Court ruled in *McNabb* v. *United States* that confessions obtained after "unreasonable delay" in a suspect's arraignment could not be used as evidence in *a federal court*.[42] In *McNabb*, five Tennessee mountaineers were arrested when federal agents closed in on their moonshining operations, and during the course of the raid one of the agents was killed. Two of the defendants were convicted of second-degree murder on the strength of their confessions and were sentenced to 45 years' imprisonment. Their incriminating statements had come after 3 days of questioning in the absence of any counsel and before they were charged with any crime. The Court overturned the *McNabb* convictions, not on the basis of the Fifth Amendment, but on the existing prompt arraignment statutes as well as on the High Court's general power to supervise the functioning of the federal judicial system.

The Federal Rules of Criminal Procedure subsequently incorporated this rule. In *Mallory* v. *United States*,[43] almost 15 years after *McNabb*, the High Court reaffirmed its prompt arraignment mandate by nullifying the death sentence imposed on a convicted rapist who "confessed" to the crime during a delay of more than 18 hours between his arrest and arraignment. The defendant, Andrew Mallory, had been arrested in the District of Columbia, and during his long period of interrogation no attempt was made to bring official charges against him—even though arraigning magistrates were available in the same building throughout the period of questioning.

In both *McNabb* and *Mallory*, the Supreme Court did not rule on whether or not the confessions had been obtained voluntarily. Rather, the cases were decided on the basis of the Court's authority to police the federal judicial system. But the Court's decision in *Mallory* received fierce criticism. By reversing the conviction on the basis of the prompt arraignment rule, the Court was saying that any evidence gathered during the delay had been acquired unlawfully and hence was inadmissible—even if it included a confession that was indeed voluntary.

The *McNabb-Mallory* prompt arraignment rule, however, would not stand the test of time. At the state level, the example set by the federal courts was never fully followed. And even the decisions in *McNabb* and *Mallory* were ultimately diluted. Less than a month after *Mallory* had been handed down, a subcommittee of the House Judiciary Committee began hearings to reverse the Supreme Court decision. Although no "corrective" legislation came out of the House, in 1968 Congress incorporated a section into the Omnibus Crime Control and Safe Streets Act that related directly to *Mallory*. The act modified the *Mallory* decision to provide that a confession made by a person in the custody of law officers was not to be inadmissible as evidence solely because of delay in arraigning the defendant, if the confession was found to be voluntary, if the weight to be given the confession was left to jury determination, and if the confession was given within 6 hours immediately following arrest. The measure also provided that confessions obtained after this 6-hour limit could be admissible if the presiding trial judge found the further delay to be not unreasonable.

Mallory v. United States

Confessions and Counsel

Prior to the 1960s, the Fifth Amendment privilege against self-incrimination and the Sixth Amendment right to counsel were not effectively linked. The *Brown* v. *Mississippi* decision in 1936 had ruled on the inadmissibility of confessions obtained by physical compulsion. In delivering the Court's opinion in that case, Chief Justice Hughes also highlighted the constitutional issue that "the state may not deny to the accused the aid of counsel." The linkage came in 1964, with the High Court's decision in ***Escobedo* v. *Illinois*.**[44]

The *Escobedo* case dated back to the night of January 19, 1960, when Manuel Valtierra, the brother-in-law of 22-year-old Danny Escobedo, was fatally shot in the back. Several hours later Escobedo was arrested without a warrant and interrogated for some 15 hours. During that time, he made no statements to the police and was released after his attorney had obtained a writ of *habeas corpus*. Eleven days after the shooting, Escobedo was arrested for a second time and again taken to a police station for questioning. Shortly after Escobedo was brought to the Chicago police station, his attorney also arrived but the police would not permit him to see his client. Both the attorney and Escobedo repeatedly requested to see each other, but both were continually denied the privilege. Escobedo was told that he could not see his attorney until the police had finished their questioning. It was during this second period of interrogation that Escobedo made certain incriminating statements

Escobedo v. Illinois: The Supreme Court ruling that when the process shifts from the investigatory to the accusatory and its purpose is to elicit a confession, the accused may be permitted to consult with his or her attorney.

that would be construed as his voluntary confession to the crime. Danny Escobedo was convicted of murder and sentenced to a 22-year prison term. After a series of appeals, his case reached the U.S. Supreme Court, which ruled in Escobedo's favor by a 5-to-4 majority.

The *Escobedo* decision required that an accused be permitted to have an attorney present during police interrogation. The majority view held that the adversary system of justice had traditionally been restricted to the trial stage, and that the system was long overdue to be hauled back into the earlier stages of criminal proceedings. It was also contended, however, that the *Escobedo* decision need not affect the powers of the police to investigate unsolved crimes. But when "the process shifts from investigatory to accusatory," the Court stated, "when its focus is on the accused and its purpose is to elicit a confession, our adversary system begins to operate, and, under the circumstances here, the accused must be permitted to consult with his lawyer."

The four dissenting justices were not convinced, and the overall tenor of their opinions was that the decision would hamper criminal law enforcement. Across the country police and prosecutors alike echoed the feelings of the dissenting justices. To interrogate a suspect behind closed doors in order to secure a confession was an aspect of policing based on centuries-old custom and usage and a deeply entrenched police practice. No longer would the well-developed "third degree" and sometimes melodramatic "good guy–bad guy" interrogation routines be as readily possible.

Miranda v. Arizona

In the final analysis, *Escobedo* seemed to raise more questions than it answered regarding police conduct during arrest and interrogation. In the Court's discussion of the conditions that existed in Danny Escobedo's interrogation and that led to the reversal of his conviction, was it being suggested that all of these conditions had to be met in order for a confession to be admissible? Were police required to warn suspects of their right to remain silent? If a suspect requested counsel but none was at hand, could a police interrogation continue? If a suspect did not wish counsel, what then? And most importantly, how were the police to determine when an investigation began to "focus," to use the Court's term, on a particular suspect?

Given these unsettled issues, by January 1966, two separate U.S. courts of appeals had interpreted *Escobedo* in diametrically opposed ways. As referee of the conflict, the U.S. Supreme Court sifted through about 170 confession-related appeals, granting *certiorari* to four cases: ***Miranda v. Arizona***, *Vignera* v. *New York*, *Westover* v. *United States*, and *California* v. *Stewart*.[45] Known by its leading case, *Miranda*, the package consolidated the appeals of four persons, all convicted on the basis of confessions made after extended questioning by police officers in which the defendants' right to remain silent had not been made known to them. In all four cases, the crimes for which the defendants had been convicted involved major felonies—Miranda had been convicted of kidnapping and rape, Vignera had been convicted of robbery in the first degree, Westover had been convicted of bank robbery, and Stewart had been convicted of robbery and first-degree murder. The convictions were reversed by the Supreme Court, and from this decision came the well-known *Miranda* warning rules, which every police officer must state to a suspect prior to any questioning:

1. "You have a right to remain silent."

2. "Anything you say can and will be used against you in a court of law."

3. "You have a right to consult with a lawyer and to have the lawyer present during any questioning."

Miranda v. *Arizona:* The Supreme Court ruling that the guarantee of due process requires that suspects in police custody be informed that they have the right to remain silent, that anything they say may be used against them, and that they have the right to counsel—before any questioning can permissibly take place.

4. "If you cannot afford a lawyer, one will be obtained for you if you so desire."

The reactions to *Miranda*, even from within the Supreme Court, were immediate. Four justices prepared a dissenting opinion, and it has been reported as well that Justice Harlan, his face flushed and his voice occasionally faltering with emotion, denounced the decision orally from the bench, terming it "dangerous experimentation" at a time of a "high crime rate that is a matter of growing concern" and a "new doctrine" without substantial precedent, reflecting "a balance in favor of the accused."[46]

Beyond the chambers of the Supreme Court, the *Miranda* decision was bitterly attacked for what was considered a handcuffing of the police in their efforts to protect society against criminals. It was asserted that more than three-fourths of the convictions in major crimes depended on confessions; and police officers and prosecutors across the country, together with some courts, echoed the belief of New York City's police commissioner, Patrick V. Murphy, that "if suspects are told of their rights they will not confess."[47]

At least one study, however, has suggested that *Miranda* had little or no effect on law enforcement. In New Haven, Connecticut, for example, some police simply did not comply with the decision in many cases.[48] Detectives gave the *Miranda* warnings only about 20 percent of the time, and few suspects were ever informed of their right to counsel. In instances when the warnings were given, the detectives had a number of ways to nullify their effect. Some altered the wording slightly: "Whatever you say may be used for or against you in a court of law." Others inserted some qualifying remarks: "You don't have to say a word, but you ought to get everything cleared up," or "You don't have to say anything, of course, but you can explain how. . . ." In the years hence, subsequent Supreme Court decisions chipped away at *Miranda*. However, its basic precepts have stood the test of time, and reciting the *Miranda* warning rules has become a routine part of police arrest practice.

Show Ups and Lineups

A final aspect of this discussion of police and the Constitution involves a variety of investigating techniques law enforcement officers employ to detect and identify criminal offenders. Among these are show ups, lineups, photographs, and other forms of "nontestimonial" material that the Supreme Court has allowed, given certain conditions, as admissible evidence.

The show up is a procedure that generally takes place shortly after a crime has been committed when a victim or witness is taken to a police station and

MIRANDA OVERRULED?

On February 8, 1999, the U.S. Court of Appeals held in *United States* v. *Dickerson* (CA4, No. 97-4750) that compliance with the *Miranda* warning rules was not an absolute prerequisite for the introduction of a defendant's confession in federal proceedings. The court pointed out that although courts throughout the United States have enforced *Miranda* for more than three decades, the decision was in fact overturned by Congress two years after it was announced. The court noted that *Miranda*'s requirements are not constitutional in scope, so Congress had the authority to overturn the decision. As such, the new ruling emphasized that the test for admissibility of a confession in federal courts is "actual voluntariness"—regardless of what the Supreme Court said in *Miranda*. This raises an interesting question: Does this decision imply that the Supreme Court can no longer impose *Miranda* on the states?

"DID YOU READ HIM HIS BOOK AND MOVIE RIGHTS?"

confronted with a suspect. In the show up, the victim or witness is not offered an array of individuals from which a suspect is to be possibly chosen, as in a lineup. Rather, it is often a one-on-one confrontation, presented in such a context as "Is he the one?" *Show up* is a term that is not consistently used by either the police or the courts; *lineup* is more popular. However, *show up* does seem to be used more often in the context of one-on-one identification. In a lineup, the suspect is placed together with several other persons and the victim or witness is then asked to pick out the suspect.

The constitutional issues in the use of lineups and show ups have generally focused on the fairness of these procedures and on the suspects' and defendants' rights to counsel during identification. In *Foster* v. *California*,[49] for example, there was only one witness to a robbery. The suspect, who was 6 feet tall, was first placed in a lineup with two other men who were several inches shorter. Also, he was wearing a leather jacket similar to the one the witness had seen one of the robbers wearing. The witness thought the suspect was indeed the robber, but was not absolutely sure. Several days later another lineup was held, and the suspect was the only one in the second lineup who had been in the earlier one. At this point the witness positively identified the suspect as the robber. The Supreme Court did not allow this type of identification procedure to stand, stating that "in effect, the police repeatedly said to the witness, 'This is the man.' "

United States* v. *Wade addressed the issue of a defendant's right to counsel during a lineup.[50] In *Wade*, the defendant had been shown to witnesses before trial at a postindictment lineup, without notice of the lineup to the accused or his attorney and without his attorney present. The Court recognized in this case that the chances of an unfair identification were so great, either through inadvertence or design, that it ruled a person who is subjected to a pretrial lineup or show up is entitled to be represented by counsel at that time. Importantly, however, the *Wade* case referred only to postindictment lineups and not to those occurring in earlier phases of the criminal justice process.

United States v. Wade: The Supreme Court ruling that a police lineup identification of a suspect, made without the suspect's attorney present, is inadmissible as evidence at a trial.

DNA and Other Nontestimonial Exemplars

DNA is a long double-stranded molecule wound in a spiral called a *helix*. Each strand in the helix contains billions of subunits, and the manner in which these are arranged determines an individual's unique genetic code, DNA profile, or "DNA fingerprint." DNA can be extracted from an individual's blood, saliva, semen or vaginal secretions, or even a speck of skin. When forensic scientists conducting criminal investigations examine DNA, they cannot focus on all of these billions of subunits. However, they can look at certain ministrands of DNA. If three of these ministrands match a suspect's, the chances are 2,000 to 1 that the police have the right person. Nine matches boost the odds to 1 billion to 1, and FBI procedures require no less than 13 matches. Quite clearly, DNA is a powerful tool in criminal investigation. DNA testing has been especially useful in rape cases, because the predator's semen is generally left behind in the victim's vagina or anus. As such, DNA evidence can serve to either convict or exonerate suspects. In fact, since 1976, no less than 10 death row inmates have had their convictions overturned on the basis of new DNA evidence. But because DNA fingerprinting is still a relatively new technique, the U.S. Supreme Court has yet to define the parameters of DNA collection and use.

With respect to other nontestimonial exemplars, the Supreme Court has maintained a firm position, as follows:

- In *Schmerber* v. *California*,[51] the Court ruled that the forced extraction of a blood sample from a defendant who was accused of driving while intoxicated was admissible at trial.
- In *United States* v. *Dionisio*,[52] the Court held that a suspect could be forced to provide voice exemplars.
- In *United States* v. *Mara*,[53] the Court held that a suspect could be compelled to provide a handwriting exemplar.
- In *United States* v. *Ash*,[54] the Court held that the Sixth Amendment does not grant the right to counsel at photographic displays conducted for the purpose of allowing a witness to attempt an identification of an offender.

The position of the Court in these cases has been that the Fifth Amendment privilege protects an accused only from being compelled to testify against himself or herself—that is, from evidence of a communicative nature. On the other hand, in *Winston* v. *Lee* the Court held that a suspect cannot be forced to undergo surgery to remove a bullet from his or her chest, even though probable cause exists that the surgery would produce evidence of a crime.[55]

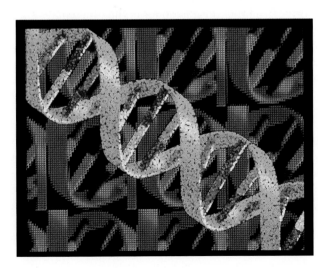

A DNA helix.

What about DNA fingerprinting? Should there be comprehensive DNA databases? Is this a good law enforcement tool or are the debates just the result of civil libertarian alarmism?

Over the past decade, anyone who watched the O. J. Simpson trial or such TV journalism broadcasts as *60 Minutes*, *20/20*, *Dateline NBC*, or *48 Hours* can agree that DNA profiling has come to be almost as important to crime fighting as conventional fingerprinting. Should we be worried about it? What would be the problem of having our DNA prints on file? After all, most of us already have our fingerprints on file for one reason or another.

The problem would appear to be this: The Fourth Amendment guarantees citizens protection from unreasonable searches and seizures. Although the framers of the Constitution did not contemplate strands of DNA when they drafted the Bill of Rights, what search could be more invasive than our very genes?

You might argue that the collection of DNA would be okay if it was limited only to convicted felons—but the process is already well beyond that. Rhode Island and Vermont established DNA repositories in 1998, and California and Connecticut are expanding theirs to include defendants found not guilty by reason of insanity.[56] Going further, when a Lawrence, Massachusetts, woman who had been comatose for more than 3 years gave birth to a baby girl in 1998, the obvi-

ous conclusion was that it had been the result of a rape. Police extracted a blood sample from the infant to obtain DNA information, and then took "voluntary" DNA samples from the male relatives of the victim, nursing home personnel, and others who might have had access to the woman. Comparing the men's DNA to that of the infant's, police believed that they could identify the rapist.[57] And in England, where a genetic database has existed since 1995 with more than 360,000 gene prints on file, suspects are routinely screened in this manner.[58]

The issue is how far the DNA inquiry will go. There are indications that by the year 2010, DNA analysis may be able to determine physical characteristics—enough to create a genetic police sketch of a suspect's appearance. The next step might be untangling the genetic hardwiring to uncover DNA strands that influence temperament and behavior, including criminal behavior. And what would be done with that information? Will we incarcerate individuals for crimes they may be predisposed to commit? All of this may sound fantastic and implausible, like something from Aldous Huxley's *Brave New World*. Maybe so, but consider this: When Huxley wrote *Brave New World* in 1931, he described in vitro fertilization of human embryos ("test tube babies"), and everyone laughed. Yet by the 1990s, it had become a common procedure for dealing with numerous types of infertility.

Exhibit 6.5 **Careers in Justice**
Police Officers

Civil service regulations govern the appointment of police officers in practically all state and local jurisdictions. In general, candidates must be U.S. citizens, usually at least 20 years of age, and must meet rigorous physical and personal qualifications. Eligibility for appointment generally depends on performance in competitive written examinations as well as on education and experience. Physical examinations include tests of vision, hearing, strength, and agility. Most police agencies also require background and psychological examinations, as well as polygraph and drug tests.

There was a time when a high school diploma was the only educational requirement for an entry-level position in policing. In recent years, however, this situation has changed. In most large police departments and many small ones, applicants are expected to have college degrees. A degree in criminal justice is preferred.

Salaries in policing vary by both state and city, and are generally linked to the cost of living in a community. For this reason, the average police officer in New York City earns far more than his or her counterpart in, say, Berrien Springs, Michigan. In 1998, the median salary for nonsupervisory positions in policing ranged from a low of $20,000 to a high of $66,000.

SUMMARY

The police have both investigative and arrest powers. Investigative powers include the power to stop and frisk, to order someone out of a vehicle, to question, and to detain. Arrest powers include the power to use force, to search, and to exercise seizure and restraint. The Constitution places restrictions on the exercise of these powers, but determining the specific intent of the Constitution in this behalf has been left to the courts.

Search and seizure refers to the search for and taking of persons and/or property as evidence of crime. The Fourth Amendment prohibits "unreasonable" searches and seizures, though it has been notably ambiguous in defining the perimeters of unreasonableness. As a result, the Supreme Court has had to define these perimeters in a variety of Fourth Amendment challenges. Court decisions have provided guidelines for the issuance of search warrants, searches incident to arrest, and the circumstances involving stop and frisk, fresh pursuit, random automobile checks, consent searches, and "plain view" seizure.

In *Terry* v. *Ohio* (1968), the Supreme Court held that police could no longer stop and frisk individuals at will. Instead, the Court ruled that the officer must have constitutionally reasonable grounds for doing so. On the other hand, the Court has tended to be quite liberal in granting police officers access to warrantless searches of automobiles. A number of recent decisions have expanded the circumstances under which officers may search vehicles and their contents. With regard to consent searches, the Court has issued a number of rulings regarding under what conditions and by whom consent can be issued, the nature of free and voluntary consent, and the viability of limited consent as a legal principle. Lastly, in the case of "plain view," the Court has ruled that evidence in an officer's "plain view" is admissible because it was not produced by a search.

The Supreme Court's exclusionary rule prohibits the use in court of any evidence seized in violation of the Fourth Amendment ban against unreasonable search and seizure. In *Weeks* v. *United States* in 1914, the Court established the exclusionary rule for federal prosecutions; *Mapp* v. *Ohio* extended this rule to the states in 1961. Since *Mapp*, however, there has been dissatisfaction with the exclusionary rule. Since the 1960s there has been a general retreat from the guidelines established in *Mapp*; the greatest setback came in 1984 when the Court established the "good faith" exception, allowing evidence gathered in questionable searches to be admitted into court depending on the circumstances of the search.

In criminal prosecutions, the Constitution prohibits forced confessions and guarantees the assistance of counsel. However, these restrictions were only recently applied to the states. The first of these provisions occurred in 1936 as part of the *Brown* v. *Mississippi* decision in which the Court ruled that state courts cannot use coerced confessions as the basis of criminal convictions. During the 1964 term, the Court ruled in *Escobeda* v. *Illinois* that the accused must be allowed to have an attorney present during the police interrogation. In addition, the Court later established in *Miranda* v. *Arizona* (1966) that police officers must issue *Miranda* warning rules to all suspects prior to questioning them. As with *Mapp*, there was dissatisfaction with the *Miranda* rule, and over the years its original strength has been diluted somewhat.

KEY TERMS

Carroll doctrine **145**	*Illinois* v. *Gates* **142**	search and seizure **140**
Chimel v. *California* **143**	*Mapp* v. *Ohio* **152**	search warrant **142**
Delaware v. *Prouse* **146**	*Minnesota* v. *Dickerson* **145**	*Terry* v. *Ohio* **144**
Escobedo v. *Illinois* **157**	*Miranda* v. *Arizona* **158**	*United States* v. *Leon* **154**
exclusionary rule **152**	"plain view" doctrine **151**	*United States* v. *Wade* **160**
Florida v. *Bostick* **149**	probable cause **142**	*Weeks* v. *United States* **152**
fruit of the poisonous tree **145**	protective sweep doctrine **151**	

QUESTIONS FOR DISCUSSION

1. Given the facts in *Chimel* v. *California*, could the prosecution have applied the doctrines of "plain view" and protective sweep?
2. What are the various rights of the accused during the pretrial phases of the criminal justice process?
3. Applying the concept of probable cause, what specifically was considered "unreasonable" about the searches and seizures in *Mapp* v. *Ohio*?

4. What are your opinions of the reasonableness of the Supreme Court decisions in *Mapp*, *Escobedo*, and *Miranda*?

MEDIA RESOURCES

1. *Miranda* **v.** *Arizona.* In 1998, the *New York Times* published two excellent articles describing how police tactics have chipped away at suspects' rights. See *New York Times*, March 29, 1998, pp. 1, 40; *New York Times*, March 30, 1998, pp. A1, B4.
2. **DNA Fingerprinting.** For those of you who wish to better understand the intricacies of DNA, genes, and chromosomes, the U.S. Department of Energy has published an excellent report titled *Primer on Molecular Genetics*. It is also on the Web: http://www.ornl.gov/hgms
3. **Search and Seizure.** Issues in search and seizure are continually being examined by state and federal courts. The Bureau of National Affairs in Washington,

D.C., publishes summaries of all major state and federal cases on a weekly basis in a document called the *Criminal Law Reporter*. It is available in most law libraries.

4. **Cocaine, Crack, and the War on Drugs.** There are libraries of information on these topics. Two books with which I am particularly familiar are James A. In-

ciardi, *The War on Drugs II: The Continuing Epic of Heroin, Cocaine, Crack, Crime, AIDS, and Public Policy* (Mountain View, Calif.: Mayfield, 1992); and James A. Inciardi, Dorothy Lockwood, and Anne E. Pottieger, *Women and Crack-Cocaine* (New York: Macmillan, 1993).

NOTES

1. *New York Times*, January 6, 1999, p. B5.
2. *Locke* v. *United States*, 7 Cr. 339 (1813).
3. *Dumbra* v. *United States*, 268 U.S. 435 (1925).
4. *Aguilar* v. *Texas*, 378 U.S. 108 (1964); *Spinelli* v. *United States*, 393 U.S. 410 (1969).
5. *Illinois* v. *Gates*, 462 U.S. 213 (1983).
6. *United States* v. *Robinson*, 414 U.S. 218 (1973).
7. *United States* v. *Watson*, 423 U.S. 455 (1976).
8. *Payton* v. *New York*, 455 U.S. 573 (1980).
9. *Chimel* v. *California*, 395 U.S. 752 (1969).
10. *Malley* v. *Briggs*, 38 CrL 3169 (1986).
11. *Terry* v. *Ohio*, 392 U.S. 1 (1968).
12. *Minnesota* v. *Dickerson*, 113 S.Ct. 2130 (1993).
13. *Carroll* v. *United States*, 267 U.S. 132 (1925).
14. *Husty* v. *United States*, 282 U.S. 694 (1931).
15. *Chambers* v. *Maroney*, 399 U.S. 42 (1970).
16. Personal communication, October 31, 1970.
17. Personal communication, June 19, 1975.
18. *Delaware* v. *Prouse*, 24 CrL 3079 (1979).
19. Louis P. Mitchell, "High Speed Pursuits," *C.J., The Americas* 2 (January 1990): 18; *Police Chief*, July 1994, pp. 59–66.
20. Geoffrey P. Alpert, "Analyzing Police Pursuit," *Criminal Law Bulletin* 27 (July-August 1991): 358–367.
21. *Wren* v. *United States*, 352 F 2d 617 (1965).
22. *United States* v. *Matlock*, 415 U.S. 164 (1974).
23. *Bumper* v. *North Carolina*, 391 U.S. 543 (1968).
24. *Schneckloth* v. *Bustamonte*, 412 U.S. 218 (1973).
25. *United States* v. *Dichiarinte*, 445 F 2d 126 (1921).
26. *Florida* v. *Jimeno*, 49 CrL 2175 (1991).
27. *Florida* v. *Bostick*, 49 CrL 2270 (1991).
28. *Harris* v. *United States*, 390 U.S. 234 (1968).
29. Steven M. Greenberg, "Compounding a Felony: Drug Abuse and the American Legal System," in *Drugs and the Criminal Justice System*, ed. James A. Inciardi and Carl D. Chambers (Beverly Hills, Calif.: Sage, 1974), p. 200.
30. Gary Kelder and Alan J. Statman, "The Protective Sweep Doctrine: Recurrent Questions Regarding the Propriety of Searches Conducted Contemporaneously With an Arrest on or Near Private Premises," *Syracuse Law Review* 30 (1979): 973–1092.
31. *Weeks* v. *United States*, 232 U.S. 383 (1914).
32. *Mapp* v. *Ohio*, 367 U.S. 643 (1961).
33. *Linkletter* v. *Walker*, 381 U.S. 618 (1965).
34. *United States* v. *Calandra*, 414 U.S. 38 (1974).
35. *United States* v. *Leon*, U.S. SupCt 35 CrL 3273 (1984); *Massachusetts* v. *Sheppard*, U.S. SupCt 35 CrL 3296 (1984).
36. *Hopt* v. *Utah*, 110 U.S. 574 (1884).
37. *Wilson* v. *United States*, 162 U.S. 613 (1896).
38. *Twining* v. *New Jersey*, 211 U.S. 78 (1908).
39. *Brown* v. *Mississippi*, 297 U.S. 278 (1936).
40. *Rogers* v. *Richmond*, 365 U.S. 534 (1961).
41. *Bram* v. *United States*, 168 U.S. 532 (1897).
42. *McNabb* v. *United States*, 318 U.S. 332 (1943).
43. *Mallory* v. *United States*, 354 U.S. 449 (1957).
44. *Escobedo* v. *Illinois*, 378 U.S. 478 (1964).
45. *Miranda* v. *Arizona*, *Vignera* v. *New York*, *Westover* v. *United States*, *California* v. *Stewart*—all 384 U.S. 436 (1966).
46. *New York Times*, June 14, 1966, p. 1.
47. Robert F. Cushman, *Cases in Constitutional Law* (Englewood Cliffs, N.J.: Prentice-Hall, 1979), p. 400.
48. Richard Ayres, "Confessions and the Court," in *The Ambivalent Force: Perspectives on the Police*, eds. Arthur Neiderhoffer and Abraham S. Blumberg (Hinsdale, Ill.: Dryden, 1976), pp. 286–290.
49. *Foster* v. *California*, 394 U.S. 440 (1969).
50. *United States* v. *Wade*, 388 U.S. 218 (1967).
51. *Schmerber* v. *California*, 384 U.S. 757 (1966).
52. *United States* v. *Dionisio*, 410 U.S. 1 (1973).
53. *United States* v. *Mara*, 410 U.S. 19 (1973).
54. *United States* v. *Ash*, 413 U.S. 300 (1973).
55. *National Law Journal*, January 25, 1999, p. A11.
56. *Time*, January 11, 1999, p. 62.
57. *Time*, January 11, 1999, p. 62.
58. *Time*, January 11, 1999, p. 62.

Elements of Criminal Justice

CHAPTER 7
POLICE MISCONDUCT

N
EW YORK — An unarmed street peddler, 22-year-old Amadou Diallo, was shot to death by four white plainclothes police officers outside his apartment in the Bronx. Diallo, an African immigrant with no criminal record, was killed during the officers' investigation of a serial rapist in the area.[1] The officers were part of the N.Y.P.D. Street Crime Unit, a special task force established as part of New York's "zero-tolerance" crime policy.

The Diallo case—clearly a tragedy but also a flagrant misuse of deadly force—raises a number of questions. What really happened in the Diallo shooting and what is a zero-tolerance crime policy? In addition to deadly force, what other kinds of police violence occur? Are there other types of police misconduct besides violence? What accounts for police misconduct and how might it be controlled?

Within the context of these questions, this chapter focuses on two areas of police misconduct: corruption and violence. Police corruption involves illegal activities for economic gain, including payment for the very services that police are sworn to carry out as part of their peacekeeping role. Police violence, in the forms of brutality and the misapplication of deadly force, involves the wrongful use of police power.

POLICE CORRUPTION

Research in the area of white-collar crime, combined with government inquiries targeting the internal operations of organized crime, labor unions, and various business enterprises, has demonstrated that work-related lawbreaking can be found within every profession and occupation. Policing is no exception, with illegal job-related activities focusing on graft, corruption, theft, and numerous other practices. In fact, crime and corruption may be considerably more widespread in policing than in most other occupations. Virtually every urban police department in the United States has experienced both organized corruption and some form of scandal, and similar problems have been uncovered in small towns and rural sheriffs' departments.

The problem lies in the fact that policing is rich in opportunities for corruption—more so than in most, if not all, other occupations. The police officer stands at the front lines of the criminal justice system in a nation where crime rates are high and where the demands for illegal goods and services are widespread. These conditions, combined with a range of numerous other variables, create a situation in which police officers are confronted daily with opportunities for accepting funds in lieu of fully discharging their duties.

Police corruption is best defined as misconduct by police officers in the forms of illegal activities for economic gain and accepting gratuities, favors, or payment for services that police are sworn to carry out as part of their peacekeeping role. It occurs in many forms, and observers and researchers of police behavior tend to agree that it is most manifest in nine specific areas: [2]

1. Meals and services
2. Kickbacks
3. Opportunistic theft
4. Planned theft and robbery
5. Shakedowns
6. Protection
7. Case fixing
8. Private security
9. Patronage

Meals and Services

Free or discount meals are available to police officers in almost every American city. A number of restaurant chains have a policy of providing meals to officers on a regular basis. Numerous diners, coffee shops, and other small restaurants have a similar policy, but in these the policy is maintained for the sake of **"police presence"** in the establishment. Many owners of diners and restaurants feel that if they can attract officers, it will extend a measure of security to their places of business. However, in some places the providing of meals, goods, and services at reduced rates or even at no cost is forced through implicit or direct coercion. In such instances, shopkeepers are reluctant to do-

Police corruption: Misconduct by police officers in the forms of illegal activities for economic gain and accepting gratuities, favors, or payment for services that police are sworn to carry out as part of their peacekeeping role.

"Police presence": The almost continuous presence of police officers in a place of business for the crime-deterrent effects it affords.

nate food or "gifts" of any sort to officers, yet they understand that it is expected of them. They comply out of fear—fear that the patrolman will "look the other way" when trouble occurs, and fear that the local precinct will search harder for violations of some kind on the business premises.

Kickbacks

Police officers have numerous opportunities to direct individuals in stressful situations to persons who—for a profit—can assist them. And police can receive a fee for referring arrested suspects to bail bonds agents and defense attorneys, for placing accident victims in contact with physicians and lawyers who specialize in filing personal injury claims, for sending tow trucks and ambulances to accident scenes, and for arranging for the delivery of bodies to specific funeral homes. Given the very nature of routine police patrol work, opportunities such as these are not uncommon, and the potential for small kickbacks on a regular basis is always present.

Opportunistic Theft

Police are presented with numerous opportunities as well to unlawfully appropriate various items of value. Such "opportunistic theft" typically involves jewelry and other goods taken from the scene of a burglary or from a suspect; narcotics confiscated from drug users and dealers; merchandise found at the scene of a fire; funds taken during a gambling raid; money and personal property removed from the bodies of drunks, crime victims, and deceased persons; and confiscated weapons.

Planned Theft and Robbery

Planned theft and robbery as a variety of police corruption refers to the direct involvement of police in predatory criminal activities. During the last two decades, either through complicity with criminals or as undertaken directly by police, it has occurred in Denver, Des Moines, Chicago, Nashville, New York, Philadelphia, Buffalo, Birmingham, Cleveland, New Orleans, Miami, and numerous other cities. Characteristically, however, planned theft and robbery by police officers, unlike some other forms of corruption, is rarely tolerated by police departments. Although there might be passive support for such activity, as soon as knowledge of this type of enterprise becomes known to the public, even corrupt departments generally react in a forceful manner.

Shakedowns

Shakedowns are forms of extortion in which police officers accept money from citizens in lieu of enforcing the law. Police have been known to shake down tavern owners by threatening to enforce obscure liquor laws, and restaurant owners and shopkeepers by threatening to enforce health regulations and zoning violations. Perhaps most common are shakedowns involving traffic violations and drug dealing (see Exhibit 7.1).

Protection

The protection of illegal activities by police has been known in this country for well over a century. Such protection usually involves illegal goods and services such as prostitution, gambling, illegal drugs, and child pornography.

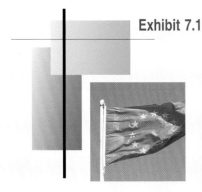

Exhibit 7.1   **International Perspectives on Crime and Justice**
Cocaine Trafficking and Police Corruption in
Latin America

Drug abuse is generally understood in terms of a limited number
of issues. First, it is a public health
problem. Illicit drugs, whether narcotics, stimulants, depressants, or
hallucinogens, have been found to
cause a range of physical and
psychosocial complications. Drug
abuse can place at risk the productivity of a potentially large segment of the population. Second,
there is the link between drug
abuse and the crime rate. The
connection between drug use and
street crime has been well documented, for the drug-taking and
drug-seeking activities of narcotics
addicts and other types of drug
users indeed affect the rates of
homicides, burglaries, larcenies,
and robberies. Further, the drug
trafficking and distribution market-
place has increased the profits
and power of criminal syndicates,
and violent crime has come to be
closely associated with the com-
petition that seems to exist at all
levels of the drug distribution
network.

Yet drug use and trafficking
have a larger effect on the social,
economic, and political organization and functioning of a nation or
community. In many parts of Latin
America, for example, cocaine
trafficking has exacerbated the effects of inflation, altered economic
planning, affected property values
and inflated wages, and shifted
government power toward wealthy
drug dealers. In *all* nations where
drug use and trafficking are commonplace, the corruption of individuals is widespread, particularly
of those charged with enforcement
of the drug laws.

*Peruvian police officers were publicly dismissed from the force after being
charged with kidnapping a Japanese business executive.*

For as long as drug enforcement has been a part of policing,
there has been drug-related corruption. Some police officers have
accepted bribes in lieu of enforcing the drug laws; others have directly participated in the actual
trafficking of illegal substances.
Yet the problem was rarely widespread and never endemic to
any given nation or police force.
All of this seemed to change,
however, with the arrival of the
cocaine era.

The high price of cocaine and
the billions of dollars accumulated
by cocaine traffickers have
brought about the wholesale corruption of law enforcement, particularly in Latin America. Human
rights groups suggest that police
abuses in Latin America and police corruption in particular are direct outgrowths of low wages. For
example:

• In Peru, a police officer with 5
years of service earns roughly
US$230 a month, well below

the $400 the government says
is necessary to cover the basic
needs of a family of four.
• In Chile, rookie police officers
earn the equivalent of $180
per month, in a country
where the average monthly
per capita income is $500. Af-
ter 10 years of service, they
earn $375.
• Police officers in Brazil earn a
monthly average of "two minimum wages," the equivalent, in
1999, of $220. This is especially
low when one considers that
prices in Brazil are higher than
those in the United States.

Observers suggest that the
problems of police corruption in
Latin America are likely to continue because of (1) the bribery
and corruption that exist in other
parts of their judicial systems,
(2) the dramatically unequal distribution of money and property in
most social sectors, and (3) the
highly pessimistic long-term economic forecasts.

SOURCES: James A. Inciardi, *The War on Drugs II: The Continuing Epic of Heroin, Cocaine, Crack, Crime, AIDS, and Public Policy* (Mountain View,
Calif.: Mayfield, 1992); *Latinamerica Press*, August 20, 1998, p. 2; *New York Times*, August 6, 1998, p. A4.

Case Fixing

As a form of corruption, case fixing has appeared at all levels of the criminal justice process and has involved not only police, but also bailiffs, court personnel, members of juries, prosecutors, and judges. Fixing a case with a police officer, however, is the most direct method, and often the least complicated and least expensive. The most common form involves a bribe to an officer in exchange for not being arrested—a practice most typically initiated by pickpockets, prostitutes, gamblers, drug users, the parents of juvenile offenders, members of organized crime, and sometimes burglars. Case fixing can also take the form of an officer perjuring himself or herself on the witness stand, reducing the seriousness of a charge against an offender, or agreeing to drop an investigation prematurely by not pursuing leads that might produce evidence supporting a criminal charge.

Traffic-ticket fixing is likely the most common form of case fixing, and often it does not involve any monetary payment. In some jurisdictions, simply "knowing" someone on the police force is all that is needed to have a summons discharged, and in other instances a call to a police chief can be effective.

Private Security

Corruption in the form of private security involves providing more police protection or presence than is required by standard operating procedures. Examples might include checking the security of private premises more frequently and intensively than is usual, escorting businesspeople to make bank deposits, or providing more visible police presence in stores or establishments in order to keep out undesirables. In such instances, payoffs are less likely to be made in cash but more typically in goods, services, and favors. This should not suggest, however, that all policing in the private sector by public police is corrupt. On the contrary, "extra-duty policing," as it has come to be known, is common in many parts of the nation.

Patronage

Patronage can occur in a variety of ways, all of which involve the use of one's official position to influence decision-making. Within the ranks of policing, corruption by patronage can occur through the granting of promotions and transfers for a fee. Arranging access to confidential department records or agreeing to alter such records may also be construed as patronage. In addition, influencing department recommendations regarding the granting of licenses is patronage.

Patronage can emerge in other ways as well. Within a police department itself, for example, inside people have been paid to falsify attendance records, influence the choice of vacations and days off, report officers as being on duty when they are not, and provide passing grades in training programs and promotion exams.

Many of the areas of police corruption just mentioned were uncovered in a single police department during a 4-year federal investigation and trial that concluded during 1999 in Camden, New Jersey.[3] The case—which erupted in early 1997 with the arrest of 9 officers and 10 residents of West New York, New Jersey, a small town across the Hudson River from Manhattan's Upper West Side—turned out to be the largest police corruption scandal in the history of New Jersey. According to prosecutors and testimony, the West New York Police Department had been on a major crime

INTERNATIONAL CORRUPTION

Corruption of some kind likely exists in every country in the world, and much of it involves police corruption. In a recent study by Transparency International, countries were ranked according to their levels of corruption. The "corruption index" is a scale from 10 (the least corrupt) to zero (the most corrupt). As indicated below, Denmark was considered the least corrupt, and Cameroon the most corrupt. The United States was about in the middle.

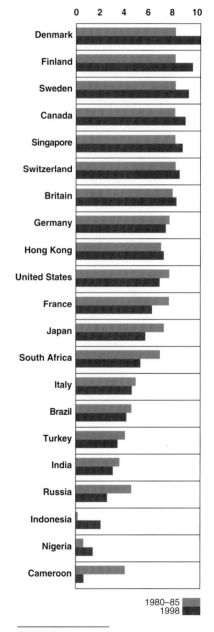

1980–85
1998

SOURCE: Transparency International.

spree for almost a decade. The police raided illegal gambling dens, stole the proceeds, and then extorted money from the operators. When community residents complained about a house of prostitution in the neighborhood, the police raided the brothel, and then took bribes and allowed it to stay in business. In addition, officers were involved in loan-sharking, the selling of official accident forms, and even stealing from suspects and corpses. Overall, federal prosecutors described the West New York Police Department as a "bustling organized crime enterprise" that had collected and shared as much as $1.5 million.

EXPLANATIONS OF POLICE CORRUPTION

A number of hypotheses as to why police corruption occurs have been offered. The three most common interpretations are that police corruption is caused by society at large, by influences within police departments, or by a disposition towards corruption in individuals who become police officers.[4]

The Society-at-Large Explanation

The society-at-large explanation comes from the late O. W. Wilson, based on his observations and experiences as Chicago's superintendent of police. As Wilson put it:

> This force was corrupted by citizens of Chicago. . . . It has been customary to give doormen, chauffeurs, maids, cooks and delivery men little gifts and gratuities. . . . It is felt that the level of service depends on these gratuities.[5]

The slippery slope hypothesis

Such practices, in turn, lead to small bribes, such as accepting money in lieu of enforcing traffic laws or minor city ordinances. Accepting small payoffs from drivers and business operators then extended to more serious crimes. Wilson called this progression the *slippery slope hypothesis*: that corruption begins with apparently harmless and well-intentioned practices and leads, eventually—in individual police officers or in departments as a whole—to all manner of crimes for profit.

The Structural Explanation

In his well-known *Behind the Shield*, the late Arthur Niederhoffer made the following comment:

> Actual policemen seem to accept graft for other reasons than avarice. Often the first transgression is inadvertent. Or, they may be gradually indoctrinated by older policemen. Step by step they progress from a small peccadillo [trifling sin] to outright shakedown and felony.[6]

Going further, this step-by-step progress results from the contradictory sets of norms that police officers see both in the world at large and in their own departments. Officers, particularly those in large cities, are exposed to a steady diet of wrongdoing. They discover, furthermore, that dishonesty and corruption are not limited to those the community views as "criminals," but also include individuals of "good reputation"—including fellow officers with whom they must establish some mutual trust and reliance. In time, they develop a cynical attitude in which they view corruption as a game in which every person is out to get a share.[7]

The Rotten-Apple Explanation

The "bad" or rotten-apple view is perhaps the most popular explanation of police corruption. It suggests that in an otherwise honest department, there are a few bad officers who are operating on their own. Corruption is the result of the moral failure of just a few officers, but it spreads, for, as the proverb suggests, "one rotten apple spoils the rest of the barrel."

In retrospect, there is likely no single explanation that accounts for all police corruption. The three discussed here are the principal views, and they likely work in conjunction with one another. The rotten-apple explanation, although the most popular, is also the most criticized, for it fails to explain *why* individual officers become corrupt.

POLICE VIOLENCE

Police violence in the form of brutality, unwarranted deadly force, and other mistreatment of citizens is not uncommon in American history. Commentaries documenting the growth and development of both the urban metropolis and the rural frontier testify amply to the unwarranted use of force throughout the ranks of policing. Law enforcement records in the trans-Mississippi West provide numerous examples of the "shoot first and ask questions later" philosophy of many American lawmen. Moreover, the brutal and sadistic application of the policeman's nightstick to demonstrate that "might makes right" appears often in the histories of urban police systems (see Exhibit 7.2).

It was not until the 1960s that the issue of police misconduct in the forms of brutality and deadly force assumed any public and political urgency, and this can be attributed to two phenomena. The first was the "criminal law revolution" carried on by the Supreme Court under the leadership of Chief Justice Earl Warren. The second was the findings of the Kerner Commission—the National Advisory Commission on Civil Disorders.

Brown v. *Mississippi* in 1936 established the Court's position on brutality, at least as far as coerced confessions were concerned.[8] It was the first time

Brown v. Mississippi

Exhibit 7.2

Historical Perspectives on Crime and Justice
"Clubber" Williams

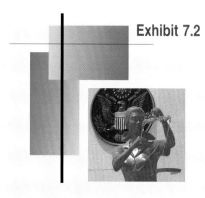

The problems of brutality, as well as those of police crime and corruption, are likely as old as policing itself. And a retrospective glance suggests that brutality and corruption were apparent from the first days of organized policing in the United States.

Among the more publicized figures in nineteenth-century police history was Alexander S. Williams, a Canadian immigrant whose career with the New York City police spanned almost three decades. Born in Nova Scotia in 1839, Williams moved to New York at midcentury in search of work as a ship's carpenter and quickly established himself in the world of shipbuilding. During the Civil War, Williams became the first Westerner to construct a ship in Japan, undertook salvage work for the U.S. government, and ultimately became a partner in a growing shipbuilding firm. Labor problems in that industry, however, quickly put an end to his business aspirations, and as an alternative he joined the New York City police force in 1866.

After only 2 years as a police officer, Williams made the first of a series of moves that would ultimately make him well known among his fellow officers, within the underworld, and to the citizens of New York. In 1868, he was assigned to the Broadway Squad in lower Manhattan, where

many police officers before him had been either seriously assaulted or murdered by the numerous gang members, street brawlers, and other violent criminals who ranged through the area. On his second day at the new post, Officer Williams positioned himself in front of the Florence Saloon—a notorious retreat at the intersection of Broadway and Houston Street that was frequented by local thieves, muggers, and other types of criminals. There he selected two of the neighborhood's toughest characters, picked fights with them, knocked them unconscious with his nightstick, and hurled their bodies through the plate glass window of their hangout. According to local folklore, 10 of their comrades came to the rescue, but Williams, a large and powerful man, stood his ground and mowed them down one after another with his hardwood club. Thereafter, he averaged a fight a day for almost 4 years. His skill with the nightstick was said to be so extraordinary and the force of his blows so powerful that he was hailed as "Clubber" Williams—a title he retained throughout his life.

Following his assignment to the Broadway Squad, Williams's career moved quickly. In July 1871 he was promoted to the rank of sergeant. Only 2 months later he became a captain, and from there he moved on to become a police inspector. His fame grew so rapidly in the city that he once commented, "I am so well known here in New York that car horses nod to me every morning." He was the star feature of police parades and received constant attention from

---

The Kerner Commission investigated the causes of urban violence that took place in the summer of 1967.

a state conviction was overturned because it had been obtained by using a confession extracted by torture.

Whereas the Supreme Court examined police violence within the context of the brutality of squad room interrogations, the Kerner Commission targeted the wider issue of street justice in all of its varied and callous forms. Known

New York City Police Commissioner Theodore Roosevelt, after his firing of "Clubber" Williams.

the daily press. He even refereed a major prizefight—in full uniform—at Madison Square Garden.

But there was another side to Alexander Williams, for he also epitomized the kinds of brutality and corruption that were characteristic of several big-city police departments during the latter part of the nineteenth century. His use of the nightstick was not limited to warding off thugs and street brawlers, but was applied to strikers and sleeping drunks as well. And Williams was also known for

clubbing spectators at parades as a means of crowd control. His technique with the nightstick reflected both sadism and brutality. Williams often spoke of how his stick could be used for knocking a man unconscious, for killing him, or for just battering him to pieces. In terms of "art for art's sake," he discussed on many occasions how a tap with the stick on the head, hands, or feet could send a current through the spine to make a prisoner stand up or lie down.

As for graft and corruption within the ranks of policing,

Williams was an entrepreneur. It was "Clubber" Williams who reportedly coined the slang term *tenderloin* as the designation for areas of vice and nightlife. When he was transferred from the not-too-lucrative downtown Broadway precinct to the area bounded by Manhattan's 14th to 42nd Streets and Fifth and Seventh Avenues, Williams was quite pleased. His new sector was so wide open as a vice resort that New Yorkers called it "Satan's Circus." But Williams give it the new nickname: As he took over his post, he commented, "I've had nothing but chuck steaks for a long time, and now I'm going to get me a little of the tenderloin."

Williams, of course, was speaking of opportunities for graft—and bountiful it was for him, for by imposing tribute on every kind of illegal activity he quickly became a wealthy man. Houses of prostitution paid him initiation fees plus monthly charges for protection; saloons paid to stay open after hours; gambling halls paid monthly contributions; and pickpockets, burglars, and other thieves paid him a percentage of the stealings.

"Clubber" Williams's exploits in police corruption and brutality came to an end during a reform movement in New York City. In 1895, he was called before a committee investigating government corruption to explain his great wealth, which included a yacht and a mansion in Connecticut. Although Williams was not indicted by the committee, the newly appointed police commissioner, Theodore Roosevelt, immediately fired Williams and put an end to his exploits.

SOURCES: A. E. Costello, *Our Police Protectors* (New York: Author's Edition, 1885); Herbert Asbury, *The Gangs of New York* (Garden City, N.Y.: Garden City, 1928); James F. Richardson, *The New York Police: Colonial Times to 1901* (New York: Oxford University Press, 1970); *Report of the Special Committee Appointed to Investigate the Police Department of the City of New York* (Albany: State of New York, Senate Documents, 1895).

more formally as the National Advisory Commission on Civil Disorders, its purpose was to investigate the causes of the rioting and destruction that occurred in Detroit, Los Angeles, Newark, New York, and 20 other urban areas during the summer of 1967. The commission concluded that there were numerous causes but ranked as the primary stimuli police practices in patrolling urban ghettos. Aggressive preventive patrol, combined with police misconduct in the forms of brutality, unwarranted use of deadly force, harassment, verbal abuse, and discourtesy were sources of aggravation among African Americans, and complaints of such practices were found in all of the locations studied.[9]

Brutality

Police brutality: The unlawful use of physical force by officers in the performance of their duties.

In the past, **police brutality** was considered to be a practice limited only to those few sadistic officers who were seen as "bad apples." However, more recent commentaries suggest that police violence is the result of norms shared throughout a police department, and that it is best understood as an unfortunate consequence of the police role. Police are given the unrestricted right to use force in situations in which their evaluation of the circumstances demands it. Yet this mandate has never been precisely defined or limited. Moreover, some officers show characteristics of the police "working personality"—the feeling of constant pressure to perform, along with elements of authoritarianism, suspicion, racism, hostility, insecurity, and cynicism. Police norms that emphasize solidarity and secrecy allow a structure in which incidents of brutality and other misconduct will not draw the condemnation of fellow officers.

Going beyond the working personality as a contributing factor to unnecessary police violence, sociologist Richard J. Lundman focused on three additional issues related to violence that apply to most police organizations:

1. Police perceptions that citizen acceptance of police authority is fundamental to effective policing
2. Police judgments of the "social value" of certain citizens
3. The conservative nature of police decision-making[10]

Police Authority   Because authority is both central and essential to the police roles of enforcing the law and keeping the peace, persons who question or resist that authority represent a challenge to officers, detectives, and the organizations they represent. Challenges are not taken lightly; they are seen as barriers to effective policing. Often police use intense verbal coercion to establish their authority quickly. Should that fail, some use physical force to elicit compliance from citizens.

Judgments of Social Value   In the view of many police officers, certain citizens—drunks, juvenile gang members, gays, sex offenders, drug users, hardened criminals—have little to contribute to society. Many officers do not consider such people worth protecting, or they protect them using different norms from those that guide their policing of other citizens. Some police even single out these people for physical abuse.

Police Decision-Making   Since police work requires officers to make quick decisions, often on the basis of only fragmentary information, both officers and their superiors tend to defend the use of violence as a means of rapid problem resolution.

Deadly Force

In common law, police were authorized to use deadly force as a last resort to apprehend a fleeing felon. This common law rule dates back to the Middle Ages, when all felonies were punishable by death, and thus the killing of the felon resulted in no greater consequence than that authorized for the punishment of the offense. This "shoot to kill" doctrine based on common law principles persists in one form or another in many jurisdictions throughout the

United States, for there are few operational guidelines in the use of deadly force by police.

The decision to use deadly force for making an arrest largely remains a matter of discretion. All jurisdictions permit officers to use lethal force in defense of themselves, and most allow firing on a fleeing felon. Yet prior to ***Tennessee* v. *Garner*** in 1985,[11] the conditions under which such force could be applied to a fleeing felon were variable. Some jurisdictions required the suspect to be a "known" felon; others required that the officer be a witness to the felony; and still others permitted deadly force when the officer had a "reasonable belief" that the fleeing individual committed the felony in question. In *Garner*, the Supreme Court held that deadly force against a fleeing felon was proper *only* when it was necessary to prevent the escape *and* if there was probable cause to believe that the suspect posed a significant threat of death or serious physical injury to the officer or others.

When it comes to explaining the use of force, both lethal and nonlethal, James J. Fyfe points out that many discussions of the topic fail to distinguish between police violence that is clearly extralegal and abusive and violence that is the unnecessary result of police incompetence. He argues that such a distinction is important because the causes and motivations for the two vary greatly. Extralegal violence involves the willful and wrongful use of force by officers who knowingly exceed the bounds of their office. Unnecessary violence, by contrast, including deadly force, occurs when well-meaning officers prove incapable of dealing with the situations they encounter without a needless or too hasty resort to force.[12]

Although the number of people killed each year by "police intervention" is relatively small, there is a widespread perception that African Americans are singled out as victims. More importantly, however, a number of studies have demonstrated that minority group members are statistically overrepresented among the victims in police killings.[13] But an explanation of the phenomenon is less clear. Radical sociologist Paul Takagi states that "police have one trigger finger for whites and another for blacks," suggesting that police are engaged in a form of genocide against minority groups.[14] This, however, seems to be a naive oversimplification of a very complex issue, for many factors are operating simultaneously. Another explanation is that communities get the number of killings by police that they deserve. Researchers Richard Kania and Wade Mackey found that police killings are statistically associated with violent crimes in a community, and they argue that "the police officer is

Tennessee v. Garner: The Supreme Court decision stating that deadly force against a fleeing felon is proper only when it is necessary to prevent the escape *and* when there is probable cause to believe that the suspect poses a significant threat to the officers or others.

Justifiable Homicides by Law Enforcement Officers

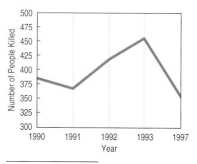

SOURCE: Uniform Crime Reports, 1997.

Racism Among Police

Have you personally ever felt treated unfairly by the police specifically because you are white/black?

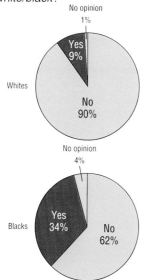

How widespread is racism against blacks among police officers?

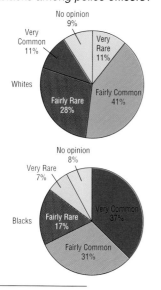

SOURCE: The Gallup Organization.

reacting to the community as he perceives it."[15] A third view is the "bad apple" theory, which puts the blame on a few uncontrollable police officers.[16]

In all likelihood, however, the reasons for the disproportionate number of minority group members killed by police involve all of these explanations. In addition, the most recent analysis of the police use of deadly force suggests that its frequency is heavily influenced by individual departmental policies on the use of force, combined with the fact that African Americans and other minorities tend to be overrepresented in the most violent and criminogenic neighborhoods.[17] (For an overview of recent research on racial/ethnic differences and people's satisfaction with police, see Exhibit 7.3.)

CONTROLLING POLICE MISCONDUCT

Without question, policing is rich in opportunities for corruption, brutality, the abuse of discretionary powers, the violation of citizens' rights, and other forms of misconduct. Furthermore, "policing the police" is difficult, for a variety of reasons. Corruption generally occurs in the most covert of circumstances and involves a willingness and cooperation on the part of many citizens. In addition, the victims of the misconduct are often reluctant, prevented, or otherwise indisposed to making the misconduct fully public. Further, police operations are in many ways invisible to disciplinary mechanisms, since officers operate alone or in small teams—beyond the observation of departmental supervisors. Finally, the "legitimatization" at the administrative levels of the internal policing of certain abusive practices, combined with the elements of secrecy and solidarity that are characteristic of all police organizations, inhibit many police agencies from making instances of misconduct a matter of public record.

This is not to say, however, that police abuses cannot be brought under greater control. There are many mechanisms that can affect police behavior for the better, including the legislature, the community, and the police system itself.

Legislative Control

State and local legislative bodies can have a specific impact on the conduct of law enforcement through a reevaluation of certain laws that create the potential for police violations and corruption. Throughout the history of the United States, criminal justice has been faced with the problem of overcriminalization due to the legislation of morality and the overregulation of civilian conduct. The laws that impose restrictions on alcohol consumption, drug use, prostitution, gambling, and other "victimless" crimes, combined with the numerous public health and other regulations over certain business enterprises, are typically the areas in which police corruption occurs. Thus, if legislatures are to control police conduct, one could argue that they might begin by decriminalizing these victimless crimes. That anything will be done in this area seems unlikely, however. The continued existence of many of the victimless crimes that generate the potential for corruption is the result of legislative unwillingness to repeal them for fear of committing political suicide. Nevertheless, a few changes have occurred. Gambling laws have been relaxed through the establishment of state-run lotteries and off-track betting; prostitution has been legalized in one jurisdiction and reduced to a minor violation in others; and a number of unreasonable restrictions placed on business owners, landlords, and the building construction industry have been eliminated. However, a major portion of police corruption is an outgrowth of the laws controlling

Exhibit 7.3   **Research in Crime and Justice**
Satisfaction With Local Police in
12 American Cities

Although police have received considerable negative attention in the media, this is generally an outgrowth of highly visible incidents of brutality and the misuse of deadly force, as well as the allegations of racially biased practices by individual officers and particular police departments. On the whole, however, it would appear that the majority of police officers *do not* conduct themselves in a corrupt, brutal, or biased fashion. Evidence for this can be found in a recent report from the Bureau of Justice Assistance that examined criminal victimization

and perceptions of community safety in 12 U.S. cities. The study was based on extensive interviews with a random selection of residents in Chicago, Kansas City (Missouri), Knoxville, Los Angeles, Madison, New York, San Diego, Savannah, Spokane, Springfield (Massachusetts), Tucson, and Washington, D.C.

A wide range of issues were examined in the survey, but most relevant to the material in this chapter were the findings on citizens' satisfaction with local police. As illustrated in the accompanying table, 90 percent of whites were satisfied with police, as compared with 76 percent of blacks and 78 percent of other groups (Asians, Native Americans, Pacific Islanders, Aluets, and Eskimos). Interestingly, levels of satisfaction varied significantly by city—from a high of 97 percent in Madison to a

low of 78 percent in Washington, D.C. The proportion of black residents who said they were satisfied with the police ranged from 97 percent in Madison to only 63 percent in Knoxville. In New York City, where police have been frequently accused of targeting minorities, 77 percent of blacks were satisfied with their local police.

Overall, the data document a high degree of support for America's neighborhood police officers, a factor that helps to promote community safety. However, the study also indicates that not everyone is happy with police performance—particularly blacks and members of other minority groups—suggesting the need for more minority officers and supervisory staff, and programs to sensitize police departments to concerns about policing in minority communities.

Percent Satisfied With Police

	Estimated Number of Residents Age 16 or Older	White	Black	Other	Total
Total	11,913,071	90%	76%	78%	85%
Chicago	1,901,575	89	69	67	80
Kansas City	330,761	90	86	84	89
Knoxville	116,356	91	63	100	89
Los Angeles	2,557,680	89	82	80	86
Madison	147,236	97	97	98	97
New York	4,973,711	89	77	77	84
San Diego	848,531	95	89	87	93
Savannah	93,110	88	81	92	86
Spokane	133,288	88	79	73	87
Springfield	102,609	90	76	82	87
Tucson	336,711	88	91	76	87
Washington, D.C.	371,503	81	75	83	78

SOURCE: Steven K. Smith, Greg W. Steadman, Todd D. Minton, and Meg Townsend, *Criminal Victimization and Perceptions of Community Safety in 12 Cities* (Washington, D.C.: Bureau of Justice Statistics, May 1999).

At the close of 1998, a survey of police shootings in the nation's largest cities was conducted by the *Washington Post*. It was found that Washington, D.C., ranked the highest, with a rate of 1.7 police shootings per 100,000 population. At the bottom was Indianapolis, with a rate of only 0.13 per 100,000.

Rank	City	Yearly Fatal Shootings by Police, 1990–1997	Rate per 100,000
1	Washington	10	1.70
2	Baltimore	8	1.10
3	Detroit	10	1.00
4	New Orleans	4	.82
5	Phoenix	8	.76
6	Jacksonville	4	.61
7	San Diego	7	.61
8	Nashville	3	.60
9	Cleveland	3	.60
10	Houston	10	.59
11	Los Angeles	20	.57
12	Milwaukee	3	.49
13	Memphis	3	.49
14	Philadelphia	7	.46
15	Chicago	12	.44
16	San Francisco	3	.41
17	New York	29	.39
18	Columbus	2	.31
19	San Antonio	3	.30
20	Dallas	3	.29
21	San Jose	2	.25
22	Austin	1	.20
23	Seattle	1	.19
24	Boston	1	.18
25	El Paso	1	.18
26	Indianapolis	1	.13

SOURCE: *Washington Post*, November 15, 1998, pp. A1, A25–A27.

Civilian review boards: Citizen-controlled boards empowered to review and handle complaints against police officers.

the possession of cocaine, crack, heroin, and numerous other drugs, and it is unlikely these will be legalized in any great hurry, if ever.

By contrast, Section 1983 of the Civil Rights Act of 1871 authorizes suits for damages for violations of one's constitutional rights. By invoking Section 1983, an individual can hold a law enforcement agency or municipality liable for an incident of police misconduct.

Civilian Review Boards

The influence of citizens on police behavior is most evident in small communities. There is closer contact between the police and members of the community, officers are typically longtime residents of the locations they patrol, police officials are often dependent on public support for their departmental finances and tenure, and police behavior in general has a higher grassroots visibility. Further, the opportunities for police abuse are less widespread in small cities, towns, and rural areas. The reverse seems to be true in large urban centers, where community control over policing is almost totally absent. There have been a number of suggestions made over the years concerning how to counter this problem, including "putting the cop back on the beat," sensitivity training for police recruits, and the establishment of civilian review boards to enforce police discipline.

Prior to 1958, all the power to discipline law enforcement personnel was in the hands of police departments, generally in the form of some internal review committee composed of one or more police officials. But during the late 1950s and early 1960s, concern about this system surfaced when the U.S. Commission on Civil Rights found that many African Americans felt powerless to do anything about police malpractice.

Led by the American Civil Liberties Union (ACLU), the National Association for the Advancement of Colored People (NAACP), and other citizen groups, public opinion urged police authorities to shift the responsibility for handling complaints to citizen-controlled outside review boards. The boards envisioned were to serve several purposes:

1. They would restrain those officers who engaged in brutality, harassment, and other abusive and even illegal practices.
2. By ensuring a thorough and impartial investigation of all complaints, they would protect other officers against malicious, misguided, and otherwise unfounded accusations.
3. They would provide blacks and other minority group members an avenue of redress, which would help restore their dwindling confidence in the police departments.
4. They would explain police procedures to citizens, review enforcement requirements with police, and initiate a genuine dialogue in place of mutual recrimination.[18]

Proposals for **civilian review boards** incensed most police officers and were bitterly fought by such organizations as the International Association of Chiefs of Police (IACP), the International Conference of Police Associations (ICPA), and the Fraternal Order of Police (FOP). Despite opposition, however, a few cities did establish and maintain civilian review boards.

Police Control

Control of police misconduct directly from within police departments is generally of two types: preventive and punitive.

Preventive control manifests itself in several areas, all of which involve numerous alterations in the structure and philosophy of a police department. First, the policy of *internal accountability* holds members of a law enforcement agency responsible for their own actions as well as for those of others. It is based on a clear communication of standards to which officers and officials will be held accountable and on an articulation of "who will be responsible for whom." Second, internal accountability becomes workable only under tight supervision of police officers by administrators, precinct commanders, and other control staff. Tight supervision involves direct surveillance of officers' work time and work products by field commanders, combined with daily logs documenting officer activity. Third, preventive control can affect areas of police misconduct through an abolition of corrupting procedures. Every large police department and many smaller ones have numerous formal procedures that inadvertently encourage corruption. For example, some policies imply levels of productivity that are all but impossible to achieve by legitimate means; others create pressures for financial contributions by officers that those officers attempt to "earn back" in corrupt ways. Vice investigators and detectives, for instance, often must "purchase" leads from informers, but funds for such purposes may be limited or unavailable. Similarly, criminal investigation work may require the use of personal autos with no provisions for expense reimbursement.

Punitive control falls into that area of policing known as internal affairs or internal policing—the purview of the so-called headhunters and shoo-fly cops who investigate complaints against police personnel or other actions involving police misconduct. Internal policing may be the responsibility of a single officer or detective, a small police unit, or an entire division or bureau, depending on the size of a department and its commitment to in-house review. Regardless of size, however, the responsibilities of internal affairs units generally include inquiries into the following:

1. Allegations or complaints of misconduct made by a citizen, police officer, or any other person against the department or any of its members
2. Allegations or suspicions of corruption, breaches of integrity, or cases of moral turpitude from whatever source—whether reported to or developed by internal policing
3. Situations in which officers are killed or wounded by the deliberate or willful acts of other parties
4. Situations in which citizens have been killed or injured by police officers either on or off duty
5. Situations involving the discharging of weapons by officers[19]

Internal policing began during the latter part of the nineteenth century, when headquarters roundsmen made inspections on a citywide basis and investigated corruption. It was not until the mid-1900s, however, that structured bureaus for internal policing came into being.[20] In the wake of a major scandal during the late 1940s, Los Angeles police chief William A. Worton formed the Bureau of Internal Affairs. Within a decade, Boston, Chicago, and Atlanta followed suit, and at the beginning of the 1960s New York City joined the trend when the police commissioner established the Inspection Service Bureau, which brought together several units that had been separately monitoring the integrity and efficiency of the police.

The special internal control units and bureaus, although permanent fixtures in big-city policing, are not without their problems. Police rank and file have always despised the activities of the headhunters and shoo-fly cops. Furthermore, internal affairs officers have sometimes been corrupt themselves, and others have been unwilling to tarnish the reputation of their departments by exposing corruption and incompetence. Finally, citizens have apparently been unwilling to file complaints and officers have been unwilling to testify against one another (see Exhibit 7.4). The product of such difficulties is an acutely low level of efficiency.

TREND IN VIEWS OF POLICE ETHICS

Those rating the honesty and ethical standards of the police as "very high" or "high."

1985	**1990**	**1994**	**1997**
47%	49%	46%	49%

SOURCES: *BJS Sourcebook*; The Gallup Organization.

Exhibit 7.4 **Legal Perspectives on Crime and Justice**
Human Rights Abuses and the "Blue Wall of Silence"

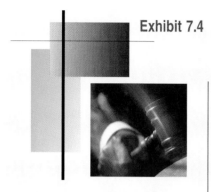

Prosecutors investigating allegations of police misconduct are aware that a "code of silence," "blue curtain," or "blue wall of silence" exists in the majority of police departments in the United States. This code of silence holds that a police officer must not provide adverse information against fellow officers, no matter what they have been accused of. Repercussions for breaking the code include ostracism, threats, and the fear that officers will not "back up" or protect those who break the code. One N.Y.P.D. officer, for example, on trial for both corruption and brutality, testified that he never feared that another officer would turn him in, for this reason:

> Cops don't tell on cops. If a cop decided to tell on me, his career is ruined. He's going to be labeled as a rat.

Another officer added:

> You first learn of the code in the Police Academy, with instructors telling you to never be a "rat." See, we're all blue. We have to protect each other no matter what.

In New York City, where the "blue wall of silence" has been especially pervasive, the assault on Haitian immigrant Abner Louima recently proved to test the limits of the code. Louima was arrested in Brooklyn on August 9, 1997, on a charge of disorderly conduct. He claimed that he was then taken to a bathroom at the 70th Precinct, sodomized with "something" (either a toilet plunger or broken-off

broomstick) by officer Justin Volpe, and warned by Volpe that "if you tell anyone about this, I'll find you and kill you." Some time later Louima was taken to a local hospital for surgery—his bladder and small intestine had been punctured.

The Louima case served as a powerful example of how police react to misconduct in their ranks. But in this instance the event was so sadistic that it tested, and ultimately broke, the "blue wall of silence." N.Y.P.D. officers testified that after the assault Volpe pranced around the precinct house with a blood-and-feces-stained stick, inviting other officers to examine it, and boasted that "I took a man down tonight." In the face of the evidence against him, Officer Volpe eventually pleaded guilty in federal court to charges of torturing Louima. (Charles Schwarz, the officer who held down the victim, was convicted of violating Louima's civil rights.)

But did the Louima/Volpe case *really* break the code of silence? Most observers say no, because Volpe himself refused to name the other officers who took part in the assault, and those who testified against Volpe took weeks to come forward, and then most likely because of the pressure of a highly publicized investigation.

Although the case against Justin Volpe was the most visible and sadistic in recent years, this should not suggest that the "blue wall" is limited to the N.Y.P.D., or that the code is something restricted just to patrol officers. During the latter half of the 1990s, Human Rights Watch conducted a lengthy and intensive investigation of police abuse in 14 U.S. cities—Atlanta, Boston, Chicago, Detroit, Indianapolis, Los Angeles, Minneapolis, New Orleans, New York, Philadelphia, Portland, Providence,

New York City residents demonstrating outside the court during Justin Volpe's trial.

San Francisco, and Washington, D.C. The Human Rights Watch report concluded:

> In all the cities we examined, and particularly in those like Philadelphia and New Orleans where police abuse and corruption have been visibly rampant, the code of silence is not limited to street officers who witness abuses and fail to report them, or who lie when asked about reported incidents. In these cases, responsibility for the "blue wall of silence" extends to supervisors and ultimately police commissioners and chiefs. Furthermore, local district attorneys, when they prosecute criminal suspects based on officers' patently fabricated justifications for searches or suspects' injuries, and who continue to cooperate with officers who commit human rights abuses rather than attempt to prosecute them on criminal charges, join in complicity.

SOURCES: Human Rights Watch, *Shielded From Justice: Police Brutality and Accountability in the United States* (Washington, D.C.: Human Rights Watch, 1998); *Newsweek*, June 7, 1999, p. 42; "Volpe Admits Louima Attack," *New York Daily News Online*, May 26, 1999.

Shifting back to the killing of Amadou Diallo, what really happened? Was it a case of police brutality, a racially motivated police execution, or just a tragic accident precipitated by a group of overzealous, trigger-happy officers?

In the months that followed the Diallo killing, the majority of New Yorkers felt that the shooting was neither racial nor intentional. Most observers agreed, however, that blacks are far more likely than whites to suffer at the hands of the police. Although the four officers were indicted for second-degree murder, even antipolice activists conceded that it had not been a deliberate killing. What actually happened may never be fully understood, but in all likelihood, the officers said something to Diallo, he moved in a manner that they interpreted as threatening, someone shouted "gun," the officers started firing, and they may have mistaken their own ricocheting bullets as return fire. Forty-one shots were fired in all, and 19 hit Diallo. It may have been hysteria, similar to the kind seen in wartime—nervous soldiers are tramping through the jungle, a sound is heard, something moves, and everyone shoots.

What were the underlying causes of the incident? One contributing factor may have been New York City's zero-tolerance crime policy, which holds that no crime—not the breaking of a window, not the theft of a pack of cigarettes, not the jumping of a subway turnstile, nothing—is too insignificant to capture the swift, decisive attention of the police. "Prosecute more petty offenders today," goes the reasoning, "and you will have fewer hard-core criminals tomorrow."

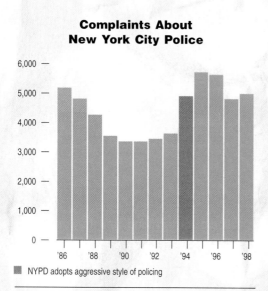

Complaints About New York City Police

NYPD adopts aggressive style of policing

SOURCE: Civilian Complaint Review Board.

Citizens love the zero-tolerance policy, because it brings down the crime rates. And New York has, indeed, become one of the safest cities in the United States. But one of the problems in implementing this policy is that it can trample on individual rights. For instance, during 1997 and 1998, officers in the Street Crime Unit frisked more than 45,000 people thought to be carrying guns—but arrested just under 10,000. Thus, although one result was that a lot of guns were taken off the street, another result was that tens of thousands of citizens were mistakenly detained.

A second problem is the manner in which zero-tolerance is applied. Black leaders and civil libertarians point out that when police put emphasis on aggressive prevention strategies, they must rely on intuition and hunches. In doing so, officers invariably lean on broad profiles in stopping and interrogating possible criminals. Those profiles are often based on prejudices, and the people most likely to be stopped are members of minority groups.

A third problem is police training, not only in the areas of police-community relations, the Constitution, and "search and seizure" issues, but also with firearms. Although the N.Y.P.D. has one of the lowest rates of police shootings in the United States, the shooting of Amadou Diallo suggests that it is still too high.

In the final analysis, there is no conflict between good crime control and respect for people's rights, but maintaining order under the rule of law is difficult to apply in practice.

Race/Ethnic Diversity in Four Big-City Police Departments, 1998–1999

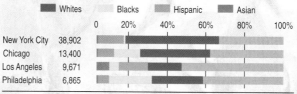

SOURCE: The Police Foundation.

Nevertheless, not all aspects of internal policing have been unsuccessful. Even in the more disorganized and inefficient of departments, a certain level of misconduct has been detected and ferreted out. Without any internal control mechanisms, police organization would probably become chaotic.

Attempts to reduce police misconduct should not be limited to efforts by the legislature, review boards, and internal policing. These treat only the symptoms of the problem. More work in the area of police professionalization also seems warranted. However, this too is an area that is problematic, for there are differing conceptions of professionalism in law enforcement. Police understand professionalism to mean more tightly defined rules and regulations, increased central control, strict discipline, and obedience. In every other organization, professionalism means that a large measure of discretion is left to

VIEWS OF POLICE BRUTALITY

In some places in the nation, there have been charges of police brutality. Do you think there is any police brutality in your area?

	Yes	No
Total	35%	60%
Whites	33	62
Blacks	45	46
Other	43	56
Large city	59	36
Medium city	40	55
Suburb	33	59
Small town	24	74
Rural	20	74

Note: "No Opinion" answers not listed.
SOURCE: The Gallup Poll.

individuals, who respond to situations with a wealth of personal expertise born of long training and experience, which, rather than organizational rules and regulations, guides them in handling various situations. In law enforcement agencies, such professionalism would come from better trained and educated officers, more sophisticated police resources, closer attention to the needs for community service and police-community relations, and more efficient and detailed policies regarding police behavior in contacts with citizens.

Properly understood, **police professionalism** implies that brutality and corruption are incompetent policing. And incompetence may be measured in terms of the following axiom: While the core of the police role is the right to use force, the skill in policing is the ability to avoid its use. With respect to corruption, professionalism engenders group norms of pride and dignity of occupation that make police intolerant of fellow officers who taint the profession.[21]

Police professionalism: The notion that brutality and corruption are incompetent policing.

SUMMARY

Police misconduct falls primarily into two areas: corruption and the excessive use of violence. Police corruption reflects illegal activities for economic gain, including payment for services that police are sworn to do as part of their law enforcement role. Police violence, in the forms of brutality and the misuse of deadly force, involves the wrongful use of police power.

Police corruption can occur in many ways, but observers and researchers in the field of police behavior agree that it is most manifest in nine specific areas: meals and services, kickbacks, opportunistic theft, planned theft, shakedowns, protection, case fixing, private security, and patronage. Policing is rich in opportunities for corruption—more so than most, if not all, other occupations.

Three major theories that attempt to explain the persistence of police corruption have gained considerable attention: the society-at-large explanation, the structural account, and the rotten-apple analogy. The society-at-large theory has attempted to locate the incidence of corruption among officers within a larger framework of relationships with citizens—specifically, those relations that involve the acceptance of gifts and gratuities for service and the waiver of minor traffic fines. The structural explanation can be seen as an extension of the society-at-large hypothesis. In this view, officers develop a cynical attitude when they begin to realize that dishonesty and criminal behaviors are not limited to lawbreaking citizens but are also found among those considered to be upstanding citizens, including officers in their own departments. Lastly, the rotten-apple theory asserts that corruption occurs among a few bad officers in an otherwise honest department. In this view, criminal behavior among officers is the result of a breakdown of morality among certain officers that has the potential to spread like a contagion through the rest of the department.

Police violence has been relatively visible throughout American history and has received much attention in recent years by the U.S. Supreme Court and the Kerner Commission. Studies have shown that police violence occurs most often when people show disrespect for officers, when police encounter certain types of offenders, and when police try to coerce confessions.

In the past, police brutality was considered to be a practice limited to a few sadistic officers. More recent commentaries suggest that while it is not particularly widespread, it appears to be an unfortunate consequence of departmental norms of conduct and the police role.

Specifically, the dangerous and often controversial role of police officers can contribute to the police "working personality" that involves a variety of performance-related pressures, elements of authoritarianism, pervasive suspicion, racism, hostility, insecurity, and cynicism. Police violence also includes the improper use of deadly force—a "shoot-to-kill" doctrine based on common law principles that persist in a few law enforcement agencies.

Attempts to control police misconduct of all varieties have emanated from the legislature, from civilian review boards, and from police agencies themselves. Perhaps the most effective method is police professionalization, which views brutality as incompetent policing and corruption beneath the dignity of effective law enforcement agents.

KEY TERMS

civilian review boards **180**
police brutality **176**
police corruption **168**

"police presence" **168**
police professionalism **185**
Tennessee v. *Garner* **177**

QUESTIONS FOR DISCUSSION

1. In what ways can civilian review boards be improved to increase their effectiveness in controlling and sanctioning police corruption and brutality?
2. Do you think that providing police with "goodwill" services contributes to corruption? Why or why not?
3. How has the war on drugs contributed to police corruption?
4. Is the problem of brutality so much a part of the police role that it can never be routed out? Why or why not?

5. In your community, what do you feel would be the best combination of activities for controlling police corruption?
6. Do you feel that corruption is *more* or *less* widespread in the ranks of policing than in other occupations and professions? Why?
7. What kinds of police misconduct have you observed? In each case, were they officer- or citizen-initiated?

MEDIA RESOURCES

1. **Human Rights and Police Abuses.** A good resource is Human Rights Watch, *Shielded from Justice: Police Brutality and Accountability in the United States* (Washington, D.C.: Human Rights Watch, 1998). This entire report can be found on the World Wide Web: http://www.hrw.org/reports98/police/toc.htm
2. **Police Violence.** Some recent insightful items on this topic include Tom Barker and David Carter, "Fluffing Up the Evidence and Covering Your Ass: Some Conceptual Notes on Police Lying," *Deviant Behavior* 11 (1990): 61–73; Craig Horowitz, "Show of Force," *New York Magazine*, September 22, 1997, pp. 29–37; Jerome Skolnick and James Fyfe, *Above the Law: Police and the Excessive Use of Force* (New York: Free Press, 1993).

3. **Police Corruption.** One of the more classic works on corruption is Herman Goldstein's *Police Corruption: A Perspective on Its Nature and Control* (Washington, D.C.: Police Foundation, 1975).
4. **Attitudes Toward Local Police.** The material discussed in Exhibit 7.3 can be found in Steven K. Smith, Greg W. Steadman, Todd D. Minton, and Meg Townsend, *Criminal Victimization and Perceptions of Community Safety in 12 Cities* (Washington, D.C.: Bureau of Justice Statistics, May 1999). This entire report can be found on the World Wide Web: http://www.ojp.usdoj.gov/bjs/press.htm

NOTES

1. Associated Press, "Four New York Officers Fire 41 Shots at Unarmed Street Peddler," February 5, 1999, 9:20 A.M. ET.
2. This discussion is based on Lawrence W. Sherman, *Scandal and Reform: Controlling Police Corruption* (Berkeley: University of California Press, 1978); Richard J. Lundman, *Police and Policing* (New York: Holt, Rinehart and Winston, 1980), pp. 142–148; Herman Goldstein, *Policing a Free Society* (Cambridge, Mass.: Ballinger, 1977), pp. 194–195; Thomas Barker and Julian Roebuck, *An Empirical Typology of Police Corruption: A Study in Organizational Deviance* (Springfield, Ill.: Thomas, 1973); Jonathan Rubinstein, *City Police* (New York: Farrar, Straus & Giroux, 1973); press releases from the Federal Bureau of Investigation; and personal observations and contacts with police in New York City, Tampa, Philadelphia, Miami, San Francisco, and Wilmington, Delaware.
3. *New York Times*, May 22, 1999, p. B5.
4. Edwin J. Delattre, *Character and Cops: Ethics in Policing* (Washington, D.C.: American Enterprise Institute for Public Policy Research, 1989), pp. 71–78.
5. From Ralph Lee Smith, *The Tarnished Badge* (New York: Arno Press, 1974), pp. 191–192.
6. Arthur Niederhoffer, *Behind the Shield: The Police in Urban Society* (Garden City, N.Y.: Doubleday, 1969), p. 70.
7. Goldstein, *Policing a Free Society*, p. 199.
8. *Brown* v. *Mississippi*, 297 U.S. 278 (1936).
9. *Report of the National Advisory Commission on Civil Disorders* (New York: Dutton, 1968).
10. Lundman, *Police and Policing*, pp. 161–164.
11. *Tennessee* v. *Garner*, U.S. SupCt 36 CrL 3233 (1985).
12. James J. Fyfe, "The Split Second Syndrome and Other Determinants of Police Violence," in *Violent Transactions*, ed. Anne Campbell and John Gibbs (New York: Basil Blackwell, 1986).
13. *U.S. News and World Report*, August 27, 1979, p. 27; *Time*, January 21, 1980, p. 32; *U.S. News and World Report*, June 2, 1980, pp. 19–22; Arthur L. Kobler, "Police Homicide in a Democracy," *Journal of Social Issues* 31 (Winter 1975): 163–184; Gerald D. Robin, "Justifiable Homicides by Police Officers," *Journal of Criminal Law, Criminology and Police Science*, June 1963, pp. 225–231; Ralph Knoohirizen, Richard P. Fahey, and Deborah J. Palmer, *The Police and Their Use of Fatal Force in Chicago* (Evanston, Ill.: Chicago Law Enforcement Study Group, 1972); Betty Jenkins and Adrienne Faison, *An Analysis of 248 Persons Killed by New York City Policemen* (New York: New York Metropolitan Applied Research Center, 1974); David Jacobs and David Britt, "Inequality and Police Use of Deadly Force: An Empirical Assessment of a Conflict Hypothesis," *Social Problems* 26 (April 1979): 403–412; Lennox S. Hinds, "The Police Use of Excessive and Deadly Force: Racial Implications," in *A Community Concern: Police Use of Deadly Force*, ed. Robert N. Brenner and Marjorie Kravitz (Washington, D.C.: U.S. Department of Justice, 1979), pp. 7–11; *Miami Herald*, March 27, 1983, p. 18A.
14. Paul Takagi, "A Garrison State in a 'Democratic' Society," *Crime and Social Justice* 1 (Spring-Summer 1974): 27–33.
15. Richard Kania and Wade Mackey, "Police Violence as a Function of Community Characteristics," *Criminology* 15 (May 1977): 27–48.
16. Kobler, "Police Homicide in a Democracy."
17. James J. Fyfe, "Police Use of Deadly Force: Research and Reform," *Justice Quarterly* 5 (June 1988): 165–205.
18. Robert M. Fogelson, *Big City Police* (Cambridge, Mass.: Harvard University Press, 1977), pp. 283–284.
19. George D. Eastman, ed., *Municipal Police Administration* (Washington, D.C.: International City Management Association, 1969), pp. 203–204.
20. Fogelson, *Big City Police*, p. 179.
21. Egon Bittner, *The Functions of Police in Modern Society* (New York: Aronson, 1975).

Part 3

THE COURTS

Chapter 8
**The American Courts and the
Right to Counsel**

Chapter 9
**The Court Process: From First
Appearance Through Trial**

Chapter 10
**Sentencing, Appellate Review,
and the Death Penalty**

CHAPTER 8

THE AMERICAN COURTS AND THE RIGHT TO COUNSEL

TELEVISION CITY — From a makeshift courtroom in a CBS studio, Judge Judith Sheindlin sneers from her bench and lectures her defendant. In a direct and confrontational style, "Judge Judy" calls the plaintiff a *nudnik,* coming off like a crazy aunt with her "don't mess with me" attitude. A few blocks away at NBC, former New York City mayor Ed Koch presides over "The People's Court." And then there are "Judge Joe Brown" and Burton Katz's "Judge and Jury" on competing networks.

What is going on here? Are these real judges and actual cases? And most importantly, are these real courts—and what kind of justice do they offer? How many different kinds of courts are there, and what are their purposes and functions?

The American courts serve the integral function of deciding in all matters of law. The issues that they address range from simple traffic violations to the more complex business of interpreting the Constitution of the United States. Accordingly, there are many different types of courts to handle the abundance of concerns of the American people. Each court system varies with regard to structure; each performs distinct operations; and each has its own jurisdictional scope. Furthermore, court systems differ across the nation and within states.

Dual court system: Courts at the state and federal levels.

To complicate matters even more, the United States has a **dual court system,** with courts at both the state and federal levels. The federal court system has a unified structure, unlike the states. Its jurisdiction spans the entire United States and covers a wide range of cases, though numerically fewer than in the states. The U.S. Supreme Court, the highest court in the nation, serves as the guardian of the Constitution.

Within this context, the purposes of this chapter are to examine how the various courts are organized and to explore the roles they play in the processing of criminal offenders. In addition, the accused's right to counsel is addressed in detail.

THE STATE COURTS

Two characteristics of the state court system are that no two are exactly alike, and the names of the various courts vary widely regardless of function. For example, all states have major trial courts devoted to criminal cases. In Ohio and Pennsylvania, these are called courts of common pleas; in California, they are known as superior courts; in New York, they are supreme courts—a designation typically used elsewhere for appeals courts. Moreover, while Michigan's major trial courts use the label of circuit court, within the corporate limits of the city of Detroit they are called the recorder's court.

The many names, functions, and types that characterize state court structures have resulted from the fact that each state is a sovereign government insofar as the enactment of a penal code and the setting up of enforcement machinery are concerned. Thus, in each of the 50 jurisdictions, the court systems grew differently—sometimes in an unplanned, sporadic way—generally guided by different cultural traditions, demographic pressures, legal and political philosophies, and needs for justice administration. Yet, despite this apparent confusion, there is nevertheless a clear-cut structure within all the state court systems. State judiciaries are divided into three, four, and sometimes five specific tiers, each having separate functions and jurisdictions.

As outlined in Figure 8.1, the courts of last resort are at the uppermost level, occupying the highest rung in the judicial ladder. These are the appeals courts. All states have a court of last resort, but depending on the jurisdiction, the specific name will vary—supreme court, supreme court of appeals, or perhaps simply court of appeals. In addition, in states such as Texas and Oklahoma, there are two courts of last resort, one for criminal cases and one for all others.

Immediately below the courts of last resort in more than half the states are the intermediate appellate courts. Located primarily in the more populous states, these courts have been structured to relieve the caseload burden on the highest courts. Like the highest courts, they are known by various names; often the names are similar to those of the courts above them in the hierarchy (appeals courts), as well as below them (superior courts).

The major trial courts are the courts of general jurisdiction, where felony cases are heard. All states have various combinations of these, and depending on the locale, they might be called superior, circuit, district, or some other designation.

Figure 8.1 State and Federal Court Structure

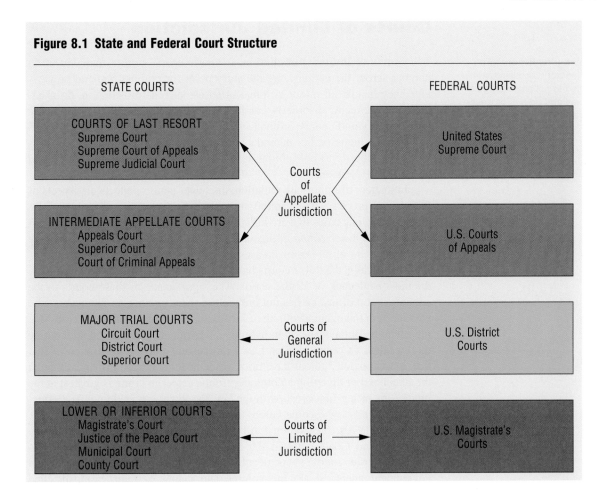

The lower courts—often referred to in legal nomenclature as inferior, misdemeanor, minor, or courts of limited jurisdiction—exist in numerous combinations in every state. Variously named county, magistrate, police, municipal, justice of the peace, and justice courts, as well as dozens of other designations, they are the entry point for most defendants being processed through the criminal justice system, and the only level at which infractions and most misdemeanors are processed.

The *jurisdiction* of each court varies by geography, subject matter, and hierarchy. Courts are authorized to hear and decide disputes arising within specific political boundaries—a city, borough, township, county, or group of counties. In addition, some courts are limited to specific matters—for example, misdemeanors or civil actions versus all other types of cases. There are family courts that decide on juvenile and domestic relations matters, probate courts whose jurisdiction is limited to the handling of wills and the administration of decedents' estates, and many others. Jurisdiction can also be viewed as limited, general, and appellate:

1. *Courts of limited jurisdiction,* the lower courts, do not have powers that extend to the overall administration of justice; they do not try felony cases, and they do not possess appellate authority.

2. *Courts of general jurisdiction,* the major trial courts, have the power and authority to try and decide any case, including appeals from a lower court.

3. *Courts of appellate jurisdiction,* the appeals courts, are limited in their jurisdiction to decisions on matters of appeal from lower courts and trial courts.

Lower courts have often been labeled inferior courts. Some have alleged that this designation comes from the lesser quality of justice and courtroom professionalism apparent in them. The term *inferior,* however, actually refers to the fact that the jurisdiction of these courts is limited.

Levels of jurisdiction in state courts

Courts of Limited Jurisdiction

Courts of limited jurisdiction: The entry point for judicial processing, with jurisdiction limited to full processing of *all* minor offenses and pretrial processing of felony cases.

The **courts of limited jurisdiction,** or lower courts—more than 13,000 in number across the nation—are the entry point for criminal judicial processing. They handle all minor criminal offenses, such as prostitution, drunkenness, petty larceny, disorderly conduct, and the myriad violations of traffic laws and city and county ordinances. In addition, they hear most civil cases and conduct inquests. For defendants charged with felonies, the lower courts have the authority to hold initial appearances and preliminary hearings, and to make bail decisions.

In matters of minor law violation, the lower court conducts all aspects of the judicial process—from initial appearance to sentencing. Given the large number of felony cases that are initially processed in this part of the state court structure, the lower courts ultimately deal, in one way or another, with more than 90 percent of all criminal cases.

Historically, the lower courts have been the most significant, yet typically the most neglected, of all the courts. The significance of these courts to the administration of justice lies not only in the sheer number of defendants who pass through them, but also in their jurisdiction over many of the offenses that represent the initial stage of an individual's criminal career. As pointed out by the President's Commission on Law Enforcement and Administration of Justice, most convicted felons have prior misdemeanor convictions, and although the likelihood of diverting an offender from a career in crime is greatest at the time of his or her first brush with the law, the lower courts do not deal effectively with those who come before them.[1]

In the 1970s, the National Advisory Commission on Criminal Justice Standards and Goals outlined the three major problems that continued to plague the lower courts: (1) neglect by bar associations, the higher courts, and government agencies; (2) the volume and nature of their caseloads; and (3) the trial *de novo* system, which precludes effective review and monitoring of the work and decisions of the lower courts by appellate tribunals.[2]

A trial *de novo* is a new trial, on appeal from a lower court to a court of general jurisdiction.

By the close of the 1990s, little had changed with respect to the operations of the lower courts. However, there are some differences in the nature of these enduring problems between rural and urban lower courts.

Justice of the Peace Courts

Justice of the peace courts, which are similar to alderman's and mayor's courts, developed at a time when a lack of effective transportation and communication tended to isolate small communities, thus preventing them from having a quick means for hearing minor criminal cases and for exercising local community authority. The **justice of the peace** was generally not required to be a lawyer and was typically best known as the person who performed marriages. The justice was either appointed or elected and usually had strong community ties. He or she heard ordinance violations, issued search and arrest warrants, determined bail, arraigned defendants, and processed civil cases involving limited dollar amounts[3] (see Exhibit 8.1).

Justices of the peace: The judges in many lower courts in rural areas, who are typically not lawyers and are locally elected.

The problems with this judicial system were, and still are, numerous. First, justices of the peace, referred to as JPs, had minimal, if any, legal training. Second, methods of compensation were problematic. In some jurisdictions, the JP was paid from the court costs he or she would assess convicted defendants. Thus, it was in the justice's interest to convict as many persons as possible.

In recent years, justice of the peace courts have been eliminated in some states and have been downgraded in others. In any event, a number of the original difficulties still persist. For example, although *Tumey* v. *Ohio* in 1927 declared that the practice of paying JPs from costs assessed defendants only when they were convicted was unconstitutional,[4] the President's Commission on Law Enforcement and Administration of Justice found the practice to be still current in some areas. Furthermore, as recently as 1977 the U.S. Supreme Court invalidated a Georgia law that provided JPs with a $5 fee for each search warrant they issued to the police.[5]

Alternatives to the JP courts in rural America are the county courts and their variants, which do not involve the more negative aspects of the justice of the peace system. As lower courts, they handle minor offenses, civil issues, and the pretrial aspects of felony processing. County justices usually have at least some legal training; the dispensing of justice occurs in more formal courts of law staffed by judges, clerks, and other personnel on state or county payrolls; and the trappings of fees for service are absent. But as with all the lower courts, they tend to reflect the shortcomings characteristic of courts of limited jurisdiction.

Municipal Courts The urban counterpart of the justice of the peace and county courts are the municipal courts, also called magistrate's courts. In jurisdictions where the judicial system has formally separated the processing of criminal and civil cases, these lower courts may be known as criminal courts or police courts.

The functions of the municipal courts are the same as those of the county courts, and many of the problems are similar. But municipal courts have the added difficulty of large caseloads and assembly-line justice. Some magistrates, in the face of heavy workloads, exercise wide discretion in ordering certain cases dismissed and in abbreviating the law. In addition, with lesser offenses such as prostitution, drunkenness, and loitering, groups of defendants are processed en masse and dispensed with quickly.

H. Ted Rubin, former judge and assistant executive director of the Institute for Court Management in Denver, Colorado, describes the Cleveland Municipal Court as follows:

> The Criminal Division of the Cleveland Municipal Court is located in the Police Building at 21st and Payne. The courtroom is well worn, crowded, and noisy. Row on row of benches are peopled with defendants out on bail, witnesses, friends and relatives of defendants, attorneys, social service personnel, and others. Most attorneys sit at the several counsel tables at the front of the room. The judge is flanked by a representative of the clerk's office to his right and two police officers. To his left is his bailiff. An assistant police prosecutor is present on one end of the judge's bench, an assistant county prosecutor on the other. A stenotype reporter was added during April 1971, and sits along the bar in front of the judge immediately next to the defendants and counsel who appear. The arraignments, hearings, and conferences which occur at the bench are largely inaudible beyond the second or third row of the spectator gallery. Witnesses generally testify from standing positions off to the side of the judge. There is little dignity to the setting. Jailed defendants are brought in and out from a door behind the judge and off to his right. People leaving the courtroom go out a door in the front of the room and off to the judge's left, where outside noise enters the courtroom as the door opens and closes.[6]

According to Rubin, the situation in the Cleveland Municipal Court in the early 1970s can be considered mild when compared with that in the New York criminal courts of the 1990s. The criminal court in Brooklyn, New York, for example, is a court of limited jurisdiction that handles minor criminal offenses as well as pretrial processing of all felony cases. Observations by the author during 1994 and 1998 showed a chaotic system of justice. On one Monday morning in one particular courtroom that dealt almost exclusively with preliminary hearings and arraignments of felony cases, the rows of benches were packed with hundreds of spectators. Presumably, these were the families, friends, and acquaintances of the defendants, together with other interested

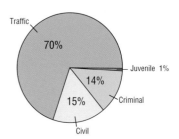

Distribution of Cases Filed in Courts of General and Limited Jurisdiction

SOURCE: Bureau of Justice Statistics.

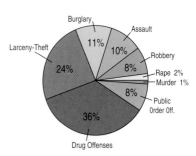

Felony Defendants in Urban Areas, by Arrest Charge

SOURCE: Bureau of Justice Statistics.

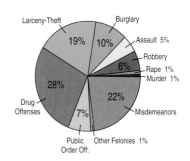

Felony Defendants in Urban Areas, by Conviction Offense

SOURCE: Bureau of Justice Statistics.

Exhibit 8.1   **Historical Perspectives on Crime and Justice**

Judge Roy Bean and the Law West of the Pecos

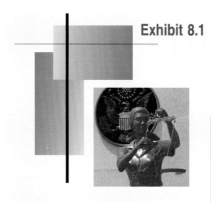

In history and folklore, Judge Roy Bean of the West Texas frontier is a familiar character. Books have been written about him, and the 1972 Warner Brothers production *The Life and Times of Judge Roy Bean* cast actor Paul Newman as the colorful seat of the rural bench. Although Bean was hardly a Paul Newman look-alike, he was a caricature and exaggeration of everything that could possibly be wrong with a rural magistrate, and his methods of distributing justice were indeed a satirical rendition of the justice of the peace court.

Born in the hills of Mason County, Kentucky, in 1825, Roy Bean's early life hardly reflected the qualities and experiences one would hope to find in a person charged with making decisions in the cause of justice. In 1847 he shot a man in a barroom brawl; several years later, he killed a Mexican army officer in a gun duel over a woman, after which he was hanged (but survived); during the Civil War he operated with Confederate irregulars; and following

the war he was a blockade runner in San Antonio.

Bean's career in frontier justice began in 1882 when he drifted across the Pecos River into West Texas, dispensing whiskey from a tent. First at a place called Eagle's Nest on the Rio Grande, and later beside a railroad bed that ran through Dead Man's Canyon just north of the Mexican border, he plied his trade as a saloonkeeper. His saloon was called the "Jersey Lilly," and the spot was Langtry, Texas—both named for actress Lillie Langtry, whom Bean idolized but had never met.

The records of Pecos County, Texas, document that Roy Bean was appointed justice of the peace on August 2, 1882, by the county commissioner's court, and that he fully qualified for the position by submitting a $1,000 bond on December 6, 1882.

As a rural magistrate, he dispensed both justice and beer from the same bar, frequently interrupting his court to serve liquor. He knew little of law or criminal procedure, and his methods of handling cases were often bizarre. Once he reportedly fined a dead man $40 for carrying a concealed weapon; on another occasion he threatened to hang a lawyer for using profanity in the courtroom.

parties, and possibly sightseers. Although many sat in a dignified manner, attempting to follow the proceedings, others conversed, ate, slept, played cards, read, or attended to other matters. Children played at their mothers' feet; an artist sketched the posture of the judge; and scores of observers listened to music through earphones.

The rumble of sound made paying attention to the matters of the court impossible. Only those in the first few rows of the courtroom, which were reserved for attorneys, could hear the words of the judge, defendant, prosecutor, bailiff, and defense. An occasional thunderclap of laughter or crying or boisterousness would alert the clerk to remind the crowd that it was a court of law.

Along the aisles, sides, and rear walls of the courtroom were dozens of police, parole, and probation officers. They complained that the docket was crowded again that day, that their case would not be heard for at least 3 hours:

Judge Roy Bean, the "Law West of the Pecos," holding court at the old town of Langtry, Texas, in 1900, trying a horse thief. This building was court-house and saloon. No other peace officers in the locality at that time.

order, Roy Bean spent much of his time worshiping Lillie Langtry. As legend tells it, his most precious moment came in the spring of 1888, when the woman whose tattered picture he carried in his pocket played in San Antonio. Free of alcoholic fumes and in a front-row seat, Bean watched the woman who had tortured his mind for years. But no one would introduce him to her, and sadly he returned to Langtry and his "Jersey Lilly," thinking only of a love he could never have.

For the next 8 years he continued his ludicrous variety of frontier justice, until he finally overstepped his bounds. In 1896, after a count of votes showed that those cast for Bean were well in excess of the Langtry population, he was removed from the bench. For the next 7 years, until his death in 1903, Bean continued as a saloonkeeper, having failed to achieve his lifelong dream of meeting Lillie Langtry. Ironically, only months after his death, she visited his saloon while on a tour through Texas. The Langtry townspeople presented her with Bean's revolver, and she kept it until her own death in 1929. Today, Roy Bean's "Jersey Lilly" still stands, and Langtry remains a small town in Texas with a population of some 75 persons.

And in one memorable trial Judge Bean freed a man accused of murdering a Chinese railroad worker because he could not find any law that made it a crime "to kill a Chinaman."

Bean's antics became so widely known that passengers passing through Langtry often stopped to look at the "Law West of the Pecos," as the judge called himself. These visits sparked more tales, which encouraged Bean to hand down more of his infamous "decisions." In fact, he spent much of his time working on the diffusion of his own legend.

But the "Law West of the Pecos" was anything but just, for Bean was ignorant, biased, and corrupt. He allowed his jurors (when he had them) to drink profusely before considering a verdict; he pocketed most of the fines he collected; he confiscated money and property from bodies brought to him in his role as coroner; he stuffed ballot boxes to ensure his reelection; and although he could hang a horse thief without batting an eye, when his friends were accused of murder, leniency always prevailed.

Besides his involvement—or lack of involvement—with law and

SOURCES: Horace Bell, *On the Old West Coast* (New York: Morrow, 1930); C. L. Sonnichsen, *Roy Bean: Law West of the Pecos* (Old Greenwich, Conn.: Devin-Adair, 1943).

"There goes another day off," said one officer. Another responded, "Doesn't pay to make an arrest any more."

Just beyond the rail that separated the bench from the spectators was the quarters of the Legal Aid lawyers. It was a long table piled high with case materials. Court personnel huddled around the table to discuss cases during the proceedings, while defendants, mothers, fathers, spouses, attorneys, police officers, and probation and parole officers hung over the rail to glance at the materials, plead their cases, or otherwise elicit information.

To the left of the magistrate's bench was a door that led to the detention pens where defendants awaited their turn. To the right of the bench, within the courtroom, was another holding area, where the faces of the accused were grim and their hands cuffed.

Justice was swift and to the point. A preliminary hearing in a felony case took only 10 minutes, or 5, or 2.

Other urban courts reflect similar styles of criminal processing. The basic problem stems from case overloads, and the result is often shorthand justice. Defendants may not be accorded the full range of procedural safeguards, and the several millions who appear annually before the urban courts run the risk of conviction and sentence in situations in which constitutional guidelines may not be fully observed.

Major Trial Courts

Courts of general jurisdiction: Courts authorized to try *all* criminal and civil cases.

The *major trial courts,* or **courts of general jurisdiction,** are authorized to try all criminal and civil cases. Such courts, numbering in excess of 3,000 across the nation, handle about 10 percent of the defendants originally brought before the lower courts who are charged with felonies and serious misdemeanors (the balance having been already disposed of at the lower court level).

In terms of nomenclature, distinctions between some types of lower courts and trial courts can often be confusing. They may be called circuit, district, or superior courts, or they may have numerous other titles. But there are some exceptions. For example, Indiana has both circuit courts and superior courts, and in Indianapolis the court is simply called "Criminal Court." While many county courts may be part of a state's lower courts, as described earlier, other county courts may actually be circuit or district courts and hence are major trial courts.

Judicial circuit: A specific jurisdiction served by a judge or court, as defined by given geographical boundaries.

Also, a given county courthouse may often serve as both a lower court and a trial court. For example, when several counties are politically grouped together in a **judicial circuit,** it is customary for a judge to hold court in each county in turn. The judge moves from county to county within the circuit, and the local county courthouse becomes the circuit court during the judge's term there; the phrase "riding the circuit" derives from this practice.[7]

The administration of criminal justice in the major trial courts tends to be less problematic than it is in the courts of limited jurisdiction. Judges are lawyers and members of the bar, and hence they are better equipped to deal with the complex issues of felony cases: Most are salaried, full-time justices and are not tarnished by the fee-for-service payment structure; the adjudication process is generally cloaked in the formalities of procedural criminal law and due process; and as courts of original jurisdiction, the trial courts are **courts of record,** which means a full transcript of the proceedings is made

Courts of record: Courts in which a full transcript of the proceedings is made for all cases.

for all cases. However, this does not mean that the trial courts are without difficulties. As seen in later chapters, there are procedural problems involving bail, indictment, plea negotiation, sentencing, and judicial discretion that can affect the fairness of trial court justice. Trial courts in other nations have problems as well, as illustrated in Exhibit 8.2.

As a final note here, some comment seems warranted to illustrate more fully the separate roles and relationships between the lower and trial courts. In some jurisdictions, *all* felonies and misdemeanors begin in the lower court. While the misdemeanor cases remain in the lower court through sentencing, felony processing shifts to the district court, the major trial court, at arraignment. This is in contrast to jurisdictions in which the *entire* felony process occurs in the trial court.

Appellate Courts

Appellate jurisdiction: Jurisdiction restricted to matters of appeal and review.

In law and criminal justice, the word *appeal* refers to the review by a higher court of the judgment of a lower court. Thus, **appellate jurisdiction** is restricted to matters of appeal and review; it cannot try cases as in the courts of general jurisdiction. However, this is not to say that the workload of these courts is light. Filings for appeal emerge not only from criminal cases, but

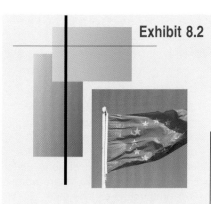

Exhibit 8.2 **International Perspectives on Crime and Justice**
Judicial Corruption
in Peru

Peru's image as a country where the rule of law and respect for human rights are problematic suffered additional humiliation during 1998. A number of judges were accused of accepting bribes from drug traffickers, and the head of the executive commission charged with reforming the entire system was charged with accumulating wealth and goods far beyond the reach of a judge's modest salary. In December 1998, a supreme court justice was dismissed by the Peruvian congress after being found guilty of handing down a judgment that favored a company with which he had dealings. A few days earlier, two judges had been caught accepting bribes by undercover investigators. One had been secretly filmed in a restaurant, pocketing a US$2,000 down payment from a drug trafficker. A public prosecutor had been caught in similar circumstances earlier in the year.

These cases brought the number of Peruvian judges and prosecutors dismissed or detained in the past year to more than 160, and to 452 over the past 4 years.

Beginning in 1993, several new systems were put into place to enhance the professionalism of the judiciary, but observers argue that little progress has been made. Critics of the system point out, furthermore, that the punishments meted out to corrupt judges have been excessively mild, sometimes amounting to only dismissal or a fine, rather than imprisonment.

The Peruvian Palace of Justice.

SOURCE: Latin American Regional Reports, *Andean Group Report,* December 15, 1998, p. 6.

from civil matters as well. In fact, the majority of appeals come out of civil suits. In the area of domestic relations alone, for example, the number of appeals filed requesting reviews of decisions rendered in matters of child custody rights, dependent support, alimony, and property settlement runs into the tens of thousands.

As a result, there are *intermediate courts of appeal* in more than half the states. If an attorney complies with the court's rules for appealing a case, the court must hear it. (This assumes that the matter is appealable—an issue discussed in Chapter 10.)

The intermediate courts of appeal serve to relieve the state's highest court from hearing every case. An unfavorable decision from an intermediate appeals court, however, does not automatically guarantee a hearing by the state

Intermediate courts of appeal

Exhibit 8.3 **Research in Crime and Justice**
The Effectiveness of Drug Courts

Drug courts represent one of the more recent trends in alternatives to incarceration, providing drug-involved offenders with less serious criminal careers an opportunity to receive drug treatment and counseling intervention through the court system. More specifically, drug courts combine intensive judicial supervision, mandatory drug testing, escalating sanctions, and treatment to help drug-involved offenders break the cycle of addiction—and the crime that often accompanies it. Drug court judges work with prosecutors, defense attorneys, probation officers, and drug treatment specialists to require appropriate treatment for offenders, monitor their progress, and ensure the delivery of other services, such as education or job skills training, to help offenders remain drug-free and crime-free.

Research suggests that drug courts have an impact on both drug use and recidivism. A National Institute of Justice evaluation of the nation's first drug court in Miami showed a 50 percent reduction in drug use and a 33 percent reduction in rearrests for drug court graduates compared with other offenders. Similar results are emerging in other jurisdictions.

By the close of 1997 there were 371 drug courts either implemented or being planned in 48 states, the District of Columbia, Guam, Puerto Rico, and two federal districts. Eighty-four of these courts have been operating for at least 2 years; 120 have been operational for less than 2 years; 4 programs became operational during 1998; and 167 are in the planning process, including 18 in Native American jurisdictions in 10 states.

SOURCES: James A. Inciardi, Duane C. McBride, and James E. Rivers, *Drug Control and the Courts* (Newbury Park, Calif.: Sage, 1996); Office of Justice Programs, *1997 Drug Court Survey Report* (Washington, D.C.: U.S. Department of Justice, 1998).

supreme court, the court of last resort in each state. It has the power to choose which cases will be placed on its docket—a characteristic of the highest court in every jurisdiction.

Reform and Unification of State Courts

The state courts have many problems. There are awkward matters of procedure—but more pertinent to this discussion are problems of organization, structure, and deployment.

For most of the twentieth century, various federal, state, and city commissions and foundations examined the state courts, and their recommendations for reorganization remained unchanged through the years:

- Unify felony and misdemeanor courts.
- Create single, unified state court systems.
- Centralize administrative responsibility.
- Abolish the justice of the peace courts.
- Increase judicial personnel.
- Improve physical facilities.

Perhaps the most pressing issue in this regard is the matter of court unification. As a study by the National Advisory Commission on Criminal Justice Standards and Goals emphasized more than two decades ago:

> State courts should be organized into a unified judicial system financed by the State and administered through a statewide court administrator or administrative judge under the supervision of the chief justice of the State supreme court.
>
> All trial courts should be unified into a single trial court with general criminal as well as civil jurisdiction. Criminal jurisdiction now in courts of limited

jurisdiction should be placed in these unified trial courts of general jurisdiction, with the exception of certain traffic violations. The State supreme court should promulgate rules for the conduct of minor as well as major criminal prosecutions.

All judicial functions in the trial courts should be performed by full-time judges. All judges should possess law degrees and be members of the bar.

A transcription or other record of the pretrial court proceedings and the trial should be kept in all criminal cases.

The appeal procedure should be the same for all cases.[8]

Court unification, however, is more easily recommended than implemented. Some unification has occurred in Arizona, Illinois, North Carolina, Michigan, Oklahoma, and Washington, and each year other states entertain proposals for a unified system. But few such proposals have been adopted due to the political, philosophical, and pragmatic dimensions involved. Local governments wish to retain control of their local courts; some judges fear that they would lose their status and discretion; nonlawyer judges fear that they would lose their jobs; political parties fear a loss of patronage opportunities; local municipalities fear the loss of revenues derived from court fines and fees; and many lawyers, judges, and prosecutors in all jurisdictions are simply resistive to change.[9]

The problem of overloaded court dockets is even more pervasive than court unification, for the costs that would be involved in expanding staff and facilities are well beyond the resources and willingness of most jurisdictions. Further, it seems that the overloading is only getting worse, principally an outgrowth of the proliferation of drug abuse, drug-related crime, and increased police activity in drug-ridden neighborhoods. The overall result has been greater numbers of drug cases coming to the attention of court systems across the nation.[10] One response to the crowding and backlogs has been the establishment of special "drug courts" in a number of jurisdictions (see Exhibit 8.3).

THE FEDERAL JUDICIARY

Unlike the state court systems, the federal judiciary has a unified structure with jurisdiction throughout the United States and its territories. But the federal court system is also complex. It has a four-tier structure similar to that in most of the states (see Figure 8.2). Although it handles fewer cases than the states, its scope is considerably greater. It has the responsibility for the enforcement of the following:

1. All federal codes (criminal, civil, and administrative) in all fifty states, U.S. territories, and the District of Columbia
2. Local codes and ordinances in the territories of Guam, the Virgin Islands, the Canal Zone, and the Northern Mariana Islands

In addition, the U.S. Supreme Court has ultimate appellate jurisdiction over the federal appeals courts, the state courts of appeal, the District of Columbia Court of Appeals, and the Supreme Court of Puerto Rico.

U.S. Commissioner's and U.S. Magistrate's Courts

Historically, U.S. commissioners occupied positions comparable to justices of the peace in the state court systems. Established by an act of Congress at the beginning of the twentieth century, commissioners had the authority to issue search and arrest warrants, arraign defendants, fix bail, hold preliminary

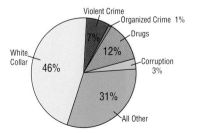

Crimes Referred by the FBI to the Federal Courts

SOURCE: General Accounting Office.

Figure 8.2 The Federal Judiciary

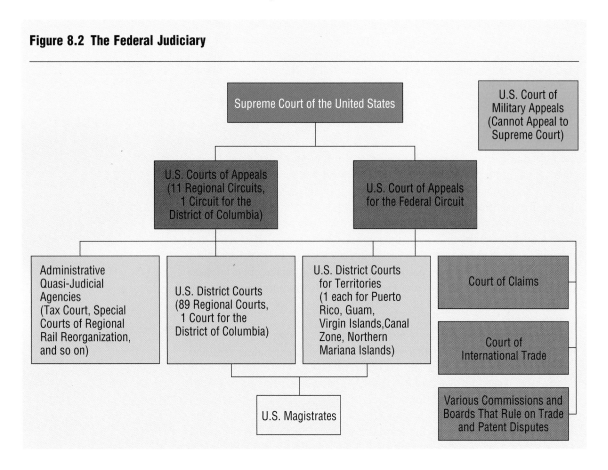

hearings, and try petty offense cases on certain federal reservations. Many of the criticisms leveled at the justice of the peace system, however, were also applicable to the U.S. commissioner's courts. In 1967, the President's Commission on Law Enforcement and Administration of Justice found that 30 percent of the more than 700 commissioners were not lawyers, that all but seven had outside employment due to the part-time nature of the work, that commissioners' private businesses often took precedence over official duties, and that the number of commissioners in many districts had no relation to the number that might be needed. The President's Commission concluded by recommending that the system be either abolished or drastically altered.[11]

On the basis of the commission's findings, together with an examination of the situation by the Senate Judiciary Committee, the federal Magistrate's Act, passed by Congress in 1968, provided for a 3-year phasing out of the office of the U.S. commissioner. The act also established **U.S. magistrates**—lawyers whose powers are limited to trying lesser misdemeanors, setting bail in more serious cases, and assisting the district courts in various legal matters. In 1976, their authority was expanded to include the issuance of search and arrest warrants, the review of civil rights and *habeas corpus* petitions, and the conducting of pretrial conferences in both civil and criminal hearings.[12] Magistrates can be both full-time and part-time jurists and all are appointed by the federal district court judges.

U.S. magistrates: Federal lower court officials whose powers are limited to trying lesser misdemeanors, setting bail, and assisting district courts in various legal matters.

U.S. District Courts

The U.S. district courts were created by the federal Judiciary Act, passed by Congress on September 24, 1789. Originally there were 13 courts, 1 for each of the original states, but now there are 95—with 89 distributed throughout the 50 states, and 1 each in the District of Columbia, Puerto Rico, Guam, the Canal Zone, the Virgin Islands, and the Northern Mariana Islands.

The **U.S. district courts** are the trial courts of the federal system and the District of Columbia—the courts of general jurisdiction. They have dominion over cases involving violations of federal laws, including bank robbery, civil rights abuses, mail fraud, counterfeiting, smuggling, kidnapping, and crimes involving transportation across state lines. The district courts try cases that involve compromises of national security, such as treason, sedition, and espionage; handle selective service violations, copyright infringements, and jurisdictional disputes; and try violations of the many regulatory codes, such as violations of the Securities and Exchange Acts, the Endangered Species Acts, the Meat and Poultry Inspection Acts, and the Foreign Agent Registration Act, among many others. In addition, district court caseloads include numerous civil actions and petitions filed by state and federal prisoners.

Each district court has one or more judges, depending on the caseload, with more than 600 judgeships authorized by law. In most cases, a single judge presides over trials, and a defendant may request that a jury be present. In complex civil matters, a special three-judge panel may be convened. In addition to U.S. magistrates, each court has numerous other officers attached to it: a U.S. attorney, who serves as the criminal prosecutor for the federal government; several assistant U.S. attorneys; a U.S. marshal's office; and probation officers, court reporters, clerks, and bankruptcy judges.

Throughout the 1980s and 1990s, the district courts had to function under near-crisis conditions. The workload increased dramatically, from 122,624 cases in 1970 to more than 300,000 by 1998. And although the level of criminal cases increased only modestly—from 45,000 to just over 55,000 filings each year dealing with everything from traffic offenses to significant violations of the U.S. Criminal Code—the number of district court judges has not been expanded in proportion to the workload. In 1982, there were 515 judges with an average load of 370 cases. In 1998, there were 647 judges with average loads of well over 400 cases.[13] To keep pace with the workload, hundreds of new judges would have to be hired, and it is unlikely that there are many highly qualified attorneys in the United States who would be willing

U.S. district courts: The trial courts of the federal judiciary.

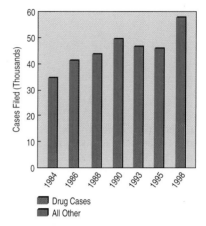

U.S. District Courts Criminal Filings, 1984–1998

SOURCE: Administrative Offices of the U.S. Courts.

National Law Journal, November 23, 1992

to work for the salary offered. In 1998, district court judges were earning $136,700.[14] Although this is no trifling salary when compared with the average national income, it is well below that of other people in the legal profession with similar credentials and experience. Yet by contrast, district court judges are already among the highest paid officials in the federal government, and if their salaries were raised significantly, many other federal salaries would have to be raised as well. The public, increasingly disenchanted with government spending and unmanageable budget deficits, probably would not stand for it.

U.S. Courts of Appeals

U.S. courts of appeals: The federal courts of appellate jurisdiction.

Appeals from the U.S. district courts move up to the next step in the federal judicial hierarchy, the **U.S. courts of appeals.** There are 13 of these courts, with more than 160 authorized judgeships. Each court is located in a circuit—described earlier in this chapter as a specific judicial jurisdiction served by the court, as defined by geographical boundaries. For example, the U.S. Court of Appeals of the First Circuit is located in Boston and serves the district courts located in Maine, Massachusetts, New Hampshire, Rhode Island, and Puerto Rico.

The 13 courts of appeals hear more than 50,000 cases each year involving both criminal and civil matters.[15] The cases heard are those appealed from the U.S. district courts—not those from state supreme or appeals courts. Almost all cases are heard by three-judge panels; a few are heard *en banc,* or "in bank," meaning the full bench of judges authorized for the court considers the appeal. In only three instances can a case appealed from one of the district courts bypass the court of appeals and go directly to the U.S. Supreme Court:

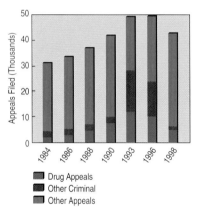

U.S. Courts of Appeals Filings, 1984–1998

SOURCE: Administrative Offices of the U.S. Courts.

1. When the ruling under appeal was decided by a special three-judge district court hearing
2. When the case involves a federal statute declared unconstitutional by a district court, and the United States is a litigant
3. When the issue under review is deemed to be of such importance that it requires immediate settlement

The U.S. Supreme Court

U.S. Supreme Court: The highest court in the nation and the court of last resort.

The **U.S. Supreme Court,** also known as the Court, High Court, and High Tribunal, is the highest court in the nation. It stands at the apex of the federal judiciary and is truly the court of last resort. The High Court is composed of nine justices: one chief justice and eight associate justices, who serve for life. They are nominated by the president of the United States and must be confirmed by the Senate.

The Jurisdictional Scope of the Supreme Court

As defined by the Constitution and spelled out in the Judiciary Act of 1789, the Supreme Court has two kinds of jurisdiction over cases—general and appellate. The Court's general jurisdiction usually involves suits between two states, issues that test the constitutionality of state laws, and matters relating to ambassadors. In such instances, the Supreme Court can serve as a trial court. In its appellate jurisdiction, the High Court resolves conflicts that raise "substantial federal questions"—typically related to the constitutionality of some lower court rule, decision, or procedure.

Selection of Cases   As the final tribunal beyond which no judicial appeal is possible, the Supreme Court has the discretion to decide which cases it will review. However, the Court *must* grant its jurisdiction in *all* of the following instances:

- When a federal court has held an act of Congress to be unconstitutional
- When a U.S. court of appeals has found a state statute to be unconstitutional
- When a state's highest court of appeals has ruled a federal law to be invalid
- When an individual's challenge to a state statute on federal constitutional grounds is upheld by a state supreme court

In all other instances, as provided by the Judiciary Act of 1925, the Supreme Court decides whether or not it will review a particular case.

The Supreme Court does not have the power and authority to review all decisions of the state courts in either civil or criminal matters. Its jurisdiction extends only to those cases where a federal statute has been interpreted or a defendant's constitutional right has allegedly been violated. Furthermore, a petitioner must exhaust all other remedies before the High Court will consider reviewing the case; that is, should a matter of "substantial federal question" emerge in a justice of the peace court, for example, the first review would not be in the Supreme Court. Rather, it would be heard as a trial *de novo* in the state trial court. Following that would be an appeal to the intermediate court of appeals (in those states where they exist), and then an appeal to the state's highest court. Only then is it eligible for review by the Supreme Court. A similar process occurs with respect to the federal court structure.

The High Court's authority to exercise its own discretion in deciding which cases it will hear is known as its *certiorari power* and comes from the **writ of** *certiorari,* a writ of review issued by the High Court ordering some lower court to "forward up the record" of a case it has tried in order that the Supreme Court can review it.

Prior to this granting of *certiorari*, the potential case must pass the **Rule of Four;** that is, a case is accepted for review only if four or more members of the High Court feel that it merits consideration by the full Court.

The Supreme Court accepts for review only cases in which its decision might make a difference to the appellant, and, as stated earlier, only those of "substantial federal question." It does not operate as a court of last resort to correct the endless number of possible errors made by other courts. Rather, it marshals its time and energy for the most pressing matters. Currently, between 6,000 and 7,000 cases are filed annually for review by the Supreme Court. However, the Court limits itself to deciding approximately 100 cases with full opinions each term.

Affirming, Reversing, and Remanding

When the Supreme Court *affirms* a case, it has determined that the action or proceeding under review is free from reversible prejudicial or constitutional error and that the judgment appealed from shall stand. Thus, if a conviction appealed from a lower court is affirmed, the conviction remains in force.

A Supreme Court decision that *reverses* or overturns a defendant's conviction or sentence does not necessarily free the appellant or impose a lighter

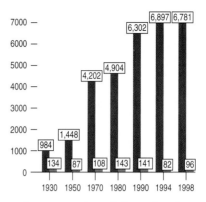

Supreme Court Caseload, 1930–1998

SOURCE: Supreme Court of the United States, Annual Report of the Director.

Writ of *certiorari*:   A writ issued by the Supreme Court ordering some lower court to "forward up the record" of a case it has tried so the High Court can review it.

Rule of Four: The decision of at least four Supreme Court justices that a case merits consideration by the full Court.

United States Supreme Court.

penalty. Rather, it *remands* or returns the case to the court of original jurisdiction for a proper judgment. Upon reversing and remanding, the trial court has several options, depending on the nature of the case. Many of the criminal cases that receive Supreme Court attention revolve around the constitutional issues of illegal search and seizure, illegal confessions, and other matters that might invoke the exclusionary rule. In such instances, the court of original jurisdiction can order a new trial, but cannot introduce the "tainted" evidence. In many of these cases, however, the prosecution may decide that without such evidence the state would have only a weak case, and it dismisses the charges. In other circumstances, the Supreme Court decision may require a *change of venue* because of pretrial publicity or community hostility that resulted in an unfair original hearing. The change of venue requires that any new trial be held in a different county or judicial district. Other Supreme Court reversals have ordered institutional authorities to remedy unconstitutional conditions of incarceration and have required that trial courts resentence certain defendants on the grounds that the original sentences constituted cruel and unusual punishment.

The Supreme Court's Mounting Problems

As the United States grew in size, complexity, and maturity, and a greater emphasis was placed on due process, human rights, and civil liberties, more and more cases began to work their way up through the appellate system. Although the number of justices on the Bench had increased by 50 percent, from six to nine, in the more than two centuries since the Court's inception, the population the Court was serving had expanded by more than 235 million—an increase of about 6,000 percent.

During the term ending in the summer of 1998, almost 7,000 petitions were received by the Court. With the crush of appeals, the nine justices have been forced to rely more and more on their clerks to review cases, and a greater number of appeals have been rendered without written opinions. Furthermore, the Court has had to become more selective in the cases it chooses to hear; or, as the former dean of Harvard Law School, Erwin N. Griswold, characterized it, the justices have been forced into "rationing justice"—ruling in only a smattering of cases, while leaving citizens without guidance on an array of questions.[16]

The increased Court workload comes not only from the simple mathematics of population growth and from the greater emphasis and awareness of civil liberties, but also from the Supreme Court's very performance. When *Mapp* v. *Ohio* in 1961 extended the exclusionary rule to the states,[17] for example, the Court opened the door to thousands of appeals involving various aspects of illegal search and seizure. Although the *Mapp* decision was clear enough in its spirit and central holding, it offered lower state and federal courts no guidance as to the specific criteria that make a search violative of the Fourth Amendment. For example, *Mapp* shed no light on such important questions as whether searches of automobiles following a traffic arrest were valid, whether search warrants issued on the basis of anonymous tips were justifiable, or whether one spouse could waive the Fourth Amendment rights of the other and consent to a search of the home. Indeed, the Court did not even tell the lower courts if the *Mapp* decision should be regarded as retroactive—that is, applicable to cases in which the trial occurred before *Mapp.* In light of the confusion surrounding *Mapp,* then, it is not surprising that research has disclosed that no two state supreme courts have reacted to *Mapp* in the same way. Some state high courts implemented *Mapp* in a very receptive fashion, while others responded to post-*Mapp* legal questions in as restrictive a manner as possible.[18]

Studies of the impact of Supreme Court decisions demonstrate that a similar phenomenon has occurred in the aftermath of every major Supreme Court decision affecting the rights of defendants. Like *Mapp,* decisions such as *Escobedo* v. *Illinois* and *Miranda* v. *Arizona* actually created more legal questions than they answered.[19] In the field of criminal law, as in all areas of law, the Court simply cannot hear enough cases to spell out all of the corollary principles that may derive from its major decisions. The very nature of the Court's work permits the justices to do little more than formulate general policy. The pressures generated by heavy caseloads and the necessity to write

The members of the Supreme Court. Standing, from left: Ruth Bader Ginsburg, David Souter, Clarence Thomas, and the Court's newest member, Stephen Breyer. Seated, from left: Antonin Scalia, John Paul Stevens, Chief Justice William H. Rehnquist, Sandra Day O'Connor, and Anthony Kennedy.

"It sort of says Judge Ginsburg—you know, moderate, careful, but you sure better have your homework done for this woman."

majority opinions that usually represent a compromise among the divergent viewpoints of individual justices make it highly likely that the Court's decisions will be uncertain and ambiguous.

THE RIGHT TO COUNSEL

In all criminal prosecutions, the accused shall enjoy the right . . . to have the assistance of counsel for his defense.
—From the Sixth Amendment

Despite the rather unambiguous language of the Sixth Amendment, for almost a century and a half after the framing of the Constitution only persons charged with federal crimes punishable by death were guaranteed the right to counsel. The right of all other defendants—both federal and state—to have the help of an attorney typically depended on their ability to retain their own defense lawyers. Beginning in the 1930s, however, all of this began to change.

Powell v. Alabama

On March 25, 1931, a group of nine African Americans, ranging in age from 13 to 21 years, were riding in an open gondola car aboard a freight train as it made its way across the state of Alabama. Also aboard the train were seven other boys and two young women, all of whom were white. At some point during the journey, and for whatever reason, a fight broke out between the two groups, during the course of which six of the white boys were thrown from the train. A message was relayed ahead reporting the incident and requesting that all of the blacks be taken from the train. As it pulled into the station at Paint Rock, a small town in northeastern Alabama, a sheriff's posse was waiting. The two white women, Victoria Price and Ruby Bates, claimed that they had been raped by a number of the black youths. All nine blacks were immediately taken into custody. Amid the hostility of a growing crowd, the youths were taken some 20 miles east and placed under military guard in the local jail at Scottsboro, the seat of Jackson County, Alabama.

The "Scottsboro boys," as they became known to history, were indicted and arraigned on March 31 and entered pleas of not guilty. Until the morning of the trial, no lawyer had been designated by name to represent any of the defendants. On April 6, a visiting lawyer from Tennessee expressed an interest in assisting any counsel the court might designate for the defense. And a local Scottsboro attorney offered a reluctant willingness to represent the defendants, whereupon the proceedings immediately began.

Of the nine young men arrested, one had not been indicted because he was only 13 years old. The remaining eight were joined into three groups for separate trials, each lasting only a single day. Medical and other evidence was presented, which established that the two women, who were alleged to be prostitutes, had not been raped. Nevertheless, the eight Scottsboro defendants were convicted of rape. Under the existing Alabama statute, the punishment for rape was to be fixed by the jury—anywhere from 10 years' imprisonment to death. The jury chose death for all eight defendants.[20]

The trial court overruled all motions for new trials and sentenced the defendants in accordance with the jury's recommendation. Subsequently, the supreme court of Alabama reversed the conviction of one defendant, but affirmed the convictions of the remaining seven. Upon appeal to the U.S. Supreme Court, the Scottsboro defendants, in ***Powell v. Alabama,***[21] alleged a denial of Fourteenth Amendment due process and equal protection of the laws because (1) they had not been given a fair trial, (2) they had been denied the right to counsel, and (3) they had been denied a trial by an impartial jury, since African Americans were systematically excluded from jury service.

In reversing the rape convictions, the Supreme Court observed that Powell and his codefendants were denied their right to the effective assistance of legal counsel and, in turn, that this denial contravened the due process clause of the Fourteenth Amendment.

The decision in *Powell,* however, was a very narrow ruling, for it limited its application to defendants who were indigent, accused of a crime for which the death penalty could be imposed, and incapable of defending themselves because of low intelligence, illiteracy, or some similar handicap. Nevertheless, *Powell* was the first in a series of Supreme Court decisions that would extend the Sixth Amendment right to counsel.[22]

Extending the Sixth Amendment Right

Six years after *Powell,* the High Court's decision in ***Johnson v. Zerbst*** held that all indigent federal defendants facing felony charges were entitled to the assistance of a government-supplied attorney.[23] Johnson, a U.S. Marine charged with passing counterfeit money, had been convicted, but without the aid of a defense attorney. He challenged his conviction and won a reversal from the Supreme Court. But *Johnson,* with its emphatic declaration of the right of federal defendants to have an attorney, provided no relief to state defendants. Although *Powell* had extended this right to those charged with capital offenses, and *Townsend v. Burke* extended the Sixth Amendment right to defendants in state cases at the time of sentencing,[24] the Court continued to withhold such aid in all other state cases. In 1942 the Supreme Court reaffirmed its early traditional position on the matter in *Betts v. Brady,*[25] ruling that in noncapital crimes, "appointment of counsel is not a fundamental right" for state felony defendants, unless "special" or "exceptional" circumstances such as "mental illness," "youth," or "lack of education" were present. In the years that followed *Betts,* the Court slowly expanded the scope of the Sixth Amendment.[26] At the same time, however, there were many cases in which the states failed to appoint counsel in compliance with *Betts,* thus leading to the most important Sixth Amendment ruling in the High Court's history.

The "Scottsboro boys"

The Alabama appellate court in 1931, shown as a vulture ready to descend on the "Scottsboro Boys."

Powell v. Alabama: The Supreme Court ruling that an indigent charged in a state court with a capital offense has the right to the assistance of counsel at trial under the due process clause of the Fourteenth Amendment.

Johnson v. Zerbst: The Supreme Court ruling that the Sixth Amendment right to counsel applies to all felony defendants in federal prosecutions.

Gideon v. Wainwright

Gideon v. Wainwright: The Supreme Court ruling that an indigent defendant charged in a state court with any noncapital felony has the right to counsel under the due process clause of the Fourteenth Amendment.

Among the Court's most significant decisions was **Gideon v. Wainwright** in 1963,[27] for not only did it extend the right to counsel to all state defendants facing felony trials, but it also dramatically demonstrated that even the least influential of citizens could persuade those in charge to reexamine the premises of justice in America.

Clarence Earl Gideon was charged with breaking and entering into the Bay Harbor Pool Room in Panama City, Florida, with the intent of committing a misdemeanor—a case of petty larceny, which, under Florida law, is considered a felony. The year was 1961, and Gideon was a 51-year-old white man who had been in and out of prisons much of his life. He was not a violent man, but he had served time for four previous felonies. He was a drifter who never seemed to settle down, making his way through life by gambling and occasional thefts. He also bore the marks of a difficult life: a wrinkled, prematurely aged face, a voice and hands that trembled, a frail body, and white hair. Those who knew him, even the officers who had arrested him, considered Gideon a harmless and rather likable human being, but one tossed aside by life.[28]

On August 4, 1961, Clarence Earl Gideon was tried on the breaking and entering charge in the Bay County, Florida, circuit court before Judge Robert L. McCrary, Jr., and the hearing began as follows:

DOES ANYONE LOVE A LAWYER?

The law, as manipulated by clever and highly respectable rascals, still remains the best avenue for a career of honorable plunder.
—Gabriel Chevalier

Doctors are just the same as lawyers; the only difference is that lawyers merely rob you, whereas doctors rob you and kill you too.
—Anton Chekhov

Lawyers, I suppose, were children once.
—Charles Lamb

THE COURT:	The next case on the docket is the case of the state of Florida, Plaintiff, versus Clarence Earl Gideon, Defendant. What says the state, are you ready to go to trial in this case?
MR. HARRIS (asst. state attorney):	The state is ready, your honor.
THE COURT:	What says the defendant? Are you ready to go to trial?
THE DEFENDANT:	I am not ready, your honor.
THE COURT:	Did you plead not guilty to this charge by reason of insanity?
THE DEFENDANT:	No sir.
THE COURT:	Why aren't you ready?
THE DEFENDANT:	I have no counsel.
THE COURT:	Why do you not have counsel? Did you not know that your case was set for trial today?
THE DEFENDANT:	Yes sir, I knew that it was set for trial today.
THE COURT:	Why, then, did you not secure counsel and be prepared to go to trial?

(The defendant answered the court's question, but spoke in such low tones that it was not audible.)

THE COURT:	Come closer up, Mr. Gideon, I can't understand you, I don't know what you said, and the reporter didn't understand you either.

(At this point the defendant arose from his chair where he was seated at the counsel table and walked up and stood directly in front of the bench, facing his honor, Judge McCrary.)

THE COURT:	Now tell me what you said again, so we can understand you, please.
THE DEFENDANT:	Your honor, I said: I request this court to appoint counsel to represent me in this trial.

THE COURT: Mr. Gideon, I am sorry, but I cannot
                                             appoint counsel to represent you in
                                             this case. Under the laws of the state
                                             of Florida, the only time the court can
                                             appoint counsel to represent a
                                             defendant is when that person is
                                             charged with a capital offense. I am
                                             sorry, but I will have to deny your
                                             request to appoint counsel to defend
                                             you in this case.

THE DEFENDANT: The United States Supreme Court
                                             says I am entitled to be represented
                                             by counsel.

Gideon, of course, was wrong, for the High Court had not said that he was entitled to counsel. In *Betts* v. *Brady,* about 20 years earlier, the Supreme Court had stated quite the opposite. The decision in *Betts* had actually denied free legal counsel to indigent felony defendants in state courts, unless "special circumstances" were present.

Judge McCrary apologetically informed Gideon of his mistake. Put to trial before a jury, Gideon heroically conducted his own defense as best as he could. He made an opening statement to the jury, cross-examined the state's witnesses, presented witnesses in his own defense, declined to testify himself, and made a short closing argument emphasizing his innocence to the charge. But Gideon's defense had been ineffective, for he was found guilty and sentenced to serve 5 years in state prison.

In the morning mail of January 8, 1962, the U.S. Supreme Court received a large envelope from Clarence Earl Gideon, prisoner number 003826, Florida State Prison, P.O. Box 211, Raiford, Florida. Gideon's petition was *in forma pauperis*—in the form of a poor man. It was prepared in pencil, with carefully formed printing on lined sheets provided by the Florida prison. Printed at the top of each sheet, under the heading Correspondence Regulations, was a set of rules ("Only 2 letters each week . . . written on one side only . . . letters must be written in English. . . ."), and the warning: "Mail will not be delivered which does not conform to these rules."[29]

Certiorari was ultimately granted to Gideon's petition. The Supreme Court assigned Washington, D.C., attorney Abe Fortas, who was later appointed to the Supreme Court by President Lyndon B. Johnson, to argue Gideon's claim. Fortas contended that counsel in a criminal trial is a fundamental right of due process enforced on the states by the Fourteenth Amendment. The Court's decision was unanimous, and in overturning *Betts,* Justice Black wrote as follows:

> Any person haled into court, who is too poor to hire a lawyer, cannot be assured a fair trial unless counsel is provided for him. This seems to us an obvious truth.

This ruling of the Supreme Court on March 18, 1963, after Gideon had served almost 2 years in prison, entitled Gideon to a new trial. He was immediately retried in the same courtroom and by the same judge as in the initial trial, but this time he was represented by counsel and was acquitted. Gideon was set free, as were thousands of other prisoners in Florida and elsewhere because they had been tried unrepresented by an attorney.[30]

In extending the right to counsel to all state defendants facing felony trials, *Gideon* also represented the beginning of a trend that would ultimately expand Sixth Amendment rights to most phases of criminal justice proceedings. On the same day as *Gideon,* the Court also delivered its opinion in *Douglas* v. *California,*[31] which stated that indigent felons were entitled to counsel, if requested, to argue their cause at the first appeal proceedings. The ruling in *Douglas* was doubly significant. Most of the Supreme Court decisions related to the Sixth Amendment right to counsel had addressed only the due process clause of the

In forma pauperis: The characterization of an appeal by a poor person.

Exhibit 8.4

Legal Perspectives on Crime and Justice
Faretta v. *California* and the Right *Not* to Have Counsel

Anthony Faretta had been accused of grand theft. At his arraignment in a California trial court, the presiding judge assigned a local public defender to represent him. But well in advance of his trial, Faretta requested that he be permitted to represent himself, arguing that the public defender's caseload was far too heavy to allow for the preparation of an effective defense. The judge approved the request, at least tentatively, but warned the defendant that he was "making a mistake." Several weeks later, still in advance of the trial date, the judge questioned Faretta about various issues in criminal procedure to inquire into his ability to conduct his own defense. On the basis of Faretta's answers and demeanor, the judge ruled that the defendant had *not* made a knowing and intelligent waiver of his right to counsel and that he did not have a constitutional right to con-

duct his own defense. Over Faretta's objections, a public defender was appointed, and the trial led to a conviction and sentence of imprisonment.

Upon review, the U.S. Supreme Court ruled in Faretta's favor. Writing for the majority, Justice Potter Stewart commented:

The Sixth Amendment does not provide merely that a defense shall be made for the accused; it grants to the accused personally the right to make his defense. It is the accused, not counsel, who must be "informed of the nature and cause of the accusation," and who must be "confronted with the witnesses against him," and who must be accorded "compulsory process for obtaining witnesses in his favor." Although not stated in the Amendment in so many words, the right to self-representation—to make one's own defense personally—is thus necessarily implied by the structure of the Amendment. The right to defend is given directly to the accused; for it is he who suf-

fers the consequences if the defense fails.

In a dissenting opinion, however, Justice Harry A. Blackmun argued that the decision in *Faretta* left open a host of other procedural issues:

Must every defendant be advised of his right to proceed *pro se* [in his or her own behalf]? If so, when must that notice be given? Since the right to assistance of counsel and the right to self-representation are mutually exclusive, how is the waiver of each right to be measured? If a defendant has elected to exercise his right to proceed *pro se,* does he still have a constitutional right to assistance of standby counsel? How soon in the criminal proceeding must a defendant decide between proceeding by counsel or *pro se?* Must he be allowed to switch in midtrial? May a violation of the right to self-representation ever be harmless error? Must the trial court treat the *pro se* defendant differently than it would professional counsel? Many of these

---

Fourteenth Amendment; *Douglas* was the first case to reference both the due process and equal protection clauses. (For a discussion of the right *not* to have counsel, see Exhibit 8.4.)

Argersinger v. Hamlin

Argersinger v. Hamlin: The Supreme Court ruling that a defendant has the right to counsel at trial whenever he or she may be imprisoned for any offense, even for 1 day, whether it is classified as a felony or as a misdemeanor.

Ever since the Supreme Court's ruling in *Gideon* v. *Wainwright*, there had been some question whether or not the constitutional right to be represented by counsel should apply not only to felony cases, but to misdemeanors as well. *Argersinger* v. *Hamlin* in 1972 addressed this issue.[32] In *Argersinger,* the defendant was an indigent charged in Florida with carrying a concealed weapon, the potential punishment for which was up to 6 months' imprisonment and/or a $1,000 fine. At the trial, the defendant was not represented by counsel and

questions . . . such as the standards of waiver and the treatment of the *pro se* defendant, will haunt the trial of every defendant who elects to exercise his right to self-representation. The procedural problems spawned by an absolute right to self-representation will far out-weigh whatever tactical advantage the defendant may feel he gained by electing to represent himself.

Without question, *Faretta* did raise a number of problematic issues. Most critical is the potential catch-22 that could emerge, whereby a judge attempts to carry out the *Faretta* mandate and at the same time knowingly allows a defendant to make a mockery of his or her own defense or antagonize the court.

Nevertheless, the High Court has continued to support the holding in *Faretta*. Moreover, in 1993, in *Godinez* v. *Moran* (113 S. Ct. 2681) the Court ruled that the standard of competency for pleading guilty or waiving the right to counsel is no higher than the competency requirement for standing trial.

A recent defendant who asserted his right not to have counsel was Theodore Kaczynski, the "Una-bomber." Charged in federal court with a variety of offenses stemming from a 17-year string of 16 bombings that killed three people and injured 29, Kaczynski wanted to base his defense on his belief that technology was destroying humanity. His request for a pro se *defense was denied on grounds that it was an attempt to delay the trial proceedings. On January 22, 1998, in order to avoid a death sentence, Kaczynski entered a plea of guilty in return for a sentence of life without parole.*

was convicted and sentenced to serve 90 days in jail. In a *habeas corpus* petition to the Florida Supreme Court, the defendant argued that because he was a poor man and had not been provided with counsel, the charge against him could not effectively be defended. The Florida appellate court rejected the claim, and the U.S. Supreme Court granted *certiorari*.

In a unanimous decision, the Court ruled that the right to counsel applied not only to state defendants charged with felonies, but also to defendants in all trials of persons for offenses serious enough to warrant a jail sentence.

Currently, there remain several areas in criminal processing—from arrest to appeal—where the courts do not mandate the assistance of counsel for the accused, including (1) preindictment lineups, (2) booking procedures, (3) grand jury investigations, and (4) appeals beyond the first review. Decisions that address the right to counsel regarding parole and correctional matters are discussed in Chapter 14.

Exhibit 8.5   **Careers in Justice**
Court Officers and Justices of the Peace

Back in the days of Judge Roy Bean, the principal function of the justice of the peace was the maintenance of order. As such, justices of the peace (JPs) had jurisdiction primarily over criminal matters. This was especially the case in the less populated parts of the country where there were no permanent trial courts. Some justices

of the peace also hung out shingles and performed marriages and minor judicial duties. With the development of America's legal system, practically all of the criminal jurisdiction held by the justices of the peace was eliminated. Much of their work now is with minor civil cases.

The requirements of justices of the peace vary widely. In Maine, for example, a justice of the peace must be an attorney, having such duties as receiving complaints and issuing search and arrest warrants. In New Hampshire, by contrast, applicants must simply be residents of New Hampshire, be

registered voters for the past 3 years, and sign a written statement under oath that they have never been convicted of a crime. Justices of the peace in New Hampshire witness signatures, take depositions, administer oaths, and perform marriages.

Salaries vary from one jurisdiction to the next. JPs in Maine, for example, receive salaries similar to those of other government lawyers. But in New Hampshire, JPs are paid on a fee basis—$5 for each oath, witness, service, or certification, and up to $50 for each deposition.

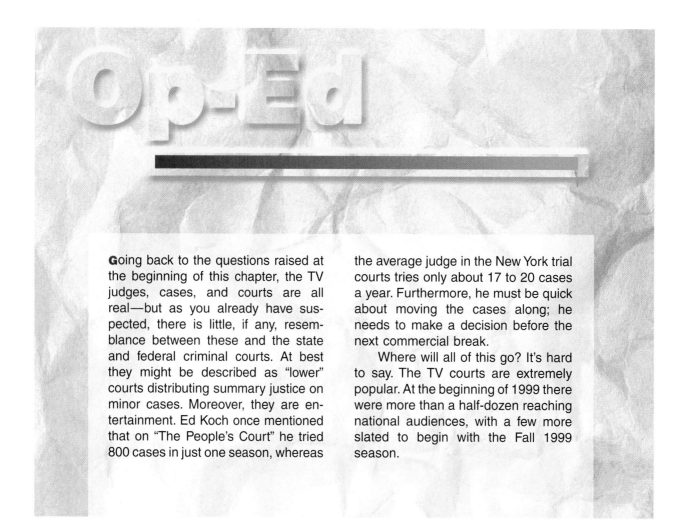

Op-Ed

Going back to the questions raised at the beginning of this chapter, the TV judges, cases, and courts are all real—but as you already have suspected, there is little, if any, resemblance between these and the state and federal criminal courts. At best they might be described as "lower" courts distributing summary justice on minor cases. Moreover, they are entertainment. Ed Koch once mentioned that on "The People's Court" he tried 800 cases in just one season, whereas

the average judge in the New York trial courts tries only about 17 to 20 cases a year. Furthermore, he must be quick about moving the cases along; he needs to make a decision before the next commercial break.

Where will all of this go? It's hard to say. The TV courts are extremely popular. At the beginning of 1999 there were more than a half-dozen reaching national audiences, with a few more slated to begin with the Fall 1999 season.

SUMMARY

The American court system has come to be a bewildering mosaic of names, structures, and functions. There are justice of the peace and municipal courts, county and city courts, superior and inferior courts, trial and appellate courts, plus a host of others. The confusion comes from a variety of sources—no two state court systems are identical, the names of courts vary regardless of function, and there are various levels of jurisdictional authority.

The variability in the structure of state court systems is a result of the constitutional guarantee that all states have sovereignty with regard to penal codes and enforcement mechanisms. Nevertheless, despite the differences among them, state court structures do possess some degree of uniformity. Common to all state court structures are appeals courts, intermediate appellate courts (in more than half the states), major trial courts, and courts of limited jurisdiction. Court jurisdiction varies by geography, subject matter, and hierarchy. The federal judiciary reflects a structure similar to that of the states.

Appellate state courts ensure that participants in lower court hearings have access to a higher court's review of the decision and proceedings in the lower court, provided, of course, that petitioners can demonstrate their case is worthy of judicial review. Caseloads in appellate courts are limited to matters of appeal and review in both civil and criminal cases. All states have a high court of appeals in one form or another, and more than half the states have an intermediate court of appeals that staves the flow of cases going directly to higher appeals courts. Major trial courts are also a part of each state's judicial structure. Authorized to try all criminal and civil cases, the major trial courts have different names in different states but are most commonly known as circuit, district, or superior courts. Courts of limited jurisdiction constitute the lower courts in all states and serve as the entry point for criminal judicial processing.

The U.S. Supreme Court stands at the apex of the federal judiciary and is the highest court in the nation. The Constitution provided the High Court with both original and appellate jurisdiction. Its original jurisdiction covers suits between two states, issues that test the constitutionality of state laws, and matters relating to ambassadors. In its appellate jurisdiction, the Court resolves conflicts that raise "substantial federal questions."

The Supreme Court is currently composed of nine justices, although the guidelines established in the Judiciary Act of 1789 allowed for only six justices. Each justice is nominated by the president of the United States and is confirmed by the Senate for a lifetime appointment. Like members of other higher courts, members of the Supreme Court have discretion over which cases will be considered for review. Nevertheless, there are a number of scenarios under which the Court must grant review to a case. These include cases in which a federal court has determined an act of Congress is unconstitutional, cases in which a U.S. court of appeals has found a state statute to be unconstitutional, cases in which a federal law was ruled invalid by a state's highest court of appeals, and cases in which an individual's challenge to a state statute on federal constitutional grounds is upheld by a state supreme court.

In recent years the Supreme Court has become overburdened by a crush of appeals. This problem has occurred mostly as a result of the greater emphasis on due process, human rights, and civil liberties. The result has been that a greater number of appeals have been administered in absence of a written opinion and that justices have become increasingly dependent on their clerks to review cases.

The Sixth Amendment holds that "in all criminal prosecutions the accused shall enjoy the right to have assistance of counsel for his defense." Despite this guarantee, for almost a century and a half after the framing of the Constitution only persons charged with capital federal crimes enjoyed the right to counsel. This situation began to change in the 1930s with the Scottsboro case. *Gideon* v. *Wainwright* in 1963 extended the right to virtually all felony defendants, while *Argersinger* v. *Hamlin* in 1972 extended the Sixth Amendment right to misdemeanor cases if imprisonment was a possible penalty.

KEY TERMS

appellate jurisdiction **198**
Argersinger v. *Hamlin* **212**
courts of general jurisdiction **198**
courts of limited jurisdiction **194**
courts of record **198**
dual court system **192**

Gideon v. *Wainwright* **210**
in forma pauperis **211**
Johnson v. *Zerbst* **209**
judicial circuit **198**
justices of the peace **194**
Powell v. *Alabama* **209**

Rule of Four **205**
U.S. courts of appeals **204**
U.S. district courts **203**
U.S. magistrates **202**
U.S. Supreme Court **204**
writ of *certiorari* **205**

QUESTIONS FOR DISCUSSION

1. What kinds of problems do you think the decisions in *Gideon* and *Argersinger* have caused for the processing of criminal cases?

2. What are the major problems with the lower courts, and how might these be remedied?

3. Is there any solution to the crush of drug cases in America's courts?

4. What types of cases fall under the jurisdiction of the U.S. Supreme Court?

MEDIA RESOURCES

1. **The Judiciary and Human Rights in Peru.** Amnesty International monitors many of the problems in Peru's judiciary. The organization has a home page on the Web: http://www.amnesty.org

2. **Drug Courts.** See James A. Inciardi, Duane C. McBride, and James E. Rivers, *Drug Control and the Courts* (Newbury Park, Calif.: Sage, 1996). In addition, several government reports on drug courts can be located through the Justice Department's Web site: http://www.ojp.usdoj.gov

3. **The Scottsboro Boys.** There are two excellent books on the Scottsboro case: Dan T. Carter, *Scottsboro: A Tragedy of the American South* (New York: Oxford University Press, 1969); James Goodman, *Stories of Scottsboro* (New York: Pantheon, 1994).

4. **Clarence Earl Gideon.** The full story of the Clarence Gideon case was published as *Gideon's Trumpet* in 1964 by *New York Times* correspondent Anthony Lewis. In addition, a 1979 made-for-television production based on the book (Samuel Goldwyn Studios' *Gideon's Trumpet,* with actor Henry Fonda in the leading role), is available on video.

NOTES

1. President's Commission on Law Enforcement and Administration of Justice, *Task Force Report: The Courts* (Washington, D.C.: U.S. Government Printing Office, 1967), p. 29.

2. National Advisory Commission on Criminal Justice Standards and Goals, *Courts* (Washington, D.C.: U.S. Government Printing Office, 1973), pp. 161–162.

3. H. Ted Rubin, *The Courts: Fulcrum of the Justice System* (Pacific Palisades, Calif.: Goodyear, 1976), p. 49.

4. *Tumey* v. *Ohio,* 273 U.S. 510 (1927).

5. President's Commission, *Task Force Report: The Courts,* p. 34; *Connally* v. *Georgia,* 429 U.S. 245 (1977).

6. H. Ted Rubin, *The Felony Processing System, Cuyahoga County, Ohio* (Denver: Institute for Court Management, 1971), pp. 16–17.

7. Murray S. Stedman, *State and Local Governments* (Cambridge, Mass.: Winthrop, 1979), p. 156.

8. National Advisory Commission, *Courts,* p. 164.

9. David W. Neubauer, *America's Courts and the Criminal Justice System* (Pacific Grove, Calif.: Brooks/Cole, 1992).

10. James A. Inciardi, Duane C. McBride, and James E. Rivers, *Drug Control and the Courts* (Newbury Park, Calif.: Sage, 1996).

11. President's Commission, *Task Force Report: The Courts,* p. 36.

12. See *United States* v. *Ford,* 41 CrL 2421 (1987).

13. Administrative Office of the United States Courts.

14. Administrative Office of the United States Courts.

15. Administrative Office of the United States Courts.

16. *U.S. News and World Report,* March 26, 1979, p. 33.

17. *Mapp* v. *Ohio,* 367 U.S. 643 (1961).

18. See Bradley C. Canon, "Reactions of State Supreme Courts to a U.S. Supreme Court Civil Liberties Decision," *Law and Society Review* 8, no. 1 (Fall 1973): 109–134.

19. *Escobedo* v. *Illinois,* 378 U.S. 478 (1964); *Miranda* v. *Arizona,* 384 U.S. 436 (1966). See Stephen L. Wasby, *The Impact of the United States Supreme Court* (Howard, Ill.: Dorsey, 1970); Theodore L. Becker and Malcolm M. Feeley, eds., *The Impact of Supreme Court Decisions,* 2d ed. (New York: Oxford University Press, 1973).

20. The full story of the Scottsboro case can be found in Dan T. Carter, *Scottsboro: A Tragedy of the American South* (New York: Oxford University Press, 1969). Also see James Goodman, *Stories of Scottsboro* (New York: Pantheon, 1994).

21. *Powell* v. *Alabama,* 287 U.S. 45 (1932).

22. See Howard N. Meyer, *The Amendment That Refused to Die* (Boston: Beacon, 1978).

23. *Johnson* v. *Zerbst,* 304 U.S. 458 (1938).

24. *Townsend* v. *Burke,* 334 U.S. 736 (1948).

25. *Betts* v. *Brady,* 316 U.S. 455 (1942).
26. See *Uveges* v. *Pennsylvania,* 335 U.S. 437 (1948); *Moore* v. *Michigan,* 355 U.S. 155 (1957); *Carnley* v. *Cochran,* 369 U.S. 506 (1962); *Hamilton* v. *Alabama,* 368 U.S. 52 (1961).
27. *Gideon* v. *Wainwright,* 372 U.S. 335 (1963).
28. Anthony Lewis, *Gideon's Trumpet* (New York: Vintage, 1964), pp. 5–6.
29. Lewis, *Gideon's Trumpet,* p. 4.
30. See Meyer, *The Amendment That Refused to Die.*
31. *Douglas* v. *California,* 372 U.S. 353 (1963).
32. *Argersinger* v. *Hamlin,* 407 U.S. 25 (1972).

Elements of
Criminal
Justice

SALEM, N.H. — In August 1998, prosecutors announced to the public that they had reached a plea agreement with Eric Jeleniewski, one of three men charged with the murder of 17-year-old Kimberly Farrah.[1] In return for his plea of guilty to the reduced charge of murder in the second degree, the defendant received a 35-year sentence. Had he been tried and convicted on the original charge of first-degree murder, a mandatory life sentence would have been imposed. The prosecutors explained that "there are risks inherent in any trial, and if we get a strong sentence like we did, we should take it." The victim's parents, however, objected to the plea bargain, arguing that justice was not served, that the case should have gone to a jury to decide.

What has happened here? What is plea bargaining? Has the adversary system of justice been corrupted? Was the defendant seduced into going to prison, or did he get off too easy? Has justice been served? And this leads to a number of other important questions. How does plea bargaining work? Is it part of the trial process? What other steps are there in the trial and what happens at each?

The processing of criminal cases through the courts from first appearance to trial involves numerous and complex steps, each of which may vary from case to case. After an accused is arrested and booked, an attorney is either retained or assigned. There is an initial appearance, where pretrial release is considered and probable cause is determined. A prosecutor's information or a grand jury's indictment brings about formal charges. An arraignment is held, and a plea is entered. Next, there are pretrial motions, jury selection, the trial, and ultimately a verdict.

Most cases, however, never make it to the advanced stages of criminal processing. Charges can be dropped at any stage in the process if there is insufficient evidence to prosecute, or if a victim decides, often for personal reasons, not to proceed with the case. The overwhelming majority of cases, however, are disposed of through a plea-bargaining process. A very small percentage ever advance to trial, and even fewer are exposed to the suspense of a jury verdict. The challenge for the courts in the American system is to ensure that justice prevails in all of these proceedings.

BAIL AND PRETRIAL RELEASE

Bail: Security posted to guarantee that a defendant in a criminal proceeding will appear and be present in court as required.

Bail is a form of security guaranteeing that a defendant in a criminal proceeding will appear and be present in court at all times as required. Thus, bail is a guarantee: In return for being released from jail, the accused guarantees his or her future appearance by posting funds or some other form of security with the court. When the defendant appears in court as required, the security is returned; if he or she fails to appear, the security is forfeited.

Excessive bail shall not be required.
—*From the Eighth Amendment*

For a defendant, bail is the bottom line of a criminal case.
—*Steven Phillips, former assistant district attorney, Bronx County, New York*

The bail system as we know it today has its roots deep in English history, well before the Norman Conquest in 1066. It emerged at a time when there were few prisons, and the only places secure enough to detain an accused awaiting trial were the dungeons and strong rooms in the many castles around the countryside. Magistrates often called upon respected local noblemen to serve as jailers, trusting them to produce the accused on the day of trial. As the land became more populated and the castles fewer in number, magistrates were no longer able to locate jailers known to them. Volunteers were sought, but to ensure that they would be proper custodians, they were required to sign a bond. Known as *private sureties,* these jailers would forfeit to the king a specified sum of money or property if they failed to live up to their obligations of keeping defendants secure and producing them in court on the day required. As the system was transferred to the New World, it shifted from a procedure of confinement to one of freedom under financial control. In current practice, it is the accused that posts the bond, or has some third party—a **surety**—post it in his or her behalf.

Surety: A third party who posts a bond for an accused.

The Right to Bail

The Eighth Amendment to the United States Constitution clearly specifies that "excessive bail shall not be required," but the extent to which the accused have any *right* to bail is a matter still under contention. The statutory right of federal defendants to have bail set in all but capital cases was established by the Judiciary Act of 1789. Furthermore, the Supreme Court held in *Hudson* v. *Parker* that a presumption in favor of granting bail exists in the Bill of Rights. Justice Horace Gray wrote in 1895:

> The statutes of the United States have been framed upon the theory that a person accused of crime shall not, until he has been fully adjudged guilty in the court of

last resort, be absolutely compelled to undergo imprisonment or punishment, but may be admitted to bail, not only after arrest and before trial, but after conviction and pending a writ of error.[2]

But Justice Gray's words carried no firm guarantees for all criminal defendants seeking release on bail. Only 1 year before, the High Court had ruled that the Eighth Amendment's bail provision placed limits only on the federal courts and did not apply to the states.[3] Since that time, the Supreme Court has decided relatively few cases involving bail, mainly because it is an issue that is moot by the time the case reaches the appellate stage of the criminal process. At the state level, the vast majority of state constitutions grant an absolute right to bail in noncapital cases.[4] However, constitutional or statutory rights to have bail set have never in practice meant an absolute right to freedom before trial. In years past, judges invariably insisted on cash bail or a surety bond from a bail bonds agent. If the defendant could not afford it, he or she remained in jail awaiting trial—for days, months, and sometimes even years.

In its principal bail ruling, **Stack v. Boyle** in 1951,[5] the Supreme Court left unsettled the constitutional status of a defendant's right to bail. But the Court did address the issue of "excessive bail," ruling that the fixing of bail must be based on standards relevant to the purpose of ensuring the presence of the defendant at trial.

Stack v. Boyle: The Supreme Court ruling that bail set at a figure higher than an amount reasonably calculated to ensure the presence of the accused at trial and at the time of final submission to sentence is "excessive" under the Eighth Amendment.

Discretionary Bail Setting

In theory, the purpose of bail is to ensure that the accused appears in court for trial. With this in mind, the magistrate is required to fix bail at a level calculated to guarantee the defendant's presence at future court hearings. This view has grown out of the historical forms of bail, as well as from the adversarial premise that a person is innocent until proven guilty and therefore ought not suffer confinement while awaiting trial. At the same time, however, there is the belief that more important than bail is the matter of societal protection. Should potentially dangerous defendants who might commit additional crimes be free to roam the community prior to trial? Judges often answer this problem by setting bail so high for some defendants that, in practice, bail becomes a mechanism for preventive detention.

In many jurisdictions, those arrested for minor misdemeanors can be released almost immediately by posting bail at the police station where they are booked. In these cases, there are fixed bail schedules and the size of the bond is relatively small. For serious misdemeanors and felonies, the amount of bail required is left to the discretion of the judge. Research has demonstrated, however, that decisions determining the size of bail are neither random nor arbitrary.

By statutory and case law, most jurisdictions have certain criteria that need to be considered in determining bail. In practice, however, there are typically only three factors that are considered in bail setting. By far, the most important is the *seriousness of the crime;* the assumption is that the more severe the offense the greater the likelihood of forfeiture of bail. The second factor is the *defendant's prior criminal record;* the rationale for this is that "recidivists" (repeat offenders) have a higher probability of forfeiting bond. In conjunction with these two factors is the *strength of the state's case.* Here the premise is that the greater the chance of conviction, the stronger the accused's interest in fleeing.[6]

Thus, if the state has a strong case against an accused with a prior felony record, and the current offense was a dangerous crime, then unquestionably, the bail set would be high.

STATUTORY BAILING CONSIDERATIONS

1. The principal's character, habits, reputation, and mental condition
2. His or her employment and financial resources
3. His or her family ties and the length of his or her residence, if any, in the community
4. His or her criminal record, if any
5. His or her previous record, if any, in responding to court appearances when required or with respect to flight to avoid criminal prosecution
6. The weight of the evidence against him or her in the pending criminal action and any other factor indicating probability or improbability of conviction
7. The sentence which may be imposed upon conviction

SOURCE: *New York State Criminal Procedure Law, Section 510.30.*

Violent offenses

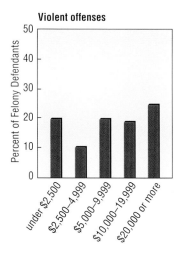

Property offenses

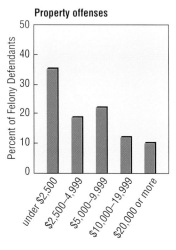

Drug offenses

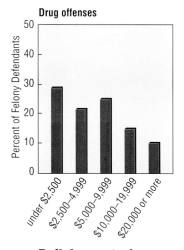

**Bail Amounts for
Felony Defendants**

SOURCE: Bureau of Justice Statistics,
National Update.

The Bail Bond Business

Once bail has been set, there are three ways it can be exercised. First, the accused may post the full amount of the bond in cash with the court. Second, many jurisdictions allow a defendant (or family and friends) to put up property as collateral and, thus, post a property bond. In either case, the money or property is returned when all court appearances are satisfied, or they are forfeited if the defendant fails to appear.

Neither cash bail nor property bonds are commonly used, however. Most defendants seldom have the necessary cash funds to meet the full bond, and the majority of courts require that the equity in the property held as collateral be at least double the amount of bond. Thus the most common method—the third alternative—is to use the services of a bail bonds agent.

Clustered around urban courthouses across the nation are the storefront offices of the bail bonds agents. Often aglow with bright neon lights, their signs boldly proclaim: BAIL BONDS—24-HOUR SERVICE. Or sometimes, during the late-night hours on local television, the viewer is confronted with the most unlikely of commercials: "Are you in trouble? Call————, 24-hour bail bond services!" In either case, the message is quite clear: that freedom is available—for a price.

Bail bonds agents, also referred to as commercial bond agents, are essentially small business entrepreneurs who serve as liaisons with the courts. For a nonrefundable fee, they post a surety bond with the court, and if the defendant fails to appear at trial, the bonds agent is responsible for the full amount of the bond.

Defendants without the funds or property necessary to meet the full amount of bail seek out a bonds agent, for the actual out-of-pocket costs usually amount to only 10 percent of the established bail. Furthermore, in actual practice the bonds agent rarely posts a cash surety with the court. Let us assume, for example, that defendant Joe Smith's bail is set at $10,000. His bonds agent charges him a nonrefundable fee of $1,000, since 10 percent is the prevailing rate. The bonds agent then purchases a surety bond from an insurance company, which typically costs 30 percent of the fee collected. Smith's cost for pretrial freedom is $1,000, of which $700 becomes the property of the bonds agent—whether or not Smith ever appears in court again. If Smith should "jump bail," the insurance company, in theory, pays the forfeiture.

Smith's case, however, is an idealized typical one and would proceed smoothly as described only if he were considered a good bail risk. If he were not, it is unlikely that the insurance company would provide a bond, or that the bonds agent would even accept him as a client. In general, the bonds agent views four types of defendants as poor risks:

1. *First felony offenders,* because they are likely to panic and leave the community
2. *Recidivists,* whose new offenses are more serious than previous ones
3. *Violent offenders,* because they can represent a personal threat to the bonds agent
4. *Those whose bail has been set at a high level,* because forfeiture would result in large financial loss, as well as damage to the agent's reputation with the insurance companies

In assessing a client's reliability, the bonds agent inquires into his or her criminal record, family situation, employment history, roots in the community, and anything else that would suggest whether the defendant has some type of "investment" in the social system. If the client is considered a bad risk, he or she will be rejected; if considered a marginal risk, the bonds agent may require her or him to post collateral—such as a house, car, or some other resource—in addition to the fee.

Bail is forfeited if the defendant fails to appear in court as required. In addition, a *capias,* or **bench warrant,** is issued by the court authorizing the defendant's arrest. Furthermore, bail jumping represents a new offense and carries criminal penalties. For example, in Maryland, which is typical of most jurisdictions, "failure to surrender after forfeiture of bail" can result in a new felony charge with penalties of 5 years' imprisonment with or without a $5,000 fine.[7]

Bench warrant: A written order, issued by the court, authorizing a defendant's arrest.

Criticisms of the Bail System

For decades, the bail system has been the subject of continuing criticism. First, bail tends to discriminate against the poor. When cash bail is set at a high level, it results in the pretrial confinement of many "low-risk" defendants who do not have the funds either to post bond or retain a bonds agent. Second, despite the Eighth Amendment safeguard against excessive bail, bail setting is totally discretionary on the part of the judge; many courts set bail at unreasonably high levels. Third, since bail is generally determined at the initial appearance, the court has little time to investigate the background of the accused and, hence, cannot adequately determine the nature of risk. Fourth, bail is often manipulated into an instrument for preventive detention. As a measure of community protection against offenders who are viewed by the courts as risks to the social welfare and safety, bail is set so high that it can rarely be met.[8]

Pretrial Detention

For defendants, the principal difficulty with the bail system is its relationship to financial well-being. Although most bail premiums paid to bonds agents are 5 to 10 percent of the face amount of the bond, rates as high as 20 percent have been reported. When bail is set at $1,000 or more, premiums of $100 to $500 become more than many defendants can afford. In a recent study of felony defendants in the nation's 75 largest counties, for example, 22 percent failed to make bail set under $2,500, 28 percent failed at $2,500 to $4,999, and 45 percent failed at $5,000 to $9,999.[9] The result of bail, then, has been the arbitrary incarceration of hundreds of thousands of persons, many of whom were innocent of any crimes. For example, when Maryland officials took over the management of the Baltimore city jail in 1991, they found a man who had already spent 16 months incarcerated awaiting trial on a shoplifting charge and a woman who had been held for 1,210 days on a contempt charge related to a child custody case.

In addition to depriving a defendant of freedom, pretrial detention prevents the accused from locating evidence and witnesses and from having more complete access to counsel. It disrupts employment and family relations. It coerces defendants into plea negotiation in order to settle the matter more rapidly. Most importantly, however, pretrial detainees are confined in city and county jails—the worst penal institutions in the country. They are overcrowded, unsanitary, and poorly equipped. Few have sufficient space for inmates to confer with counsel or visit with families. Defendants awaiting trial are indiscriminately mixed with convicted felons, with a result, as the late Supreme Court Justice William D. Douglas once remarked, "equivalent to giving a young man an M.A. in crime."[10] Finally, jails are populated by many violent offenders, and scores of detainees each year are beaten, raped, and murdered.

Preventive Detention

Stack v. *Boyle* in 1951 made it explicitly clear that the purpose of bail is "to assure the defendant's attendance in court when his presence is required." At the same time, the Supreme Court also noted that bail is not "a means for punishing defendants nor protecting public safety." In these words, the High Court has made its position on preventive detention unmistakable, at least by implication; at the same time, however, it has not ruled whether the practice is constitutionally impermissible. As a result, many magistrates use bail as a mechanism for preventive detention. For those who are considered dangerous offenders or where there is a likelihood of repeated crimes during the pretrial period, prohibitively high money bail is set for the ostensible purpose of ensuring an accused's appearance in court.

The legal consequences of pretrial detention, whether preventive or otherwise, can be disastrous. Research has demonstrated repeatedly that detainees are more likely to be indicted, convicted, and sentenced more harshly than released defendants. Furthermore, in its work on pretrial release the American Bar Association noted that the conviction rate for jailed defendants materially exceeded that of bailed defendants. In terms of the sentence imposed on those convicted, the bailed defendant was far more likely to receive probation; a jailed counterpart, having been unable to confer more fully with counsel, to seek out witnesses and evidence in his or her behalf, and most importantly, to demonstrate reliability in the community, went to prison more frequently.

There are some factors, such as strong evidence of guilt or a serious prior criminal record, that necessarily lead to high bail and hence detention. These factors, of course, and not just pretrial detention, can also cause a court to find a defendant guilty and sentence him or her to prison rather than probation. However, one study that took these factors into consideration still found a strong relationship between detention and unfavorable disposition.[11] Moreover, in an experimental mock jury study of criminal trial judgments, it was found that "jurors" were more likely to convict "defendants" who had been kept in jail prior to trial than those who had been released.[12]

There is an additional problem with preventive detention. Some courts have used it as a method of punishing defendants for the crimes for which they were charged. This is a serious abuse of judicial discretion, for punishment without conviction is patently illegal. Nevertheless, there are differing opinions on the matter.

Release on Recognizance

At the beginning of the 1960s, increasing dissatisfaction with the bail bond system led to experimentation with alternative forms of pretrial release. Early in the decade, New York industrialist Louis Schweitzer's concern for youths who were detained while awaiting trial led to his establishment of the Vera Foundation. The foundation, later called the Vera Institute of Justice, conducted an experiment with pretrial release based on the notion that "more persons can successfully be released . . . if verified information concerning their character and roots in the community is available to the court at the time of bail determination."[13] Known as the Manhattan Bail Project and begun in 1961, the effort was made possible through the cooperation of the New York criminal courts and law students from New York University. The students interviewed defendants, looking for information that would support a recommendation for pretrial release, including the following factors: (1) present or recent residence at the same address for 6 months or more; (2) current or recent employment for 6 months or more; (3) relatives in New York City with whom the defendant is in contact; (4) no previous conviction of a crime; and (5) residence in New York City for 10 years or more. For those who met the criteria, the students would recommend **release on recognizance (ROR)** to the judge. ROR simply meant that the defendant would be released on his or her own obligation without any requirement of money bail. The obligation was one of record entered into before the court with the condition to appear as required. If the judge agreed with the project's recommendation, the accused was released, subject to some follow-up contacts to ensure that the defendant knew when he or she was due to make a court appearance. Not all defendants were eligible for ROR. Those arrested for such charges as murder, robbery, rape, and other serious crimes were excluded, as were defendants with long criminal histories.

The Vera Institute's pioneer effort in release on recognizance was an immediate success in that four times as many defendants were released. Follow-up studies demonstrated that few released defendants defaulted on their obligation, and the ROR programs modeled after the Manhattan Bail Project were also deemed successful. In the years since, ROR programs have expanded dramatically, and other forms of pretrial release have emerged as well. Under the *10 percent cash bond plans,* for example, the court sets bail as it normally

The Manhattan Bail Project

Release on recognizance (ROR): The release of an accused on his or her own obligation rather than on a monetary bond.

10 percent cash bond plans

CRIMINAL OFFENSES AND I-BOND RELEASES IN COOK COUNTY, ILLINOIS

Release permitted in cases of:
Aggravated assault
Battery
Burglary
Drug possession and delivery
Forgery
Gambling
Prostitution
Theft
Weapons use

Release prohibited in cases of:
Armed violence
Arson
Child pornography
Home invasion
Kidnapping
Murder
Residential burglary
Robbery
Sexual assault

Information: A formal charging document drafted by a prosecutor and tested before a magistrate.

Indictment: A formal charging document returned by a grand jury, based on evidence presented to it by the prosecutor.

Presentment: A written notice of accusation issued by a grand jury, based on its own knowledge and observation.

Grand jury: A body of persons who have been selected according to law and sworn to hear the evidence against accused persons and to determine whether there is sufficient evidence to bring those persons to trial, to investigate criminal activity generally, and to investigate the conduct of public agencies and officials.

would. However, the accused is permitted to deposit 10 percent of the bond directly with the court, eliminating the need for a bonds agent. When the accused appears for trial, 90 percent of the deposit is returned, with the remainder held to support the operating costs of the program.[14] For example, should the bail be set at $2,000, the defendant deposits a $200 cash bond with the court; when he or she appears for trial, $180 is returned. In this way, the financial incentive to appear shifts from the bonds agent to the accused.

The size of the deposit and the proportion that is returned varies from one jurisdiction to another. Some require only a 5 percent deposit; others, such as Atlantic City, New Jersey, return the entire deposit upon appearance. Whatever the arrangement, the purposes were to make bail possible for those who were not eligible for ROR and at the same time to eliminate the bonds agent from the administration of bail.

Both the 10 percent cash bond and the ROR programs have been successful, and a larger portion of defendants are released who might otherwise have awaited trial in detention facilities. Nevertheless, there have been difficulties. A case in point is the Cook County (Chicago) no-cash "I-bond" program. The I-bond procedure was established during the mid-1980s when a U.S. district court judge found local jail officials to be in contempt of a 1982 federal court order requiring that a bed be available for each inmate. When jail officials could not reduce the crowding, the judge ordered that defendants be released on bond requiring no cash. During the late 1980s and early 1990s, with tens of thousands of drug arrests in the county each year, use of the I-bond program became widespread and indiscriminate. The result was that one in every four defendants freed from the Cook County jail on the no-cash bond system was rearrested on new charges at least once within the following 6 months.[15] In effect, the combination of increased drug enforcement, crowded jails and courts, and widespread use of no-cash bonds served to practically decriminalize such offenses as burglary, prostitution, and drug sales.

THE GRAND JURY

Following the initial court proceedings, prosecution is instituted by an information, indictment, or presentment. The **information** is a document filed by the prosecutor that states the formal charges, the statutes that have been violated, and the evidence to support the charges. The filing of the information generally occurs at the preliminary hearing and the judge determines whether there is "probable cause" for further processing. The **indictment** is a formal charging document returned by a grand jury, based on evidence presented to it by the prosecutor. Slightly different from the indictment is the **presentment,** which is a written notice of accusation issued by a grand jury. The presentment comes not from evidence and testimony provided by the prosecution, but rather from the initiative of the grand jury, based on its own knowledge and observation. In actual practice, however, the terms *indictment* and *presentment* have come to be substantially interchangeable.

The **grand jury** system apparently originated in England in 1166, when King Henry II required knights and other freemen drawn from rural neighborhoods to file with the court accusations of murder, robbery, larceny, and harboring of known criminals. In time, the English grand jury came to consist of not fewer than 12 nor more than 23 men. Furthermore, not only did they tender criminal accusations, but they considered them from outsiders as well. The jurors heard witnesses and, if convinced that there were grounds for trial, returned an indictment.[16] Historically, therefore, the purposes of the grand jury were to serve as an investigatory body and to act as a buffer between the state and its citizens in order to prevent the Crown from unfairly invoking the criminal process against its enemies.

After the American Revolution, the grand jury was incorporated into the Fifth Amendment to the Constitution, which provides that "no person shall be held to answer for a capital or otherwise infamous crime, unless on a presentment or indictment of a grand jury." Despite this Fifth Amendment guarantee, however, the Supreme Court ruled in **Hurtado v. California** more than a century ago that the grand jury was merely a form of procedure that the states could abolish at will.[17]

The American grand jury has retained the common law size of 12 to 23 persons, and the jury's purposes remain unchanged: to investigate and to protect citizens from unfair accusations. Currently, most of the states and the federal system use grand juries, and members are generally selected from voting registers. However, many of the territories west of the Mississippi River that achieved statehood late in the nineteenth century did not adopt the grand jury system, choosing instead the prosecutor's information.

Hurtado v. California: The Supreme Court ruling that the due process clause of the Fourteenth Amendment does not require states to use grand jury indictments or presentments in capital cases.

Operation of the Grand Jury

There are essentially two types of grand juries: investigatory and accusatory. The *investigatory grand jury* looks into general allegations of unlawful activity within its jurisdiction in an effort to discover if there is enough information to justify initiating criminal prosecutions against anyone. An investigatory grand jury may sit for as little as 1 month and as many as 18 months, and it most often examines suspicions and allegations regarding organized crime and official corruption. More common is the *accusatory grand jury,* a body impaneled for a set period of time—generally 3 months—that determines whether there is sufficient evidence against persons already charged with particular crimes to warrant criminal trials. It is the indictment by the accusatory grand jury that parallels the prosecutor's filing of an information, and it is the accusatory grand jury that serves as a screening body to decide whether cases already in the early stages of the criminal justice process are worthy of being tried.

Investigatory and accusatory grand juries

Since grand juries are either investigating or accusing bodies, and do not determine guilt or innocence, many of the elements of due process are absent. For example:

- Grand jury sessions are private and secret.
- Witnesses, having been subpoenaed by the prosecutor, are sworn and heard one by one, and excused as soon as they are finished testifying.
- Ordinarily the accused is not present, unless compelled to testify or invited to serve as a witness.
- In most jurisdictions, the defense counsel has no right to be present; if present, the defense counsel has no right to cross-examine witnesses.
- In some jurisdictions, written transcripts are not required.

When the members of a grand jury agree that an accused should be tried for a crime, they issue a **true bill.** That is, they endorse the validity of the charge or charges specified in the prosecutor's bill, thus returning an indictment. If they fail to find probable cause, they issue a *no bill* and the accused is released. Since the grand jury proceeding is not a trial, only a majority vote—not a unanimous one—is required for a true bill. For decisions of the Supreme Court regarding grand jury proceedings, see Exhibit 9.1.

True bill: A grand jury's endorsement of the charge or charges specified in the prosecutor's bill.

Grand Juries on Trial

Historically, the grand jury was created to stand between government and the citizen as a protection against unfounded charges and unwarranted prosecutions. Critics maintain, however, that the grand jury process has now become

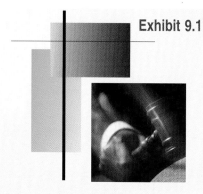

Exhibit 9.1

Legal Perspectives on Crime and Justice
Grand Jury Procedure and the Supreme Court

Prosecutors have wide discretion in the conduct of grand jury proceedings. They may introduce almost any evidence to support their cases, for the Supreme Court has generally refused to impose substantive limits on a grand jury's exercise of discretion. One exception to this course occurred in 1906, in *Hale* v. *Henkel* (201 U.S. 43 [1906]). In this decision, the Court ruled that "a grand jury may not indict upon current rumors or unverified reports." At the same time, however, the justices did agree that indictments could be based on other information—however unreliable—as long as it was not called "rumor." The Court's position on this latter point became more explicit half a century later in the case of *Costello* v. *United States* (350 U.S. 359 [1956]).

The principal in the case was Frank Costello, well known to the federal judiciary as an associate of such underworld figures as Charles "Lucky" Luciano and Vito Genovese. Furthermore, as a syndicate racketeer who had consolidated gambling interests throughout the United States during the 1930s, he had the continuous attention of the Internal Revenue Service.

Early in the 1950s, Frank Costello was indicted by a federal investigatory grand jury for willfully attempting to evade payment of federal income taxes for the years 1947 through 1949. The indictments, however, were based on hearsay evidence. Three FBI agents who had no personal knowledge of Costello's finances appeared before the grand jury and "summarized his net worth on the basis of witnesses who were not called to testify." The agents produced "exhibits," which included newspaper stories about Costello's activities. They also made "computations" based on the "exhibits" to demonstrate that Costello and his wife had received a far greater income during those years than they had reported.

After a trial in which 144 witnesses testified and 368 exhibits were introduced, Costello was convicted. The Supreme Court upheld the indictments against Costello, and in so doing, established a precedent that grand juries may issue indictments based on hearsay evidence—evidence learned through others and not within the personal knowledge of the witness offering it as testimony.

Almost two decades later, the Supreme Court addressed the role of the exclusionary rule in grand jury proceedings, in *United States* v. *Calandra* (414 U.S. 338 [1974]). The case involved the

search of John Calandra's place of business in Cleveland, Ohio. Federal agents, armed with a valid search warrant, were seeking evidence of bookmaking records and gambling paraphernalia. They found none, but during the course of the search they did discover evidence of a loan-sharking operation. Subsequently, a special federal grand jury was convened and Calandra was subpoenaed to answer questions based on the evidence seized. Calandra refused on Fifth Amendment grounds, as well as on the basis that the search and seizure exceeded the scope of the warrant and was in violation of the Fourth Amendment. The district court ordered the evidence suppressed and the U.S. court of appeals affirmed, holding that the exclusionary rule may be invoked by a witness before a grand jury to bar questioning based on illegally obtained evidence.

On an appeal to the U.S. Supreme Court brought by the prosecution, the lower court ruling was reversed. The Court based its decision to allow the evidence to be used on what it found to be the purpose of the exclusionary rule: "The rule is a judicially-created remedy designed to safeguard Fourth Amendment rights generally through its deterrent effects rather than a personal constitutional right of the party aggrieved."

Ex parte *proceeding*

an instrument of the very prosecutorial misconduct it was intended to buffer the citizen against.

One complaint concerns the *ex parte* nature of grand jury proceedings. An *ex parte* is a "one-party" proceeding, meaning that the accused and his or her attorney are not permitted to be present during the grand jury hearing. Under this circumstance, the accused cannot cross-examine witnesses or object to testimony or evidence.

Criticisms leveled against grand juries also suggest abuses of their power as they relate to the granting of immunity. The Fifth Amendment protects individuals against self-incrimination. Traditionally, the government could compel a witness to testify and still protect his or her Fifth Amendment privilege by providing **transactional immunity.** This meant the witness was granted immunity against prosecution in return for testifying. Pursuant to a federal statute in 1970, however, the government adopted a new form of immunity, **use immunity.** This is a limited immunity that prohibits the government only from using the witness's compelled testimony in a subsequent criminal proceeding. If a grand jury witness has been granted use immunity, his or her compelled testimony cannot be used against him or her as direct evidence or as an "investigatory lead" in a subsequent criminal proceeding. At the same time, the prosecutor has an affirmative duty to prove that the evidence he or she proposes to use against the immunity-granted witness was derived from a source wholly independent of the compelled testimony. However, as supported by the Supreme Court's 1972 decision in *Kastigar* v. *United States,*[18] a witness can be indicted on the basis of evidence gathered because of, but "apart" from, his or her testimony. For example, if a grand jury witness has been given use immunity and the compelled testimony reveals that he or she was a participant in a bank robbery, the witness may nevertheless be prosecuted for that crime if the prosecution is able to produce at trial evidence wholly independent of the witness's grand jury testimony. In the final analysis, then, use immunity is not total immunity.

Grand juries also possess *contempt power,* which can be used to compel witnesses to provide testimony needed for criminal investigations. Witnesses who refuse to testify can be jailed for an indefinite period of time until they "purge" themselves of contempt by providing the requested information. This would seemingly result in the abridgment of certain constitutional guarantees.

Other criticisms of the grand jury are that it is really an extension of the prosecution, helping to create "plea bargaining chips," and that it is cumbersome, expensive, and sometimes forces defendants to spend more time in jail awaiting trials.[19]

Transactional immunity: Immunity against prosecution given to a grand jury witness in return for testifying.

Use immunity: A limited immunity that prohibits the government only from using a grand jury witness's compelled testimony in a subsequent criminal proceeding.

In *Kastigar* v. *United States,* the Supreme Court ruled that in any subsequent prosecution of an immunized witness, the government must demonstrate that evidence presented is derived from sources independent of testimony given under a grant of immunity.

Contempt power of grand juries

WILL WORK FOR IMMUNITY FROM PROSECUTION

THE PLEA

After the formal determination of charges through either the information or indictment, the defendant is arraigned, at which time he or she is asked to enter a plea. The four basic pleas, as noted in Chapter 4, are not guilty, guilty, *nolo contendere,* and standing mute. There is also the special plea of not guilty by reason of insanity, as well as other special pleas involving statute of limitations and double jeopardy.

Plea of Not Guilty

The plea of *not guilty,* the most common entry at arraignment, places the full burden on the state to move ahead and prove beyond a reasonable doubt the case charged against the defendant. Under the principles of American jurisprudence, even the "guilty" are morally and legally entitled to make such a plea. In the adversary system of justice, it is the right of everyone charged with a crime to rely on the presumption of innocence. *Standing mute* at arraignment by failing or refusing to enter a plea is presumed to be an entry of not guilty.

Guilty Plea

The guilty plea, whether negotiated or not, has several consequences. It functions not only as an admission of guilt but also as a surrender of the entire array of constitutional rights designed to protect a criminal defendant against unjustified conviction, including the right to remain silent, the right to confront witnesses, the right to a trial by jury, and the right to be proven guilty by proof beyond a reasonable doubt.[20]

Nolo Contendere

Nolo contendere: A plea of "no contest" or "I do not wish to contest," with the same implication as a guilty plea.

The **nolo contendere** plea, which means "no contest," or, more specifically, "I will not contest it," is essentially a guilty plea. It carries with it the surrendering of certain constitutional rights, and conviction is immediate. However, there is one important difference between a *nolo contendere* and a guilty plea. With *nolo contendere,* there is technically no admission of guilt, which protects the accused in civil court should the victim subsequently sue for damages.

The *nolo contendere* plea is not an automatic option at arraignment. It is acceptable in the federal courts and in about half the states, and it may be entered only at the discretion of the judge and the prosecutor. Generally, this plea is entered for the benefit of the accused, but in at least one instance, it carried an unintended consequence for perhaps the whole nation. On August 7, 1973, the *Wall Street Journal* reported that Spiro T. Agnew—at the time vice president of the United States under Richard M. Nixon—was the target of an investigation by a U.S. attorney concerning allegations of kickbacks by contractors, architects, and engineers to officials of Baltimore County, Maryland. The alleged violations of conspiracy, extortion, bribery, and tax statutes were supposed to have extended from the time Agnew was a Baltimore County executive in 1962 through his years in the vice presidency. After several sessions of plea negotiation between Agnew's attorneys and the Justice Department, it was agreed that Agnew would resign the vice presidency and plead *nolo contendere* to a single charge of income tax evasion. In return, the Justice Department would not proceed with indictment on the other charges. On October 10, 1973, Agnew announced his resignation and entered his plea. It was accepted by Federal District Judge Walter Hoffman, and Agnew received a $10,000 fine and 3 years' unsupervised probation.

Seven years later, Judge Hoffman recalled the case and remarked that accepting Agnew's plea had been a "wise decision." Had he not accepted the plea, Agnew would have been indicted, tried, and, upon conviction, probably would have appealed. This would have meant that the case would still have been pending when President Nixon resigned from the presidency on August 9, 1974. As Hoffman put it, "When Nixon resigned, Agnew would automatically have been President of the United States."[21]

Insanity Plea

The plea of *not guilty by reason of insanity* is generally not to the advantage of the accused, for it is an admission of guilt with the contention that the commission of the crime is not culpable in the eyes of the law because of the insanity of the defendant at the time he or she committed the act. More typically, a dual plea of not guilty and not guilty by reason of insanity is entered, which implies, "the burden is on the government to prove that I did the act upon which the charge is based, and, even if the government proves that at trial, I still claim I am not culpable because I was legally insane at the time."[22]

Not all jurisdictions have a separate insanity plea, nor do all have the dual plea of not guilty–not guilty by reason of insanity. In these instances, a plea of not guilty is entered and it is the burden of the defense to raise the issue of insanity. However, even in jurisdictions where the statutes allow the insanity plea, the accused and his or her counsel must present an *affirmative defense*. In law, this defense amounts to something more than just a mere denial of the prosecution's allegations. Thus, while the burden of proving the guilt of the accused is on the state, evidencing insanity at the time of the commission of the offense generally rests with the defendant.

In recent years there has been considerable opposition to the insanity plea. However, studies suggest that the general public drastically overestimates the incidence of successful insanity pleas, primarily because the insanity cases are among the most highly publicized. In reality, comparatively few defendants enter pleas of not guilty by reason of insanity. Furthermore, the insanity defense rarely wins. Of the millions of criminal cases disposed of each year in state and federal courts, less than one-tenth of 1 percent involve insanity pleas, only one in four of such pleas lead to acquittals, and the majority of these involve misdemeanor charges.[23]

An affirmative defense is one that amounts to something more than the mere denial of the prosecution's allegations; it requires the defense to provide new material and evidence in support of its position.

Pleas of Statute of Limitations

Every state has laws known as "statutes of limitations," which bar prosecution for most crimes after a certain amount of time has passed; that is, the suspect must be accused within a reasonable period of time after the offense was committed. The reasons for these statutes are numerous. After the passage of time, for example, defendants may be unable to establish their whereabouts at the time of the crime, or evidence or witnesses supporting their innocence might be lost. Furthermore, during the long period of time since the offense the offender may have become a law-abiding citizen who presents no further threat to the community, and conviction and sentencing would serve little purpose.

Statutes of limitations can be quite complex. Generally, such statutes do not apply to murder prosecutions. Furthermore, statutes for other offenses may be *tolled* (suspended) by reason of circumstances, such as the defendant's absence from the state. And finally, in most jurisdictions the plea of statute of limitations must be entered at arraignment; otherwise the accused will be deemed to have waived that particular defense.[24]

Double Jeopardy

Double jeopardy: Multiple prosecutions for the same offense and/or multiple punishments for the same crime; prohibited by the Fifth Amendment.

To restrain the government from repeatedly prosecuting an accused for one particular offense, the prohibition against **double jeopardy**—two trials for one offense—was included in the Constitution. The Fifth Amendment provides in part: "Nor shall any person be subject for the same offense to be twice put in jeopardy of life or limb."

The Supreme Court has held that this guarantee protects the accused against both multiple prosecutions for the same offense and multiple punishments for the same crime. However, to whom and when the Fifth Amendment guarantee applies are matters that have taken the Supreme Court almost two centuries to clarify.

United States v. *Perez* in 1824 denied double jeopardy protection in cases in which a jury failed to agree on a verdict.[25] In 1896, the Court ruled in *United States* v. *Ball* that if a conviction is set aside for some reason other than insufficient evidence, the defendant may be tried again for the same offense.[26] *Wade* v. *Hunter* in 1949,[27] following a similar line, declared that the double jeopardy clause did not apply in certain circumstances of mistrial.

Palko v. Connecticut: The Supreme Court ruling that the due process clause of the Fourteenth Amendment does not require the states to observe the double jeopardy guarantee of the Fifth Amendment.

Benton v. Maryland: The Supreme Court ruling that overruled *Palko* and extended the double jeopardy protection to state actions.

As noted earlier in some detail in Chapter 4, the application of the double jeopardy clause to state criminal trials was rejected by the Supreme Court in the 1937 case of **Palko v. Connecticut.**[28] Some three decades later, however, in **Benton v. Maryland,**[29] the majority opinion declared that the double jeopardy clause applied to the states through the due process clause of the Fourteenth Amendment. Finally, in **Downum v. United States,**[30] the Court declared that double jeopardy begins at the point when the second trial jury is sworn in.

Downum v. United States: The Supreme Court ruling that double jeopardy begins at the point where the second trial jury is sworn in.

Plea Bargaining

Plea bargaining, which can occur at any point during the pretrial and trial phases, is one of the most commonly accepted practices in criminal justice processing. Furthermore, it is generally believed that more than 90 percent of criminal convictions result from negotiated pleas of guilty. Plea bargaining takes place between the prosecutor and the defense counsel or the accused, and involves discussions that aim toward an agreement under which the defendant will enter a plea of guilty in exchange for some prosecutorial or judicial concession. These concessions are of four possible types:

1. The initial charges may be reduced to some lesser offense, thus ensuring a reduction in the sentence imposed.

2. In instances of multiple criminal charges, the number of counts may be reduced.

3. A recommendation for leniency may be made by the prosecutor, thus reducing the potential sentence from one of incarceration to probation.

4. In instances where the charges involve a negative label, such as child molesting, the complaint may be altered to a less repugnant one, such as assault.

Although plea bargaining would appear to compromise the integrity of the criminal justice process, it has received the blessing of the U.S. Supreme Court. The High Court once commented that although there may be neither a constitutional nor a statutory basis for plea bargaining, the practice can nevertheless serve the interests of both the accused and the court. This formal recognition of the previously unacknowledged custom of plea negotiation, however, occurred only in 1970. In **Brady v. United States,**[31] the Court upheld the use of plea bargaining, advising that it provided a "mutuality of advantage" for the state and for the defendant. In later declarations, the Supreme Court also built a number of safeguards into the bargaining process. In 1971, it maintained that the promise of a prosecutor made during plea negotiations must be kept;[32] and in 1976, the Court ruled that to be valid, a guilty plea had to be *voluntarily* made and entered with full knowledge of its implications.[33]

PRETRIAL MOTIONS

All pleas of not guilty (other than those dismissed on statute of limitations or double jeopardy grounds) result in the setting of a trial date. Prior to the actual commencement of the trial, however, and sometimes prior to arraignment, both the defense and the prosecution may employ a number of motions. A **motion** is a formal application or request to the court for some action, such as an order or rule. The purpose of motions is to gain some legal advantage, and most are initiated by the defense. The number and type of motions vary by the nature and complexity of the case, and it is the court's role to decide whether each should be granted or denied. Without question, the court's decision in these matters can have a considerable impact on the outcome of a proceeding.

Motion: A formal application or request to the court for some action.

Motion for Discovery

It is always in the best interests of the defense to know in advance what witnesses and kinds of evidence the prosecution plans to introduce at trial. The motion for discovery is a request to examine the physical evidence, evidentiary documents, and lists of witnesses in the possession of the prosecutor. Although some jurisdictions may resist such a motion, discovery is a matter of constitutional law. The Supreme Court's decision in the 1963 case of *Brady* v. *Maryland* held that a prosecutor's failure to disclose evidence favorable to the accused upon request violates due process.[34] However, in *Moore* v. *Illinois* some years later,[35] the Court also ruled that there was no constitutional requirement for the prosecution to fully disclose the entire case file to the defense.

Motion for Change of Venue

Venue, from the Latin meaning "neighborhood," refers to the county or district—not the jurisdiction—wherein a case is to be tried. A motion for a change of venue is a request that the trial be moved from the county, district, or circuit in which the crime was committed to some other place. The jurisdiction does not change; the original trial court simply moves if the motion is granted.

Either the defense or the prosecution can introduce such a motion. Typically, however, it is a move made by the defense in the case of sensational or highly publicized crimes when it is felt that the accused cannot obtain a fair trial in the particular locale of the court.

Motion for Suppression

Mapp v. *Ohio, Escobedo* v. *Illinois,* and *Miranda* v. *Arizona* collectively served to make suppression one of the most common of pretrial motions in criminal cases.[36] The motion for suppression is a request to have evidence excluded from consideration. Typically, it is filed by the defense to prohibit evidence that was obtained as the result of an illegal search and seizure or wiretap or to challenge the validity of a confession.

Motion for a Bill of Particulars

A *bill of particulars* is a written statement that specifies additional facts about the charges contained in the information or indictment. As a motion filed by the defense, it is a request for more details from the prosecution. The motion is not made for the purpose of discovering evidence or of learning exactly how much the prosecution knows, and it is not designed to suggest an insufficient indictment. Rather, the motion for a bill of particulars asks for details about what the prosecution claims in order to give the accused fair notice of what must be defended. For example, if a neighborhood bookmaker who operates illegal lotteries and off-track betting schemes is charged with possession of gambling paraphernalia, the defense might wish to know which of the confiscated materials (policy slips, betting cards, and so on) the prosecutor intends to use as the basis of his or her action.

A bill of particulars is a written statement that specifies additional facts about a charge.

Motion for Severance of Charges or Defendants

Many legal actions involve multiple charges against one defendant. The accused may have been arrested, for example, for a number of different crimes resulting from a single incident—an auto theft, for example, followed by destruction of property, resisting arrest, and assault upon a police officer. Or the accused may be charged with multiple counts of the same offense—perhaps several sales of dangerous drugs during a given period of time. In both instances, and for the sake of expediency, the prosecution may consolidate these multiple charges into a single case. The defense, however, may feel that different tactics are required for dealing with each charge. Thus, the *motion for severance of charges* requests that each specific charge be tried as a separate case.

Similarly, many proceedings involve more than one person charged with participation in the same crime—perhaps four codefendants in a bank robbery. There are times when the best interests of one or more of the accused are served by separate trials. Defendant Joe Smith, for example, may wish a trial by jury; defendant Sarah Jones may wish to place the blame on her co-defendants. Thus, the *motion for severance of defendants* requests that one or more of the accused be tried in separate proceedings.

It should be pointed out here that recent research has demonstrated that *joinders* (of charges and/or defendants) may have prejudicial effects. In several mock jury experiments, for example, "jurors" were presented with cases in which "defendants" were charged with individual or multiple charges. When defendants had joined trials, there was a greater tendency to convict. When charges were joined, jurors confused the evidence among the charges and made more negative inferences about the character of the defendant.[37]

Motion for Continuance

The *motion for continuance* requests that the trial be postponed to some future date. Such a motion is filed by the defense or the prosecution on the grounds that there has not been sufficient time to prepare the case. There may, for example, have been difficulty in gathering evidence or locating witnesses.

The witness stand in the Edgefield County courthouse, Edgefield, South Carolina.

This motion is used by some defense attorneys as a stalling tactic to enhance the accused's chances. As one lawyer in Brooklyn, New York, commented:

> If you can delay a case long enough, victims' memories begin to fail, witnesses begin to lose interest, and the court wants to move on to other things. Sometimes you end up working out a better plea, and on two separate occasions we actually managed to get the cases dismissed because of lack of witnesses.[38]

Motion for Dismissal

As a matter of common practice, at arraignment, defense attorneys make a motion for dismissal of charges on the grounds that the prosecution has failed to produce sufficient evidence to warrant further processing. Justified or not, this is an almost automatic motion filed by most defense attorneys. In practically all instances, however, such a motion is denied by the judge. There are other situations, though, where the motion for dismissal is fully warranted and is granted by the presiding magistrate. A previously granted motion for suppression, for example, may have weakened the state's case. Here it could be the defense or the prosecution who files the motion.

Other pretrial motions may include requests to inspect grand jury minutes, to determine sanity, or to discover statements made by prosecution witnesses. By far, however, the most common are the motions for suppression and dismissal.

Time From Arrest to Disposition in State Court Cases

SOURCE: Bureau of Justice Statistics.

Speedy trial: The Sixth Amendment guarantee that protects an accused from indefinite incarceration prior to coming to trial.

Sixth Amendment: Amendment to the Constitution guaranteeing the right to:

- A speedy and public trial, by an impartial jury, in the district where the offense was committed
- Notice of charges
- Confrontation with witnesses
- Compulsory process for obtaining witnesses
- Assistance of counsel

The Constitution offers no clues as to what its framers had in mind when they incorporated the concept of "speedy trial" into the Bill of Rights.

It should be emphasized here that if a motion by the defense results in the dismissal of a case, the prosecution has the legal authority to reinstate the case. Charges can be filed, dismissed, and refiled, for there is no double jeopardy connected with the pretrial process. As noted in *Downum* v. *United States* and reaffirmed by the Supreme Court in *Serfass* v. *United States,*[39] in a jury trial, jeopardy attaches when the jury is impaneled and sworn; in a bench trial, jeopardy attaches when the court begins to hear evidence.

SPEEDY AND PUBLIC TRIAL

It is no surprise that the right to a **speedy trial** appears in the Constitution of the United States. Without it, persons accused of crimes would have no protection against indefinite incarceration prior to coming to trial. Like all other provisions in the Bill of Rights, the guarantee of a speedy trial is a measure devised solely to ensure the rights of individual defendants, rather than to protect the state from delays that might be caused by the accused.

Putting the speedy trial clause of the **Sixth Amendment** into practice, however, has been difficult. *First,* since the early days of the Constitution, the criminal justice system has become more complex. Many procedural steps have been added to criminal proceedings in order to guarantee a fair hearing for the accused. *Second,* increasing numbers of persons are accused of violations of the law each year, making delays inevitable. Furthermore, in many metropolitan areas where crime rates are high, it is difficult for some defendants to receive any trial at all, not to mention a speedy one. *Third,* the criminal law has become more detailed and elaborate over the years. Some state statutes have become so highly specific that the evidence-gathering process in many cases has evolved into a time-consuming task. *Fourth,* the requirement that the judicial contest be conducted with promptness must be balanced against the right of an accused as well as of a prosecutor to have ample time to prepare their cases before going to trial. *Fifth,* some trials are inexcusably delayed by either the prosecution or the defense for the purpose of achieving their own objectives. A prosecutor, for example, may seek several continuances, hoping to put off a trial until an accused's codefendant is convinced to "strike a deal" and become a witness for the state. A defense attorney may employ the same delaying tactics in anticipation of witnesses' loss of interest in the case. *Sixth,* some delays result from little more than prosecutors' apathy or lack of concern for defendants' rights and humanity. And *seventh,* there is no consensus among the states as to the meaning of "speedy trial." Statutory time limits vary by jurisdiction and by the nature of the offense charged. Here are three examples:

- In California, the period between arraignment and trial must not exceed 56 days.[40]
- In Alabama, the time limit between arrest and trial is set at 12 months for misdemeanors and at 3 years for all felonies—except capital offenses, for which there is no limit.[41]
- In Maine, there is a flexible standard of "unnecessary delay"—whatever that might mean.[42]

The Supreme Court and Speedy Trial

The Constitution offers no clues as to what its framers had in mind when they incorporated the concept of "speedy trial" into the Bill of Rights. As a result, the Supreme Court has attached a standard of *reasonableness* to the right, which represents an attempt at a balancing of interests—weighing the effects of delays against their causes and justifications. The Court emphasized this posture as early as 1905, when it ruled that the right to a speedy trial was only a "relative" matter "consistent with delays and dependent on circumstances."[43]

Speedy Trial and the States

Speedy trial, a constitutional guarantee at the federal level since the framing of the Bill of Rights, was not made applicable to the states until relatively recently. The vehicle was ***Klopfer* v. *North Carolina*,**[44] decided in 1967.

The petitioner in this somewhat unusual case was Peter H. Klopfer, a professor of zoology at Duke University. Klopfer had been indicted by the state of North Carolina for criminal trespass as the result of a sit-in at a segregated motel and restaurant. At trial, however, the jury failed to agree on a verdict. This resulted in a mistrial, thus necessitating a new trial. But after a year had passed and the second trial had not been ordered, Professor Klopfer demanded that his case either be tried immediately or dismissed. Rather than complying with the petitioner's demands, the presiding judge instead granted the prosecutor's request for a *nolle prosequi*. At the time, this allowed the prosecutor to place the indictment in an inactive status without bringing it to trial—and thus retaining it for use at any time in the future. On appeal to the North Carolina Supreme Court, Klopfer argued that the trial judge's action denied his Sixth Amendment right, which he regarded as applicable to the states. The Carolina appeals court ruled that a defendant's right to a speedy trial did not encompass "the right to compel the state to prosecute him." Thus, still in limbo with this "suspended" trespass indictment, Klopfer petitioned the U.S. Supreme Court.

The Court ruled in favor of Professor Klopfer, and more. First, it unanimously struck down the recalcitrant North Carolina law that allowed indefinite postponement of a criminal prosecution without dismissal of an indictment. At the same time, the High Court extended the speedy trial clause to the states.

***Klopfer* v. *North Carolina*:**　The Supreme Court ruling that the Sixth Amendment right to a speedy trial applies in state as well as federal proceedings.

The Right to a Public Trial

The Sixth Amendment provides not only for a speedy trial, but for a *public trial* as well—a guarantee with its roots in our heritage of English common law. (For a detailed look at a trial that became *very* public, see the discussion of the Scopes "monkey trial" in Exhibit 9.2.)

The traditional Anglo-American distrust for secret trials evolved from the notorious use of the practice by the Spanish Inquisition and the French monarchy's use of the *lettre de cachet*. In the hands of despotic groups, these institutions became instruments of political and religious suppression through their ruthless disregard of the accused's right to a fair trial.

Although all jurisdictions have adopted the Sixth Amendment right to a public trial through state constitutions, by statute, or by judicial decisions, there have been exceptions in the recent past. *In re Oliver,*[45] decided in 1948, was one of the very few cases addressed by the Supreme Court on the right to a public trial. The issue in *Oliver* stemmed from the actions of a Michigan judge serving in the role of a one-person grand jury. The judge's actions were described in the High Court's opinion:

> In the case before us, the petitioner was called as a witness to testify in secret before a one-man grand jury conducting a grand jury investigation. In the midst of petitioner's testimony the proceedings abruptly changed. The investigation became a "trial," the grand jury became a judge, and the witness became an accused charged with contempt of court—all in secret. . . .
>
> Following a charge, conviction, and sentence, the petitioner was led away to prison—still without any break in the secrecy. Even in jail, according to undenied

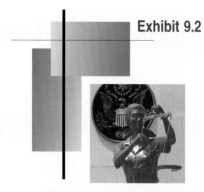

Exhibit 9.2   **Historical Perspectives on Crime and Justice**
The Scopes "Monkey Trial"

Anti-evolution books being sold during the Scopes "monkey trial."

One of the more curious and notable cases in the annals of criminal justice history occurred during the 1920s in the remote mountain town of Dayton, Tennessee, a community of less than 2,000 persons some 100 miles southeast of Nashville. The accused was 24-year-old John Thomas Scopes, a high school teacher charged with a relatively minor criminal offense in violation of a Tennessee statute. The Scopes case caught the attention of the entire world, and today it is still considered by many to be among the country's most famous criminal trials.

At the root of *Tennessee* v. *Scopes* was a movement of religious conservatism that had emerged early in the twentieth century in parts of the South and Midwest. This conservative movement was a reaction to the developing liberal theology that was attempting to recast Christian teaching in light of the scientific and historic thought of the time. By 1909, those who saw the orthodox truths of Christianity to be in danger organized a protest against the new "modernists" in a 12-volume publication called *The Fundamentals.* In this work, five points of doctrine were set forth as fundamental: the Virgin birth, the physical resurrection of Christ, his substitutional atonement on the Cross, the physical second coming of Christ, and the *total* infallibility of the Holy Scriptures. Those who believed in the strict letter of the Bible and refused to accept any teachings, including those of science and philosophy, that seemed to conflict with it began in 1921 to call themselves

Fundamentalists. They came primarily from the Baptists and Presbyterians, but many came from other Protestant denominations as well. The modernists, in contrast, tried to reconcile their beliefs with scientific thought—to discard that which was out of date, to retain what was essential and intellectually respectable, and generally to mediate between Christianity and the skeptical spirit of the age.

During the early 1920s, Fundamentalist politicians introduced bills into the legislatures of nearly half the states that were designed to forbid the teaching of Charles Darwin's theory of evolution. These efforts failed in most states, but in Tennessee, Oklahoma, and Mississippi the Fundamentalists fully succeeded in writing their anachronistic views into law. The Tennessee legislature, dominated by Fundamentalists, approved a bill known as the Butler Act, which specifically provided as follows:

It shall be unlawful for any teacher in any of the universities, normals [colleges of education] and all other public

schools of the State, which are supported in whole or in part by the public school funds of the State, to teach any theory that denies the story of the Divine creation of man as taught in the Bible, and to teach instead that man has descended from a lower order of animals.

This statement sets the scene for the Scopes trial, which pitted the beliefs of religious fundamentalism against the principles of scientific modernism.

Shortly after the new Tennessee law had become official, the American Civil Liberties Union (ACLU)—questioning the constitutionality of legislation that prohibited the teaching of evolution—began agitating for a test case. After some persuasion, John T. Scopes, a biology instructor at the Dayton, Tennessee, high school, volunteered for the challenge. It was during the late spring of 1925, and after only a few lectures on evolution, young Scopes was arrested for "undermining the peace and dignity of the State."

Attorney General A. T. Stewart of the Eighteenth Judicial Circuit of Tennessee was in charge of the prosecution. Well known to the judiciary in that region as a shrewd courtroom lawyer, Stewart was also an impassioned rabble-rousing orator. A number of local attorneys who had volunteered their services without pay also were attached to the state's case as lawyers *pro hac vice* ("for this occasion"). When the eminent statesman William Jennings Bryan offered to assist in the prosecution, what might have been only a minor criminal case in a rural county court suddenly became an international media event. At the time, Bryan was a distinguished figure in the minds of most Americans. He had been a member of the U.S. House of Representatives, the Democratic nominee for the U.S. presidency three times, and President Woodrow Wilson's Secretary of State. After his retirement from politics he had become a chief spokesman for the Fundamentalist movement, drafting legislative resolutions banning the teaching of Darwinian theory in public school systems.

With Bryan's appearance in the case, the ACLU secured for Scopes the services of three attorneys, including the acclaimed Clarence Seward Darrow. As a defense lawyer, Darrow's abilities were considered unparalleled. His reputation had reached national proportions in 1924, when he rep-

resented Nathan Leopold and Richard Loeb in a Chicago courtroom. Although both Leopold and Loeb had been convicted and sentenced to terms of life plus 99 years for kidnapping and murder, Darrow's courtroom approaches, including the presentation of novel forms of evidence based on psychiatric examinations, had been viewed as unique for the time.

In the minds of the public the Scopes trial was characterized as a battle between religious conservatism on the one hand and twentieth-century skepticism on the other. As the day of the trial approached, revivalists of every sort flocked to Dayton, ready to defend their faith against the onslaught of "science" and "foreigners"—yet at the same time curious to know what evolutionary theory was really all about. The hearings convened amid a circus atmosphere of hot dog and lemonade vendors, booksellers, hundreds of newspaper reporters, photographers, Western Union telegraph operators, and more than 30,000 curiosity seekers. Worldwide attention focused on the small Tennessee town. To many observers, it was "the trial of the century."

What followed was a most peculiar and bitter trial. Referred to in the media as the Scopes "monkey trial," it began on July 10, with a heated denouncement of evolutionary theory by Attorney General Stewart. He called it an "insidious doctrine" that was "undermining

the faith of Tennessee's children and robbing them of their chance of eternal life." Bryan charged that Darrow's only purpose in accepting the case was to slur the Bible, and Darrow spoke of his opponent's position as simply "fool religion." The litigation continued for days, with little accomplished in terms of legal precedent.

On the afternoon of July 20, the trial finally approached its climax when the defense requested that William Jennings Bryan be placed on the stand as an expert on the Bible. Bryan consented. Popular historian Frederick Lewis Allen has described the scene:

> So great was the crowd that afternoon that the judge had decided to move the court outdoors, to a platform built against the courthouse under the maple trees. Benches were set out before it. The reporters sat on the benches, on the ground, anywhere, and scribbled their stories. On the outskirts of the seated crowd a throng stood in the hot sunlight which streamed down through the trees. And on the platform sat the shirt-sleeved Clarence Darrow, a Bible on his knee, and put the Fundamentalist champion through one of the strangest examinations which ever took place in a court of law.

Soaring to awesome heights of hyperbole, Bryan declared that the Bible *must* be taken literally. Preaching fire and brimstone, he asserted that only those who believed in the letter of the Scriptures could ever be saved. What then followed was a savage encounter. Darrow asked Bryan about Jonah and the whale, Joshua and the sun, the date of the Great Flood, and the significance of the Tower of Babel. Bryan affirmed his belief that the world was created in 4004 B.C.; that it had taken the Lord but 6 days; that the Flood occurred around 2348 B.C.; that Eve had

From ape to man.

literally been fashioned out of Adam's rib; that the Tower of Babel was directly responsible for the diversity of languages in the world; that Joshua had moved the sun; and that a "big fish" had swallowed Jonah. He had fallen into Darrow's trap; it had quickly become clear that the naive religious faith of the Fundamentalists could not face Reason as prosecutor. Bryan was laughed off the witness stand by a hooting audience. Several days later, humiliated and morose at what was an absurd end to his remarkable career, Bryan died suddenly of a heart attack.

In the end, the presiding judge expunged Bryan's testimony from the record and barred Clarence Darrow from placing any scientific evidence before the jury. Scopes was convicted and fined $100. On appeal to the Tennessee Supreme Court, the antievolution law was upheld, but Scopes was exonerated on a technicality, thus preventing further appeal to the U.S. Supreme Court.

In theory, Fundamentalism had won. The Tennessee law stood (and would not be repealed for more than 40 years). But in reality, the conservative religious movement and the Tennessee courts and legislature had suffered a crushing defeat. Observers everywhere viewed the trial with amazement, wondering how long such ignorance would continue to control the Tennessee judicial system. It appeared too that there was another defeat as well—one involving democracy. As columnist Walter Lippmann put it at the time, the people of Tennessee had used the power of democracy to prevent their own children from learning "not merely the doctrine of evolution, but the spirit and method by which learning is possible." In so doing, he continued, they had revealed the "deep destructive confusion" that lay within the dogma of democratic majority rule.

In the decades that followed, the Scopes "monkey trial" has not been forgotten. Hundreds of books and articles have been written about the events that took place in Dayton, Tennessee, during July 1925. As for the issue that initiated the Scopes trial, it never passed into obscurity. Even at the end of the twentieth century, discussions continued across the United States as to whether both biblical and scientific explanations of creation should be taught in public school classrooms.

SOURCES: Frederick Lewis Allen, *Only Yesterday: An Informal History of the 1920s* (New York: Harper & Row, 1931); Leslie H. Allen, *Bryan and Darrow of Dayton* (New York: Arthur Lee, 1925); L. Sprague de Camp, *The Great Monkey Trial* (Garden City: Doubleday, 1968); Louis Gasper, *The Fundamentalist Movement* (Paris: Mouton, 1963); Ronald Steel, *Walter Lippmann and the American Century* (Boston: Little, Brown, 1980).

allegations, his lawyer was denied an opportunity to see and confer with him. And that was not the end of the secrecy. His lawyer filed in the state supreme court this *habeas corpus* proceeding. Even there, the mantle of secrecy enveloped the transaction and the state supreme court ordered him sent back to jail without ever having seen a record of his testimony, and without knowing all that took place in the secrecy of the judge's chambers. In view of this nation's historic distrust of secret proceedings, their inherent dangers to freedom, and the universal requirement of our federal and state governments that criminal trials be public, the Fourteenth Amendment's guarantee that no one shall be deprived of his liberty without due process of law means that at least an accused cannot be thus sentenced to prison.

The Court further held that the failure to give the accused a reasonable opportunity to defend himself against the contempt charge was a denial of due process of law. Yet curiously, despite the justices' pronouncement in behalf of the petitioner, *Oliver* did not expressly incorporate the Sixth Amendment right to a public trial within the meaning of the Fourteenth Amendment. This did not occur until 20 years later, in a footnote to *Duncan* v. *Louisiana*,[46] discussed in the next section.

THE JURY

As a criminal prosecution approaches the trial date, a pretrial hearing is held, at which point the pretrial motions are heard and dealt with by the judge. At the same time, the court also asks whether the accused wishes a trial by judge or a trial by jury.

The trial by judge (or judges), more commonly referred to as a *bench trial,* is one in which the decision of guilty or not guilty is made by the presiding judge. In some jurisdictions the decision regarding trial by judge may be dictated by state requirements. Under Tennessee statutes, for example, the accused is not prevented from waiving his or her right to a trial by jury;[47] in Idaho, however, this waiver is permitted only in nonfelony cases.[48]

When defendants are in a position to exercise a choice, there are several circumstances under which the bench trial would probably be more desirable. For example, the crime may be so reprehensible or so widely publicized that finding a neutral jury could be difficult if not impossible. Or the nature of the defense may be too complex or technical for persons untrained in law to fully comprehend. Also, the presiding judge may have a previous record of favorable decisions in like cases. In addition, there is the possible effect of the defendant's appearance and past record on the jury:

> The general appearance of the defendant may be such that a jury may become more prejudiced against him. The defendant may have a serious past criminal record subjecting him to possible impeachment should he take the witness stand in his own defense, and the probability of the jury convicting the defendant on his past record rather than on the evidence contended in the present charge is great. Or the defendant may be a part of an organized criminal syndicate, or minority group of which local feeling is against, and the jury may convict the accused by association rather than on the facts of the case. A judge is considered less inclined to be affected by any of these situations than a jury.[49]

A crime analyst displaying evidence at a murder trial.

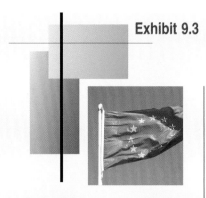

Exhibit 9.3

International Perspectives on Crime and Justice
Law and Disorder in the Italian Courts

In the village of Muro Lucano, a small community in southern Italy, an 18-year-old woman brought an accusation of rape against her driving instructor, Carmine Cristiano. She claimed that during her driving lesson, Cristiano drove her to an isolated spot, forced her out of the car, and then raped her. At trial in 1996, he argued that the sex had been consensual. The court seemed to believe him, for he was convicted of a lesser charge of "indecent exposure in a public place." The woman then appealed, and Cristiano was convicted and sentenced on the original charge of rape. In 1999, however, Italy's highest criminal appeals court, the Court of Cassa-

tion in Rome, overturned the conviction—for a most unusual reason: Pointing out that the victim was wearing jeans at the time of the alleged offense, the court stated that it was "common knowledge" that jeans "cannot even be partly removed without the effective help of the person wearing them," and that it is "impossible, if the victim is struggling with all her force."

Not surprisingly, the decision drew expressions of outrage throughout Italy, the United States, and other parts of the world. Alessandra Mussolini, a member of the Italian Parliament and the granddaughter of the former fascist leader Benito Mussolini, commented that "the judges obviously have no sensitivity to the psychology of rape—no understanding of how victims think or how real life works." How the Italian courts will ultimately resolve cases of this type is difficult to forecast.

A judge in an Italian trial court.

SOURCE: *New York Times,* February 16, 1999, p. A6.

The reasons for selecting a trial by jury are perhaps even more compelling. The jury serves as a safeguard against overzealous prosecutors and biased judges, and it affords the accused the benefit of commonsense judgment as opposed to the perhaps less sympathetic reactions of a single magistrate. (For an example of an Italian court's biased opinion, see Exhibit 9.3.)

The Right to Trial by Jury

The trial by jury is a distinctive feature of the Anglo-American system of justice, dating back more than 7 centuries. When the Magna Carta was signed in the year 1215, it contained a special provision that no freeholder would be deprived of life or property except by judgment of his or her peers. This common law principle was incorporated into the Constitution of the United States. Article III contains this simple and straightforward statement: "The trial of all crimes, except in cases of impeachment, shall be by jury." Article III is reaffirmed by the Sixth Amendment, which holds that "in all criminal prosecutions, the accused shall enjoy the right to a speedy and public trial by an impartial jury."

In federal cases, where Article III applies directly, the Supreme Court has been unrelenting in its view that a jury in criminal cases must contain

12 persons and reach a unanimous verdict. Curiously, however, for almost two centuries after the framing of the Constitution, the right to a trial by jury "in all criminal prosecutions" was not fully binding in state trials. Despite Article III and the Sixth Amendment, some state statutes denied the right to many defendants. What ultimately brought the right to a jury trial to the states was *Duncan v. Louisiana,*[50] decided in 1968.

The setting was Plaquemines Parish, Louisiana, an oil-rich community about 50 miles northwest of New Orleans. At the time, Plaquemines Parish had long been bossed by the skillful political leader Leander H. Perez, a virulent segregationist whose philosophies and opinions seemingly influenced local folkways. Gary Duncan, a 19-year-old African American youth, had been tried in the local court on a charge of simple battery—a misdemeanor punishable by a maximum of 2 years' imprisonment and a $300 fine. His crime had involved no more than slapping the elbow of a white youth. He was convicted, fined $150, and sentenced to 60 days in jail. Duncan had requested a trial by jury, but this was denied on the authority of the Louisiana constitution, which granted jury trials only in cases in which capital punishment or imprisonment at hard labor could be imposed. Duncan appealed to the U.S. Supreme Court, contending that his right to a jury trial was guaranteed by the Sixth and Fourteenth Amendments.

In a 7-to-2 decision, the Court ruled in favor of Duncan, thus incorporating the Sixth Amendment right to a jury into the due process clause of the Fourteenth Amendment. In the words of Justice Byron White:

> Because we believe that trial by jury in criminal cases is fundamental to the American scheme of justice, we hold that the Fourteenth Amendment guarantees a right of jury trial in all criminal cases which—were they to be tried in federal court— would come within the Sixth Amendment's guarantee. Since we consider the appeal before us to be such a case, we hold that the Constitution was violated when appellant's demand for jury trial was refused.

An unresolved issue in the case related to a segment of Justice White's opinion in *Duncan.* He had pointed out that so-called petty offenses were traditionally tried without a jury. That would continue to be so, but beyond that he offered no distinction between serious and petty offenses in state cases. Two years later the court brought this matter to rest when it defined a petty offense as one carrying a maximum sentence of 6 months or less.[51]

Jury Selection

Historically, trial juries—sometimes referred to as *petit juries* to differentiate them from grand juries—have typically consisted of 12 jurors. In all federal prosecutions, 12-member juries are required, but not in all state prosecutions. In *Williams* v. *Florida,*[52] decided in 1970, the Court ruled that it was proper for states to use juries composed of as few as six persons, at least in noncapital cases.

Jury selection involves a series of procedural steps, beginning with the preparation of a master list of eligible jurors. Eligibility requirements generally include citizenship and literacy. In addition, there are restrictions against minors, persons with serious felony convictions, and occupational groups such as physicians, attorneys, police officers, legislators, the clergy, and several others, depending on the rules of the jurisdiction. Others, such as the aged, disabled, mothers with young children, and persons whose employers will not allow it, may be exempted from jury service on the basis of hardship. Not too many exemptions can be allowed in preparing the master list, however, because an "impartial" jury in constitutional terms means a representative cross section of a community's citizens. This is why the Supreme Court in 1975

Duncan v. Louisiana: The Supreme Court ruling that the Fourteenth Amendment's guarantee of due process requires states to provide trial by jury to persons accused of serious crimes.

struck down a Louisiana law that barred women from juries unless they specifically requested, in writing, to participate.[53]

In current practice, the basis of the master list in many communities is the local voter registration roll. This source, at least in theory, is considered to be representative of the population, and it is readily available. However, studies of voting behavior have demonstrated that registration lists are highly biased as sources of jury pools. From 30 percent to 50 percent of those eligible in various jurisdictions do not register to vote. Furthermore, one study found the registration rates for low-income persons to be only 61.2 percent, compared to 85 percent for those with considerably high incomes.[54] Similarly, members of racial minorities, young people, and the poorly educated more frequently ignore the electoral process or have been excluded from it by legal or extralegal means. To mitigate this difficulty, some communities have initiated the use of multiple-source lists, supplementing voter registration lists with names drawn from rosters of licensed drivers and telephone directories.

The *Venire*

Venire: A writ that summons jurors.

From the master list of eligible jurors, names are randomly selected for the *venire.* The *venire,* or *venire facias,* is the writ that summons jurors. More commonly, however, the *venire* refers to the list of potential jurors who are eligible for a given period of service. These summoned jurors become members of a jury pool, and they are interviewed to confirm their eligibility and availability. Those who remain in the pool are paid for their time; the current rate ranges from $15 to $30 per day.

The procedure through which members of the jury pool become actual trial jurors begins with the selection of a *jury panel.* In a felony prosecution that requires 12 jurors, as many as 30, and sometimes more than 100, are selected for the panel. Their names are drawn at random by the clerk of the court, and from there they move on to the *voir dire* examination.

The *Voir Dire*

Voir dire: An oath sworn by a juror regarding his or her qualifications.

A ***voir dire,*** meaning "to speak the truth," is an oath sworn by a prospective juror regarding his or her qualifications as a juror. The *voir dire* examination involves questioning by the prosecutor, defense attorney, and sometimes the judge in order to determine a candidate's fitness to serve as a juror. The inquiry focuses on the person's background, familiarity with the case, associations with persons involved in the case, attitudes about certain facts that might arise during the trial, and any other matters that may reflect upon his or her willingness and ability to judge the case fairly and impartially. A potential juror who is deemed unacceptable to either the prosecutor or the defense is eliminated through either the challenge for cause or the peremptory challenge.

Challenge for cause

The *challenge for cause* means that there is a sound legal reason to remove a potential juror, and whoever makes such a challenge—either the defense attorney or the prosecutor—must explain to the judge the nature of the concern. Typically, challenges for cause allege that the prospective juror would be incapable of judging the accused fairly. Such challenges are controlled by statute, and the decision to remove a juror is vested with the court. Also, there is technically no limit on the number of challenges for cause that may be made.

Peremptory challenge

A *peremptory challenge* is an objection to a prospective juror for which no reason must be assigned. It can be made for any reason or no reason at all and is totally within the discretion of the attorney making it. Peremptory challenges generally reflect the biases and strategies of the defense and the prosecution. Clarence Darrow, perhaps the greatest defense attorney of the twentieth century, once advised his colleagues to avoid affluent jurors, "because, next to the Board of Trade, the wealthy consider the penitentiary to be the most important of all public buildings."[55] In contrast is an excerpt from a training manual for Texas district attorneys:

What to Look for in a Juror

1. You are not looking for a fair juror, but rather a strong biased, and sometimes hypocritical individual who believes that defendants are different from them in kind, rather than degree.

2. You are not looking for any member of a minority group which may subject him to oppression—they almost always empathize with the accused.

3. You are not looking for the free thinkers and flower children.[56]

In short, many attorneys use these challenges to try to obtain partial jurors, not impartial ones; they hope to impanel jurors sympathetic to their side.

The practice of systematically excluding minorities from juries was sanctioned by the Supreme Court in 1965 through its ruling in *Swain* v. *Alabama*.[57] In 1986, the Supreme Court overruled *Swain* in part, holding that prosecutors may not exclude blacks from juries because of concern that they will favor a defendant of their own race. The case was **Batson v. Kentucky,**[58] in which the prosecutor, in the trial of an African American man, used his peremptory challenges to strike all four black persons on the *venire,* and a jury composed of only white persons was selected. The defendant was convicted. On appeal to the U.S. Supreme Court, it was held that the equal protection clause of the

Batson v. Kentucky: The Supreme Court ruling that a prosecutor's use of peremptory challenges to exclude from a jury members of the defendant's race solely on racial grounds violates the equal protection rights of the defendant.

"Your honor, the defense would like to excuse juror No. 3."

Exhibit 9.4

Gender Perspectives on Crime and Justice
J.E.B. v. *Alabama ex rel. T.B.*

In *J.E.B.* v. *Alabama,* a paternity and child support case rather than a criminal matter, an Alabama prosecutor used 9 of the state's 10 peremptory challenges to remove all the men from the jury, based on the belief that male jurors would likely be sympathetic to the man who was denying paternity. The defendant's lawyer used his peremptory challenges to remove women from the jury. However, because there were twice as many women as men in the jury pool that day, an all-female jury remained after the two sides had used all their challenges. J.E.B. protested, saying the state violated the equal protection clause of the Fourteenth Amendment

when it used its peremptory challenges to strike jurors solely because they were men. The court rejected J.E.B.'s claim, and jurors in the case found him to be the father of the child and directed him to pay child support. J.E.B. appealed to the U.S. Supreme Court, which ruled in his favor by a 6-to-3 majority.

Justice Sandra Day O'Connor, speaking for the majority, commented in the case that "to say that gender makes no difference as a matter of law is not to say that gender makes no difference as a matter of fact"—suggesting that women might also suffer in some kinds of cases if their lawyers were barred from using peremptory challenges to choose sympathetic juries. She cited, for example, a case that would involve a "battered wife on trial for wounding her abusive husband." Although stereotypes affect jurors of both sexes, many experts contend that women are most often harmed by gender classifications.

According to the common stereotypes, female jurors help the state's case in crimes against children, but are usually more sympathetic overall to criminal defendants and are considered to be less capable than men in understanding complex financial cases.

In contrast to the remarks of Justice O'Connor, Justice Antonin Scalia, along with Chief Justice William Rehnquist and Justice Clarence Thomas, accused the majority of politically correct "anti-male-chauvinist oratory." Scalia further stated:

> In order not to eliminate any real denial of equal protection, but simply to pay conspicuous obeisance to the equality of the sexes, the court imperils a practice that has been considered an essential part of fair jury trial since the dawn of the common law. The Constitution of the United States neither requires nor permits this vandalizing of our people's traditions.

SOURCE: *J.E.B.* v. *Alabama ex rel. T.B.,* 55 CrL 2003 (1994).

J.E.B. v. *Alabama ex rel. T.B.*: The Supreme Court ruling that the exercise of peremptory challenges on the basis of gender violates the equal protection clause of the Fourteenth Amendment.

Fourteenth Amendment is violated when a defendant is put on trial before a jury from which members of his or her race have been purposely excluded. The High Court reasoned that although a defendant has no right under the equal protection clause to a jury composed in whole or part of persons of his or her own race, the clause forbids the prosecutor from challenging potential jurors solely on account of their race or on the assumption that black jurors as a group will be unable impartially to consider the state's case. In 1994, in *J.E.B.* v. *Alabama ex rel. T.B.,*[59] the Supreme Court expanded the teachings of *Batson* v. *Kentucky* beyond race, to include gender (see Exhibit 9.4).

Challenges notwithstanding, the *voir dire* examination continues until the required number of jurors has been selected. In many jurisdictions where the 12-person jury is used, as many as 24 may be accepted. The additional jurors serve as alternates. They sit through the entire trial and are available to take the place of a regular jury member should he or she become ill, be forced to withdraw, or become disqualified while the trial is in process. Potential jurors who are successfully challenged return to the original jury pool, and new ones are drawn from the panel and subjected to *voir dire.* Those ultimately selected are sworn in and become the trial jury.

The *voir dire* can be brief or it can be time-consuming. In prosecutions of misdemeanors and many felonies where there has been little pretrial publicity and trial proceedings are anticipated to be fairly routine, there may be few challenges and the *voir dire* may last only a few hours or even less. In other cases, the examination can continue for days, weeks, or even months.

It is the challenges for cause that lengthen the *voir dire* proceedings. Any and every potential juror can be thus challenged. Peremptory challenges, on the other hand, are controlled by statute. In New York, for example, the maximum permitted is 3, except in such serious cases as murder, where as many as 20 are allowed, and where there are multiple defendants.

The *voir dire* can be a crucially important part of a criminal proceeding. Its purpose is to do more than merely choose a fair and impartial jury—as significant as this may be. Its primary functions are to educate the citizen as to the role of the juror and to develop jury-attorney rapport. Moreover, the *voir dire* provides the defense and the prosecution with the opportunity to attempt to influence jurors' attitudes and perhaps their later vote. One prosecutor put it this way:

> There is much more to a *voir dire* than the simple process of questioning and selecting jurors. In addition to the gamesmanship and psychology, a *voir dire* is an opportunity for the attorneys to educate their juries about the theories of their cases. It is also an opportunity to plant seeds of doubt that they hope will produce a favorable verdict. It is a chance to predispose jurors to be receptive to the attorney's case.[60]

THE CRIMINAL TRIAL

The trial is the climax of the criminal proceeding, and it begins as soon as the jury is sworn in. The only matter that remains in doubt before commentary and testimony can begin is the judge's decision as to whether or not to sequester the jurors for the entire trial. **Sequestration** involves removal of the jurors (and alternates, if any) from all possible outside influence. They are

Sequestration: The removal of the jurors (and alternates, if any) from all possible outside influences.

JURY ROOM

© 1999 Joseph Farris

"The jury is being sequestered."

housed in a hotel or motel for the duration of the trial; they are generally forbidden all visitors; and the newspapers they read, as well as the television programs they watch, are fully censored.

Few juries are sequestered for an entire trial, for most criminal prosecutions fail to generate a line of newspaper copy or even a second of television news time. Only if there is continuing media coverage that has the potential for influencing a juror's decision is sequestration ordered. If the judge does so rule, however, sequestration places a tremendous hardship on the jury members.

The procedures used in criminal trials are for the most part the same throughout the United States, and the process consists of the following steps:

- Opening statements
- Presentation of the state's case
- Presentation of the defense's case
- Rebuttal and surrebuttal
- Closing arguments
- Charging the jury
- Deliberation and verdict

In bench trials, this process is altered only minimally. First, those steps involving the jury are eliminated. Second, the tactics and strategies of the defense and prosecuting attorneys are simplified and much of the dramatic effect is removed.

Opening Statements

The first step in a trial proceeding is the reading of the criminal complaint by the court clerk, followed by opening statements—first by the prosecution and then by the defense.

The prosecutor's statement is an attempt to provide the jury with an outline of the case and how the state intends to prove, beyond a reasonable doubt, that the defendant did indeed commit the crime or crimes charged in the indictment. This outline generally includes a description of the crime, the defendant's role in it, and a discussion of the evidence and witnesses to be presented. In addition, the prosecutor is likely to address the meaning of "beyond a reasonable doubt." Reasonable doubt is fair doubt based on reason and common sense and growing out of the testimony of the case; it is doubt arising from a candid and impartial investigation of all the evidence and testimony presented. The purpose of the prosecutor's analysis here is to distinguish between reasonable doubt and vague apprehension, and at the same time to emphasize that the state's object is to prove guilt beyond a *reasonable* doubt—not beyond *all* doubt.

Although the prosecutor has considerable freedom as to what is said in the opening statement, no references may be made to evidence that is known to be inadmissible, and no comment may be made concerning the defendant's prior criminal record (if any exists). To make such a comment would be considered a *prejudicial error*—an error of such substance that it compromises the rights of the accused. Prejudicial errors that cannot be corrected by any action by the court are often the bases for appeals. Furthermore, they can result in a **mistrial,** a discharging of the jury without a verdict. A mistrial is the equivalent of no trial at all.

The defense attorney's opening statement is an address to the jury that focuses on how the defense will show that the state has a poor case, and that proof of guilt beyond a reasonable doubt cannot be demonstrated. It is not uncommon for defense attorneys to stress that the accused is innocent until proven guilty and that the burden of proof is fully on the prosecution.

Mistrial: A trial that has been terminated without a verdict and declared invalid by the court because of some circumstance that creates a substantial and uncorrectable prejudice to the conduct of a fair trial.

Frank Cotham

"LIAR! LIAR! PANTS ON FIRE!"

Defense attorneys and prosecutors often vary their strategies for opening statements, as dictated by the nature of the case, evidence, and witnesses. One approach is to keep opening remarks short and vague, letting the particulars of the case emerge during the course of the trial. Such a tactic makes few promises to the jury, but it allows flexibility. Such flexibility can be important because it enables the attorney, during the final summation, to structure an argument uncompromised by promises that he or she could not deliver. An alternative is a detailed opening statement, eloquently expressed and forcefully presented, that conditions the jury to accept the evidence that is ultimately delivered. This can be a risky technique, but it is highly rewarding if the promises made can be kept during the course of the trial.

In a jury trial, the prosecutor always delivers an opening statement. Without it, the jurors would have no framework within which to consider the evidence and testimony. The defense attorney, however, may choose to make no statement at all—out of necessity perhaps, if the defense strategy cannot be determined until the content of the state's case is revealed; or as part of the strategy, which is not to be revealed until the proper time. Opening statements are infrequently used in bench trials; they are less effective, since the seasoned judge has handled perhaps hundreds of similar cases in the past.

Presentation of the State's Case

In order to give the accused the opportunity to provide an informed defense, it is the state that presents its case first in the adversary system of justice. The prosecutor begins by presenting evidence and questioning witnesses.

Evidence: Any species of proof, through the media of witnesses, records, documents, concrete objects, and circumstances.

The Rules of Evidence   Generally, **evidence** is any species of proof, through the media of witnesses, records, documents, concrete objects, and circumstances. Specifically, evidence is of four basic types:

1. *Real evidence* is physical objects, such as a murder weapon, stolen property, fingerprints, DNA, the physical appearance of the scene of the crime, the physical appearance of a person when exhibited to the jury, wounds, or other items. Real evidence may be the original objects or facsimile representations, such as photographs, models of the crime scene, tire tracks, or other duplicates of objects that are either unavailable or unusable in their original form.

2. *Testimonial evidence* is the sworn, verbal statements of witnesses. All real evidence is accompanied by testimonial evidence, in that objects presented in evidence are explained by someone qualified to discuss them. Conversely, however, not all testimonial evidence is accompanied by real evidence.

3. *Direct evidence* is eyewitness evidence. Testimony that a person was seen painting a fence, for example, is direct evidence that the person painted a fence.

4. *Circumstantial evidence,* or indirect evidence, is evidence from which a fact can be reasonably inferred. Testimony that a person was seen with paint and a paint brush in the vicinity of a newly painted fence is circumstantial evidence that the person painted the fence.

These four types necessarily overlap, since all are ultimately presented through testimony. Furthermore, *all* evidence must be competent, material, and relevant. Evidence is *competent* when it is legally fit for admission to court. The testimony of an expert witness on a scientific matter is deemed competent, for example, if the court accepts his or her credentials as a reflection of proficiency in the subject area. In contrast, testimonial evidence on ballistics presented by an automobile mechanic would be considered incompetent; or an individual who has been convicted of perjury might be considered incompetent to testify. In common law, a person was considered to be "incompetent" to testify against his or her spouse, under the theory that by being compelled or even allowed to do so would undermine the marriage and thus be detrimental to the public welfare. In 1980, however, the Supreme Court ruled in *Trammel* v. *United States* that a criminal defendant could no longer invoke the "privilege against adverse spousal testimony," as long as the testimony is voluntary and does not compromise a confidential marital communication.[61]

Evidence can be deemed incompetent if it is based on *hearsay.* Under most circumstances the hearsay rule prohibits a witness from testifying about statements not within his or her personal knowledge—that is, about secondhand information. There are two exceptions to this rule. The first is an admission of criminal conduct made by the defendant to the witness. Such hearsay testimony is allowed because the accused is present in court to challenge it. The other exception is the "dying declaration" of a crime victim that has been told to or overheard by the witness; it is based on the presumption that a person who is about to die will not lie.[62]

To be admissible in a court of law, evidence must also be material and relevant, and there is only a slight distinction between the two. Evidence is *material* when it has a legitimate bearing on the decision of the case. Evidence is *relevant* when it is applicable to the issue in question. For example, evidence of a defendant's bad character on previous occasions is immaterial (unless he or she is submitting his or her good character in evidence). By contrast, the fact that an accused has stolen property in the past is irrelevant to whether or not he or she has murdered someone (assuming, of course, that the accused is not being tried on multiple charges of theft and murder).

Examination of Witnesses The state's presentation begins with the *direct examination* of witnesses. This consists only of eliciting facts from the witness in some chronological order. The first witness called is generally one who can establish the elements of the crime. Subsequent witnesses introduce physical, direct, and indirect evidence, and expert testimony.

After the prosecutor has completed his or her interrogation of a witness through direct examination, the defense is permitted (but not required) to cross-examine the witness. The purpose of *cross-examination* is to discredit the testimony, by either teasing out inconsistencies and contradictions or attacking the credibility of the witness. The prosecution can ask further questions of the witness through a *redirect examination,* as can the defense with a *recross-examination.* This examination procedure continues until all of the state's witnesses have been called and evidence presented.

Objections During the examination of any witness, whether it be by the prosecutor or the defense counsel, the opposing attorney can *object* to the introduction of evidence or testimony that he or she considers to be incompetent, immaterial, or irrelevant. Objections can also be made to "leading questions" (ones that inherently instruct or at least suggest to the witness how to answer), to eliciting a witness's opinions and conclusions, to being argumentative, and to "badgering" (abusing) a witness.

If the objection is *sustained* (consented to), the examiner is ordered to withdraw the question or cease the mode of inquiry, and the jury is instructed to disregard whatever was deemed inappropriate. If the objection is *overruled* (rejected), the examining attorney may continue with the original line of questioning.

Motion for Directed Verdict

Following the presentation of the state's case, it is not uncommon for the defense attorney to enter a motion for a directed verdict. With this, the defense moves that the judge enter a finding of acquittal on the grounds that the state failed to establish a *prima facie* case of guilt against the accused. If the judge so moves, he or she directs the jury to acquit the defendant. Even in the absence of a motion by the defense, the trial judge can order a directed verdict. Furthermore, the judge can do so not only on the grounds that the state failed to prove its case, but also because the testimony of the prosecution witnesses was not credible or because the conduct of the prosecutor was not proper. Conversely, *a judge cannot direct the jury to convict the accused.*

A *prima facie* case is one supported by sufficient evidence to warrant submission to the jury for the rendering of a verdict.

Presentation of the Defense's Case

At the outset, the defense attorney has the option of presenting many, some, or no witnesses or evidentiary elements on behalf of the accused. In addition, the defense must decide whether the accused will testify on his or her own behalf. The Fifth Amendment right against self-incrimination does not require it, but if the defendant chooses to testify, the prosecution then has the option of cross-examination.

Once these matters are decided, the defense's presentation follows the procedures outlined for the state's presentation: direct examination, cross-examination, redirect examination, and recross-examination. In addition, the rules of evidence and right to make objections apply equally to the defense as to the prosecution.

It is a common misconception that during this stage of the trial the burden of proof shifts to the defense. *This is not so.* The responsibility of proving guilt beyond a reasonable doubt always remains with the prosecution. What shifts to the defense is the "burden of going forward with the evidence." This means that since the prosecution has presented its suit to the jury, it becomes the defense's responsibility to offer its own argument for the jury to consider.

Rebuttal and Surrebuttal

When the defense "rests" (concludes its presentation), the prosecutor may elect to introduce new witnesses or evidence in an effort to refute the defense's case. Known as the *prosecutor's rebuttal,* the same format of examination and cross-examination, redirect and recross-examination is followed. In turn, the counsel for the accused may put forth a *surrebuttal,* which is a rebuttal of the prosecutor's rebuttal.

Closing Arguments

The *summation,* or closing arguments, gives each side the opportunity to recapitulate all the evidence and testimony offered during the trial. The arguments are made directly to the jury, and the defense emphasizes a posture of innocence while the state proffers the opposite view. Closing arguments are often quite eloquent and dramatic.

The summation ceremonies begin with the defense attorney, who points out any weaknesses or flaws in the prosecutor's theory and evidence. Counsel for the accused argues that proof "beyond a reasonable doubt" has not been established and reminds the jurors that they will have to live with their decision and consciences for the rest of their lives. Since the burden of proof rests with the state, the prosecutor is entitled to the final argument. For both the defense and the prosecution, perhaps the most vital element to be offered is *persuasion.*

Charging the Jury

Charging the jury: An order by the judge directing the jurors to retire to the jury room, consider the facts of the case and the evidence and testimony presented, and from their deliberations return a just verdict.

Charging the jury involves an order by the judge that directs the jurors to retire to the jury room, consider the facts of the case and the evidence and testimony presented, and from their deliberations return a just verdict. Regarded by many as the single most important statement made during the trial, it includes instructions as to the possible verdicts, the rules of evidence, and the legal meaning of "reasonable doubt." The instructions contained in the charge, furthermore, are often arrived at through consultation by the defense and the prosecution with the judge, and from statutory instructions as contained in the jurisdiction's code of criminal procedure.

In some states, the judges are permitted to review thoroughly all the evidence that has been presented to the jury. They are free to summarize, for example, the testimony of each witness. This can be useful to jurors, especially if the trial has been long and complex. But it also can be hazardous, for a judge has opinions about innocence and guilt, and these can inadvertently influence the jury. However, the judge is not permitted to express opinions as to the accused's culpability, the strengths and weaknesses of evidence, and whether or not some fact was proven. Any violations of this rule could result in a mistrial.

Finally, the members of the jury are instructed that they cannot communicate with anyone as to the facts of the case. Further sequestration might be ordered, which would place the jurors under the supervision of a court officer until a verdict is reached.

Jury Deliberations

Every jury has a *foreperson,* who serves as the nominal leader of the group. He or she is chosen by the jurors during the trial or after retirement to the jury room. In New York the first juror selected in the *voir dire* becomes the leader. Whether this person becomes the *actual* leader is another matter, depending on personality factors and the dynamics of group interaction.

Once the jury has retired, it is traditional for the foreperson to sit at the head of the table and call for a vote. With the exceptions of Oregon and Louisiana, unanimous verdicts are required by law. If such a verdict is acquired, the deliberations are finished. Typically, however, it is not that simple. In one study undertaken by the University of Chicago, for example, one vote was all that was necessary to reach a unanimous verdict in only 30 percent of the cases.[63]

Should deliberations fail to generate a unanimous decision, the dilemma is referred to as a deadlocked or "hung" jury. There are several consequences of such a situation: The jury is dismissed in open court, the judge declares a mistrial, and the prosecution can either retry the case or dismiss the charges. Deadlocked juries result from differences of opinion over the strengths and weaknesses of evidence, varying perceptions of innocence and guilt, and the meaning of "reasonable doubt." The deadlocked jury is not a common occurrence. Reports indicate that few criminal trials end with a hung jury, with most resulting in a negotiated consensus.[64]

The "hung" jury

Verdict and Judgment

When the jury reaches a verdict, it returns to the courtroom to announce its decision: "We, the jury, duly impaneled and sworn, find the defendant guilty [or not guilty] as charged." In cases involving multiple counts, the jury may find the accused guilty of some and innocent of others.

Exhibit 9.5   **Careers in Justice**
Legal Assistants

Legal assistants, also known as paralegals, assist attorneys in the delivery of legal services. Through formal education and training, legal assistants develop expertise in substantive and procedural law, thus qualifying them to do various types of legal work under the supervision of an attorney.

In all 50 states, legal assistants are prohibited from "practicing law." As such, they cannot give legal advice, represent a client in court, set a fee, or accept a case—all of which are generally considered components of the practice of law. Working under the supervision of an attorney, however, legal assistants perform any function delegated by an attorney, including the following:

- Conducting client interviews and maintaining general contact with clients
- Locating and interviewing witnesses
- Conducting investigations and statistical and documentary research
- Conducting legal research
- Drafting legal documents, correspondence, and pleadings
- Summarizing depositions, interrogatories, and testimony
- Attending depositions, court or administrative hearings, and trials with the attorney

- Authoring and signing correspondence

In addition to working in private law firms, legal assistants are found in courts, corporations, insurance companies, government offices, and administrative agencies. Some legal assistants establish their own businesses, working for attorneys on a contract basis.

It is estimated that there are more than 750 educational programs offering paralegal training, including associate degree programs offered at community colleges and universities; bachelor degree programs that combine paralegal studies with other disciplines, often criminal justice; and certificate programs offered in schools of continuing education.

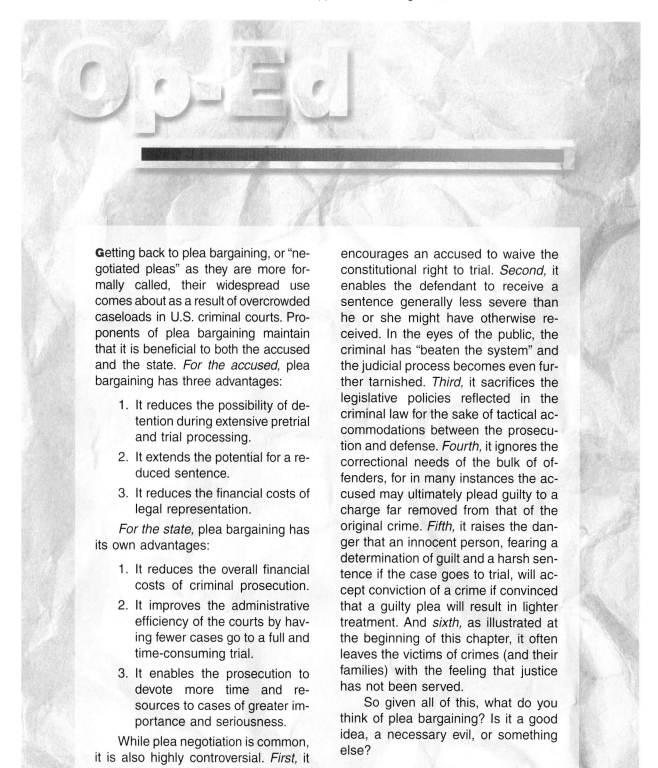

Getting back to plea bargaining, or "negotiated pleas" as they are more formally called, their widespread use comes about as a result of overcrowded caseloads in U.S. criminal courts. Proponents of plea bargaining maintain that it is beneficial to both the accused and the state. *For the accused,* plea bargaining has three advantages:

1. It reduces the possibility of detention during extensive pretrial and trial processing.

2. It extends the potential for a reduced sentence.

3. It reduces the financial costs of legal representation.

For the state, plea bargaining has its own advantages:

1. It reduces the overall financial costs of criminal prosecution.

2. It improves the administrative efficiency of the courts by having fewer cases go to a full and time-consuming trial.

3. It enables the prosecution to devote more time and resources to cases of greater importance and seriousness.

While plea negotiation is common, it is also highly controversial. *First,* it encourages an accused to waive the constitutional right to trial. *Second,* it enables the defendant to receive a sentence generally less severe than he or she might have otherwise received. In the eyes of the public, the criminal has "beaten the system" and the judicial process becomes even further tarnished. *Third,* it sacrifices the legislative policies reflected in the criminal law for the sake of tactical accommodations between the prosecution and defense. *Fourth,* it ignores the correctional needs of the bulk of offenders, for in many instances the accused may ultimately plead guilty to a charge far removed from that of the original crime. *Fifth,* it raises the danger that an innocent person, fearing a determination of guilt and a harsh sentence if the case goes to trial, will accept conviction of a crime if convinced that a guilty plea will result in lighter treatment. And *sixth,* as illustrated at the beginning of this chapter, it often leaves the victims of crimes (and their families) with the feeling that justice has not been served.

So given all of this, what do you think of plea bargaining? Is it a good idea, a necessary evil, or something else?

Jury nullification: The refusal or marked reluctance on the part of a jury to convict, because of the severe nature of the sentence involved, or when a jury otherwise "nullifies" the force of strict legal procedure.

One of the more enduring issues in criminal trials is the problem of **jury nullification.** It occurs when juries do not follow the court's interpretation of the law in every instance, disregard what they have been told about the law or certain aspects of evidence, consider the application of certain laws to be unjust, refuse to convict because they consider the penalties too severe, or otherwise "nullify" or suspend the force of strict legal procedure. Instances of jury nullification have occurred in cases of battered spouses who kill, political crimes, and mercy killings.

Jury nullification can be both inadvertent or by design. If a verdict of guilty is returned and it is the court's opinion that it is an erroneous decision, the judge can refuse to abide by it. He or she can *direct* the jury to acquit, or "arrest" the guilty verdict and enter a judgment of acquittal. However, as mentioned earlier, a trial judge does *not* have the authority to direct a jury to convict or enter a judgment arresting a verdict of not guilty.

Lastly, jurors can be *polled.* At the request of the defense or the prosecution, the judge (or the bailiff) asks each juror if the verdict announced is his or her individual verdict. Polling the jury is done to determine whether any juror has been pressured by fellow jury members into voting a particular way.

Polling the jury

Posttrial Motions

With a judgment of not guilty, the defendant is immediately released—unless other charges are still pending. With a guilty verdict, most jurisdictions allow the defense to file motions to set aside the judgment or to file motions for a new trial.

The *motion in arrest of judgment* asks that no judgment be pronounced because of one or more defects in the record of the case. Possible defects might be that the trial court had no jurisdiction over the case; the verdict included conviction on a charge that was not tested in the indictment or information; or there was error "on the face of the record." This last term refers to any faults of procedure that may have occurred during the pretrial process.

Motion in arrest of judgment

The *motion for a new trial,* which can be made only by the defense, can be based on numerous grounds. The defense may claim that the jury received evidence outside of the courtroom; that the jury was guilty of misconduct during deliberations; that the court erred in overruling an objection or permitting the introduction of certain evidence; that the jury charge was made improperly; that the prosecution was guilty of misconduct; that there is a suspicion of *jury tampering* (bribes or threats made to a juror to influence his or her vote); or that newly discovered evidence is available for review.

Motion for a new trial

Jury tampering

If either motion is sustained, new proceedings will be initiated. Any new trial that results, however, does not represent double jeopardy, for the defendant's motion is an allegation that the proceedings should be declared utterly invalid.

SUMMARY

The movement of defendants through the criminal courts is quite complex. The process is characterized by many stages and checks and balances, while beset with numerous difficulties. Early in the process is the matter of pretrial release. Bail has been the traditional mechanism of temporary release. The amount of bail set is determined by a number of factors, including the seriousness of the crime, the defendant's prior criminal record, and the strength of the state's case. The bail system has been heavily criticized on the grounds that it discriminates against the poor and that the bail bonds industry promotes inequity and corruption. As a result, several states have abolished the bail bonds business, and numerous other jurisdictions are debating its future. Nonetheless, the majority of states still view it as a viable and effective means to ensure that defendants appear in court.

Stack v. *Boyle* noted that bail was not a means for punishing defendants or protecting society, but rather a means of assuring the accused's attendance in court. Nevertheless, high bail is often set for the purposes of pre-ventive detention. Moreover, for those who cannot make bail, pretrial detention has negative effects on their criminal processing. Release on recognizance has become a popular alternative to bail and has been generally effective.

Following the initial court proceedings, an information or indictment initiates prosecution. An information is filed by a prosecutor, while an indictment is handed down by a grand jury. The purposes of the grand jury are to investigate and to protect citizens from unfair accusations. Since grand juries do not determine guilt or innocence, many of the elements of due process are absent. The Supreme Court has generally refused to impose substantive criteria on the grand jury's exercise of discretion.

After the formal determination of charges, the defendant is arraigned, at which time he or she is asked to enter a plea. The basic pleas are those of guilty, not guilty, *nolo contendere,* and standing mute. In addition, there are special pleas of insanity, statute of limitations, and the issue of double jeopardy.

Prior to the actual trial a number of motions can be filed by the defense or prosecution: discovery, change of venue, suppression, bill of particulars, severance, continuance, and dismissal. Then there is the matter of a "speedy trial" as guaranteed by the Sixth Amendment. There are many legitimate reasons for delays in formally trying a defendant, but the Supreme Court has held that if a defendant is denied a speedy trial, the remedy is dismissal of the charges.

Criminal defendants have a constitutional right to a trial by jury, a right extended to the states through *Duncan* v. *Louisiana* in 1968. Potential jurors are selected from voter registration rolls or multiple source lists. The *voir dire* examination functions to determine a candidate's fitness to serve, and jurors can be eliminated through challenges by the defense and prosecution. Two Supreme Court cases—*Batson* v. *Kentucky* and *J.E.B.* v. *Alabama ex rel. T.B.*—have ensured that neither the prosecution nor the defense may remove a potential juror on the basis of race or gender.

The criminal trial has many steps: opening statements, presentation of the state's and defense's cases, rebuttal and surrebuttal, closing arguments, charging the jury, and deliberation and verdict. There may be posttrial motions for arrest of judgment or for a new trial. Each of these steps affects the next step in the trial process. When deliberations among jurors fail to reach a unanimous decision, the dilemma is referred to as a "hung jury." There are several possible consequences to this situation: The jury may be dismissed in open court, the judge may declare a mistrial, and the prosecution must decide whether to retry the case or dismiss the charges.

KEY TERMS

bail **220**
Batson v. *Kentucky* **245**
bench warrant **223**
Benton v. *Maryland* **232**
charging the jury **252**
double jeopardy **232**
Downum v. *United States* **232**
Duncan v. *Louisiana* **243**
evidence **250**
grand jury **226**
Hurtado v. *California* **227**

indictment **226**
information **226**
J.E.B. v. *Alabama ex rel. T.B.* **246**
jury nullification **254**
Klopfer v. *North Carolina* **237**
mistrial **248**
motion **233**
nolo contendere **230**
Palko v. *Connecticut* **232**
presentment **226**
release on recognizance (ROR) **225**

sequestration **247**
Sixth Amendment **236**
speedy trial **236**
Stack v. *Boyle* **221**
surety **220**
transactional immunity **229**
true bill **227**
use immunity **229**
venire **244**
voir dire **244**

QUESTIONS FOR DISCUSSION

1. Should the bail bonds business be abolished? Why or why not?
2. Do grand juries play too large a role in criminal justice proceedings? Is their power justified? Why or why not?
3. Given the respective roles of the defense and the prosecution, is the deliberate seeking of biased jurors legal or ethical?
4. What are the potential consequences of a defendant's waiver of rights?
5. Should criminal trials be televised?

MEDIA RESOURCES

1. **Plea Bargaining and Crime Victims.** The National Center for Victims of Crime has taken a strong stand with regard to plea bargaining. Web site address: http://www.nvc.org
2. **The Scopes Monkey Trial.** The most recent book on the "great monkey trial" is Edward J. Larson, *Summer of the Gods: The Scopes Trial and America's Continuing Debate Over Science and Religion* (New York: Basic Books, 1997). *Inherit the Wind,* a 1960 film version of the trial story, is available in most video stores.
3. **African Americans and the Criminal Justice System.** See David Cole, *No Equal Justice* (New York: New Press, 1999).
4. **Current Court Cases.** Materials on recent trials and court decisions can be found on the "Court TV" Web site. Web address: courttv.com/index.html
5. **Bail and Bounty Hunters.** See Jonathan Drimmer, "When Man Hunts Man: The Rights and Duties of Bounty Hunters in the American Criminal Justice System," *Houston Law Review* 33 (1996): 731–793.

1. Associated Press, August 31, 1998.
2. *Hudson* v. *Parker,* 156 U.S. 277 (1895).
3. *McKane* v. *Durston,* 153 U.S. 684 (1894).
4. Patricia M. Wald, "The Right to Bail Revisited: A Decade of Promise Without Fulfillment," in *The Rights of the Accused,* ed. Stuart S. Nagel (Beverly Hills, Calif.: Sage, 1972), pp. 175–205.
5. *Stack* v. *Boyle,* 342 U.S. 1 (1951).
6. See Paul Wice, *Freedom for Sale* (Lexington, Mass.: Lexington, 1974); Frederick Suffet, "Bail Setting: A Study of Courtroom Interaction," *Crime and Delinquency,* October 1966, pp. 318–331. Also see John S. Goldkamp and Michael R. Gottfredson, "Bail Decision Making and Pretrial Detentions," *Law and Human Behavior* 3 (1979): 227–249; Ilene H. Nagal, "The Legal/Extra-Legal Controversy: Judicial Decisions in Pretrial Release," *Law and Society Review* 17 (1983): 481–515.
7. Annotated Code of Maryland, Article 27, Section 12B.
8. See James G. Carr, "Bailbondsmen and the Federal Courts," *Federal Probation* 57 (March 1993): 9–13.
9. *Pretrial Release of Felony Defendants* (Washington, D.C.: Bureau of Justice Statistics, 1991).
10. *New York Times,* April 4, 1963, p. 37.
11. Brian A. Reaves, *Pretrial Release of Federal Felony Defendants* (Washington, D.C.: Bureau of Justice Statistics, 1994).
12. P. Koza and A. N. Doob, "The Relationship of Pretrial Custody to the Outcome of a Trial," *Criminal Law Quarterly* 17 (1975): 391–400.
13. Charles E. Ares, Anne Rankin, and Herbert Sturtz, "The Manhattan Bail Project," *New York University Law Review* 38 (January 1963): 68.
14. Tyce S. Smith and James E. Reilley, "The Illinois Bail System: A Second Look," *John Marshall Journal of Practice and Procedure* (Fall 1972): 33.
15. *Chicago Tribune,* September 2, 1990, pp. 1, 10; September 3, 1990, pp. 1, 2; September 4, 1990, pp. 1, 10.
16. Marvin E. Frankel and Gary P. Naftalis, *The Grand Jury: An Institution on Trial* (New York: Hill and Wang, 1977), pp. 3–17.
17. *Hurtado* v. *California,* 110 U.S. 516 (1884).
18. *Kastigar* v. *United States,* 406 U.S. 441 (1972).
19. Charlotte Allen, "Grand Illusion," *Insight,* February 17, 1992, pp. 6–11.
20. National Advisory Commission on Criminal Justice Standards and Goals, *Courts* (Washington, D.C.: U.S. Government Printing Office, 1973), p. 13.
21. *New York Times,* October 5, 1980, p. 33.
22. Thomas C. Marks and J. Tim Reilly, *Constitutional Criminal Procedure* (North Scituate, Mass.: Duxbury, 1979), p. 136.
23. Henry J. Steadman, Margaret A. McGreevy, Joseph P. Morrissey, Lisa A. Callahan, Pamela Clark Robbins, and Carmen Cirincione, *Before and After Hinckley: Evaluating Insanity Defense Reform* (New York: Guilford, 1993).
24. David A. Jones, *The Law of Criminal Procedure* (Boston: Little, Brown, 1981), p. 398.
25. *United States* v. *Perez,* 9 Wheat. 579 (1824).
26. *United States* v. *Ball,* 163 U.S. 662 (1896).
27. *Wade* v. *Hunter,* 336 U.S. 684 (1949).
28. *Palko* v. *Connecticut,* 302 U.S. 319 (1937).
29. *Benton* v. *Maryland,* 395 U.S. 784 (1969).
30. *Downum* v. *United States,* 372 U.S. 734 (1963).
31. *Brady* v. *United States,* 397 U.S. 742 (1970).
32. *Santobello* v. *New York,* 404 U.S. 257 (1971).
33. *Henderson* v. *Morgan,* 426 U.S. 637 (1976).
34. *Brady* v. *Maryland,* 363 U.S. 83 (1963).
35. *Moore* v. *Illinois,* 408 U.S. 786 (1972).
36. *Mapp* v. *Ohio,* 367 U.S. 643 (1961); *Escobedo* v. *Illinois,* 368 U.S. 478 (1964); *Miranda* v. *Arizona,* 384 U.S. 436 (1966).
37. See Sarah Tanford, Steven Penrod, and Rebecca Collins, "Decision Making in Joined Criminal Trials: The Influence of Charge Similarity, Evidence Similarity, and Limiting Instructions," *Law and Human Behavior* 9 (1985): 319–337; Kenneth S. Bordens and Irwin A. Horowitz, "Joinder of Criminal Offenses," *Law and Human Behavior* 9 (1985): 339–353.
38. Personal communication, September 15, 1971.
39. *Serfass* v. *United States,* 420 U.S. 377 (1975).
40. California Penal Code, Section 1382 (1).
41. *Code of Alabama,* Title 15, Section 3-1.
42. *State* v. *Brann,* 292 A.2d 173 (Me. 1972).
43. *Beavers* v. *Haubert,* 198 U.S. 77 (1905).
44. *Klopfer* v. *North Carolina,* 386 U.S. 213 (1967).
45. *In re Oliver,* 333 U.S. 257 (1948).
46. *Duncan* v. *Louisiana,* 391 U.S. 145 (1968).
47. *Tennessee Code Annotated,* Title 40-2504.
48. 74 *Idaho Code,* Title 19-1902.
49. Gilbert B. Stuckey, *Procedures in the Criminal Justice System* (Columbus, Ohio: Merrill, 1976), p. 91.
50. *Duncan* v. *Louisiana,* 391 U.S. 145 (1968).
51. *Baldwin* v. *New York,* 399 U.S. 66 (1970).
52. *Williams* v. *Florida,* 399 U.S. 78 (1970).
53. *Taylor* v. *Louisiana,* 419 U.S. 522 (1975).
54. Laura Rose Handman, "Underrepresentation of Economic Groups in Federal Juries," *Boston University Law Review* 57 (January 1977): 198–224.
55. Melvyn B. Zerman, *Beyond a Reasonable Doubt: Inside the American Jury System* (New York: Crowell, 1981), p. 181.
56. In Zerman, *Beyond a Reasonable Doubt,* p. 181.
57. *Swain* v. *Alabama,* 380 U.S. 202 (1965).
58. *Batson* v. *Kentucky,* 106 S. Ct. 1712 (1986).
59. *J.E.B.* v. *Alabama ex rel. T.B.,* 55 CrL 2003 (1994).
60. Steven Phillips, *No Heroes, No Villains: The Story of a Murder Trial* (New York: Vintage, 1978), pp. 136–137.
61. *Trammel* v. *United States,* 445 U.S. 40 (1980).
62. Jones, *Law of Criminal Procedure,* p. 475.
63. *New York Times,* June 7, 1981, p. 25.
64. Zerman, *Beyond a Reasonable Doubt,* p. 102.

Elements of Criminal Justice

**SENTENCING,
APPELLATE REVIEW,
AND THE DEATH
PENALTY**

Death Row Segregation

C HICAGO, ILL. — In what death penalty opponents considered an extraordinary move, prosecutors arranged for the release of 43-year-old Anthony Porter, who had spent 16 years on death row and had come within just minutes of being executed for a double murder. It appears that Porter was not the killer after all.[1] Throughout the city people were incredulous, especially over allegations that the investigation had been sloppy and that the police might have intimidated a witness into naming Porter as the killer. Moreover, Porter's release in 1999 was the 10th time in less than 20 years that an Illinois inmate was freed because he turned out to be innocent. Nationwide, moreover, at least 77 inmates have been exonerated and released from death rows during the past 25 years.

The Porter case raises a number of questions. What kind of punishment philosophy fosters execution? Is execution "cruel and unusual punishment" and is it justified at any time? What does the U.S. Supreme Court have to say about the death penalty? What other kinds of sentencing alternatives are available for serious offenders?

In the sentencing phase of the criminal justice process, the obligation of the court is transformed from providing due process in the determination of guilt or innocence to the allocation of sanctions for those who have been proven guilty. Appellate review is granted to those individuals who have been found guilty, but who nevertheless claim that procedural or judgmental errors were made during their movement through the court system. On appeal, it becomes the obligation of the defendant to prove why a conviction should be overturned. Both the sentencing and appeals processes are challenging in that the court must create an equilibrium between justice and law. Judges must apply the appropriate sentence for the offender, but at the same time ensure justice for society. Discretion is also given to judges to hear those appeals in which they believe a defendant was denied due process. Thus, sentencing and appeal can be considered among the most controversial aspects of criminal justice processing. And without question, the sentence of death continues to be the most debated sanction in contemporary times.

SENTENCING

Life for life, eye for eye . . .
—*Exodus 21:23–24*

What should be done with criminal offenders after they have been convicted? The answer is a difficult one for a sentencing judge, because the administration of justice has a variety of conflicting goals: the rehabilitation of offenders, the discouragement of potential lawbreakers, the isolation of criminals who pose a threat to community safety, the condemnation of extralegal conduct, and the reinforcement of accepted social norms. Objectives as varied as these tend to generate such contradictory suggestions as the following:

"The punishment should fit the crime."

"The public demands a prison sentence."

"The purpose of justice is individualized sentencing."

"The sentence should be a warning to others."

"Rehabilitate offenders so they can be returned to society."

"Lock them up and throw away the keys."

The burden of the judge is to choose one or more of these various goals while subordinating all others.

Sentencing Objectives

Throughout the history of the United States, there has been no single and clearly defined rationale to serve as a guiding principle in sentencing. For more than 200 years, the public has alternated between revulsion at inhumane sentencing practices and prison conditions on the one hand and overly compassionate treatment on the other. While the former practices are denounced as "barbaric" and "uncivilized" and the latter as "coddling criminals," the fate of convicted offenders has repeatedly shifted according to prevailing national values and current perceptions of danger and the fear of crime. As a result, sentencing objectives are based on at least five competing philosophies: retribution, vengeance, incapacitation, deterrence, and rehabilitation.

Retribution: A sentencing philosophy seeking to create an equal or proportionate relationship between the offense and the punishment.

Retribution The **retribution** philosophy involves creating an equal or proportionate relationship between the offense and the punishment. It is concerned exclusively with making the punishment fit the crime and is as old as recorded history. It can be found in Exodus (21:23–25) and Leviticus (24:17–22), with such prescriptions as "When one man strikes another and kills him, he shall be put to death," and "Eye for eye, tooth for tooth, hand for hand, foot for foot, burning for burning, wound for wound." Retribution rests on the notion that criminals are wicked people who are responsible for their actions and deserve to be punished. At the same time, however, it asserts that the state shall act as the instrument of the community's collective response, thus incorporating the idea that the victims of crime cannot make reprisals against the offending parties. Yet as a sentencing philosophy, retribution presents an ethical dilemma. In a democratic society built on the principles of individual rights and civil liberties, penalties based on "getting even" seem to represent a contradiction in values.

Vengeance   In contrast with retribution, **vengeance** is the desire to punish criminals because society gains some measure of satisfaction from seeing or knowing that they are punished.[2] Like retribution, vengeance also presents an ethical dilemma. Should it be accepted as a valid rationale for punishment? The U.S. Supreme Court's decision in *Payne* v. *Tennessee* suggests that it may already have been.[3] In Payne, decided in 1991, the Court held that at a capital sentencing proceeding, the Constitution does not forbid the admission of evidence or prosecutorial argument concerning the personal characteristics of the victim or the impact of the crime on the victim's family. In other words, the decision permitted *victim impact statements* at sentencing hearings. As Chief Justice William Rehnquist put it: "Victim impact evidence is simply another form or method of informing the sentencing authority about the harm caused by the crime in question." One could reasonably argue that permitting the victim, or members of the victim's family, to testify at sentencing as to the personal harm the offender has caused is tantamount to eliciting requests for vengeance from a sentencing judge or jury.

Vengeance: A sentencing philosophy seeking satisfaction from knowing or seeing that offenders are punished.

In *Payne* v. *Tennessee*, the Supreme Court permitted the use of victim impact evidence in the penalty phase of capital trials.

Victim impact statements

Incapacitation   Unlike retribution, **incapacitation** is simply the removal of dangerous persons from the community. Also referred to as the "restraint" or "isolation" philosophy, its object is community protection rather than revenge. By removing the offender from society through execution, imprisonment, or exile (as is the case with the deportation of foreign nationals upon conviction of certain crimes), the community is thus protected from further criminal activity.

As with retribution, incapacitation as a punishment philosophy is problematic. If the goals are crime prevention and community protection, then the sanctions would have to be quite severe to be effective. Regardless of the offense, life imprisonment with no parole and execution are the only forms of restraint that can guarantee the elimination of future offenses against the community. The alternative—temporary incarceration until such times as the community can be reasonably assured the offender will no longer commit crimes—is impossible to predict.

Incapacitation: A sentencing philosophy seeking to remove the offender from society.

Deterrence   The most widely held justification for punishment is reducing crime. Thus, as a sentencing philosophy, **deterrence** refers to the prevention of criminal acts by making examples of persons convicted of crimes. Deterrence can be both general and specific. *General deterrence* seeks to discourage would-be offenders from committing crimes; *specific deterrence* is designed to prevent a particular convicted offender from engaging in future criminal acts.

The notion of punishment as a deterrent is best illustrated in the words of an eighteenth-century judge who reportedly stated to a defendant at sentencing, "You are to be hanged not because you have stolen a sheep but in order that others may not steal sheep."[4] Belief in the efficacy of deterrence, however, seems mainly based on conjecture, faith, and emotion, and there is overwhelming evidence to suggest that the deterrent effect of punishment is,

Deterrence: A sentencing philosophy seeking to prevent criminal acts by making an example of persons convicted of crimes.

"The court hopes that you'll look at your life sentence as a wake up call."

at best, weak.[5] High rates of violent crime in the nation's cities as well as high levels of recidivism among many offender populations are ample evidence of this. On the other hand, specific deterrence does seem to affect the behavior of many white-collar criminals and first-time misdemeanants whose arrests and convictions cause them embarrassment and public disgrace and threaten their careers and family life.

Rehabilitation: A sentencing philosophy seeking to reintegrate the offender into society.

Rehabilitation   From a humanistic point of view, the most appealing basis for sentencing and justification for punishment is that future crime can be prevented by changing the offender's behavior. The **rehabilitation** philosophy rests on the premise that persons who commit crimes have identifiable reasons for doing so and that these can be discovered, addressed, and altered. Rehabilitation suggests to the offender that "crime does not pay" and that "there is a better way." Its aim is to modify behavior and reintegrate the lawbreaker into the wider society as a productive citizen.

The goal of rehabilitation has wide support, for in contrast with other sentencing philosophies, it takes a positive approach to eliminating offense behavior. Unlike the false hope of deterrence or the temporary measures of retribution and incapacitation, proponents argue that rehabilitation is the only humanitarian mechanism for altering the criminal careers of society's casualties.

Yet the efficacy of rehabilitation has been seriously questioned. Some suggest that since the causes of crime are not fully understood, efforts at behavioral change are of questionable value. Others maintain that since the availability of rehabilitative services in many institutions and community-based programs is either minimal or nonexistent, then "correction" as such has only little limited practical potential. Still a third group espouses a "nothing works" philosophy, arguing that rehabilitation has not demonstrated and never will demonstrate its ability to prevent or reduce crime.

Statutory Sentencing Structures

Regardless of the sentencing philosophy of the presiding judge, the actual sentence imposed is influenced to some degree by the statutory alternatives that appear in the penal codes, combined with the facilities and programs available in the correctional system. Thus, the competing objectives of retribution, vengeance, incapacitation, deterrence, and rehabilitation may be diluted to some degree, since the judicial sentencing responsibility must be carried out within the guidelines provided by legislative sentencing authority.

Statutory sentencing guidelines, which have generally evolved over long periods of time and often reflect the changing nature of legislative philosophy, appear in each state's criminal code. No two state codes are quite alike—the punishments they designate for specific crimes vary, and the methods establishing the parameters for sentencing can also differ. Furthermore, some statutes give judges wide latitude in sentencing, while others do not. In some states—Tennessee, for example—the penal code designates the range of punishments for each specific crime. Others, such as Idaho, follow the Tennessee model for some crimes, but extend almost total discretion to the judge for others. And in other states, such as New York, crimes are first classified according to their severity (for example, rape in the first degree is a class B felony, while incest is a class E felony) and then are assigned punishments according to their felony or misdemeanor class.

Although statutory guidelines provide a range of sentencing alternatives, judges also have discretion in many instances to deviate from the legislative norm, on the premise that sentences should be individualized. Conversely, there are situations in which sentencing discretion can be taken away from the judge. For example, a person convicted of rape in the first degree in the state of New York faces a statutory period of imprisonment of no less than 6 years and no more than 25 years, since the crime is a class B felony. Assume that the judge imposes the maximum of 8 to 25 years, his or her philosophy being that the defendant is a dangerous criminal from which society must be protected for as long as is legally possible. Under Section 70.40 of the New York penal law, however, this offender can be released on parole after serving the minimum sentence—6 years. In addition, under Section 241 of the New York correction law, the governor always has the power to reduce a sentence or grant a pardon.

A judge's authority and discretionary power to determine a sentence is, in a few jurisdictions, delegated by statute to the jury, but only for certain types of crimes. North Carolina, for example, is one of several states in which the jury makes the sentencing decision in capital cases. In addition, 13 jurisdictions provide for jury-determined sentences in some noncapital cases. The wisdom of this practice, however, has been called into serious question.

TWO WORDS THAT HELPED TO LENGTHEN A SENTENCE

In 1984, defendant Harold Coleman was facing 35 years in prison after convictions of burglary, theft, and being a habitual criminal. However, following an outburst at his sentencing hearing during which he called the presiding judge a "prick" and an "asshole," another 7 years was added to his sentence. The judge remarked that "he called me a few choice names that didn't reflect well on the judiciary, and you can't let them get by with this." Coleman's attorney commented that "I don't think it was worth the satisfaction my client got."

SOURCE: *National Law Journal*, September 3, 1984, p. 11.

Author Melvyn Zerman has commented that the sentencing decision is the most formidable demand that can be made of a jury and that it often occurs at a time when the jurors are both mentally and physically weak.[6] Even more to the point, the National Advisory Commission on Criminal Justice Standards and Goals has argued as follows:

> The practice has been condemned by every serious study and analysis in the last half century. Jury sentencing is nonprofessional and is more likely than judge sentencing to be arbitrary and based on emotions rather than the needs of the offender or society. Sentencing by juries leads to disparate sentences and leaves little opportunity for development of sentencing policies.[7]

Whatever theory of sanctions ultimately guides the sentencing of the defendant, and depending on the statutory requirements of the jurisdiction, the alternatives for the presiding judge include fines, probation or some other community-based program, imprisonment, or the death penalty.

Sentencing Alternatives: Fines

Fines are imposed either in lieu of or in addition to incarceration or probation. They are the traditional means of dealing with most traffic infractions and many misdemeanors, and the sentence "$30 or 30 days" has often been heard in courtrooms across America over the years.

Fines can also be imposed for felonies, instead of or in addition to some other sentence. They can involve many thousands of dollars and sometimes twice the amount of the defendant's gain from the commission of the crime. However, since *Williams* v. *Illinois* in 1970 and *Tate* v. *Short* the following year,[8] the use of fines has been curtailed somewhat. In *Williams*, the Supreme Court ruled that no jurisdiction could hold a person in jail or prison beyond the length of the maximum sentence merely to work off a fine they were unable to pay—a practice that was allowed at that time in 47 states. In *Tate*, the

*"It's not fair. In my one-year sentence, I'll be serving an extra day
because it's leap year!"*

Court held that the historic "$30 or 30 days" sentence was an unconstitutional denial of equal protection, because limiting punishment to a fine for those who could pay, but expanding punishment for the same offense to imprisonment for those who could not, violated the Fourteenth Amendment.

During the 1980s and 1990s, several jurisdictions have experimented with ways of making fines a more meaningful sentencing option. In many instances, judges are adjusting fines to correspond with both the financial means of the offender and the seriousness of the crime. These fines are referred to as *day fines* because they are figured as multiples of the offender's daily net income.

Sentencing Alternatives: Imprisonment

For a convicted offender who receives a sentence of imprisonment, there are numerous types of sentences on the statute books; some have elicited considerable controversy. Sentences can be termed *indeterminate, determinate, definite, "flat," "fixed," indefinite, intermittent,* or *mandatory,* plus a host of other names, many of which have been confused and mislabeled in the literature. In practice, there are three major types: the indeterminate, the determinate, and the definite sentence.

The Indeterminate Sentence   The most common sentence is the **indeterminate sentence,** which has a fixed minimum and a fixed maximum term for incarceration, rather than a definite period. The actual amount of tine served is determined by the paroling authority. Sentences of 1 to 5 years, $7\frac{1}{2}$ to 15 years, 10 to 20 years, or 15 years to life are indeterminate.

The statutory sentencing guidelines for forcible rape in New York are truly indeterminate. For example, the crime of rape in the first degree calls for a period of incarceration of not less than 6 years and not more than 25 years, with the minimum fixed at one-third of the maximum. Within those guidelines, the judge can impose a sentence, for example, of 7 to 21 years. Thus, the offender must serve at least 7 years, after which the paroling authority may release him at any time prior to the completion of his maximum sentence.

The philosophy behind the indeterminate sentence is based on a purely correctional model of punishment, the underlying premise being that the sentence should meet the needs of the defendant. After incarceration begins, at least in theory, the rehabilitation process is initiated, and the inmate should be confined until there is substantial evidence of "correction." At that point, it becomes the responsibility of the paroling authority to assess the nature and extent of such rehabilitation and release the defendant if the evidence so warrants it. Thus, the indeterminate sentence rests on the notion that the length of imprisonment should be based on progress toward rehabilitation and makes the following assumptions (all of which are disputable and are not widely held by corrections specialists):

1. Criminals are personally or socially disturbed or disadvantaged, and therefore their commission of crime cannot be considered a free choice. If this is the case, then setting terms commensurate with the severity of the crime is not logical.

2. Indeterminate sentences allow "effective" treatment to rectify sociopsychological problems, which are the root of crime.

3. Readiness for release varies with the individual and can be determined only when the inmate is in the institution, not before.[9]

In recent years, the practice of indeterminate sentencing has received considerable criticism. For example, the following arguments have been made against this form of sentencing:

Indeterminate sentence: A sentence of incarceration having a fixed minimum and a fixed maximum term of confinement, rather than a definite period.

Criticisms of indeterminate sentencing

- Since the causes of crime and criminal behavior are not readily understood, they cannot be dealt with under the premise of indeterminate sentencing.
- Rehabilitation cannot occur within the prison setting, regardless of the nature of the sentencing.
- The indeterminate sentence is used as an instrument of inmate control, put into practice through threats of disciplinary reports and, hence, extended sentences.
- Sentences within the indeterminate model can vary by judge and by jurisdiction, resulting in unfair and disparate terms of imprisonment.
- An offender's uncertainty as to how long his or her prison term may last can lead to frustration, violence, and riot.[10]

The Determinate Sentence   The growing concerns over indeterminate sentencing have generated considerable interest in the **determinate sentence.** Known also as the "flat," "fixed," or "straight" sentence, it has no set minimum or maximum, but rather a fixed period of time. The term of the determinate sentence is established by the legislature—say, 15 years—thus removing the sentencing discretion of the judge. However, under determinate sentencing guidelines, the court's discretion to choose between prison, probation, a fine, and some other alternative is not affected. Only the length of the sentence is taken away from judicial discretion, if the judge imposes imprisonment.

In some instances, the determinate sentence can, in effect, become an indeterminate sentence. Under determinate sentencing statutes, inmates are still eligible for parole after a portion of their terms have been served. Thus, in a state where parole eligibility begins after one-half of the term has expired, a determinate sentence of 10 years really ranges from a minimum of 5 years to a maximum of 10.

> **Determinate sentence:** A sentence of incarceration for a fixed period of time, but with possible reduction by parole.

The Definite Sentence   The first application of indeterminate sentencing policies in the United States appeared in 1924.[11] Prior to that time, a regular feature of incarceration was the **definite sentence**—one having a fixed period of time with no reduction by parole. This type of sentence fell out of favor, however, because those interested in rehabilitation found it to be too rigid and insensitive to defendants' individual characteristics and needs.

In contemporary statutes, the definite sentence is occasionally seen with respect to punishments for minor misdemeanors. It is rarely imposed with felonies, however, although life sentences with no eligibility for parole are in a sense definite sentences. For example, the *Delaware Code* reads:

> **Definite sentence:** A sentence of incarceration having a fixed period of time with no reduction by parole.

> Any person who is convicted of first-degree murder shall be punished by death or by imprisonment for the remainder of his or her natural life without benefit of probation or parole or any other reduction.[12]

The diminished appeal of the indeterminate sentence, combined with concerns over street crime and the "coddling" of criminals, has led to renewed interest in definite sentencing guidelines. In 1975, Maine became the first state to abandon the indeterminate sentencing system. At the same time, it also abolished parole. Under its new "flat" sentencing laws, terms of imprisonment are, in effect, definite sentences. Similarly, the "three strikes and you're out" (or "*in*") laws calling for life imprisonment without parole upon conviction of a third felony are a form of definite sentence (see Exhibit 10.1).

Other Sentencing Variations   In addition to the three basic sentences of imprisonment—the indeterminate, the determinate, and the definite—a number of variations and adaptations have been receiving increased attention in recent years.

Exhibit 10.1 | **Research in Crime and Justice**

The Use of the "Three-Strikes" and "Two-Strikes" Laws

Public concern over violent crime has always encouraged the passage of new laws mandating lengthy sentences for repeat felons. The newest of these initiates, known as "Three Strikes and You're Out" laws, mandate that certain (or all) offenders convicted of three felonies face life in prison.

In 1994, California voters approved what has been considered the most sweeping of the three-strikes laws, and the following list reflects some of the felony crimes which now qualify as "strikes" under California law:

1. Murder, voluntary manslaughter, or attempted murder
2. Mayhem (the infliction of serious bodily injury)
3. Rape, sodomy by force, or oral copulation by force
4. Any felony punishable by death or life imprisonment
5. Sexual abuse or lewd acts on a child
6. Kidnapping
7. Robbery with use of a deadly weapon
8. Carjacking with use of a deadly weapon

Although an offender's first two strikes must fall under the above serious felony categories, the crime that triggers the life sentence (the third strike) can be *any* felony. Furthermore, once an individual accrues a second stroke, sentences are doubled and these

Strike two or strike three?

terms must be served in prison rather than on probation. In addition, earned "good time" is limited.

By 1998, some 23 states had enacted three-strikes laws similar (but with modifications) to the California legislation. Research indicates, however, that only Georgia and California have made much use of the statutes. Most jurisdictions use the three-strikes idea sparingly because of concern with long-term incarceration costs. An additional issue has been the potential for increases in the number of jury trials, because instead of plea bargaining, defendants facing a third conviction are almost certain to request a jury trial.

What has been the California experience? From 1994 when the law was passed through July 30,

1998, well over 4,000 California offenders had been convicted on a third strike and were sentenced to 25 years to life. But interestingly, one-third of these sentence enhancements were for nonviolent offenses. Moreover, 192 persons "struck out" for marijuana possession, but only 40 for murder, 25 for rape, and 24 for kidnapping. Translated into dollars and cents, at a cost of $21,885 per year per inmate, it is costing California taxpayers $4.2 million annually to protect society from the marijuana smokers as compared to $1.9 million for the murderers, rapists, and kidnappers *combined.* In early 1999, furthermore, a California inmate, serving 25 years to life for shoplifting a $20 bottle of vitamins, failed to persuade the U.S. Supreme Court to hear his argument that the three-strikes law imposes constitutionally "cruel and unusual punishment."

Georgia has one-upped other states, by instituting a two-strike law. As part of this legislation, Georgia has enumerated what it calls the "seven deadly sins," which include most of the offenses listed earlier that qualify for a third strike in California. A first conviction earns a minimum of 10 years without parole; a second conviction earns life without parole. As of the middle of 1998, Georgia had almost 1,000 two-strike convictions.

Advocates for the enhanced sentencing claim that it is an effective deterrent that has reduced crime. The reality, however, is that crime rates had begun to fall before the laws were passed, typically due to community policing techniques and the booming economy of the 1990s.

SOURCES: *New York Times,* January 20, 1999, p. A12; Peter C. Patch, "The Three Strikes Law and Control of Crime in California," *ACJS Today* 17 (Nov/Dec 1998): 1, 3; *New York Times,* April 12, 1995, p. 21; *USA Today,* November 13, 1998, p. 3A.

Intermittent sentence: A sentence to periods of confinement interrupted by periods of freedom.

Mandatory sentence: A statutory requirement that a certain penalty shall be set and carried out in all cases upon conviction for a specified offense or series of offenses.

In New York and several other jurisdictions, there is the sentence of intermittent imprisonment. Under the New York statute, the **intermittent sentence** is a term to be served on certain days or periods of days as specified by the court.[13] For example, a defendant who pleaded guilty to the felonious possession of 74 pounds of marijuana was sentenced to an intermittent term of 60 days, to be served on consecutive weekends, followed by 5 years' probation.[14] It is a sanction used in instances where the nature of the offense warrants incarceration, but where the defendant's characteristics and habits suggest full-time imprisonment to be inappropriate. It should also be noted that a sentence of intermittent imprisonment is *revocable.* That is, should the offender fail to report to the institution on the days specified, he or she can be returned to court and resentenced to a more traditional term of imprisonment.

Also, a variety of determinant sentence known as the **mandatory sentence** has been the subject of extensive discussion since the middle of the 1970s. Mandatory sentences limit judicial discretion; they are penal code provisions that require the judge to sentence persons convicted of certain specified crimes to prison terms. Under these statutes, which are intended to guarantee that recidivists, violent offenders, and other serious criminals face the strictness and certainty of punishment, neither probation nor other alternative sentences are permitted.

Disparities in Sentencing

Sentencing disparities have long since been a major problem in criminal justice processing. The basis of the difficulty is threefold:

1. The structure of indeterminate sentencing guidelines
2. The discretionary powers of sentencing judges
3. The mechanics of plea bargaining

The statutory minimum and maximum terms of imprisonment combined with fines, probation, or other alternatives to incarceration create a number of sentencing possibilities for a specific crime. With judicial discretion in sentencing, sanctions can vary widely according to the jurisdiction, the community, and the punishment philosophy of a particular judge. The dynamics of plea bargaining enable various defendants accused of the same crime to be convicted and sentenced differently. These problems exist, furthermore, both within an individual court and across jurisdictions, since sentencing statutes can differ drastically from one state to the next.

Consider, for example, the range of sentences possible for conviction of burglary in the first degree (or its equivalent) in the following states:

Percent of felons

State Court Sentences

■ Prison
■ Jail
■ Probation

Percent of felons

Federal Court Sentences

■ Prison
■ Jail
■ Probation

SOURCE: Bureau of Justice Statistics.

- *Idaho:* imprisonment for not less than 1 year nor more than 15 years, or probation[15]
- *New York:* imprisonment for not less than 3 years and not more than 25 years, or probation, or a fine[16]
- *West Virginia:* imprisonment for not less than 1 year nor more than 10 years, or probation (for a first felony conviction)[17]
- *Delaware:* 2 to 20 years' imprisonment, or a suspended sentence, or probation, or a fine (payable in installments)[18]
- *Alabama:* imprisonment for not less than 10 years, or probation[19]

Statistical comparisons of sentencing tendencies in various jurisdictions demonstrate that disparities have been widespread. In the Detroit Recorder's Court, for example, sentencing dispositions were sampled from 10 judges over a 20-month period. It was found that one judge imposed prison terms upon as many as 90 percent of the defendants he sentenced, while another ordered such sentences in only 35 percent of his cases. Another magistrate consistently imposed prison sentences twice as long as those of the most lenient judge; and judges who were the most severe for certain crimes were the most lenient in others.[20] Recent analyses have also demonstrated that a conviction for automobile theft in one jurisdiction may result in more time in prison than a rape conviction in numerous other states, and that some prisoners sentenced for armed robbery end up doing more time in the penitentiary than convicted murderers.

The consequences of disparities in sentencing can be significant, and not only for the convicted, but also for the court and correctional systems and the entire administration of justice. *First,* the wide variations in sentencing make a mockery of the principle of evenhanded administration of the criminal law, thus calling into question the very philosophy of justice in America. *Second,* disparities have a rebound effect on plea bargaining and court scheduling. On the one hand, defendants may opt for a negotiated plea rather than face trial before a judge known to be severe. On the other, substantial delays often result from the granting of continuances sought by defense attorneys who hope that numerous reschedulings will ultimately bring their cases before lenient judges. Known as "judge-shopping," the practice is so widespread that at one time in the District of Columbia court of general sessions, giving a defendant the judge of his or her choice became part of the plea negotiation arrangements.[21] *Third,* prisoners compare their sentences, and an inmate who believes that he or she received an unfair sentence or was the victim of judicial prejudice often becomes hostile, resistant to correctional treatment and discipline, and even riot-prone. *Fourth,* the image of the courts and of the process of justice is even further denigrated (see Exhibit 10.2).

Sentencing Reform

The criticisms of sentencing disparities are directed not only toward judicial discretion, but also toward the statutes that make far-reaching discretion possible. Criminal laws that allow jurists to impose terms of "not more than" 5 years, or 10 years, or 30 years proclaim, in effect, that sentencing judges are answerable only to their consciences. The measures that have been proposed or adopted in various jurisdictions to remedy the problem of sentencing disparities remove that key phrase "not more than" from the penal laws, reducing judicial discretion. Mandatory sentencing statutes, with their stipulations of fixed penalties, are in part the result of calls for better community protection, but they also clearly decrease the court's discretion.

A less extreme model for eliminating the abuses of discretion is the *presumptive fixed sentence,* in use in some jurisdictions and under consideration in several others. The objectives of presumptive sentencing are (1) to reduce disparities by limiting judicial discretion without totally eliminating it, and (2) to increase community protection by imposing a sentence the offender is required to serve.

More stringent than the indeterminate sentence but less rigid than the determinate sentence, the presumptive fixed sentence is a good combination of the two. A state legislature would set a minimum and maximum term, with a limited range, for a particular crime. The judge would impose a fixed determinate sentence within that range, decided on the basis of mitigating circumstances and the offender's characteristics. This sentencing scheme also eliminates the need for parole.[22]

For example, a presumptive sentence for the crime of burglary in the first degree might have a lower legislative limit of 3 years and an upper limit of 10, with a fixed sentence of 5 years as set by the judge. Through this model, imprisonment becomes mandatory, a defined range of terms is established by

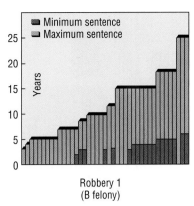

Robbery 1
(B felony)

Disparate Sentencing

In a study of 41 New York judges from across the state, the judges were asked to review files on actual cases and then indicate the sentences they would impose.

In this case, an elderly man was robbed at gunpoint by a heroin addict. The defendant was convicted of first-degree robbery. He was unemployed, lived with his pregnant wife, and had a minor criminal record. Each bar in the figure represents one judge's hypothetical sentence. (His actual sentence was 0–5 years.)

SOURCE: *New York Times.*

Exhibit 10.2   **Historical Perspectives on Crime and Justice**
A Consequence of Sentencing Disparity?

One of the more celebrated cases of disparate sentencing practices involved the conviction of a 20-year-old youth on charges of conspiracy to commit a felony and assault with the intent to rob. The year was 1924, and the youth, although AWOL from the U.S. Navy, had no prior criminal record. His codefendant, Edgar Singleton, was a 31-year-old former convict and umpire for a local baseball team. The two had collaborated to rob a grocery store in Mooresville, Indiana, but the victim resisted, the attempt was thwarted, and both were quickly arrested.

Fearing the strictness and certainty of punishment handed down at the county court in Martinsville, Indiana, Singleton obtained a change of venue, received a term of 2 to 10 years, and was paroled after less than 2 years. The youth,

however, threw himself on the mercy of the local court—but nevertheless received sentences of 2 to 14 years and 10 to 20 years.

Embittered by unequal justice and the inequitable sentence, the

John Dillinger.

youth rebelled against his warders at the Indiana State Reformatory. He attempted escape on three occasions, was charged with numerous disciplinary violations, and as a result was denied parole when first eligible in 1929. Later that year, he was transferred to Indiana State Prison, where he met a score of experienced criminals who taught him the fine art of bank robbery.

On May 22, 1933, just a few days before his thirtieth birthday, after having spent his entire young adult life in prison, he was finally paroled. Based on the tutelage provided by his inmate associates, he began a professional career in bank robbery. During the next 13 months, he engineered a score of armed holdups at banks and stores across the Midwest. His efforts netted him many hundreds of thousands of dollars, but in the process he killed at least 15 people. On July 2, 1934, when he was a young man of only 31 years, FBI agents shot him to death as he exited a theater in Chicago, Illinois. His name was John Dillinger.

SOURCES: L. L. Edge, *Run the Cat Roads* (New York: December, 1981); J. Edgar Hoover, *Persons in Hiding* (Boston: Little, Brown, 1938); John Toland, *The Dillinger Days* (New York: Random House, 1963).

statute, and a degree of judicial discretion remains At the same time, such disparity-producing guidelines as Delaware's 2 to 20 years' imprisonment for the same crime, or Alabama's imprisonment "for not less than" 10 years, or other terms "as the judge sees fit to impose" would be eliminated.

Federal Sentencing Guidelines

In an attempt to reduce disparities at the federal level, in 1985 Congress created the Federal Sentencing Commission. It was a nine-member committee whose task was to establish sentencing guidelines that would reduce judicial discretion and thereby ensure more equal punishments. After 2 years of work, the new guidelines were put into force effective November 1, 1987. They promulgated the greater uniformity that was hoped for and at the same time tended to send more defendants to prison (although for shorter periods of time). For example, the following table shows the case for first offenders:

Crime	Average Time Served Prior to Guidelines	Sentences Under New Guidelines
Kidnapping	7.2 to 9 years	4.2 to 5.2 years
First-degree murder	10 to 12.5 years	30 years to life in all cases
Income tax evasion ($5,000 or less)	4 to 10 months for the only 30% who serve time	Virtually all are subject to some confinement for 1 to 7 months
Drug dealing (1 oz. of cocaine)	21 to 27 months for the only 33% who serve time	Virtually all serve 21 to 27 months

NOTE: Comparisons apply only to the 15% of federal defendants who go to trial; plea negotiations not included.

SOURCE: Sentencing Guidelines and Policy Statements for the Federal Courts, 41 CrL 3087 (1987).

Although the new federal guidelines held the promise of sentence reform, they were attacked immediately because of the way that the U.S. Sentencing Commission had been formed. The commission was an independent body within the judicial branch of government, but it was argued that the act of writing the guidelines was essentially legislative. As such, this represented an unconstitutional delegation of authority by Congress and a violation of the separation-of-powers doctrine. The **separation-of-powers doctrine** is a major principle of American government whereby power is distributed among three branches of government—the legislative, the executive, and the judicial. The officials of each branch are selected by different procedures, have different terms of office, and are independent of one another. The separation is not complete, however, in that each branch participates in the functions of the other through a system of checks and balances. Yet most importantly, the doctrine serves to ensure that the same person or group will not make the law, interpret the law, and apply the law.

By early 1988, hundreds of federal judges had faced the question of the guidelines' constitutionality. Slightly more than half had struck them down, in most instances on separation-of-powers grounds. It was at that point that the U.S. Supreme Court agreed to rule on the matter. In 1989, decided by an 8-to-1 majority, the Court held that the creation of the Federal Sentencing Commission was neither an unconstitutional delegation of legislative discretion nor a violation of the separation-of-powers doctrine.[23]

Separation-of-powers doctrine: The principle that power is distributed among three branches of government—the legislative, the executive, and the judicial—for the purpose of ensuring that no one person or group will make the law, interpret the law, and apply the law.

Truth in Sentencing

The amount of time offenders spend in prison is almost always shorter than the time they are sentenced to serve by the courts. This is the result of "good time" (time off for good behavior) and parole, combined with many correctional systems' efforts to release prisoners early to relieve overcrowding. A recent Department of Justice study, for example, found that prisoners released in 1996 served on average 30 months in jail or prison—only 44 percent of their actual sentences.[24] In response to this situation, a number of states have passed **truth in sentencing** laws that require offenders to serve a substantial portion of their sentences. Under these laws, parole eligibility and good-time credits are either eliminated or restricted, thus reducing the discrepancy between the sentence imposed and the actual time served.

Although the first truth in sentencing law was passed almost two decades ago, it was not until the second half of the 1990s that the movement was fully under way. By 1998, some 40 states and the District of Columbia had truth

Truth in sentencing: Laws that require offenders to serve a substantial portion of their sentences.

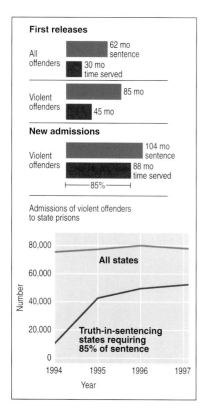

Discrepancy Between Sentence and Time Served: State Prisons, 1997

SOURCE: U.S. Department of Justice.

Presentence investigation: An investigation into the background and character of a defendant that assists the court in determining the most appropriate sentence.

Allocution: the right of a convicted offender to address the court personally prior to the imposition of sentence.

Concurrent and consecutive sentences

in sentencing laws in place, and most require inmates to spend 85 percent of their sentences in prison.

The Sentencing Process

Sentencing is generally a collective decision-making process that involves recommendations of the prosecutor, the defense attorney, the judge, and sometimes the presentence investigator. In jurisdictions where sentence bargaining is part of the plea negotiation process, the judge almost invariably imposes what has been agreed on by the prosecution and the defense.

In the federal system and the majority of state jurisdictions, a **presentence investigation** may be conducted prior to actual sentencing. This is undertaken by the court's probation agency or presentence office, and the resulting report is a summary of the defendant's present offense, previous criminal record, family situation, neighborhood environment, school and educational history, employment record, physical and mental health, habits, associates, and participational activities. The report may also contain comments as to the defendant's remorse, and recommendations for sentencing by the victim, the prosecutor, and the officer who conducted the investigation.

Although presentence investigations are not mandatory in all jurisdictions, the American Bar Association has recommended that they be used for every criminal case. Furthermore, as noted by the Administrative Offices of the U.S. Courts, the value of presentence reports goes well beyond their use in determining appropriate sentences. For example:

- They aid probation and parole officers in their supervision of offenders.
- They aid correctional personnel in their classification, treatment, and release programs.
- They furnish parole boards with useful information for release decision-making.
- They can serve as a database for systematic research.[25]

Following the submission of the presentence report to the judge, a sentencing hearing is held. In common law, and in most jurisdictions, a convicted offender has the right to address the court personally prior to the imposition of sentence. Known as **allocution,** this practice is available so that the court can identify the defendant as the person judged guilty, the defendant can be given the opportunity to plead a pardon, move for an arrest of judgment, or indicate why judgment ought not be pronounced. The specific matters a defendant might state at the allocution are limited and would not include attempts to reopen the question of guilt. Rather, some of the claims included in allocutions have been that the offender has become insane since the verdict was rendered, that he or she has received a pardon for the offense in question, that the defendant is not the person against whom there was a finding of guilt, and in the case of a woman, especially if a death sentence is to be pronounced, that the punishment be adjusted or deferred because of a possible pregnancy.

The presiding judge then imposes the sentence. As noted earlier, the most typical sanctions include fines, imprisonment, probation, or some combination thereof, or death. In instances when the defendant receives multiple sentences for several crimes, the judge may order that terms of imprisonment be served concurrently or consecutively. *Concurrent sentences* are those that are served simultaneously. For example, if the defendant is convicted of both burglary and assault, and is given two terms of 5 years' imprisonment to be served concurrently, both terms are satisfied after 5 years. *Consecutive sentences* are successive—one after another.

As noted in Chapter 9, in the discussions of bail and pretrial detention, it often happens that a defendant comes before a judge for sentencing having already spent weeks, months, and sometimes even years in a local jail or detention facility awaiting trial. This period of detention, referred to as "jail time," is generally deducted from the period of imprisonment imposed. When the conviction is for a misdemeanor or minor felony and the period of pretrial detention closely matches the probable term of imprisonment, the judge may impose a sentence of "time served." That is, the accumulated jail time represents the sentence, and the defendant is released. When the jail time spent awaiting trial is not counted as part of the final sentence, it is commonly referred to as "dead time."

"Jail time"

"Time served"

"Dead time"

THE DEATH PENALTY IN AMERICA

The Eighth Amendment ban against cruel and unusual punishment

For the greater part of U.S. history, the death penalty was used as a punishment for crime, with little thought given to its legitimacy or justification. It was simply accepted as an efficient mechanism for dealing with criminal offenders. When the framers of the Constitution created the Eighth Amendment ban against cruel and unusual punishment, the death penalty itself was apparently not an issue. From the earliest days of the colonial experience, capital punishment was considered neither cruel nor unusual. Under the criminal codes of 1642 and 1650 enacted for the New Haven colony, for example, a total of 11 offenses—some of which do not even appear as misdemeanors in contemporary statutes—called for the death sentence:

1. If any person within this Government shall by direct, express, impious or presumptuous ways, deny the true God and His attributes, he shall be put to death.

2. If any person shall commit any willful and premeditated murder he shall be put to death.

3. If any person slayeth another with a sword or dagger who hath no weapon to defend himself, he shall be put to death.

4. If any man shall slay, or cause another to be slain by lying in wait privily for him or by poisoning or any other such wicked conspiracy, he shall be put to death. . . .

5. If any man or woman shall lie with any beast or brute creature by carnal copulation they shall be put to death, and the beast shall be burned.

6. If any man lieth with mankind as he lieth with a woman, they shall be put to death, unless the one party were forced or be under fourteen years of age, in which case he shall be punished at the discretion of the Court of Assizes.

7. If any person forcibly stealeth or carrieth away any mankind, he shall be put to death.

8. If any man bear false witness maliciously and on purpose to take away a man's life, he shall be put to death.

9. If any man shall traitorously deny his Majesty's right and titles to his Crowns and Dominions, or shall raise armies to resist his authority, he shall be put to death.

10. If any man shall treacherously conspire or publickly attempt to invade or surprise any town or towns, fort or forts, within this Government, he shall be put to death.

11. If any child or children, above sixteen years of age, and of sufficient understanding, shall smite their natural father or mother, unless thereunto provoked and forced for their self-protection from death or maiming, at the complaint of said father and mother, and not otherwise, there being sufficient witnesses thereof, that child or those children so offending shall be put to death.[26]

The death penalty inherently violates the constitutional ban against cruel and unusual punishment and the guarantee of due process of law and equal protection of the laws. The imposition of the death penalty is inconsistent with the fundamental values of our democratic system. . . . Capital punishment is an intolerable denial of civil liberties.
—The American
Civil Liberties Union, 1992

Anyone can avoid the death penalty by not committing murder.
—Professor Ernest van den Haag, 1990

Death cases are indeed different in kind from all other litigation. The penalty, once imposed, is irrevocable.
—Justice John Paul Stevens, 1981

The infamous electric chair, also referred to in underworld lingo as the "hot seat," "hot chair," "hot shot," "Old Sparky" (in Florida), "Gruesome Gertie" (in Louisiana), or simply, the "chair."

Within such a context, execution upon conviction of numerous crimes was indeed quite unusual. The definition of what was cruel punishment similarly eluded rigid guidelines. Consider, for example, the punishment for treason under the English common law—the very sanction that the leaders of the American Revolution risked by signing the Declaration of Independence:

> That you and each of you, be taken to the place from whence you came, and from thence be drawn on a hurdle to the place of execution where you shall be hanged by the neck not till you are dead; that you be severally taken down, while yet alive, and your bowels be taken out and burned before your faces—that your heads be then cut off, and your bodies cut into four quarters, to be at the king's disposal. And God have mercy on your souls.[27]

What the framers of the Constitution likely had in mind, however, when they spoke of "cruel and unusual" punishments were the many more grisly forms of execution that had periodically appeared throughout human history. Down through the ages criminals have been burned at the stake, crucified, boiled in flaming oil, impaled, and flayed, to name only a few.

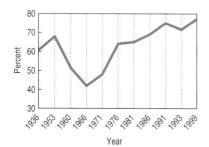

Support for the Death Penalty (for murder) in the United States

Percent responding "yes."

SOURCE: Gallup Poll.

Capital Punishment and Discrimination

In 1967, the President's Commission on Law Enforcement and Administration of Justice commented that the death penalty "is most frequently imposed and carried out on the poor, the Negro, and the members of unpopular groups."[28] Such an observation was no surprise to those who had watched closely the pattern of the imposition of capital punishment over the years, nor to the many African Americans, especially in the South, who had been systematically victimized by death sentences for well over a century and a half. In Virginia during the 1830s, for example, there were 5 capital crimes for whites but at least 70 for blacks.[29] In 1848 the Virginia legislature required the death penalty for any offense committed by a black for which 3 or more years' imprisonment might be imposed as punishment for a white.[30] Pursuant to the South Carolina Black Codes in 1825, burning at the stake was permitted and even carried out—a punishment that had originally been reserved for executing heretics in medieval Europe.[31] And from 1882 through 1903, at least 1,985 African Americans were hanged or burned alive by the Ku Klux Klan and other southern lynch mobs—often when there was no offense at all or even the mere suspicion of one.

Even the most superficial analysis of executions under civil authority reflects a clear overrepresentation of blacks. In 1965, for example, sociologist Marvin E. Wolfgang and law professor Anthony Amsterdam began a study to determine the relationship between ethnicity and sentencing for rape in 11 southern and border states where rape was a capital offense. Their findings supported the notion that African Americans were treated with undue severity.

> Among the 823 blacks convicted of rape, 110, or 13 percent, were sentenced to death; among the 442 whites convicted of rape, only 9, or 2 percent, were sentenced to death. *The statistical probability that such a disproportionate number of blacks could be sentenced to death by chance alone is less than one out of a thousand.*[32]

There were 3,859 prisoners executed under civil authority in the United States from 1930 through 1967. When these cases are studied, it becomes even more evident that capital punishment was used as an instrument for racial discrimination. In this period, about 55 percent of those executed for all crimes were either black or members of some other minority group. Of the 455 executed for rape alone, 90 percent were nonwhite.

Cruel and Unusual Punishment

Historically, the Supreme Court's position on the death penalty has been grounded in the broader issue of "cruel and unusual" punishment as prohibited by the Eighth Amendment. When adopting the Eighth Amendment ban, it is likely that the framers of the Constitution had intended to outlaw punishments that were outside both the mainstream of penalties typically imposed in the new nation and the moral judgments of the people. Thus the purpose of the amendment may have been to prevent any return to the screw and the rack, rather than to outlaw any sanctions then in common use. But this can be viewed only as conjecture, for the High Court itself, for more than a century, offered little as to the nature and scope of the ban.

The notion that punishment could be cruel and unusual was argued by three of the justices in 1892. The case was *O'Neil* v. *Vermont*,[33] in which the petitioner stood to serve 19,915 days (almost 55 years) in jail for 307 separate illegal sales of liquor. The Court found that since the Eighth Amendment did not limit the states, no federal question was involved, and the sentence imposed by the Vermont court was affirmed. However, in a strong dissenting opinion, Justice Stephen J. Field argued that punishment would necessarily be cruel and unusual when it did not fit the crime to which it was attached.

U.S. JURISDICTIONS WITHOUT A DEATH PENALTY	
Alaska	Michigan
District of Columbia	Minnesota
	North Dakota
Hawaii	Rhode Island
Iowa	Vermont
Maine	West Virginia
Massachusetts	Wisconsin

DEATH PENALTY JURISDICTIONS WITH NO EXECUTIONS	
Connecticut	New York
Kansas	South Dakota
New Hampshire	Tennessee
New Jersey	U.S. Government
New Mexico	U.S. Military

Weems **v.** *United States:* The Supreme Court ruling that a sentence disproportionate to the offense is in violation of the Eighth Amendment ban against cruel and unusual punishment.

After *O'Neil,* the issue remained dormant for almost two decades until *Weems* **v.** *United States,*[34] decided in 1910. The case was significant for the Eighth Amendment ban, for in its ruling the Court struck down a sentence involving a heavy fine, 15 years at hard labor, the wearing of chains, the life-long loss of certain rights, plus several other sanctions—all for the offense of making false entries in official records. The High Court had found the sentence disproportionate to the offense, and as such, *Weems* was the first case decided on Eighth Amendment grounds.

By 1958, the Court had agreed that the constitutional prohibition could have no fixed and unchanging meaning. Rather, any challenges brought to the Court must necessarily be viewed in terms of "evolving standards of decency."

Death and the Supreme Court

On the issue of capital punishment per se, the Supreme Court's interpretation of the Eighth Amendment has remained flexible. As to the method of execution, the Court offered some preliminary guidelines well over a century ago. In *Wilkerson* v. *Utah,*[35] decided in 1878, the justices agreed that public shooting was neither cruel nor unusual. At the same time, however, it was noted that the constitutional amendment would oppose such punishments as drawing and quartering, burning alive, and other punishments of torturous death. *In re Kemmler,*[36] decided in 1890, held that death by electrocution reflected humane legal intentions and hence did not offend the Eighth Amendment.

Subsequent to *Kemmler,* the Court remained essentially silent on the constitutionality of capital punishment for almost eight decades. Meanwhile, throughout the 1950s and well into the 1960s, the NAACP Legal Defense and Education Fund combined its efforts with those of the American Civil Liberties Union (ACLU) to wage an all-out legal attack against capital punishment. The two organizations came to the aid of many prisoners who had been sentenced to death. Briefs were prepared, appeals were filed, and data were collected on the disproportionate use of the death penalty for African American offenders. The courts reflected an increasing willingness to review capital cases and to reverse lower court decisions, with the result that many state authorities became reluctant to schedule and perform executions.

In 1963, Justice Arthur J. Goldberg suggested that capital punishment may be a per se violation of the Eighth Amendment. Although he was not speaking for the majority of the Court at the time, his statement, combined with mounting pressure for a decision on the constitutionality of the death penalty, served to further the NAACP-ACLU effort. The penalty was ultimately challenged on a variety of legal grounds, and on June 3, 1967, the impending execution of more than 500 condemned prisoners throughout the country came to a halt, while courts and governors waited to see what the High Court would decide.

Witherspoon **v.** *Illinois:* The Supreme Court ruling that states cannot exclude from juries in capital cases *all* persons opposed to the death penalty.

Witherspoon* v. *Illinois The first of these challenges reached the Supreme Court in *Witherspoon* **v.** *Illinois,*[37] and the decision in 1968 was the first indication that the death penalty might be in trouble. In *Witherspoon,* an Illinois court had permitted a verdict of guilty and a sentence of death to be handed down by a jury from which the state had deliberately and systematically excluded all persons who had any scruples against capital punishment. The Court sustained Witherspoon's challenge, ruling that the "death-qualified" jury was indeed unconstitutional (see Exhibit 10.3). Coming at almost the same time was the High Court's decision in *United States* v. *Jackson,*[38] which invalidated the death penalty provisions of the Federal Kidnapping Act (better known as the Lindbergh Law).

Furman v. Georgia   In the fall of 1971, *Furman* v. *Georgia, Jackson* v. *Georgia,* and *Branch* v. *Texas* were brought before the High Court on the challenge that the death sentences ordered were "cruel and unusual" because of the arbitrary and discriminatory manner in which such sanctions had been imposed in the past for the crimes of murder and rape. The leading case was *Furman* v. *Georgia,*[39] which involved the death sentence following William Furman's conviction for a murder that had occurred during the course of a burglary attempt. The decision as to whether Furman's sentence should be life or death had been left to the jury, and his conviction and sentence had been affirmed by all of the Georgia courts.

The Supreme Court's *Furman* decision on June 29, 1972, was a most complex one. It was announced in a nine-opinion *per curium* (unsigned) statement that summarized the narrow argument of the five justices in the majority. In addition, each of the nine justices issued a separate concurring or dissenting opinion. Only Justices Brennan and Marshall were willing to hold that capital punishment was unconstitutional per se. Justices Douglas, Stewart, and White adopted a more narrow view, arguing that the state statutes in question were unconstitutional because they offered judges and juries no standards or guidelines to consider in deciding between life and death. As Justice Stewart put it, the result was that the punishment of death was tantamount to being "struck by lightning." In other words, all state and federal death penalty statutes were deemed too arbitrary, capricious, and discriminatory to withstand Eighth Amendment scrutiny. The position taken by Justices Douglas, Stewart, and White presented the common ground of agreement with Justices Brennan and Marshall, thus constituting the five-justice majority.

Gregg v. Georgia   By effectively invalidating all existing state death penalty statutes, *Furman* also served to remove more than 600 persons from death row. But nevertheless, the Court's decision in *Furman* did provide two avenues by which states could enact new capital punishment laws. First, they could establish a two-stage procedure consisting of a trial at which the question of culpability could be determined, followed by an additional proceeding for those found guilty, during which evidence might be presented to make the decision for death or life more informed and procedurally sound. Or second, states could remove the discretion from the jury by making death the mandatory punishment for certain crimes.

In the wake of *Furman,* 35 states passed new capital statutes. Ten chose the mandatory route while 25 selected the two-stage procedure. By 1976, both approaches were brought before the Supreme Court, and the constitutionality of the death penalty was again argued.

The issue in *Gregg* **v.** *Georgia* was Georgia's new bifurcated trial structure.[40] Following a conviction of guilt in first-degree murder cases, the nature of punishment was decided in a separate proceeding. The Georgia statute required the judge or jury to consider any aggravating or mitigating circumstances in the life-or-death decision, including the following conditions:

- The defendant had a prior conviction for a capital felony or a substantial history of serious assaultive criminal convictions.
- The murder was committed during the course of a rape, an armed robbery, a kidnapping, a burglary, or arson.
- The defendant created a grave risk of death to more than one person.
- The defendant killed for profit.
- The victim was a judicial officer or a prosecutor killed during or because of his exercise of official duty.
- The victim was a police officer, corrections employee, or firefighter who was engaged in the performance of his duties.

Furman **v.** *Georgia:*   The Supreme Court ruling that statutes that leave arbitrary and discriminatory discretion to juries in imposing death sentences are in violation of the Eighth Amendment.

Gregg **v.** *Georgia:*   The Supreme Court ruling that (1) the death penalty is not, in itself, cruel and unusual punishment; and (2) a two-part proceeding—one for the determination of innocence or guilt and the other for determining the sentence—is constitutional and meets the objections noted in *Furman* v. *Georgia.*

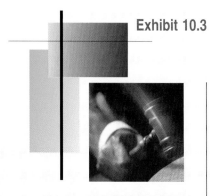

Exhibit 10.3 **Legal Perspectives on Crime and Justice**
Witherspoon v. *Illinois* and the "Death-Qualified" Jury

In capital cases, prosecutors seek jurors who will consider imposing the death penalty. Under current laws, a person can be excluded from serving on a capital jury if personal opposition to the death penalty will impair the performance of his or her duties as juror. Who then, is left to sit on the capital jury? It has been argued that these jurors—empowered to impose a sentence of death—are biased in favor of the death penalty, and as such, conviction prone. Consequently, they have been dubbed "death-qualified jurors," "automatic death penalty jurors," or even "hanging jurors."

Why the death qualification process? It seemingly emerged as a direct result of cases in which a conviction called for an automatic and mandatory sentence of death. And because of the automatic death sentence, jurors opposed to the death penalty acquitted defendants who appeared to be guilty. To alleviate this problem, jurors opposed to the death penalty were removed from the *venire* pool, and prosecutors no longer had to deal with what they considered to be biased jurors.

Currently, mandatory death sentences are no longer permitted, and the Supreme Court requires

that capital cases be divided into two stages—one phase for the determination of guilt or innocence and a second for sentencing. But there is still a compelling reason to continue the death qualification process. If jurors opposed to the death penalty are not screened out, the jury faces the possibility of not reaching consensus in the determination of guilt; those opposed to the death penalty may not be inclined to return a guilty verdict knowing that the defendant could receive a death sentence in the sentencing phase.

The potentially biasing effects of death qualification were brought to the forefront in *Witherspoon* v. *Illinois.* In 1968, defendant Witherspoon contended that his jury did not represent the community, that its members were highly supportive of the death penalty, and were therefore conviction prone. At the time, current Illinois law read that a person opposed to the death penalty for any reason was to be excluded from a capital jury. Because of this, nearly half of the *venire* were disqualified. The resulting jury convicted Witherspoon, and subsequently handed down a sentence of death.

The U.S. Supreme Court held that a death-qualified jury, as was selected in Witherspoon's case, could not constitutionally put a person to death. The Court reasoned that a death sentence under those circumstances would deprive Witherspoon of life without due process of law in accordance with the Fourteenth Amendment.

The death qualification process was then modified to allow individuals with "reservations about the death penalty," but who could "follow the law," to serve in the sentencing phase of a capital case.

In the most recent decision relating to death-qualified juries, the Supreme Court voted to uphold the practice of death qualification. *Lockhart* v. *McCree,* decided in 1986, examined ample social science research which almost unanimously agreed that death-qualified juries are more conviction prone than regular juries. The main issue in *Lockhart* was whether or not there can be death qualification for the guilt phase of a bifurcated trial or only for the penalty phase. The defendant in this case felt that because his jury was death-qualified from the beginning, his guilt was determined by a jury that was inclined to convict. He contended that there is no necessity for death qualification before the sentencing phase, and that the only result is bias in the state's favor.

In the majority opinion, Chief Justice Rehnquist admitted that death-qualified juries were somewhat more conviction prone, but stated that this does not violate the defendant's right to an impartial jury. In addition, it was decided that death-qualified juries do not represent a distinct group (such as women or African Americans), so that they do not violate the fair cross-section requirement of the Sixth Amendment.

SOURCES: *Gregg* v. *Georgia,* 428 U.S. 153 (1976); *Witherspoon* v. *Illinois,* 391 U.S. 510 (1968); *Lockhart* v. *McCree,* 106 U.S. 1758 (1986); T. Brown, "Who's Qualified to Decide Who Dies?" *Nebraska Law Review* 65 (1986): 558–583.

- The defendant directed another person to kill as his agent.
- The murder was committed in a wantonly vile, horrible, or inhumane manner because it involved torture, depravity of mind, or an aggravated battery.
- The defendant was a prison escapee.
- The murder was committed in an attempt to avoid arrest.[41]

By a 7-to-2 majority, the decision in *Gregg* upheld the Georgia law, reasoning as follows:

> The new Georgia sentencing procedures, by contrast, focus the jury's attention on the particularized nature of the crime and the particularized nature of the individual defendant. While the jury is permitted to consider any aggravating or mitigating circumstances, it must find and identify at least one statutory aggravating factor before it may impose a penalty of death. In this way is the jury's discretion channeled. No longer can a jury wantonly and freakishly impose the death sentence; it is always circumscribed by the legislative guidelines.

Coker v. Georgia   During the years following the decision in *Gregg,* the Supreme Court continued in its refusal to hold categorically that the death penalty per se constituted cruel and unusual punishment. However, in a series of rulings from 1977 through 1980, the Court did place limitations on the imposition of capital sentences. In **Coker v. Georgia,**[42] decided in 1977, it was held that the death sentence could not be imposed for rape, because such punishment was grossly disproportionate to the injury caused the victim. And without expressly stating so, the Court strongly implied in *Coker* that a death sentence was inappropriate except as punishment for murder.

Coker v. *Georgia:*   The Supreme Court ruling that the sentence of death for the crime of rape is an excessive and disproportionate penalty forbidden by the Eighth Amendment.

The Return of Capital Punishment

On June 2, 1967, Luis Jose Monge was put to death in Colorado for the crime of murder. He was the last person to be executed in the United States prior to the suspension of capital punishment later that year, and for a full decade capital punishment ceased to exist throughout the United States. With the decision of *Gregg,* however, made on the eve of the nation's two-hundredth birthday, the Supreme Court upheld the constitutionality of capital punishment. By 1977, more than 400 persons were on death row, with the first execution occurring during the early weeks of that year.

The prisoner was Gary Mark Gilmore, a convicted murderer who had been sentenced to death by a Utah court. The Gilmore case attracted national headlines, not only because it was the first probable execution in a decade, but also because of the many bizarre events associated with it. The initial sensation came late in 1976 when Gilmore fired his attorneys, abandoned his appeal, and requested that his execution be carried out at the earliest possible date. He even appeared before the justices of the U.S. Supreme Court to argue that he had a "right to die."

Attorneys then petitioned the Utah courts, indicating that Gilmore was insane, that he was incapable of representing himself, and that his death wish was "tantamount to suicide." But the state court rejected this argument, and all pending appeals were dismissed. Gilmore's mother then petitioned the U.S. Supreme Court, maintaining that her son was incompetent to waive his right to appeal. The stay of execution she requested was denied, however, on the basis that she had no legal standing to seek relief for her son.

The case of Gary Mark Gilmore then began to take on a tragically comic air. On the morning of November 16, 1976, Gilmore attempted suicide by taking an overdose of sedatives. At almost the same moment, some 40 miles south of the prison in a small apartment just outside Provo, Utah, 20-year-old Nicole Barrett also took an overdose of drugs. The suicide pact had been arranged as part of a pathetic love affair that Gilmore had been carrying on with the young mother of two. But Gilmore survived the ordeal, as did Barrett.

Counsel was then appointed to help Gilmore secure an execution date. It was later revealed that this attorney had a financial interest in Gilmore's death, having secured the exclusive right to act as the condemned man's biographer

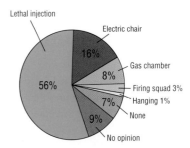

"Apart from your opinion about the death penalty, what form of execution do you consider to be the most humane?"

SOURCE: Gallup Poll.

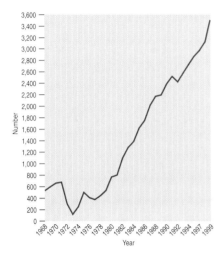

Number of Persons on Death Row, Year End, 1968–1999

SOURCE: Bureau of Justice Statistics; NAACP Legal Defense and Education Fund, Inc.

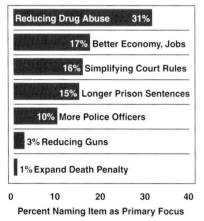

0   10   20   30   40

Percent Naming Item as Primary Focus

Police Chiefs Place Death Penalty Last in Reducing Violent Crime

SOURCE: Death Penalty Information Center.

DEATH ROW INMATES SEEK EXECUTION

Eleven of the 68 inmates put to death in 1998 had dropped their appeals and opted for speedier executions. Their reasons included:

- The appeals process, which can take 10 years or more
- Loathing the idea of a life sentence, which is the usual alternative to death
- Atoning for their sins and gaining spiritual closure

and agent; a six-figure contract had been negotiated for publication and motion picture rights to the story of Gilmore's life and death. "Gary Gilmore" T-shirts also appeared, and media bidding wars began for exclusive interviews and stories.

Independent legal groups challenged the courts with collateral legal suits, but angered over the new delays, Gilmore staged yet another unsuccessful suicide attempt. The Supreme Court elected not to intervene in any further litigation, and an execution date was finally set. As the day approached, the media and pro- and anti-death groups began a death watch outside the walls of the prison. During his final hours, Gilmore refused any interviews. There was another stay of execution, but it lasted only a few hours. Gilmore was scheduled to die before a firing squad, and while he was being led to the execution chamber, mobile television crews attempted to position themselves to record the gunshots signaling Gilmore's demise. When asked by Warden Samuel W. Smith if he had any last words, Gilmore offered nothing philosophical or dramatic—simply, "Let's do it!" Finally, just after dawn on January 17, 1977, Gilmore was strapped to a wooden chair in a cold and shadowy prison warehouse. At 8:07 A.M., a signal was given to marksmen hidden behind a cubicle 30 feet from the prisoner. Four .30-caliber bullets ripped through his chest, and Gary Mark Gilmore became the first person to be executed in an American prison in almost a decade.[43] (For a discussion of the number of women executed in recent history, see Exhibit 10.4.)

Methods of Execution

In a series of decisions spanning the period from 1878 through 1953, the Supreme Court has upheld as constitutional such methods of execution as hanging, shooting, electrocution, and the use of lethal gas.

As of 1999, some 38 states had a death penalty in force. A number of states allow for more than one mode of execution. While electrocution is generally instantaneous, the use of lethal injection is considered by many to be more humane. Another method, the well-known "gas chamber," seems to be a grim process. An eyewitness described the execution of Luis Jose Monge in 1967:

> According to the official execution log unconsciousness came more than five minutes after the cyanide splashed down into the sulfuric acid. Even after unconsciousness is declared officially, the prisoner's body continues to fight for life. He coughs and groans. The lips make little pouting motions resembling the motions made by a goldfish in a bowl. The head strains back and then slowly sinks down to the chest. And in Monge's case, the arms, though tightly bound to the chair, strained through the straps and the hands clawed torturously as if the prisoner were struggling for air.[44]

Interestingly, in 1994 a federal district court ruling declared execution by lethal gas to be in violation of the Eighth Amendment ban against cruel and unusual punishment. In making the decision, presiding Judge Marilyn Hall Patel stated that California's gas chamber at San Quentin Prison, where almost 200 prisoners had been executed since 1938, was a "brutal relic with no place in civilized society and must be immediately shut down."[45] Rejecting the state's assertion that cyanide gas causes virtually instant unconsciousness, Judge Patel cited doctors' reports and witnesses' accounts of numerous past executions as evidence that dying inmates remain conscious for up to a minute or longer. In that time, she said, the inmate is likely to suffer intense physical pain, mainly an "air hunger" similar to strangulation or drowning. The ruling required the use of lethal injection for all future executions in California.

Execution by cyanide gas is still permitted, however, in Arizona, Maryland, Missouri, and Wyoming.

In four states—Delaware, Montana, New Hampshire, and Washington—the official methods of execution include hanging. In Delaware, many a defense attorney has vividly described execution via the hangman's noose in an attempt to sway jurors away from imposing a death sentence. This was

---

Exhibit 10.4   Gender Perspectives on Crime and Justice
Women on Death Row

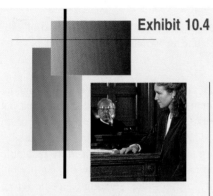

Throughout U.S. history, the rate at which women have been sentenced to death and actually executed has remained quite small in comparison to men. Women account for only 13 percent of all murder arrests, and only 1.9 percent of the death sentences imposed. Actual executions of female offenders in America have been quite rare, totaling only 559 documented instances since the first occurred in 1632. These 559 executions constitute less than 3 percent of the total of 19,200 confirmed executions in the United States since 1608. Only three women have been executed since the death penalty was reinstated in 1976: Judy Buenoano in Florida on March 30, 1998, Karla Faye Tucker in Texas on February 3, 1998, and Velma Barfield in North Carolina on November 2, 1984. Prior to this, the last woman offender executed was Elizabeth Ann Duncan, in California, on August 8, 1962.

During the past quarter-century only 123 death sentences have been imposed on female offenders, and of these only 45 sentences remained in effect as of January 1, 1999. In addition to the three that resulted in execution,

the rest were either reversed or commuted to life imprisonment. Of the 45 women on death row, a slight majority were there as the result of killings associated with other crimes—robberies, burglaries, drug deals, and the like. Of the others, however, 10 had murdered their husbands or boyfriends (or had arranged for the killing), 7 had murdered their children or grandchildren, 2 had killed both husband and children, and 1 had murdered a relative. What this suggests is that women are far more likely than men to end up on death row for family-related murders. This should not imply that killings by women are less serious or gruesome. Among the methods these women used to murder their victims are shooting with an AK-47, slicing with a box cutter, injecting with drain cleaner, and beating with a baseball bat. Or consider Kelly O'Donnell, sentenced for killing a Philadelphia man in 1992. O'Donnell and her boyfriend dismembered their victim, pieces of whom were found in trash bags along the shores of the Delaware River, and on the street where she lived. One of the victim's eyes and eyelids, furthermore, were found in a pencil case in O'Donnell's apartment.

With the exception of 38-year-old Karla Faye Tucker, women have rarely made headlines for being put to death. The murder for which Tucker was convicted and sentenced to death had been

especially vicious. On June 12, 1983, she killed two people with a pickax, and boasted, just after the killings, that she had experienced a surge of sexual pleasure every time she swung the weapon. But that was not why her case received so much attention. What was troubling to many was that during her years on death row she went from a strung-out killer with a pickax to a penitent, committed Christian. Her supporters, who included Bianca Jagger, Pope John Paul II, and televangelist Pat Robertson, argued that it was a different Karla Faye Tucker who was scheduled to die—she was not the same person who committed the ax murders so many years earlier.

Interestingly, many prosecutors around the country spoke of "equality for women" when Karla Faye Tucker was executed, suggesting that women had indeed achieved equal rights in capital litigation, that they were being held just as accountable for their actions as men are. Given the small percentage of women who are on death row and the even smaller number who are actually executed, one could argue that there may be gender bias at work, that women are screened out of the death penalty track. But on the other hand, it must also be remembered that women commit only a small fraction of the kinds of murders that qualify for capital punishment.

SOURCES: *New York Times,* February 8, 1998, Section 4, pp. 1, 3; Victor L. Streib, "Death Penalty for Female Offenders: January 1, 1973, to the Present" (Web site address: http://www.law.onu.edu/faculty/streib/femdeath.htm).

DEATH PENALTY ATTITUDES AMONG COLLEGE STUDENTS

	Percent agreeing*
Pro statements:	
Capital punishment is a deterrent to crime	79.8%
Convicted murderers are given too many appeals	91.8
The death penalty helps make society safer	70.0
Drug dealers should be executed	40.3
Only guilty people are sentenced to die	25.0
Anti statements:	
It costs less to keep someone in prison for life than it does to execute him or her	32.2%
The death penalty is society's way of getting revenge	52.8
Minorities are more likely to be executed than are whites	53.5
Mentally retarded murderers shouldn't be executed	51.5
The race of the victim plays a major role in whether the accused will be given the death penalty	50.8

*Strongly, moderately, and slightly agree categories were combined.

SOURCE: Brian K. Payne and Victoria Coogle, "Examining Attitudes About the Death Penalty," *Corrections Compendium,* April 1998.

The hospital-type gurney used in Texas executions by injection. Restraints rest on top of the gurney, and an intravenous needle is visible at the observation window. Murderer Charles Brooks, Jr., was the first criminal in the United States to be executed by this method, on December 7, 1982.

most effectively done in the case of Mark McKinney, convicted of a 1980 homicide:

> He will walk thirteen steps to the gallows. He will stand, and a hood, black in color, will be placed over his head. A noose with thirteen knots will be dropped over his shoulders and pulled around his neck. There will be an executioner, whom we do not know, who will stand removed, and Mark will stand over a trap door. The executioner will push a button which will cause the trap door to spring open, and Mark will drop between four to six feet. The rope will constrict around his neck, causing him to die.[46]

For inmates sentenced to death under federal statues, the method of execution is governed by the law of the state in which the punishment is to be carried out.

Lethal Injection Among the most virulent arguments regarding the nature of execution emerged in 1977 when a number of states enacted statutes that put to rest their electric chairs, gas chambers, and gallows. In their place was death by lethal injection, referred to by many death row inmates as "the ultimate high."

Proponents of the new process argued that it would be a more palatable way of killing—it would be instantaneous, and the prisoner would simply fall asleep. Opponents denied its humanity, arguing that sticking a needle into a vein can be tricky, with the prospect of repeated attempts upon a struggling prisoner posing "a substantial threat to tortuous pain." The American Medical Association also took a stand on the matter, instructing its members not to take part in such executions, arguing that the role of the physicians was to protect lives, not take them.[47]

Despite the arguments, the new method of execution went forward. On December 7, 1982, Charles Brooks, Jr., was put to death in Huntsville, Texas, becoming the first person to die by a state-sanctioned lethal injection. First a catheter was placed into a vein in his left arm; through the catheter a saline solution flowed—a sterile saltwater used routinely as a medium for drug injections. Brooks was then given doses of barbiturates and potassium chloride, which paralyzed him, stopped his breathing, and guaranteed his death.[48] Ironically, on Brook's arm above the catheter through which the deadly concoction flowed was a tattoo that read, "I was born to die."

By the middle of the 1980s, the debate over the humanity of lethal injections quelled, while others argued against the brutal nature of electrocution. By the 1990s, however, injection had become the primary mechanism,

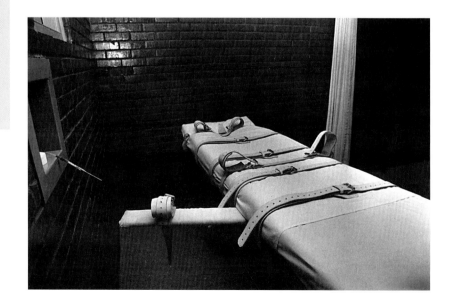

followed immediately by electrocution. (For an international perspective on the death penalty, see Exhibit 10.5.)

The Death Penalty Debate

The arguments for or against capital punishment historically have revolved around the issues of economics, retribution, public opinion, community protection, deterrence, irreversibility, discrimination, protection of the criminal justice system, brutalization, and cruel and unusual punishment.

The *economic argument* for capital punishment holds that execution is far less expensive than maintaining a prisoner behind bars for the remainder of his or her natural life. However, death sentences are invariably appealed, and these too can be costly. In fact, every available quantitative study of this argument demonstrates that because of all of the additional appeals and their procedural safeguards that are constitutionally required in capital cases, the death penalty costs taxpayers substantially more than life imprisonment.[49]

The *retribution argument* asserts that the kidnapper, murder, and rapist, as vile and despicable human beings, deserve to die. This is simply a matter of individual opinion, and differences in philosophy appear even within the Supreme Court. In *Furman*, Justice Thurgood Marshall spoke against this position. At the same time, however, the Court stated that while retribution was no longer a dominant objective, "neither is it a forbidden objective nor one inconsistent with our respect for the dignity of men."

Public opinion has been a motivating factor in the reenactment of death penalty statutes. When the California Supreme Court declared the state's death penalty law unconstitutional in February 1972, letters and telegrams opposing the decision poured into the legislature and governor's office. In a referendum held later that year, 5 months after *Furman*, California voters overwhelmingly approved an amendment to the state constitution that made capital punishment mandatory for selected crimes.[50] In the years hence, throughout the United States, every poll conducted on the matter found the vast majority of Americans to favor the death penalty for murder.

The *community protection argument* made by supporters of the death penalty maintains that such a "final remedy" is necessary to keep the murderer from further ravaging society. Counter to this position is the claim that life imprisonment could achieve the same goal. Yet, as has been pointed out by a number of studies, paroled murderers have lower rates of recidivism than other classes of offenders. For example, in a recent study of 558 death-sentenced inmates, four were actually later found to be innocent; and of 239 that were eventually released from prison, just 20 percent committed new crimes and only one of these was a homicide. The conclusion of the study was that these inmates did not pose a subsequent "disproportionate danger" to society.[51]

Related to this is the *deterrence argument,* held by retentionists, that capital punishment not only prevents the offender from committing additional crimes, but deters others as well. With respect to deterrence in general, the work of Franklin E. Zimring and Gordon J. Hawkins demonstrated that punishment is an effective deterrent for those who are not predisposed to commit crimes, but a questionable deterrent for those who are criminally inclined.[52] A number of studies have also been done specifically on the deterrent effects of capital punishment. One research strategy for such studies has been to compare the homicide rates in states that have death penalty provisions with states that do not. Another has been to examine murder rates in given areas both before and after an execution. And still a third approach has been to analyze crime rates in general as well as murder rates in particular in jurisdictions before and after the abolition of capital punishment. These studies have consistently produced no evidence that the death penalty deters homicide.[53]

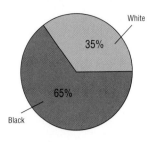

Race of victim in all murder cases

White 35%

Black 65%

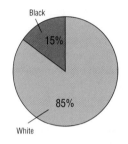

Race of victim in all murder cases where district attorney sought death penalty

Black 15%

White 85%

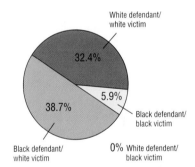

Percentage of cases where death penalty was sought, by race of defendant and victim

White defendant/ white victim 32.4%

Black defendant/ black victim 5.9%

Black defendant/ white victim 38.7%

White defendent/ black victim 0%

The Death Penalty and Accusations of Racial Bias: The Chattahoochee Study

A look at prosecution for the death penalty since 1973 in the Chattahoochee judicial district, which covers six counties in western Georgia and includes Columbus, the state's second largest city.

SOURCES: Death Penalty Information Center; Southern Christian Leadership Council.

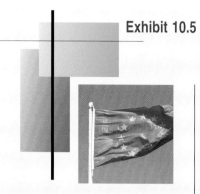

Exhibit 10.5 **International Perspectives on Crime and Justice**
Punishment Under Taliban Islamic Rule

Taliban militiamen use a tank to knock down a wall on top of a man (not visible) convicted of raping a 12-year-old boy in Kabul, Afghanistan. The punishment was devised by the Taliban to punish homosexual acts, a crime in Islam. After 30 minutes the rubble is removed and anyone who survives is exonerated.

Little was known of Afghanistan's Taliban Islamic movement until September of 1996, when its followers stormed the capital city of Kabul. The Taliban is a religious militia that fosters an extremist interpretation of Islam. International attention came to the Taliban because of its treatment of women, who are now prohibited from going to school or work, earning money, and leaving their homes unless accompanied by a close male relative. Furthermore, women in Afghanistan run the risk of being beaten for not wearing the head-to-toe *burqu*, an all-enveloping garment required by the Taliban.

Punishment under the Taliban would also appear to be extreme by Western standards. In 1996, for example, a case of public stoning for adultery reached the international media. The couple were placed blindfolded in small dug-out pits with only their heads and chests showing The first stone was cast by the Muslim cleric who had judged them, followed by a cascade of stones thrown by

Taliban fighters. It was more than 10 minutes before the two were finally dead.

On a January morning in 1999, thousands of people watched as a Taliban tank knocked over a 15-foot brick wall, sending it crashing down on a 60-year-old man sentenced to death for sodomizing a 12-year-old boy. When the rubble was cleared away half an hour later, the man was found dead. Under Taliban law, homosexuality is a

capital offense punishable by the wall-toppling method, but if the offender survives the sentence is commuted. Several men have been sentenced to death by this means, and a few have actually survived.

On the same day as the wall-toppling execution, the hands and feet of a number of thieves were amputated in the main stadium of the city of Kabul. Elsewhere in the Islamic world, similar methods of punishment are known to occur.

SOURCES: *World Press Review*, August 1997, p. 36; *New York Times International*, November 3, 1996, p. 8; *New York Times International*, January 19, 1999, p. A4.

The *irreversibility argument* put forth by those opposed to the death penalty contends that there is always the possibility that an innocent person might be put to death. Retentionists maintain that although such a risk might exist, there are no documented cases of such an occurrence in recent years. But in counterpoint, it was noted in the opening sentences of this chapter that at least 77 inmates have been exonerated and released from death rows during the past 25 years. This suggests that there might have been other innocent inmates who were not as fortunate to have their convictions overturned before their death sentences were carried out.

The *discrimination argument* against capital punishment contends that the death penalty is a lottery system, with the odds stacked heavily against those less capable of defending themselves. As Justice Thurgood Marshall wrote in his concurring opinion in *Furman* v. *Georgia:*

It also is evident that the burden of capital punishment falls upon the poor, the ignorant, and the underprivileged members of society. It is the poor, and the members of minority groups who are least able to voice their complaints against capital punishment. Their impotence leaves them victims of a sanction which the wealthier, better-represented, just-as-guilty person can escape. So long as the capital sanction is used only against the forlorn, easily forgotten members of society, legislators are content to maintain the status quo, because change would draw attention to the problem and concern might develop. Ignorance is perpetuated and apathy soon becomes its mate, and we have today's situation.

The most recent statistics available on the social characteristics of death row inmates suggest that the death penalty continues to be administered in a selective and discriminatory manner. The federal courts have rejected this claim, however, even when arguments have been grounded in precise statistical studies. In *McCleskey* v. *Zant*,[54] a 1984 Georgia case, the U.S. District Court held that statistical data "are incapable of producing evidence on whether racial factors play a part in the imposition of the death penalty in any particular case."

The *protection of the criminal justice system argument* against capital punishment holds that equity in the administration of justice is hindered by the very bearing of capital statutes. As noted by the President's Crime Commission:

> Whatever views one may have about the efficacy of the death penalty as a deterrent, it clearly has an undesirable impact on the administration of justice. The trial of a capital case is a stirring drama, but that is perhaps its most dangerous at-

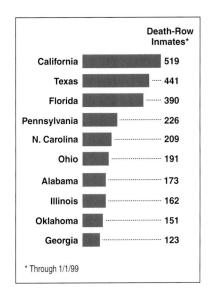

	Death-Row Inmates*
California	519
Texas	441
Florida	390
Pennsylvania	226
N. Carolina	209
Ohio	191
Alabama	173
Illinois	162
Oklahoma	151
Georgia	123

* Through 1/1/99

Death Row Inmates, as of January 1, 1999
Ranked first among the states with the largest death row populations, California is now searching for ways to expedite the appeal process.

SOURCES: Death Penalty Information Center; *U.S. Dept. of Justice.*

Jimmy Lee Gray in his death row cell in Mississippi State Prison. Executed on September 2, 1983, Gray had been convicted of kidnapping and raping a 3-year-old girl and murdering her by suffocation in mud. At the time of the kidnapping, Gray was on parole from an Arizona prison, where he had served 7 years of a 20-year sentence for the 1968 slaying of his 16-year-old fiancee. Ironically, Gray, whose mother even urged her son's execution, died through suffocation by lethal gas.

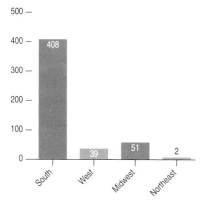

Executions by Region, 1976–1998

SOURCE: Death Penalty Information Center.

tribute. Selecting a jury often requires several days; each objection or point of law requires excessive deliberation because of the irreversible consequences of error. The jury's concern with the death penalty may result in unwarranted acquittals and there is increased danger that public sympathy will be aroused for the defendant, regardless of his guilt of the crime charged.[55]

The *brutalization argument* holds that executions actually cause homicides, rather than deter them. In this behalf, William J. Bowers has extensively analyzed numerous studies of both the short-term and long-term effects of executions on homicide rates. He demonstrated that executions cause a slight but discernible increase in the murder rate. This "brutalizing effect," he added, typically occurs within the first 2 months after an execution and dissipates thereafter. Bowers's explanation is that the effect is most likely to occur among those who have reached a state of "readiness to kill"—a small subgroup of the population composed of individuals on the fringe of sanity for whom the suggestive or imitative message of the execution is that it is proper to kill those who betray, disgrace, or dishonor them.[56]

And finally, the *cruel and unusual punishment argument* maintains that the death penalty is a violation of the constitutional right guaranteed by the Eighth Amendment. Abolitionists and retentionists differ, however, in their interpretations of the cruel and unusual punishment clause. The former hold that capital punishment in all circumstances is cruel and unusual. The latter insist that a sentence of death is forbidden by the Eighth Amendment only when it is a disproportionate punishment for the crime committed.

APPELLATE REVIEW

"An appeal is when you ask one court to show its contempt for another." This brief utterance from the essays of the early twentieth-century American journalist and humorist Finley Peter Dunne, although cynical and irreverent in tone, is essentially what an **appeal** is all about. More accurately, an appeal is a complaint to a superior court of an injustice done or error committed by a lower court, whose judgment or decision the higher tribunal is called upon to correct or reverse.

Despite the fact that appellate procedures exist throughout the federal and all of the state court structures, the right of appeal was unknown in common law, and such a right was not incorporated into the Constitution. Furthermore, the constitutionality of a state's denial of appellate review has never been decided by the U.S. Supreme Court, and the High Court has noted on many occasions that such review is not constitutionally required.[57]

The Defendant's Right to Appeal

At the appellate stage, the presumption of innocence has evaporated, and it becomes the defendant's obligation to show why a conviction should be overturned. Thus the nature of the adversary system changes, the burden of proof shifting from the prosecution to the defense.

All jurisdictions have procedural rules requiring that objections to the admission (or exclusion) of evidence, or to some other procedure, be made by the defense either at a pretrial hearing or at the time evidence or other procedure becomes an issue at trial. Failure to make a timely objection results in an automatic forfeiture of the claim for appeal purposes. Such a requirement has been instituted in order that trial judges can make rules and develop facts that will appear in the record and thus enable the appeals court to conduct an adequate review.

Appeal: A complaint to a superior court of an injustice done or an error committed by a lower court, whose judgment or decision the higher tribunal is called upon to correct or reverse.

The Plain Error Rule   The notable exception to the timely objection requirement is the *plain error rule,* incorporated into Federal Rules of Criminal Procedure and with an equivalent in all state jurisdictions. Under this rule, "plain errors or defects affecting substantial rights" of defendants become subject to appellate review even though they may not have been properly raised at trial or during some prior appeal.[58] Thus, a denial of the right to counsel at trial, the admission of an involuntary confession, or the negation of some other constitutional guarantees—even in the absence of a timely objection—are considered "plain errors" and hence appealable.

The Automatic Reversal Rule   On numerous occasions, the Supreme Court has held that certain constitutional errors are of such magnitude that they require automatic reversal of a conviction: hence the *automatic reversal rule.* The Fourteenth Amendment guarantee of due process, for example, ensures the defendant a fair trial before an impartial judge. Pursuant to this guarantee, the Court ruled in *Tumey* v. *Ohio,*[59] decided in 1927 by a unanimous vote, that an accused is denied due process when tried before a judge with a direct, personal, pecuniary interest in ruling against him. At issue in *Tumey* was the fact that the petitioner had been tried in a city court, whose judge was the mayor and from which fines were deposited in the city treasury. The High Court found the lower court's error to be of such significance that it mandated an automatic reversal of Tumey's conviction.

The Harmless Error Rule   In *Chapman* v. *California,*[60] decided in 1967, the Supreme Court established the *harmless error rule,* holding that a denial of a federal constitutional right can at times be of insufficient magnitude to require a reversal of a conviction on appeal. Known also as the *Chapman* rule, the "harmless error" doctrine has been applied by the Supreme Court and other appellate courts in numerous areas of constitutional dimension: evidence seized in violation of the Fourth Amendment, denial of counsel at a preliminary heating, in-court identifications based on invalid pretrial identification procedures, and obtaining a confession from a defendant after indictment without expressly informing the defendant of his or her right to counsel.[61] When a court considers an error to be harmless, it is indicating that the mistake was not prejudicial to the rights of the accused and thus made no difference in the subsequent conviction or sentence.

The Invited Error Rule   Although uncommon, there have been instances when, during the course of a proceeding, the defense requests the court to make a ruling that is actually erroneous, and the court does so. Under the *invited error rule,* the defense cannot take advantage of such an error on appeal or review.

The Prosecution's Right to Appeal

Neither the federal government nor the states may appeal the acquittal of a defendant. Nor can the prosecution appeal the conviction of some lesser offense (say, murder in the second degree or manslaughter) when the original indictment was for a greater one (murder in the first degree). In either case, such an action is barred by the double jeopardy clause of the Fifth Amendment.

However, there are two instances in which the prosecution may initiate appellate review. First, should a defendant successfully appeal and his or her conviction is reversed on some matter of the law, the prosecution may contest the correctness of that legal ruling to the next higher court or even to the U.S. Supreme Court. Such was the case in *Delaware* v. *Prouse,*[62] which involved a seizure of marijuana following a random "spot check" of the defendant's driver's license and vehicle registration. Upon conviction, the defendant appealed to the Delaware

Exhibit 10.6

Careers in Justice

Advocacy for the Abolition of the Death Penalty

Although most Americans consider the death penalty to be the appropriate punishment for first-degree murder, there are many who do not. Furthermore, scores of individuals are so opposed to the death penalty that they devote part of their free time—or even their entire careers—to advocating the abolition of capital statutes and helping death row inmates to have their sentences appealed. For those interested in this type of advocacy, there are literally dozens of anti–death penalty organizations. The following are among the most visible:

- **Death Penalty Information Center.** The Death Penalty Information Center is a nonprofit organization serving the media and the public with analysis and information on capital punishment. Founded in 1990, the center prepares in-depth reports, issues press releases, conducts briefings for journalists, and serves as a resource for those working on the issue. Web site address: http://www.essential.org/dpic
- **Amnesty International.** The object of Amnesty International is to foster the observance of human rights throughout the world. One of its mandates is opposition to the death penalty as well as to torture or other cruel, inhuman, or degrading treatment or punishment of prisoners or other detailed persons. Web site address: http://www.amnesty.org
- **American Civil Liberties Union.** The ACLU is a 50-state network with offices in most major cities and more than 300 chapters in smaller towns. The ACLU has some 60 staff attorneys and 2,000 volunteer attorneys who handle almost 6,000 cases annually. The mission of the ACLU is to assure that the Bill of Rights is preserved, and in this context it maintains that capital punishment is a violation of the Eighth Amendment ban against cruel and unusual punishment. Web site address: http://www.aclu.org

Supreme Court, which overturned the lower court ruling on the basis of illegal search and seizure. The prosecution then appealed to the U.S. Supreme Court, to argue the constitutionality of the state's random license check practices.

Alternatively, some jurisdictions permit the prosecution to initiate appeals from both convictions and acquittals, solely for the purpose of correcting any legal errors that may have occurred during trial.

Appellate Review of Sentences

Although appeals are commonly filed to review either real or imagined errors in court procedure, sentences, for the most part, are unappealable. This is so because each jurisdiction has statutes that mandate a range of penalties for each specific crime. Although a convicted offender might consider the sentence imposed to be unfair, it is legal as long as it falls within statutory guidelines.

There are, however, a number of circumstances under which sanctions have been appealed and reversed, including the following: (1) if the sentence was not authorized by statute and thus was illegal; (2) if the sentence was based on sex, ethnicity, or socioeconomic status and was, therefore, a violation of due process; (3) if the sentence had no relationship to the purposes of criminal sanctions; and (4) if the sentence was cruel and unusual. Note that in these four potential instances, the bases for appeal are not simply issues of sentencing "excess," but rather, straightforward matters of constitutional rights.

It has been argued for many decades that all sentences should be subject to some form of appeal. The fact that sentences are discretionary within a jurisdiction's statutory guidelines and, as such, are lawful should not automatically suggest that they are therefore unappealable. Discretion, after all, can be abused.

Currently, approximately 14 states have appellate bodies that generally review a term handed down by a sentencing judge. State appeals courts, on the other hand, are generally reluctant to review sentences. Not wishing to second-guess the sentencing judge, these higher courts feel that the magistrate who presided at the trial and pronounced the sentence had the most information available and was in the most qualified position to determine the penalty.

The Appeal Process

After conviction, appeals are not automatic. There are specific procedural steps that must be followed. First, within a specified period of time (from 30 to 90 days) subsequent to conviction, the petitioner must file with the court a notice of appeals. Second, and again within a specified period of time, the petitioner must submit an "affidavit of errors" setting forth the alleged errors or defects in the trial (or pretrial) proceedings that are the subjects of the appeal. If these requirements are followed, the higher court must review the case. Appeals are argued on the basis of the affidavit of errors and sometimes through oral argument. In either case, the subject matter of the appeal must be limited to the contents of the original proceeding. Thus, no new evidence or testimony can be presented, for an appeal is not a trial. However, if new evidence is discovered that was unknown or unknowable to the defense at the time of the trial, that can be made the basis of an appeal.

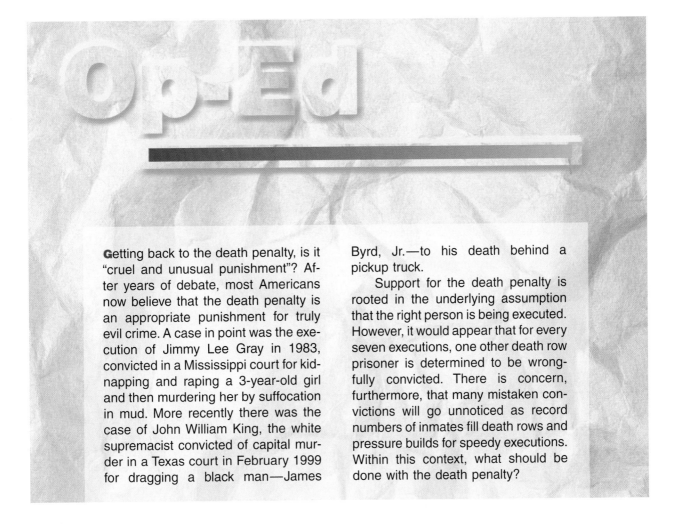

Getting back to the death penalty, is it "cruel and unusual punishment"? After years of debate, most Americans now believe that the death penalty is an appropriate punishment for truly evil crime. A case in point was the execution of Jimmy Lee Gray in 1983, convicted in a Mississippi court for kidnapping and raping a 3-year-old girl and then murdering her by suffocation in mud. More recently there was the case of John William King, the white supremacist convicted of capital murder in a Texas court in February 1999 for dragging a black man—James Byrd, Jr.—to his death behind a pickup truck.

Support for the death penalty is rooted in the underlying assumption that the right person is being executed. However, it would appear that for every seven executions, one other death row prisoner is determined to be wrongfully convicted. There is concern, furthermore, that many mistaken convictions will go unnoticed as record numbers of inmates fill death rows and pressure builds for speedy executions. Within this context, what should be done with the death penalty?

SUMMARY

After the verdict, the business of the court is not complete. First there is the matter of sentencing. Throughout American history, there has been no single and clearly defined rationale to serve as a guiding principle in sentencing. As a result, even contemporary sentencing objectives are seemingly based on at least five competing philosophies: retribution, vengeance, incapacitation, deterrence, and rehabilitation. Sentencing alternatives include fines, probation or some other community-based program, imprisonment, or the death penalty.

The death penalty is the most terminal form of punishment. When the framers of the Constitution incorporated the Eighth Amendment ban against cruel and unusual punishment, the death penalty was apparently not at issue. Under colonial philosophy, capital punishment was considered neither cruel nor unusual.

The Supreme Court's interpretation of the Eighth Amendment has been flexible. The Court has ruled on various forms of punishment but has generally been silent regarding the constitutionality of capital punishment. *Furman* v. *Georgia* in 1972 invalidated state death penalty statutes on Eighth Amendment grounds, but it enabled the states to enact new capital punishment laws. Executions resumed, and the number of persons on death rows across the nation began to grow. Meanwhile, the death penalty debate continues, with arguments for and against capital punishment revolving around issues of economics, retribution, public opinion, community protection, deterrence, irreversibility, discrimination, protection of the criminal justice system, brutalization, and cruel and unusual punishment.

At the appellate stage of the criminal justice process, the presumption of innocence has evaporated with the finding of guilt. It then becomes the defendant's obligation to show why a conviction should be overturned. There are grounds on which the defense can initiate an appeal, but the prosecution cannot appeal the acquittal of a defendant because of the double jeopardy clause of the Fifth Amendment. However, should an accused successfully appeal and have his or her conviction reversed on some matter of law, the prosecution may contest the correctness of that legal ruling to the next highest court or even to the U.S. Supreme Court.

KEY TERMS

allocution **273**
appeal **287**
Coker v. *Georgia* **279**
definite sentence **266**
determinate sentence **266**
deterrence **261**
Furman v. *Georgia* **277**

Gregg v. *Georgia* **278**
incapacitation **261**
indeterminate sentence **265**
intermittent sentence **268**
mandatory sentence **268**
presentence investigation **272**
rehabilitation **262**

retribution **260**
separation-of-powers doctrine **271**
truth in sentencing **271**
vengeance **261**
Weems v. *United States* **276**
Witherspoon v. *Illinois* **277**

QUESTIONS FOR DISCUSSION

1. Should vengeance be accepted as a rationale for punishment?
2. How might mandatory sentencing statutes lead to increased prosecutorial discretion and court delays?
3. What argument in favor of capital punishment seems most valid? Should capital punishment be abolished? Will it be?
4. Would "three strikes" laws make the certainty of punishment more realistic? Do they affect the crime problem?
5. What is "truth in sentencing"?

MEDIA RESOURCES

1. **Women and the Death Penalty.** Victor L. Streib's report, "Death Penalty for Female Offenders," is updated on a regular basis and can be found on the Internet. Web address: http://www.law.onu.edu/faculty/streib/femdeath.htm

2. **"Three Strikes and You're Out."** See John Clark, James Austin, and Alan Henry, "Three Strikes and You're Out: A Review of State Legislation," *National Institute of Justice Research in Brief,* September 1997.

3. **Attitudes About the Death Penalty.** Detailed findings of a recent survey among college students can be found in Brian K. Payne and Victoria Coogle, "Examining Attitudes About the Death Penalty," *Corrections Compendium*, April 1998. This publication can be obtained through the American Correctional Association. Web site address: http://www.corrections.com/aca

4. **Minorities and the Death Penalty.** The Death Penalty Information Center has prepared an excellent report titled "The Death Penalty in Black & White: Who Lives, Who Dies, Who Decides," by Richard C. Dieter, June 1998. Contact the Center's Web site for a copy. Internet address: http://www.essential.org. dpic

NOTES

1. *New York Times,* February 6, 1999, p. A7.
2. Kenneth C. Haas, "The Triumph of Vengeance Over Retribution: The United States Supreme Court and the Death Penalty," *Crime, Law and Social Change: An International Journal* 21 (1994):127–154.
3. *Payne* v. *Tennessee,* 49 CrL 2325 (1991).
4. Quoted in Sanford H. Kadish and Monrad G. Paulsen, *Criminal Law and Its Processes* (Boston: Little, Brown, 1969), p. 85.
5. See Franklin E. Zimring and Gordon J. Hawkins, *Deterrence* (Chicago: University of Chicago Press, 1973).
6. Melvyn Bernard Zerman, *Beyond a Reasonable Doubt: Inside the American Jury System* (New York: Crowell, 1981), p. 170.
7. National Advisory Commission on Criminal Justice Standards and Goals, *Courts* (Washington, D.C.: U.S. Government Printing Office, 1973), p. 110.
8. *Williams* v. *Illinois,* 399 U.S. 235 (1970); *Tate* v. *Short,* 401 U.S. 395 (1971).
9. Walter S. Carr, "Sentencing Practices, Problems, and Remedies," *Judicature* 53 (1969): 14.
10. See Marvin E. Frankel, *Criminal Sentences: Law Without Order* (New York: Hill and Wang, 1973); Karl Menninger, *The Crime of Punishment* (New York: Viking, 1968); Nigel Walker, *Sentencing in a Rational Society* (London: Penguin, 1972).
11. Harry Elmer Barnes, *The Repression of Crime* (New York: Doran, 1926), p. 220.
12. *Delaware Code,* Title 11, Section 4209.
13. State of New York, *Penal Law,* 40-85.
14. *People* v. *Warren,* 79 Misc 2d 777, 360 NYS 2d 961 (1974).
15. *Idaho Code,* 18-1403, 19-2601.
16. State of New York, *Penal Law,* 40-70.00, 80.00, 140.30.
17. *West Virginia Code,* Chapter 61, Section 3-11; Chapter 62, Section 12-2.
18. *Delaware Code,* Title 11, Sections 826, 4204-5.
19. *Code of Alabama,* 13-2-40, 15-22-50.
20. President's Commission on Law Enforcement and Administration of Justice, *The Courts* (Washington, D.C.: U.S. Government Printing Office, 1967), p. 23.

21. President's Commission, *Courts,* p. 24.
22. Marvin Zalman, "The Rise and Fall of the Indeterminate Sentence," *Wayne Law Review* 24 (1978): 857.
23. *Mistretta* v. *United States,* 44 CrL 3061 (1989).
24. Paula M. Ditton and Doris James Wilson, "Truth in Sentencing in State Prisons," *Bureau of Justice Statistics Special Report,* January 1999.
25. Administrative Offices of the U.S. Courts, Division of Probation, "The Selective Presentence Investigation Report," *Federal Probation* 38 (December 1974): 48.
26. From Barnes, *Repression of Crime,* pp. 44–45.
27. George Ryley Scott, *The History of Capital Punishment* (London: Torchstream, 1950), p. 179.
28. President's Commission, *Courts,* p. 28.
29. C. Spear, *Essays on the Punishment of Death* (London: Green, 1844), pp. 227–231.
30. David A. Jones, *The Law of Criminal Procedure* (Boston: Little, Brown, 1981), p. 543.
31. Jones, *Law of Criminal Procedure,* p. 544.
32. Marvin E. Wolfgang and Marc Riedel, "Race, Judicial Discretion, and the Death Penalty," *Annals of the American Academy of Political and Social Science* 407 (May 1973): 129.
33. *O'Neil* v. *Vermont,* 114 U.S. 323 (1892).
34. *Weems* v. *United States,* 217 U.S. 349 (1910).
35. *Wilkerson* v. *Utah,* 99 U.S. 130 (1878).
36. *In re Kemmler,* 136 U.S. 436 (1890).
37. *Witherspoon* v. *Illinois,* 391 U.S. 510 (1968).
38. *United States* v. *Jackson,* 390 U.S. 570 (1968).
39. *Furman* v. *Georgia, Jackson* v. *Georgia, Branch* v. *Texas,* 408 U.S. 238 (1972).
40. *Gregg* v. *Georgia,* 428 U.S. 153 (1976).
41. *Georgia Code,* 26-1101, 1311, 1902, 2001, 3301 (1972).
42. *Coker* v. *Georgia,* 433 U.S. 583 (1977).
43. This account of the Gilmore case is based on Louis R. Katz, *The Justice Imperative* (Cincinnati: Anderson, 1980), pp. 348–349); *New York Times,* January 18, 1977, pp. 1, 21; *New York Times,* January 12, 1977, pp. 1, 12; *New York Times,* January 11, 1976, pp. 1, 14; *New York Times,* January 16, 1977, pp. 1,

48; *New York Times,* December 1, 1976, p. 18; *New York Times,* January 17, 1976, pp. 1, 24.

44. Quoted in Austin Sarat and Neil Vidmar, "Public Opinion, The Death Penalty, and the Eighth Amendment: Testing the Marshall Hypothesis," *Wisconsin Law Review* (1976): 206.

45. *Fierro* v. *Gomez,* 56 CrL 1085 (1994).

46. Wilmington (Delaware) *News-Journal,* February 17, 1985, p. A16.

47. *American Medical News,* July 11, 1980, p. 13.

48. *Time,* December 20, 1982, pp. 28–29. See also *Texas Monthly,* February 1983, pp. 100–105, 170–176, 182.

49. See M. Garey, "The Cost of Taking a Life," *University of California–Davis Law Review* 18 (1985): 1221–1270.

50. *National Observer,* November 18, 1972, p. 2.

51. James W. Marquart and Jonathan R. Sorensen, "A National Study of the *Furman*-Committed Inmates," *Loyola of Los Angeles Law Review* 23 (1989): 5–28.

52. Zimring and Hawkins, *Deterrence.*

53. See Thorsten Sellin, ed., *Capital Punishment* (New York: Harper & Row, 1967); Karl F. Schuessler, "The Deterrent Influence of the Death Penalty," *Annals of the American Academy of Political and Social Science* 284 (November 1952): 54–62; Hugo Adam Bedau and Chester M. Pierce, eds., *Capital Punishment in the United States* (New York: AMS Press, 1976), pp. 299–416.

54. *McCleskey* v. *Zant,* 34 CrL 2429 (1984).

55. President's Commission, *Courts.*

56. See William J. Bowers, "The Effect of Execution Is Brutalization, Not Deterrence," in *Challenging Capital Punishment,* ed. Haas and Inciardi, pp. 49–89.

57. For example, in *McKane* v. *Durston,* 153 U.S. 684 (1894); *Griffin* v. *Illinois,* 351 U.S. 12 (1956).

58. *Federal Rules of Criminal Procedure,* Rule 52 (b).

59. *Tumey* v. *Ohio,* 273 U.S. 510 (1927).

60. *Chapman* v. *California,* 386 U.S. 18 (1967).

61. See Peter W. Lewis and Kenneth D. Peoples, *The Supreme Court and the Criminal Process* (Philadelphia: Saunders, 1978), p. 515.

62. *Delaware* v. *Prouse,* 440 U.S. 648 (1979).

CORRECTIONS

Chapter 11
The American Prison Experience

Chapter 12
**Behind the Walls: A Look Inside
the American Penitentiary**

Chapter 13
**The Conditions of Incarceration
and the Constitutional Rights
of Prisoners**

Chapter 14
Community-Based Corrections

CHAPTER **11**

THE AMERICAN PRISON
EXPERIENCE

AUBURN, N.Y. — After his first visit to the new prison in Auburn, N.Y., Lewis Dwight, founder of the Boston Prison Society, made the following observations:

> At Auburn we have a more beautiful example of what may be done by proper discipline, in a prison well constructed. It is not possible to describe the pleasure which we feel in contemplating this noble institution, after wading through the fraud, and the material and moral filth of many prisons. We regard it as a model worthy of the world's imitation.[1]

Lewis Dwight's comments about Auburn Prison are certainly optimistic. Does this mean that the correctional system in New York finally developed a model penitentiary—or is there something wrong with this picture? And this question raises a host of others. When did the prison system in the United States begin and how did it develop? Have correctional philosophies changed over the years? What are jails, and are there differences between prisons and jails? Are jails just smaller prisons? Who goes to jail, and what are the conditions that jail inmates face?

William Penn

AMERICAN PRISONS IN PERSPECTIVE

The American prison system had its beginnings during the second half of the seventeenth century in Philadelphia. In 1682, William Penn, a religious reformer and the founder of Pennsylvania, made sweeping changes in the administration of justice in the territory under his control. He limited the death penalty in Pennsylvania to cases of murder, called for fines and imprisonment as penalties for most offenses, and urged flogging for adultery, arson, and rape. These were mild sanctions compared to the executions, brandings, mutilations, and other severe punishments that existed throughout the other colonies. (For a discussion of punishment in the American colonies, see Exhibit 11.1.) Penn also influenced the construction of county jails, which were designed to be workhouses for convicted felons. The first of these was the High Street Jail

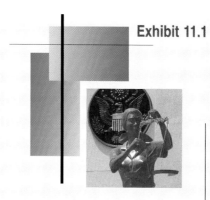

Exhibit 11.1   **Historical Perspectives on Crime and Justice**
Punishment in the American Colonies

Historically and cross-culturally, the range of punishments imposed has been vast. Over the centuries, the sanctions even for less serious crimes were exceedingly harsh, and the litany of punishments down through the ages has often been referred to as the story of "man's inhumanity to man."

In early societies the death penalty was a universal form of punishment. It was commonly applied both as a deterrent and a means for removing an offender from the community. Criminal codes from the ancient East to the modern West included capital statutes for offenses as trivial as adultery and petty theft. As recently as the early nineteenth century in England there were 200 capital crimes—ranging from murder and rape to larceny and disturbing the peace. Corporal punishment, in the form of mutilation, branding, whipping, and torture, was also commonplace for a variety of punitive purposes. Ban-

ishment and transportation were alternatives to capital punishment. Banishment served to rid the community of undesirables, who were never to return, under penalty of certain death. Other punishments have included forced labor, sterilization, excommunication from the Church, loss of property and inheritance rights, disfigurement, and imprisonment.

With the growth of the American colonies, many of the punishments that had been common throughout medieval Europe found their way to the New World. Capital statutes endured for numerous offenses, as did banishment—and corporal punishments in the form of branding, flogging, and mutilation persisted. A curious variety of additional sanctions also appeared in colonial tradition: the ducking stool, the stocks and pillory, the brank, the scarlet letter, and the bilboes. These methods were imposed for minor offenses, and although they are generally associated with early American life, most had originated in Western Europe as means to shame and humiliate offenders.

The *ducking stool,* as its name implies, was a chair fastened to a long lever and situated at the bank

in Philadelphia, erected in 1682; others appeared in the decades that followed. But even before Penn's death in 1718, the workhouse idea failed due to overcrowding and inadequate conditions.

The Walnut Street Jail

During the eighteenth century, the Quakers of Pennsylvania placed their commonwealth in the forefront of correctional history. In 1787, they formed the Philadelphia Society for Alleviating the Miseries of Public Prisons and quickly addressed the conditions of their local jails. In 1776, a new prison-workhouse opened on Philadelphia's Walnut Street to receive prisoners from the overcrowded High Street Jail. In 1790, influenced by the work of John Howard, the society transformed the new structure on Walnut Street into the first American penitentiary.

As recently as 1915, the stocks were used for publicly humiliating conscientious objectors.

of a river or pond. The victim, generally a village gossip or scold, was repeatedly submerged in the water before a jeering crowd. The *stocks and pillory,* common in almost every early New England community, were wooden frames with holes for the head, hands, and feet. They were located in the town square, and the culprit—generally a wife beater, petty thief, vagrant, Sabbath-breaker, drunkard, adulterer, or unruly servant—would be open to public scorn. But confinement in the stocks and pillory often resulted in much more than simple humiliation. The offenders were often whipped or branded while being detained, and most were pelted by passersby. Some were even stoned to death. Those secured to the pillory generally had their ears nailed to the frame and were compelled to tear themselves loose (or have their ears cut off) when their period of detention concluded.

The *brank,* also called the "gossip's helm" or the "dame's bridle," was a cage placed about the head. It had a spiked plate or flat dish of iron that was placed in the mouth over the tongue thus inflicting severe pain if the offender spoke. As the structure of the device would suggest, it had been designed for gossips, perjurers, liars, and blasphemers, but in colonial New York it was also used for husband beaters and village drunkards.

The *scarlet letter,* made famous by Nathaniel Hawthorne's novel of the same name, was used for a variety of offenses. The adulterous wife wore an *A,* cut from scarlet cloth hand sewn to her upper garments. The blasphemer wore a *B,* the pauper a *P,* the thief a *T,* and the drunkard a *D.* And finally there were the *bilboes,* wherein the citizen convicted of slander and libel was shackled by the feet to a wooden stake.

SOURCES: Alice Morse Earle, *Curious Punishments of Bygone Days* (Montclair, N.J.: Patterson Smith, 1969); Harry Elmer Barnes, *The Story of Punishment: A Record of Man's Inhumanity to Man* (Montclair, N.J.: Patterson Smith, 1972).

The **Walnut Street Jail** was both a prison and a workhouse, and it covered about 2 acres. Those convicted of the most serious crimes were confined without labor in 16 solitary cells, each 6 feet wide and 8 feet long, with an inner iron door, an outer wooden door, and wire across the single window. The prisoners were fed a rather peculiar diet of pudding made from molasses and maize. A large pipe extending from each cell to a sewer served as a toilet, while a stove in the corridor provided heat. Offenders confined for less serious crimes were lodged together in rooms 18 by 20 feet. Together they worked in a large stone structure at shoemaking, carpentry, weaving, tailoring, and nailmaking. Women worked at spinning cotton, preparing hemp and wool, washing, and mending. Vagrants and unskilled prisoners beat hemp or picked moss and oakum (jute fiber used for caulking ships). Male prisoners were credited with the prevailing wage but were charged the costs of their trials, fines, and maintenance. Women were not given wages, nor were they charged for their maintenance. No irons or guard weapons were permitted. Except for female prisoners, silence was enforced in the shops and at meals, but some low-toned conversation was permitted in the night quarters before bedtime. Religious instruction and weekly services were offered.[2]

Throughout the 1790s, the Walnut Street Jail was considered a model prison. Officials from other states and from throughout Europe visited to observe its cellular confinement pattern and workhouse program, returning to their homes to praise its design and procedures. By the beginning of the nineteenth century, however, Philadelphia's acclaimed jail had begun to deteriorate, primarily due to overcrowding. Work activity had become impossible to continue, discipline had become difficult, and riots were common.

The Separate System

The solitary confinement of hardened offenders in the Walnut Street Jail was based on the notion that recidivism could be prevented and offenders reformed by eliminating evil association in congregate prison quarters. Confinement in an isolated cell would give the convict an opportunity to contemplate the evils of his past life, thereby leading him to resolve "in the spiritual presence of his Maker" to reform his future conduct.[3] More specifically, the defenders of this **separate system** argued, it possessed a number of wholesome virtues, as follows:

- The protection against possible moral contamination through evil association
- The invitation to self-examination and self-reproach in solitude
- The impossibility of being visited by anyone (other than an officer, a reformer, or members of the clergy)
- The great ease of administration of discipline
- The possibility of a great degree of individuality of treatment
- The minimal need for disciplinary measures
- The absence of any possibility of mutual recognition of prisoners after discharge
- The fact that the pressures of loneliness would make convicts eager to engage in productive labor, during which time they could be taught a useful trade[4]

Such was the basis for the construction of Western Penitentiary near Pittsburgh in 1826, and of Eastern Penitentiary near Philadelphia in 1829. Eastern Penitentiary epitomized the Pennsylvania correctional philosophy and its architecture was adapted to the principle of solitary confinement.[5] It had seven wards housing 844 individual cells, all radiating from a common center like

Eastern Penitentiary, Philadelphia, Pennsylvania, as it appeared in its early years. _____

the spokes of a wheel. To each individual cell on the lower floor of each ward was attached a small exercise yard, which the prisoner could visit twice daily for short periods. In the interim, he washed, ate, and slept in his cell, seeing no one other than the prison officials and reformers from the outside community. Massive walls surrounded the entire institution and divided its parts so as to eliminate all contact and make escape impossible.

However, the abominable simplicity of the separate system was also a dehumanizing experience. As one commentator described it:

> He was given a hot bath, and a prison uniform. Then his eyes were bandaged, and he was led blindfolded into the rotunda, where, still not seeing, he heard the rules of the house explained by the superintendent. And still blindfolded, he was led to his living grave. The bandage was taken from his eyes. He saw a cell less than twelve feet long, less than eight feet wide, and if he was to live on the ground floor, he saw a little courtyard, the same size, highly walled, opening out of it, in which he sometimes might exercise. In that cell, and that courtyard, he stayed without any change, for three, ten, twenty years or for life. He saw only the guard who brought his food to him, but who was forbidden to speak to him. He got no letters, saw none of his family. He was cut off from the world. When the cholera raged in Philadelphia in 1843, it was months before the prisoners got a hint that an epidemic had visited the city. After the slave had been three days in his cell, he was allowed to work, if he wished, and the fact that nearly all prisoners asked for something to do proved to the inspectors that reform was beginning. If they did not choose to work they might commune with their corrupt hearts in a perfectly dark and solitary punishment cell.[6]

The Pennsylvania plan never gained widespread popularity in the United States. It was the basis of temporary experimentation in New Jersey and Rhode Island, but by the latter part of the nineteenth century it had been abandoned, even in Pennsylvania.

The Silent System

Silent system: A prison system whereby inmates experience confinement under a rigid rule of absolute silence at all times.

The demise of the separate system was due not so much to the destructive effects of long-term solitary confinement as to the emergence of a different pattern of prison administration in New York State. Known as the **silent system** and established at Auburn Prison in 1823, it was considered to be the most economically sound of penitentiary programs. And it was *this* system, *back in 1823,* that Lewis Dwight was referring to in the remarks at the beginning of this chapter.

As opposed to the outside cells with individual exercise yards at Eastern Penitentiary, prisoners at Auburn were confined in banks of inside cells each measuring only 7 feet by 312 feet. Inmates were employed in congregate shops during the day under a rigid rule of absolute silence at all times and with solitary confinement only at night. Hard labor was considered essential to the reformation of character and to the economic solvency of the prison. Perpetual silence was seen as mandatory while inmates were in close proximity in order to avoid their corruption of one another and to reduce any opportunities for the hatching of plots for insurrection, escape, or riot. Furthermore, all prisoners were totally separated from the outside world; communication with relatives and friends was forbidden.[7]

The attractiveness of the silent system was primarily due to its economic advantages. Small inside cells were cheaper to construct. Also, industrial production within a setting of large congregate work areas was far greater and more efficient than the limited output possible under the Pennsylvania plan of handicraft construction in separate confinement.

Prison Industries

The Auburn model became the major pattern of prison administration for the rest of the nineteenth century. Sing Sing Prison in New York followed the Auburn plan in 1825, and more than 30 other states built similar institutions in the years that followed. However, the rule of absolute silence was soon relaxed, for conditions within most penitentiaries made it impractical. Not only had most of the institutions become overcrowded, but more importantly, the Industrial Revolution had arrived and factory workshop production had been introduced to exploit cheap inmate labor and to make the penitentiaries self-sustaining. Production became the paramount goal of prisons, and the necessity for communication within the industrial shops served to make the perpetual silence rule counterproductive.[8]

Prisoners marching in lockstep at Joliet Penitentiary, Illinois, in 1900.

Contract labor and the piece-price system were the earliest forms of prison industry. Under the **contract system,** the labor of the inmates was leased to an outside contractor, who furnished the machinery and raw materials and supervised the work. The only responsibility of the prison administration under such an arrangement was to guard the convicts. The **piece-price system** was a variation on this. Under this plan, the contractor supplied the raw material and received the finished product, paying the prison a specified amount for each unit produced. Under both plans the prisoners were invariably exploited, overworked, and otherwise abused. Contractors often short-changed convicts in their work tallies, and prison officials were known to force inmates to work long hours, under deplorable conditions, and for little or no pay.

Even more severe was the **lease system,** under which contractors assumed complete control over the prisoners, including their maintenance and discipline. Convicts were taken from the institutions and employed in agriculture, quarrying, bridge and road construction, mining, and in turpentine camps or sugar cane plantations. The forced labor resembled slavery, and prisoners received little, if any, compensation for their work.[9]

Alternatives to the contract labor practices were the **state account** and **state-use systems.** Under the state account plan, inmate production was directed and supervised by prison officials, the manufactured goods were sold on the open market, and the convicts received a small share of the profits. The state-use plan produced articles in prison that were subsequently used in state-supported institutions and bureaus. Related to these was the public works system of prison labor, under which inmates were employed in the construction and repair of public streets, highways, and structures. The well-known Sing Sing Prison, for example, from which came such terms as the "big house" and "up the river" (because it was in Ossining, on the eastern shore of the Hudson River, 30 miles north of New York City), was constructed by a team of 100 inmates from Auburn under the public works system.[10]

Most nineteenth-century prisons also included farming as a form of prison labor. As a separate form of the state-use philosophy, prison agriculture was viewed as a necessary part of institutional procedure. The raising of crops and vegetables was a means of hard inmate labor, and at the same time it reduced the cost of inmate maintenance.

Contract system: A form of prison industry in which the labor of inmates is leased to an outside contractor, who furnishes the machinery and raw materials and supervises the work.

Piece-price system: A variation of the contract system of prison industry in which the contractor supplies the raw material and receives the finished product, paying the prison a specified amount for each unit produced.

Lease system: A form of prison industry under which contractors assume complete control over prisoners.

State account system: A form of prison industry in which inmate production is directed by prison officials, goods are sold on the open market, and inmates receive a share of the profits.

State-use system: A form of prison industry in which inmate-produced goods are used in state institutions and bureaus.

The Reformatory Era

From the institutional backwater of the mid-nineteenth century emerged a *treatment* philosophy of corrections. This was an ideology that viewed many forms of offense behavior as manifestations of various social "pathologies," psychological "maladies," and inherited "predispositions" that could be "corrected" by some form of therapeutic or rehabilitative intervention. This new treatment ideology led to the *reformatory era* in American corrections, which endured from 1870 through 1910. The influences that led to the reformatory idea came from numerous theorists and practitioners in many parts of the world, but the movement was affected most directly by the work of Captain Alexander Maconochie in Australia and Sir Walter Crofton in Ireland.

In 1840, Captain Alexander Maconochie, a geographer with England's Royal Navy, was placed in charge of Norfolk Island, a penal colony for habitual felons located 1,000 miles off the coast of Australia. Conditions were so bad at Norfolk that it has been said that "men who were reprieved wept with sorrow that they had to go on living, and those doomed to die fell on their knees and thanked God for the release that was to be theirs."[11] Maconochie eliminated the brutality of the system and implemented a correctional scheme that rested on five postulates:

The reformatory era in American corrections

Alexander Maconochie

1. Sentences should not be for a period of time, but for the performance of a determined and specified quantity of labor; in brief, time sentences should be abolished, and task sentences substituted.

2. The quantity of labor a prisoner must perform should be expressed in a number of "marks" that he must earn, by improvement of conduct, frugality of living, and habits of industry, before he can be released.

3. While in prison he should earn everything he receives; all sustenance and indulgences should be added to his debt of marks.

4. When qualified by discipline to do so he should work in association with a small number of other prisoners, forming a group of six or seven, and the whole group should be answerable for the conduct and labor of each member of it.

5. In the final stage, a prisoner, while still obliged to earn his daily tally of marks, should be given a proprietary interest in his own labor and be subject to a less rigorous discipline in order to prepare him for release into society.[12]

"Mark system": Started by Alexander Maconochie at Norfolk Island, a system by which inmates earn early release by hard work and good behavior.

This "apparatus," as Captain Maconochie called it, removed the "flat" term of imprisonment and replaced it with a **"mark system,"** whereby an inmate could earn early release by hard work and good behavior. But the scheme was not looked on favorably by Maconochie's superiors. He was removed as administrator after only a brief time, his accomplishments were disclaimed, and the colony quickly returned to its former brutalizing routine.

But what had occurred at Norfolk Island had not gone unnoticed. Drawing on Maconochie's notion that imprisonment could be used to prepare a convict for eventual return to the community, Sir Walter Crofton of Ireland implemented what he called his "indeterminate system." Also known as the *"Irish system,"* it called for four distinct stages of treatment: (1) solitary confinement at monotonous work for 2 years, followed by (2) congregate labor under a marking system that regulated privileges and determined the date of discharge, then by (3) an intermediate stage during which inmates were permitted to work on outside jobs, and finally (4) conditional release under a **"ticket-of-leave."**[13] This ticket, which could be revoked if the convict failed to live up to the conditions of this temporary release, was the first attempt at what has come to be known as parole.

Sir Walter Crofton's "Irish system"

"Ticket-of-leave": Started by Sir Walter Crofton of Ireland, a system of conditional release from prison that represented an early form of parole.

Maconochie's "mark system" and Crofton's "Irish system" were overwhelmingly endorsed at the American Prison Congress in 1870. The result was the opening of the first reformatory in the United States in 1876, at Elmira, New York, as an institution for youths and young adults serving their first term of imprisonment. Zebulon Brockway, the first superintendent of Elmira, listed the essentials of a successful reformatory system:

1. The material structure establishment itself. . . . The general plan and arrangements should be those of the Auburn System plan, modified

Sing Sing Prison, on the eastern shore of the Hudson River, 30 miles north of New York City, from which the expression "up the river" comes.

and modernized; and 10 percent of the cells might well be constructed like those of the Pennsylvania System structures. The whole should be supplied with suitable modern sanitary appliances and with abundance of natural and artificial light.

2. Clothing—not degradingly distinctive but uniform, yet fitly representing the respective grades or standing of the prisoners. . . . Scrupulous cleanliness should be maintained and the prisoners appropriately groomed.

3. A liberal prison dietary designed to promote vigor. Deprivation of food, by a general regulation, is deprecated. . . .

4. All the modern appliances for scientific physical culture; a gymnasium completely equipped with baths and apparatus; and facilities for field athletics.

5. Facilities for manual training sufficient for about one-third of the population. . . . This special manual training covers, in addition to other exercises in other departments, mechanical and freehand drawing; cardboard constructive form work; clay modeling; cabinet making; clipping and filing; and iron molding.

6. Trade instruction based on the needs and capacities of individual prisoners.

7. A regimental military organization with a band of music, swords for officers and dummy guns for the rank and file of prisoners.

8. School of letters with a curriculum that reaches from an adaptation of the kindergarten . . . up to the usual high school course; and, in addition, special classes in college subjects. . . .

9. A well-selected library for circulation, consultation, and for occasional semi-social use.

10. A weekly institutional newspaper, in lieu of all outside newspapers, edited and printed by the prisoners under due censorship.

11. Recreating and diverting entertainments for the mass of the population, provided in the great auditorium; not any vaudeville or minstrel shows, but entertainments of such a class as the middle cultured people of a community would enjoy. . . .

12. Religious opportunities . . . adapted to the hereditary, habitual, and preferable denominational predilection of the individual prisoners.

13. Definitely planned, carefully directed, emotional occasions; not summoned, primarily, for either instruction, diversion, nor, specifically, for a common religious impression, but, figuratively, for a kind of irrigation.[14]

The program established at Elmira quickly spread to other states, but the reformatory movement as a whole proved to be a relative failure and disappointment for its advocates. Many of Brockway's principles were never put into effect; prison employees were too conditioned to the punishment ideology to support the new concepts; safe and secure custody continued to be regarded as the most important institutional activity; the reformatories quickly became overcrowded and staff shortages prevented the development of academic programs; and, hard-core offenders were housed in the new structures, thus turning them into the more typical penal environments.[15]

By 1910 the reformatory experiment was abandoned. Nevertheless, it left an important legacy for corrections in the years to come. The indeterminate sentence, conditional release, educational programs, vocational training, and the other rehabilitative ideals fostered by the reformatory became fully a part of the correctional ideology of later decades.

The Twentieth-Century Industrial Prison

WAGES PAID IN SELECTED STATES FOR INMATE LABOR FOR PRISON CONSTRUCTION	
State	**Hourly Rate**
Alabama	$.15 to .25
California	.30 to .90
Delaware	.50 to 3.00
Indiana	.65 to 1.25
Louisiana	.03 to .20
Michigan	.50 to 5.00
Oklahoma	.18 to .45
Wisconsin	.08 to .47

SOURCE: U.S. General Accounting Office.

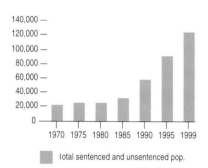

■ Total sentenced and unsentenced pop.

Federal Prison Inmate Population, 1970–1999

SOURCE: U.S. Department of Justice.

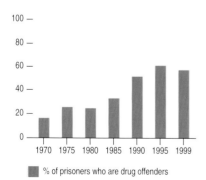

■ % of prisoners who are drug offenders

Proportion of Federal Prison Inmates Sentenced as Drug Offenders, 1970–1999

SOURCE: U.S. Department of Justice.

By the early years of the twentieth century, the American prison system had evolved into a growing number of institutions similar to Sing Sing and Auburn. With many reflecting the architecture of medieval dungeons and Gothic castles, they were fortresslike structures, operated on the principles of mass congregate incarceration and rigid discipline and security. Their most distinctive feature, furthermore, was the use of inmate labor for the production of industrial goods for sale on the open market. This practice was widely encouraged not only because of the belief in hard labor as a correctional tool, but also because of the economics of creating a self-sustaining prison system.

Yet as the industrial prison was developing into a prudent financial operation, so too was opposition to inmate labor. Prison industries under the contract, piece-price, lease, and state account systems were seen as threats to free enterprise. With the formation of the American Federation of Labor in 1880, labor and its political lobbyists organized a formal attack on the industrial prison. The culmination of the assault came during the years of the Great Depression with the passage of numerous federal and state statues.[16] Even before the economic strains of the depression occurred, the Hawes-Cooper Act of 1929 disallowed certain prison-made goods from being shipped to other states.

Humanitarian concerns as well aided in the demise of the prison industrial complex. Contract labor systems were often no more than exploitation motivated by corruption and greed. Although the philosophy of the time supported the notion that offenders needed discipline and hard labor to teach them the lessons of deterrence and salvation, reformers nevertheless opposed the misuse of convict workers.

The abolition of contract labor was in many ways desirable, but there was little to take the place of free-market prison enterprise. State-use and public works programs survived, but a majority of convicts were left idle. The reduction in institutional self-support and maintenance led to the gradual decay of prison structures and conditions. Eventually many state penitentiaries began shifting back to their original purposes of punishment and custody.

After the depression years, through World War II, and into the second half of the twentieth century, there was great turmoil within state prison systems. Referred to as the "period of transition" in American corrections,[17] it was a time when clinicians and reformers were introducing new treatment ideas against a backdrop of growing apathy and decaying institutions. Some segments of the public subscribed to the rehabilitative goals of correctional ideology; others wished prisons to be no more than secure places to house criminal offenders.

The 1960s and 1970s reflected even greater contrasts. Emphasis was placed more on the needs of individual prisoners, and many of the ideas generated during the reformatory era were put into place. Academic and vocational programs were established; social casework and psychiatric treatment approaches were designed and implemented; many prison facilities were expanded; special institutions were built and equipped for youthful offenders; more concern was demonstrated for the separation of hard-core from amateur criminals; a variety of changes made prison life somewhat more humane and productive; and state and federal judges reflected a greater awareness of prisoners' rights by providing easier access to the courts for those seeking remedies against cruel and unusual punishment. At the same time, however, there was growing unrest within the nation's institutions. The majority of state penitentiaries were still the walled fortresses of decades past—solemn monuments to the ideas of nineteenth-century penology. Prison administrators were faced with the contradictions of "rehabilitation" within a context of mass overcrowding, personnel shortages, and demands for better security. It was also a time of militancy and violence within the nation's correctional institutions. The awareness of prisoners' rights under conditions that seemed to be getting worse instead of better led to riots—in the East, the Midwest, the South, and the far West.

Exhibit 11.2 **Gender Perspectives on Crime and Justice**
Differences Between Male and Female Inmates

In recent years, researchers and policy makers have argued that women offenders not only need more services to put them on a par with men, but in many instances women require different services as well. A recent survey by the Bureau of Justice Statistics clarifies why women may need different services.

Women and men inmates differ in their patterns of drug use and drug-related crime. Women were somewhat more likely than men to have used drugs in the month before the offense that resulted in their incarceration and to have been under the influence of drugs at the time of the offense. They were also more likely then men to have used crack in the month before the incarceration offense. Women were considerably more likely than men to have committed crimes in order to obtain

money to purchase drugs, and were also more likely than men to be serving sentences for drug offenses.

Women inmates have important, and often unique, health-related needs. At least 6 percent are pregnant when they enter prison. Also, a slightly higher proportion of women than men report being HIV-positive.

Female inmates are more than 3 times as likely as incarcerated men to report having experienced physical or sexual abuse at some time prior to incarceration. Research suggests that 43 percent of the women inmates report having been victims of sexual or physical abuse prior to admission, with most having been victimized before the age of 18.

Women are more likely than men to have children for whom they act as caretakers until the time of their incarceration. They were more likely than men to have children under the age of 18 who are being cared for primarily by their grandparents while their mothers are incarcerated. Further, the burden on grandparents is greater when a child's mother is

incarcerated than when a father is incarcerated because mothers usually care for the children of incarcerated fathers.

Female inmates are less likely than male inmates to have been sentenced in the past. Almost three-fourths of women inmates have been sentenced previously. Among inmates with prior records, women inmates are more likely than men to have been sentenced previously for a nonviolent offense.

Women are less likely than men to have been incarcerated for violent crimes. Women are about as likely to be serving time for a violent offense as for a property or drug offense. In contrast, almost half of male inmates are incarcerated for a violent offense.

Men and women incarcerated for violent crimes differ in their patterns of violence. Women incarcerated for violent crimes are nearly twice as likely as their male counterparts to have committed homicide, more than twice as likely to have victimized a relative or intimate, and more likely to have victimized men.

SOURCE: Adapted from Office of Justice Programs, "The Women's Prison Association: Supporting Women Offenders and Their Families," National Institute of Justice *Program Focus,* December 1998.

Throughout the 1980s and 1990s, the future of the American prison system still remained unclear. Diagnosticians, reformers, social scientists, and civil libertarians continued their efforts to make prisons more humane, structured for the rehabilitation of offenders. Yet the growing "law and order" approach toward offenders combined with perceptions of inefficiency within the criminal justice system served only to harden public attitudes toward the treatment of both male and female criminals. (For an idea of the differences between today's male and female prison inmates, see Exhibit 11.2.)

THE FEDERAL PRISON SYSTEM

The most diversified prison system in the United States emerged at the federal level, and many of the reforms and rehabilitative measures that were introduced in state institutions following the depression years were modeled after federal practices. The federal system is also the most recently developed, although its roots date back to the signing of the Declaration of Independence.

Beginning in 1776 and for more than a century, all federal offenders were confined in state and territorial institutions. The criminal law of the U.S. government was not particularly well developed at that time, and the few federal prosecutions that occurred were limited to the areas of counterfeiting, piracy and other crimes on the high seas, and felonies committed on Indian reservations. By the 1880s, however, the number of federal prisoners in state penitentiaries numbered more than 1,000, with an additional 10,000 housed in county jails. This situation created pressure on federal authorities to take a more active role in the field of corrections.[18]

As a result of the Mann Act of 1910 (which prohibited the transportation of women in foreign and interstate commerce for immoral purposes), the Harrison Act of 1914 (which regulated the distribution and sale of narcotics), the Volstead Act of 1919 (which prohibited the manufacture, transportation, and sale of alcoholic beverages), and the National Motor Vehicle Theft Act of 1919 (which banned the interstate transportation of stolen vehicles), the number of persons convicted of federal crimes during the 1920s grew rapidly. The result was the creation of the *Federal Bureau of Prisons,* signed into law on May 14, 1930. It called for the "proper classification and segregation of Federal prisoners according to their character, the nature of the crimes they have committed, their mental condition, and such other factors as should be taken into consideration in providing an individualized system of discipline, care, and treatment."[19]

Subsequently, the bureau established a graded system of institutions, including maximum-security penitentiaries for the close custody of the most serious felons, medium-security facilities for the better rehabilitative prospects, reformatories for young and inexperienced offenders, minimum-security open camps for those requiring little custodial control, detention centers for those awaiting trial and disposition, and a variety of halfway houses and community treatment centers. Despite the many negative opinions about its fortresslike

FEDERAL DRUG SEIZURES (IN POUNDS)					
	Total	Heroin	Co-caine	Mari-juana	Hash-ish
1990	737,318	1,794	235,214	483,248	17,062
1991	926,635	3,030	246,324	499,070	178,211
1992	1,093,334	2,551	303,260	783,475	4,048
1993	1,046,203	3,514	244,302	772,307	26,080
1994	1,065,241	2,824	282,086	778,715	1,616
1995	1,576,865	2,569	234,105	1,308,171	32,020
1996	1,720,805	3,324	254,367	1,430,096	33,018
1997	1,784,344	3,044	243,272	1,484,306	53,722

SOURCE: *Sourcebook of Criminal Justice Statistics, 1997.*

Courtesy Penthouse Magazine

"The defendant will kindly report to the federal minimum-security prison at his earliest convenience."

Alcatraz Island Penitentiary, the bureau evolved into the acknowledged leader in American correctional practice. By the late 1990s, the bureau had grown to the point where it operated an integrated system of 93 adult and juvenile correctional facilities nationwide, holding more than 123,000 inmates.

JAILS AND DETENTION CENTERS

A jail is not a prison. **Prisons** are correctional institutions maintained by the federal and state governments for the confinement of convicted felons. **Jails** are facilities of local authority for the temporary detention of defendants awaiting trial or disposition on federal or state charges, and of convicted offenders sentenced to short-term imprisonment for minor crimes. Historically, however, jails have been somewhat more than this—they have been used for the holding of many types of outcasts, suspects, and offenders.

Prisons: Correctional institutions maintained by federal and state governments for the confinement of convicted felons.

Jails: Local facilities for temporary detention.

Gaols, Hulks, and the Origins of American Jails

The jail is the oldest institution for incarcerating offenders, dating to perhaps as early as the fourth-century England, when Europe was under the rule of the Roman Empire. But little is known of the jails of that period other than that they were places for the accused and that there were separate quarters for women and men.

Even more wretched were the notorious hulks of eighteenth- and nineteenth-century England. In 1776, when transportation to the American colonies was terminated, a series of acts passed by George II ordered that the excess prison populations be placed in *hulks*, abandoned or unusable sailing vessels, generally of the man-of-war (warship) variety, permanently anchored in rivers and harbors throughout the British Isles. Within, they were similar to prisons and other places of detention. For security, inmates were often chained in irons. Hulks were overcrowded and dirty, and they quickly degenerated into human garbage dumps.

The American jail as we know it today is more likely rooted in the twelfth century, when places of detention had to be provided for prisoners awaiting trial in the English courts. Known as *gaols* (pronounced "jails"), they were often only a single room or two in a castle, market house, or the gaoler's own dwelling. The inmates were known as gaolbirds (jailbirds), from the large cagelike cells often used to confine groups of the prisoners like "birds in a cage."

By the seventeenth century, England's gaols had come to house both accused persons and convicted criminals. In addition to those awaiting trial, the jails held minor offenders sentenced to short-term imprisonment; debtors who were detained until they paid their creditors; vagrants, beggars, and other rogues and vagabonds who were considered public nuisances; and prisoners awaiting transportation to the colonies, execution, mutilation, branding, or placement in the stocks or pillory. The conditions were abominable, and inmates were abused and exploited by their keepers.

The English jail tradition came with the colonists to the New World. Jails first appeared in the Virginia colony in 1626 and were established in Pennsylvania as promulgated by the *Charter and Laws* of the Duke of York on September 25, 1676:

> Every town shall provide a pair of stocks for offenders, and a pound for the impounding of cattle; and prisons and pillories are likewise to be provided in these towns where the several courts of sessions are to be holden.

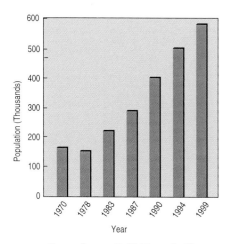

American Jail Population (average daily census), 1970–1999

SOURCE: Bureau of Justice Statistics.

Thus, the conventional English detention jail was introduced into America. The city and county jails in the colonies, and later in the states, maintained the characteristics of their prototypes. They were overcrowded and poorly maintained, prisoners were exploited by their warders, and both suspected and convicted offenders were kept unsegregated within their walls. It was not until the conversion of Philadelphia's Walnut Street Jail into a prison in 1790 and the development of the penitentiary system during the following century that jails and prisons across America became distinct custodial entities.

Contemporary Jail Systems

Jails, in current terminology, include a variety of facilities and structures. Depending on the jurisdiction and locale, they might be called "lockups," workhouses, detention centers, stockades, or town, city, and county jails. Regardless of the particular nomenclature, however, all are institutions of temporary or short-term detention. Some are small and able to hold only a few inmates; others can house many hundreds, even thousands, of prisoners.

Jail systems vary widely in terms of organization and jurisdictional authority. There are county jails under the jurisdiction of the local sheriff and city jails under the authority of the chief of police. There are other independent units, not tied to any jail "system" as such. In some large communities, there are complex arrangements of authority between several segments of local government. In many urban areas, for example, each police precinct has its own "lockup," which holds suspects during the questioning and booking stages of processing. In this phase, the jailing authority is in the hands of the precinct captain and the city police commissioner. Prisoners are then shifted to one of many city or county jails or detention centers. There are also statewide

systems, such as in Alaska, Connecticut, Delaware, Rhode Island, and Vermont, where all jails fall under the authority of a single state agency. Finally, there is the federal system, with its numerous detention centers throughout the United States under the jurisdiction of the Federal Bureau of Prisons.

The Jail Population

The jail is the portal of the criminal justice system. Except for defendants who are bailed while still in initial police custody, most arrestees are placed in jail, even if only for a short period of time.

As of January 1, 1999, there are more than 3,500 jails across the nation holding an estimated 580,000 inmates. Of this population, 90 percent were men and less than 1 percent were juveniles. Survey data reflect the traditional, twofold function of the jail: as a place for the temporary detention of the unconvicted and as a confinement facility where many convicted persons, primarily misdemeanants, serve out their sentences. As of 1999, half of all jail inmates were unconvicted, either not arraigned or arraigned and awaiting trial. The balance were either sentenced offenders or convicted offenders awaiting sentence.

Jail Conditions

For more than two centuries, jails have been described as "cesspools of crime," the "ultimate ghetto," "dumping grounds," and "festering sores in the criminal justice system." And what was said about American jails in the 1780s still applies today.[20] Most jails were, and are still, designed to allow for a minimum of staff while providing secure confinement for inmates. Most cells are large, cagelike rooms that hold significant numbers of prisoners at any given time. Although some structures have separate quarters for violent offenders, "drunk tanks" for the intoxicated, and alternative facilities for youthful offenders, many maintain all inmates in common quarters. The only exception here is the separation of sexes, which is almost universal.

Sanitary facilities are often poor and degrading, especially in older jails. Common open toilets prevent personal privacy; the large percentage of drunks and others who spew vomit and urine on the toilets and floors make for unhealthy and unwholesome circumstances; poor plumbing often results in repeated breakdowns and clogged facilities; and the inadequate availability of showers and washrooms inhibits personal cleanliness. To add to these potential health problems, many jails fail to provide appropriate medical care or even a physical examination at admission, thus increasing the possibility of disease. (For a glimpse of the grim conditions in Brazilian jails, see Exhibit 11.3.)

Jails are poorly staffed. Whatever personnel are available are often untrained. This can result in a lack of attention to inmate needs and mistreatment by other prisoners or correction officers.

Most jail inmates have little to occupy their time. Some of the larger detention centers have libraries and exercise areas, but in the main, recreational and academic facilities are not provided. Furthermore, the concepts of "treatment" and "rehabilitation" are not part of the American jail tradition.

New York City's *Rikers Island Penitentiary* is the largest penal colony in the nation, and perhaps the world. Built in 1933 to house sentenced offenders, some of its cell blocks are the length of a football field. By the mid-1990s, Rikers Island was home to almost 16,000 inmates, most of whom were in

AMERICAN JAIL INMATES AND DRUGS		
Type of Drug	% Who Ever Used Drugs	% Who Used in Month Before Arrest
Any drug	77.7%	43.9%
Major drug		
Cocaine or crack	50.4	23.6
Heroin	18.2	7.0
LSD	18.6	1.6
PCP	13.9	1.7
Methadone	4.8	.6
Other drug		
Marijuana	70.7	31.3
Amphetamines	22.1	5.4
Barbiturates	17.2	3.3
Methaqualone	14.7	.8
Other drugs	11.0	2.4

SOURCE: Bureau of Justice Statistics.

Rikers Island Penitentiary

Exhibit 11.3 **International Perspectives on Crime and Justice**
Jails and Prisons in Brazil

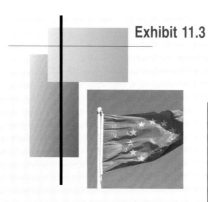

Dating back to the Portuguese colonial administration, Brazilian jails and prisons had some of the worst conditions in the Western world. Currently, although conditions vary significantly from state to state and from institution to institution, in most they tend to be appalling. Many facilities hold 2 to 5 times more inmates than they were designed for. In some facilities, the overcrowding has reached inhuman levels, with inmates jammed together in a tight crowd. The densely packed cells and dormitories in these places offer such sights as prisoners tied to windows to lessen the demand for floor space, and prisoners being forced to sleep on top of hole-in-the-floor toilets.

In most prisons, the distribution of living space is relatively unregulated, so that the burden of overcrowding falls disproportionately on certain prisoners. In general,

prisoners who are poorer, weaker, and less powerful tend to live in correspondingly less habitable accommodations. Typically, the disciplinary and holding cells—which are as likely to hold prisoners needing protection from other prisoners as they are to hold those being punished—are the most cramped and uncomfortable areas.

While certain prisons are crowded far beyond their capacities, the most overcrowded penal facilities in Brazil are generally the police lockups. Rather than being used as places of short-term detention for newly arrested criminal suspects, as they are supposed to be, police lockups in many Brazilian states hold inmates for long periods, even years. In states where the prison authorities are able to limit the transfer of additional inmates from lockups to the prisons, the police end up being left in charge of a significant proportion of the inmate population. Indeed, in the most extreme cases the police have become a *de facto* prison authority, supplementing or nearly replacing the conventional prison system.

Another serious problem is inmate-on-inmate violence. In the

detention because they were either denied or unable to make bail. Currently, Rikers has 10 separate buildings, each holding a separate population of offenders. Six are designated for male detainees (one of these is a high-security facility and another is for juveniles). Of the remaining four buildings comprising Rikers, one is for detained, convicted, and sentenced women; one is for inmates with HIV infection or AIDS; one is for inmates with contagious diseases; and one is for convicted and sentenced men. In addition, two floating detention centers are docked off the northern tip of Rikers Island. Each of these converted Staten Island ferries has an inmate capacity of 162 and serves as an annex to one of the other jails on the island, all housing adult male detainees. Rikers facilities other than institutions housing inmates include a bakery, central laundry, tailor shop, print shop, maintenance and transportation divisions, marine unit, K-9 unit, and a power plant. Any airline passengers flying into New York City's La Guardia Airport can get an excellent view of Rikers: It is to the immediate right as the plane approaches the landing strip.

In fairness to those sheriffs, police chiefs, wardens, and other jail administrators who have made attempts to upgrade the personnel and conditions in the facilities under their authority, it must be stated here that not all detention

Crowding in a Rio de Janeiro detention center.

most dangerous prisons, powerful inmates kill others with impunity, while even in relatively secure prisons extortion and other lesser forms of mistreatment are common. A number of factors combine to cause such abuses, among them the prisons' harsh conditions, lack of effective supervision, abundance of weapons, lack of activities, and, perhaps most importantly, the lack of inmate classification. Indeed, violent recidivists and persons held for first-time petty offenses often share the same cell in Brazil.

On the positive side of the balance, Brazilian penal facilities normally offer generous visiting policies, allowing prisoners regular face-to-face visits with their family and friends, and even conjugal visits. Not all facilities, however, are equally commendable in this regard, and certain systemic abuses can also be identified. The primary obstacle to inmates' visits is the humiliating treatment of visitors, who may be subject to poorly regulated strip searches and even, according to some inmates' allegations, invasive vaginal searches.

Women inmates are generally spared some of the worst aspects of the men's prisons—enjoying greater access to work opportunities, suffering less custodial violence, and being provided with greater material support—but they also bear special burdens. Most notably, women in many states face discrimination with regard to conjugal visiting rights. While male prisoners tend to be freely granted such visits, with little or no control exercised by state authorities, women prisoners are sometimes denied them or allowed them only under extremely tight restrictions. In addition, despite the Brazilian constitutional requirement that women prisoners be permitted to keep their nursing babies during the entire lactation period, women confined in some penal facilities lose their infants immediately after delivering them.

SOURCE: Adapted from "Behind Bars in Brazil," *Human Rights Watch,* 1998.

centers across America suffer from all the deficiencies mentioned in this discussion. Many jurisdictions have provided funds for the construction of modern, humane jails. Recent court decisions have legislated change in others. And too, there are independent jailers and wardens who have extended themselves to make the best of what otherwise might have been intolerable situations.

There have been numerous suggestions for improving local jails, including state inspection; the provision of social casework services; the development of educational, medical, and drug treatment programs; the use of volunteers to structure and supervise recreational services; and reorganization and cost sharing by state and local governments. Some of these approaches are beginning to be implemented.

In the final analysis, most of the problems of jails stem form overcrowding. It was once estimated that the daily population of American jails could be reduced by 50 percent, without endangering the public, by making the following changes:

1. Wider use of release on recognizance

2. Preferential trial scheduling for those in jail

Exhibit 11.4 **Careers in Justice**
Federal Bureau of Prisons

The Federal Bureau of Prisons employs staff in more than 200 job categories at more than 80 locations nationwide, and offers excellent benefits and competitive salaries. Qualifications for positions vary in the type of education and work experience required.

Correctional officers are the largest part of the workforce, and all Bureau of Prisons institutions routinely have vacancies for this position. Correctional officers supervise inmates and enforce the rules and regulations of a correctional institution. To qualify for this position at the entry level, you must have successfully completed at least one of the following:

- A bachelor's degree in any field of study
- At least 3 years of qualifying general work experience such as supervisor, teacher, counselor, parole/probation worker, worker with juvenile delinquents, welfare/social worker, firefighter, clergyman, emergency medical technician, air traffic controller, sales person in commissioned sales, security guard, manager, or day care facility worker
- A combination of undergraduate education and qualifying

general work experience, as previously described, that equals at least 3 full years

For a higher level position in this area you must have one of these qualifications:

- At least 6 months of graduate education in criminal justice or a social science
- At least 1 full year of specialized work experience in correctional work, law enforcement, or mental health facility work
- A combination of graduate education and specialized work experience, as previously described, that equals at least 1 full year

Correctional treatment specialists develop, evaluate, and analyze program needs and other data about inmates. The work they perform is similar to that of a social worker. To qualify, you must have successfully completed undergraduate education that includes 24 semester hours of a social science (which would qualify most criminal justice majors) plus 1 year of professional casework experience, or 2 years of graduate education in a social science, or at least 2 years of a combination of graduate education and professional casework experience.

For more information, contact the Bureau of Prisons on the Internet (Web site address: http://www.bop.gov).

3. Use of citations rather than jail terms for more offenses
4. Creation of installment plans for those who go to jail because they cannot pay their fines
5. Use of work-release for jail inmates

Although these alternatives have been implemented widely in many jurisdictions, apparently they have not been enough. The jail population of some 580,000 inmates in 1999 represented a 100 percent increase since 1985, up some 300,000 inmates.

Op-Ed

Getting back to Lewis Dwight's comments about Auburn Prison that were quoted in the opening sentences of this chapter, Auburn was anything but the model penitentiary he described. As noted earlier in this chapter, the attractiveness of Auburn was in its economic advantages. The small cells were cheap and easy to construct, and the industrial output in a setting of large congregate work areas was efficient and profitable. But remember, Dwight's observations were made back in 1823 during the days of the Auburn "silent system."

The hard and unremitting labor, perpetual silence, and unquestioning obedience were maintained by severe corporal punishments such as flogging, the "douche," and the "water cure." Of these, flogging was considered the most effective method of gaining compliance and was generally done with a rawhide whip or a "cat" made of wire strands. The "douche" involved the continuous dumping of frigid water from a great height onto the body of the prisoner. The "water cure" had several variations. At times it consisted of a strong, fine stream of water turned onto sensitive parts of the prisoner's body; on other occasions, water came only one drop at a time onto the prisoner's head, the

process sometimes lasting for days. These were common punishments for breaking the silence rule. The technique of talking out of the side of one's mouth—often depicted in the gangster movies of the 1930s and 1940s—had its origin in "silent" prisons, where it was a means of getting around the silence rules.

Prison stripes and the lockstep were also features of prison life devised at Auburn. Striped uniforms served to degrade convicts and to make them conspicuous should they escape. The lockstep, which was originated for the purpose of making supervision easier, was a bizarre marching formation. Prisoners were required to line up behind one another, with their hands on the shoulders or under the arms of the person in front. The line then moved rapidly toward its destination as the prisoners shuffled their feet in unison, without lifting them from the ground with their eyes focused on the guard. Another feature of Auburn was the "prison-within-a-prison," or "hole," which was an area where prisoners were put into total isolation for violation of some institutional rule. So on the basis of these remarks, was Auburn a model prison, even in its day?

SUMMARY

The American prison experience began during the eighteenth century in Philadelphia. The Walnut Street Jail was the nation's first penitentiary. Throughout the 1790s its structure and separate system characterized it as a model

prison. The separate system approach was based on the notion that recidivism could be eliminated by obstructing "evil associations" between prisoners through separate living quarters. The decline of the Walnut Street Jail occurred in the beginning of the nineteenth century, largely because of overcrowding, periodic riots, and inadequate disciplinary control. This system was subsequently rivaled by New York's silent system as it emerged at Auburn Prison in 1823. The silent system prevailed over a system of separate quarters for primarily economic reasons. This system allowed for smaller cells and large, congregate work areas while attempting to accomplish the same objective: prevention of corruption through obstructing communication among inmates. Ultimately, a desire for greater profits extracted from cheap inmate labor served to weaken the silent system, since perpetual silence on the workfloor was counterproductive.

The work of Captain Alexander Maconochie in Australia and Sir Walter Crofton in Ireland influenced America's reformatory era. Maconochie was responsible for inventing the "mark system," through which an inmate could receive early release if he worked hard and exhibited good behavior. Crofton's "Irish system" built on Maconochie's earlier work, but in addition it established four stages through which inmates must successfully pass before receiving a conditional release. Based on these systems, the first reformatory was opened at Elmira, New York, in 1876, but by 1910 this correctional experience was abandoned.

As corrections moved from the mid-1800s into the early years of the twentieth century, the American prison system had evolved into an expanding hoard of maximum-security institutions. This period first witnessed active prison industries, then idle convict populations. Following the depression years, new treatment ideas were introduced against a backdrop of growing apathy and decaying institutions. The 1960s through the 1990s saw even greater contrasts—an emphasis on individual prisoners' needs and rights in settings of unrest and massive overcrowding.

The emergence and growth of the federal prison system has been a much more recent phenomenon. From 1776 through 1891, all federal prisoners were housed in state and territorial institutions. Following the passage of the Mann Act (1910), the Harrison Act (1914), the Volstead Act (1919), and the Motor Vehicle Theft Act (1919), the number of federal prisoners in state institutions grew rapidly, ultimately forcing the birth of the first federal penitentiaries. The Federal Bureau of Prisons was created in 1930 and became responsible for the development of a graded system of federal institutions that ranged from maximum- to minimum-security facilities and camps.

The jail is a detention facility quite distinct from a prison. Unlike prisons, which are run by state and federal governments, jails are administered by local authorities and house only those individuals who are awaiting trial or who are convicted of relatively minor crimes and receive comparatively short sentences. The jail is one of the oldest known institutions for detaining offenders, dating back to the fourth-century England. Jails first appeared in the United States in 1626 and were modeled after the English detention facility. Today, jails vary greatly depending on the area and the demands of the local criminal justice system. One nearly universal similarity, however, is the overcrowded and inadequate living conditions characteristic of most jails today.

KEY TERMS

contract system **301**	piece-price system **301**	state account system **301**
jails **307**	prisons **307**	state-use system **301**
lease system **301**	separate system **298**	"ticket-of-leave" **302**
"mark system" **302**	silent system **300**	Walnut Street Jail **298**

QUESTIONS FOR DISCUSSION

1. How did the Industrial Revolution affect the evolution of prisons in the United States?
2. What are the differences between jails and prisons?
3. Would the *silent* and *separate* systems of imprisonment be appropriate for today's prisoners? Which types of prisoners? Why?
4. How might jails be reformed?

MEDIA RESOURCES

1. **Women Inmates.** See Office of Justice Programs, "The Women's Prison Association: Supporting Women Offenders and Their Families," National Institute of Justice *Program Focus,* December 1998.

2. **Federal Bureau of Prisons.** The Bureau of Prisons has an extensive Web site with information about the bureau's systems, institutions, inmates, and employment. (Web site address: http://www.bop.gov)

3. **Rikers Island.** The New York City Department of Correction has put together a good Web site with some interesting historical material on the city jail system, including its history, programs, and current statistics. (Web site address: http://www.ci.nyc.ny.us/html/doc/home.html)

4. **Human Rights Watch.** Human Rights Watch monitors prison conditions around the world, and has numerous reports that can be accessed from their Web site. (Web address: http://www.hrw.org/hrw/reports98)

NOTES

1. From a letter by Lewis Dwight, founder of the Boston Prison Society, written shortly after the full implementation of the "silent system" at Auburn in 1823; cited by Harry Elmer Barnes, *The Story of Punishment: A Record of Man's Inhumanity to Man* (Montclair, N.J.: Patterson Smith, 1972), pp. 136–137.)

2. Orlando F. Lewis, *The Development of American Prisons and Prison Customs, 1776–1845* (Albany: Prison Association of New York, 1922), pp. 26–28.

3. Harry Elmer Barnes, *The Repression of Crime* (New York: Doran, 1926), p. 162.

4. Barnes, *Repression of Crime.*

5. See Negley K. Teeters and John D. Shearer, *The Prison at Philadelphia: Cherry Hill* (New York: Columbia University Press, 1957); William Crawford, *Report on the Penitentiaries of the United States* (Montclair, N.J.: Patterson Smith, 1969), pp. 1–2.

6. Margaret Wilson, *The Crime of Punishment* (New York: Harcourt, Brace, 1931), pp. 219–220.

7. Lewis, *Development of American Prisons,* pp. 80–95.

8. See Blake McKelvey, *American Prisons: A History of Good Intentions* (Montclair, N.J.: Patterson Smith, 1977), pp. 116–149.

9. See J. C. Powell, *The American Siberia* (Chicago: Smith, 1891).

10. McKelvey, *American Prisons,* p. 14.

11. John V. Barry, "Alexander Maconochie," *Journal of Criminal Law, Criminology, and Police Science* 47 (July–August 1956): 145–161.

12. John V. Barry, "Captain Alexander Maconochie," *The Victorian Historical Magazine* 27 (June 1957): 5.

13. McKelvey, *American Prison,* p. 37.

14. Zebulon Brockway, *Fifty Years of Prison Service* (Montclair, N.J.: Patterson Smith, 1969), pp. 419–423.

15. Harry Elmer Barnes and Negley K. Teeters, *New Horizons in Criminology* (Englewood Cliffs, N.J.: Prentice-Hall, 1959), p. 428.

16. Frank Flynn, "The Federal Government and the Prison Labor Problem in the States," *Social Science Review* 24 (March–June 1950): 19–40, 213–236.

17. Harry E. Allen and Clifford E. Simonsen, *Corrections in America* (New York: Macmillan, 1981), pp. 51–53.

18. Paul W. Tappan, *Crime, Justice, and Correction* (New York: McGraw-Hill, 1960), p. 619.

19. 2818 U.S. Code 907, cited by Tappan, *Crime, Justice and Correction,* p. 620.

20. Ronald Goldfarb, *Jails: The Ultimate Ghetto of the Criminal Justice System* (Garden City, N.Y.: Anchor, 1976), p. 3; George Ives, *A History of Penal Methods* (Montclair, N.J.: Patterson Smith, 1970); Joseph F. Fishman, *Crucibles of Crime: The Shocking Story of the American Jail* (Montclair, N.J.: Patterson Smith, 1969); *Newsweek,* August 18, 1980, pp. 74, 76; *New York Times,* August 14, 1987, pp. B1, B3; *New York Times,* August 30, 1990, pp. A1, B2; Wayne N. Welsh, Henry N. Pontell, Matthew C. Leone, and Patrick Kinkade, "Jail Overcrowding: An Analysis of Policy Makers' Perceptions," *Justice Quarterly* 7 (June 1990): 341–370; Joel A. Thompson and G. Larry Mays, eds., *American Jails: Public Policy Issues* (Chicago: Nelson-Hall, 1991).

CHAPTER **1 2**

BEHIND THE WALLS: A LOOK INSIDE THE AMERICAN PENITENTIARY

F

LORENCE, COLO. — Situated in the arid, remote, high desert near Florence, Colorado, there is a triangular, two-story, high-tech prison known as ADX. Officially known as the Federal Bureau of Prisons' Administrative Maximum Facility, some inmates refer to it as the "Alcatraz of the Rockies" while others call it the "hellhole of the Rockies." Some observers call it "the end of the line."

Built in 1994 in response to the growing number of violent predatory criminals being housed in federal prisons, this "supermax" facility has the unique mission of confining "the worst of the worst"—some 400-plus inmates from all over the federal prison system considered so dangerous that no other penitentiary can hold them. The mere existence of ADX raises an interesting set of questions. Is this prison really necessary, and who is confined there? What is a "supermax" prison like, and is there more than one? And there are other questions. How many different kinds of prisons are there? What goes on in prisons? Do they actually rehabilitate offenders?

Total institutions: Places that furnish barriers to social interchange with the world at large.

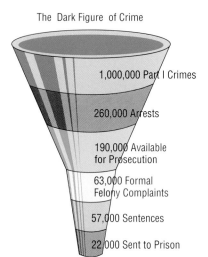

The Dark Figure of Crime

1,000,000 Part I Crimes

260,000 Arrests

190,000 Available for Prosecution

63,000 Formal Felony Complaints

57,000 Sentences

22,000 Sent to Prison

The Criminal Justice Funnel

Prisons, psychiatric hospitals, and nursing homes all share something in common—they are often referred to as "total institutions." **Total institutions** are places that furnish barriers to social interchange with the world at large.[1] In total institutions, large groups of persons live together, day and night, in a fixed area and under a tightly scheduled sequence of activities imposed by a central authority. In total institutions there are "subjects" and "managers." Subjects are the large class of individuals who have restricted contact with the world outside the walls. Managers, who are socially integrated into the outside world, are the small class that supervise the subjects. In total institutions the social distance between subjects and managers is great and communication is restricted. Each group conceives of the members of the other in terms of narrow, hostile stereotypes, resulting in the development of alternative social and cultural worlds that remain in continuous conflict with one another. In total institutions there is an elaborate system of formal rules intended to achieve the organization's official aim and to maintain the distance between subjects and managers. Correctional institutions are total institutions organized to protect the community against what are conceived to be intentional dangers to it. Correctional institutions include penitentiaries and reformatories, as well as a multitude of training schools, ranches, farms, and camps. Regardless of the designations, however, all are generally referred to as "prisons."

TYPES OF PRISONS

It has been traditional in the United States to divide correctional institutions into three or more levels of custody, according to their construction and measures of custody and control.

Maximum-Security Prisons

Maximum-security prisons: Correctional institutions designed to hold the most aggressive and incorrigible offenders.

The best-known prisons in the United States are likely Sing Sing, Attica, San Quentin, Leavenworth, Joliet, and the now-closed Alcatraz Island Penitentiary (see Exhibit 12.1). These are **maximum-security prisons.** They are walled fortresses of concrete and steel and house the most serious, most aggressive, and most incorrigible of offenders. Many maximum-security prisons also have segregated "supermax" units for "the worst of the worst" that the offender population has to offer.

Most maximum-security prisons have a common design. Housing anywhere from many hundreds to several thousands of inmates, secure custody and control are the guiding principles. They are enclosed by massive concrete walls, sometimes as high as 30 feet, or by a series of double or triple perimeter fences topped with barbed wire or razor ribbon, and often electrically charged. Located along the outer-perimeter walls are well-protected guard towers, strategically placed to provide guards with open fields of fire and observation of prison yards and the outside areas surrounding the prison.

Inside cells: Cells constructed back-to-back, with corridors running along the outside shell of the cell house.

A characteristic feature of the maximum-security prison is the inside cell block. **Inside cells** are constructed back-to-back, with corridors running along the outside shell of the cell house. In contrast to outside cells, which are affixed to the outside walls of the cell house, inside cells are considered more secure. Whereas escape through the window or wall of an outside cell would place an inmate in the prison yard, such escape from an inside cell would leave the prisoner still within the cell block.

Each tier of cells is called a *cell block* and the cell house may contain as many as 10 such blocks. The cell blocks are self-contained security enclosures,

Exhibit 12.1 **Historical Perspectives on Crime and Justice**
Alcatraz Island Penitentiary

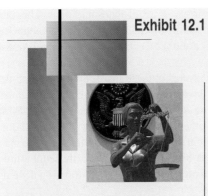

During the early years of the Great Depression, an unusual crime wave had spread across the American Midwest. Banks that had weathered the stock market crash of 1929 were being robbed at the rate of two a day. The outlaws operated with flair and skill. Armed with machine guns, they recreated a frontier pattern of rapid assault followed by elusive retreat. The millions of citizens caught in the drab round of idleness and poverty that characterized the times responded to the criminal exploits with acceptance and admiration. The bandits became folk heroes and such names as John Dillinger, Frank Nash, Charles "Pretty Boy" Floyd, Bonnie Parker, Clyde Barrow, and George "Baby Face" Nelson quickly found their way into American folklore. But to the Federal Bureau of Investigation they were "public enemies"; to FBI Director J. Edgar Hoover they were "public rats," "the lowest dregs of society," "vermin in human form," "slime," "vermin spewed out of prison cells," and "scum from the boiling pot of the underworld."

The 1930s crime wave, the public enemies, and the vibrant rhetoric had ushered in a new phase in twentieth-century penology. It was a thesis built on the belief that some criminals were so incorrigible that they should be repressed and disciplined with absolute inflexibility. Many thought that

Alcatraz Island Penitentiary might be the answer to the problem.

Originally named by eighteenth-century Spanish explorers *Isla de los Alcatraces* (Island of Pelicans) after the birds that then roosted there, Alcatraz has an area of 12 acres and rises steeply to 136 feet above San Francisco Bay. In 1859 a U.S. military prison was built on the island, and in March 1934 it was taken over by the Federal Bureau of Prisons.

Alcatraz became the most repressive maximum-security facility in the nation. Its six guard towers, equipped with .30-caliber carbines and high-powered rifles, could observe every square foot of the island. Barbed-wire barriers dotted the shorelines, and each entrance to the cell house had a three-door security system.

There were 600 one-man cells, built into three-tiered cell blocks. Measuring 8 feet by 4 feet, each cell contained a fold-up bunk hooked to the wall, fold-up table and chair, shelf, washbasin, toilet, and shaded ceiling light. Cell block D was the disciplinary barracks—solitary confinement for the more difficult offenders. It included "the Hole," a series of smaller cells with solid steel walls, floors, and doors; there were no furnishings and its inmates were locked into total darkness.

Each day at Alcatraz began at 6:30 A.M. with the clanging of a bell and a burst of electric light. Inmates had 20 minutes to dress, make their beds, and head out to breakfast and then work. Recreation was limited to an exercise yard and a small library. There was no commissary. Prisoners were allowed three packs of cigarettes each week. Newspapers

and radio were denied in order to intensify the sense of isolation. One letter could be written each week and three could be received, but with severe restrictions: Correspondence could not be carried on with nonrelatives, and the content was restricted to family matters. One visit per month, from a family member or attorney, was permitted. Work was limited to cooking, cleaning, maintenance, and laundry. Security was rigid, with one guard for every three inmates.

With its policy of maximum security, combined with minimum privileges and total isolation for America's "public enemies," Alcatraz did have a number of underworld aristocrats and spectacular felons, including Arthur "Doc" Barker, last surviving son of Ma Barker's murderous brood; kidnapper George "Machine Gun" Kelly; Alvin Karpis, the most evasive bank robber of the 1930s; and bootlegger, murderer, and syndicate boss Al "Scarface" Capone. But for the most part, comparatively few big-time gangsters ever went to Alcatraz; many of the island's inmates were actually first offenders.

From its earliest days, the concept behind Alcatraz had generated considerable opposition from social scientists and prison administrators. It was closed in 1963 because it was too costly to operate and too typical of the retributive justice that no longer had any stature in the federal prison system. Today, Alcatraz Island Penitentiary is part of the Golden Gate National Recreation Area, having shifted over a four-decade period from a dead-end prison to a public tourist attraction.

SOURCES: E. E. Kirkpatrick, *Voices From Alcatraz* (San Antonio: Naylor, 1947); James A. Johnston, *Alcatraz Island Prison* (New York: Scribner's, 1949); John Kobler, *Capone: The Life and World of Al Capone* (New York: Putnam, 1971); L. L. Edge, *Run the Cat Roads* (New York: Dembner, 1981).

When they locked me in my cell that very first day it suddenly hit me all at once. "This is it, asshole," I said to myself, "you're gonna die in this place." I was scared, lonely, and depressed and really feeling sorry for myself. But I didn't die. I became just like all the other shit-heads, pissholes, and zombies— playing the games, doing the time, falling into the routine ... sleep, eat, work, sleep, eat, work, "yes sir," "no sir," "I'm sorry sir," "I must have been mistaken sir. ..."

—Former inmate,
Leavenworth Penitentiary

often partitioned off from one another by a series of gates and pens. This creates a complex of miniature prisons within the penitentiary, thus enhancing the overall security. Such a pattern is doubly effective, since each cell house is similarly separated from all others.

The emphasis on escape-proof measures in these institutions also includes tool-proof steel construction, multiple lock devices, frequent *shake-downs* (searches) and counts, infrared sensing devices, and closed-circuit TV. More modern maximum-security prisons are beginning to move away from the construction of these double- and triple-security patterns, and particularly the massive outside walls, because of their prohibitive cost. In place of those measures, officials are increasing the use of sophisticated technological intrusion devices.

Medium-Security Prisons

While reproducing the basic pattern of maximum-security prisons, there is somewhat less emphasis on internal fortification in medium-security facilities. They are rarely fortresslike structures with high stone walls. Rather, the perimeters are marked by a series of fences and enclosures with fewer guard towers. Outside cells are characteristic, and in the newer structures, banks of dormitories and other congregate living quarters are becoming common.

The inmates placed in medium-security institutions are those who are considered less dangerous and escape-prone than those in the more security-oriented institutions. Their internal movements within the facility are less controlled, and surveillance is less vigilant. However, these prisons generally do have a maximum-security unit, available for those inmates who become custodial problems or threats to the safety of other prisoners.

Minimum-Security Prisons

Correctional institutions of minimum-security design operate without armed correctional officers, without walls, and sometimes even without perimeter fences. The inmates of these facilities are considered to be low security risks: the most trustworthy and least violent offenders, those with short sentences, and white-collar criminals. A great deal of personal freedom is allowed, dormitory living is the common practice, educational release is encouraged, and the level of surveillance is low.[2]

Minimum-security facilities that cater to white-collar criminals, built on what has become known as the "cottage plan," have often been criticized as being more likely country clubs than prisons. Yet despite the attractiveness of their physical layout and resources, they are nevertheless "total institutions" and serve as effective barriers to the outside world.

Open Institutions

As a departure from the traditional maximum-, medium-, and minimum-security prisons, which are essentially closed institutions, there are variations in the minimum-security plan that serve as "prisons without walls." These are the prison farms, camps, and ranches, the vocational training centers, and the forestry settlements that are relatively recent innovative reforms. The modern counterparts of the nineteenth-century reformatories for youthful offenders and young adult felons, they provide instructive work for inmates within an environment more conducive to behavioral change.

These **open institutions** have numerous advantages over more traditional correctional facilities. They relieve the problem of overcrowding in other types

Open institutions: "Prisons without walls," such as correctional camps, farms, and ranches.

of institutions; they are less costly to construct and maintain; and they enable various types of prisoners to be separated, thus reducing the opportunities for contamination of attitudes. Furthermore, they have economic and community service advantages. Prisoners in the open camps produce crops and dairy products for use in the state correctional system and other government facilities. Ranches employ inmates in cattle raising and horse breeding. Forestry camps are used to maintain state parks, fight forest fires, and aid in reforestation. Finally, these camps and farms avoid many of the drawbacks of the traditional total institutions, for regulation and regimentation is more relaxed and greater freedom of movement is possible.

Women's Institutions

Historically, there have been few women prisoners. Prior to the beginning of the twentieth century, women represented less than 1 percent of the adult felon prison population. This changed somewhat over the years, and from 1970 through the end of the 1990s the proportion of women in state and federal correctional institutions increased from 2.9 percent to 6.9 percent. This low population of women has resulted, for most of the past 200 years of U.S. history, in a series of rather disjointed and arbitrary policies for the incarceration of female offenders.

Not until 1873, in Indianapolis, Indiana, was the first separate prison for women opened in the United States. Prior to that time, women were confined in congregate quarters with men or held in isolation within small sections of men's penitentiaries and supervised by male warders.[3] During the last 50 years, and especially in the past two decades, the number of correctional facilities for women has increased dramatically. And, in spite of considerable progress, these institutions reflect both the best and the worst elements of the American prison system.

Today, although they are often referred to as reformatories and state farms, women are confined in separate maximum- and minimum-security prisons, in isolated wings of men's penitentiaries, in coeducational facilities (discussed later in this chapter), and in open institutions. Some states have no correctional facilities for women, using in their place, under a contract arrangement, the institutions of other jurisdictions.

As the general population of prison inmates has grown, so too has the number of women behind bars—in many ways a reflection of tougher drug laws and mandatory sentencing policies. A recent survey of women inmates found that the majority were serving time for drug or drug-related charges and only one-fifth were classified as violent offenders.[4] Despite the growing numbers of incarcerated women, many states have failed to adequately reform their antiquated, gender-typed policies and programs targeting female offenders. Many state institutions for women do not provide the range of opportunities and privileges available at most institutions for men. Moreover, women's vocational training and work opportunities continue to reflect gender-based notions of "women's work." A disproportionate number of women inmates are still involved in cleaning and kitchen work while male inmates are involved in farming, forestry, and maintenance. Further, vocational training programs at women's prisons continue to offer classes in cosmetology, data processing, food preparation, and nurse's aide training. The gender-typed nature of vocational programming is particularly problematic, since these types of jobs are notorious for their lack of benefits and low wages, making it difficult for women inmates (73 percent of whom are single parents) to achieve economic independence after release. Only a few of the nation's correctional institutions for women offer training in such areas as auto servicing, plumbing, and heating/air conditioning repair.

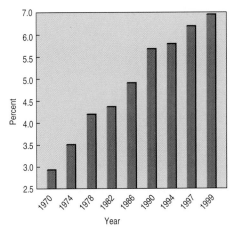

Proportion of Female Inmates in State and Federal Correctional Institutions, 1970–1999

SOURCE: Bureau of Justice Statistics.

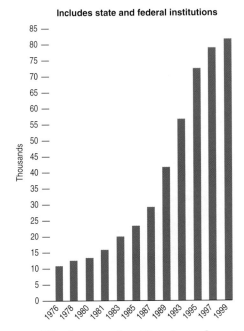

The Increasing Number of Women Behind Bars

SOURCE: Bureau of Justice Statistics.

CORRECTIONAL ORGANIZATION AND ADMINISTRATION

The central administration of correctional systems in the United States reflects a wide diversity of organizational patterns within complex state power structures. But it was not always this way. Until the beginning of the twentieth century, prisons were administered by state boards of charities, boards of inspectors, state prison commissions, boards of control made up of "prominent citizens," or individual prison keepers.[5] Generally, however, most prisons in most states operated as independent fiefdoms. Few jurisdictions had a state department of corrections. Individual wardens received their appointments directly from governors through the system of political patronage, and institutional staff held their positions by virtue of their political connections. While governors made hiring and budgetary decisions, the leadership roles and the administrative procedures of individual institutions were under the absolute control of the wardens. Today, every state has some form of centralized department of corrections that establishes policy for all institutions within its jurisdiction.

Prison Administration

The two most common forms of correctional systems are those that are subdivisions of some larger state department, such as justice or welfare, and those that are independent structures. The U.S. Bureau of Prisons, for example, is a division of the Department of Justice; Florida's department of corrections is a separate state agency; in Vermont and Tennessee, corrections falls under a department of institutions; and in Virginia, corrections is a segment of the department of public welfare. California, Arkansas, Texas, and numerous other states, however, have independent departments of corrections with lines of authority running directly to the governor's office.

At the top of the administrative hierarchy of any department of corrections is the commissioner of corrections. This executive works directly under the governor to establish policy, shape the direction of institutional procedures, negotiate annual budgetary allotments for the various institutions, and make major personnel decisions.

The head of each prison, generally appointed by the commissioner of corrections, is a warden, director, principal keeper, or superintendent, depending on state nomenclature. The duty of the warden or superintendent is to manage the prison. In the larger institutions, the warden may be assisted by one or more associates: a deputy warden in charge of discipline, security, inmate movement and control, and prison routine; a second deputy in charge of prison programs, records, library services, mail and visitation, recreation, and release procedures; an industries manager in charge of prison industries, farms, production, and supplies; and a medical supervisor in charge of prison health services and sanitation.

Prison Personnel

In addition to wardens, their deputies, and other administrators, prison personnel include both professional and custodial staff. The *professional staff* are the physicians, nurses, dentists, chaplains, psychiatrists, psychologists, clerks and secretaries, teachers, counselors, and dietitians who deal with the institutional paperwork and serve the medical, spiritual, and treatment needs of the

Sex

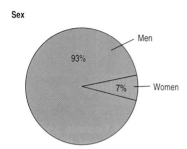

Race

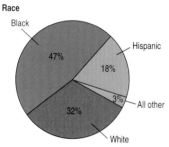

Age

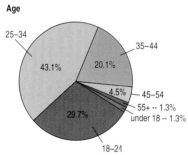

Commitment Offense

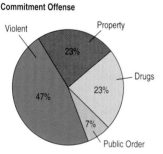

Education

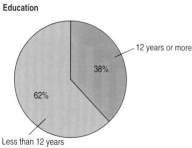

The U.S. Prison Population

SOURCE: Bureau of Justice Statistics.

offender population. The size of the professional staff varies with that of the institution and with its particular orientation (custody versus rehabilitation). In larger prisons, professionals constitute about one-third of the workforce. The *custodial staff* is made up of the correctional officers and their supervisors, whose functions fall into the areas of inmate security, movement, and discipline. Invariably, however, their roles go considerably further.

Prison guards, more currently referred to as correction, correctional, or custodial officers, work in a maligned profession. Guarding is considered a tainted occupation because people find the surveillance and repression that are characteristic of prison life to be repugnant. The popular media are in large part responsible for creating and sustaining this image. Contemporary cinema and television dramas often portray the correctional officer as evil and savage. Late-night TV movies such as *The Big House* (1930), *White Heat* (1949), *Inside the Walls of Folsom Prison* (1951), *Birdman of Alcatraz* (1962), and *Cool Hand Luke* (1967), to name but a few, have shown prison guards as bigoted, corrupt, brutal, and morally base. More recently, the Earle Owensby films of the 1970s as well as *Escape From Alcatraz* (1978), *Brubaker* (1980), *Bad Boys* (1983), *The Shawshank Redemption* (1994), and *Sleepers* (1996) have continued the tradition. Segments of the prison literature, particularly those that have appeared as emotional statements against the prison system—such as Eldridge Cleaver's *Soul on Ice* and George Jackson's *Soledad Brother*—have also presented the prison guard in a most negative way.[6]

Without question, there are many corrupt and brutal prison guards. But to put them all in a common mold would be no more accurate than suggesting that "all convicts are evil," "all police are dishonest," or "all politicians are criminals." In fact, if the popular image of the guard were accurate, most prisons would not function.

Correctional officers' duties are onerous and difficult, and they must be performed under the most unpleasant of circumstances. Their careers unfold while they are locked up in an unattractive and depressing environment. Outnumbered by a legion of hostile, restless, and sometimes desperate and violent inmates, they must always be watchful and always appear vigilant, alert, strong, competent, and self-confident.

Within this closed setting, and faced with few means for carrying out their custodial duties, correctional officers must resort to a number of unconventional mechanisms for maintaining the internal order of the prison. Some become brutal and sadistic. A few become indispensable to the inmate black market, providing illegal services and contraband or serving as "mules" to carry drugs into the prison. And still others develop a system of punishments and rewards to exact inmate compliance. Most, however, use the spirit of compromise to accomplish their mission. They overlook a number of infractions. Inmates may be allowed to remain out of their cells without authorization, to pass letters back and forth, to cook food stolen from the prison kitchen, to smoke in unauthorized areas, or to possess trivial contraband items. In return, they are expected to refrain from violence, to perform their assigned tasks, and to be civil toward the guards.[7]

PRISON CROWDING IN SELECTED FEDERAL FACILITIES			
Facility	Year Opened	Rated Capacity	Current Population
Atlanta	1902	1,429	2,281
Leavenworth	1906	1,197	1,803
Lewisburg	1932	678	1,091
Lompoc	1959	1,035	1,591
Marion	1963	482	290
Terre Haute	1940	741	1,094

SOURCE: Bureau of Prisons, 1999.

INSTITUTIONAL ROUTINES

At the beginning of 1999, there were more than 1.2 million persons housed in federal and state correctional institutions in the 50 states, the District of Columbia, and the U.S. territories. The institutions in which these prisoners were being held included the full range of correctional facilities—from maximum-security walled fortresses, to minimum-security cottages and reformatories, to "open" forestry camps and ranch settlements. The physical conditions of these institutions also covered the entire range of alternatives—from the best to the worst that the American prison system has to offer. Although many new correctional facilities have been built over the years, the majority are old and in varying stages of decay, with conditions that are often appalling.

Prison Facilities

In 1975, studies by the Federal Bureau of Prisons revealed that of the hundreds of state institutions in operation at that time, 47 percent had been built since 1949, 32 percent dated from the period between 1924 and 1948, and the balance had been put into operation during 1923 or earlier.[8] Furthermore, 24 of the prisons—most of them large maximum-security facilities—had been in continuous use since before 1874. By the late 1990s, with proper upkeep of the institutions difficult, further deterioration had become apparent. Today, Clinton Prison in New York, Joliet in Illinois, and California's San Quentin are more than 125 years old; Michigan's Jackson Prison and Pennsylvania's Eastern Penitentiary have been housing inmates for more than a century and a half; and if current trends in prison use continue, both Auburn and Sing Sing in New York may celebrate their bicentennials as still-operational institutions. All of these ancient institutions have made improvements over the years: Many of the original cell blocks have been abandoned or modernized, new structures have been added, and sanitary and other facilities have been renovated to reflect more humanitarian standards. Nevertheless, in their basic order and design, the more than 100 correctional institutions built during the nineteenth and early twentieth centuries, together with the many more built during the 1920s and 1930s, continue to operate as grim monuments to the penal philosophy of the unyielding past.

One of the major reasons that many antiquated prisons continue to remain in use is overcrowding. Put simply, state governments are economically not in the position to build a new prison to completely replace an older one that is already filled beyond capacity. As such, new prisons typically do not replace older ones, but act to complement them by accommodating inmate overloads.

Classification

Classification: The process through which the educational, vocational, treatment, and custodial needs of the offender are determined.

The prison experience generally begins with **classification.** In its broadest sense, classification is the process through which the educational, vocational, treatment, and custodial needs of the offender are determined. At least theoretically, it is the system by which a correctional agency reckons differential handling and care, fitting the treatment and security programs of the institution to the requirements of the individual.

The most rudimentary forms of correctional classification were seen when the practice developed of imprisoning people after conviction. Separating the guilty from the not-guilty was itself a process of classifying those accused of criminal behavior. The separation of debtors from criminals was a type of classification by legal status. Early forms of classification included the separation of men from women, youth from adults, and first offenders from habitual criminals. The reformatory movements of the late nineteenth century, the differentiation between maximum- versus medium- and minimum-security prisons, and the designation of Alcatraz as a superpenitentiary for the most incorrigible felons were all examples of rudimentary classification schemes. As correctional systems continued to evolve, the separation of the "feebleminded," the "tubercular," the "venereally diseased," the "sexually perverted," the drug addicted, and the aged and "crippled"—as they were referred to for a good

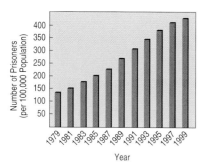

Rates of Imprisonment, 1979–1999

SOURCE: Bureau of Justice Statistics.

part of the twentieth century—from the general prison population or into special institutions was also based on the principle of classification. (For a brief
discussion of why HIV/AIDS-infected inmates are segregated, see Exhibit 12.2.)

The classification process may range from a physical examination and a
single interview to an extensive series of psychiatric and psychological tests,
academic and vocational evaluations, orientation sessions, medical and dental
checkups, and numerous personal interviews. Some classification programs
may also include analyses of athletic abilities and recreational interests, and
contacts with religious advisers.

Exhibit 12.2   **International Perspectives on Crime and Justice**
Prisoners, HIV/AIDS, and Harm Reduction   WWW.
Around the World

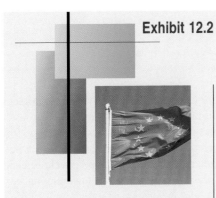

AIDS (acquired immunodeficiency
syndrome) was the most publicized disease of the twentieth century. It is best defined as a severe
manifestation of infection with HIV
(human immunodeficiency virus),
a virus that destroys or incapaci-
tates components of the immune
system. The actual causes of
death among people with AIDS include a variety of infections and
other diseases that an otherwise
healthy immune system can effectively cope with.

HIV is transmitted when virus
particles or infected cells gain direct access to the bloodstream.
This can occur during all forms of
sexual intercourse that involve the
transmission of body fluids, as
well as oral-genital intercourse
with an infected partner. The virus
can also be transmitted through
shared injection equipment among
injection drug users, and it can be
passed to unborn or newborn children by infected mothers, as well
as through transfusions from an
infected blood supply.

In various parts of the world,
HIV prevalence in many prisons is
already high—higher than in the
population at large, and still

increasing. Prison conditions are
ideal places for the transmission
of HIV infection through drug use
and sex.

Because drug injection paraphernalia are so scarce in prisons,
they are typically shared. In addition, the needles and syringes are
often ingenious homemade devices—crafted from such things
as ball-point pens and eye drop-
pers—and are likely to contain
significantly large amounts of
blood and virus from the previous
user. A recent survey in a Lower
Saxony (Germany) women's
prison found that a third of those
sampled were injection drug
users, 5 percent of whom were
infected with HIV. In Thailand, a
country that has endured one of
the fastest spreads of the HIV epidemic in Asia, the transmission of
the virus was fueled to a great extent by drug injectors moving in
and out of prison.

Sexual contacts among men
are common in prisons around the
world. Estimates vary considerably. A survey in Rio de Janeiro,
Brazil, suggested that 73 percent
of male prisoners had had sex
with other men while in prison,
and surveys in Zambia, Australia,
England, and Canada reflect infection rates up to 12 percent—figures that are probably low
because of denial and underreporting. Sex between men in
prison includes unprotected anal
sex, which is a high-risk factor for

transmission of HIV. The risk is
even greater if lubrication is not
used and if sex is forced. Condoms are not available in prisons
as a rule. In women's prisons
where there are male prison staff,
sex between men and women
may also take place, creating a
risk of HIV transmission.

Tattooing is common in prisons
and equipment is frequently
shared, creating an additional risk
of HIV transmission. There are
similar risks where skin piercing is
practiced. The practice of "blood
brotherhood" rites in some prisons, furthermore, clearly presents
a high risk of HIV infection.

A number of harm reduction
approaches can slow the spread
of HIV and AIDS infection among
prison populations. "Harm reduction" includes a variety of programs and policies designed to
reduce the harm associated with
drug use and sexual behaviors.
For the reduction of HIV infection,
the appropriate harm reduction
policies would include drug treatment, AIDS prevention education,
condom distribution, and providing
bleach for the disinfection of drug
injection and tattooing paraphernalia. Treatment and education are
already available in many prisons.
However, because of the strict
custodial and contraband policies
that exist in virtually all correctional institutions, it is doubtful that
condom and bleach distribution
are likely to occur.

SOURCE: James A. Inciardi and Lana D. Harrison, *Harm Reduction: National and International Perspectives* (Thousand Oaks, Calif.: Sage, 1999).

Subsequent to the testing and interview period, reports are prepared by the various diagnosticians and incorporated into the inmate's case file. Summaries of the prisoner's social and family background, work history, criminal record, prior institutionalization (if any), current offense, and any other relevant background data are also included. A classification board or committee then evaluates the case and makes its recommendations. This board can range from one counselor or social worker to as many as 15 persons, including teachers, psychologists, physicians, researchers, members of the administrative and custodial staffs, and persons from numerous other fields. This board then integrates and discusses the various data and plans the inmate's correctional career. It also takes responsibility for *reclassification* should the inmate's needs or situation change.

Prison Programs

Institutional programs include a variety of activities, all of which can affect, either directly or indirectly, the rehabilitation of offenders and their successful reintegration into the free community. There are *treatment programs,* for example, which focus on behavioral change. These attempt to remove what are often considered "defects" in an inmate's socialization and psychological development and that are necessarily responsible for some lawbreaking behaviors. There are *academic* and *vocational programs,* which attempt to provide inmates with the skills necessary for adequate employment after release. There are *recreational programs,* which have humanitarian, medical, social-psychological, and custodial motives; they are structured to ease the pressures of confinement, making inmates more receptive to rehabilitation and less depressed, hostile, and asocial. There are *work programs,* which serve many of the humanitarian and rehabilitative needs of the offender, yet at the same time are related to the successful economic functioning of the institution. And finally, there are *medical* and *religious programs,* which also have implications for institutional management and reintegration of the offender into the community.

Health and Medical Services   The number and types of programs and services available to inmates vary widely by both jurisdiction and institution. Every prison has some form of health and medical program, although some are quite rudimentary. All reception centers have comprehensive medical facilities, with separate hospital units and some with well equipped operating rooms. Similar facilities are also present in the larger prisons and reformatories.

Smaller institutions use a range of medical and health alternatives. Some have small hospital units with a full-time physician or nurse, and paraprofessionals who are on hand for the day-to-day care of minor illnesses and injuries. Where a physician is not a full-time member of the institutional staff, one is drawn from the local community to visit on a routine basis. All but the largest prisons and reception centers contract out for the services of dentists and opticians.

The importance of sufficient medical care for prison inmates cannot be overstated. Poor diet, alcoholism and drug abuse, and histories of inadequate medical attention are disproportionately evident among those entering the nation's correctional system. Furthermore, the potential for the rapid spread of even the most minor illnesses is high within a population that is confined in such close quarters (see Exhibit 12.3). The prison medical unit also has responsibility for monitoring sanitary conditions and inmate dietary needs, for these too are directly related to the well-being of the institution as a whole.

Exhibit 12.3 **Legal Perspectives on Crime and Justice**
Controlling the Spread of HIV/AIDS in Prisons

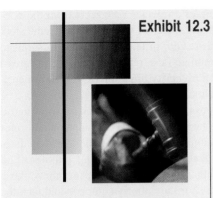

Although such HIV/AIDS risk behaviors as drug use and sex generally occur at lower frequencies among inmates than in street populations, strategies have nevertheless been implemented in correctional settings in an effort to prevent the transmission of HIV. The most common HIV control strategies include mandatory testing of inmates for HIV, segregating infected inmates from the general prison population, establishing special health care units for HIV-positive and AIDS symptomatic inmates, offering HIV prevention and risk reduction programs, distributing condoms to sexually active inmates, and granting "medical parole" for the terminally ill.

A number of these strategies, however, result in the disclosure—either directly or indirectly—of an inmate's infection status. Many state jurisdictions, for example, segregate all HIV-positive inmates because the procedure serves to protect infected inmates from other prisoners who fear AIDS and to prevent the spread of HIV by inmates who refuse to take proper precautions. Some inmates have argued that segregation is punitive, particularly for those who show no symptoms of the disease.

A number of inmates have challenged segregation policies in the courts, but most have been unsuccessful. Most courts have concluded that the fact that a prisoner is carrying a contagious disease is enough to distinguish his or her situation from that of noninfected prisoners. Furthermore, so long as prison officials cite such interests as protecting HIV-positive inmates from the general population, preventing the spread of AIDS, or treating those infected with the virus, it is unlikely that the courts will declare segregation policies violative of the Constitution.

SOURCE: James A. Inciardi, "HIV Risk Reduction and Service Delivery Strategies in Criminal Justice Settings," *Journal of Substance Abuse Treatment* 13 (1996): 1–8.

Religious Programs   The availability of spiritual services to prison inmates has a long history in American corrections. Solitary meditation was the theoretical basis of reform in Philadelphia's Walnut Street Jail almost two centuries ago, and penitence was encouraged by frequent visits by missionaries and local clerics. Over the years, various Christian denominations and other religious organizations have devoted their time to the spiritual needs of inmates and have provided ongoing programs of religious instruction.

Contemporary institutions generally retain Protestant, Roman Catholic, and sometimes Jewish chaplains, or at least a nondenominational cleric, on a full- or part-time basis, for religious counseling and worship services. In some small institutions where there are no educational programs or rehabilitative services, the prison chaplain represents the only available treatment component.

Education Programs   Most Americans have confidence in education as a mechanism for upgrading skills and understanding, for shaping attitudes, and for promoting social adjustment. It is not surprising, then, that academic education and vocational training are regarded as the primary programs in correctional institutions.

In *academic education programs,* the emphasis is on the acquisition of basic knowledge and communicative skills. Most institutions have some sort of prison school, and in most state correctional systems education for inmates is a matter of legislative mandate. Courses of instruction vary from one institution to the next, ranging from literacy programs to high school equivalency studies to college-level learning with degree-awarding curricula.

Prison schools, however, are beset with numerous difficulties. Many institutions are short on classroom facilities and useful teaching aids; there is a lack of qualified instructors, which forces a reliance on rejects from the public school system and on inmate teachers, scores of whom are undereducated; many inmates lack motivation, which results in teachers being pressured to make the classes effortless and to complete false reports on inmate progress; and the realities of prison discipline and security often interfere with inmates' courses of instruction or curtail enrollments.

Vocational training programs focus on preparing inmates for meaningful postrelease employment. Most of the larger institutions and many small ones have a number of such programs, including automobile repair and maintenance, welding, sheet metal work, carpentry and cabinetmaking, plumbing and electricity, and radio and television repair. As with academic programs, these too have some problems. Many prison shops are poorly equipped and lack the appropriate technical staff; in others the machinery and fittings have long since become outmoded; and in some, the training is in fields in which work is unavailable in the outside world. Furthermore, inmates acquiring skills in such areas as plumbing, electrical work, carpentry, and masonry are often barred upon release from joining unions because of their criminal records.

Although almost one-fourth of the U.S. prison population participates in academic and vocational education programs, at least half of all state prisons have made significant budget cuts in educational programs. Generally, cutbacks appear to be motivated by shrinking state budgets and the ballooning costs associated with increases in the inmate population. Nevertheless, limiting funds for education programs may prove to be a costly choice for states in the long run. A study by the Alabama Council on Vocational and Technical Education compared inmates who participated in academic or vocational programs with those who did not over the course of 5 years. Inmates who had participated in some form of educational training had an average recidivism rate of 5 percent compared to the 35 percent rate averaged by nonparticipants.[9]

Prison Labor and Industry   Closely related to vocational training in correctional institutions are the prison work and industrial programs. At least in theory, these can provide numerous opportunities for inmates to do the following:

- Earn wages while serving their terms
- Develop regular work habits
- Gain experience in machine operation, manufacturing, and other specialized skills
- Ease the boredom of institutional confinement

Despite these praiseworthy possibilities, however, most prison work programs generally fail to provide most, if not all, of these opportunities. First, many penitentiaries and other correctional institutions have no such programs. Those that do are open to fewer than 25 percent of the prison population and they provide wages that are extremely low. Second, the jobs made available to inmates in many jurisdictions are typically dull and irrelevant. The major industries include printing and the production of auto tags, road signs, brooms, clothing, and similar articles. Furthermore, many nonindustrial prison jobs are restricted to such meaningless tasks as cleaning, laundry, and other simple maintenance work.

There are several reasons for this situation. First, state use is the chief outlet for prison-made products. This situation is the result of state and federal legislation that barred prison industrial production from competing with private enterprise. Second, prison industrial plants are costly to construct, equip, maintain, and keep up to date. And third, to house an inmate in a correctional institution is prohibitively expensive, ranging from annual expenditures of

$10,000 per inmate in some jurisdictions to as much as $25,000 in others. This rebounds on prison inmates in that their wages are kept low, with most of the profits going into state treasuries.

On the more optimistic side, not all states and institutions suffer equally from these problems. A number of prisons have modernized their industrial plants or constructed totally new ones in an effort to make inmate work more instructive, meaningful, and efficient. Florida's Union Correctional Institution, for example, has its own inmate-operated slaughterhouse and cement block plant. In Texas, where local laws do not prohibit the sale of its prisons' products in markets within the state, prison industries have moved into some highly technical areas and generate many millions of dollars each year. Indeed, faced with the costly challenges of increasing prison populations, many states have begun shifting from the nineteenth-century legacy of rock busting, ditch digging, and license plate stamping to highly profitable prison labor programs.

For example, a garment factory staffed exclusively by death row inmates in Huntsville, Texas, has received considerable notice from prison administrators throughout the nation who are anxiously looking for ways to keep death row inmates occupied. The Huntsville garment factory employs 115 workers, with plans to accommodate 85 more. In exchange for work, inmates are given larger cells, freedom to visit with other death row friends during the day, and they go unshackled to meet their families on visitor's day.[10] At least a dozen states are using inmates as operators on their tourist information phone lines. The Iowa tourist line, for example, is staffed by 14 male hard-timers who are serving life sentences at the maximum-security prison in Fort Madison. Inmates in Iowa earn 30 to 55 cents an hour and take about 1,200 calls a day.[11] In federal prisons, all prisoners are required to participate in daily work activities as long as they are medically able. Approximately one-fifth of the federal prisoners meet their work requirements through participation in UNICOR, the industrial arm of Federal Prison Industries.[12]

Clinical Treatment Programs Academic education and vocational training are often viewed as the primary rehabilitative tools a correctional institution has to offer. It is felt that if inmates can learn the necessary skills and training to secure and maintain gainful employment after release, then their need to return to careers in crime will be eliminated or at least reduced. In this sense, academic and vocational programs can also be viewed as treatment programs, for correctional treatment has generally meant the explicit activities designed to alter or remove conditions operating on offenders that are responsible for their behavior.[13] In a more clinical sense, however, institutional treatment programs are those effects specifically oriented toward helping inmates resolve those personal, emotional, and psychological problems that are related to their lawbreaking behavior.

Counseling, social casework, psychological and psychiatric services, and group therapy represent the core of clinical treatment programs in prisons. *Counseling* refers to the relationship between the counselor and the prisoner-client in which the counselor attempts to understand the prisoner-client's problems and to help him or her solve the problems by discussing them together, rather than by giving advice or admonition. *Social casework* is a process that (1) develops the prisoner-client's case history, (2) deals with immediate problems involving personal and familial relationships, (3) explores long-range issues of social adjustment, and (4) provides supportive guidance for any anticipated plans or activities.

Psychological and *psychiatric services* provide more intensive diagnosis and treatment aimed at (1) discovering the underlying causes of individual maladjustments, (2) applying psychiatric techniques to effect improved behavior, and (3) providing consultation to other staff members. These three modes of treatment involve direct interaction between clinician and prisoner-patient on an individual, one-to-one basis. Treatment in a group setting includes one or more clinicians plus several prisoner-patients.

Group treatment programs have been variously referred to as "group psychotherapy," "group therapy," "group guided interaction," "group counseling," and numerous other terms that are often used interchangeably. However, only two basic kinds of therapy are actually involved when the "group" label is used: group psychotherapy, which is individual therapy in a group setting; and "group" therapy in its truest sense, which is designed to change groups, not individuals.

These four models of clinical treatment—counseling, casework, psychological and psychiatric services, and group therapy—are employed to deal with the general issues associated with criminality and to bring about behavioral change. They are also used to address the problems of specific kinds of offenders, such as sexual deviates and substance abusers. However, these clinical treatment services are not available in most institutions, and only a modest number of prisons have a resident psychiatrist. More common in contemporary correctional facilities are counselors. These, however, generally deal with inmates' confrontations with the day-to-day pressures of institutional life rather than with any long-term treatment goals. Counselors, moreover, rarely have any clinical training or experience. The position of correctional counselor is an entry point to a criminal justice career, and for most counselors, it is their first job after college graduation.

Drug Abuse Treatment

Much of the increased activities and backlogs in the criminal justice system are an outgrowth of the nation's war on drugs. This is particularly apparent in correctional agencies and facilities. In New York, for example, almost 50 percent of the state's more than 70,000 prison inmates were initially arrested for drug-related offenses.[14] In Florida, prison admissions increased by 250 percent from the 1980s to the 1990s, with those for drug-related crimes swelling by more than 2,000 percent.[15] And nationally, it would appear that perhaps three-fourths of all inmates have histories of substance abuse.[16]

One approach to the phenomenon has been to increase prison capacity. The other approach has been to expand drug abuse treatment services. Virtually all of the states and the federal system have some sort of drug treatment services for inmates. Furthermore, most are expanding the capacities of existing programs as well as implementing new ones.

In addition to the four models of clinical treatment described earlier, prison-based drug rehabilitation strategies also include the *therapeutic community*. More commonly referred to as a "TC," the therapeutic community is a total treatment environment established in a separate residential unit of a prison. TC participants are kept removed from other inmates and are assigned to separate work, school, and recreational programs as well. The purpose is to create a partnership between prisoner-clients and clinicians. The work supervisors, teachers, counselors, correctional officers, and other staff members involved with TC residents become part of the treatment regimen and are regarded as agents of behavioral change. Group and individual therapy represents the core of the treatment model, but the peer pressure characteristic of the therapy sessions appears during other daily routines as well.

Currently, the therapeutic community is among the most popular approaches for the treatment of drug abuse. Its application within the prison setting has been primarily for substance abusers, although some non-drug-abusing offenders are also involved. However, few correctional institutions have therapeutic communities, because of the lack of special facilities as well as staff

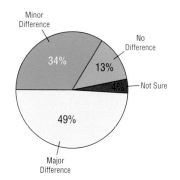

What Effect Do Prison Treatment Programs Have on the Reduction of Drug-Related Crimes?

SOURCE: University of Maryland, Center for Substance Abuse Research.

The therapeutic community

A view of "The KEY," Delaware's prison-based therapeutic community.

shortages and a concentration of efforts on custodial issues—concerns that tend to limit all varieties of institutional treatment. During the closing years of the 1980s, however, funding from the Bureau of Justice Assistance and other federal agencies rekindled the interest in TCs in correctional environments, creating a movement that is expected to continue well into the next century (see Exhibit 12.4).

PRISON DISCIPLINE

Over the years, lists of inmate rules have grown long, reaching far into every aspect of inmate life. Regulations in South Dakota prisons, for example, number well into the hundreds. Some rules are of a general nature, pertaining to the orderly operation and safety of the institution:

> Orders shall be obeyed promptly. . . .
> Fighting is prohibited. . . .
> Locking devices will not be tampered with. . . .

Others are of questionable value:

> Long sleeved sweat shirts will not be worn under a short sleeved shirt. . . .
> Only one cribbage board per man.[17]

In New York's Attica Prison, there is even a regulation governing the number of times an inmate may kiss a visitor:

> They have locked up guys in the place for felonious kissing in the visiting room. If a guy kisses his wife six times it is felonious kissing.[18]

Although one may consider the rules to be too numerous and many quite trivial, they found their way into inmate handbooks for very specific reasons. Some were designed to prevent disturbances, violence, and escapes; others serve to ensure the health and safety of both inmates and staff; still others were imposed to maintain the orderly movement of prisoners and the flow of institutional life and procedure. Many regulations, however, are punitive in nature or, as in the military, are deemed necessary to provide regimentation, to

Exhibit 12.4

Research in Crime and Justice
A Model Prison Therapeutic Community

There are many phenomena in the prison environment that make rehabilitation difficult. Not surprisingly, the availability of drugs is a problem. In addition, there is the violence associated with inmate gangs—often formed along racial lines for the purposes of establishing and maintaining status and "turf," retaining unofficial control over certain sectors of the prison for distributing contraband, and providing "protection" for other inmates. And finally, there is the prison subculture—a system of norms and values contending, among other things, that "people in treatment are faggots," as one maximum-security inmate so emphatically put it.

In contrast, the therapeutic community (or simply "TC") is a total treatment environment isolated from the rest of the prison population—separated from the drugs, the violence, and the norms and values that militate against treatment and rehabilitation. The primary clinical staff of the TC are typically former substance abusers who themselves were rehabilitated in therapeutic communities. The treatment perspective is that drug abuse is a disorder of the whole person—that the problem is the *person* not the drug, that addiction is a *symptom* not the essence of the disorder. In the TC's view of recovery, the primary goal is to change the negative patterns of behavior, thinking, and feeling that predispose drug use. As such, the overall goal is a responsible drug-free lifestyle.

Recovery through the TC process depends on positive and negative pressures to change, and this is brought about through a self-help process in which relationships of mutual responsibility to every resident in the program are built. Or as TC researcher George De Leon once described it:

The essential dynamic in the TC is mutual self-help. Thus, the day-to-day activities are conducted by the residents themselves. In their jobs, groups, meetings, recreation, personal, and social time, it is residents who continually transmit to each other the main messages and expectations of the community.

In addition to individual and group counseling, the TC process has a system of explicit rewards that reinforce the value of earned achievement. As such, privileges are *earned*. In addition, TCs have their own specific rules and regulations that guide the behavior of residents and the management of their facilities. Their purposes are to maintain the safety and health of the community and to train and teach residents through the use of discipline. TC rules and regulations are numerous, the most conspicuous of which are total prohibitions against violence, theft, and drug use. Violation of these cardinal rules typically results in immediate expulsion from the TC.

Although prison-based TCs are few in number, preliminary evaluations have been positive. Moreover, inmates in TCs see them as safe places to finish their time and learn positive values. In addition to their potential for treatment, correctional administrators view TCs as excellent tools for prison management, since they tend to be the cleanest, safest, and most orderly parts of a prison.

One of the best-known and most effective prison TCs is

Delaware's KEY program, first established in 1988. Follow-up studies of KEY graduates found that they have significantly lower rates of rearrest and drug relapse than those drug-involved offenders who received no treatment.

The effectiveness of the Delaware prison program, furthermore, has not gone unnoticed. On September 10, 1996, in a press release on drug abuse treatment for state prisoners from the U.S. Department of Justice, the effectiveness of the KEY was referenced as a model program for use by other states. The following day, in his address announcing an appropriation of $27 million for residential drug treatment for prisoners, President Bill Clinton also referenced the effectiveness of the Delaware program.

Drug Treatment Outcome in Delaware Prisons

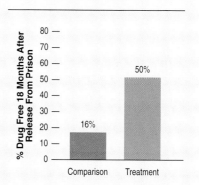

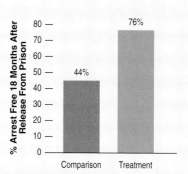

SOURCE: Center for Drug and Alcohol Studies, University of Delaware, 1998.

SOURCE: James A. Inciardi, Steven S. Martin, Clifford A. Butzin, Robert M. Hooper, and Lana D. Harrison, "An Effective Model of Prison-Based Treatment for Drug-Involved Offenders," *Journal of Drug Issues* 27 (1997): 261–278.

further preserve order, and to define the boundaries of inmate status. Conversely, a variety of regulations have evolved with the idea of creating a self-respecting prison community and inculcating standards that will contribute to successful adjustment after release. Finally, as corrections specialists Harry Allen and Clifford Simonsen have suggested, many rules have resulted from the *"convict bogey"* syndrome—an exaggerated fear of prisoners requiring unnecessarily severe discipline.[19]

A major issue in inmate regulation is *prison contraband*. Contraband is officially defined as any item that can be used to break a rule of the institution or to assist in escape. Such articles as drugs, knives, guns, bombs, and vaulting poles are contraband. In practice, however, contraband becomes anything that the custodial staff designates as undesirable, and the banning power is unrestricted.

Contraband is uncovered by periodic searches of prisoners and their cells or dormitories, and rule-breaking is either observed or discovered directly by a custodial officer or indirectly through inmate informers. In many instances, the violations are more or less ignored; sometimes the guard will simply give the inmate a warning and, if minor contraband is involved, confiscate it. In more serious cases, there are formal disciplinary proceedings with many due process safeguards.

The major disciplinary violations in prisons, at least those that result in formal hearings, involve drugs, gambling, sex, fighting, stealing, and refusing to work. Most inmates are fairly sophisticated when it comes to hiding serious

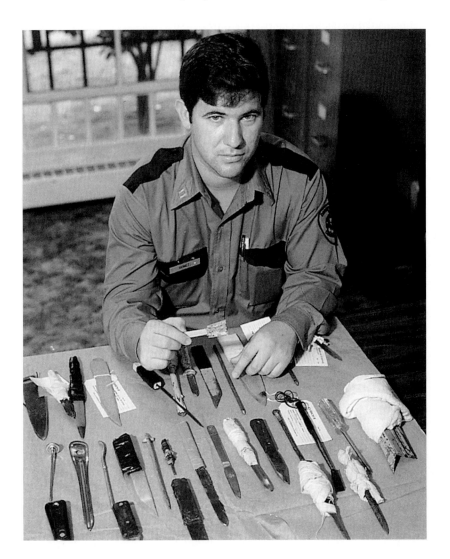

Prison guard with confiscated tools and weapons.

contraband items such as drugs or weapons. Penalties for violations include solitary confinement, temporary loss of privileges, temporary "keeplock" (being locked in the cell during recreation periods), or loss of "good time" (time off for good behavior). Numerous disciplinary violations can also affect an inmate's parole date, since institutional conduct is a factor taken into account in parole release decisions.

SEX IN PRISON

Aside from the loss of liberty itself, perhaps the most obvious area of deprivation associated with prison life is heterosexual activity. Isolation from the opposite sex implies a frustration of sexual desires and drives at a time when, for many inmates, those impulses are quite strong. Some prisoners remain abstinent, or rely wholly on sexually fantasies and masturbation, while others partake in voluntary or involuntary homosexual contacts or rape. However, the data on these activities are only fragmentary, and any conclusions are at best tentative.

Same-Gender Sex

Several decades ago, lawyer-sociologist Paul W. Tappan commented that homosexual behavior is a universal concomitant of sex-segregated living; that it is a perennial problem in camps, boarding schools, one-sex colleges, training schools, and correctional facilities; and that from a biological point of view homosexuality is normal behavior in the distorted institutional environments that characterize our nation's prisons.[20] Whether Tappan's argument can be applied equally to all sex-segregated environments is difficult to document. Within the prison setting, however, same-gender sexual contacts indeed occur, although perhaps not to the extent that popular images would suggest.

Based on the few studies that have examined the question of sexual behavior among prison inmates, estimates can be made that between 30 and 45 percent of inmates have experienced same-gender sex, with the variations associated with the intensity of custodial surveillance, the characteristics of the inmate population, and the average length of confinement in a given prison.[21]

A recent study in Delaware suggested that although same-gender sexual contacts might not be widespread, they nevertheless occur.[22] During the early months of 1994, 101 clients in a prison therapeutic community (TC) were interviewed at length regarding their sexual histories and practices, and their sexual activities while in prison during the 1-year period prior to entering the TC. Although only 2 percent admitted to having sex with other men while in prison, almost all stated that they had "heard" of it occurring and half reported having observed it.

The patterns of sexual practices tend to differ between male and female inmates. Among males, sex seldom involves a close relationship between the parties; rather, it is often a response to physical needs. Prostitution is a frequent type of male homosexual association. Also, there are cases in which a male who is particularly vulnerable to sexual attacks will enter into a relationship with another male who agrees to protect him from the assaults of others.[23]

While there have been only a few studies of sex in women's prisons, most of the sex that takes place appears to be consensual. Interviews with inmates at the Women's Correctional Institution in New Castle, Delaware, suggest that many inmates form long-standing relationships with one another—friendships rather than pseudo-marriages. Sexual contacts are usually oral-genital and/or involve mutual masturbation. Women have indicated that they wanted to "get a woman" while in prison, and many brag about their sexual conquests to other women and most talk about their need to "get off." For women who are bound to a heterosexual identity, sexual gratification usually comes by way of masturbation. Nevertheless, homosexuality among women does not appear to carry the same stigma as it does among male inmates.

Despite data that suggest that one-third of prison inmates engage in same-gender sexual practices, whether regularly or at least periodically, both inmates and institutional personnel agree that the most frequently observed form of sexual release is solitary masturbation (see Exhibit 12.5).

Conjugal Visitation

Conjugal visitation has been promoted as a means of reducing same-gender sexual contacts in prison, as well as of raising inmate morale and maintaining

Conjugal visitation: The practice of permitting inmate and spouse to spend time together in private quarters on prison grounds, during which time they may engage in sexual relations.

Exhibit 12.5 **Gender Perspectives on Crime and Justice**
Sexual Assault in Prison

In recent years, considerable attention has been given to the matter of so-called *homosexual rape* in correctional institutions. It is generally believed that sexual attacks are quite common in men's prisons, yet the data on this are only fragmentary. Some people have argued that the impressions of sexual activity in prison—that behind prison walls the incidence of male-on-male rape is high, and that sexual assault is the most characteristic form of prison sex—are essentially unfounded assumptions. The only recent study in this regard is that conducted in Delaware, as noted earlier in this chapter. Of the inmates interviewed, 24 percent reported having seen an average of two rapes during their incarceration careers, 36 percent had heard of a rape occurring in the previous year, but only one inmate reported having been raped and only five reported attempted rapes.

Rape and coerced sex in women's prisons has received little research attention. Since the 1960s, women inmates have complained of having been forced into sexual relations with guards and other administrators. However, with few advocates and limited access to law libraries, women have had few means for filing official complaints. More recently, however, the problem has become more visible. The most notable case involved the indictments of 14 prison officials in the Georgia Department of Correction, following charges brought by more than 150 female inmates claiming they were forced to engage in sex. Following years of rumors about forced abortions, prostitution rings, and nonconsensual sex in the Georgia women's prisons, federal investigators were finally brought in to look into the charges. It would appear that guards procured sex from inmates by offering them privileges or threatening them with rule violations and classification changes. Correction officers and administrative officials were also forcing those women who became pregnant to undergo abortions, often by threatening to send them to

a harsher prison or taking away their accrued good time.

While the research on the incidence of rape in prison remains tentative, there seems to be agreement that such attacks are more often power plays than sources of sexual release. For example, Leo Carroll's analysis of interracial rape in male prisons suggests blacks often sexually assault whites in retaliation for 300 years of social oppression and to demonstrate their manhood and dominance. As one of Carroll's informants explained it:

> To the general way of thinking it's 'cause we're confined and we've got hard rocks. But that ain't it at all. It's a way for the black man to get back at the white man. It's one way he can assert his manhood. Anything white, even a defenseless punk, is part of what the black man hates. It's part of what he's had to fight all his life just to survive, just to have a hole to sleep in and some garbage to eat. . . . It's a new ego thing. He can show he's a man by making a white guy into a girl.

SOURCES: *National Law Journal,* September 20, 1993, p. 8; Leo Carroll, "Humanitarian Reform and Biracial Sexual Assault in a Maximum Security Prison," *Urban Life* 5 (January 1977): 422. See also "From Thief to Cellblock Sex Slave: A Convict's Testimony," *New York Times,* October 19, 1997, Section 4, p. 7.

family ties. During the conjugal visit, inmate and spouse are permitted to spend time together in private quarters on prison grounds, during which they may engage in sexual relations.

Conjugal visitation has been well known in European and Latin American countries for quite some time, and it has likely always occurred in some American prisons, although on an informal and haphazard basis. As an official correctional program, however, its first appearance in the United States was in 1900 at the Mississippi State Penitentiary at Parchman. In 1968, conjugal visiting began as an experiment at California's Tehachapi facility and was later expanded to other California institutions. More recently, New York, New Jersey, North Carolina, and Texas have also introduced conjugal visitation on an experimental basis. Reports on both the Mississippi and California programs have been positive.[24]

Those who favor conjugal visiting argue that it decreases same-gender sex within the prison, that it helps to preserve marriages, and that it strengthens family relationships.[25] Yet there has been opposition to conjugal visiting. Opponents argue that such visits can serve only the minority of inmates who have spouses, thus raising the question of fairness; that appropriate visitation facilities are typically lacking; that children may be born to men who cannot support them; and that the situation would pose potential security risks.[26]

In recent years, two factors have served to refocus correctional thinking about conjugal visitation. The first issue relates to women. Historically, the majority of programs in the United States have been available only to male inmates; the idea that the same heterosexual opportunities should be extended to women inmates was to some a "shocking" idea.[27] An early exception to this pattern has been New York State's Family Reunion Program, begun in 1976 and established at Bedford Hills Correctional Facility for women the following year. The program allows overnight visits for selected inmates and members of their immediate families. The "family member" is typically a spouse but can also be a parent or a child.

Fueled by the growing number of incarcerated women over the last two decades, many more correctional systems have developed structured arrangements whereby women inmates can have meaningful visits with family members in general, and with their children in particular. In Massachusetts, for example, where the majority of women inmates are mothers with young children, a program established in 1985 permits overnight visits with children.[28] A similar program exists in Delaware's Women's Correctional Institution.

Coeducational Prisons

Since 1973, prisons housing both men and women have proliferated throughout the United States. Coeducational facilities currently operate in a number of states and the federal system. In these institutions, inmates eat, study, and work together, and associate with each other generally, except with regard to sleeping arrangements.

The philosophy behind the establishment of these institutions was that men tend to behave better in the presence of women, have fewer fights, take more pride in their appearance, and are less likely to engage in same-gender sexual contacts. Furthermore, it was felt that for both male and female prisoners, the more normal social environment hastens community reintegration.[29] Preliminary studies and the testimony of coed facility administrators suggest that these expectations have been met. Both violence and forced homosexuality have declined, attendance in work and education programs has increased, and inmates seem to return home with more self-esteem and higher expectations.[30]

Yet not everyone has been thrilled about the coeducational experiments. The coed program at Oklahoma's Jess Dunn Correctional Center, which began in 1986, was ended after only 2 years as the result of jealousies over certain male and female inmates pairing off, as well as for the six pregnancies that occurred during that period.[31] For similar reasons, male and female inmates have been separated at the California Youth Authority's Camarillo coeducational compound. Under regulations promulgated in mid-1990, coed activities became limited to school and Sunday worship, with strict separation at all other times.[32]

As for the future of coeducational custody, it is difficult to predict. Expansions are necessarily restricted, however, since women represent such a small proportion of the federal and state correctional populations.

THE INMATE SOCIAL SYSTEM

The primary task of prisons, despite any arguments to the contrary, is custody. The internal order of the prison is maintained by strictly controlling the inmates and regimenting every aspect of their lives. In addition to their loss of freedom and basic liberties, goods and services, heterosexual relationships, and autonomy, they are deprived of their personal identities. Upon entering prison, inmates are stripped of their clothing and most of their personal possessions; and they are examined, inspected, weighed, documented, and given a number. Thus, prison becomes painful, both physically and psychologically:

> Unable to escape either physically or psychologically, lacking the cohesion to carry through an insurrection that is bound to fail in any case, and bereft of faith in peaceful innovation, the inmate population might seem to have no recourse but the simple endurance of the pains of imprisonment. *But if the rigors of confinement cannot be completely removed, they can at least be mitigated by the patterns of social interaction established among the inmates themselves.*[33]

The rigors and frustrations of confinement leave but a few paths open to inmates. They can bind themselves to their fellow captives in ties of mutual aid and loyalty, in opposition to prison officials. They can wage a war against all, seeking their own advantage without reference to the needs and claims of others. Or they can simply withdraw into themselves. Ideally these alternatives exist only in an abstract sense, and most inmates combine characteristics of the first two extremes:

> The population of prisoners does not exhibit a perfect solidarity yet neither is the population of prisoners a warning aggregate. Rather, it is a mixture of both and the society of captives lies balanced in an uneasy compromise.[34]

It is within this balance of extremes that the inmate social system functions.

Prisonization

Exposure to the social system of the *prison community* is almost immediate, for all new inmates become quickly aware of the norms and values that are shared by their fellow captives. The internalization of the prison norms and values has been described as **prisonization:**

> Every man who enters the penitentiary undergoes prisonization to some extent. The first and most obvious integrative step concerns his status. He becomes at once an anonymous figure in a subordinate group. A number replaces a name. He

Prisonization: The socializing process by which the inmate learns the rules and regulations of the institution and the information rules, values, customs, and general culture of the penitentiary.

wears the clothes of the other members of the subordinate group. He is questioned and admonished. He soon learns that the warden is all-powerful. He soon learns the ranks, titles, and authorities of various officials. And whether he uses the prison slang and argot or not, he comes to know its meanings. Even though a new man may hold himself aloof from other inmates and remain a solitary figure, he finds himself within a few months referring to or thinking of keepers as "screws," the physician as the "croaker," and using the local nicknames to designate persons. He follows the examples already set in wearing his cap. He learns to eat in haste and in obtaining food he imitates the tricks of those near him.

After the new arrival recovers from the effects of the swallowing-up process, he assigns a new meaning to conditions he had previously taken for granted. The fact that food, shelter, clothing, and a work activity had been given him originally made no especial impression. It is only after some weeks or months that there comes to him a new interpretation of these necessities of life. This new conception results from mingling with other men and it places emphasis on the fact that the environment should administer to him. This point is intangible and difficult to describe in so far as it is only a subtle and minute change in attitude from the taken-for-granted perception. Exhaustive questioning of hundreds of men reveals that this slight change in attitude is a fundamental step in the process we are calling prisonization.[35]

Thus, prisonization refers to the socializing process by which the inmate learns the rules and regulations of the institution and the informal rules, values, customs, and general culture of the penitentiary.

The concept of prisonization comes from Donald Clemmer, who was a staff sociologist at Menard Penitentiary in Chester, Illinois, and is based on his studies of the male prison subculture during the 1930s. His thesis maintains that prisoners share the common experience of enforced confinement, and from this come many influences that tend to draw them together in a common cause against their keepers. The close physical proximity in which inmates must live destroys much, if not all, of their privacy; prison regulations and routine press them toward conformity; and their isolation limits their range of experience. Furthermore, institutional life fosters a monotonous equalitarianism among inmates. Prisoners occupy similar cells; they wear the same clothes and eat the same food; and they do the same things at the same time and according to the same rules, regulations, and potential for disciplinary punishment. Within such a setting, prison life holds little for inmates, but what it does offer they share in common. And all of this happens under the same structure of authority—one that is direct, immediate, inescapable, and sometimes brutal. Everything that prisoners have, or fail to have, is traceable to that structure. Food and clothing, rules and regulations, pleasures and pains, sorrows and cruelties, and indignities and brutalities—all seem to come from the same source. The inmate community, then, has a common hatred—the prison administration—against which it can direct its hostilities.

In presenting this notion of prisonization, Clemmer maintains that prison values could be taken on to a greater or lesser degree. Once they were internalized, however, the prisonized inmate became immune, for the most part, to the influences of conventional value systems. This suggests that the process of prisonization transforms the nonviolent inmate into a fully accredited convict; it is a *criminalization* process that militates against any reform or rehabilitation.

Prisonization as "criminalization"

Some people have argued against Clemmer's thesis. They point to evidence that suggests that inmates are first prisonized and then "deprisonized" immediately prior to release; others hold that prisonization itself is a myth.[36] Most observers agree, however, that some form of prisonization process does indeed occur, but that it is affected by an inmate's priority, duration, frequency, and intensity of contact with the prison subculture and the values of varying segments of the inmate population. This point of view is most likely correct, for circumstances, regulations, population characteristics, and administrative authority structures vary widely from one institution to the next. Furthermore, socialization into the inmate worlds of the more repressive maximum-security prisons across the nation seems to most closely resemble what Clemmer originally described as "prisonization."

The Inmate Code

Regardless of the degree of prisonization experienced by an inmate, every correctional institution has a subculture. Every prison subculture has its system of norms that influence prisoners' behavior, typically to a greater extent than the institution's formally prescribed rules. These subcultural norms are informal, unwritten rules, but their violation can evoke sanctions from fellow inmates ranging from ostracism to physical violence or death. The informal rules, furthermore, are referred to as the **inmate code,** and generally include at least the following:

1. *Don't interfere with the interests of other inmates.* Concretely, this means that inmates never "rat on a con" or betray each other. It also includes these directives: "Don't be nosy," "Don't put a guy on the spot," and "Keep off a man's back." There are no justifications for failing to comply with these rules.

2. *Keep out of quarrels or feuds with fellow inmates.* This is expressed in the directives "Play it cool" and "Do your own time."

3. *Don't exploit other inmates.* Concretely, this means, "Don't break your word," "Don't steal from the cons," "Don't welsh on debts," and "Be right."

4. *Don't weaken; withstand frustration or threat without complaint.* This is expressed in such directives as "Don't cop out" (cry guilty), "Don't suck around," "Be tough," and "Be a man."

5. *Don't give respect or prestige to the custodians or to the world for which they stand.* Concretely, this is expressed by "Don't be a sucker" and "Be sharp."[37]

Although the inmate code is violated regularly, most prisoners adhere to its major directives. But they do so not because it represents a "code of honor," but for other, more serious considerations—the very same reasons why professional thieves follow the underworld code:

> **Inmate code:** The unwritten rules of the prison subculture, which, if violated, can result in sanctions ranging from ostracism to death.

Entertainment at California's Folsom Prison.

Honor among thieves? Well—yes and no. You do have some old pros who might talk about honor, but they're so well heeled and well connected that they can afford to be honorable. But for most people, it's a question of "do unto others"— you play by the rules because you may need a favor someday, or because the guy you skip on, or the guy you rap to the cops about—you never know where he'll turn up. Maybe he's got something on you, or maybe he ends up as your cell-mate, or he says bad things about you—you can't tell how these things could turn out.[38]

The Social Order of Women's Prisons

Most studies of prison communities and inmate social systems have been undertaken in men's institutions, and the findings are not fully applicable to women's prisons. Fewer women are convicted of crimes, and a greater proportion of those who are found guilty are placed on probation. Those who do receive terms of imprisonment have typically been convicted of homicide, aggravated assault, check forgery, shoplifting, and violations of the drug laws, with few serving time for burglary and robbery. Women's prisons have an even greater proportion of minority group members than have institutions for men, but fewer women have had prior prison experiences. Finally, the cottage system is the model more typically followed in women's prisons. Although few women inmates are confined in cells, the more "open" nature of the women's institution often requires more frequent security checks and, hence, close custodial supervision. All of these factors combine to affect the character of the social order of female correctional institutions.

In some ways, the social system in women's prisons is similar to that in the all-male penitentiary. There are social roles, argot, an inmate code, and accommodation between captive and captor. But in other ways the social system of women inmates is not as clearly defined, for it is a microsociety made up of four main groups.[39] There are the "squares" from conventional society, who are having their first experience with custodial life. Many of these are members of the middle class. They see themselves as respectable persons and view prisons as places to which only "criminals" go. Their convictions have generally been for embezzlement or situational homicides. There are the "professionals," who are career criminals and who view incarceration as an occupational hazard. Expert shoplifters fall into this group. They adopt a "cool" approach to prison life that involves taking maximum advantage of institutional amenities without endangering their chances for parole or early release. The third group, and perhaps the largest, is made up of habitual criminals who have had numerous experiences with prison life since their teenage years. Some are prostitutes who have assaulted and robbed their clients, many are thieves, and others are chronic hard drug users and sellers. For them, institutional life provides status and familial attachments. Finally, there is the custodial staff, which reflects the same values and attributes as in men's institutions.[40]

THE EFFECTIVENESS OF CORRECTIONAL TREATMENT

The treatment approach to the management and control of criminal offenders was used in the United States early in its history, and by the middle of the twentieth century the idea of "changing the lawbreaker" had become a dominant force in correctional thinking. Most offenders were still "punished," but at the same time classification exercises assigned them to "programs" and "supervision" designed for their reintegration into law-abiding society.

Yet throughout the history of corrections in America there has also been a tendency among advocates of both the punishment and treatment philosophies to commit themselves to unproven techniques. Correctional and reform approaches were often founded on intuition and sentiment, rather than on an awareness of prior success or failure. This began to change, however, when the rehabilitative ideal emerged as a strong force in correctional thinking. Attempts were made not only to test the efficacy of existing programs, but also to design and evaluate experimental and innovative approaches. Research strategies were devised, outcome measures were specified, data were prudently collected and judiciously analyzed, and the findings were invariably circulated.

Throughout the 1950s and for the better part of the 1960s, a vast body of literature began to accumulate offering testimony on the successes and failures of therapeutic approaches. In the main, however, they projected a rather gloomy outlook for the rehabilitative ideal. One of the early disappointments, for example, was the well-known Cambridge-Somerville Youth Study. Begun in 1935 and often described as the most energetic experiment in the prevention of delinquency, it attempted to test the impact of intensive counseling on young male delinquents. For 10 years the research continued, using an experimental group of youths who had access to counseling and a control group who did not. When the findings of the experience were published in 1951, it was learned that there were no significant differences between the outcomes of the treatment and the control groups. This led the evaluators to the natural conclusion that there was no evidence that counseling could make a positive contribution to the rehabilitation of delinquents.[41] In subsequent years, numerous researchers in Europe and the United States surveyed the field of correctional evaluation. Their conclusions were overwhelmingly negative—that the treatment of offenders had questionable results.[42] But still, the focus on treatment continued and the findings of the studies were ignored by all but the social-behavioral research communities.

This apparent disregard of negative results could be readily understood. The research had typically been carried out by members of the academic community. The findings were prepared in a technical format, and, perhaps more importantly, they appeared almost exclusively in professional and scientific journals, government reports, academic symposia, and books published by university presses. For the general public and the nation's legislators and opinion makers, these sources of information were as remote as medieval parchments hidden in the cellars and garrets of some ancient moated castle.

The Martinson Report

During the late 1960s and early 1970s, the programs to abolish poverty and racial injustice had not lived up to their expectations. There were riots, many were angered over American involvement in Vietnam, and crime rates were increasing at a rapid pace. Furthermore, there was growing opposition to the many Supreme Court decisions that some claimed, and others denied, were "handcuffing police" and "coddling criminals." During much of this period, researchers in New York had been undertaking a massive evaluation of prior efforts at correctional intervention.

The idea for the research went back to early 1966, when the New York State Governor's Special Committee on Criminal Offenders decided to commission a study to determine what methods, if any, held the greatest promise for the rehabilitation of convicted offenders. The findings of the study were to be used to guide program development in the state's criminal justice system. The project was carried out by researchers at the New York State Office of Crime Control Planning, and for years they analyzed the literature on hundreds of correctional efforts published between 1945 and 1967.

The findings of the project were put together in a massive volume that was published in 1975.[43] Prior to the appearance of the in-depth report, *Public Interest* published an article by one of the researchers, Robert Martinson, titled "What Works?—Questions and Answers About Prison Reform."[44] In it he reviewed the purpose and scope of the New York study and implied that with few and isolated exceptions, *nothing works!*

There was little that was really new in Martinson's article. In 1966, Professor Walter C. Bailey of the City University of New York had published the findings of a survey of 100 evaluations of correctional treatment programs with the final judgment that "evidence supporting the efficacy of correctional treatment is slight, inconsistent, and of questionable reliability."[45] But the Martinson article created a sensation, for it appeared in a visible publication and attracted attention in the popular media at a time when politicians and opinion makers were desperately searching for some response to the widespread public fear of street crime. Furthermore, as political scientist James Q. Wilson explained:

> Martinson did not discover that rehabilitation was of little value in dealing with crime so much as he administered a highly visible coup de grace. By bringing out into the open the long-standing scholarly skepticism about most rehabilitation programs, he prepared the way for a revival of an interest in the deterrent, incapacitative, and retributive purposes of the criminal justice system.[46]

Martinson also created a sensation within the research and treatment communities—mostly negative. He was criticized for bias, major distortions of fact, and gross misrepresentation.[47] And for the most part, his critics were correct. Martinson had failed to include all types of treatment programs; he tended to ignore the effects of some treatment programs on some individuals; he generally concentrated on whether the particular treatment method was effective in all the studies in which it was tested; and he neglected to study the new federally funded treatment programs that had begun after 1967.

In all fairness to Martinson, though, his work cannot be overlooked. While he may have been guilty of overgeneralization, most correctional treatment programs were demonstrating little success, and indeed, many were not working. Furthermore, his essay had an impact in other ways. It pushed researchers and evaluators to sharpen their analytical tools for the measurement of

Federal Intensive Confinement Center for women in Bryan, Texas.

success and failure. Yet simultaneously, it ushered in an "abolish treatment" era characterized by a "nothing works" philosophy.

New Approaches to Correctional Treatment

Going beyond the "what works," and "nothing works" rhetoric of the 1970s and early 1980s, questions still remain as to how effective correctional treatment really is. Probably no one actually knows.

Since the very beginnings of the American prison experience, new strategies have been implemented in an effort to improve the overall value of correctional treatment. The "silent" and "separate" systems of the nineteenth century were among the first approaches, as were later reformatory and classification schemes. Among the more recent innovations in correctional treatment is what some jurisdictions refer to as "shock incarceration" and others call "boot camp." **Shock incarceration** is a 3- to 6-month regimen of military drill, drug treatment, physical exercise, hard labor, and academic work in return for having several years removed from an inmate's sentence. Available to young nonviolent offenders, the idea is to "shock" budding felons out of careers in crime by imposing large amounts of rigor and order in what appear to be chaotic and otherwise purposeless lives. But even this promising alternative is not perfect.

Shock incarceration: A 3- to 6-month regimen of military drill, drug treatment, physical exercise, hard labor, and academic work in return for having several years removed from an inmate's sentence.

Obstacles to Effective Correctional Treatment

Despite any advances in correctional techniques and program services, there are numerous obstacles that prevent most prisons from becoming effective agencies of rehabilitation, including the following:

1. Many institutions are old and antiquated.

2. Maximum-security prisons are, for the most part, too large or overcrowded.

3. Prison cells and many medium-security dormitories are unsuitable for human habitation.

4. Correctional institutions are typically understaffed and personnel often lack proper training.

5. The proper segregation of inmates is not widely enforced.

6. Inmate unemployment is common, and too many prisoners are assigned to what has become known as "idle company."

Exhibit 12.6   Careers in Justice
The Corrections Connection

The Corrections Connection Network is an excellent online resource for students studying correctional issues as well as for those interested in working in the corrections field. In addition to weekly updates on correctional matters and news from the front lines in the corrections field, the network has numerous bulletin boards and links to related correctional sites. Among these are postings of available positions in the corrections field in all 50 states. (Web site address: http://www.corrections.com)

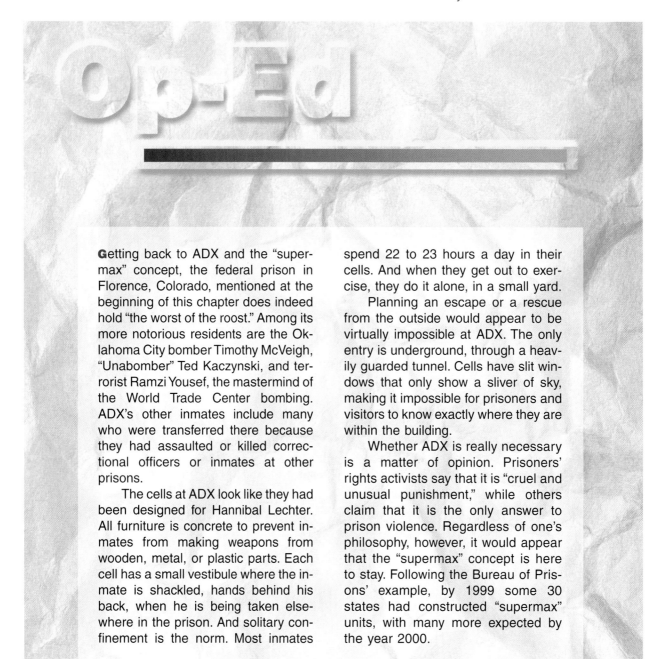

Getting back to ADX and the "super-max" concept, the federal prison in Florence, Colorado, mentioned at the beginning of this chapter does indeed hold "the worst of the roost." Among its more notorious residents are the Oklahoma City bomber Timothy McVeigh, "Unabomber" Ted Kaczynski, and terrorist Ramzi Yousef, the mastermind of the World Trade Center bombing. ADX's other inmates include many who were transferred there because they had assaulted or killed correctional officers or inmates at other prisons.

The cells at ADX look like they had been designed for Hannibal Lechter. All furniture is concrete to prevent inmates from making weapons from wooden, metal, or plastic parts. Each cell has a small vestibule where the inmate is shackled, hands behind his back, when he is being taken elsewhere in the prison. And solitary confinement is the norm. Most inmates spend 22 to 23 hours a day in their cells. And when they get out to exercise, they do it alone, in a small yard.

Planning an escape or a rescue from the outside would appear to be virtually impossible at ADX. The only entry is underground, through a heavily guarded tunnel. Cells have slit windows that only show a sliver of sky, making it impossible for prisoners and visitors to know exactly where they are within the building.

Whether ADX is really necessary is a matter of opinion. Prisoners' rights activists say that it is "cruel and unusual punishment," while others claim that it is the only answer to prison violence. Regardless of one's philosophy, however, it would appear that the "supermax" concept is here to stay. Following the Bureau of Prisons' example, by 1999 some 30 states had constructed "supermax" units, with many more expected by the year 2000.

7. Institutional discipline is often too rigid.
8. Prison life tends to be monotonous and oppressive.
9. Parole policies are sometimes unfair or inefficient.
10. Comprehensive classification and program strategies are not universally available.
11. The prisonization and criminalization processes apparent in many correctional facilities bar many inmates from achieving any motivation for treatment.

By the close of the 1990s, attempts at prison reform had accomplished little to remove these obstacles. Moreover, given the sentencing philosophies that serve to increase the already overpopulated prisons, it would appear that the American penitentiary in the year 2000 will resemble that of the 1970s, 1980s, and 1990s.

SUMMARY

Total institutions such as prisons are places that furnish barriers to social interchange with the world at large. There are a variety of types of prisons differentiated by their level of security. Maximum-security prisons are best characterized by their massive concrete walls, rows of razor wire, strategically located guard towers, and their overwhelming emphasis on custody and control of inmates. Medium-security facilities tend to be less fortresslike than maximum-security institutions and place fewer restrictions on inmate movement; additionally, inmates housed there are considered less dangerous and unlikely to attempt an escape. Minimum-security facilities operate with little emphasis on controlling inmate movement, instead allowing a great deal of personal freedom and low levels of surveillance. Often, minimally secure facilities do not have walls, armed guards, or fences. Open institutions include such correctional facilities as prison farms, work camps, and ranches. Prisons are administratively structured like other large organizations. The physical facilities of correctional institutions vary from one place to another. Most prisons, however, are rather old, and many are deteriorated. As a result, upkeep tends to be difficult.

The prison experience begins with classification, a process through which the educational, vocational, treatment, and custodial needs of offenders are determined. Prison programs focus on health and medical services, religious needs, academic education and vocational training, labor and industry, recreation, and clinical and drug abuse treatment.

Aside from the loss of liberty itself, perhaps the most obvious deprivation associated with prison life is the loss of heterosexual activity. As a result, same-gender sexual relationships and sexual assaults occur behind prison walls. The conjugal visit has been promoted as a means for reducing sexual frustrations in correctional institutions. Furthermore, coeducational facilities are being expermented with for the purpose of reducing both homosexuality and violence.

Every prison has an inmate social system, characterized by an argot, social roles, and an inmate code. Exposure to the social system of the prison community begins almost immediately after the prisoner enters the institution. All new inmates become quickly aware of the norms and values that are shared by their fellow inmates. The internalization of these prison norms and values is known as prisonization. As aspects of the institutional subculture, prevailing norms and informal rules are often referred to as the inmate code. Typical codes include norms of noninterference, strength/masculinity, loyalty to inmates, and rules that discourage the direct exploitation of other inmates.

Evaluative studies of correctional treatment programs have not been favorable to the notion of rehabilitation. Research findings during the 1960s and early 1970s resulted in a "nothing works" and "abolish treatment" era in corrections. Indeed, many obstacles to treatment are present in the structure of correctional facilities themselves. Many researchers still intent on providing treatment to inmates have been quick to point out that numerous factors compromise even the most effective treatment strategies, citing problems in the following areas: overcrowding; institutional age, physical structure, and size; understaffing; poor staff training; inefficient parole policies; improper segregation; and institutional rigidity.

KEY TERMS

classification **324**
conjugal visitation **335**
inmate code **339**

inside cells **318**
maximum-security prisons **318**
open institutions **320**

prisonization **337**
shock incarceration **343**
total institutions **318**

QUESTIONS FOR DISCUSSION

1. In what ways is life in prison similar to life in the military or on the college campus?
2. What are the general characteristics of prison life?
3. What impact might the changing nature of female crime have on the social order of women's prisons?
4. What steps should be taken to change prison into environments more suitable for rehabilitation and reform?
5. Are "supermax" prisons necessary and appropriate?

MEDIA RESOURCES

1. **The Corrections Connection Network.** This is an excellent Web site with all types of information and sources in the corrections field, including news and events, bulletin boards, employment and educational opportunities, to name but a few. Web site address: http://www.corrections.com

2. *The Shawshank Redemption.* This is an excellent film about prison life and is available on video. A thorough review of the film by James J. Sobel of the State University of New York at Albany can be found in the *Journal of Criminal Justice and Popular Culture* 4 (1996): 15–17.

3. **Women in Prison.** The entire December 1998 issue of *Corrections Today,* published by the American Correctional Association, is devoted to women offenders.

4. **Prison Life.** There are many excellent books on this topic. Among the most recent are John Irwin and James Austin, *It's About Time: America's Imprisonment Binge* (Belmont, Calif.: Wadsworth, 1997); Elliott Currie, *Crime and Punishment in America* (New York: Henry Holt, 1998).

NOTES

1. Erving Goffman, *Asylums* (Garden City, N.Y.: Anchor, 1961), pp. 1–8.
2. National Advisory Commission on Criminal Justice Standards and Goals, *Corrections* (Washington, D.C.: U.S. Government Printing Office, 1973), p. 345.
3. Paul W. Tappan, *Crime, Justice, and Correction* (New York: McGraw-Hill, 1960), p. 653.
4. *Corrections Compendium,* January 1994, pp. 1–7.
5. Blake McKelvey, *American Prisons: A History of Good Intentions* (Montclair, N.J.: Patterson Smith, 1977), pp. 150–196.
6. Eldridge Cleaver, *Soul on Ice* (New York: McGraw-Hill, 1968); George Jackson, *Soledad Brother: The Prison Letters of George Jackson* (New York: Bantam, 1970).
7. James B. Jacobs and Harold G. Retsky, "Prison Guard," *Urban Life* 4 (April 1974): 5–29; Gresham M. Sykes, *The Society of Captives: A Study of a Maximum Security Prison* (New York: Atheneum, 1965), pp. 40–62; Edgar May, "Prison Guards in America: The Inside Story," *Corrections Magazine* 2 (December 1976): 3–5, 40, 45.
8. U.S. Department of Justice, *Census of State Correctional Facilities, 1974* (Washington, D.C.: U.S. Government Printing Office, 1975).
9. *Corrections Compendium,* March 1994, pp. 4–6.
10. *New York Times,* January 12, 1994, p. A14.
11. *Newsweek,* April 25, 1994, p. 8.
12. *1992 Annual Report of the Federal Bureau of Prisons.*
13. Don C. Gibbons, *Changing the Lawbreaker: The Treatment of Delinquents and Criminals* (Englewood Cliffs, N.J.: Prentice-Hall, 1965), p. 136.
14. *DOCS Today* (New York State Department of Correctional Services, April 1998).
15. *Drug Enforcement Report,* August 23, 1991, p. 6; *Alcoholism and Drug Abuse Week,* September 11, 1991, p. 3.
16. *Sourcebook of Criminal Justice Statistics* (Washington, D.C.: Bureau of Justice Statistics, 1995).
17. Leonard Orland, *Justice, Punishment, Treatment* (New York: Free Press, 1973), pp. 263–269.
18. Hans Toch, *Living in Prison: The Ecology of Survival* (New York: Free Press, 1977), p. 100.
19. Harry E. Allen and Clifford E. Simonsen, *Corrections in America* (New York: Macmillan, 1981), pp. 57, 375.
20. Tappan, *Crime, Justice, and Correction,* pp. 678–679.
21. Joseph Fishman, *Sex in Prison* (New York: National Library Press, 1934); Donald Clemmer, *The Prison Community* (New York: Rinehart, 1958), pp. 249–273; Sykes, *Society of Captives;* Peter C. Buffum, *Homosexuality in Prisons* (Washington, D.C.: U.S. Government Printing Office, 1972); John H. Cagnon and William Simon, "The Social Meaning of Prison Homosexuality," *Federal Probation* 32 (March 1968): 23–29.
22. Christine A. Saum, Hilary L. Surratt, James A. Inciardi, and Rachael E. Bennett, "Sexual Behavior in a Male Correctional Facility" (Paper presented at the Annual Meeting of the American Society of Criminology, Miami, Florida, November 14–18, 1994).
23. Sykes, *Society of Captives,* pp. 95–99; Clemmer, *The Prison Community;* Leo Carroll, *Hacks, Blacks, and Cons: Race Relations in a Maximum Security Prison* (Lexington, Mass.: Heath, 1974).
24. Columbus B. Hopper, "The Evolution of Conjugal Visiting in Mississippi," *Prison Journal* 69 (1989): 103–109; Lawrence A. Bennett, "Correctional Administrators' Attitudes Toward Private Family Visiting," *Prison Journal* 69 (1989): 110–114; Bonnie E. Carlson and Neil Cervera, "Inmates and Their Families: Conjugal Visits, Family Contact, and Family Functioning," *Criminal Justice and Behavior* 18 (1991): 318–331.

25. Pauline Morris, *Prisoners and Their Families* (New York: Hart, 1965), p. 90.

26. Donald Johns, "Alternatives to Conjugal Visits," *Federal Probation* 35 (March 1971): 48.

27. Norman S. Hayner, "Attitudes Toward Conjugal Visits for Prisoners," *Federal Probation* 36 (March 1972): 43.

28. *USA Today,* February 7, 1985, p. 3A; *New York Times,* September 18, 1988, p. 28.

29. J. G. Ross, E. Heffernan, J. R. Sevick, and F. T. Johnson, *Assessment of Coeducational Corrections* (Washington, D.C.: U.S. Government Printing Office, 1978).

30. *Newsweek,* January 11, 1982, p. 66.

31. *New York Times,* November 15, 1988, p. A16.

32. *Los Angeles Times,* July 24, 1990, p. A3; *Los Angeles Times,* July 29, 1990, p. A29.

33. Sykes, *Society of Captives,* p. 82.

34. Sykes, *Society of Captives,* p. 83.

35. Clemmer, *The Prison Community,* p. 299.

36. For a review and commentary of the various studies and points of view of prisonization, see Gordon Hawkins, *The Prison: Policy and Practice* (Chicago: University of Chicago Press, 1976), pp. 56–80.

37. Gresham M. Sykes and Sheldon L. Messenger, "The Inmate Social System," in *Theoretical Studies in the Social Organization of the Prison* (New York: Social Science Research Council, 1960), pp. 6–8.

38. From James A. Inciardi, *Careers in Crime* (Chicago: Rand McNally, 1975), p. 70.

39. Esther Heffernan, *Making It in Prison: The Square, the Cool and the Life* (New York: Wiley, 1972).

40. For descriptive material on women's prisons, see Kathryn W. Burkhart, *Women in Prison* (New York: Doubleday, 1973); Jocelyn Pollock-Bryne, *Women, Prison, and Crime* (Pacific Grove, Calif.: Brooks/Cole, 1990).

41. Edwin Powers and Helen Witmer, *An Experiment in the Prevention of Delinquency* (New York: Columbia University Press, 1951).

42. See, for example, Walter C. Bailey, "Correctional Outcome: An Evaluation of 100 Reports," *Journal of Criminal Law, Criminology, and Police Science* 57 (June 1966): 153–160; Roger Hood, "Research on the Effectiveness of Punishments and Treatments," in European Committee on Crime Problems, *Collected Studies in Criminological Research* (Strasbourg: Council of Europe, 1967).

43. Douglas Lipton, Robert Martinson, and Judith Wilks, *The Effectiveness of Correctional Treatment: A Survey of Treatment Evaluation Studies* (New York: Praeger, 1975).

44. Robert Martinson, "What Works?—Questions and Answers About Prison Reform," *Public Interest* 35 (Spring 1974): 22–54.

45. Bailey, "Correctional Outcome."

46. James Q. Wilson, " 'What Works?' Revisited: New Findings on Criminal Rehabilitation," *Public Interest* 61 (Fall 1980): 3–17.

47. See, for example, Carl B. Klockars, "The True Limits of the Effectiveness of Correctional Treatment," *Prison Journal* 55 (Spring–Summer 1975): 53–64; Ted Palmer, "Martinson Revisited," *Journal of Research in Crime and Delinquency* 12 (July 1975): 133–152.

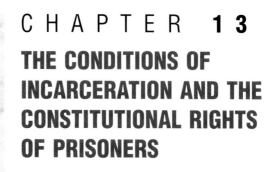

C H A P T E R **1 3**

THE CONDITIONS OF INCARCERATION AND THE CONSTITUTIONAL RIGHTS OF PRISONERS

TRENTON, N.J. — New Jersey gubernatorial candidate Tom J. Farer offered an interesting array of suggestions for dealing with the growing tide of violent crime. One of his propositions for dealing with the growing populations of prisoners was to establish colonies, on islands, whose perimeters could be easily guarded.[1] Custodians would be located on the outside; the colonies would be "trust territories"; there would be democratic elections; and only abuses would be subject to outside interference. Farer noted that his idea stemmed from the British experiments with transportation of criminals to colonial territories such as Australia, Botany Bay, Norfolk Island, and Van Diemen's Land (now Tasmania).

Would something like this be feasible? What would likely happen if Farer's experiment were to be tried? Would it be a violation of prisoners' rights? And for that matter, what kinds of rights do prisoners have?

Prior to the 1960s, prison inmates in the United States had virtually no legal rights, nor had they avenues for redressing wrongs committed against them while in the custody of the state. The Supreme Court's 1871 decision in *Ruffin* v. *Commonwealth* defined the legal status of inmates for nearly a century:

> A convicted felon is one whom the law in its humanity punishes by confinement in the penitentiary instead of death. . . . For the time being, during his term of service in the penitentiary, he is a slave of penal servitude to the State . . . for the time being, the slave of the State.[2]

By characterizing inmates as "slaves of the state," the High Court's decision permitted extensive administrative discretion over the lives of inmates. Both punishment and privileges were decided and dispensed by prison staff often without explanation or merit. The courts, furthermore, supported a **hands-off doctrine** regarding correctional matters. Inmate petitions for hearings regarding the adequacy of prison environments, constitutional deprivations, and the general conditions of incarceration were repeatedly denied by the federal courts.

It was only during the 1960s that the courts began to depart from their traditional "hands-off" policy. Following the decision in *United States ex rel. Gereau* v. *Henderson,*[3] prisoners were given the right to be heard in court regarding such matters as the widespread violence that threatened their lives and security, the problems of overcrowding, the nature of disciplinary proceedings, the conditions affecting health and safety, the regulations governing visitation and correspondence, and the limitations on religious observance, education, work, and recreation.

Appellate courts quickly became the instruments of change in American correctional policy. But only a few years after the prisoners' rights movement began, there was a major correctional tragedy that symbolized the problems in prisons and the degraded conditions of inmate life. The happening was the inmate uprising at New York's Attica Correctional Facility on September 9, 1971. Although the Attica riot occurred almost three decades ago, it continues to serve as a painful reminder of the conditions and contexts that generate conflict and violence in prisons, and the lessons learned from Attica continue to remain salient as American corrections moves into the twenty-first century.

Hands-off doctrine: The refusal of the courts to hear inmate complaints about the conditions of incarceration and the constitutional deprivations of penitentiary life.

ATTICA, 1971

For prisoners at Attica in late 1971, "correction" meant little more than daily degradation and humiliation. They were locked in cells for 14 to 16 hours each day; they worked for wages that averaged 30 cents a day, at jobs with little or no vocational value; and they had to abide by hundreds of petty rules for which they could see no justification. In addition, their mail was read, their radio programs were screened in advance, their reading material was restricted, their movements outside their cells were tightly regulated, they were told when to turn lights out and when to wake up, their toilet needs had to be taken care of in the full view of patrolling officers, and their visits from family and friends took place through a mesh screen and were preceded and followed by strip searches probing every opening of their bodies.

In prison, inmates found deprivations worse than they had encountered on the street: Meals were unappetizing and not up to nutritional standards. Clothing was old, ill-fitting, and inadequate. Most inmates could take showers only once a week. State-issued clothing, toilet articles, and other personal items had to be supplemented by purchases at a commissary where prices did not reflect the meager wages inmates were given to spend. To get along in the prison's economy, inmates resorted to "hustling."

The sources of inmate frustration and discontent did not end there. Medical care, while adequate to meet acute health needs, was dispensed in a callous, indifferent manner by doctors who feared and despised most of the convicts they treated; inmates were not protected from unwelcome homosexual advances; even the ticket to freedom for most inmates—parole—was burdened with inequities or at least the appearance of inequity.

For officers, "correction" meant a steady but monotonous 40-hour-a-week job, with a pension after 25 years' service. It meant maintaining custody and control over an inmate population that had increasing numbers of young blacks and Puerto Ricans from the urban ghettos who were unwilling to conform to the restrictions of prison life and who were ready to provoke confrontation—men whom the officers could not understand and were not trained to deal with. It meant keeping the inmates in line, seeing that everything ran smoothly, and enforcing the rules. It did not mean, for most officers, helping inmates to solve their problems or to become citizens capable of returning to society. For the correctional officers, who were always outnumbered by inmates, there was a legitimate concern about security; but that concern was not served by policies that created frustration and tension far more dangerous than the security risks they were intended to avert.

Above all, for both inmates and officers, "correction" meant an atmosphere charged with racism. Racism was manifested in job assignments, discipline, self-segregation in the inmate mess halls, and in the daily interactions between inmate and officer and inmate and inmate. There was no escape within the walls from the growing mistrust outside the walls between white middle America and the residents of urban ghettos. Indeed, at Attica racial polarity and mistrust were magnified by the constant reminder that the "keepers" were white and the "kept" were largely black or Spanish-speaking. The young black inmate tended to see the white officer as a symbol of a racist, oppressive system that put him behind bars. The officer, his perspective shaped by his experience on the job, knew blacks only as belligerent unrepentant criminals. The result was a mutual lack of respect that made communication all but impossible.[4]

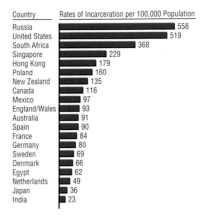

Country	Rates of Incarceration per 100,000 Population
Russia	558
United States	519
South Africa	368
Singapore	229
Hong Kong	179
Poland	160
New Zealand	135
Canada	116
Mexico	97
England/Wales	93
Australia	91
Spain	90
France	84
Germany	80
Sweden	69
Denmark	66
Egypt	62
Netherlands	49
Japan	36
India	23

Incarceration Rates for Selected Nations

SOURCE: The Sentencing Project.

The Uprising and Revolt

The majority of Attica's inmates were housed in four main cell blocks: A, B, C, and D Blocks. Each block had three tiers of cells, and each group of about 40 cells was referred to as a "company."

The uprising against the conditions in Attica was not the result of a planned revolt inspired by a core of inmate revolutionaries. Rather, it was the product of building dissatisfactions and frustrations and was sparked by two related incidents.

Tensions had been growing between inmates and correctional officers amid a setting of rising expectations of improved conditions. But the anticipated changes in the prison environment seemed to be slow in coming. During the summer of 1971 there had been a number of organized protest efforts, but these accomplished no more than the disciplining of the organizers.

On September 8, an incident occurred that provoked the particular resentment and anger of inmates in two companies of Block A. An exercise-yard misunderstanding led to an unusually intense confrontation between officers and inmates, during which a lieutenant was struck by inmate Leroy Dewer. The officers were forced to back down. That evening, however, Dewer and another inmate were removed from their cells and placed in solitary confinement. It was widely believed that the two were subsequently beaten by several of the guards.

Sattler/Bunte/Munich

On the following morning, September 9, officers found the men of 5-Company, to which one of the inmates involved in the Dewer incident belonged, to be especially belligerent and troublesome. Thus, they decided to return the members of 5-Company to their cells immediately after breakfast without allowing them their usual time in the exercise yard. This decision came at a point when the inmates were lined up in one of the prison's many "tunnels."

Attica's four cell blocks form a square enclosing a large open area. Narrow corridors ("tunnels") running from the middle of one block to the block opposite divide the central area into four exercise yards. The tunnels intersect at a junction that is called "Times Square," inside of which is a locking device that controls access to all of the cell blocks.

As the inmates of 5-Company were being escorted through the tunnels back to their cells, several attacked the officer on duty. Others joined in, and after an initial outburst of violence, the Block A inmates regrouped and set upon the locked gate at Times Square. A defective weld, unknown to officers and inmates alike, broke and the gate gave way. This gave the prisoners access to Times Square and the keys that unlocked the gates to all other directions. From Times Square the inmates spread throughout the prison, attacking officers, taking hostages, and destroying property.

By afternoon, the New York state police had regained control of part of the prison, but most of the inmates assembled in one of the exercise yards along with their 39 hostages, whom the rioters threatened to kill if their demands were not met.

The Negotiations and Assault

Initially, the rebellious inmates released a series of five demands, including complete amnesty and safe transportation to a "nonimperialistic" country. These were quickly rejected, however, and more serious negotiations began. New York's commissioner of corrections, Russell Oswald, ultimately came up with a 28-point proposal that represented major advances in penal reform. It included a general liberalization of prison life, combined with provisions for more adequate food, political and religious freedom, realistic rehabilitation programs, reductions in cell time, removal of most communications censorship, recruitment of black and Hispanic correctional officers, better education and drug treatment programs, and more adequate legal assistance services. In addition, Oswald agreed to recommend the application of the New York State minimum wage law standards to all work done by inmates.

During riots at Attica Prison, prisoners raise their hands in clenched fists as a show of unity.

But for 4 days the negotiations dragged on because of one major stumbling block: amnesty. During the initial revolt, one of the correctional officers, William Quinn, suffered serious skull injuries at the hands of the inmates. Two days later he died. Without total amnesty, the inmates realized, there would be murder charges—which would subject any prisoner already serving a life sentence to a possible death sentence.

Governor Nelson Rockefeller was asked to make a personal appearance at Attica to help with the negotiations and prevent a bloodbath, but he refused. Instead, he authorized Commissioner Oswald to end the rebellion by force if necessary.

On the morning of September 13, 1971, a local state police troop commander planned and led an assault to retake Attica Prison. Within 15 minutes, the Attica uprising was over. The state troopers, however, had killed 29 inmates and 10 officer hostages and wounded hundreds more. It was the bloodiest 1-day encounter between Americans since the Civil War.[5]

IN PURSUIT OF PRISONERS' RIGHTS

The Attica revolt was a dramatic symbol of the enduring struggle that had been developing for almost a decade. Prior to the 1960s, it was a matter of law that offenders were deemed to have forfeited virtually all rights and to have retained only those expressly granted by statute or correctional authority. Thus,

inhuman conditions and practices were permitted to develop and continue in many correctional systems, despite the Eighth Amendment's ban on cruel and unusual punishment. The courts, furthermore, generally refused to intervene in correctional matters. Their justifications were twofold:

> Judges felt that correctional administration was a technical matter to be left to experts rather than to courts, which were deemed ill-equipped to make appropriate evaluations. And, to the extent that courts believed the offenders' complaints involved privileges rather than rights, there was no special necessity to confront correctional practices, even when they infringed on basic notions of human rights and dignity protected for other groups by constitutional doctrine.[6]

The Writ of *Habeas Corpus*

Whenever an individual is being confined in an institution under state or federal authority, he or she is entitled to seek *habeas corpus* relief. This is guaranteed by Article 1, Section 9, of the U.S. Constitution, which states: "The privilege of the writ of *habeas corpus* shall not be suspended."

By applying for a writ of **habeas corpus,** the person seeking relief is challenging the lawfulness of his confinement. *Habeas corpus* is a Latin term that means "you should have the body." In practice, *habeas corpus* relief involves a writ issued by a court commanding the person who holds another in captivity to produce the prisoner in court so that the legality of the prisoner's confinement can be adjudicated.[7]

Traditionally, the writ was limited to contesting the legality of confinement itself. However, in *Coffin v. Reichard,*[8] decided in 1944, the Sixth Circuit U.S. Court of Appeals held that suits challenging the conditions of confinement could be brought under the federal *habeas corpus* statute.

Although the U.S. Supreme Court has never fully resolved the question of whether the writ of *habeas corpus* is available to seek relief from allegedly unconstitutional conditions of confinement, most federal courts have elected to follow the logic of *Coffin v. Reichard.*[9] Nevertheless, from the prisoner's perspective, the process of bringing a *habeas* petition to a federal court is unwieldy and time-consuming. This is because the law requires inmates of state institutions to exhaust all state judicial and administrative remedies before they apply for the federal writ of *habeas corpus.* Thus, most prisoners remain effectively barred from the most direct mechanism for challenging the conditions of their confinement.

Habeas corpus: A writ that directs the person holding a prisoner to bring him or her before a judicial officer to determine the lawfulness of imprisonment.

Civil Rights and Prisoners' Rights

The civil rights movement of the late 1950s and early 1960s created a climate more conducive to a serious reexamination of the legal rights of prisoners. The specific vehicle that opened the federal courts to inmates confined in state institutions was **Section 1983** of the Civil Rights Act of 1871, which provides:

> Every person who, under color of any statute, ordinance, regulation, custom, or usage of any State or Territory subjects, or causes to be subjected, any citizen of the United States or other person within the jurisdiction thereof to the deprivation of any rights, privileges, or immunities secured by the Constitution and laws shall be liable to the party injured in an action at law, suit in equity or other proper proceeding for redress.

The long-dormant Section 1983 was resurrected in ***Monroe v. Pape,***[10] decided by the Supreme Court in 1961 and holding that citizens could bring Section 1983

Section 1983: The section of the Civil Rights Act of 1871 used by state prisoners as a vehicle for access to the federal courts to litigate inmate rights.

Monroe v. Pape: The Supreme Court ruling that citizens can bring Section 1983 suits against state officials in federal courts without first exhausting state judicial remedies.

Inmate No. 3409, buried in a small cemetery on the grounds of New York's Green Haven Prison in 1962, remains but a number in death as in life. His name was John Baldwin.

suits against state officials to the federal courts without first exhausting state judicial remedies.

Three years later the High Court made it clear that the *Pape* holding applied to state prisoners who could articulate cognizable constitutional claims against state prison officials or employees.[11] However, the Court later held that although a Section 1983 suit is a proper remedy to make a constitutional challenge to the *conditions* of prison life, it could not be used to challenge the *fact* and *length* of custody.[12]

The major advantages of a Section 1983 suit, as opposed to a *habeas corpus* petition, are that a Section 1983 suit does not require that available state remedies be exhausted before the federal district courts will have jurisdiction,

Petitions Filed in U.S. District Courts by State Prisoners, 1977–1997

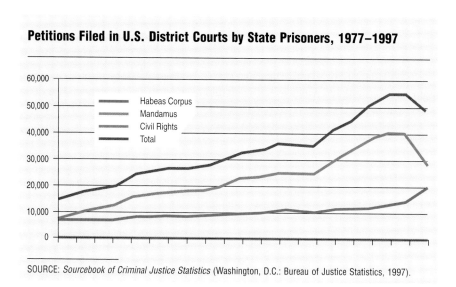

SOURCE: *Sourcebook of Criminal Justice Statistics* (Washington, D.C.: Bureau of Justice Statistics, 1997).

and that an award of money damages is possible. However, the remedy of release from imprisonment is not available under a Section 1983 suit—only the writ of *habeas corpus* can secure such release.

LEGAL SERVICES IN PRISON

In *ex parte Hull,*[13] a state prison regulation required that all legal documents in an inmate's court proceedings must be submitted to an institutional official for examination and censorship before they are filed with the court. The Supreme Court found this and similar prison regulations invalid, holding that whether a petition is properly drawn and what allegations it must contain were issues for the court, not the prison authorities, to decide.

Johnson v. Avery

In spite of the rule established by *Hull,* an inmate's right of access to the courts proved to be more theoretical than actual. In many prison systems, disciplinary actions against inmates pursuing legal remedies, or wholesale confiscation of a prisoner's legal documents, were quite common. Furthermore, court access was either curtailed or totally inhibited because most prison officials withheld from inmates any services related to their legal needs. In most instances, inmates seeking remedies were provided with no more than a few outdated law books and occasionally the services of a notary public. Since most prisoners were indigent and lacked the funds to secure the help of an attorney, the courts were essentially closed to them. Many correctional institutions had "jailhouse lawyers"—inmates who claimed legal expertise and who provided advice and counsel to their fellow prisoners, with or without compensation. Yet even this aid was severely restricted by prison officials, thus further denying inmates their basic constitutional right of access.

Johnson v. Avery in 1969 acknowledged and resolved a number of these problems.[14] The case involved the constitutionality of a Tennessee prison regulation with the following provision:

No inmate will advise, assist or otherwise contract to aid another, either with or without a fee, to prepare writs or other legal matters. . . . Inmates are forbidden to set themselves up as practitioners for the purpose of promoting a business of writing writs.[15]

The petitioner in *Johnson* was a jailhouse lawyer serving a life sentence who had spent almost a year in solitary confinement for repeatedly violating the rule against writ writing.

In its analysis of the Tennessee rule, the Supreme Court addressed the fact that many prisoners are illiterate and are frequently unable to find legal help from sources beyond the prison walls. Thus, the justices held, unless the state could provide some reasonable alternative type of legal assistance to inmates seeking postconviction relief, a jailhouse lawyer must be permitted to aid inmates in filing *habeas corpus* petitions.

Although the decision in *Johnson* was a significant one, it failed to delineate many of the specifics of inmates' mechanisms for legal access. In the years that followed, the Supreme Court began to address this vagueness—giving inmates access to law books and other legal documents and

Johnson v. Avery: The Supreme Court ruling that unless a state provides some reasonable legal assistance to inmates seeking postconviction relief, a jailhouse lawyer must be permitted to aid inmates in filing *habeas corpus* petitions.

TV OR NO TV

Johnson v. *Avery* also held that the Eighth Amendment's prohibition against cruel and unusual punishment could be applied to a variety of prisoner complaints. Shortly after the High Court decision, Georgia correctional officials began providing air conditioning and television to inmates under the threat of having their prisons declared "unconstitutional." A quarter of a century later, jurisdictions across the United States began curtailing recreation for prisoners in an effort to make "hard time" harder. The most common activity eliminated was television watching.

SOURCES: *National Review,* March 16, 1992, pp. 36–38; *New York Times,* October 17, 1994, pp. 1, 11.

the right to the legal assistance of a jailhouse lawyer not only for seeking *habeas corpus* relief, but also for filing civil rights actions against prison officials.[16]

Jailhouse Lawyers

Jailhouse lawyers are inmates claiming to have some legal knowledge, who counsel and assist other inmates in the preparation of legal documents such as *habeas corpus,* pleadings, and appeals to higher courts. For years, however, prison regulations forbade inmates from both assisting and receiving this kind of help in the preparation of legal materials. The rules were an outgrowth of several factors. Initially, the rule was a reflection of the general custodial attitude toward prison inmates. That is, the convict was a ward of the state who possessed no civil rights, and the privilege of obtaining legal help from other convicts was simply unthinkable. In addition, there were a number of security issues involved. "Writ writers," as they were often called, were seen as potential troublemakers. Officials often felt that the jailhouse lawyer, in advising inmates of their legal rights, might create dissatisfactions within the prison population that could lead to belligerence and revolt. Furthermore, the phenomenon of inmates conferring about legal matters was interpreted by some as plotting against administrative authority. Finally, there was the fear that jailhouse lawyers would provide their clients with inferior representation and false hopes of success while they flooded the courts with spurious claims.

Most of these administrative and custodial concerns had some basis in fact, but in general the problems that jailhouse lawyers caused in correctional institutions were more often ones of inconvenience than of discipline and security. Since *Johnson* v. *Avery* and numerous subsequent state and federal court decisions, the activities of jailhouse lawyers in many jurisdictions have been relatively unrestricted.

During the past few years, public and private agencies have begun to furnish grants to law schools for the development of legal aid programs for prisons and jails. But as Justice William O. Douglas pointed out in his concurring opinion in *Johnson,* such programs rest on a shifting law school population and often fail to meet the daily needs and demands of inmates. As a result, the jailhouse lawyer remains a significant figure in many American prisons. In some states, for example, jailhouse lawyers are permitted — and even encouraged — to work *with* volunteer law students and paralegals, usually under the supervision of an attorney, in providing legal advice to the inmate population.[17] (See Exhibit 13.4 at the end of this chapter.)

CONSTITUTIONAL RIGHTS AND CIVIL DISABILITIES

Historically, persons convicted of serious crimes could lose much more than their liberty or their lives. Under the early English common law, an offender, in addition to being sentenced, was also "attaint." Under this status, he lost all of his civil rights and forfeited his property to the Crown. Furthermore, his entire family was declared corrupt, which made them unworthy to inherit his property. The U.S. Constitution forbids *bills of attainder,* and similar provisions against the attainder or its effects are found in the constitutions and statutes of the states. Yet in spite of these, every state has enacted civil disability laws that affect convicted offenders. Depending on the jurisdiction, civil disabilities may include losses of the rights to vote, hold public office, sit on a jury, be bonded, collect insurance or pension benefits, sue, hold or inherit

Bills of attainder

property, receive worker's compensation, make a will, marry and have children, or even remain married. The most severe disability is the loss of all civil rights, or **civil death.**

 Technically, a civil right is a right that belongs to a person by virtue of his or her citizenship. Since civil rights include constitutional rights, it would seem that state statutes and provisions placing civil disabilities on convicted and imprisoned offenders would be in direct conflict with the Constitution. However, the Supreme Court has not interpreted these statutes as complete denials of prisoners' civil rights, but as restrictions and conditions of their expression. And with respect to many rights that have some direct bearing on the Constitution, the Court's position in recent years has been to remove a number of these restrictions.

Civil death: The loss of all civil rights.

Religion

The First Amendment of the Constitution provides that "Congress shall make no law respecting an establishment of religion, or prohibiting the free exercise thereof." Generally, or at least historically, freedom of religion was rarely a problem in correctional institutions. In fact, participation in religious instruction and worship services was always encouraged. Infringements on this right began only with the rise of minority religions and the demands of their members to have the same rights as those of conventional faiths.

 The leading cases involving religious expression occurred with the growing influence of the Black Muslim movement within prisons during the 1960s. Issues such as the right to attend services, obtain literature, and wear religious medals were raised by the Black Muslims because, unlike Protestant or Catholic inmates, the Black Muslims had been denied the right to engage in such practices. The threshold question was the recognition of the Muslim faith as a religion. This was quickly answered by a federal court in 1962 with its decision in *Fulwood* v. *Clemmer* and other cases,[18] with the assertion that

Fulwood v. *Clemmer*

Cruz v. Beto

Black Muslims retain the same constitutional protection offered to members of other recognized religions. However, although these cases established the Black Muslims' right to hold religious services, the courts have refused to extend that right in specific circumstances. In some institutions and at certain times, for instance, assemblages of Black Muslims were considered by custodial authorities to be revolutionary in character and to represent "clear and present dangers" to security. In several decisions, the courts ruled that although Black Muslims had the right to worship, their right to hold religious services could be withheld if they represented potential breaches of security.[19] (For a glimpse at how prisons in Hong Kong deal with religious, ethnic, and culturally based dietary preferences, see Exhibit 13.1.)

Other cases involving religious freedom in prisons dealt with inmate access to clergy, special diets, and the right to wear religious medals. A case to reach the U.S. Supreme Court in this regard was *Cruz* v. *Beto* in 1972.[20] Cruz, a Buddhist, had been barred from using the chapel in a Texas prison and was placed in solitary confinement for sharing his religious material with other inmates. The Court ruled that the Texas action was "palpable discrimination" in violation of the equal protection clause of the Fourteenth Amendment. On the other hand, the federal courts have held that placing limits on the practice of "satanism" is not a violation of prisoners' First Amendment rights.[21]

Prison Mail

Prison officials in the United States have traditionally placed certain restrictions on inmates' use of the mails. These restrictions generally include limiting the number of persons with whom inmates may correspond, opening and reading incoming and outgoing material, deleting sections from both incoming

---

Exhibit 13.1 **International Perspectives on Crime and Justice**
Food and Drink in Hong Kong Prisons

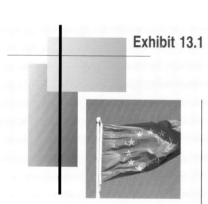

Inmates everywhere complain about food, but it would appear that they have little to complain about in Hong Kong prisons. According to Human Rights Watch observers, meals are ample, well balanced, and varied. Vegetables, fruit, meat, and fish are provided in sufficient amounts, and kitchen areas are clean. Correctional officers taste the food before each meal, and record their reactions in a log book.

In order to meet the needs of inmates' religious and culturally based dietary preferences, the prisons provide different diets for different groups. In particular, they offer an "Asian" (Chinese) diet, a vegetarian diet to comply with Buddhist religious beliefs, an Indian/Pakistani diet, and a European diet. In addition, prisoners needing special diets for medical reasons, such as diabetes, are also accommodated.

A Vietnamese protester stands on the roof of Victoria Prison in Hong Kong to protest his pending deportation to Vietnam.

SOURCE: Human Rights Watch, 1999.

and outgoing mail, and refusing to mail for an inmate or forward to an inmate certain types of correspondence. The reasons for these restrictions follow security and budgetary requirements. Contraband must be intercepted, escape plans must be detected, and material that might incite the inmate population in some way must be excluded. Furthermore, correctional budgets do not allow for the unlimited use of the mails. Prisons have also used the goal of rehabilitation to justify certain restrictions on inmate correspondence.

The courts have generally accepted these justifications for mail censorship and limitation, and in years past have rarely intervened in prison mail regulations. More recently, however, a range of situations have been examined by the courts, with major rulings in *Wolff* v. *McDonnell* and *Procunier* v. *Martinez,* both decided by the Supreme Court in 1974.[22]

In *Wolff,* at issue was whether prison officials could justifiably open correspondence from an inmate's attorney. The Court ruled that officials are permitted to open a communication from an attorney to check for contraband, but (1) it must be done in the presence of the inmate and (2) the contents must not be read. ***Procunier* v. *Martinez*** dealt with the broader issue of censorship of nonlegal correspondence. The Supreme Court held that prison mail censorship is constitutional only when two criteria are met: (1) The practice must further substantial government interests such as security, order, or rehabilitation; and (2) the restrictions must not be greater than necessary to satisfy the particular government interest involved.

Importantly, ***Thornburgh* v. *Abbott,***[23] decided by the Supreme Court in 1989, partially overruled the Court's earlier holding in *Martinez.* In *Abbott,* the mail censorship regulations of the Federal Bureau of Prisons were upheld. But what was most significant was that the High Court jettisoned the "substantial government interests" test of *Martinez* in favor of a "reasonableness" standard as the proper analysis to be applied when courts evaluate prison restrictions on incoming mail or publications. In *Abbott,* the *Martinez* standard was held to apply only to outgoing mail, which in the High Court's opinion presented a security concern of a "categorically lesser magnitude" than incoming mail. By rejecting the *Martinez* "substantial government interests" test as the foundation for reviewing incoming publications and correspondence, *Abbott* reversed much of the existing case law on prison mail censorship, since most of those cases involved inmate challenges to restrictions on incoming mail. As such, *Thornburgh* v. *Abbott* has been considered by a number of constitutional scholars to be an example of the Supreme Court's retreat to a modified hands-off doctrine.

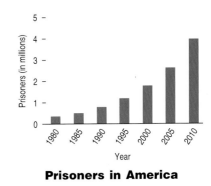

Prisoners in America

SOURCE: U.S. Department of Justice.

Procunier* v. *Martinez: The Supreme Court ruling that prison mail censorship is constitutional only when the practice furthers government interests in security and rehabilitation and when the restrictions are no greater than necessary to satisfy the particular government interest involved.

Thornburgh* v. *Abbott: The Supreme Court ruling that federal prison regulations restricting prisoners' receipt of publications from outside prison pass First Amendment muster if they are reasonably related to legitimate penological interests.

Rehabilitative Services

There is agreement among many clinicians, legislators, and members of the general public that in addition to confinement, one purpose of imprisonment is rehabilitation. Furthermore, in the constitutions and statutes of many states, the rehabilitation of prison inmates is at least implied, if not directly stated. The courts, however, while supporting the rehabilitative ideal, have not defined rehabilitative treatment as a constitutional right.[24] While the courts may not have extended constitutional status to the right to treatment, they have taken a strong stand against several "rehabilitative" practices of questionable moral and legal status. During the early 1970s, for example, a number of behavior modification techniques were imposed on inmates, ostensibly for their therapeutic value. In one case that reached the federal courts in 1973, severely nauseating injections were used to produce an aversion to minor infractions of prison rules.[25] In this case, it was ruled that the procedure was not "treatment" but "punishment"—and cruel and unusual as well, in violation of the Eighth Amendment.

However, the courts have supported some prison requirements that mandate enrollment in certain institutional programs (such as class attendance by illiterate inmates) and disciplinary measures for those who refuse to participate.[26] Similarly, the Supreme Court held in 1990 that the due process clause of the Fourteenth Amendment permits a state to treat prison inmates who have serious mental illnesses with antipsychotic medication against their will, if they are dangerous to themselves or others and the treatment is in their medical interests.[27]

Medical Services

In principle, inmates have a right to "adequate" and "proper" medical care on several grounds. The right is protected by common law and state statutes, by the Civil Rights Act of 1964, by the due process clauses of the Fifth and Fourteenth Amendments, and by the Eighth Amendment ban against cruel and unusual punishment. Prisoners have made claims regarding the adequacy and nature of medical care received, improper and inadequate care, and the total denial of medical and health services.

In *Estelle v. Gamble,*[28] the U.S. Supreme Court enunciated its position on the medical rights of inmates:

> Deliberate indifference to serious medical needs of prisoners constitutes the "unnecessary and wanton infliction of pain" proscribed by the Eighth Amendment. This is true whether the indifference is manifested by prison doctors in their response to the prisoner's needs or by prison guards in intentionally denying or delaying access to medical care or intentionally interfering with the treatment once prescribed.

Beyond this statement, the High Court has generally left the specifics of medical rights to the lower courts.

Estelle v. Gamble: The Supreme Court ruling that the deliberate indifference of prison officials or personnel to the serious medical needs of inmates constitutes cruel and unusual punishment proscribed by the Eighth Amendment.

Prisoner Labor Unions

Although the courts have recognized the rights of prison inmates to adequate medical care, religious expression, and access to the courts, their opinions on the issue of prisoner collective bargaining have been a different matter. In a number of institutions across the nation, inmates have sought to establish what are typically referred to as "labor unions," organized for the purposes of advocating increased pay for inmate labor, improving safety and working conditions, increasing inmate participation in handling matters affecting their welfare, ending contract labor, expressing dissatisfaction with prison programs, and gaining official recognition for inmate workers as public employees having statutory rights under state labor laws.[29] For prisoners, then, unions could operate as channels for communicating complaints that might otherwise not be brought into the open and to official notice. For prison officials, however, unions represent a foundation for concerted inmate actions that could represent significant threats to institutional safety and control.

Throughout the 1970s, prisoner unions attempted to organize in a number of jurisdictions. It was not until *Jones v. North Carolina Prisoners' Labor Union* in 1977,[30] however, that the Supreme Court ruled on the matter. The case began when the North Carolina Prisoners' Labor Union (PLU), whose statewide membership included about 2,000 inmates, alleged that correctional regulations were in violation of First and Fourteenth Amendment rights by denying it the opportunity to hold meetings, solicit additional members, and receive organizational materials from the outside and distribute them in-house.

The Supreme Court disagreed with the contentions of the PLU, however, holding that inmates have no constitutional right to organize a prisoners'

Jones v. North Carolina Prisoners' Labor Union: The Supreme Court ruling that prison regulations prohibiting the organized activities of inmate labor unions are not violative of the freedom of association clause of the First Amendment.

labor union, and hence, prison regulations that prohibit the organized activities of an inmate union do not violate the freedom of association clause of the First Amendment. The High Court went on to emphasize that prison regulations may constitutionally ban union solicitation, group meetings of members, and bulk mail privileges of the organization as long as such regulations are reasonable and rationally related to such legitimate objectives as maintenance of security, prevention of escapes, safety of inmates and prison personnel, and the rehabilitation of inmates.

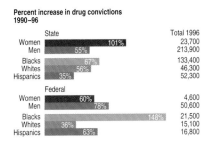

PRISON DISCIPLINE AND CONSTITUTIONAL RIGHTS

Many readers may be familiar with the story of *Papillon*. Written by French novelist Henri Charrière, it told the story of two convicts confined to several French penal colonies and of the determination of one to escape. The colonies included several camps in French Guiana, and Devil's Island—a patch of rock less than a mile in circumference 10 miles off the Guiana coast. Most striking in *Papillon* were the severe disciplinary procedures for escape attempts and other rule violations: slow starvation; confinement for years at a time in small, dark, vermin-infested cells; or even a short interlude with what Frenchmen called "the widowmaker"—the infamous guillotine.[31]

Many may think of such practices as utterly foreign to American soil, or at least far removed in time from contemporary standards. But only a few short years ago, long after the French penal colonies were abolished, discipline at least as barbaric as the Devil's Island tradition was practiced in the very heart of America.

The Arkansas Prison Scandal

In 1966, Winthrop Rockefeller, grandson of industrialist and philanthropist John D. Rockefeller, was elected governor of Arkansas. As a candidate, he had pledged to eliminate corruption in state government and to hire a professional penologist to reform the state prison system. The following year, the late Thomas O. Murton, a professor of criminology from Southern Illinois University, was put in charge of the Arkansas prisons.

What Murton found was a prison system that had been operating on fear for more than a century.[32] The traditional methods of instilling inmate compliance included beatings, needles under the fingernails, starvation, and floggings with the "hide" — a leather strap 5 inches wide and 5 feet long. At Tucker Prison Farm, there was a contraption known as the "Tucker telephone" used to punish inmates and to extract information:

> The telephone, designed by prison superintendent Jim Bruton, consisted of an electric generator taken from a crank-type telephone and wired in sequence with two dry-cell batteries. An undressed inmate was strapped to the treatment table at Tucker Hospital while electrodes were attached to his big toe and to his penis. The crank was then turned, sending an electrical charge into his body. In "long distance calls" several charges were inflicted — of a duration designed to stop just short of the inmate's fainting. Sometimes the "telephone" operator's skill was defective, and the sustained current not only caused the inmate to lose consciousness but resulted in irreparable damage to his testicles. Some men were literally driven out of their minds.[33]

For more than 50 years, many had boasted that the Arkansas prison system was a symbol of efficiency, for no state appropriations were needed to

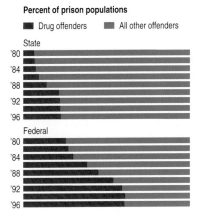

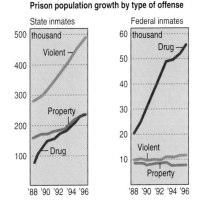

Drugs and Punishment

The war on drugs has changed the profile of prison populations in America, both demographically and in terms of the crimes being punished.

SOURCE: U.S. Department of Justice.

support the convicts. But Murton found that this was so only because of the exploitation of inmate labor. Furthermore, the control of inmates, work assignments, promotion, food rations, bed assignments, visiting privileges, commissary privileges, laundry and clothing procedures, and the very survival of the inmate had been delegated to a select few powerful convicts who operated the prison. To make such a system operable, these "trusties" had been granted many privileges, including graft obtained from all inmate goods and services, freedom to sell liquor and narcotics, to gamble and lend money, to live in squatter shacks outside the prison and spend nights with women, and to profit from the illegal trafficking in prison produce. Thus, there were no traditional custodial officers. Rather, the institutions were run by a powerful structure of convict guards who used bribery and torture to maintain the status quo and to profit from the inmate slavery. In Arkansas's Cummins Prison Farm, it was alleged that inmates had been routinely murdered as punishment for disciplinary infractions and then buried in a remote cow pasture. The total number of these killings was estimated to be more than 100.[34]

The barbaric conditions in the Arkansas prisons came to national attention in January 1968 as a result of Murton's discoveries and efforts at reform. However, for fear that Murton was damaging Arkansas's image with the scandal, he was fired on March 2, 1968, and placed under house arrest. Governor Rockefeller at a press conference the following day simply explained that Murton had been a "poor prison administrator."

In the years following Murton's departure, the Arkansas prisons were in constant turmoil. On several occasions, inmates protesting prison conditions were shot at by prison officials.[35] Explanations for the continuing difficulties focused on racial conflicts and efforts at integration.

When the courts finally listened to the Arkansas prisoners, the savage discipline and inhumane conditions were more fully acknowledged. A federal court decision, **Holt v. Sarver** in 1970,[36] declared the entire Arkansas prison system to be in violation of the Eighth Amendment ban against cruel and unusual punishment (see Exhibit 13.2).

Holt v. *Sarver:* The federal court decision declaring the Arkansas prison system to be in violation of the Eighth Amendment.

Solitary Confinement

Solitary confinement has been variously referred to as "isolation" or "segregation" in "the hole" or in a "strip cell." It is the total separation of an inmate from the general prison population in a special cell of meager size and comfort, combined with the revocation of all prisoner privileges and constitutional rights, and often with a restricted diet or other physical abuse. Placement in "solitary" generally occurs for serious violations of prison regulations, such as escape attempts, forced sexual advances, assaulting prison staff or other inmates, or being excessively troublesome.

As with other aspects of prisoners' rights, prior to the 1960s the courts maintained their hands-off doctrine with respect to inmate complaints concerning isolated confinement. During the past three decades, however, numerous actions concerning the practice have been brought to the courts by both state and federal inmates. Some suits have argued that the very practice of solitary confinement is unconstitutional. The federal courts, however, have flatly rejected this contention.

Despite the courts' unwillingness to ban solitary confinement on constitutional grounds, they have taken a stand on how it can be imposed and administered. Using standards established by the Supreme Court for interpreting what constitutes cruel and unusual punishment,[37] the federal courts have examined the duration of an inmate's confinement, the physical conditions of the cell, the hygienic conditions of the inmate, the exercise allowed, the diet provided, and the nature of the infraction that resulted in punitive isolation.

Exhibit 13.2 **Legal Perspectives on Crime and Justice**
Excerpts From the Court Opinion in *Holt* v. *Sarver*

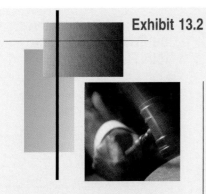

For the ordinary convict a sentence to the Arkansas Penitentiary today amounts to a banishment from civilized society to a dark and evil world completely alien to the free world, a world that is administered by criminals under unwritten rules and customs completely foreign to free world culture.

After long and careful consideration the Court has come to the conclusion that the Fourteenth Amendment prohibits confinement under the conditions that have been described and that the Arkansas penitentiary system as it exists today, particularly at Cummins, is unconstitutional.

Such confinement is inherently dangerous. A convict, however cooperative and inoffensive he may be, has no assurance whatever that he will not be killed, seriously injured, or sexually abused. Under the present system the state cannot protect him. Apart from physical danger, confinement in the penitentiary involves living under degrading and disgusting conditions. This Court has no

patience with those who still say, even when they ought to know better, that to change those conditions will convert the prison into a country club; the Court has not heard any of those people volunteer to spend a few days and nights at the penitentiary incognito.

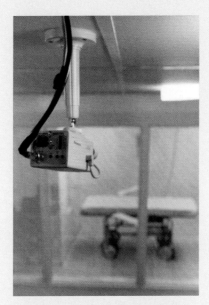

A television camera mounted on the ceiling of the witness room is pointed toward the death chamber at Cummins Prison in Varner, Ark. The camera is intended to provide live images of executions to the warden's office.

The peril and degradation to which Arkansas convicts are subjected daily are aggravated by the fact that the treatment which a convict may expect to receive depends not at all upon the gravity of his offense or the length of his term. In point of fact, a man sentenced to life imprisonment for first-degree murder and who has a long criminal record may expect to fare better than a country boy with no serious record who is sentenced to two years for stealing a pig.

It is one thing for the State to send a man to the penitentiary as a punishment for crime. It is another thing for the State to delegate the governance of him to other convicts and to do nothing meaningful for his safety, well-being, and possible rehabilitation. It is one thing for the State not to pay a convict for his labor; it is something else to subject him to a situation in which he has to sell his blood to obtain money to pay for his own safety, or for adequate food, or for access to needed medical attention.

However constitutionally tolerable the Arkansas system may have been in former years, it simply will not do today as the twentieth century goes into its eighth decade.

SOURCE: *Holt* v. *Sarver*, 309 F. Supp. 362 (E.D. Ark. 1970).

The courts have been reluctant, however, to establish rigid criteria for deciding on the unconstitutionality of solitary confinement. In one case, for example, the "strip cells" in California's Soledad Prison were deemed "cruel and unusual" due to their poor sanitary conditions.[38] In another, by contrast, since the inmate was not denied the minimum necessities of food, water, sleep, exercise, toilet facilities, and human contact, a federal court held that the deprivation of a comb, pillow, toothbrush, and toothpaste for 7 to 10 days in a segregation cell with continuous lights, a few mice and roaches, and no reading material was not unconstitutional.[39] Furthermore, although the stereotyped solitary confinement meal of "bread and water" has been disapproved of by the courts,[40] it has been deemed satisfactory when supplemented by a full meal every third day.[41]

Exhibit 13.3 | **Historical Perspectives on Crime and Justice**
Old Red Hannah

John Smith, colored, house breaking, twenty lashes.

John Brown, horse stealing, twenty lashes and one hour in the pillory.

—*Delawarean,* May 27, 1876

The semiannual whipping and pillorying of criminals convicted at the present term of the court, for theft and other crimes, took place on Saturday. The attendance was small, probably not exceeding one hundred people, most of whom were boys. The following are the names of the "candidates," and the offenses for which they were sentenced:

Joseph Derias, colored, horse stealing, twenty lashes, one hour in the pillory.

Scott Wilson, larceny of clothing, twenty lashes.

John Carpenter, colored, four cases of larceny (ice cream freezers, carriage reins, and a cow). He received ten lashes in each case.

John Conner, larceny of tomatoes, five lashes.

For centuries, the whipping post was a conspicuous part of Delaware's penal tradition. The first person to suffer the sanction was Robert Hutchinson, convicted of petty theft and sentenced to 39 lashes on June 3, 1679. Each town and county had its own whipping post, but the one that earned a prominent place in the annals of American corrections was the notorious "Red Hannah." As the Wilmington *Journal Every Evening* once described it:

In days gone by, the whipping post down in Kent County stood out brazenly in the open courtyard of the county jail not far from the old state house. It looked like an old-time octagonal pump without a handle. It had a slit near the top of it in which the equally old-time pillory boards might be inserted

The Lash

Whipping (or flogging) has been a common sanction in most Western cultures. In American tradition, it was used as a punishment for crimes and for preserving discipline in domestic, military, and academic environments. And curiously, although whipping has been viewed by most as uncivilized brutality, its final abolition in American penal practice has been only recent. In Delaware, for example, whipping was a constitutionally permissible punishment for specified crimes from the seventeenth through most of the twentieth century (see Exhibit 13.3). Furthermore, in many jurisdictions, flogging was a form of convict discipline.

The end of whipping as an official means of enforcing prison rules and regulations evolved from an Arkansas case, ***Jackson v. Bishop***,[42] decided by a federal circuit court in 1968. In the Arkansas prison system, whipping was the primary disciplinary measure. Facilities for segregation and solitary confinement were limited, and inmates had few privileges that could be withheld from them as punishment. Prison regulations, furthermore, allowed whipping

Jackson v. Bishop: The federal court decision declaring that whipping is in violation of the eighth Amendment.

when needed for punitive use. There also were iron shackles for holding the prisoners while they were being whipped. That whipping post was painted red from top to bottom. Negro residents bestowed upon it the name of "Red Hannah." Of any prisoner who had been whipped at the post it was said, "He has hugged Red Hannah!"

Red Hannah was a survivor. Despite public and local congressional pressure to ban whipping in the state, during the second half of the twentieth century, almost 300 years after Robert Hutchinson received his 39 lashes, old Red Hannah was still very much alive.

In 1963, the statutes that permitted whipping were challenged in the Delaware Supreme Court. The case was *State* v. *Cannon,* and the presiding judge held that the use of flogging to punish certain crimes did *not* violate either state or federal bans on cruel and unusual punishment. However, Red Hannah was ultimately laid to rest in 1973, when the statute authorizing the use of the lash was finally repealed by the Delaware legislature. Still, every 2 years or so a

group of 10 to 15 Delaware legislators will introduce a bill to bring back the whipping post. The most recent effort was in 1997.

The Whipping Post and Pillory at New Castle, Delaware.

SOURCES: Robert G. Caldwell, *Red Hannah: Delaware's Whipping Post* (Philadelphia: University of Pennsylvania Press, 1947); *Delawarean,* May 27, 1876, p. 3; *Journal Every Evening,* August 2, 1938, p. 8; *State* v. *Cannon,* 55 Del. 587 (1963).

for such infractions as homosexuality, agitation, insubordination, making or concealing weapons, participating in or inciting a riot, and refusing to work when medically able to do so. Using the criteria of "broad and idealistic concepts of dignity, civilized standards, humanity, and decency," the court declared whipping to be a violation of the Eighth Amendment ban on cruel and unusual punishment.

Prison Disciplinary Proceedings

Throughout the history of corrections, disciplinary actions against prison inmates have often been arbitrary administrative operations controlled solely by wardens, their deputies, or other custodial personnel. Without a formal hearing, and at the discretion of an institutional officer, inmates could be placed in solitary confinement, lose some or all of their privileges, or be deprived of good-time credits. Even in those correctional settings where disciplinary hearing committees were convened to review serious infractions of prison regulations, decisions could be made entirely on the basis of a custodial officer's testimony. Evidence was generally not required, prisoners were rarely permitted to speak in their own behalf, and the rules of due process were typically ignored. When the prisoners' rights movement first brought these practices to the attention of the federal courts during the 1960s, the due process clauses of the Fifth and Fourteenth Amendments were applied sparingly and only in specific circumstances. The position of the courts seemed to be that due process should prevent only "capricious" or "arbitrary" actions by prison administrators.

During the 1970s, however, the courts began to focus on the specific procedures used in prison disciplinary proceedings, seeking to resolve the wider issue of due process requirements. The principal case was ***Wolff v. McDonnell***,[43] decided by the U.S. Supreme Court in 1974. The ruling in *Wolff* held the following:

1. Advance written notice of the charges against an inmate must be provided to him at least 24 hours prior to his appearance before the prison hearing committee.

2. There must be a written statement by the fact finders as to the evidence relied upon and the reasons for the disciplinary action.

3. The prisoner should be allowed to call witnesses and present documentary evidence in his defense, providing such actions would cause no undue hazards to institutional safety or correctional goals.

4. The inmate must be permitted representation by a counsel substitute (a fellow inmate or staff member) when the prisoner is illiterate or when the complexity of the case goes beyond the capabilities of the person being charged.

5. The hearing committee must be impartial (suggesting that those involved in any of the events leading up to the hearing—such as the charging or investigating parties—may not serve as members of the committee).

In establishing these requirements, the full spectrum of due process was *not* extended. The Court made it clear that neither retained or appointed counsel, nor the right to confrontation and cross-examination, were constitutionally required. The decision stressed some additional points. First, the ruling in *Wolff* did not apply retroactively. Second, in writing the Court's opinion, Justice White emphasized that the limitations on due process imposed by the decision were "not graven in stone"; future changes in circumstances could require further "consideration and reflection" of the Court. Third, the due process requirements set forth applied only to proceedings that could result in solitary confinement and the loss of good time. Left unresolved were the procedures to be observed if other penalties were to be imposed.

In recent years, the High Court has not gone much beyond *Wolff* in protecting inmates' rights in prison disciplinary proceedings. A case in point is *Superintendent, Massachusetts Correctional Institute at Walpole* v. *Hill*,[44] decided in 1985. As noted earlier, *Wolff* set forth certain safeguards that must be provided when a disciplinary hearing may result in the loss of good-time credits, but that ruling did not require either judicial review or a specific quantum of evidence to support a disciplinary board's decision. The matter of evidence was the issue addressed in *Hill*, and here the Court ruled that only "some evidence" was necessary. In the *Hill* case, the evidence consisted of a correctional officer's report that he had heard a commotion, discovered an inmate who had apparently been assaulted, observed three other inmates, including those in this case, fleeing down an enclosed walkway, and noticed no other

---

***Wolff* v. *McDonnell*:** The Supreme Court ruling that the due process clause of the Fourteenth Amendment protects, in part, state prisoners facing loss of good-time credit or punitive confinement.

Question: Exactly how much evidence is *indeed* required by the due process clause to support a prison disciplinary hearing board's finding of guilt? Proof beyond a reasonable doubt? Clear and convincing evidence? Substantial evidence? A preponderance of evidence?

Answer: In *Superintendent, Massachusetts Correctional Institute at Walpole* v. *Hill*, the Supreme Court ruled that such a decision will pass constitutional muster if there is "some evidence" to support the board's conclusions.

inmates were in the area. Justice Sandra Day O'Connor, in delivering the Court's opinion, emphasized that although the evidence presented in the disciplinary proceeding was "meager," it was nevertheless sufficient to meet due process requirements.

THE CONDITIONS OF INCARCERATION

The Arkansas prison scandal in 1968 pointed to many problems within that state's correctional system. Not only was there corruption and brutality, but, as a federal court noted, there was also confinement under degrading and disgusting conditions. Although Arkansas during the 1960s may have been unique in its sanctioned administration by convicts under a system of unwritten rules, its general prison conditions were not an isolated phenomenon. Similar problems of overcrowding and extreme physical danger were commonplace all across the nation.

In general, the courts have held that most aspects of prison life are dictated by the needs of security and discipline, thus giving custodial authorities wide discretion in their regulation of inmate comforts. At the same time, however, the federal courts have monitored some conditions of confinement, taking the position that while offenders are sent to prison for punishment, prison should not impose extra punishments of a barbaric and uncivilized nature. For example, prison overcrowding itself has not been declared unconstitutional. Yet, as was pointed out in *Costello* v. *Wainwright* in 1975,[45] overcrowding can be a factor, when combined with other conditions, in declaring the circumstances of incarceration to be in violation of the Constitution. Thus, the federal courts have indicated that it is their duty to protect inmates from conditions of confinement that serve to add punitive measures

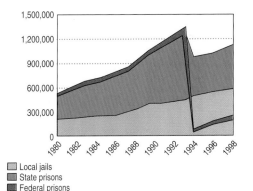

☐ Local jails
☐ State prisons
■ Federal prisons

Number of Inmates in Custody, 1980–1998

SOURCE: Bureau of Justice Statistics, 1998.

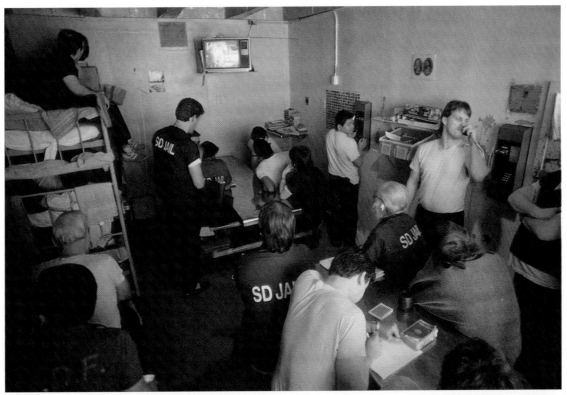

Overcrowding at a San Diego jail.

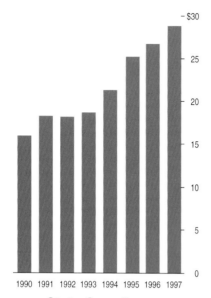

State Spending on Corrections in the U.S.

Includes capital expenditures

SOURCE: National Association of State Budget Officers.

Ruiz v. Estelle: The federal court decision declaring the Texas prison system to be unconstitutional.

to those already meted out by a sentencing court. The courts have also ruled, as in the 1974 case of *People* v. *Lovercamp*,[46] that the situations and circumstances some inmates face inside prison walls may serve as a defense for the crime of escape.

The Texas Prison Suit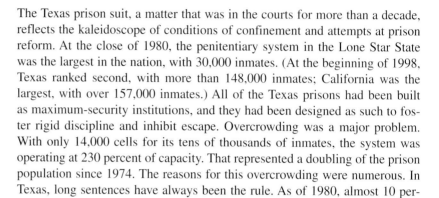

The Texas prison suit, a matter that was in the courts for more than a decade, reflects the kaleidoscope of conditions of confinement and attempts at prison reform. At the close of 1980, the penitentiary system in the Lone Star State was the largest in the nation, with 30,000 inmates. (At the beginning of 1998, Texas ranked second, with more than 148,000 inmates; California was the largest, with over 157,000 inmates.) All of the Texas prisons had been built as maximum-security institutions, and they had been designed as such to foster rigid discipline and inhibit escape. Overcrowding was a major problem. With only 14,000 cells for its tens of thousands of inmates, the system was operating at 230 percent of capacity. That represented a doubling of the prison population since 1974. The reasons for this overcrowding were numerous. In Texas, long sentences have always been the rule. As of 1980, almost 10 percent of the inmates were serving life sentences; an additional 45 percent had terms of 10 years or more. Since 1977, the Texas legislature has passed several laws ordering mandatory sentences for a variety of offenses and requiring inmates convicted of certain crimes to serve at least one-third of their terms before becoming eligible for parole.

Overcrowding was not the only problem in the Texas prison system; there was also violence. During 1981, 11 prisoners were slain by fellow inmates, and during one 7-day period, more than 70 inmates and correctional officers were injured in a series of altercations. Two factors contributing to this violence were understaffing and the use of prisoners in supervisory roles and as building tenders, turnkeys, and counters. A Texas statute specifically prohibited the use of inmates in such administrative and supervisory capacities, but it was generally ignored by institutional officials. Furthermore, and ironically, for a long time these inmate supervisors *were permitted to carry weapons*— weapons that would have been denied them outside the prison walls.[47]

In June 1972, ***Ruiz* v. *Estelle*** was instituted as a class action suit in behalf of all past, present, and future Texas Department of Corrections inmates.[48] After many years of discovery efforts, a trial finally began on October 2, 1978. At its conclusion, the court had heard 349 witnesses and had received 1,565 exhibits into evidence. The case involved issues of overcrowding, inmate security, and numerous prison services. Presiding over the case was federal judge William Wayne Justice.

In 1980, Judge Justice declared the Texas prison system to be unconstitutional. The court ordered the addition of new facilities to alleviate overcrowding; the abolition of arrangements that placed some prisoners in charge of others; the placement of any new prisons near urban areas of 200,000 population; changes in the staff-to-inmate ratio; the limiting of inmate populations; an adherence to the due process rights guaranteed by *Wolff*; and improved medical, educational, occupational, and mental health services.

Despite the ruling in *Ruiz*, many Texas officials maintained that their prison system was the best in the nation, and the Texas Department of Corrections sought relief in the U.S. court of appeals on the argument that the reforms ordered by Judge Justice were beyond the jurisdiction of his court and should not be required. In 1982, the court of appeals upheld the lower court order,[49] but the reforms were not immediately forthcoming. By 1983, conditions in the Texas system had gotten worse, and there were allegations of corruption, graft, and mismanagement.

Shakedown in a Texas prison.

By the 1990s, however, some dramatic changes had become evident. At the close of 1992, Judge Justice approved a settlement between the state and its inmates. As part of the settlement, Texas officials agreed to monitor inmate population levels and take steps to relieve overcrowding—by building more prisons and increasing capacity in others.[50] Texas also implemented a wide range of treatment alternatives for drug-involved offenders, and established in-prison therapeutic communities for thousands of inmates.[51]

The New Mexico Inmate Massacre

In 1971, the Attica riot distinguished itself as the bloodiest 1-day encounter between Americans since the Civil War. On February 1, 1980, New Mexico State Penitentiary distinguished itself for having the most gruesome prison riot in U.S. history. Nearly a thousand inmates seized the institution and took 15 correctional officers as hostages. Prisoners threatened to kill all of the captives if state officials refused to meet their demands for improved conditions.[52]

The New Mexico institution, built in 1957 for 850 convicts, had been housing almost 1,200. A 1977 lawsuit by inmates described the prison as unsanitary and lacking medical facilities, and an investigation in 1979 found the facility to be dangerously understaffed and the correctional officers poorly

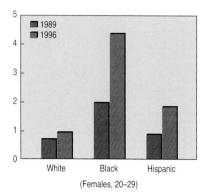

(Females, 20–29)

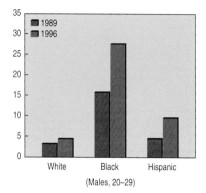

(Males, 20–29)

Percentage of Americans Under Control of the Criminal Justice System,* 1989 and 1996

*In prison or jail, or on probation or parole.

SOURCE: The Sentencing Project.

Lockdown: A situation in which inmates are confined to their cells around the clock—denied exercise, work, recreation, and visits.

trained. When the riot broke out, only 18 officers were on duty. Inmates looted the prison hospital for drugs and set fires that gutted all five cell blocks. They had essentially two demands: relief of overcrowded conditions and an end to harassment by guards. The prison was quickly retaken by police and the National Guard, but not before many inmates had died from drug overdoses, burns, and smoke inhalation.

But the New Mexico incident was not just another prison riot. It was unmatched in savagery in terms of the nature of inmate violence. Investigators found that during the riot, there had been a seven-man inmate execution squad to exact revenge on convict informers. One prisoner was beheaded; another was found with a metal rod driven through his head; several had their arms and legs cut off or their eyes gouged out; and still others were charred by blowtorches or beaten beyond recognition.[53] In all, 33 fellow prisoners were brutally slain.

In the wake of the holocaust, numerous reforms were proposed, but several years later, the New Mexico State Penitentiary appeared to be no less a slaughterhouse. The trials of those charged with the killings inspired further bloodshed. As one prison official explained:

> Everybody is a potential witness against everybody else. No one knows who will testify against them, and that breeds tension.[54]

From Texas and New Mexico to Attica and Beyond

Despite federal court intervention and concerted plans for change, conditions in many prisons across the nation have remained unconstitutional and in a constant state of chaos. In the aftermath of the riot at Attica Correctional Facility in 1971, a number of reforms were proposed and implemented. But as the years passed, conditions there began to deteriorate again. By the early 1980s, Attica had become overcrowded; it had absorbed inmates from two state hospitals for the criminally insane; most of the population were violent offenders; and the number of assaults on correctional officers was steadily increasing. In September 1981, just a few days before the tenth anniversary of the riot, one officer who had been on duty during the 1971 rebellion commented that tensions at Attica once again were reaching the boiling point. "We have all the ingredients for a disaster here," he remarked. Another officer said, "This place could go right now."[55] Throughout the 1990s, the same comments were being heard.

While Attica has not again exploded, it has undergone a series of disturbances and strikes the likes of which might be called "prison riots in slow-motion." In addition, there have been scores of prison disturbances every year in federal and state penitentiaries throughout the nation. At the same time, a number of institutions have been experiencing lengthy **lockdowns,** situations in which inmates are confined to their cells around the clock—denied exercise, work, recreation, and visits. Lockdown status typically results from inmate violence, and is intended to separate prisoners from one another in an effort to prevent further violence.

The reasons for the numerous riots and other disturbances are twofold. The conditions of confinement, combined with the very fact of confinement, produce anger, frustration, and emotions that are difficult to control. Furthermore, penitentiaries are dangerous places. They contain many predatory felons, and it is often a matter of survival of the fittest. Seeking protection and status, many inmates join gangs. But the very presence of gangs within prison walls means additional violence, resulting from struggles over power, turf, and contraband.

REFORM VERSUS LAW AND ORDER

While the 1960s ushered in the era of prisoners' rights and the 1970s witnessed agitation for prison reform, calls for "law and order" in the 1980s and 1990s brought into focus a dilemma for American corrections that had been evolving for decades. Initially, civil libertarians had agitated for the rights of prison inmates. The federal courts responded by casting aside the hands-off doctrine and strengthening mechanisms for inmates in their attempts to file suits against their keepers. Prisoners were no longer the complete slaves of the state, and they slowly won significant victories with respect to legal and medical services, religious expression, access to the media, and their general treatment inside penitentiary walls. Moreover, the courts began to take a more balanced look at the conditions of incarceration. The result was that correctional systems in most jurisdictions were declared unconstitutional and ordered to reform.

At the same time, however, a slow erosion of the rights of the accused, combined with calls for strict and certain punishment of criminal offenders, led to an unprecedented escalation in the size of prison populations. The ultimate consequence was an American corrections system that, while in the throes of reform, deteriorated at a more rapid rate.

Added to this state of affairs were indications that there was an emergent trend aimed at limiting the rights of prisoners. In 1979 the Supreme Court handed down its ruling in *Bell* v. *Wolfish,*[56] a decision upholding the constitutionality of "double-bunking," broad room search powers, frequent body cavity searches, and other restrictions imposed on federal pretrial detainees on the ground that such restrictions were rational responses to legitimate security concerns. Writing for the majority, Justice William H. Rehnquist commented that he did not see "some sort of 'one man, one cell' principle lurking in the Due Process Clause of the Fifth Amendment." The High Court upheld the double-bunking, in part, on the ground that pretrial detainees would rarely remain incarcerated for more than 60 days.

Bell v. *Wolfish*

Then there was ***Rhodes*** v. ***Chapman,***[57] decided by the Supreme Court in 1981. The suit, filed in 1975, came from Kelly Chapman, an armed robber being held at the Southern Ohio Correctional Facility in Lucasville. Chapman argued that the one-man cell he shared with another prisoner gave him only 32 square feet of personal living space, an area approximately 4 feet wide and 8 feet long. That was less, he contended, than Ohio law required for 5-week-old calves in feed lots. The district court agreed that the double-celling violated the Eighth Amendment and subsequently ordered Lucasville to reduce its inmate population. Governor James Rhodes of Ohio filed an appeal for the state, but the lower federal court's decision was affirmed by the U.S. court of appeals.

Rhodes v. ***Chapman:*** The Supreme Court ruling that cell overcrowding, in and of itself, is neither cruel nor unusual.

In an 8-to-1 decision, the Supreme Court reversed the lower court ruling, holding that the double-celling was *not* unconstitutional at the Ohio prison. The court was not claiming that double-celling was itself constitutional, but rather, that given the nature of other services and conditions at the institution, the cell overcrowding was neither "cruel and unusual" nor the cause of physical or mental injury. Thus, as Justice Brennan pointed out, the Court had used the "totality of circumstances" test and found the double-celling to be constitutional. Since the original ruling, *Rhodes* v. *Chapman* has resulted in a reduction—but not a drastic reduction—in the number of cases in which prisoners successfully challenged overcrowding on Eighth Amendment grounds.

In ***Hudson*** v. ***Palmer,***[58] decided by the Supreme Court in 1984, it was made clear that prison inmates had little, if any, privacy rights. On September 16, 1981, Ted S. Hudson, an officer at the Bland Correctional Center at

Hudson v. ***Palmer:*** The Supreme Court ruling that a prisoner has no reasonable expectation of privacy in his prison cell entitling him to Fourth Amendment protection.

Bland, Virginia, along with a fellow officer, conducted a shakedown search of inmate Russel Palmer's prison locker and cell. Looking for contraband, the officers discovered a ripped pillowcase in a trash can near Palmer's cell bunk. Charges were instituted against Palmer for destroying state property, and he was ordered to reimburse the state for the material destroyed.

In petitioning the U.S. district court, Palmer asserted that Hudson had intentionally destroyed letters from his wife, pictures of his children, legal papers, and other noncontraband items. He also claimed that the search of his cell and the destruction of the noncontraband items were violations of his Fourth Amendment rights. The High Court ruled that a prisoner has no reasonable expectation of privacy in his prison cell entitling him to the protection of the Fourth Amendment against unreasonable searches. The Court noted that it would be impossible to accomplish the prison objectives of preventing the introduction of weapons, drugs, and other contraband into the premises if inmates retained a right of privacy in their cells.

Wilson v. Seiter: The Supreme Court ruling that an inmate alleging that the conditions of his confinement violate the Eighth Amendment's prohibition against cruel and unusual punishment must show deliberate indifference on the part of the responsible prison officials.

The evisceration of the rights of prisoners continued into the 1990s. A key case in this behalf was **Wilson v. Seiter,**[59] decided in 1991. In *Seiter,* the Supreme Court ruled that prisoners filing lawsuits over inhumane living conditions must show not only that conditions are so deplorable as to violate the Constitution, but also that prison officials have acted with *"deliberate indifference" to basic human needs.* This standard of "deliberate indifference" previously applied only in medical care cases, as ordered by *Estelle* v. *Gamble* in 1976. The *Seiter* decision made it considerably more difficult for prisoners to prevail in Eighth Amendment lawsuits.

It would be difficult to predict how correctional systems will fully deal with prison overcrowding and the other problematic conditions of incarceration. Some jurisdictions have instituted procedures for early parole, while others have placed a portion of their excess prisoners in local jails. But these are only temporary measures. Moreover, the early paroling of convicted offenders is unpopular with the public; the placement of prison inmates in local facilities further strains the already excessive jail populations; and neither approach addresses the basic need for better institutional conditions. A number of states and the federal system have allocated funds for new prison construction. But correctional facilities are costly to build, equip, and properly staff; the prison population continues to expand; and the funding for new institutions must come from increased taxation. Yet although citizens continue to ask for more swift and certain punishment for criminal offenders, they tend to be unwilling to bear the financial and social burden for new prison construction. As both taxpayers and the victims of crime, they feel that they would be paying twice for the misbehavior of lawbreakers.

Privatization of corrections: The construction, staffing, and operation of prisons by private industry for profit.

One approach to the problem has been the **privatization of corrections**—the construction, staffing, and operation of prisons by private industry, for profit. Such an approach might be highly cost-effective, but there has been strong opposition to the privatization model. Opponents raise a variety of moral, legal, and ethical questions, including whether it is appropriate for the state to hand over incarceration to a profit-making organization, how liability and disciplinary issues will be handled, and whether private firms will end up lobbying for more and longer prison sentences instead of alternatives to incarceration.[60] Yet despite the debate, the private prison movement gained considerable ground during the 1990s. Private prisons began in Florida in 1982, and by the late 1990s the federal government, 32 states, Puerto Rico, and the District of Columbia are authorized to contract for private corrections. Moreover, 19 private companies had contracts to operate almost 100 secure adult facilities in the United States, including medium- and maximum-security prisons, designed for more than 50,000 prisoners.

Op-Ed

What about the prison "islands" and "trust territories" suggested by candidate Farer in the opening paragraphs of this chapter? Could they be like the Botany Bay and Norfolk Island colonies, and could they work?

To begin with, conditions were so brutal and inhumane at the early colonies that, as Judge John V. Barry of Melbourne commented many years ago:

> Men who were reprieved wept with sorrow that they had to go on living, and those who were doomed to die thanked God for the release that was theirs.

One could readily argue that the conditions and brutalities at Botany Bay and the other penal settlements would not recur in Farer's trust terri-Consider, for example, some of the occurrences at our nation's prisons. Correctional institutions are very violent places. Prisoners assault and kill one another. There is rape and racial unrest. There is drug abuse. The strong prey upon the weak, and there are rivalries and jealousies. Let us not forget the Arkansas prison scandal of the 1960s, in which convicts were executed by fellow inmate-guards. Let us not forget the massacre at the New Mexico State Penitentiary in 1980, where prisoners systematically beheaded, incinerated, and otherwise butchered dozens of fellow inmates. Furthermore, an unsupervised penal colony would quickly become a well-armed camp, with weapons fashioned from ordinary tools and equipment.

Taking the discussion one step further, aside from whether or not penal colonies could work is the question of *where* the colonies could be established. Where indeed? How about Hawaii? If the locals wouldn't mind moving to the mainland, it might be ideal. It is far removed from the continental United States, the weather is excellent, recreational opportunities are abundant, the soil is rich and fertile, and the islands are large enough to house the nation's entire penitentiary population. If that could not be worked out, surely authorities could identify other possible locations. At the very least, there are likely few Americans who would oppose the establishment of penal colonies at such locations as Gatlinburg, Tennessee; Marcus Hook, Pennsylvania; Burnt Fly Bog, New Jersey; or one of the many other locations in the U.S. with little or no socially redeeming value.

Exhibit 13.4 **Careers in Justice**
Jailhouse Lawyers and the Prison Law Project

Jailhouse lawyers are inmates claiming to have some legal knowledge, who counsel and assist other inmates in the preparation of legal documents such as *habeas corpus,* pleadings, and appeals to higher courts. Although you have to be an inmate to be a jailhouse lawyer, others can work in their behalf. The Prison Law Project of the National Lawyers Guild is one of the mechanisms available to assist jailhouse lawyers.

In 1971, the National Lawyers Guild—a New York City human rights advocacy group composed of attorneys, legal workers, and law students—began to recognize the role played by jailhouse lawyers in providing legal services to prisoners. Since then, members of the guild who participate in its Prison Law Project provide a variety of services, including these:

- Assisting jailhouse lawyers in their efforts to provide quality legal services to inmates
- Encouraging prisoners to educate themselves regarding the law, to develop legal skills, and to use their knowledge and skills to assist their fellow prisoners in advancing their legal interests

- Producing and distributing educational materials concerning the substantive law of prisoners' rights; procedures and strategies for litigation, politics of law, society, and incarceration; and related topics
- Advocating for the adoption of laws, regulations, and policies that encourage and accommodate the work of jailhouse lawyers
- Providing legal services, support, and assistance to jailhouse lawyers and other prisoners
- Educating the general public regarding prison and criminal law issues

SOURCE: National Lawyers Guild.

SUMMARY

For the better part of U.S. history, prisoners were considered "slaves" of the state. Upon conviction, defendants experienced "civil death." The conditions in prison were generally brutal, and inmates had no recourse. The Supreme Court, furthermore, maintained a hands-off doctrine regarding correctional matters, refusing even to consider inmates' complaints.

The Constitution guarantees that all individuals confined to correctional institutions under state or federal authority have the right to file *habeas corpus* petitions with the courts to challenge the lawfulness of their confinement. It was not until 1944 in *Coffin* v. *Reichard,* however, that inmates could use *habeas corpus* petitions to challenge anything other than the legality of their confinement. The prisoners' rights movement began in 1961 when the High Court ruled in *Monroe* v. *Pape* that the long-dormant Section 1983 of the Civil Rights Act of 1871 was an appropriate mechanism for challenging the constitutionality of the conditions of prison life. Through

a rush of petitions to the federal courts, convicts secured favorable decisions regarding legal services, the use of jailhouse lawyers, religious expression, media and mail services, medical programs, rehabilitative services, disciplinary proceedings, and the use of solitary confinement and corporal punishment.

During this period of prisoners' rights activity, however, many institutions across the nation continued to maintain archaic conditions. In the late 1960s, the Arkansas prison scandal erupted, and it demonstrated that, as stated in a federal court's opinion in *Holt* v. *Sarver,* "a sentence to the Arkansas Penitentiary today amounts to a banishment from civilized society." In 1971, news from New York's Attica Prison reached the press around the world. Attica's inmates revolted because of the conditions of incarceration, and the siege to recover the prison resulted in the deaths of scores of inmates and correctional officers. In 1980, New Mexico State Prison distinguished itself for having the most gruesome riot in U.S.

history. A year later, the entire Texas prison system was declared unconstitutional.

Throughout the 1990s, riots continued to erupt in the nation's prisons and jails, though none gained the notoriety of Attica or New Mexico. Nevertheless, riots continue to present a major problem to corrections officials—one that is not easily dealt with, as the conditions of overcrowding continue to overwhelm institutional capacities. The persistent problems across the nation continue to be overcrowding, inadequate programming, and a general lack of inmate safety. One solution that has gained considerable popularity among lawmakers in the 1990s has been the somewhat controversial privatization of corrections.

KEY TERMS

civil death **359**

Estelle v. *Gamble* **362**

habeas corpus **355**

hands-off doctrine **350**

Holt v. *Sarver* **364**

Hudson v. *Palmer* **373**

Jackson v. *Bishop* **366**

Johnson v. *Avery* **357**

Jones v. *North Carolina Prisoners' Labor Union* **362**

lockdown **372**

Monroe v. *Pape* **355**

privatization of corrections **374**

Procunier v. *Martinez* **361**

Rhodes v. *Chapman* **373**

Ruiz v. *Estelle* **370**

Section 1983 **355**

Thornburg v. *Abbott* **361**

Wilson v. *Seiter* **374**

Wolff v. *McDonnell* **368**

QUESTIONS FOR DISCUSSION

1. How are inmates' rights to proper and adequate medical care protected by the Constitution?

2. Discuss the constitutional debate over smoking in prisons and jails. What is your point of view?

3. Should prisoners have any rights at all?

MEDIA RESOURCES

1. **"Supermax" Prisons.** A recent discussion of the problems of "supermax" prisons can be found in Spencer P. M. Harrington, "Caging the Crazy: 'Supermax' Confinement Under Attack," *The Humanist* 57 (January–February 1997): 14–20.

2. **Prison Conditions in Hong Kong.** Human Rights Watch has prepared a detailed report on numerous phases of prison organization and conditions in Hong Kong. (Web address: http://www.hrw.org/research/hongkong/hk-cov.htm)

3. **Prison Conditions on Video.** There are two films available on video that present deplorable prison conditions. The first is *Brubaker* (132 minutes), 1980; based on the Arkansas prison scandal; with Robert Redford, Morgan Freeman, and Yaphet Kotto. Another is *Papillon* (150 minutes), 1973; based on Henri Charrière's attempts to escape from Devil's Island; with Steve McQueen, Dustin Hoffman, and Anthony Zerbe.

4. **Prisoners' Rights.** A good review article on the topic is Fred Cohen, "The Law of Prisoners' Rights," *Criminal Law Review* 24 (July–August 1988): 321–349.

5. **Attica.** The details of the riot at Attica Prison appear in Tom Wicker, *A Time to Die* (New York: Ballantine, 1975).

NOTES

1. From James A. Inciardi, "From Botany Bay to Burnt Fly Bog," *Transaction*, August 1982, pp. 12–14.

2. *Ruffin* v. *Commonwealth*, 62 Va. (21 Gratt.) 790, 796 (1871).

3. *United States ex rel. Gereau* v. *Henderson*, 526 F. 2d 889 (1976). For a history of the hands-off doctrine, see Kenneth C. Haas, "Judicial Politics and Correctional Reform: An Analysis of the Decline of the

Hands-Off Doctrine," *Detroit College of Law Review* (Winter 1977–1978): 795–831.

4. *Attica: The Official Report of the New York State Special Commission on Attica* (New York: Bantam, 1972), pp. 3–15.

5. See Tom Wicker, *A Time to Die* (New York: Ballantine, 1975).

6. National Advisory Commission on Criminal Justice Standards and Goals, *Corrections* (Washington, D.C.: U.S. Government Printing Office, 1973), p. 18.

7. David A. Jones, *The Law of Criminal Procedure* (Boston: Little, Brown, 1981), p. 574.

8. *Coffin* v. *Reichard,* 143 F.2d 443 (1944).

9. See Kenneth C. Haas, "The Comparative Study of State and Federal Judicial Behavior Revisited," *Journal of Politics* 44 (August 1982): 729–739.

10. *Monroe* v. *Pape,* 365 U.S. 167 (1961).

11. *Cooper* v. *Pate,* 378 U.S. 546 (1964).

12. *Preiser* v. *Rodriquez,* 411 U.S. 475 (1973).

13. *Ex parte Hull,* 312 U.S. 546 (1941).

14. *Johnson* v. *Avery,* 393 U.S. 483 (1969).

15. Cited by Kenneth C. Haas and Anthony Champagne, "The Impact of *Johnson* v. *Avery* on Prison Administration," *Tennessee Law Review* 43 (Winter 1976–1977): 275.

16. *Younger* v. *Gilmore,* 404 U.S. 15 (1971); *Wolff* v. *McDonnell,* 418 U.S. 539 (1974); *Procunier* v. *Martinez,* 416 U.S. 396 (1974); *Bounds* v. *Smith,* 430 U.S. 817 (1977).

17. Kenneth C. Haas and Geoffrey P. Alpert, "American Prisoners and the Right of Access to the Courts," in *The American Prison: Issues in Research and Policy,* ed. Lynne Goodstein and Doris MacKenzie (New York: Plenum, 1989), pp. 68–72.

18. *Fulwood* v. *Clemmer,* 206 F. Supp. 370 (D.C. Cir. 1962).

19. *Jones* v. *Willingham,* 248 F. Supp. 791 (D. Kan. 1965); *Cooke* v. *Tramburg,* 43 N.J. 514, 205 A.2d 889 (1964).

20. *Cruz* v. *Beto,* 405 U.S. 319 (1972).

21. *Childs* v. *Duckworth,* CA 7, 33 CrL 2120 (1983).

22. *Wolff* v. *McDonnell,* 418 U.S. 539 (1974); *Procunier* v. *Martinez,* 416 U.S. 396 (1974).

23. *Thornburgh* v. *Abbott,* 109 S. Ct. 1874 (1989).

24. *O'Connor* v. *Donaldson,* 422 U.S. 563 (1975); *Wilson* v. *Kelley,* 294 F. Supp. 1005 (N.D. Ga. 1968); *Padgett* v. *Stein,* 406 F. Supp. 287 (M.D. Pa. 1976).

25. *Knecht* v. *Gillman,* 488 F.2d 1136 (8th Cir. 1973).

26. *Rutherford* v. *Hutto,* 377 F. Supp. 268 (E.D. Ark. 1974); *Jackson* v. *McLemore,* 523 F.2d 838 (8th Cir. 1975).

27. *Washington* v. *Harper,* 110 S. Ct. 1029 (1990).

28. *Estelle* v. *Gamble,* 429 U.S. 97 (1976).

29. Barbara B. Knight and Stephen T. Early, *Prisoners'*

Rights in America (Chicago: Nelson-Hall, 1986). p. 113.

30. *Jones* v. *North Carolina Prisoners' Labor Union,* 433 U.S. 119 (1977).

31. For further study of Devil's Island and the other French penal colonies, see George J. Seaton, *Isle of the Damned* (New York: Farrar, 1951); Aage Krarup-Nielson, *Hell Beyond the Seas* (New York: Dutton, 1940); Mrs. Blair Niles, *Condemned to Devil's Island* (London: Jonathan Cape, 1928).

32. Tom Murton, "Too Good for Arkansas," *Nation,* January 12, 1970, pp. 12–17.

33. Tom Murton and Joe Hyams, *Accomplices to Crime: The Arkansas Prison Scandal* (New York: Grove, 1969), p. 7.

34. *Newsweek,* February 12, 1968, pp. 42–43.

35. Thomas O. Murton, *The Dilemma of Prison Reform* (New York: Holt, Rinehart and Winston, 1976), pp. 35–38.

36. *Holt* v. *Sarver,* 309 F. Supp. 362 (E.D. Ark. 1970).

37. *Wilkerson* v. *Utah,* 99 U.S. 130 (1878); *Weems* v. *United States,* 217 U.S. 349 (1910); *Trop* v. *Dulles,* 356 U.S. 86 (1958); *Robinson* v. *California,* 370 U.S. 660 (1962).

38. *Jordan* v. *Fitzharris,* 257 F. Supp. 674 (N.D. Cal. 1966).

39. *Bauer* v. *Sielaff,* 372 F. Supp. 1104 (E.D. Pa. 1974).

40. *Landman* v. *Royster,* 333 F. Supp. 621 (E.D. Va. 1971).

41. *Novak* v. *Beto,* 453 F.2d 661 (5th Cir. 1972).

42. *Jackson* v. *Bishop,* 404 F.2d 571 (8th Cir. 1968).

43. *Wolff* v. *McDonnell,* 418 U.S. 539 (1974).

44. *Superintendent, Massachusetts Correctional Institute at Walpole* v. *Hill,* 471 U.S. 491 (1985).

45. *Costello* v. *Wainwright,* 397 F. Supp. 20 (M.D. Fla. 1975).

46. *People* v. *Lovercamp,* 43 Cal. App.3d 823, 118 Cal. Rptr. 110 (1974).

47. Fred Cohen, "The Texas Prison Conditions Case: *Ruiz* v. *Estelle,*" *Criminal Law Bulletin* 17 (May–June 1981): 252–257.

48. *Ruiz* v. *Estelle,* 74–329 (E.D. Tex., Dec. 19, 1980).

49. *Ruiz* v. *Estelle,* F.2d 115 (5th Cir. 1982).

50. *New York Times,* December 13, 1992, p. 42.

51. *Texas Criminal Justice Treatment Initiative,* Texas Department of Criminal Justice, Commission on Alcohol and Drug Abuse, 1993; *Austin American-Statesman,* January 16, 1994, pp. A1, A19.

52. *New York Times,* February 2, 1980, p. 1; *U.S. News and World Report,* February 18, 1980, p. 68.

53. Kinesley Hammett, *Holocaust at New Mexico State Penitentiary* (Lubbock, Texas: Boone, 1980).

54. *Newsweek,* September 7, 1981, p. 11.

55. *New York Times,* September 1, 1981, p. 34.

56. *Bell* v. *Wolfish,* 441 U.S. 520 (1979).

57. *Rhodes* v. *Chapman,* 452 U.S. 337 (1981).

58. *Hudson* v. *Palmer,* U.S. SupCt 35 CrL 3230 (1984).

59. *Wilson* v. *Seiter,* 49 CrL 2264 (1991).

60. Ira P. Robbins, "Privatization of Corrections: Defining the Issues," *Judicature* 69 (April–May 1986): 325–331; U.S. General Accounting Office, *Private Prisons: Cost Savings and Bureau of Prison's Statutory Authority Need to be Resolved,* February 1991; Christine Bowditch and Ronald S. Everett, "Private Prisons: Problems Within the Solution," *Justice Quarterly* 4 (September 1987): 441–453.

CHAPTER 14

COMMUNITY-BASED CORRECTION

Elements of Criminal Justice

ALBANY, N.Y. — In his State of the State address on January 5, 1999, Governor George E. Pataki proposed that New York become the 16th state to abolish parole.[1] Calling it "a failed system of penal rehabilitation" because of the growing number of offenders who commit serious violent crimes while on parole, Pataki suggested that parole boards be eliminated and that all offenders receive "flat" sentences instead.

Given Governor Pataki's remarks and the trend across the nation, is abolishing parole a feasible and desirable idea? But more importantly, what *is* parole? How is it different from probation? What other forms of "community corrections" are there? Do any of them work?

Community-based correction: Rehabilitative activities and programs within the community that have effective ties with the local government.

The concept of community-based correction has often been interpreted to mean that a fundamental dichotomy exists between incarceration in a correctional facility and residence in the community. This would suggest, then, that the term "community-based correction" refers to all of those correctional alternatives that occur within the free community. But this definition tends to be a bit misleading, for it oversimplifies the nature of community correction. More precisely, **community-based correction** refers to all those activities and programs within the community that have effective ties with local government. These activities are generally of a rehabilitative rather than a punitive nature and can include coordination with employment, educational, social, and clinical social service programs. Many of these programs also involve supervision by a community or governmental agency. Prevalent forms of community-based correction include pretrial diversion programs, probation and parole, education and work-release projects, furlough, restitution, and halfway houses.

Community-based correctional strategies represent a crucial part of the administration of justice in America for a number of humanitarian, fiscal, and practical reasons. *First,* humanitarian considerations dictate that numerous first offenders and others who pose no risk to the community should not be subject to the generally debilitating conditions of incarceration. *Second,* there is the concern among many reformers that exposure to prison life—the loss of liberty and self-esteem, the potential for physical harm, and the fact that prisons often serve as "schools of crime"—markedly decreases the likelihood that offenders will be successfully rehabilitated and integrated back into the community. This concern seems particularly salient for first-time, petty offenders, many of whom are reformable. *Third,* it is less expensive to house offenders in the community rather than in correctional facilities. *Fourth,* many community-based programs, particularly service programs, provide benefits to the community. *Fifth,* with the growing problems of prison crowding, reducing and/or eliminating the periods of confinement for less seriously involved offenders seems a pragmatic approach. *Sixth,* community-based correction allows for the development and evaluation of new, innovative approaches for handling offenders. The development of new programs seems particularly important, given the increasing number of offenders for whom prison appears to have no appreciable deterrent effect.

CRIMINAL JUSTICE DIVERSION

Diversion: The removal of offenders from the application of the criminal law at any stage of the police or court processes.

Criminal justice **diversion** refers to the removal of offenders from the application of the criminal law at any stage of the police and court processes.[2] It implies the formal halting or suspending of traditional criminal proceedings against persons who have violated criminal statutes, in favor of processing them through some noncriminal disposition or means. Thus, diversion occurs prior to adjudication; *it is a preadjudication disposition.*

The Development of Diversion

Diversion is not a new practice in the administration of justice. It has likely existed in an informal fashion for thousands of years, since the inception of organized law enforcement and social control. In both ancient and modern societies, informal diversion has occurred in many ways: A police officer removes a public drunk from the street to a Salvation Army shelter; a magistrate releases with a lecture an individual who assaulted a neighbor during the course of an argument; a prosecutor decides to *nolle pros.* a petty theft. These are problematic, however, because they are generally discretionary decisions, undertaken at random and off the record, and they tend to be personalized, standardless, and inconsistent. Furthermore, they serve only to remove offenders from the application of criminal penalties with no attempt to provide appropriate jurisprudential alternatives. In the case of *nolle pros.,* for example, once a prosecution has formally begun and the case is a matter of court record, the prosecutor can declare that he or she will "no further prosecute" the case, either (1) as to some of the counts, (2) as to some of the defendants, or (3) altogether.

Although these haphazard and unsystematic practices will continue, more formalized diversion activities impose social-therapeutic programs in lieu of conviction and punishment. These latter seem to have emerged within the juvenile justice system during the early part of the twentieth century. Among the first was the *Chicago Boys' Court,* founded in 1914 as an extralegal form of probation.

The Boys' Court system of supervision placed a young defendant under the authority of one of four community agencies: the Holy Name Society, the Chicago Church Federation, the Jewish Social Service Bureau, or the Colored Big Brothers. After a time, the court requested a report of the defendant's activities and adjustment, and if they were favorable, he would be officially discharged from the court having no criminal record.[3]

Later developments in youthful diversionary programs included New York City's Youth Counsel Bureau. This agency was established during the early 1950s for handling juveniles alleged to be delinquent or criminal but not deemed sufficiently advanced in their misbehavior to be adjudicated and committed by the court.[4] The bureau provided counseling services and discharged those whose adjustment appeared promising. In many instances, the youthful defendants not only avoided criminal convictions, but arrest records as well.

Patterns of Diversion

As criminal justice diversion continued to evolve, the arguments in its favor increased. It was felt that its practice would reduce court backlog, provide early intervention before the development of full-fledged criminal careers, ensure some consistency in selective law enforcement, reduce the costs of criminal processing, and enhance an offender's chances for community reintegration. More importantly, however, it had been the conclusion of many social scientists and penal reformers that the criminal justice process, which was designed to protect society from criminals, often contributed to the very behavior it was trying to eliminate. This typically came about as a result of the following:

1. Forcing those convicted of criminal offenses to interact with other, perhaps more experienced criminals, thus becoming socialized to a variety of criminal roles, learning the required skills and the criminal value system.
2. Denying convicted felons the opportunity to play legitimate roles.
3. Changing the individual's self-concept to that of a criminal. This occurs as a result of an individual being told by the courts that he or she is a criminal and being placed in an institution where inmates and correctional officers define the individual as a criminal.

Primarily as a result of massive federal funding allocated by the Law Enforcement Assistance Administration for the prevention and reduction of crime, diversion programs of many types emerged and expanded throughout the nation during the 1970s. Most, however, were designed for youths, for minor crimes (such as assaults, simple thefts, and property damage resulting from neighborhood disputes), and for special offenders whose crimes were deemed to be related to problem drinking or narcotics use.

Youth Service Bureaus Specifically recommended by the President's Commission on Law Enforcement and Administration of Justice in 1967 and begun in California during 1971, youth service bureaus became common by the mid-1970s. They are similar in concept to New York's original Youth Counsel Bureau, but many operate as adjuncts to local police departments. They offer counseling, tutoring, crisis intervention, job assistance, and guidance with school and family problems for truants, runaways, and delinquent youths.

Public Inebriate Programs In municipalities where public intoxication has remained a criminal offense, several diversionary alternatives to prosecution have been structured for public inebriates. Some are placed in alcohol detoxification centers rather than in jails. Others are referred before trial to community service agencies for more intensive treatment and care.

Civil Commitment Based on a medical model of rehabilitation, civil commitment programs were founded on the notion that some types of criminality result from symptoms of illness rather than malicious intent. Such offenders as drug users, sexual deviants, and the mentally ill might be diverted either before or after trial to a residential setting for therapeutic treatment. Civil commitment programs have been most common in California, New York, and the federal system, for the treatment of drug abusers.

Citizen Dispute Settlement Citizen dispute settlement programs were designed to deflect from the criminal justice system complaints related to family and neighborhood quarrels and evolving from petty crimes, simple assaults, property damage, threats, and bad checks. Cases are diverted to mediation by a disinterested third party at the family or neighborhood level, and identified problem areas receive help through arbitration combined with help from local community service agencies.

Treatment Alternatives to Street Crime Treatment Alternatives to Street Crime, better known as TASC, is a program designed to serve as a liaison between the criminal justice system and community treatment programs. As a program for substance-abusing arrestees, probationers, and parolees, its more than 120 sites in 25 states make it the most widely supported form of court diversion in the United States.[5]

Mentoring Diversion Programs Many jurisdictions have "mentoring programs" for first-time nonviolent drug offenders. In the Oakland, California, program, for example, participants must stay drug- and arrest-free, and go back to school and either earn a high school equivalency degree or satisfactorily complete 8 to 12 credits at a local community college. If these conditions are met, their records are cleared of all felony charges.[6]

The Impact of Diversion

It is difficult to assess the overall value and impact of the national diversion effort. Many programs have never been evaluated, and estimations of their effectiveness have been based on little more than clinical intuition and hunch. Among those that have undergone rigorous assessment, the findings have ranged from promising to bleak. The experience with the numerous Treatment Alternatives to Street Crime (TASC) programs have been quite positive. Evaluations from the 1970s through the 1990s have demonstrated TASC to be highly productive in (1) identifying populations of drug-involved offenders in need of treatment; (2) assessing the nature and extent of their drug use patterns and specific treatment needs; (3) effectively referring drug-involved offenders to treatment; (4) serving as a link between criminal justice and treatment systems; and (5) providing constructive client identification and monitoring services for the courts, probation, and other segments of the criminal justice system.[7] Similarly, positive outcomes are beginning to emerge with the new diversion mentoring programs.[8]

As jail and prison populations continue to grow beyond capacity, diversion programs continue to remain popular regardless of the lack of published data on their effectiveness. Overall, they permit judges to impose intermediate sanctions yet avoid incarcerating offenders.

PROBATION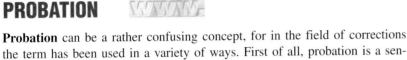

Probation can be a rather confusing concept, for in the field of corrections the term has been used in a variety of ways. First of all, probation is a sentence. It is a sentence of conditional release to the community. More specifically, as defined by the American Bar Association, probation is a sentence not involving confinement that imposes conditions and retains authority in the sentencing court to modify the conditions of sentence or to resentence the offender if he or she violates the conditions.[9]

In addition to being a disposition, the word *probation* has also been used to refer to a status, a system, and a process.[10] As a status, probation reflects the unique character of the probationer: He or she is neither a free citizen nor a confined prisoner. As a system, probation is a component in the administration of justice, as embodied by the agency or organization that administers the probation process. As a process, probation refers to the set of functions, activities, and services that characterize the system's transactions with the courts, the offender, and the community. This process includes the preparation of reports for the courts, the supervision of probationers, and the obtaining and providing of services for them (see Exhibit 14.1).

Probation: A sentence not involving confinement that imposes conditions and retains authority in the sentencing court to modify the conditions or sentence or to resentence the offender if he or she violates the conditions.

Probation can be a *disposition*, a *status*, a *system*, and a *process*.

The Probation Philosophy

The premise behind the use of probation is that many offenders are not dangerous and represent little, if any, menace to society. It has been argued that when defendants are institutionalized, the prison community becomes their new reference point. They are forced into contact with hard-core criminals, the prison experience generates embitterment and hostility, and the "ex-con" label becomes a stigma that impedes social adjustment. Probation, on the other hand, provides a more therapeutic alternative. The term comes from the Latin *probare,* meaning "to test or prove," and the probationer is given the opportunity to demonstrate that if given a second chance, more socially acceptable behavior patterns will result.

The probation philosophy also includes elements of community protection and offender rehabilitation. Probationers are supervised by agents of the court or probation agency. These are trained personnel with dual roles. They are present to ensure that the conditions of probation are fulfilled and to provide counseling and assistance in community reintegration. Furthermore, as with all types of community-based correction, it is generally agreed that the rehabilitation of offenders is more realistically possible in the natural environment of the free community than behind prison walls.

While these are the ideal philosophical underpinnings of probation, several more pragmatic issues have also entered into its use as an alternative to imprisonment. First, and as noted in the previous chapter, correctional institutions throughout the nation have become painfully overcrowded. With the

Exhibit 14.1 **Historical Perspectives on Crime and Justice**
The Roots of Probation

In the month of August, 1841, I was in court one morning, when the door communicating with the lock-room was opened and an officer entered, followed by a ragged and wretched looking man, who took his seat upon the bench allotted to prisoners. I imagined from the man's appearance, that his offense was that of yielding to his appetite for intoxicating drinks, and in a few moments I found that my suspicions were correct, for the clerk read the complaint, in which the man was charged with being a common drunkard. The case was clearly made out, but before sentence had been passed, I conversed with him for a few moments, and found that he was not yet past all hope of reformation. He told me that if he could be saved from the House of Correction, he never again would taste intoxicating liquors; there was such an earnestness in that tone, and a look of firm resolve, that I determined to aid him; I bailed

him, by permission of the Court. He was ordered to appear for sentence in three weeks from that time. He signed the pledge and became a sober man; at the expiration of this period of probation, I accompanied him into the courtroom. The Judge expressed himself much pleased with the account we gave of the man, and instead of the usual penalty—imprisonment in the House of Corrections—he fined him one cent

John Augustus, the "first probation officer."

and costs, amounting in all to $3.76, which was immediately paid. The man continued industrious and sober, and without doubt has been by this treatment, saved from a drunkard's grave.

—John Augustus

The foregoing incident, during the latter part of 1841, gave birth to the concept of probation in the United States. John Augustus was a Boston shoemaker, and his method was to bail an offender after conviction, to provide him with friendship and support in family matters, as well as job assistance. When the defendant was later brought to court for sentencing, Augustus would report on his progress toward reformation and request that the judge order a small fine and court costs in lieu of a jail sentence. As such, John Augustus could be considered the first probation officer. By 1858, he had bailed almost 2,000 defendants. His efforts led to the first probation statute, passed in Massachusetts in 1878. By 1900, four other states had enacted similar legislation, and probation became an established alternative to incarceration. Currently, probation exists in most jurisdictions throughout the world.

SOURCE: John Augustus, *A Report of the Labors of John Augustus, for the Last Ten Years, in Aid of the Unfortunate* (Boston: Wright & Hasty, 1852), reprinted as *John Augustus, First Probation Officer* (New York: National Probation Association, 1939).

almost prohibitive costs of new prison construction, probation is seen by many as a more economically viable correctional alternative. Second, and also as a matter of simple economics, the probation process is considerably cheaper than the prison process. The cost of maintaining an inmate in prison has been estimated to average $25,000 per year. Probation costs approximately one-tenth of that amount. Third, within some sectors of the criminal justice community, imprisonment is being viewed more and more as cruel and unusual punishment. Prisons are dangerous places to live. Inmates are physically, sexually, and emotionally victimized on a regular basis. Probation, within this context, is considered to be the more humane avenue of correctional intervention.

Suspended Sentences and Conditional Release

There are a variety of terms that tend to be used interchangeably with probation but represent things that are quite different. The best known of these is the **suspended sentence,** a disposition that in and of itself implies supervision of the offender with a set of specified criteria and goals. The suspended sentence is a quasi-freedom that can be revoked at the pleasure of the court. Suspended sentences, furthermore, are of two types: *suspension of imposition* of sentence and *suspension of execution* of sentence. In the case of suspension of imposition, which is infrequently used, there may be verdict or plea, but no sentence is pronounced. The presiding magistrate releases the defendant on the general condition that he or she stay out of trouble and make restitution for the crime. With the suspension of execution, the sentence is prescribed but is postponed or not carried out. In a number of jurisdictions, a sentence can be suspended, and this suspension is followed by an order for probation.

Suspended sentence: A court disposition of a convicted person, pronouncing a penalty of a fine or commitment to confinement, but unconditionally discharging the defendant or holding execution of the penalty in abeyance upon good behavior.

The Presentence or Probation Investigation

Probation in the United States is administered by hundreds of independent government agencies, each jurisdiction operating under different laws and many with widely varying philosophies. In some jurisdictions, such as Hawaii and Delaware, a single state authority provides services for all probationers. In other jurisdictions, probation descends from county or municipal authority, functioning under state laws and guidelines, but is administered by the lower courts. In some areas, such as South Carolina, probation and parole are combined into a single state unit. In the federal system, probation is administered as an arm of the federal district courts.

The presentence investigation is one of the basic services provided by the probation agency, and such reports are generally mandatory if probation appears to be a possible sentence. In their examination of the backgrounds and characteristics of defendants, these reports can vary widely in depth, content, and usefulness. The norm includes the characteristics of the offender, the circumstances of his or her offense, an evaluative summary, and a recommendation.

Studies have demonstrated that in most sentences involving probation, there is a high correlation between the presentence or probation officer's recommendation and the judge's sentencing decision.[11] This should not suggest, however, that judicial decision-making is dictated by the content of a presentence report recommendation. Rather, there are a number of more logical factors at work. First, since probation is one of the most common sentences, the simple laws of chance are operative. Second, most criminal convictions occur as the result of guilty pleas. The details of the plea negotiation and the prosecutor's sentencing recommendation are generally known to the presentence investigator, and these typically influence his or her recommendation. Third, presentence or probation officers tend to be aware of the sentencing recommendations that will be acceptable to specific judges for given kinds of cases, and they often take the path of least resistance.[12]

The U.S. Supreme Court has upheld the validity of the presentence investigation as meeting the due process requirements of the Constitution.[13] However, the Court has provided defendants with some safeguards in this matter. In the 1977 case of *Gardner* v. *Florida,*[14] for example, the Court ruled that

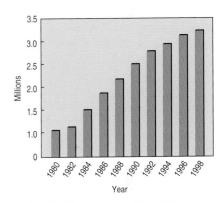

Probationers in the U.S., 1980–1998

SOURCE: Bureau of Justice Statistics.

a defendant is denied due process when a sentence is based, even in part, on confidential information contained in a presentence report that the defendant is not given the opportunity to deny or explain.

Conditions of Probation

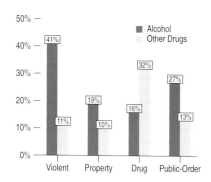

Percentage of Adult Probationers Reporting Alcohol or Other Drug Use at the Time of the Offense

SOURCE: Bureau of Justice Statistics, 1998.

Most states have statutory restrictions on the granting of probation. In some jurisdictions, defendants convicted of such crimes as murder, kidnapping, and rape are ineligible for probation, as are second and third felony offenders. Others tend to be less specific, but structure their penal codes in such a manner as to preclude a sentence of probation for most serious offenders. In Alabama, for example, persons convicted of crimes that typically call for sentences of death or imprisonment for 10 years or more are ineligible for probation.[15]

Thus, in most jurisdictions, probation is a statutory alternative to imprisonment for most felony convictions. Judges differ, however, in their approaches to granting it. As noted earlier, both plea bargaining and factors contained in the presentence report enter into the decision. In addition, there are such elements as the prosecutor's recommendation, anticipated community reaction, political consideration, court backlog, the availability of space in the prison system, and the judge's own feelings toward the particular offense or the offender.

Upon the granting of probation and as part of their probation agreement, defendants are required to abide by a variety of regulations and conditions. These conditions are fairly standard from state to state. Typically, the conditions exhort the probationer to live a law-abiding and productive life, to work, to support his or her dependents, to maintain contact with the supervising probation officer, and to remain within the jurisdiction of the court.

Special conditions of probation may also be imposed, by either the sentencing judge or the supervising probation agency. Many of these have been challenged by probationers as "improper," but most have been upheld by state appellate courts. State and federal court decisions have affirmed the correctness of such special requirements as undergoing treatment for drug abuse,[16] abstaining from the use of alcohol,[17] serving a short jail sentence prior to release on probation with no credit for prior confinement,[18] refraining from operating a motor vehicle during the period of probation,[19] submitting to a search by the supervising probation officer,[20] and payment of restitution.[21]

Since the beginning of the 1980s, a new condition of probation has become common. In more than half the states, probation clients are being assessed a fee for services. Supervision services typically range from $10 to $30 per month, with presentence investigation costs running $100 to $300.[22] Although there are waivers for the indigent, nonpayment must be sanctioned by the court or probation agency. Texas is among the most successful states in collecting fees from probationers. Officials estimate that probation departments in Texas collect fees from at least 90 percent of all misdemeanor probationers and 65 percent of all felony offenders on probation. Collected fees have paid in excess of 50 percent of the cost of basic supervision.[23]

Generally, conditions of probation are considered constitutional and proper unless they bear no reasonable relationship to the crime committed or the defendant's probationary status. Thus, placement in a drug treatment program becomes an appropriate condition of probation only when the defendant's offense is considered to be a consequence of a drug abuse problem. Conversely, abstinence from alcohol would be an improper condition for probationers who never had problems with drinking. Furthermore, in 1987 the Supreme Court ruled that state regulations permitting probation officers to conduct searches of probationers' homes, without warrants and upon "reasonable grounds" (rather than probable cause) to believe that contraband might be found, do not violate the Fourth Amendment.[24] However, while warrantless searches of probationers, their automobiles, and premises are permissible conditions if carried out by probation officers with just cause, the courts have ruled that such searches cannot be extended to all law enforcement officers.[25]

Restitution Programs

Among the more widely endorsed conditions of probation in recent years is **restitution:** requiring offenders to compensate their victims for damages or stolen property (monetary restitution) or donate their time to community service (community service restitution).

> **Restitution:** A condition of probation requiring offenders to compensate their victims for damages or to donate their time in service to the community.

The rationales for restitution are numerous. First, while fines imposed go into court or government treasuries, monetary restitution goes directly to the victims of crime, compensating them for injuries, time lost from work, and other losses. Second, it forces the offender to take personal responsibility for his or her crime. Third, it has the potential for reconciling victims and offenders. Fourth, it can be incorporated into a probation program without the need for additional programs and expenditures. And fifth, it provides a vehicle for including the victim in the administration of justice.[26]

Despite these apparent virtues, restitution does have critics. It has been suggested that restitution can be a punitive sanction rather than a rehabilitative one, since it places an additional burden on offenders that they might not ordinarily have. Even more importantly, it carries the potential for nullifying any deterrent effects of punishment by allowing criminals to "write a check" and "pay a fee" for their offenses. Finally, it can be argued that restitution serves only the interests of those of reasonable financial ability, thus prohibiting such an option to the indigent. Although in many ways this latter argument is true, there are a number of alternatives that make restitution available to offenders at all levels of the socioeconomic ladder. There are, for example, community service restitution outlets through which juvenile vandals can work to repair the damage they have caused, drunk drivers can work in alcohol detoxification centers, and other offenders can work in hospitals, nursing homes, or juvenile counseling programs.[27]

Probation Services

At least in theory, probation service incorporates the casework approach. During the probationer's initial interview with his or her probation officer, an evaluation is made to determine what type of treatment supervision is most appropriate. Based on information contained in the presentence investigation and on his or her skills in counseling and problem solving, the officer plans a treatment schedule designed to allow the probationer to make a reasonable community adjustment. This diagnostic aspect of probation intake examines the probationer's peer relationships, family problems, work skills and history, educational status, and involvement with drug or alcohol abuse. During the course of the probation period, the office works with the offender in these designated areas as required. The treatment may be limited to one-to-one counseling, or it may involve referral to community service agencies for drug abuse treatment, vocational skill enhancement, or job assistance. Because probationers are convicted criminal offenders and one of the officer's roles involves community protection, a second function of the intake interview is to determine what level of community supervision appears necessary. Such supervision can involve regular visits to the probationer's home and place of employment and can require the client to report to the probation office on a weekly, semimonthly, or monthly basis.

Although many probation agencies do operate in the manner outlined, in practice few probationers receive such individualized treatment and supervision, for many different reasons. *First,* the educational backgrounds, skills, and experiences of probation officers vary widely. A number of agencies require graduate education and related experience for a career in probation work, but others have no such prerequisites. Furthermore, in some states high school graduates with no training in counseling, psychology, social work, or any other behavioral field have managed to secure work in the probation area. *Second,* as with members of any occupation or profession, many probation officers have little dedication or interest in their work. This often results in apathy toward their clients' needs and problems, an avoidance of responsibility, and the "stealing of time" during business hours.

A *third* problem is the low level of career mobility in probation work. Combined with moderate to low salaries in many jurisdictions are limited opportunities for advancement. This results in frustration, dissatisfaction, cynicism, and high staff turnover. Additionally, there is the issue of caseload size. Workloads range from a dozen probationers per officer in a few agencies to more than 300 per officer in others. The treatment and supervision aspects of probation become even further diluted by the requirements to perform presentence investigations. In consequence, treatment sometimes becomes reduced to making a telephone call every other week to determine if a job is being maintained, and supervision amounts to as little as one mail contact each month to determine if the probationers are residing where they say they are.

Fourth, and finally, as is the case in police work, probation officers can differ dramatically in approaches to their work and attitudes toward their clients. There are probably many who can successfully mediate their dual roles as clinicians and supervisors. However, there are also many "social workers" and "rule enforcers" who operate only from these diverse ends of the spectrum. In addition, there are the "legalists," who stress the upholding of law for its own sake; there are "company agents," who focus almost exclusively on their upward mobility in the probation organization; and there are the stereotyped "civil service hacks," who seem to think of little else than the number of years left until retirement and in the meantime work hard at getting the lion's share of days off, sick pay, fringe benefits, lunch hours, and coffee breaks. Each of these types can hurt a probationer's potential for readjustment.

Shock Probation

Shock probation: Brief incarceration followed by suspension of sentence and probation.

In 1965, the Ohio state legislature passed the first **shock probation** law in the United States, allowing judges to incarcerate an offender for a brief part of the sentence, suspend the remainder, and place him or her on probation. Under the Ohio statute, shock probation (also known as a *mixed* or *split sentence*) is not part of the original sentence. Rather, the defendant can file a petition requesting it between 30 and 60 days after sentencing, or the judge can order it in the absence of any petition. Its "shock" value comes from the contention that the staggering effect of exposure to prison or jail can be a significant deterrent to crime. Eligibility for shock probation procedures follows the same statutory guidelines that govern the granting of probation in general.

Sentiments regarding the suitability of shock probation as a rehabilitative tool have been mixed. From a positive standpoint, it represents a way for the courts to do the following:

- Impress offenders with the seriousness of their actions without a long prison sentence

- Release offenders found by the institutions to be more amenable to community-based treatment than was realized by the courts at the time of sentence
- Arrive at a just compromise between punishment and leniency in appropriate cases
- Provide community-based treatment for rehabilitable offenders, while still observing their responsibilities for imposing deterrent sentences where public policy demands it[28]

In addition, since imprisonment is only short-term, it inhibits absorption of the offender into the "hard rock" inmate culture. At the same time, the fiscal costs of shock probation are significantly lower than those of a full period of incarceration.

Opponents of shock probation argue vigorously that it is counterproductive as a rehabilitative tool. First, its deterrent effect is limited or totally negated by the job loss and broken community ties that occur with incarceration, however brief. Second, the purpose of probation is to avoid incarceration, not supplement it. Third, even a short period of incarceration has the potential for contaminating offenders through exposure to hardened criminals and the hostilities and resentment of prison life. Fourth, it stigmatizes offenders for having been in jail or prison and may add to their confusion of status and self-concept. Fifth, and perhaps most importantly, prison and probation are at opposite ends of the punishment and rehabilitation scale; they are mutually exclusive and therefore should not be mixed.[29]

Although shock probation may be functional from the perspective of the criminal justice system in terms of the lower costs of probation versus imprisonment and the alleviation of prison overcrowding, there is no evidence yet to demonstrate that it reduces recidivism. Several empirical studies have examined the shock probation experience, but the findings remain inconclusive.[30] In the opinion of the National Institute of Justice, shock probation and split sentences *do not* reduce repeat offending.[31]

Intensive Probation Supervision

Intensive probation supervision is a program of closer surveillance and more exhaustive services that place a probationer under tighter control than he or she might experience under regular probation. Although it is not a particularly new concept, it has received considerable attention in recent years because of the dual purposes it appears to serve in these times of over-crowded penitentiaries and escalating criminal justice costs. First, it restrains the growth of prison populations and associated costs by controlling selected offenders in the community. Second, and at the same time, it satisfies at least a part of society's demand that offenders be punished for their crimes.[32]

The degrees of surveillance vary considerably from one intensive probation supervision to another. In general, all involve small caseloads and frequent contacts between the probationer and probation officer in the home, on the job, and at the probation office.

As for the effectiveness of intensive probation supervision, the data appear to be inconclusive. An evaluation of the program in Montgomery County (Dayton), Ohio, from its inception in 1984 through the middle of 1986 generated results that were clearly mixed.[33] A comparison of the performance of 163 intensive probationers with that of 130 regular probationers found that while 66 percent of the intensive probationers were not rearrested during the follow-up period and 74 percent were not convicted of new crimes, these results are not all that different from the regular probationers—67 percent of whom were not rearrested and 78 percent of whom were not convicted of new crimes.

Intensive probation supervision: A program of closer surveillance and more exhaustive services that place a probationer under tighter control than he or she might experience under regular probation.

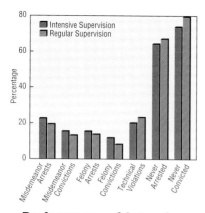

**Performance of Intensive
and Regular Probationers in
Montgomery County, Ohio**

SOURCE: Adapted from Susan B. Noonan
and Edward J. Latessa, "Intensive Probation:
An Examination of Recidivism and Social
Adjustment," *American Journal of Criminal
Justice* 11 (1987): 45–61.

A study of 14 intensive probation supervision programs in nine states for the years 1986 through 1991 produced far more ambiguous results.[34] For example, no clear relationship was found to exist between frequency of contact with probationers and recidivism. Nor was there any indication that probationers in intensive supervision were rearrested for less serious crimes than their counterparts. Intensive supervision programs did, however, succeed in altering offender perceptions about crime commission. Those in intensive programs believed their chances of getting caught for a crime while on probation were high, particularly if the crime involved drug use. They also believed that, if caught, they would be treated more harshly than those on regular probation. Finally, the study found that while intensive supervision programs were not necessarily more cost-effective than regular probation, they were considerably cheaper than housing offenders in prison.

Probation Violation and Revocation

Since probation is a conditional release, it does not guarantee absolute freedom. Arrests for new crimes or technical violations of the conditions of probation can result in *revocation of probation* and the imprisonment of the offender.

As noted earlier in this chapter, the conditions of probation are established by statute, and special conditions can be applied by the sentencing court. There has been little argument as to whether a new arrest constitutes a violation of probation. Furthermore, the appellate courts have given the lower courts considerable latitude in imposing conditions of probation. Thus, such technical violations as nonpayment of a fine imposed as a condition of probation, failure to pay off civil judgments for fraud although able to pay, failure to make child support payments, failure to report to one's probation officer, and driving while intoxicated, to name only a few, have been grounds for violation and revocation. *Absconding* from probation supervision—that is, failing to report and concealing oneself from the probation authorities—represents another serious violation of probation.

The issue of probation violation tends to underscore the tremendous discretionary authority that is at the disposal of the probation officer. Technical violations generally come to the attention of only the supervising officer. If the defendant fails to report, reverts to the use of drugs, consorts with known criminals, refuses to remain gainfully employed, or fails to live up to other conditions of the probation contract, the officer has several options. He or she can cite the probationer for violation, make continued and more intensive counseling and supervision efforts in order to bring about community adjustment, or simply "look the other way." Thus violation proceedings are initiated by the probation officer, and these generally begin only when revocation is the course decided on. It should be emphasized, however, that although the probation officer or department can recommend revocation, *only the court has the authority to revoke probation.*

In the event of a new arrest, a warrant may be lodged against the probationer in order to prevent his or her release on bail. If the violation is only technical, a warrant may also be issued and the violator taken into custody by either the police or probation authorities. Some jurisdictions issue such detainers as a matter of course; others do so only when there is evidence to believe that the probationer would abscond if left in the community pending a revocation hearing.

Once revocation is the direction decided on by the probation authorities, the offender is given notice of such, the probation officer prepares a violation report, and a formal court hearing is scheduled. Until only recently, revocation hearings reflected few procedural safeguards. In 1967, however, the U.S. Supreme Court held in ***Mempa v. Rhay*** that a probationer has a constitutional right to counsel at any revocation proceeding where the imposition of

Mempa v. Rhay: The Supreme Court ruling that the right to counsel applies to state probation revocation hearings at which deferred sentence may be imposed.

sentence had been suspended but would be enjoined following revocation.[35] In 1972, the Court ruled in **Morrissey v. Brewer** that when the potential for parole revocation is at issue, an informal inquiry is required to determine if there is probable cause to believe that the parolee had indeed violated the conditions of parole.[36] The Court added the mandate of a formal revocation hearing as well, within minimum due process requirements (see Exhibit 14.2).

Morrissey v. Brewer: The Supreme Court ruling that a parolee facing revocation is entitled to both a preliminary hearing to determine whether he or she actually violated parole and a final hearing to consider not only the facts in question, but also, if there was a violation, what to do about it.

Exhibit 14.2 **Legal Perspectives on Crime and Justice**
Morrissey v. *Brewer*

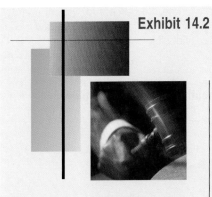

The decision in *Morrissey* v. *Brewer* related to parole revocation, but because parole and probation revocation are similar in nature, it had potential significance for both types of proceedings.

In 1967, John Morrissey was convicted in an Iowa court of falsely drawing checks, and was sentenced to a maximum term of 7 years' imprisonment. He was released on parole the following year, but within 7 months Morrissey was cited for violation of his parole. He was arrested—and admitted to purchasing an automobile without permission, obtaining credit under an assumed name, having become involved in an automobile accident, and failing to report these and other matters to his parole officer. He maintained that he had not contacted his parole officer due to sickness.

One week later, the parole violation report was reviewed, parole was revoked, and Morrissey was returned to prison. On a *habeas corpus* petition to the U.S. district court, Morrissey claimed that he had been denied due process under the Fourteenth Amendment in that his parole had been revoked without a hearing. The district court denied his petition, the U.S. court of appeals affirmed the lower court decision, and the U.S. Supreme Court granted *certiorari*.

The Court began its opinion stating that the revocation of parole is not part of a criminal prosecution and thus the full panoply of rights due a defendant in such a proceeding does not apply. However, the Court went on to state that parole revocation involves the potential termination of an individual's liberty, and therefore certain due process safeguards are necessary to ensure that the finding of a parole violation is based on verified facts to support the revocation.

In establishing procedural safeguards, the Court considered parole revocation to be a two-stage process: (1) the arrest of the parolee and a preliminary hearing, and (2) the revocation hearing. In designating a preliminary hearing for all parole violators, the Court held as follows:

Such an inquiry should be seen in the nature of a preliminary hearing to determine whether there is probable cause or reasonable grounds to believe that the arrested parolee had committed acts which would constitute a violation of parole condition.

The Court also specified that at this preliminary review, the hearing officer should be someone not involved in the case, and that the parolee should be given notice of the hearing and the opportunity to be present during the questioning of persons providing adverse information regarding the alleged violation. Subsequently, a determination should be made to decide if the parolee's continued detention

is warranted. In reference to the revocation hearing, the Court held:

The parolee must have an opportunity to be heard and to show, if he can, that he did not violate the conditions or if he did, that circumstances in mitigation suggest the violation does not warrant revocation. The revocation hearing must be tendered within a reasonable time after the parolee is taken into custody. A lapse of two months as the state suggests occurs in some cases would not appear to be unreasonable.

And in terms of due process at revocation hearings, this is what the Supreme Court had to say:

Our task is limited to deciding the minimum requirements of due process. They include (a) written notice of the claimed violation of parole; (b) disclosure to the parolee of evidence against him; (c) opportunity to be heard in person and to present witnesses and documentary evidence; (d) the right to confront and cross-examine adverse witnesses (unless the hearing officer specifically finds good cause for not allowing confrontation); (e) a "neutral and detached" hearing body such as a traditional parole board, members of which need not be judicial officers or lawyers; and (f) a written statement by the fact finders as to the evidence relied on and reasons for revoking parole.

SOURCE: *Morrissey v. Brewer*, 408 U.S. 471 (1972).

Exhibit 14.3

Research in Crime and Justice
The Rand Study of Probation Effectiveness

The Rand study, commissioned by the National Institute of Justice and conducted by the Rand Corporation during the 1980s, examined 1,672 felony cases from California's Los Angeles and Alameda counties. During the 40-month follow-up period of the research, 65 percent of those placed on probation were rearrested. Almost 80 percent of these, or 51 percent of the entire sample, were convicted of new crimes. Of the sample, 18 percent were reconvicted of serious violent crimes, and 34 percent were

reincarcerated. Charges were filed against 53 percent of the felony probationers: 19 percent had only one charge, 12 percent had two charges, and 22 percent had three or more charges against them. As the accompanying

figure illustrates, 51 percent of the entire study population experienced a filing for property crime, 24 percent for violent crime, and 14 percent for a drug law violation.

Charges Filed Against Probationers: The Rand Study

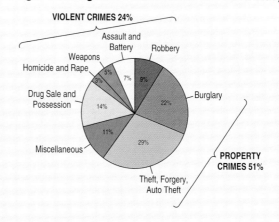

SOURCE: Joan Petersilia, Susan Turner, James Kahan, and Joyce Peterson, *Granting Felons Probation: Public Risk and Alternatives* (Santa Monica, Calif.: Rand, 1985).

Gagnon v. Scarpelli: The Supreme Court ruling that the holding in *Morrissey v. Brewer* also applies to probationers and that neither probationers nor parolees are entitled to counsel as a matter of right at revocation hearings.

Although *Morrissey* was a parole case, its significance for probationers came the following year with ***Gagnon v. Scarpelli.***[37] In *Gagnon,* the High Court extended the holding in *Morrissey* to probationers and also held that both probationers and parolees have a constitutionally limited right to counsel during revocation proceedings.

The Effectiveness of Probation

Probation is by far the most widely used criminal sanction. There are many reasons for this, most of which evolve from the economic and humanitarian considerations that characterize the probation philosophy. In addition, some observers believe that probation is the most effective phase of the criminal justice process. This notion, however, can be called into serious question. The vast majority of the studies on probation effectiveness are at least two decades old. Moreover, they may not be meaningful as indicators of the success of probation. Further, more recent data even contradict the findings of the earlier research.

One of the largest studies of probation effectiveness, commonly known as the Rand study, found that most felony offenders placed on probation were still a considerable threat to the community (see Exhibit 14.3).[38] The Rand study, however, was descriptive of only one population. In 1986, researchers at Southeast Missouri State University replicated the Rand effort for the state of Missouri.[39] A total of 2,083 felons from the most urban population in

Missouri were tracked for the same 40-month period used by Rand, with very different results. In Missouri, only 22 percent of the probationers were re-arrested and 12 percent were convicted of new crimes. This suggests that the effectiveness of probation tends to vary from one jurisdiction to the next and that individual studies of probation effectiveness may not be representative of felony probation in general.

PAROLE

Parole, from the French meaning "word of honor" and first used in 1846 by the Boston penal reformer Samuel G. Howe,[40] refers to the practice of allowing the final portion of a prison sentence to be served in the free community.

In practice, parole actually refers to two operations: (1) "parole release," the procedures used to establish the actual periods of confinement that prisoners serve, and (2) "parole supervision," the conditions and provisions that regulate parolees' postprison lives until the final discharge from their sentence.

For at least a century, parole has been an established part of American correctional theory and practice. It has had the ostensible purposes of ensuring that imprisonment is tailored to the needs of the inmate, ameliorating the harshness of long prison sentences, and hastening the offender's reintegration into the community when it appears that he or she is able to function as a law-abiding citizen. In addition, it has had the more subtle designs of alleviating the crowded conditions of correctional institutions and assisting in maintaining prisons' social control through the threat of parole denial for instances of misbehavior.

Parole: The status of being released from a penal or reformatory institution in which one has served a part of his or her maximum sentence, on the condition of maintaining good behavior and remaining in the custody and under the guidance of the institution or some other agency approved by the state until a final discharge is granted.

The Origins of Parole

As a combination and extension of penal practices, parole has a long history. It seems to have first appeared in a most rudimentary form when the British economy declined during the latter part of the sixteenth century.[41] In the colonies, the need for cheap labor was critical. The British government began granting reprieves and stays of execution to felons physically able to work so they could be transported to the New World. The pardoned convicts became indentured servants, whose labor was sold to the highest bidder in the colonies. The newly arrived felons were required to work off their indenture, and the only other condition of their pardon was that they did not return to England.

Captain Alexander Maconochie of Norfolk Island, Australia, however, was the "father of parole" in its purest form. Maconochie established a "mark system" whereby an inmate could earn early release by hard work and good behavior. Sir Walter Crofton's "Irish system" was a refinement of Maconochie's ideas, by which inmates could earn a conditional release through a "ticket-of-leave."

The concept of parole continued to evolve in the United States with the principles of *"good-time" laws* and indeterminate sentencing. The notion underlying good-time laws was modest. If, in the opinion of prison authorities, inmates maintained an institutional record of hard work and good conduct, they could be released after a shorter period than that imposed by the sentencing court. The purposes of the laws, however, were somewhat more complex. They were attempts to assist in the reformation of criminals, combined with endeavors to mitigate the severity of the penal codes; to solve the problems of prison discipline; and to get good work from inmates, thereby increasing the profits of the prison industries and contract labor.[42]

Parole Administration

Parole versus probation

The terms *parole* and *probation* have often been mistakenly used interchangeably, but as is already apparent, there are many differences between the two. Probation involves a sentence by the court to community supervision in lieu of imprisonment; parole is a conditional release from a correctional institution after a period of imprisonment has already been served. Beyond this preliminary distinction, there are other administrative differences. First, the authority to both grant and revoke probation falls within the realm of the courts. The authority to grant and revoke parole is held by an administrative board that can be (1) an independent state agency, (2) a unit within some larger state department, or (3) the same body that regulates the state's correctional institutions. Second, the supervision of probationers can be the function of a single court, a county agency, a state department or division, or some combination thereof in any given jurisdiction. Parole supervision services, however, are under the authority of a single state agency in all instances but are not necessarily under the leadership of the parole board.

The advantages and disadvantages of the various models of parole administration have been heavily debated. Which model is actually followed, however, is generally a matter of state politics. In recent years, as both parole and correctional agencies have become more professionalized, the trend has been to combine administration of the two.

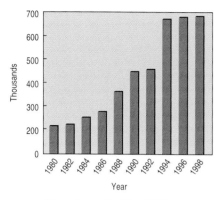

Parolees in the U.S., 1980–1998

SOURCE: Bureau of Justice Statistics.

The Parole Board   The functions of parole boards are essentially four-fold: (1) to select and place prisoners on parole; (2) to provide continuing control over parolees in the community; (3) to discharge parolees from supervision when they complete their sentences; and (4) to review parole violations and determine whether revocation and return to prison is appropriate. Thus the overall task of the parole board is the implementation of indeterminate sentencing.

Parole Officers   The characteristics of parole officers, or "agents" as they are referred to in some jurisdictions, vary widely. Some states require a graduate degree in an appropriate field; others expect only a high school diploma. Furthermore, what has already been stated regarding probation officers can be applied to parole officers, for in many ways the requirements and skills are similar.

Eligibility for Parole

There are numerous statutory restrictions on the granting of parole. As a result, inmates are not automatically paroled as a matter of right. Parole eligibility, then, refers to the earliest date that an inmate can be considered for parole. However, due to the nature of their offenses and sentences, some prisoners can never be paroled.

A key factor in the determination of parole eligibility are the statutes regarding good time. Good time, as explained earlier, refers to the number of days deducted from a sentence for good behavior, meritorious service, particular kinds of work, or other considerations. Some states have a fixed formula for allocating good time, such as 2 or 3 days for each month served. In others it is left to the discretion of the prison authorities, but cannot exceed a certain portion of the term imposed by the court. Good time, however, is not a matter of right; it must be earned, and as noted in Chapter 13, in the discussion of prison disciplinary proceedings, it can be forfeited for poor behavior.

Adults in Jail, on Probation, in Prison, or on Parole in the U.S., 1980–1998

SOURCE: Bureau of Justice Statistics.

The Parole Hearing   Parole hearings are generally private and are attended only by the inmate, the board, a representative of the institution in which the inmate is incarcerated, and a stenographer or stenotypist to record the proceedings. The board reviews the inmate's case as well as any institutional reports that may have been submitted; it questions the inmate regarding his or her adjustment, plans if released, and perhaps the circumstances of the inmate's offense; and then it offers the inmate an opportunity to make a statement on his or her own behalf. The inmate is then dismissed, and the board discusses the case and makes its decision.

The specific procedures used by different boards vary. In years past, one board member examined the institutional records and interviewed each inmate under consideration. He or she would then make a recommendation, and the entire board would either ratify or modify the recommendation in an executive session. Currently, several models exist. Some boards meet *en banc* for every case; others break up into groups to hold hearings in different parts of the jurisdiction. Since the mid-1970s, the U.S. Board of Parole and many of the larger states have been using hearing examiners, who make recommendations on which the board acts. Regardless of the particular procedure, parole authorities have been given wide discretion as to how hearings are actually conducted. This discretion, furthermore, has been uniformly supported by the courts. In *Menechino* v. *Oswald*,[43] the U.S. court of appeals ruled that the due process clause did not apply to parole hearings since inmates, who are already imprisoned, do not have "present private interests" that require protection. The following year, though, the court did hold that written reasons for the denial of parole must be given to an inmate.[44] Finally, in 1979, the U.S. Supreme Court in *Greenholtz* v. *Inmates of Nebraska Penal and Correctional Complex* affirmed previous decisions that parole hearings need not have all the elements of due process that are required at criminal trials.[45]

Parole Selection   An overview of contemporary parole practice suggests that many release decisions often reflect variable, arbitrary, and sometimes whimsical standards. A variety of legislative mandates, for example, express the vague policy that a prisoner should be paroled only when such action is not incompatible with the welfare of the community.[46] More specific criteria have included such factors as the offender's prior criminal record, his or her personality and physical condition, social history, employment record, intelligence, family status, institutional conduct, parole plan, prior probation or parole history, and his or her stated intentions for the future, among others. Yet questions exist as to how these variables should be weighted in determining if or when a prisoner should be released. Factors that are deemed significant may be emphasized although they may indeed have no significance at all.

In a number of settings the decision to release falls within a political arena. The recommendations of a sentencing judge, a prosecuting attorney, or an active press can invariably affect the paroling process when such gestures have implications for the political power base held by a member of the parole board. Moreover, in some state jurisdictions and the federal system, crime victims are permitted to testify at the release hearings of inmates convicted of victimizing them—a practice with a probable impact on parole decision-making.

Finally, predictions of human behavior are especially problematic when the subjects under review have already demonstrated a reduced capacity to function in a socially approved manner. Selection decisions may totally bypass all those considered less likely to succeed. Indeed, conservative parole boards have been known to release only those prisoners who are seen to be good risks while denying parole to the remainder.[47]

WHO ARE THE BEST PAROLE RISKS?

Who, indeed, do the best on parole without repeating the crimes for which they were initially convicted? Rapists? Robbers? Prostitutes? Burglars? Check forgers? Shoplifters? Who?

Actually, it's none of the above. Quite surprisingly, the answer is murderers. There are several explanations. Many murderers tend to be first offenders who have committed crimes of passion and emotion. Another explanation is *age:* Since the majority of convicted murderers serve long prison sentences, they tend to be older when released—well beyond the high-crime-risk years of adolescence and young adulthood. Finally, the "felony murders" whom one would expect to be repeaters—the killers-for-hire, robber-murderers, and serial killers—never really get the chance, at least not on the street. Most of these end up on death row or receive terms of life without parole.

American Law Institute Guidelines Given the lack of specific criteria for parole decision-making in many jurisdictions, the American Law Institute in its *Model Penal Code* has suggested an alternative approach. Rather than determining who should be paroled, the emphasis should be on who ought not to be paroled, using the following primary reasons for denial:

1. There is a substantial risk that he will not conform to the conditions of parole.
2. His release at that time would depreciate the seriousness of his crime or promote disrespect for law.
3. His release would have a substantially adverse effect on institution discipline.
4. His continued correctional treatment, medical care, or vocational or other training in the institution would substantially enhance his capacity to lead a law-abiding life when released at a later date.[48]

Even this, however, has problems, since it includes no criteria for determining when the inmate denied parole should ultimately be released.

Mandatory Release One final matter here is the issue of repeated denials of parole in spite of an inmate's eligibility for conditional release. It is not uncommon, for example, for a parole board to request a recommendation from the district attorney or chief prosecutor from the county in which a defendant was convicted. Depending on the nature of the case, the prosecutor's parole recommendation can influence the board's decision. Similarly, there can be opposition to an inmate's parole by the police, the news media, the victims of the crime, and the public at large.

In cases where inmates are serving indeterminate sentences and parole is repeatedly denied, or in certain types of definite ("flat") sentences, another factor comes into play—good-time credits. As noted earlier, **good time** refers to the number of days deducted from a sentence for good behavior, meritorious service, particular kinds of work, or other considerations. Moreover, good time falls into three categories. There is *statutory good time,* which is given automatically when inmates serve their time without problems. In addition, there is *earned time* for participation in work, educational, or treatment programs. In a few jurisdictions there is *meritorious time,* earned for some exceptional act or service (such as firefighting or other life-saving efforts).

Almost all jurisdictions provide for some type of good time, ranging from 4.5 days per month in the federal system to 75 days a month in Alabama.[49] Although the maximum number of good-time days are fixed by statute, in some jurisdictions "earned time" credits are applied beyond this upper limit. In Florida, for example, where there is no parole and the maximum amount of good time is 30 days per month, many inmates serve an average of less than a third of their original sentences.[50] Florida correctional officials explain that despite the statutory limitations, most drug offenders earn time off at a rate of 5 days for every day served.

The accumulation of good-time days ultimately results in **mandatory release**—release as a matter of law. In New York and Missouri, inmates who are mandatory releasees are subject to the same conditions as parolees and are under the supervision of a parole officer. In all other jurisdictions, however, mandatory release is *unconditional.*

Conditions of Parole As with probationers, all individuals released on parole are released under a series of conditions, the violation of which can result in revocation and return to prison. These are the "dos and don'ts" of parole, and they originated under the ticket-of-leave system.

Parole conditions are fairly uniform from state to state and can be grouped into two general areas: *reform conditions,* which urge parolees toward a

Good time: The number of days deducted from a sentence for good behavior, meritorious service, particular kinds of work, or other considerations.

Mandatory release: A release from prison required by statute when an inmate has been confined for a time period equal to his or her full prison sentence minus statutory "good time" if any.

noncriminal way of life; and *control conditions,* which enable the parole agency to keep track of them. The most common conditions include the following:

- *Reform Conditions:*
  Comply with the laws
  Maintain employment and support dependents
  Refrain from use of drugs
- *Control Conditions:*
  Report to parole officer upon release and periodically thereafter
  Cooperate with the parole officer
  Get permission (or notify) to change employment or residence

In addition, as with probationers, there may be special conditions of parole geared to the particular treatment and control needs of a given person.

In many jurisdictions, the list of parole regulations tends to be extreme, designed to control almost every aspect of the parolee's life. Since 1970, however, a number of states, such as Alaska, Connecticut, Massachusetts, and Ohio, have abandoned a number of the restrictions, including regulations on marriage and divorce, association with undesirables, motor vehicle usage, and alcohol use.

Parole Supervision and Services

Like probation officers, parole officers are responsible for supervising, aiding, and controlling the clients assigned to their caseloads. As counselors, officers serve to ease parolees' reentry into society and to aid them in overcoming any obstacles to community adjustment. In addition to individual counseling, they may help in the development of employment plans and job readiness, work with families in the resolution of problems, and orchestrate referrals to community agencies for the handling of certain persistent difficulties. Some parole agencies have special units that focus on such areas as alcoholism, drug use, and unemployment, or on the more unique concerns presented in the supervision of mentally ill or retarded offenders.

Parole officers, in addition to being counselors, also have the duty to police the behavior of those under their supervision. In many states, parole officers are armed peace officers, and as such, one officer put it this way:

> It's a rather contradictory bag to be in. We're what you might call "gun-carrying social workers." Or better yet, how about if we refer to it as the discipline of "authoritarian casework"?

Although quasi–law enforcement responsibilities are apparent in probation supervision, they are considerably more pronounced with respect to parole. Parolees tend to be more dangerous and serious offenders. Many have been incarcerated for long periods of time, with intensive exposure to prison violence and the inmate culture. Furthermore, the stigma of the ex-con label and former inmate status lessen the potential for community adjustment. All of these combine to stress the law enforcement role of the parole officer and hinder the effective pursuit of rehabilitative goals.

Parole Violation and Revocation

The violation and revocation process in parole is very similar to that described for probation. After a new arrest or serious technical violation, a warrant is issued and the parolee is taken into custody. Pursuant to the Supreme Court decision in *Morrissey* v. *Brewer,* the delinquent parolee is given a measure of due process during his or her preliminary and revocation hearings, and the parole board can make one of two decisions: "restore to supervision" or "return to prison."

Should parole be revoked, the next issue involves exactly how much time the parolee must serve in prison. This decision is made by the parole board either at the revocation hearing or during the next board meeting at the institution. A bitterly disputed matter in this regard is whether *"street time"*—the period spent under parole supervision prior to violation—should be credited against the remaining sentence. In some jurisdictions, the parole board establishes the violator's "date of delinquency"—the point at which the violation occurred. From that date on, any time served on the street is considered *"dead time."* Thus, if an inmate with a 15-year sentence is paroled after 3 years, serves 2 years in the community in good standing but is then declared delinquent, 5 years of the sentence will be considered as having been completed. The parole board may put a 3-year "hold" on the offender, meaning that he or she will be eligible for parole consideration in 3 years. However, in other jurisdictions, the time spent on the street in good standing is not credited in this manner.

This issue has also been addressed with respect to probation violation, and in regard to both probation and parole revocation, the denial of street-time credit represents a nonjudicial increase in sentence. This argument notwithstanding, the courts have consistently upheld the right of states to deny street-time credits. They have done so on the theory that since the probationer or parolee was not physically in custody, he or she was not "serving a sentence."[51]

"Street time"

"Dead time"

Parole Discharge

Individuals can be discharged from parole in a number of ways. First, they can "max out." That is, they can reach their **maximum expiration date**—the date their entire full sentence formally terminates. Second, in more than half the states and the federal system, parolees can be discharged by the parole board prior to their maximum expiration date. In this instance, however, a number of jurisdictions require that some minimum parole period must be served. In Ohio, for example, discharge can occur after 1 year of satisfactory supervision and after 5 years, in the case of a life sentence. Under New York's *executive clemency statute,* if the time remaining on the maximum sentence at the time of parole is more than 5 years, the board can issue a discharge after 5 consecutive years of satisfactory supervision. Third, discharge can occur through commutation of sentence or pardon by the governor. Pardon also represents the chief mechanism through which the civil rights lost upon conviction and imprisonment can be restored in about half the states. In the balance, they are automatically restored upon release from the penitentiary, discharge from parole, or at the final expiration of sentence. In Hawaii, Indiana, Massachusetts, Michigan, and New Hampshire, however, a defendant's civil rights are not lost upon conviction of a felony offense. (For an overview of parole in Canada, see Exhibit 14.4.)

Maximum expiration date: The date on which the full sentence ends.

TRENDS IN COMMUNITY-BASED CORRECTION

As of 1999, the prison population in the United States well exceeded 1.2 million. Moreover, there were more than 690,000 parolees and mandatory releasees under the supervision of parole authorities, an additional 400,000 under the supervision of various community agencies, plus more than 3 million

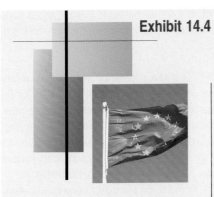

Exhibit 14.4   **International Perspectives on Crime and Justice**
Parole in Canada

Despite calls from many sources for its abolition, Canada has retained a system of parole to govern release from prison, at least for the minority of adult inmates with lengthy sentences. Most inmates will be released at the discretion of correctional officials on a program typically called a temporary absence (TA), to live in the community until the end of their sentences with varying levels of supervision.

If the sentence is 6 months or longer, inmates in most parts of Canada can apply for a hearing before the parole board. Federal inmates apply to the National Parole Board, which has members across the country to hold hearings as needed in penitentiaries. Provincial parole boards can be found in Ontario, Quebec, and British Columbia. In other areas, the National Parole Board has agreed to hear the cases of provincial inmates, but the number is small because of the common use of TAs. Inmates are eligible for full parole after serving one-third of the sentence. If repeatedly denied parole, they are released after two-thirds and are subject to parole supervision for the remaining third. In rare cases, federal inmates who constitute a demonstrable risk to the public can be held until the end of the sentence but then they are released without parole supervision.

The parole component of the system draws considerable public contempt, notable even in a criminal justice system that does not enjoy widespread public support. Parole is not a public process in Canada, but the media or other interested parties can apply to observe specific hearings of the National Parole Board and the British Columbia Board of Parole; the results of decisions are in the public domain and victim involvement in the process has increased in recent years. As in the United States, high-profile crimes committed by parolees draw criticism to the parole process. Civil litigation against the parole board and/or correctional officials has been launched by surviving family members of people murdered by parolees, but no case has yet come to trial.

Young offenders do not qualify for parole unless they were tried in adult court. Instead, they can apply for a judicial review of their custody sentence if there are reasons to believe that early release is desirable. The decision is made by the judge, who can reduce but not extend the length of a custody term.

SOURCE: Alison Hatch Cunningham and Curt Taylor Griffiths, *Canadian Criminal Justice: A Primer* (Toronto: Harcourt Brace, 1997).

under court-ordered probation. Given the overcrowding in contemporary prisons and the pressures on state correctional systems to remedy the unconstitutional conditions of many of their facilities, combined with the trend toward mandatory prison sentences for violent offenders and drug traffickers, the character of inmate populations across America will likely undergo some change. More and more, prisons and penitentiaries will become places for holding the serious criminals, at least for a time, and there will be an increased use of community corrections for other types of offenders. Thus probation, court diversion, and other forms of community-based supervision and service will become even more significant in the overall correctional spectrum. The criminal justice system has long since begun its attempts to meet this challenge of community-based supervision. However, many issues and alternatives remain problematic, casting considerable doubt over the effectiveness and future use of community supervision.

Furlough and Temporary Release

As a generic concept, the **furlough** is an authorized, unescorted absence from a correctional institution for a specified period of time.[52] It is a temporary release from prison granted for the purpose of enabling inmates to reestablish

Furlough: An authorized, unescorted absence from a correctional institution for a specified period of time.

community contacts and family ties on a gradual basis. It has emerged in a variety of forms, including the home furlough, work release, and educational release.

Home Furlough   A home furlough is a short leave of absence from the institution, often taken on weekends, and lasting anywhere from 24 hours to a week. It serves a number of rehabilitative, humanitarian, and pragmatic purposes. It is a mechanism of release transition whereby inmates can begin the normalization of family relationships, reestablish contacts with the outside community, and prepare for eventual permanent release. In addition, prison administrators view the furlough as an avenue for better institutional management, feeling that the promise of a home visit for good behavior fosters better compliance with custodial regulations.

Virtually unknown before the late 1960s, home furloughs have been adopted by most states as well as the federal system. Eligibility criteria vary, however, from one jurisdiction to the next. In some states, it is a matter of legislative statute and applies only to inmates who are within 1 year of parole eligibility or conditional release and who have not been convicted of any escape, absconding, or violent offenses. In others, eligibility is a matter of legislative, judicial, or correctional policy, with the criteria ranging from highly specific to hopelessly vague.[53]

Work Release   In many ways similar in concept and purpose to the home furlough, work release is an alternative to total incarceration whereby inmates are permitted to work for pay in the free community but must spend their nonworking hours back at the institution. Work release is not a recent correctional innovation; it was initiated under Wisconsin's Huber Law (introduced by Senator Henry A. Huber for the temporary release of jailed misdemeanants) in 1913. However, the idea has been only slowly accepted, and it was not until the early 1970s that work release became a widespread correctional practice for felony offenders.[54] Eligibility criteria are similar to those adopted for home

"We'll continue this tomorrow. I'm on a work-release program and I have to be back in my cell by six o'clock."

furloughs, restricting release to those nearing parole or conditional release who do not represent significant risk to the community.

In addition to the advantages of furloughs in general, work release offers the benefit of potentially reshaping an offender's self-image and promoting the process of decarceration. Furthermore, releasees can assume some financial responsibilities by paying their own transportation to and from the institution, contributing to their room and board, supplementing any welfare benefits that are being given to their families, and beginning payments on any court-ordered restitution. Thus, work release can also serve in the interests of the taxpaying community.

However, work release has been faced with many obstacles to its effective implementation. It has been opposed on the grounds that prisoners take jobs away from law-abiding citizens; releasees have been exploited by some employers who feel that "cons" should not be paid at normal wage levels; and prison-based training has not always been usable in the modern employment market. The distance between many correctional institutions and active job centers has also restricted work-release efforts. Many prisons are in isolated rural areas, and it is generally neither feasible nor cost-effective to transport inmates daily over long distances. This has been mitigated, to some extent, by the nightly housing of inmates in jails and detention centers located near their job sites. Some jurisdictions have provided for residential work-release centers. These offer not only living facilities for working inmates, but also counseling and supervised recreation during evening and weekend hours.

Study Release   As a natural extension of the work-release principle, study release is offered to minimum-security, parole-eligible inmates with the motivation for vocational or academic enrichment. Following the criteria and regulations of a state's work-release project, study release provides opportunities for full-time, on-site participation in vocational school and college programs.

Experiences With Temporary Release   Temporary release programs also have their critics, and crimes committed by inmates on work release or home furlough are quickly made conspicuous. During 1988, for example, there were few Americans who were unaware of the name of Willie Horton—sentenced to life without parole in Massachusetts for a homicide in 1974 only to be released on a weekend furlough during which he committed a brutal rape.[55] Following the Horton incident, Massachusetts revoked work-release privileges for all inmates convicted of first-degree murder.

"I'm sentencing you to 25 years in prison with no hope of parole until after 3 p.m. tomorrow afternoon!"

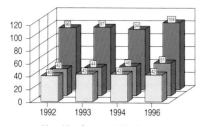

■ Mean Max. Sentence in Months
■ % of Sentence Served
□ Mean Months Served (in prison/jail)

**Time Served by Violent
Offenders in State Prisons**

SOURCE: *Truth in Sentencing Report*, Bureau of Justice Statistics, 1999.

In spite of incidents of bad publicity, the concept of temporary release continued to hold promise as a form of partial incarceration, as a bridge between the prison and open society, and as another treatment mechanism in the spectrum of community-based correctional services. Perhaps many of the difficulties in existing programs might be eliminated, or at least minimized, with better screening of candidates and monitoring of releasees. However, the kind of public outrage that can be generated when even a few isolated violent crimes are committed by persons who are supposed to be behind bars provides little support for its use as an acceptable correctional tool. This, combined with many unresolved questions as to whether temporary release actually reduces recidivism, and the political realities associated with rehabilitative risk taking at the potential expense of public safety, suggest only a guarded prognosis for the implementation of such programs on a continuing basis.

In contrast are the *halfway houses* and *prerelease centers* that have been developing since the 1960s. Designed for inmates who are just a few months away from their parole dates, these residential facilities in urban locations provide individual counseling, vocational guidance, and job placement. Residents are required to abide by minimum-security regulations, attend counseling and therapy sessions, and actively seek employment when ready.

Whether halfway houses are effective mechanisms for community reintegration is open to question. Studies of their experience found significant levels of escape, recidivism, and returns to prison for disciplinary violations. But, since recidivism seemed to be no higher among prerelease center residents than among other newly released inmates, it has been recommended that the halfway house concept be expanded. There seems to be little likelihood that this will occur, however, not only because of the sensitive political nature of the concept, but also due to the opposition of many communities to "placing convicts in our backyards."

Exhibit 14.5   **Careers in Justice**
Parole Officer

Parole officers provide counseling, agency and employment referrals, and services related to offenders' risks and needs. Extensive field and public relations contacts are required. Parole officers work extensively with trial judges, prosecutors, police, and other criminal justice personnel. Parole officers also conduct investigations on parolees' backgrounds and behaviors. In addition, because parole officers are armed peace officers in many jurisdictions, they make arrests, transport parole violators, and testify at violation hearings. While most parole officers work in the community, some work in correctional institutions preparing pre-parole summaries for those inmates about to be released.

The minimum qualifications for parole work in most jurisdictions include a bachelor's degree from an accredited educational institution, in criminal justice, law enforcement, social service, communications, or a related field, and no legal prohibition against carrying a firearm. In lieu of the educational requirement, a few jurisdictions accept 2 years' experience in probation or some other area of social service. By contrast, some jurisdictions require a master's degree, or a bachelor's degree plus 2 years' experience in social service.

Starting salaries for parole officers vary by jurisdiction, with a range of $22,000 to more than $30,000 per year.

Op-Ed

When Governor George Pataki proposed that New York become the 16th state to abolish parole, he was echoing the feelings of many other politicians and law enforcement officials who had seriously pondered its abolition. As early as 1938, FBI Director J. Edgar Hoover had commented that the biggest job of law enforcement was the chasing down of the "canny recidivists," "mad dogs," and "predatory animals" who have been "cloaked by the mantle of parole."

The antagonism toward parole is probably greater than toward any other correctional policy. And this is not surprising, given some of the stories in the media about paroled sex offenders and other violent predatory criminals who commit unspeakable acts after they are released from prison.

In counterpoint, however, there is no proof that eliminating parole reduces crime. Furthermore, without parole many offenders could end up spending less time in the penitentiary, since "flat" sentences result in automatic release at the end of a set term. As such, having no parole option decreases the state's ability to keep dangerous offenders in the institution. And here is one final thought. Of all of the states that have eliminated parole in recent years, three of them—Colorado, Connecticut, and Florida—have reestablished the equivalent of parole boards, for a very clear reason: Abolition failed to increase the amount of time served, because prisons had become so crowded that many inmates had to be released early.

SUMMARY

Community-based correction involves programs and activities within the community that are generally of a rehabilitative, nonpunitive nature. Such correctional approaches include criminal justice diversion, probation and conditional release, restitution programs, and furlough and temporary release.

Criminal justice diversion refers to the removal of offenders from the application of the criminal law at any stage of the police or court processes. Diversion as such began with the Chicago Boys' Court in 1914. Today its use is widespread for both juvenile and adult offenders, but its impact is difficult to assess. Both researchers and penal reformers have generally agreed that diversion programs are an essential part of correctional programming, since the experience of incarceration for many individuals often contributes to the very behaviors it was designed to eliminate. Diversion typically includes programs like youth service bureaus, public inebriate programs, civil commitment, citizen dispute settlement, and Treatment Alternatives to Street Crime (TASC).

Probation is a judicial disposition, a status, a system, and a process. As an alternative to imprisonment, it is the most widely used adjudication disposition, encompassing elements of both community protection and offender rehabilitation. Probation was initially developed in recognition of the fact that a large number of offenders pose little, if any, threat to the community. It was later developed with the notion that these offenders could be spared the stigmatizing experience of prison and still be successfully punished for their crimes. Additionally, the appeal of probation has also been economic, since the costs of placing an individual on probation are considerably less than incarceration. Today, many jurisdictions vary their probation programming to meet the security, punishment, and rehabilitative needs of individual offenders. Such programs include restitution, shock probation, and intensive probation supervision.

Parole, common in the United States for at least a century, refers to the practice of allowing the final portion of a prison sentence to be served in the community. In contrast to probation, which involves community supervision in lieu of imprisonment, parole occurs after some part of the prison term has been completed. Also, the power to grant parole is not held by the courts, as is the case with probation, but is determined by an administrative board that can be an independent state agency,

a unit in a larger state department, or part of the body that regulates the state's correctional institutions.

Both probation and parole are subject to conditions, the violation of which may result in incarceration. The U.S. Supreme Court, through a series of decisions during the 1970s, has established guidelines regarding the due process requirements at probation and parole revocation proceedings.

Other forms of community-based correction include temporary release programs, restitution, and halfway houses. Temporary release programs include furlough, work release, and study release. Furlough involves a short leave of absence from a correctional facility that is intended to ease the transition from institutional to community life. Work release, not unlike home furlough, allows inmates to work in the community for a certain number of hours while they spend their nonworking hours in a correctional institution. Study release programs, though not as widespread as work release, allow inmates to pursue vocational or academic schooling outside the correctional facility.

KEY TERMS

community-based corrections **382**
diversion **382**
furlough **401**
Gagnon v. *Scarpelli* **394**
good time **398**

intensive probation supervision **391**
mandatory release **398**
maximum expiration date **400**
Mempa v. *Rhay* **392**
Morrissey v. *Brewer* **393**

parole **395**
probation **385**
restitution **389**
shock probation **390**
suspended sentence **387**

QUESTIONS FOR DISCUSSION

1. What are the differences between probation and parole in terms of organization and administration, eligibility and selection, supervision and services, and conditions and revocation?
2. What is your opinion of home furlough and work release? Should they be abolished? Why or why not?

3. Should parole be abolished? Why or why not?
4. How do you feel about community-based correction? Is this a helpful way to deal with nonviolent offenders? Why or why not?

MEDIA RESOURCES

1. **What Works.** The National Institute of Justice has prepared an interesting summary report on the effectiveness of various types of criminal justice programs. See Lawrence W. Sherman, Denise C. Gottfredson, Doris L. MacKensie, John Eck, Peter Reuter, and Shawn D. Bushway, "Preventing Crime: What Works, What Doesn't, and What's Promising," National Institute of Justice, *Research in Brief*, July 1998.
2. **Corrections in Canada.** For an indepth examination of corrections in Canada, see Alison Hatch Cunningham and Curt Taylor Griffiths, *Canadian Criminal*

Justice: A Primer (Toronto: Harcourt Brace, 1997). There is also a useful Web site associated with this book. Web address: http://www.cjprimer.com
3. **Probation and Parole Data.** The Bureau of Justice Statistics has complied a number of reports on probationers and parolees, which may be obtained through its Web site. (Web address: http://www.ojp.usdoj.gov)
4. **Parole Watch.** Parole Watch is a Web site, with links to other sites, that monitors current parole issues and tracks violent parolees. (Internet address: http://parolewatch.org/welcome.htm)

NOTES

1. *New York Times,* January 10, 1999, p. 11.
2. Duane C. McBride, "Criminal Justice Diversion," in *Crime and the Criminal Justice Process,* ed. James A. Inciardi and Kenneth C. Haas (Dubuque, Iowa: Kendall/Hunt, 1978), p. 246.
3. Jacob M. Braude, "Boys' Court: Individualized Justice for the Youthful Offender," *Federal Probation* 12 (June 1948): 9–14.
4. Daniel Glaser, James A. Inciardi, and Dean V. Babst, "Later Heroin Use by Marijuana-Using, Heroin-Using, and Non–Drug-Using Adolescent Offenders in New York City," *International Journal of the Addictions* 4 (June 1969): 145–155.
5. James Swartz, "TASC—The Next 20 Years," pp. 127–148 in *Drug Treatment and Criminal Justice,* ed. James A. Inciardi (Newbury Park, Calif.: Sage, 1993).
6. *Criminal Justice Drug Letter,* January 1999, pp. 1, 6.
7. James A. Inciardi, Duane C. McBride, and James E. Rivers, *Drug Control and the Courts* (Thousand Oaks, Calif.: Sage, 1996), pp. 35–53.
8. *Criminal Justice Drug Letter,* January 1999, pp. 1, 6.
9. American Bar Association Project on Standards for Criminal Justice, *Standards Relating to Probation* (New York: Institute for Judicial Administration, 1970), p. 9.
10. National Advisory Commission on Criminal Justice Standards and Goals, *Corrections* (Washington, D.C.: U.S. Government Printing Office, 1973), p. 312.
11. James A. Inciardi, "The Impact of Presentence Investigations on Subsequent Sentencing Practices" (Paper presented at the Annual Meeting of the American Sociological Association, New York, N.Y., August 1976).
12. Robert M. Carter and Leslie T. Wilkins, "Some Factors in Sentencing Policy," *Journal of Criminal Law, Criminology, and Police Science* 58 (December 1967): 503–514.
13. *Williams* v. *New York,* 347 U.S. 241 (1949).
14. *Gardner* v. *Florida,* 430 U.S. 349 (1977).
15. *Code of Alabama,* 15-22-50.
16. *Cox* v. *States,* 283 S.E. 2d 716 (Ga Ct. App. 1981).
17. *People* v. *Mitchell,* 178 Cal. Rptr. 188 (Cal. Ct. App., 1981).
18. *State* v. *Behrens,* 285 N.W. 2d 513 (Neb. Sup. Ct., 1979).
19. *State* v. *Wilson,* 604 P. 2d 739 (Idaho Sup., 1980).
20. *Wood* v. *State,* 378 So. 2d 111 (Fla. Dist. Ct. App., 1980).
21. *State* v. *Alexander,* 267 S.E. 2d 397 (N.C. Ct. App., 1980).
22. Denny C. Langston, "Probation and Parole: No More Free Rides," *Corrections Today,* August 1988, pp. 90–93.
23. Peter Finn and Dale Parent, "Texas Collects Substantial Revenues From Probation Fees," *Federal Probation* 57 (June 1993): 17–18.
24. *Griffin* v. *Wisconsin,* 483 U.S. 868 (1987).
25. See *Barber* v. *State,* 387 So. 2d 540 (Fla. Dist. Ct. App., 1980).
26. See Gilbert Geis, "Restitution by Criminal Offenders: A Summary and Overview," in *Restitution in Criminal Justice,* ed. Joe Hudson and Burt Galaway (Lexington, Mass.: Lexington, 1977), pp. 246–264.
27. Richard Lawrence, "Restitution Programs Pay Back the Victim and Society," *Corrections Today,* February 1990, pp. 96–98; Michael Courlander, "Restitution Programs: Problems and Solutions," *Corrections Today,* July 1988, pp. 165–167.
28. Paul C. Friday and David M. Petersen, "Shock of Imprisonment: Comparative Analysis of Short-Term Incarceration as a Treatment Technique" (Paper presented at the InterAmerican Congress of the American Society of Criminology and the Inter-American Association of Criminology, Caracas, Venezuela, November 1972).
29. Friday and Petersen, "Shock of Imprisonment"; Harry E. Allen and Clifford E. Simonsen, *Corrections in America* (New York: Macmillan, 1981), p. 161; National Advisory Commission, *Corrections,* p. 321.
30. See David M. Petersen and Paul C. Friday, "Early Release From Incarceration: Race as a Factor in the Use of 'Shock Probation,' " *Journal of Criminal Law and Criminology* 66 (March 1975): 79–87; Joseph A. Waldron and Henry R. Angelino, "Shock Probation: A Natural Experiment on the Effect of a Short Period of Incarceration," *Prison Journal* 57 (Spring–Summer 1977): 52.
31. Lawrence W. Sherman, Denise C. Gottfredson, Doris L. MacKensie, John Eck, Peter Reuter, and Shawn D. Bushway, "Preventing Crime: What Works, What Doesn't, and What's Promising," National Institute of Justice, *Research in Brief,* July 1998.
32. Billie S. Erwin and Lawrence A. Bennett, "New Dimensions in Probation: Georgia's Experience with Intensive Probation Supervision," National Institute of Justice, *Research in Brief,* January 1987.
33. Susan B. Noonan and Edward J. Latessa, "Intensive Probation: An Examination of Recidivism and Social Adjustment," *American Journal of Criminal Justice* 11 (1987): 45–61. See also, Frank S. Pearson, "Evaluation of New Jersey's Intensive Supervision Program," *Crime and Delinquency* 34 (October 1988): 437–448.
34. Joan Petersilia and Susan Turner, "Evaluating Intensive Supervision Probation/Parole: Results of a Nationwide Experiment," National Institute of Justice *Research in Brief,* May 1993, pp. 1–10.

35. *Mempa* v. *Rhay,* 398 U.S. 128 (1967).

36. *Morrissey* v. *Brewer,* 408 U.S. 471 (1972).

37. *Gagnon* v. *Scarpelli,* 411 U.S. 778 (1973).

38. Joan Petersilia, Susan Turner, James Kahan, and Joyce Peterson, *Granting Felons Probation: Public Risk and Alternatives* (Santa Monica, Calif.: Rand, 1985).

39. Johnny McGaha, Michael Fichter, and Peter Hirschburg, "Felony Probation: A Re-Examination of Public Risk," *American Journal of Criminal Justice* 11 (1987): 1–9.

40. G. I. Giardini, *The Parole Process* (Springfield, Ill.: Thomas, 1959), p. 9.

41. Harry Elmer Barner, *The Story of Punishment: A Record of Man's Inhumanity to Man* (Montclair, N.J.: Patterson Smith, 1972), pp. 68–80.

42. See E. C. Wines, "Commutation Laws in the United States," *Report of the Prison Association of New York,* 1868, pp. 154–170.

43. *Menechino* v. *Oswald,* 430 F. 2d 403 (2d Cir., 1970).

44. *Johnson, U.S. ex rel.* v. *Chairman, New York State Board of Parole,* 363 F. Supp. 416, aff'd, 500 F. 2d 925 (2d Cir., 1971).

45. *Greenholtz* v. *Inmates of Nebraska Penal and Correctional Complex,* 422 U.S. 1 (1979).

46. See, for example, *Tennessee Code,* 40-3614.

47. James A. Inciardi and Duane C. McBride, "The Parole Prediction Myth," *International Journal of Criminology and Penology* 5 (August 1977): 235–244.

48. Don M. Gottfredson, Peter B. Hoffman, Maurice H. Sigler, and Leslie T. Wilkins, "Making Paroling Policy Explicit," *Crime and Delinquency* 21 (January 1975): 36.

49. Su Park Davis, "Good Time," *Corrections Compendium,* May 1990, pp. 1, 4–11.

50. James Austin, "The Consequences of Escalating the Use of Imprisonment," *Corrections Compendium,* September 1991, pp. 1, 4–8.

51. See Richard C. Hand and Richard G. Singer, *Sentencing Computation Laws* (Washington, D.C.: American Bar Association, 1974).

52. E. Eugene Miller, "Furloughs as a Technique of Reintegration," in *Corrections in the Community,* ed. E. Eugene Miller and M. Robert Montilla (Reston, Va.: Reston, 1977), p. 201.

53. *Corrections Compendium,* January–February 1990, pp. 9–15.

54. Elmer H. Johnson and Kenneth E. Kotch, "Two Factors in Development of Work Release: Size and Location of Prisons," *Journal of Criminal Justice* 1 (March 1973): 44–45.

55. *Time,* November 14, 1988, p. 20.

Part 5

JUVENILE JUSTICE

Chapter 15
The Juvenile Justice System

Elements of
Criminal
Justice

WASHINGTON, D.C. — The U.S. Department of Justice reported that the nation's homicide rate fell in 1997 to its lowest level in 30 years, with particularly significant drops recently among those in the crime-prone age groups of 14-to-17 years and 18-to-24 years. Nevertheless, the Justice Department added, young Americans with firearms were still killing each other at a relatively high rate.[1] Specifically, while firearms killings by people 25 and older dropped 50 percent between 1980 and 1997, the number of killings by those under 25 decreased by almost the same proportion.

What explains the changing rates of homicide by youths? Will such a trend continue, or will the numbers of serious crimes by youths shift again as the nation enters the twenty-first century?

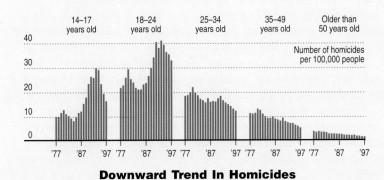

Downward Trend In Homicides

Homicides have decreased nationally, especially those committed by teenagers.

SOURCE: Bureau of Justice Statistics.

In response to the changes and severity of youth crime in the United States, the juvenile justice system has been forced to reevaluate its guiding principles. Considerable debate has centered on the proper role of the justice system in dealing with youthful offenders—whether the juvenile, no matter how serious the crime, needs protection and rehabilitation, or whether the punishment should fit the crime, regardless of the offender's age.

To understand the paradoxical character of juvenile justice processing in the United States, a number of questions must be addressed. Who is a juvenile? What is the jurisdiction of the juvenile justice system? Why are juveniles treated differently from adults? What is the philosophy that characterizes juvenile justice? Why is it that some juveniles who are not necessarily "delinquent" are nevertheless dealt with by the juvenile courts? How is juvenile justice different from the rest of the criminal justice system? And since a special justice system has been designed for youths, why are many juvenile cases transferred to the adult criminal courts?

THE NATURE OF JUVENILE JUSTICE

An *adult* is a person who reached "the age of majority"—some "magic number" (usually 18) that indicates that the individual is legally responsible for his or her actions and behavior. An adult has the right to vote, to marry, to hold government office, and to enter into contracts. Furthermore, if an adult should violate the criminal law or be accused of a crime, he or she is processed through a justice system that is grounded in the due process of law guaranteed by the Constitution of the United States.

A *juvenile* is a person who has not reached the age of majority—and therefore is deemed to have a "special status."[2] Juveniles are held to an alternative standard of behavior than are adults. Children are required to attend school from the ages of 6 to 16; they are expected to obey their parents; they are forbidden to drink alcohol, smoke cigarettes, or drive motor vehicles; they may not marry without parental permission; they cannot enter into business or financial contracts; and they are not permitted to vote, enter the military, or run away from home. Some jurisdictions may place other restrictions on juveniles, such as curfews, or laws against "incorrigible" or "immoral" behavior. But like adults, children can be charged with violations of the criminal law. Yet because of their special status of being below the age of majority, an alternative system has evolved for dealing with juvenile lawbreakers.

The juvenile justice system in the United States was designed with the philosophy that the special status of children requires that they be protected and corrected, not necessarily punished. But as the system evolved, it failed to accord to juveniles any individual rights. For after all, in American society a juvenile is essentially in the "custody" of parents or guardians, or failing either, the state.

Beyond the philosophical orientation stemming from the special status of children, there are other differences between adult and juvenile justice systems. For adults to fall within the jurisdiction of the criminal courts, there is only one mechanism: They must be charged with some violation of the criminal law. A young person's coming to the attention of the juvenile courts, however, can occur through a variety of ways. First, and quite logically, the juvenile may be found to have violated the criminal law. Second, he or she can be charged with having committed a **status offense**—an act declared by statute to be a crime because it violates the behavior standards expected of children. Because of their status, only juveniles can be charged with the offenses of running away, truancy, or being incorrigible. Third, a child may fall within the jurisdiction of the court because of the behavior of an adult. Should a juvenile be the victim of abuse, neglect, or abandonment by a parent or guardian, the courts may intervene.

Single parent/family breakdown	26%
Drugs	21%
No jobs	17%
Poor housing	15%
Poor education	7%
All these factors	5%
Don't know	5%

0   5   10   15   20   25   30

The Roots of Delinquency

Where judges place the greatest blame for the delinquency of today's youth.

SOURCE: *National Law Journal,* August 8, 1994.

Status offense: An act declared by statute to be a crime because it violates the standards of behavior expected of children.

Perhaps the major difference between the adult and juvenile justice systems involves the purpose and nature of the sanctions imposed when intervention occurs. As noted in Chapter 10, five competing philosophies circumscribe sentencing in the adult courts: retribution, vengeance, incapacitation, deterrence, and rehabilitation. By contrast, the actions taken in the juvenile courts, at least in theory, are those considered to be "in the best interests of the child." The juvenile justice system, then, has been structured in the notion that every child is treatable and that judicial intervention will result in positive behavioral change. One would thus assume that juvenile court sanctions are based on a rehabilitation model and do not include any other sentencing objectives.

The Emergence of Juvenile Justice

From the early days of colonial America through the better part of the nineteenth century, juvenile offenders were handled in essentially the same way as adults. Children beyond the age of reason (about 7 years old) were held to adult standards of behavior. For criminal offenses, they were subject to the same sanctions, placed in the same institutions, and hung from the same gallows.

Parens Patriae

During the latter part of the nineteenth century there was an increasing awareness of explanations of criminal behavior suggesting that the roots of crime and delinquency were not necessarily to be found within individual offenders but, rather, were products of the culture and greater environment in which they lived. This new awareness, coupled with concern for the abuse and neglect of children both in and out of institutions, led to the emergence of a juvenile justice philosophy based on the established concept of ***parens patriae***, meaning "the state as parent."

Parens patriae: A philosophy under which the state takes over the role of parent.

Reformers merged the concept of *parens patriae* with the medical model of treatment to establish a system of juvenile justice in the United States designed to reform and rehabilitate young offenders. The underlying philosophy was that if a child "went astray," it was the parents who had failed. The court could take over the role of the parent, diagnose the problem, and prescribe the appropriate treatment. It did not matter what the child had done. His or her deviant behavior was merely a symptom of the problem. The court was not to blame the child or bring a finding of guilt, but to identify and treat the underlying problem. Moreover, the youth's welfare was to be the central concern of the court. This would not only protect the future of the child, but also permit an informal court process that considered the entire history and background of the child's difficulties, without being hampered by the limitations and requirements of official criminal procedure. Thus, juvenile processing would be a civil rather than a criminal matter.

The early juvenile justice reform efforts were heavily promoted by a number of penologists, philanthropists, and women's organizations—a group who have become known as the *"child savers."* The child savers movement crystallized in the passage of the **Illinois Juvenile Court Act** in 1899, which established the first statewide juvenile court system in the United States. The Illinois statute mandated a system that was to "secure for each minor such care and guidance, preferably in his own home, as will serve the emotional, mental and physical welfare of the minor and the best interests of the child; to preserve and strengthen the minor's family ties whenever possible." Only when necessary was the court to provide "custody, care, and discipline as nearly as possible equivalent to that which should be given by his parents."[3]

Illinois Juvenile Court Act: Legislation that established the first statewide juvenile court system in the United States.

Youths dealing cocaine in New York City.

Modern Juvenile Courts

By 1945, a juvenile court system was present in every state jurisdiction in the United States. Currently, there are approximately 3,000 courts across the nation hearing juvenile cases. While they all reflect the same general underlying philosophy, their sophistication and procedures tend to vary. Some systems are highly organized, having extensive and well-trained support staffs and large probation and treatment components. Others are less so, relying for their services on the resources of the adult criminal courts and correctional systems. Moreover, exactly where juvenile cases are heard within a jurisdiction's overall court structure varies greatly. In a number of states, such as Utah and Wyoming, there are *autonomous* juvenile courts, in which the court is organizationally separated from all others and the judges spend all of their time on juvenile matters. More commonly, as in New York and Delaware, for example, there are *coordinated juvenile courts,* wherein the proceedings occur in the state's family or domestic relations courts. Most jurisdictions, however, have *designated juvenile courts.* In these, judges who preside over criminal and civil cases also hear juvenile cases. On the latter occasions, the judge becomes the juvenile court.

Autonomous, coordinated, and designated juvenile courts

Juvenile courts, regardless of how they may be organized, have a jurisdiction defined in terms of a youth's age and alleged offense. Typically, the maximum age is 18, although age 16 is the upper limit in some locations. Furthermore, juvenile courts have authority over delinquency and status offenses. **Delinquency** involves criminal law violations, such as those listed in the FBI's *Uniform Crime Reports,* that would be considered crimes if committed by an adult. As such, a **delinquent** is a juvenile offender who has been adjudicated by an officer of a juvenile court. Status offenses, as noted earlier, are specific acts (truancy, running away) and general conditions (incorrigibility, uncontrollable behavior) that are unique to the status of being a juvenile. Although delinquents and status offenders compose the great majority of the juvenile justice population, there is yet a third category: dependent and neglected children, the deprived, and the abused. These juveniles are victims rather than offenders, and the court's intent is to provide assistance "in their best interests."

Delinquency: Criminal law violations by a juvenile that would be considered crimes if committed by an adult.

Delinquent: A juvenile offender who has been adjudicated by an officer of a juvenile court.

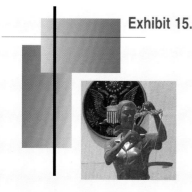

Exhibit 15.1 Historical Perspectives on Crime and Justice
The House of Refuge

The New York City House of Refuge, composed of a bleak set of barracks leased from the federal government, was the first house of correction for juveniles in the United States. It was dedicated on January 1, 1825, to its first nine inmates. Its founder, Reverend John Stanford, stated to his charges:

> You are to look at these walls which surround the building, not so much as a prison, but as a hospitable dwelling, in which you enjoy comfort and safety from those who once led you astray. And, I may venture to say, that in all probability, this is the best home many of you ever enjoyed. You have no need for me to tell you, that the consideration of all these favors should stimulate you to submission, industry, and gratitude. You are not placed here for punishment, but to produce your moral improvement.

Although the philosophy that led to the establishment of the New York City House of Refuge may have been praiseworthy at the time, in actual practice the institution was a juvenile prison. Structured to hold children securely, its interior was designed to implant the notions of order and rationality. Rooms were small and windowless and, much like jail cells, their doors were of iron-lattice slab. The treatment also paralleled that of a penitentiary. As children were admitted, they were given identical clothing and hair-

cuts. "Troublemakers" were always punished. The milder sanctions included either a diet of bread and water or the depriving of meals altogether. More serious cases received bread and water coupled with solitary confinement, manacling with a ball and chain, or whipping with a cat-o'-nine-tails. The most troublesome offenders were typically shipped off to sea.

The House of Refuge grew rapidly, accepting not only those children who had been adjudicated for delinquent acts, but also the poor, the destitute, the orphaned, the incorrigible, and others who were simply in danger of getting into trouble. Rather than a house of "refuge," the institution had become a reformatory for delinquents and a repository for street waifs that New York had nowhere else to put. But to the society at large, the House of Refuge was a model juvenile institution. A "refuge movement" began, and by the late 1840s similar facilities had been established in most eastern U.S. cities. By then, however, New York had already begun to phase out the refuge system.

In 1854, a facility large enough to hold more than a thousand juveniles was opened on Randall's Island—a small strip of land in New York's East River northeast of Manhattan. It was the *new* House of Refuge. Although it had retained the original name, it represented the state's first of many juvenile reformatories yet to come. In practice, youths placed in the Randall's Island facility were in prison at hard labor. In 1901, reformers exposed the Randall's Island refuge as an immense "chamber of horrors." Crusading journalists declared that beyond the waters of the East River and behind the bastions of Randall's Island lay a barbaric prison colony. An investigation was launched, but the House of Refuge somehow endured, at least for a time. Finally, in 1935, the edifice on Randall's Island was closed, the inmates were moved to a new juvenile prison recently built by the New York State Department of Corrections some 50 miles north of New York City, and the House of Refuge passed into history—remaining only as a curious anecdote in the annals of juvenile justice.

SOURCES: B. K. Pierce, *A Half Century With Juvenile Delinquents: The New York House of Refuge and Its Times* (New York: Appleton, 1869); Homer Folks, *The Care of Destitute, Neglected and Delinquent Children* (New York: Macmillan, 1902); Negley K. Teeters and John Otto Reinemann, *The Challenge of Delinquency* (Englewood Cliffs, N.J.: Prentice-Hall, 1961); David J. Rothman, *The Discovery of the Asylum* (Boston: Little, Brown, 1971); Robert S. Pickett, *House of Refuge: Origins of Juvenile Reform in New York State, 1815–1857* (Syracuse: Syracuse University Press, 1969).

PROCESSING JUVENILE OFFENDERS

Each year, more than a million juveniles are arrested by the police in the United States. The offenses cover all crime categories, from the most serious violent crimes of murder, forcible rape, and robbery, to such status offenses as running away, truancy, and curfew violations. Although perhaps a third of these offenses result in release with no more than a warning, the majority are referred to the courts for official processing. However, given the less formal nature of juvenile justice combined with the dynamics of police discretion, it was once estimated that for each arrest of a juvenile about 500 "probable cause" arrest situations occur.[4] (For a geographical analysis of juvenile homicides, see Exhibit 15.2.)

Youths and the Police

Police officers who encounter status offenders or juveniles involved in delinquent activities have several alternatives at their disposal. First, the officer may simply release the youth with a reprimand. Second, the officer may take the youth to the police station, where a "juvenile card" that briefly describes the incident is prepared. The parents may be called in for a discussion, after which the youth is released.

This discretionary power of the police is generally unreviewed. The style of the officer, the circumstances of the incident, and the policies of the department typically play a role in the decision to release or to detain juveniles. Studies have demonstrated, however, that numerous other factors can come into play: the attitude of the victim; the juvenile's prior record; the seriousness of the offense; the age, sex, race, and demeanor of the offender; the likelihood of adequate parental handling of the matter; the time and location of the incident; the availability of a service agency for referral; and the officer's perception of how the case will be handled by the court.[5] Consideration of these factors by a police officer, consciously or otherwise, is more likely to result in an "on the street disposition," or no action at all. Beyond these, there is the third option—taking the juvenile into custody. Yet even in this event, the police still have alternatives. Some law enforcement agencies in large urban areas have their own diversion and delinquency prevention programs to which they may send a juvenile, while status offenders may be brought to social service agencies for counseling and treatment. With felony offenses, and particularly those involving violence, there is the fourth police option—referral to the juvenile court.

Petition and Intake

The mechanism for bringing juveniles to the attention of the courts is through a **petition,** as opposed to an arrest warrant. This can be filed by the police, a victim, parents, school officials, or a social worker. Like an arrest warrant, the petition specifies the alleged offense or delinquency, the name and address of the child, the names and residences of his or her parents, and a description of the circumstances of the offense. This petition initiates the formal judicial processing of a juvenile.

After the petition is filed, an **intake hearing** is conducted by the court as a preliminary examination into the facts of the case. However, it is not presided over by a judge nor does it occur in open court. Rather, the hearing officer is usually a referee with a background in social work or one of the behavioral sciences, an attorney, a probation officer, or someone else assigned by the

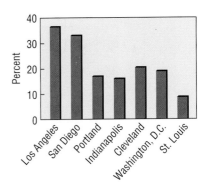

Drug Use Among Juvenile Arrestees

Percentages based on positive urinalysis for cocaine, opiates, PCP, marijuana, or amphetamines

SOURCE: National Institute of Justice.

Smoking crack-cocaine.

Petition: In juvenile proceedings, a document alleging that a youth is a delinquent, a status offender, or a dependent child and asking that the court assume jurisdiction over the juvenile.

Intake hearing: An early stage in juvenile court proceedings in which a court officer makes a legal judgment of the probable cause of the petition.

Exhibit 15.2   **Research in Crime and Justice**
The Geography of Juvenile Homicide

Each year, the Federal Bureau of Investigation collects from a large sample of police agencies a detailed report on each homicide that occurred in their jurisdictions. Based on these data, in 1997 the Department of Justice prepared an analysis of juvenile homicide for the year 1995. Overall, some 2,300 juveniles were implicated in 1,900 homicides that year, and 30 percent of their victims were juveniles.

The analysis also indicated that of all homicides that occurred in 1995—regardless of the age of the offender—2,600 of the victims were under age 18. The general

Figure 1

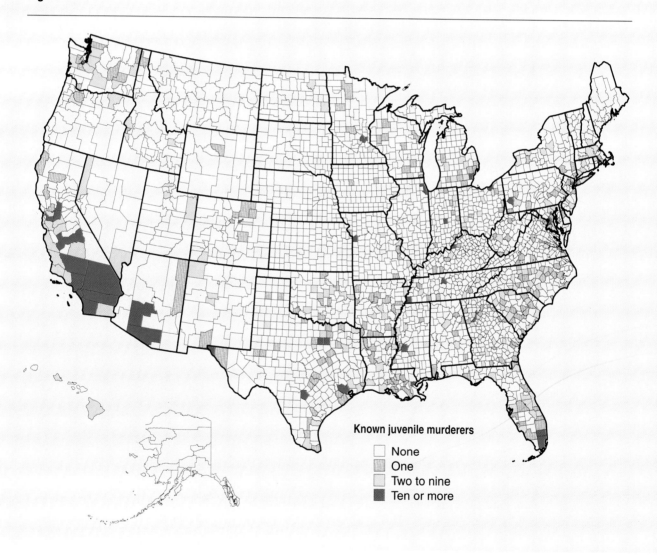

Known juvenile murderers

- None
- One
- Two to nine
- Ten or more

juvenile court. The purpose of this hearing is to protect the interests of the child and to quickly dispose of cases that do not require the time and expense of formal court processing.

In effect, the intake officer makes a legal judgment of the probable cause of the petition, and this may be the only time that the sufficiency of the evidence is evaluated. The officer may also conduct a brief investigation into the background of the juvenile, have an informal hearing with the child and parents, or discuss the case with the police and attorneys. Depending on the

characteristics of both the juvenile offenders and the juvenile victims of homicide were essentially the same as those seen in all homicides: The overwhelming majority of both victims and offenders were males; about two-thirds of the victims and offenders were either family members or acquaintances; and most of the killings were the result of differences of opinion in personal or social relations. What is most striking, however, are the similarities in the geographical distribution of both the juvenile murderers and the juvenile victims of murder. As illustrated in Figure 1, for example, juvenile murderers were concentrated in just a few specific areas, with as many as 25 percent in the counties that contain the cities of Los Angeles, Chicago, Houston, Detroit, and New York City. At the same time, and as illustrated in Figure 2, one-third of all juvenile victims of murder—regardless of the age of the offenders—occurred in 10 counties, most of which are the same as those illustrated in Figure 1.

Figure 2

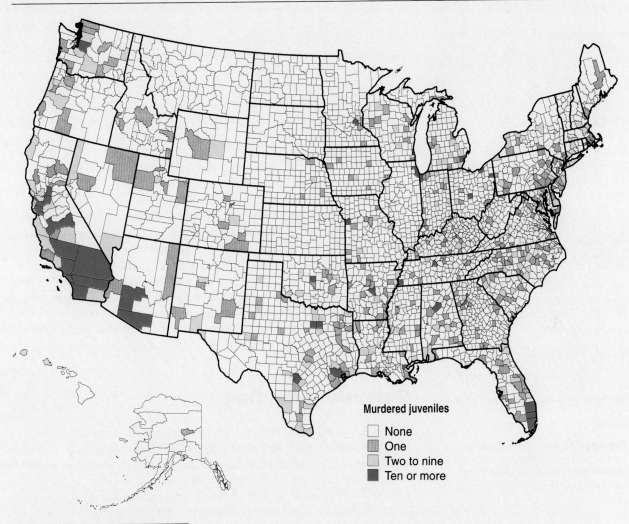

Murdered juveniles
- None
- One
- Two to nine
- Ten or more

SOURCE: Milissa Sigmund, Howard N. Snyder, and Eileen Poe-Yamagata, *Juvenile Offenders and Victims: 1997 Update on Violence* (Washington, D.C.: National Center for Juvenile Justice, 1997).

hearing officer's judgment of the sufficiency of the evidence, the seriousness of the offense, and the need for court intervention, there are three alternatives:

1. The hearing officer can dismiss the case, in which instance the matter is over—no further court processing is required and the child can go home.
2. The officer can make an informal judgment, such as arbitration, restitution, or referral to some social agency.
3. The officer can authorize an inquiry before the juvenile court judge.

JUVENILE ARRESTS, 1997

Total	**2,838,300**
Murder and nonnegligent manslaughter	2,500
Forcible rape	5,500
Robbery	39,500
Aggravated assault	75,900
Burglary	131,000
Larceny-theft	493,900
Motor vehicle theft	66,600
Arson	10,000
Other assaults	241,800
Forgery and counterfeiting	8,500
Fraud	11,300
Embezzlement	1,400
Stolen property (buying, receiving, possessing)	39,500
Vandalism	136,500
Weapons (carrying, possessing, etc.)	52,200
Prostitution and commercialized vice	1,400
Sex offense (except forcible rape and prostitution)	18,500
Drug abuse violations	220,700
Gambling	2,600
Offenses against the family and children	10,200
Driving under the influence	19,600
Liquor law violations	158,500
Drunkenness	24,100
Disorderly conduct	215,100
Vagrancy	3,100
All other offenses (except traffic)	468,000
Suspicion	1,600
Curfew and loitering	182,700
Runaways	196,100

SOURCE: *Uniform Crime Reports.*

Detention hearing: The stage in juvenile court proceedings in which it is determined whether a child is to be released to a parent or guardian or retained in custody.

Although the intake process represents an excellent mechanism for screening juvenile cases, it is not without its problems and shortcomings. First, the "social service" worker in charge of the hearing is making legal judgments about probable cause. The hearing decision, in large measure, determines the immediate future of the child. Yet most hearing officers have no formal legal training and may be ill-prepared to deal with the complexities of law. In some jurisdictions, such as California, there has been an increasing trend to involve prosecutors in screening hearings.[6] Although this addresses the issue of legal judgments, it can also change the focus and effect of juvenile court intake procedures.

Second, as is the case with plea negotiation in the adult criminal courts, the intake hearing places pressures on the juvenile and his or her parents to proceed in a particular way. Statutes in most jurisdictions hold that if a child maintains his or her innocence or the parents so demand it, the case must be sent before a judge. However, the child's liability in the matter might not be disputed in an effort to avoid formal court inquiry.

Third, there are the issues of reliability and objectivity of case file data. The file begins at intake and the hearing officer gathers facts about the case and the juvenile. Quite often, none of these are verified. The file may contain opinions of the intake officer, the police, and the victim that cannot be effectively challenged. Yet this file information is generally accepted by the court as accurate. It is permanently entered and used as "fact" throughout the remainder of the process.

Fourth, there is the matter of discretion. Hearing officers, like police and judges, can exercise a considerable degree of discretion as to how a case ought to be handled. Decisions are often based on opinions as well as the factors used in deciding to take the juvenile into custody—both of which may be tainted by bias, resulting in the potential for arbitrary and discriminatory judgments.[7]

Such difficulties as these, however significant, do not warrant the elimination of the juvenile intake process. Rather, they suggest areas of needed improvement. In the final analysis, intake continues to serve the dual purposes of protecting the juvenile from exposure to the formal adjudication process and preserving court resources for more serious cases. The intake procedures in the juvenile court thus fulfill much the same role as does plea negotiation in the adult court.

Detention and Bail

Subsequent to the intake decision that recommends a hearing before the juvenile court judge, most state statutes require a **detention hearing** to determine whether the child should be released to a parent or guardian or retained in custody. The issues addressed might include such considerations as whether there is a need to protect the child, whether the child presents a serious threat to the community, or the likelihood that the child will return to court for adjudication.

In theory, the temporary detention of juveniles should meet three basic objectives:

1. Secure custody with good physical care that will offset the damaging effects of confinement
2. A constructive and satisfying program of activities to provide the juvenile with a chance to identify socially acceptable ways of gaining satisfaction
3. Observation and study to provide screening for undetected mental or emotional illnesses as well as diagnoses upon which to develop appropriate treatment plans[8]

New Orleans youth with semiauto-matic weapon purchased from a drug dealer, used for protection.

Should these goals be met, the detention experience might actually aid both the child and the court. In practice, however, most children in detention are housed in facilities that provide little more than security. Many are held in police lockups or local jails; even at the close of the 1990s, for some tens of thousands of juveniles annually, temporary detention occurred in secure state correctional facilities and local jails for adults.[9]

If the detention hearing decision is to release the juvenile, the question of bail arises. Although there is a trend in some states to establish bail procedures in the juvenile courts, the federal courts have deemed it unnecessary to rule on the matter. On the one hand, there are liberal statutory alternatives for juveniles, including release on recognizance or release to parents. On the other, there is considerable opposition to the use of bail bonds and other financial conditions of release.[10] A bail agreement is a contract that is not binding on a minor. Moreover, children are unlikely to have the independent financial means to make bail, thus making it necessary for them to rely on others for the needed funds or collateral. This would provide the juvenile with little personal motivation to appear in court as required. And finally, as is the case with adult defendants, bail tends to discriminate against the poor.

Adjudication and Disposition

At the **adjudication inquiry,** which is generally closed to the public and the media, the judge determines whether the facts of the case and the child's behavior warrant a formal hearing by the court. This inquiry is similar in purpose to the intake hearing, but now it is a magistrate who rules on the need for further processing. The magistrate can dismiss the case, order a formal adjudication hearing, or refer the juvenile elsewhere.

Adjudication inquiry: The stage in juvenile court proceedings in which a judge determines whether the facts of the case warrant a formal hearing by the court.

Adjudication hearing: The stage in juvenile court proceedings in which a judge presides on behalf of the child to determine whether he or she actually committed the alleged offense.

Disposition hearing: The stage in juvenile court proceedings in which the judge exercises his or her discretionary authority to choose among a variety of alternatives for resolving a case.

In re Gault: The Supreme Court ruling that extended some—but not all—due process privileges to juvenile court proceedings.

In recent years, the juvenile justice system in the United States has sought out any number of alternatives for avoiding the official adjudication of youths. The major mechanism is diversion out of the court system into community agencies for counseling and treatment. However, a youth may refuse diversion and request a formal adjudication hearing.

The **adjudication hearing** is not a trial. Given the *parens patriae* roots of juvenile justice processing, the adjudication hearing is legally classified as a civil rather than a criminal proceeding. The judge presides on behalf of the child to determine if he or she actually committed the alleged offense, and, if so, to use the misconduct described to determine if the youth's parents are providing adequate care, supervision, and discipline. The judge relies on any clinical, social, or diagnostic reports that may have been prepared. Should the judge determine that no misconduct occurred, the case is dismissed. If youthful misconduct is apparent, the youth is "adjudicated delinquent" and a disposition hearing is scheduled.

At **disposition hearings,** juvenile court judges have extremely broad discretion. They have the authority to dismiss a case, give the juvenile a warning, impose a fine, order the payment of restitution, require the performance of community service, refer the offender to a community agency or treatment facility, place the child on probation under the supervision of a court officer, place the child on some informal probationary status, put the child in a foster home, enter an order against the parents for the protection of the child, or mandate commitment into a juvenile institution. In practice, the most common dispositions are probation, court-sponsored restitution programs, and institutional commitment.

JUVENILES AND THE CONSTITUTION

The juvenile court process, as noted earlier, is not a criminal proceeding. It is not a matter of "*State* v. *Child*": There is no prosecutor who acts on behalf of the state to prove the guilt of the youth, and there is no jury. Rather, it is a civil process designed, at least in theory, to aid and protect the child. But is the youthful defendant in the juvenile court protected by the Bill of Rights? Does the juvenile have the same constitutional rights enjoyed by adult defendants in criminal trials? For the most part, the answers are no, and until the Supreme Court's decision in *Kent* v. *United States* in 1966,[11] juvenile courts seemed to accord few, if any, rights at all. In *Kent,* for the first time in its long history, the High Court evaluated juvenile court proceedings and the constitutionally guaranteed rights of children. The Court noted that youths involved in juvenile proceedings were being deprived of constitutional rights and denied the rehabilitation promised under juvenile court philosophy.

Due Process and Juvenile Proceedings

The issue in *Kent* did not give the Court the opportunity to render a decision on the content of juvenile delinquency proceedings. The next year, however, the Court did have the occasion to do so. The case was ***In re Gault,***[12] an appeal involving the detention of a 15-year-old in a state industrial school for allegedly having made an obscene telephone call. The *Gault* decision extended to juvenile court proceedings the requirement of notice of charges, the right to counsel, the right to confrontation and cross-examination of witnesses, the privilege against self-incrimination, and the rights to a transcript of proceedings and appellate review.

EXPULSIONS FOR GUNS

Federal law requires a student to be expelled for bringing a firearm to school. Expulsion rates for the 1997–98 school year:

Highest	Rate per 100,000 Students	Students Expelled
South Dakota	32.7	49
Delaware	22.6	29
Oregon	22.6	135
Tennessee	19.9	192
Washington	17.8	190
Missouri*	17.2	179
Idaho	16.2	42
Georgia	14.2	203
Arizona	12.3	111
Alaska	12.2	17
Lowest		
Wyoming	0.0	0
North Dakota	0.8	1
Hawaii	1.4	3
Connecticut	1.6	9
Utah	1.8	8

*May include other weapons, like knives.

SOURCE: *U.S. Department of Education.*

Subsequent to *Gault,* additional rights were applied to juvenile proceedings. In the case of ***In re Winship,***[13] addressed by the Supreme Court in 1970, it was held that proof "beyond a reasonable doubt" was required for an adjudication of delinquency. Prior to that, in juvenile matters guilt needed to be established only by the lower "preponderance of evidence" standard. In ***Breed v. Jones,***[14] decided in 1975, the Fifth Amendment protection against double jeopardy was extended to juveniles. ***McKeiver v. Pennsylvania,***[15] on the other hand, held that due process of law does not require a jury in juvenile court hearings. However, the Supreme Court was careful to note in *McKeiver* that there "is nothing to prevent a juvenile court judge in a particular case where he feels the need is demonstrated from using an advisory jury."

Although *Gault* changed the juvenile court into a *court of law* with due process safeguards, there have been numerous transitional problems. During the pre-*Gault* era, there was no need for prosecutors, since the sufficiency of the evidence was not in dispute—only the needs of the child. There was no need for defense attorneys, since due process requirements were not at issue. Probation or hearing officers simply prepared the cases and presented them to the court. The adjudication hearing was an informal one where the evidence was not usually questioned. And typically, there was pressure on juveniles to admit their guilt so as to initiate the rehabilitation process.

Gault introduced defense attorneys to the adjudication hearing and prosecutors for the sake of balance. Hearings became more formal and greater attention was paid to legal sufficiency. Although this initiated more focused attention on the issue of "justice," particularly in those courtrooms and cases where it was needed, in many juvenile courts it also brought about conflict— conflict that was not necessarily in the best interest of the juvenile. Many defense attorneys who attempted to turn adjudication hearings into adversarial proceedings found themselves confronted with magistrates who fully adhered to the *parens patriae* philosophy. Through both subtle and obvious methods, they influenced attorneys to cooperate with the court and to repress their adversarial roles.

Police Encounters and Juvenile Rights

While *Gault* addressed the rights required at the adjudication stage of the juvenile justice process, the High Court left other due process issues to the state and lower federal courts. For the most part, many of these issues have remained unsettled, particularly with regard to juvenile rights and police encounters. The Court has not ruled specifically, for example, on the applicability of the *Miranda* safeguards to the juvenile process.[16] Although *Gault* held the privilege against self-incrimination applicable to juveniles in the same way it is applicable to adults, elsewhere in its opinion the Court qualified the scope of its ruling in general:

> We do not in this opinion consider the impact of these constitutional provisions upon the totality of the relationship of the juvenile and the state. We do not even consider the entire process relating to juvenile "delinquents." For example, we are not here concerned with the procedures or constitutional rights applicable to the pre-judicial stages of the juvenile process.

In 1968, the National Conference of Commissioners on Uniform State Laws drafted the *Uniform Juvenile Court Act* and recommended its enactment in all states.[17] The purpose of the act was to encourage uniformity of purpose, scope, and procedures in the juvenile justice system. One of its provisions dealt with the issue of self-incrimination. Jurisdictions that adopted

In re Winship: The Supreme Court ruling that required proof "beyond a reasonable doubt" for an adjudication of delinquency.

Breed* v. *Jones: The Supreme Court ruling that extended the Fifth Amendment protection against double jeopardy to juveniles.

McKeiver* v. *Pennsylvania: The Supreme Court ruling that due process does not require a jury in juvenile court hearings.

The Uniform Juvenile Court Act

the Uniform Juvenile Court Act, in whole or in part, have similar provisions. Moreover, following *Gault* other jurisdictions enacted statutes designed to implement the *Miranda* safeguards during the investigatory stage of juvenile proceedings.

Juveniles and **Miranda**

Thus, it would appear that in most jurisdictions, juveniles have the protections accorded by *Miranda*. The more perplexing issue, however, focuses on a juvenile's waiver of his or her *Miranda* rights. Does a minor—without the guidance of a parent, attorney, or other friendly adult—have the competence to make an intelligent, voluntary waiver of these rights? In *Fare* v. *Michael C.,*[18] the Supreme Court said yes, given the "totality of circumstances." Moreover, in *West* v. *United States,*[19] the U.S. court of appeals set forth the following circumstances to be considered in determining the validity of a minor's waiver of *Miranda* rights:

1. Age of the accused
2. Education of the accused
3. Knowledge of the accused as to both the substance of the charges and the nature of his or her rights to consult with a parent or attorney and to remain silent
4. Whether the juvenile was held incommunicado or was allowed to consult with relatives
5. Whether the interrogation was held before or after the filing of the formal charges
6. Methods of interrogation
7. Length of the interrogation
8. Whether the juvenile refused voluntarily to give statements on prior occasions
9. Whether the accused had repudiated an extralegal statement given at a later date

A juvenile is legally capable of waiving his or her rights under the Fourth, Fifth, and Sixth Amendments depending on these conditions and whether the juvenile is able to comprehend the meaning and possible effect of any statements given to the police.

In light of Supreme Court action in 1985, juveniles' rights under the Fourth Amendment protection against illegal search and seizure are less clear. Almost two decades earlier, when the opinion in *Gault* emphasized that it was concerned only with due process requirements at the adjudicatory stage of juvenile proceedings, and not with those at the pre-judicial stages, it also reiterated a point made in *Kent*—that the purpose was not to extend to the juvenile process all of the rights required in adult criminal proceedings. Nevertheless, the state courts interpreted *Gault* to require the application of the Fourth Amendment and the exclusionary rule to juvenile cases, and no court has held the rule to be inapplicable.

In loco parentis: A position in reference to a child of that of lawful guardian or parent.

On the other hand, there is the principle of ***in loco parentis***—literally, "in the place of the parent." The principle emerges with reference to searches of students and their lockers by school officials. The Supreme Court has long since held that the Fourth Amendment does not protect individuals from searches conducted by private persons acting on behalf of the government. When searches of students occur, four questions emerge:

Juveniles and the Fourth Amendment

1. Is the school official acting as a private individual, or as a government agent?
2. Is the official authorized to conduct a search on the basis of his or her *in loco parentis* relationship to the student?
3. Does the *in loco parentis* relationship give to a school official a parent's immunity from the Fourth Amendment?
4. Is the search reasonable?

These questions were addressed by the Supreme Court in *New Jersey* v. *T.L.O.*,[20] decided in 1985. The Court held that in spite of the *in loco parentis* relationship, schoolchildren have legitimate expectations of privacy and public school officials are not exempt from the Fourth Amendment ban. Nevertheless, the Court added, school officials, with reasonable grounds to believe that the law or school rules are being violated, may conduct reasonable searches if needed to maintain safety, order, and discipline in the school (see Exhibit 15.3).

One could interpret the decision in *T.L.O.* as the signal of a retreat from the trend to give juveniles full procedural due process rights. Whatever the trend, state and federal court decisions since the mid-1960s have opened the juvenile courts to defense lawyers and prosecutors and have instilled greater regard for the rights of juvenile defendants. It would appear that the days of the closed, protected, benevolent, and sometimes unfair system based on the philosophy of *parens patriae* are now little more than history.

New Jersey v. **T.L.O.:** The Supreme Court ruling that school officials, with reasonable grounds to believe that the law or school rules are being violated, may conduct reasonable searches if needed to maintain safety, order, and discipline in a school.

CRITICAL ISSUES IN JUVENILE JUSTICE

Much like criminal justice, juvenile justice in America has often been described as a "system." There are similar diagrams and flowcharts that depict juvenile justice as a system—how the various agencies and components fit together as each case is being processed and what decisions are possible at each stage. In many ways, at least on the surface, juvenile justice seems indeed to function as a system. Juveniles violate laws; police take juveniles into custody; detention facilities admit juveniles; juveniles and their parents or guardians appear at hearings in court; attorneys are present in behalf of juveniles and the state; judges enter rulings; and adjudicated youths are placed on probation, assigned to group homes, or committed to institutions. Yet juvenile justice is an imperfect system, suffering from the same lack of unity of purpose and organized interrelationships that is apparent within the adult system. Beyond this, juvenile justice also has a number of unique problems—problems that raise some serious questions about the efficacy and fairness of a process that is structured to handle children "in their best interests."

Status Offenders

In New York they are "persons in need of supervision" (PINS); in Illinois they are "minors otherwise in need of supervision" (MINS); in Colorado they are "children in need of supervision" (CHINS); in Florida they are also "children in need of supervision," but by a different acronym (CINS); in New Jersey they are "juveniles in need of supervision" (JINS); in Montana they are "youths in need of supervision" (YINS); and elsewhere they are known, however informally, as "ungovernable" or "unruly" or "wayward." Whatever the name or acronym, these are the **status offenders**—the runaways, truants, and other "incorrigibles" who, because of their special status as children, can be brought to the attention of the juvenile courts for certain kinds of noncriminal behavior.

The creation of the PINS, CHINS, and other designations was an outgrowth of a movement during the 1960s and 1970s to decriminalize status offense behavior. Prior to that time, such acts fell under statutory definitions of "delinquency."[21] The need for decriminalizing status offenses was obvious. Children who were runaways, curfew violators, truant, or otherwise "incorrigible" were handled in the same manner as juvenile law violators, given the same delinquent status, and housed in the same reform and industrial schools. A case in point involved New York's Girls' Term Court. Under the state's Wayward Minor Act of 1923, the juvenile courts had jurisdiction over youths ages

Status offenders: Youths who, because of their special status as children, can be brought to the attention of the juvenile courts for certain kinds of noncriminal behavior.

Exhibit 15.3 **Legal Perspectives on Crime and Justice**
New Jersey v. *T.L.O.*

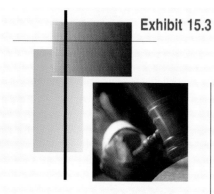

A teacher at a New Jersey high school discovered T.L.O., a 14-year-old freshman, and her companion smoking cigarettes in a school lavatory in violation of a school rule. The two girls were taken to an office, where they were questioned by a vice principal. When T.L.O. denied smoking and claimed that she was not a smoker, the vice principal demanded to see her purse. Upon opening it, he observed cigarettes and the rolling papers typically associated with marijuana use. He then searched the purse thoroughly and found marijuana, a pipe, plastic bags, a substantial amount of money, an index card listing students who owed money to T.L.O., and two letters that implicated T.L.O. in marijuana dealing. The police were called, and delinquency charges were brought against T.L.O. in juvenile court. The court denied T.L.O.'s motion to suppress the evidence found in her purse on Fourth Amendment grounds, declared the search to be a reasonable one, and adjudicated T.L.O. to be delinquent. T.L.O. appealed the decision. Eventually, the New Jersey Supreme Court reversed the decision in T.L.O.'s favor and ordered that the evidence be suppressed, holding that the search of the purse was unreasonable. On subsequent appeal to the U.S. Supreme Court, entered by the Reagan administration in

behalf of the state of New Jersey, the High Court ruled in favor of New Jersey, and stated the following:

1. The Fourth Amendment's prohibition on unreasonable searches and seizures applies to searches conducted by public school officials and is not limited to searches carried out by law enforcement officers. Nor are school officials exempt from the Amendment's dictates by virtue of the special nature of their authority over schoolchildren. In carrying out searches and other functions pursuant to disciplinary policies mandated by state statutes, school officials act as representatives of the State, not merely as surrogates for the parents of students, and they cannot claim the parent's immunity from the Fourth Amendment strictures.

2. Schoolchildren have legitimate expectations of privacy. They may find it necessary to carry with them a variety of legitimate, noncontraband items, and there is no reason to conclude that they have necessarily waived all rights to privacy in such items by bringing them onto school grounds. But striking the balance between schoolchildren's legitimate expectations of privacy and the school's equally legitimate need to maintain an environment in which learning can take place requires some easing of the restrictions to which searches by public authorities are ordinarily subject. Thus, *school officials need not obtain a warrant before searching a student who is*

under their authority. Moreover, school officials need not be held subject to the requirement that searches be based on probable cause to believe that the subject of the search has violated or is violating the law. Rather, the legality of the search should depend simply on reasonableness, under all the circumstances of the search.

The Court's ruling in *T.L.O.* left a number of questions unanswered. There were no views expressed on whether evidence obtained by school authorities through an *illegal* search could be used in court; whether the standard announced also applied to searches of desks and lockers; what standard would apply to searches undertaken at the request of police; and whether authorities require "individualized suspicion" before searching a particular student.

As for 14-year-old T.L.O.—as she was designated in court records—by the time the High Court delivered its opinion in early 1985 she was 18 years old. When the incident originally took place, in 1980 at New Jersey's Piscataway High School, T.L.O. was ordered expelled. That action was postponed, however, given the litigation. Moreover, as the case moved up the judicial ladder, a New Jersey trial court affirmed the juvenile court's original finding that there had been no Fourth Amendment violation. At the same time, however, the trial court also vacated T.L.O.'s adjudication of delinquency. In June 1984, T.L.O. was graduated from Piscataway High School.

SOURCE: *New Jersey* v. *T.L.O.*, 105 S.Ct. 733 (1985).

16 to 21 who had been arrested on criminal charges or who were "developing habits and associations that may lead to crime." This latter category was for status offenders, and the Girls' Term Court handled the females as

wayward minors.[22] The court procedures followed the *parens patriae* concept of informal hearings and individualized planning, but many of the Girls' Term "respondents," as they were called, were status offenders who were mixed with hard-core delinquent offenders in state prisons. Moreover, "respondents" who earned early release from these institutions were supervised in the community by the New York State Division of Parole—the adult parole authority—by the same parole officers, under the same conditions, and reporting to the same offices that were used for convicted felons. The results were sometimes disastrous. A former New York parole officer recalled a particularly tragic case:

> I'll never forget Carlyle. It was during the 1960s, and the Girls' Term system really worked against her. She was a bright and beautiful child, and a woman by the time she was sixteen. She did well in school, but her parents—wealthy New York socialites—just couldn't deal with the way Carlyle slept around, particularly with *older* men. When she contracted the "clap" from one of her sex partners, Mr. and Mrs. B. really flipped. In the hope of scaring Carlyle into straightening out, they hauled her off to Girls' Term Court. But the judge sent her to Westfield State Farm for "correction." There she was brutally raped and sodomized on more than one occasion. She also made some new friends there—heroin addicts, hookers, and some pretty vicious people. *I* know, I was supervising *all* of them. To make a long story short, Carlyle ended up as a heroin addict, a junky prostitute, and on her twenty-first birthday we found her dead of a drug overdose in a sleazy Times Square hotel.[23]

While the decriminalization of status offenses in most states was a positive step, what seems warranted is the total repeal of status offender jurisdiction and shifting the care and management from the juvenile courts to the social service delivery network. In many jurisdictions, status offenders continue to be detained or incarcerated with hard-core offenders—sometimes including detention in adult jails and state correctional facilities.

Perhaps the most significant problem faced by the juvenile courts is the sheer number of status offenders. About 40 percent of juvenile court dispositions involve status offenders, and the attention and resources spent on them reduce the ability of the courts to effectively deal with serious criminal offenders. Perhaps this accounts for the apparently misplaced priorities in some juvenile sentences. Nationally, some status offenders are more likely to be incarcerated than are juvenile burglars.

A move toward the repeal of the current process was the passage in 1974 of the *Juvenile Justice and Juvenile Delinquency Prevention Act*.[24] This federal legislation specified that states' receipt of federal funds for delinquency programs was dependent on their reform of status offender management. It required by 1985 the deinstitutionalization of status offenders, their removal from the justice system, and the detaining and incarceration of delinquents in separate facilities from adults. Currently, while a few jurisdictions have complied with the mandates of the Juvenile Justice and Juvenile Delinquency Prevention Act and most have separated status offenses from the former delinquency classifications, tens of thousands of status offenders continue to be incarcerated each year in the most unfavorable of conditions.

The Juvenile Justice and Juvenile Delinquency Prevention Act   *1974*

Juveniles in the Adult Courts

Although federal and state laws have specified the ages at which the criminal courts gain jurisdiction over young offenders, for as long as there have been juvenile court systems in the United States there have also been statutory exceptions.

Waiver of jurisdiction: The process by which the juvenile court relinquishes its jurisdiction over a child and transfers the case to a court of criminal jurisdiction for prosecution as an adult.

***Kent* v. *United States*:** The Supreme Court ruling that the wavier of jurisdiction is a critically important stage in juvenile proceedings and must be attended by minimum requirements of due process and fair treatment.

AGES AT WHICH CRIMINAL COURTS ASSUME JURISDICTION OVER YOUNG OFFENDERS

Age 16	Age 17
Connecticut	Georgia
New York	Illinois
North Carolina	Louisiana
Vermont	Massachusetts
	Michigan
	Missouri
	South Carolina
	Texas

Age 18	
Alabama	Nebraska
Alaska	Nevada
Arizona	New Hampshire
Arkansas	New Jersey
California	New Mexico
Colorado	North Dakota
Delaware	Ohio
District of	Oklahoma
Columbia	Oregon
Florida	Pennsylvania
Hawaii	Rhode Island
Idaho	South Dakota
Indiana	Tennessee
Iowa	Utah
Kansas	Virginia
Kentucky	Washington
Maine	West Virginia
Maryland	Wisconsin
Mississippi	Wyoming
Minnesota	Federal districts
Montana	

Not altogether inconsistent with the *parens patriae* philosophy upon which the juvenile court system was founded, such statutes were grounded in the notion that certain young offenders—specifically, those accused of serious felonies—were simply not amenable to the guardianship and special form of treatment found in the juvenile courts. That is, such youths were deemed unwilling to follow the advice of the juvenile court and submit to its authority. By the late 1940s, however, many states had changed their statutes in favor of young offenders, granting to the juvenile courts exclusive jurisdiction over youths regardless of the offenses involved.[25]

In recent decades, there has been a reversal in this trend. With the *Gault* decision in 1967 combined with increased rates of juvenile crime since the 1960s, many state jurisdictions lowered the age at which youths could be tried as adults. Although such changes had the coincidental effect of extending the full complement of the rights of the accused to some juveniles, the actual purpose of the new statutes was to subject youths found guilty of serious offenses to the same sentences and punishments that would befall adults convicted of the same crimes.

The process of transferring a case from the juvenile to the adult criminal court has become known as **waiver of jurisdiction.** The effect of such a transfer is to deny a youth the protection and ameliorative treatment afforded by the juvenile process. Although state and federal statutes specify the ages at which the criminal courts gain jurisdiction over young offenders (generally 17 or 18), they also provide for waivers of jurisdiction—the provisions of which vary widely. In California and Oregon, for example, waivers can be applied to all juveniles age 16 and over, regardless of the offense involved. By contrast, in the states of Alabama, Colorado, and Pennsylvania, waivers can occur for juveniles as young as 14 years, but only in the case of felony offenses. And in Florida and Texas there is the equivalent of the "three strikes and you're out" law, except that it translates into "three strikes and you are an adult."[26]

The waiver statutes in a number of other jurisdictions permit extremely young children to be tried in the adult courts. In Mississippi and Illinois the age is 13. In Indiana, 10-year-olds charged with murder can be transferred to the criminal courts. In New Hampshire and Wyoming, waivers are permitted but no age is indicated in their statutes, which theoretically means that 7- or 8-year-olds can face official criminal proceedings. Ironically, depending on the jurisdiction, children may commit crimes so serious that they do not understand their gravity, but they come before the courts as adults. Yet if they steal candy and comic books from a convenience store, they are still "youths" in the eyes of the law and their understanding of the nature of their crimes is not at issue.

Although the decision to waive jurisdiction is critical in its effect on a juvenile offender's subsequent treatment, for a long time youths had no protection against procedural arbitrariness in the waiver process. Change finally occurred in 1966 with ***Kent* v. *United States*,** the first Supreme Court evaluation of the constitutionality of juvenile court proceedings.[27] The ruling in *Kent* held that there must be waiver hearings, and although such hearings need not conform to all the requirements of a criminal trial, they must measure up to the essentials of due process and fair treatment.

Although *Kent* accorded a measure of constitutional safeguards to waiver proceedings, the question remains as to whether any juvenile should be dealt with in the adult criminal courts. On the one hand, there is the pragmatic issue of community protection and the state's right to wage war against its enemies. On the other, there is the more abstract and philosophical consideration of confinement in a penitentiary as an appropriate treatment for what is defined under the state statutes as delinquent behavior.

Of even greater significance is the matter of juveniles and capital punishment. Sixteen states currently permit the execution of criminals ages 16 and 17, and for eight more the minimum age is unspecified. Although the majority of nations around the world have set 18 as the minimum age for capital punishment, since 1977 a total of 12 offenders have been executed in the United States for crimes committed while they were still juveniles.

As of 1999, there were 73 residents of death row in America who were juveniles at the time of their capital offense.[28] Opponents of the death penalty argue that the execution of any juvenile is "cruel and unusual punishment" in violation of the Eighth Amendment. Moreover, they hold, a child's behavior is different from that of an adult. On the other hand, supporters of the death penalty insist that youthful offenders should not be permitted to wrap themselves in the shield of age in order to escape responsibility for their crimes. Interestingly, the U.S. Supreme Court remained silent on the matter of juveniles and the death penalty until only recently. In *Thompson* v. *Oklahoma*,[29] decided in 1988, the Court put forth the somewhat narrow ruling that a state may not execute a person who was less than age 16 at the time of the offense, unless the legislature had spoken clearly on the matter by setting a minimum age for the death penalty. In **Stanford v. Kentucky,**[30] however, decided in 1989, the Court made the more specific ruling that the imposition of the death penalty for a crime committed at 16 or 17 years of age does not constitute a violation of the Eighth Amendment ban against cruel and unusual punishment.

Interestingly, one of the few recent empirical studies of the juvenile death penalty found that in general, the public is unwilling to sentence juveniles to death—even when it feels that the circumstances warrant it. More specifically, the data suggest that juvenile murder cases resulting in a death sentence tend to involve more heinous crimes than those of the adults receiving the same sentence.[31]

Juvenile Detention

The temporary detention of youths pending juvenile court action presents significant problems for both juvenile justice officials and those youths held in custody. The Supreme Court's ruling in **Schall v. Martin** sanctioned the practice of preventive detention for certain juvenile arrestees. In that case, on December 13, 1977, 14-year-old Gregory Martin, along with two other youths, had been arrested on charges of robbery, assault, and weapons violations. For 15 days Martin had been held in detention, after which he was adjudicated a juvenile delinquent and placed on probation. While still in detention, however, Martin instituted a *habeas corpus* class-action suit on behalf of *all* youths being held in preventive detention pursuant to New York's Family Court Act. When the case reached the U.S. Supreme Court in 1984, it was held that preventive detention was permissible with respect to an accused juvenile delinquent when there was evidence that he or she presented a "serious risk" of committing a crime before adjudication of the case. The New York procedure was upheld because it served the legitimate purpose of community protection and because there were numerous procedural safeguards in the New York Juvenile Court Act intended to safeguard against erroneous deprivations of liberty.

Schall v. *Martin* is the most significant case addressing the issue of juvenile detention, not just because it validated the constitutionality of New York's statute, but also because of the perspective on juvenile justice reflected in the High Court's opinion:

> Juveniles, unlike adults, are always in some form of custody. Children, by definition, are not assumed to have the capacity to take care of themselves. They are

THE HANGING OF A CHILD

In 1786, a 12-year-old girl was sentenced to be hanged in New London, Connecticut, for the killing of a playmate. A local clergyman who witnessed the child's execution described her last few days of life:

About a fortnight before her execution she appeared to realize her danger, and was more concerned for herself. She continued nearly in the same state until the Monday night before her execution, when she appeared greatly affected, saying that she was distressed for her soul. She continued in tears most of Tuesday, and Wednesday, which was the day of execution. At the place of execution she said very little, appeared afraid and seemed to want somebody to help her. She then passed into that state which never ends.

SOURCE: From Henry Channing, "God Admonishing His People of Their Duty as Parents and Masters" (Sermon preached at New London, December 20, 1786).

Stanford v. Kentucky: The Supreme Court ruling that the imposition of the death penalty for a crime committed at age 16 or 17 does not constitute cruel and unusual punishment merely because of the accused's age.

Schall v. Martin: The Supreme Court ruling that preventive detention is permissible for accused juvenile delinquents when there is evidence that the youth presents a serious risk of committing a crime before adjudication of the case.

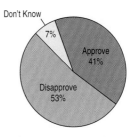

Death Penalty for Juveniles?

Percentage of judges who support letting youths face the death penalty

SOURCE: *National Law Journal.*

assumed to be subject to the control of their parents, and if parental control falters, the State must play its part as *parens patriae.* In this respect, the juvenile's liberty interest may, in appropriate circumstances, be subordinated to the State's *parens patriae* interest in preserving and promoting the welfare of the child.[32]

In addition to its contention that preventive detention acts in behalf of the welfare of a child, the Court also noted that such detention is for a limited period of time, as most youths are released after only a few days. And therein lies the dilemma for both youths "in trouble" and the juvenile justice system as a whole. Jails and detention centers, particularly those that mix juveniles with adults, can be depressing and exceedingly dangerous places. For example:

- In California, a 15-year-old girl arrested for assaulting a police officer hanged herself after 4 days of isolation in jail.
- In Illinois, a 17-year-old boy was taken into custody and detained for owing $73 in unpaid traffic tickets, only to be tortured and beaten to death by his cellmates.
- In a West Virginia jail a truant was murdered by an adult inmate; in an Ohio jail a teenage girl was raped by a guard.
- In Kentucky, 15-year-old Robbie Horn hanged himself in a jail where he had been held for only 30 minutes. His offense: arguing with his mother.[33]

Although one might argue that the foregoing are just isolated cases, in fact no one really knows the full extent of the problem. As is the case with crime victims in the general population, victimizations within jails are reported only infrequently. What is known, however, is the relative extent to which youths find themselves in contact with jail populations—both juvenile and adult.

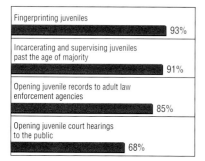

Options Requested

What judges seek as options for dealing with troubled youths

SOURCE: *National Law Journal.*

Juvenile Corrections

Although data periodically emerge as to the number of juveniles held in jails and correctional institutions, relatively little is known about the extent of juvenile delinquency and youth crime, the number of status offenders and the nature of their "misbehavior," the size and character of the juvenile justice population as a whole, the dispositions that result from both informal and formal juvenile hearings, and the recidivism rates of adjudicated youths. The reason is that in many jurisdictions juvenile laws require that records of youthful offenders be sealed or destroyed to protect minors from being labeled as criminals. In fact, findings from a U.S. Bureau of Justice Statistics survey indicated that 26 states do not retain police and court records pertaining to juveniles.[34] As a result, any conclusions as to the nature and effectiveness of juvenile corrections are at best tentative.

Diversion The juvenile due process requirements derived from *Kent, Gault,* and *Winship,* combined with rising costs of operating correctional institutions, have resulted in the wider use of community-based treatment for adjudicated juveniles. A recent trend has been the greater use of diversion programs, with many young offenders being placed in remedial education and drug abuse treatment programs, foster homes, and counseling facilities.

Probation Probation is by far the primary form of community treatment in the juvenile justice system, and the probation process for youths is essentially the same as that for adults. At any given time as many as 500,000

Fingerprinting juveniles
93%

Incarcerating and supervising juveniles past the age of majority
91%

Opening juvenile records to adult law enforcement agencies
85%

Opening juvenile court hearings to the public
68%

Major Changes in the System Favored by Juvenile Court Judges (percent in favor)

SOURCE: *National Law Journal,* August 8, 1994.

youths are on probation in the United States. The tendency toward such wide-spread use of juvenile probation evolved from the same rationales as diversion, combined with the findings of studies conducted decades ago that found that most juvenile probationers had been discharged from supervision under favorable circumstances.[35] In other words, most had finished their probation time with no new arrests or technical violations or at least none severe enough to warrant revocation of probation. For most juveniles on probation, however, supervision is generally minimal. Therefore, violations of the conditions of probation rarely come to the attention of court officials.

"Boot Camps"   As mentioned briefly in Chapter 12, one of the more recent innovations in correctional treatment is what some jurisdictions refer to as "boot camps" and others call "shock incarceration." The juvenile boot camp is a 3- to 6-month regimen of military drill, physical exercise, hard labor, and sometimes drug treatment and academic work in return for having several years removed from an individual's sentence, in lieu of a traditional prison sentence, or as part of a sentence of probation. Available to young nonviolent offenders, the idea is to "shock" budding felons out of careers in crime by imposing large amounts of rigor and order in what appear to be chaotic and otherwise purposeless lives. Boot camp programs have been designed for both adults and juveniles, and as illustrated in Exhibit 15.4, for young women offenders as well.

Correctional Institutions   Finally, there are the juvenile correctional institutions, which are generally of two types. There are the *cottage systems* similar to many of the nation's facilities for women offenders. They are typically structured as campuslike environments with dormitory rooms rather than cells. For serious juvenile offenders, there are *secure training and industrial schools,* which generally resemble medium-security penitentiaries for adults.

Nearly all juvenile correctional facilities have a variety of treatment programs—counseling on an individual or group basis, vocational and educational training, recreational and religious programs, and medical and dental facilities. A number of these institutions also provide legal services for juveniles, and a few have drug abuse treatment programs. Regardless of the settings and available services, juvenile facilities are still places of confinement that militate against rehabilitation in the same ways as adult penitentiaries do.

As to the effectiveness of juvenile corrections, and the juvenile justice process as a whole, the lack of comprehensive evaluative information leads only to speculation. However, data from the largest follow-up study of juveniles ever conducted provide at least a few insights. In 1985, researchers at the University of Pennsylvania's Center for Studies in Criminology and Criminal Law released a report on a study of 13,160 Philadelphia male youths born in 1958.[36] Data on each youth were gathered from schools, the police, and the juvenile court, and the findings, however tentative, were nevertheless significant because they were based on a generalizable urban population.

Of the 13,160 juveniles in the 1958 birth cohort, 4,315—or 33 percent—had at least one police contact prior to reaching age 18. Of these, 42 percent were one-time offenders, 35 percent were nonchronic recidivists, and the remaining 23 percent were chronic recidivists. The 4,315 offenders had committed a total of 15,248 delinquent acts and, significantly, the chronic recidivists were responsible for almost two-thirds of all the delinquencies. In other words, most of the offenses had been committed by the 992 chronic delinquents. An analysis of the juvenile court dispositions of all of the delinquent youths and their subsequent recidivism suggested that lenient treatment for serious crimes early on in delinquent careers tended only to exacerbate subsequent lawbreaking behavior.

1,000,000	The number of students who brought a gun to school during 1998
63%	The proportion of students carrying guns to school who said they had threatened to harm another student

SOURCE: *Time,* June 29, 1998, p. 25.

Exhibit 15.4   **Gender Perspectives on Crime and Justice**
Female "Boot Camps"

Although the boot camp is thought to be a recent innovation in correctional treatment, its roots are more than a century old, dating back to the efforts of Zebulon Brockway at New York's Elmira Reformatory in 1876. Part of the Brockway regimen for reforming wayward youths included regimental military organization, hard work, and educational opportunities (see Chapter 11). The contemporary boot camp concept was introduced in Georgia in 1983, followed by Oklahoma in 1984. They quickly became popular, because the idea of rigorous training, hard work, and military-style discipline was appealing to legislators and the public at large as a "get tough" approach for young offenders. By the close of the 1990s, almost 100 boot camps were operating in some 30 jurisdictions.

Boot camps for women began in the early 1990s in Massachusetts. Other states soon followed, with the program content similar to that seen in the men's camps. In the North Carolina boot camp, for example, the young women sent there can expect an extremely rigorous schedule. The minute a "trainee," as they are called, steps out of the department of correction's van, drill instructors begin

barking orders, putting her in a state of confusion designed to make her ready to listen and learn and not be manipulative. For 3 months, the young women trainees rise each morning at 4:30 A.M. and go to bed at 9 P.M. They spend more than 7 hours a day working, usually clearing land or cleaning property for government agencies, and at least 2 hours in school. For the remaining 7.5 hours that they are awake, the women are engaged in physical training, drill, and exercise designed to instill self-confidence and discipline.

Despite their popularity, it is generally held that boot camps for

both women and men are ineffective. Studies have found that drill instructors routinely use forms of corporal punishment under the guise of "on the spot" correction that result in serious injury; younger trainees who had difficulty understanding boot camp commands were being physically and psychologically harmed; mentally and physically disabled youths were not receiving adequate care; and those graduating from boot camp programs were rearrested more often than similar youths who were either incarcerated or placed on probation.

Young women inmates in a wilderness boot camp.

SOURCES: Peter Katel, Melinda Liu, and Bob Cohn, "The Bust in Boot Camps," *Newsweek,* February 21, 1994, p. 26; Howard W. Polsky and Jonathan Faust, "Boot Camps, Juvenile Offenders, and Culture Shock," *Child and Youth Care Forum* 22 (1993): 403–415; *Criminal Justice Newsletter,* November 17, 1997, p. 5; Associated Press, "U.S. Justice Department Says Boot Camps Do More Harm Than Good," June 1, 1998.

The study suggested that the majority of delinquents were one- or two-time offenders, that most of the serious delinquencies were perpetrated by a small group of hard-core offenders, and that the juvenile justice system in the United States might have had a greater effect on reducing subsequent delinquent behavior if it took somewhat stronger measures with young offenders when they first came to its attention.

Op-Ed

At the beginning of the 1990s, a number of influential criminal justice researchers and politicians met to discuss future trends in juvenile crime and violence. Many of them saw a "crime storm" on the horizon—a new breed of "superpredators," as they called them, who would soon be reaching their teens. Even the Federal Bureau of Investigation predicted that the annual number of juvenile arrests for violent crimes would increase from 125,000 in 1990 to almost 300,000 by 2005.

Predictions had been made on the basis of social trends and simple demographics. The trends included the increasing rates of violence among youths, the rising number of adolescents who were using drugs, and the wider availability of guns among juveniles in both urban and rural communities. The demographics were even more clearcut. Youths in the 15-to-19 age cohort tend to be more crime-prone than most other age groups, and the number of 15-to 19-year-olds would be increasing by 21 percent by the year 2005.

By 1999, had the forecasts been accurate, the storm of youth crime should have hit. But the skys were still clear. Although gun-related homicides by youths were up, overall violent crime was down. So what had happened?

The pessimistic projections about youth crime stemmed from a "historical fact" about youth crime long held to be sacred theory among many academic criminologists and demographers: *Teenagers commit a lot of crimes, and more teenagers would mean more crime.* The problem with this conventional wisdom is that you just can't predict the criminal potential of groups of people who are just toddlers now, or not even born yet. Too many things can intervene. With respect to the 1990s, few had anticipated the falloffs in the inner-city crack markets, the booming economy and high rates of employment, the effectiveness of community policing programs, and the growth in youth crime prevention initiatives.

Perhaps the chaos will still arrive. John J. Dilulio, a professor of politics and public affairs at Princeton University, has commented that the dip in the crime rate may just be the "lull before the crime storm."

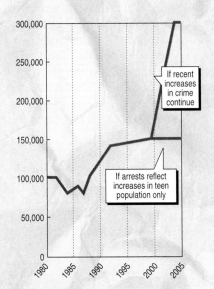

Troubling Projections

The number of youths ages 15 to 19 will increase by 21 percent by the year 2005, pushing up the crime rate. Crime could rise even faster if recent trends like inner-city drug use and wider availability of guns continue.

SOURCE: Federal Bureau of Investigation.

Exhibit 15.5 Careers in Justice
Juvenile Probation Officer

The duties of juvenile probation officers are not unlike those of other probation officers, as described in Chapter 14. Specifically, juvenile probation officers are responsible for the guidance and supervision of youths under age 18 who have been referred to by local courts, police departments, and social agencies as a result of having committed a crime or for having been designated as a status offender. Juvenile probation officers ensure that youths who are placed on probation abide by the rules of probation, receive appropriate court-related services, and are referred to other community services when necessary. They coordinate with schools, agencies, employment and training programs, substance abuse treatment, and other services within the community. Juvenile probation officers sometimes supervise truancy cases as well.

For those who wish to work in the criminal justice field, probation work (juvenile and adult) is an excellent entry-level position. It provides individuals with (1) broad exposure to most aspects of state and local criminal justice operations and procedures, (2) the requisite experience for higher level criminal justice positions, and (3) access to employment opportunities in other criminal justice agencies.

In most jurisdictions, the minimum qualifications for juvenile probation work are U.S. citizenship and a bachelor's degree in criminal justice or one of the social or behavioral sciences.

SUMMARY

The juvenile justice system in the United States was designed with the philosophy that, as minors, young offenders have a "special status" that requires they be protected and corrected and not necessarily punished. Given this special status, juveniles can come to the attention of the courts as delinquents, for having violated the criminal law; as status offenders, for having departed from the behavior expected of youths; and as dependent or neglected children, for having been the victims of abuse, neglect, or abandonment.

Juvenile justice processing is grounded in the notion of *parens patriae,* a position that holds a child's natural protectors have been either unwilling or unable to provide the appropriate care. Thus, the state must take over the role of parent. Historically, as an outgrowth of *parens patriae,* juvenile offenders were rarely treated with the "due process of law" accorded to adults by the Bill of Rights.

Much of juvenile justice processing is informal, with a wide degree of discretion permitted at every stage. Police who take juveniles into custody have the options of releasing youths with a reprimand, referring them to police-based diversion programs, or detaining them for court processing. Similar discretionary alternatives are apparent in the juvenile courts. The actual court process is considered a civil matter. Moreover, it is not a trial, there is no jury, and the judge presides *in behalf* of the child.

It was not until 1966 that the Supreme Court first evaluated juvenile court proceedings and the constitutional rights of children. During that year, *Kent* v. *United States* brought the juvenile justice system within the framework of the Constitution and the Bill of Rights. Subsequently, *In re Gault* in 1967, *In re Winship* in 1970, and *Breed* v. *Jones* in 1975 extended basic due process rights to juvenile court proceedings.

Although juvenile justice philosophy and procedure have attempted to provide fair and beneficial treatment for children, the system as a whole suffers from a number of serious difficulties. First, the persistence of status offender laws in many jurisdictions places nondelinquent youths in contact with criminals and reduces the ability of the juvenile courts to more effectively deal with youths involved in serious criminal conduct. Second, there are many questions as to the wisdom of transferring delinquents to the adult courts for formal criminal processing. Third, the widespread practice of confining juveniles in detention facilities has placed the health and welfare of many youths at high risk. Fourth, regardless of the disposition of juvenile delinquents and status offenders, little is known as to the effectiveness of juvenile correctional approaches.

KEY TERMS

adjudication hearing **422**
adjudication inquiry **421**
Breed v. *Jones* **423**
delinquency **415**
delinquent **415**
detention hearing **420**
disposition hearing **422**
Illinois Juvenile Court Act **414**

in loco parentis **424**
In re Gault **422**
In re Winship **423**
intake hearing **417**
Kent v. *United States* **428**
McKeiver v. *Pennsylvania* **423**
New Jersey v. *T.L.O.* **425**

parens patriae **414**
petition **417**
Schall v. *Martin* **429**
Stanford v. *Kentucky* **429**
status offenders **425**
status offense **412**
waiver of jurisdiction **428**

QUESTIONS FOR DISCUSSION

1. Given the *parens patriae* philosophy of the juvenile justice system in the United States, would delinquent youths be better off in the adult criminal courts with its strict guarantees of due process of law?
2. Do status offender laws serve any real purpose for today's youth? Should such laws be fully abolished? Why?
3. Should youths who commit murders be given capital sentences, placed on death row, and executed?
4. How might contemporary juvenile correctional programs and procedures be best upgraded or reformed? What ought to be done with juvenile offenders?
5. Should "boot camps" be eliminated?

MEDIA RESOURCES

1. **Juvenile Justice.** The School of Criminology and Criminal Justice at Florida State University has constructed a number of useful Web links. (Web site address: http.//www.fsu.edu/~crimdo/jd.html)
2. **Juvenile Arrests.** For an analysis of the most recent juvenile arrest data, see Howard N. Snyder, "Juvenile Arrests 1997," *OJJDP Juvenile Justice Bulletin,* December 1998.
3. **Youth, Guns, Gangs, and Violence.** Two interesting books are available on these topics: Joseph F. Sheley

and James D. Wright, *In the Line of Fire* (New York: Aldine, 1995); Malcolm W. Klein, *The American Street Gang* (New York: Oxford, 1995).
4. **Status Offenders.** See Randall G. Shelden, John A. Horvath, and Sharon Tracy, "Do Status Offenders Get Worse? Some Clarifications on the Question of Escalation," *Crime and Delinquency* 35 (April 1989): 202–216.

NOTES

1. *New York Times,* January 4, 1999, p. A13.
2. President's Commission on Law Enforcement and Administration of Justice, *Task Force Report: Juvenile Delinquency and Youth Crime* (Washington, D.C.: U.S. Government Printing Office, 1967); pp. 2–3.
3. Illinois Juvenile Court Act, *Illinois Statutes,* 1899, Section 131.
4. Norval Morris and Gordon Hawkins, *The Honest Politician's Guide to Crime Control* (Chicago: University of Chicago Press, 1969), p. 91.
5. Irving Piliavin and Scott Briar, "Police Encounters With Juveniles," *American Journal of Sociology* 70 (September 1964): 206–214.
6. H. Ted Rubin, "The Emerging Prosecutor Dominance of the Juvenile Court Intake Process," *Crime and Delinquency* 26 (July 1980): 299–318.

7. See Charles E. Silberman, *Criminal Violence, Criminal Justice* (New York: Random House, 1978), pp. 309–370.
8. H. Ted Rubin, *Juvenile Justice: Policy, Practice, and Law* (Santa Monica, Calif.: Goodyear, 1979), pp. 86–108.
9. *Prison and Jail Inmates at Mid-Year, 1998,* Bureau of Justice Statistics, March 1999.
10. Rubin, *Juvenile Justice,* pp. 86–108.
11. *Kent* v. *United States,* 383 U.S. 541 (1966).
12. *In re Gault,* 38 U.S. 1 (1967).
13. *In re Winship,* 397 U.S. 358 (1970).
14. *Breed* v. *Jones,* 421 U.S. 519 (1975).
15. *McKeiver* v. *Pennsylvania* 403 U.S. 548 (1971).
16. *Miranda* v. *Arizona,* 384 U.S. 436 (1966).

17. The Uniform Juvenile Court Act has been reprinted in its entirety in Samuel M. Davis, *Rights of Juveniles: The Juvenile Justice System* (New York: Clark Boardman, 1983), pp. A1–A53.
18. *Fare* v. *Michael C.,* 442 U.S. 707 (1979).
19. *West* v. *United States,* 399 F.2d 467 (5th Cir. 1968).
20. *New Jersey* v. *T.L.O.,* 105 S.Ct. 733 (1985).
21. Herbert A. Bloch and Frank T. Flynn, *Delinquency: The Juvenile Offender in America Today* (New York: Random House, 1956), p. 471.
22. Bloch and Flynn, *Delinquency,* p. 471.
23. Personal communication, September 17, 1985.
24. *Juvenile Justice and Juvenile Delinquency Prevention Act of 1974* (P.L. 933-415).
25. Negley K. Teeters and John Otto Reinemann, *The Challenge of Delinquency* (Englewood Cliffs, N.J.: Prentice-Hall, 1950), pp. 290–313.
26. National Conference of State Legislatures, 1997.
27. *Kent* v. *United States,* 383 U.S. 541 (1966).
28. Amnesty International, *The Program to Abolish the Death Penalty,* March 16, 1999.
29. *Thompson* v. *Oklahoma,* 43 CrL 4084 (1988).
30. *Stanford* v. *Kentucky,* 45 CrL 3203 (1989).
31. Gennaro Vito and Thomas J. Keil, "Selecting Juveniles for Death: The Kentucky Experience, 1976–1986," *Journal of Contemporary Criminal Justice* 5 (1989): 181–198.
32. *Schall* v. *Martin,* 35 CrL 3103 (1984).
33. *Newsweek,* May 27, 1985, pp. 87–89.
34. *New York Times,* October 21, 1985, p. A17.
35. For example, see Frank Scarpitti and Richard Stephenson, "A Study of Probation Effectiveness," *Journal of Criminal Law, Criminology, and Police Science* 59 (1968): 361.
36. Paul E. Tracy, Marvin E. Wolfgang, and Robert M. Figlio, *Delinquency in Two Birth Cohorts: Executive Summary* (Philadelphia: Center for Studies in Criminology and Criminal Law, The Wharton School, University of Pennsylvania, 1985). This effort was a replication of the original *Delinquency in a Birth Cohort* study, which followed up more than 10,000 Philadelphia youths born in 1945. See Marvin E. Wolfgang, Robert M. Figlio, and Thorsten Sellin, *Delinquency in a Birth Cohort* (Chicago: University of Chicago Press, 1972).

GLOSSARY

Abettor A person who, with the requisite criminal intent, encourages, promotes, instigates, or stands ready to assist the perpetrator of a crime.

Accessory after the fact A person who, knowing that a felony has been committed, receives, relieves, comforts, or assists the felon to hinder apprehension or conviction.

Accessory before the fact A person who abets a crime but is not present when the crime is committed.

Adjudication hearing The stage in juvenile court proceedings in which a judge presides on behalf of the child to determine if he or she actually committed the alleged offense.

Adjudication inquiry The stage in juvenile court proceedings in which a judge determines whether the facts of the case warrant a formal hearing by the court.

Administrative law A branch of public law that deals with the powers and duties of government agencies.

Adversary system of justice A system in which the innocence of the accused is presumed and the burden of proof is placed on the court.

Allocution The right of a convicted offender to address the court personally prior to the imposition of sentence.

Appeal A complaint to a superior court of an injustice done or an error committed by a lower court, whose judgment or decision the higher tribunal is called upon to correct or reverse.

Appellate jurisdiction Jurisdiction restricted to matters of appeal and review.

Argersinger* v. *Hamlin The Supreme Court ruling that a defendant has the right to counsel at trial whenever he or she may be imprisoned for any offense, even for 1 day, whether it is classified as a felony or as a misdemeanor.

Arrest The action of taking a person into custody for the purpose of charging with a crime.

Arson The willful or malicious burning or attempt to burn, with or without intent to defraud, any dwelling, other building, vehicle, or personal property.

Assault An intentional attempt or threat to physically injure another.

Assault and battery An assault carried into effect by doing some violence to the victim.

Bail Security posted to guarantee that a defendant in a criminal proceeding will appear and be present in court as required.

Barron* v. *Baltimore The Supreme Court ruling that the Bill of Rights was added to the Constitution to protect citizens only against the action of the federal, not state or local, government.

Batson* v. *Kentucky The Supreme Court ruling that a prosecutor's use of peremptory challenges to exclude from a jury members of the defendant's race solely on racial grounds violates the equal protection rights of the defendant.

Bench warrant A written order, issued by the court, authorizing a defendant's arrest.

Benton* v. *Maryland The Supreme Court ruling that overruled *Palko* and extended the double jeopardy protection to state actions.

Bill of Rights The first 10 amendments to the Constitution of the United States, which restrict government actions.

Booking The police administrative procedures for officially recording an arrest.

Brady* v. *United States The Supreme Court ruling that upheld the use of plea negotiations.

Breaking and entering The forcible entry into a building or structure, with the intent to commit a crime therein.

Breed* v. *Jones The Supreme Court ruling that extended the Fifth Amendment protection against double jeopardy to juveniles.

Carrier's Case The 1473 legal ruling whereby a person in possession of another's packaged goods, who opens the package and misappropriates its contents, is guilty of larceny.

Carroll doctrine The ruling, from the Supreme Court's decision in *Carroll* v. *United States,* that warrantless searches of vehicles are permissible where reasonable suspicion of illegal actions exists.

Case law Law that results from court interpretations of statutory law or from court decisions where rules have not been fully codified or have been found to be vague or in error.

***Certiorari,* writ of** A writ issued by the Supreme Court ordering some lower court to "forward up the record" of a case it has tried so the High Court can review it.

Charging the jury An order by the judge directing the jurors to retire to the jury room, consider the facts of the case and the evidence and testimony presented, and from their deliberations return a just verdict.

Chimel* v. *California The Supreme Court ruling that a search incident to a lawful arrest in a home must be limited to the area into which an arrestee might reach in order to grab a weapon or other evidentiary items.

Civil death The loss of all civil rights.

Civilian review boards Citizen-controlled boards empowered to review and handle complaints against police officers.

Civil law The body of principles that determines private rights and liabilities.

Classification The process through which the educational, vocational, treatment, and custodial needs of the offender are determined.

Clearance rate The proportion of crimes that result in arrest.

Coker **v.** *Georgia* The Supreme Court ruling that the sentence of death for the crime of rape is an excessive and disproportionate penalty forbidden by the Eighth Amendment.

Common law Customs, traditions, judicial decisions, and other materials that guide courts in decision-making but have not been enacted by the legislatures into statutes or embodied in the U.S. Constitution.

Community-based corrections Rehabilitative activities and programs within the community that have effective ties with the local governments.

Community policing A collaborative effort between the police and the community to identify the problems of crime and disorder and to develop solutions from within the community.

Conjugal visitation The practice of permitting inmate and spouse to spend time together in private quarters on prison grounds, during which time they may engage in sexual relations.

Conspiracy Concert in criminal purpose.

Constitution The institutions, practices, and principles that define and structure a system of government, and the written document that establishes or articulates such a system.

Constitutional law The legal rules and principles that define the nature and limits of governmental power, and the duties and rights of individuals in relation to the state.

Contract system A form of prison industry in which the labor of inmates is leased to an outside contractor, who furnishes the machinery and raw materials and supervises the work.

Courts of general jurisdiction Courts authorized to try *all* criminal and civil cases.

Courts of limited jurisdiction The entry point for judicial processing, with jurisdiction limited to full processing of *all* minor offenses and pre-trial processing of felony cases.

Courts of record Courts in which a full transcript of the proceedings is made for all cases.

Crime An intentional act or omission in violation of criminal law, committed without defense or justification, and sanctioned by the state as a felony or misdemeanor.

Crime control model The model of the criminal justice system that views the repression of criminal conduct as its most important function.

Crime Index The sum of Part I offenses reported in a given place for a given period of time.

Crime rate The number of Part I offenses that occur in a given area per 100,000 inhabitants living in that area.

Criminal justice process The agencies and procedures set up to manage both crime and the persons accused of violating the criminal law.

Criminal law The branch of jurisprudence that deals with offenses committed against the safety and order of the state.

Defense Any number of causes and rights of action that serve to mitigate or excuse guilt in a criminal offense.

Definite sentence A sentence of incarceration having a fixed period of time with no reduction by parole.

Delaware **v.** *Prouse* The Supreme Court ruling that police may not randomly stop motorists, without any probable cause to suspect crime or illegal activity, to check their driver's licenses and auto registrations.

Deliberation The full and conscious knowledge of the purpose to kill.

Delinquency Criminal law violations by a juvenile that would be considered crimes if committed by an adult.

Delinquent A juvenile offender who has been adjudicated by an officer of a juvenile court.

Detention hearing The stage in juvenile court proceedings in which it is determined whether a child is to be released to a parent or guardian or retained in custody.

Determinate sentence A sentence of incarceration for a fixed period of time, but with possible reduction by parole.

Deterrence A sentencing philosophy seeking to prevent criminal acts by making an example of persons convicted of crimes.

Deviance Conduct that the people of a group consider so dangerous, embarrassing, or irritating that they bring special sanctions to bear against the persons who exhibit it.

Disposition hearing The stage in juvenile court proceedings in which the judge exercises his or her discretionary authority to choose among a variety of alternatives for resolving a case.

Diversion The removal of offenders from the application of the criminal law at any stage of the police or court processes.

Domestic violence Activities of a physically aggressive nature occurring among members of the family, current or former spouses or lovers, live-ins, and others in close relationships, resulting from conflicts in personal relations.

Double jeopardy Multiple prosecutions for the same offense and/or multiple punishments for the same crime; prohibited by the Fifth Amendment.

Downum **v.** *United States* The Supreme Court ruling that double jeopardy begins at the point where the second trial jury is sworn in.

Dual court system Courts at the state and federal levels.

Due process of law A concept that asserts fundamental principles of justice and implies the administration of laws that do not violate the sacredness of private rights.

Duncan v. Louisiana The Supreme Court ruling that the Fourteenth Amendment's guarantee of due process requires states to provide trial by jury to persons accused of serious crimes.

Durham Rule Legal standard by which an accused is not held criminally responsible if he or she suffers from a diseased or defective mental condition at the time the unlawful act is committed.

Entrapment The inducement of an individual to commit a crime not contemplated by him or her.

Escobedo v. Illinois The Supreme Court ruling that when the process shifts from the investigatory to the accusatory and its purpose is to elicit a confession, the accused may be permitted to consult with his or her attorney.

Estelle v. Gamble The Supreme Court ruling that the deliberate indifference of prison officials or personnel to the serious medical needs of inmates constitutes cruel and unusual punishment proscribed by the Eighth Amendment.

Evidence Any species of proof through the media of witnesses, records, documents, concrete objects, and circumstances.

Exclusionary rule The constitutional guarantee that prohibits the use in court of illegally obtained evidence.

Federal Bureau of Investigation The chief investigative body of the Justice Department, with jurisdiction extending to all federal crimes that are not the specific responsibility of some other federal enforcement agency.

Felony A crime punishable by death or imprisonment in a state or federal penitentiary.

Felony-murder doctrine Principle maintaining that if a death occurs during the commission of a felony, the person committing the primary offense can also be charged with murder in the first degree.

Florida v. Bostick The Supreme Court ruling that police officers' conduct in boarding stopped passenger buses and approaching seated passengers to ask them questions and to request consent to search their luggage does not constitute a Fourth Amendment "seizure" in every instance, but instead must be evaluated in each case.

Fruit of the poisonous tree The doctrine that evidence seized illegally is considered "tainted" and cannot be used against a suspect.

Full enforcement The tenacious enforcement of every statute in the criminal codes.

Furlough An authorized, unescorted absence from a correctional institution for a specified period of time.

Furman v. Georgia The Supreme Court ruling that statutes that leave arbitrary and discriminatory discretion to juries in imposing death sentences are in violation of the Eighth Amendment.

Gagnon v. Scarpelli The Supreme Court ruling that the holding in *Morrissey* v. *Brewer* also applies to probationers and that neither probationers nor parolees are entitled to counsel as a matter of right at revocation hearings.

Gideon v. Wainwright The Supreme Court ruling that an indigent defendant charged in a state court with any noncapital felony has the right to counsel under the due process clause of the Fourteenth Amendment.

Gitlow v. New York The Supreme Court ruling that the First Amendment prohibition against government abridgment of the freedom of speech applies to state and local governments as well as to the federal government.

Good time The number of days deducted from a sentence for good behavior, meritorious service, particular kinds of work, or other considerations.

Grand jury A body of persons who have been selected according to law and sworn to hear the evidence against accused persons and to determine whether there is sufficient evidence to bring those persons to trial, to

investigate criminal activity generally, and to investigate the conduct of public agencies and officials.

Gregg v. Georgia The Supreme Court ruling that (1) the death penalty is not, in itself, cruel and unusual punishment; and (2) a two-part proceeding—one for the determination of innocence or guilt and the other for determining the sentence—is constitutional and meets the objections noted in *Furman* v. *Georgia.*

Griswold v. Connecticut The Supreme Court ruling that a right of personal privacy is implicit in the Constitution.

habeas corpus A writ that directs the person holding a prisoner to bring him or her before a judicial officer to determine the lawfulness of imprisonment.

Hands-off doctrine The refusal of the courts to hear inmate complaints about the conditions of incarceration and the constitutional deprivations of penitentiary life.

Hate crime Offenses motivated by hatred against a victim because of his or her race, ethnicity, religion, sexual orientation, handicap, or national origin.

Holt v. Sarver The federal court decision declaring the Arkansas prison system to be in violation of the Eighth Amendment.

Homicide The killing of one human being by another.

Hudson v. Palmer The Supreme Court ruling that a prisoner has no reasonable expectation of privacy in his prison cell entitling him to Fourth Amendment protection.

Hurtado v. California The Supreme Court ruling that the due process clause of the Fourteenth Amendment does not require states to use grand jury indictments or presentments in capital cases.

Illinois Juvenile Court Act Legislation that established the first statewide juvenile court system in the United States.

Illinois* v. *Gates The Supreme Court ruling that magistrates, in establishing probable cause for the issuance of a search warrant, may make a common-sense decision, given all the circumstances set forth in the affidavit, whether there is a fair probability that contraband can be found in a particular place.

Incapacitation A sentencing philosophy seeking to remove the offender from society.

Indeterminate sentence A sentence of incarceration having a fixed minimum and a fixed maximum term of confinement, rather than a definite period.

Indictment A formal charging document returned by a grand jury based on evidence presented to it by the prosecutor.

In forma pauperis The characterization of an appeal by a poor person.

Information A formal charging document drafted by a prosecutor and tested before a magistrate.

In loco parentis A position in reference to a child of that of lawful parent or guardian.

Inmate code The unwritten rules of the prison subculture, which, if violated, can result in sanctions ranging from ostracism to death.

Inquiry system of justice A system in which all participants in a proceeding are obliged to cooperate with the court in its inquiry into the crime.

Inquisitorial system of justice A system in which the accused is considered guilty until he or she is proven innocent.

In re Gault The Supreme Court ruling that extended some—but not all—due process privileges to juvenile court proceedings.

In re Winship The Supreme Court ruling that required proof "beyond a reasonable doubt" for an adjudication of delinquency.

Inside cells Cells constructed back-to-back, with corridors running along the outside shell of the cell house.

Intake hearing An early stage in juvenile court proceedings in which a court officer makes a legal judgment of the probable cause of the petition.

Intensive probation supervision A program of closer surveillance and more exhaustive services that place a probationer under tighter control than he or she might experience under regular probation.

Intermittent sentence A sentence to confinement interrupted by periods of freedom.

Interpol An international police organization of 177 member countries that serves as a depository of intelligence information on wanted criminals.

Jackson* v. *Bishop The federal court decision declaring that whipping is in violation of the Eighth Amendment.

Jails Local facilities for temporary detention.

J.E.B.* v. *Alabama ex rel. T.B. The Supreme Court ruling that the exercise of peremptory challenges on the basis of gender violates the equal protection clause of the Fourteenth Amendment.

Johnson* v. *Avery The Supreme Court ruling that unless a state provides some reasonable legal assistance to inmates seeking postconviction relief, a jailhouse lawyer must be permitted to aid inmates in filing *habeas corpus* petitions.

Johnson* v. *Zerbst The Supreme Court ruling that the Sixth Amendment right to counsel applies to all felony defendants in federal prosecutions.

Jones* v. *North Carolina Prisoners' Labor Union The Supreme Court ruling that prison regulations prohibiting the organized activities of inmate labor unions are not violative of the freedom of association clause of the First Amendment.

Judicial circuit A specific jurisdiction served by a judge or court, as defined by given geographical boundaries.

Jury nullification The refusal or marked reluctance on the part of a jury to convict, because of the severe nature of the sentence involved, or when a jury otherwise "nullifies" the force of strict legal procedure.

Justices of the peace The judges in many lower courts in rural area, who are typically not lawyers and are locally elected.

Kent* v. *United States The Supreme Court ruling that the waiver of jurisdiction is a critically important stage in juvenile proceedings and must be attended by minimum requirements of due process and fair treatment.

Klopfer* v. *North Carolina The Supreme Court ruling that the Sixth Amendment right to a speedy trial applies in state as well as federal proceedings.

Lambert* v. *California Ruling whereby the Supreme Court held that due process requires that ignorance of a duty must be allowed as a defense when circumstances that inform a person as to the required duty are completely lacking.

Larceny The taking and carrying away of the personal property of another, with the intent to deprive permanently.

Lease system A form of prison industry under which contractors assume complete control over prisoners.

Lockdown A situation in which inmates are confined to their cells around the clock—denied exercise, work, recreation, and visits.

Malice aforethought The intent to cause death or serious harm, or to commit any felony whatsoever.

Mandatory release A release from prison required by statute when an inmate has been confined for a time period equal to his or her full prison sentence minus statutory "good time," if any.

Mandatory sentence A statutory requirement that a certain penalty shall be set and carried out in all cases upon conviction for a specified offense or series of offenses.

Manslaughter The unlawful killing of another, without malice.

Mapp **v.** *Ohio* The supreme Court ruling that evidence obtained in violation of the Fourth Amendment must be excluded from use in state as well as federal trials.

"Mark system" Started by Alexander Maconochie at Norfolk Island, a system by which inmates earn early release by hard work and good behavior.

Maximum expiration date The date on which the full sentence ends.

Maximum-security prisons Correctional institutions designed to hold the most aggressive and incorrigible offenders.

McKeiver **v.** *Pennsylvania* The Supreme Court ruling that due process does not require a jury in juvenile court hearings.

Mempa **v.** *Rhay* The Supreme Court ruling that the right to counsel applies to state probation revocation hearings at which deferred sentence may be imposed.

Mens rea **(criminal intent)** A person's awareness of what is right and wrong under the law, with an intention to violate the law.

Minnesota **v.** *Dickerson* The Supreme Court ruling that established the "plain feel" doctrine; that is, an object a police officer detects on a suspect's person during the course of a valid protective frisk under *Terry* v. *Ohio* may be seized without a warrant if the officer's sense of touch makes it immediately apparent to the officer that the object, though not threatening in nature, is contraband.

Miranda **v.** *Arizona* The Supreme Court ruling that the guarantee of due process requires that suspects in police custody be informed that they have the right to remain silent, that anything they say may be used against them, and that they have the right to counsel—before any questioning can permissibly take place.

Misdemeanor A crime punishable by no more than a $1,000 fine and/or 1 year of imprisonment, typically in a local institution.

Misprision of felony The concealment of a felony committed by another.

Mistrial A trial that has been terminated without a verdict and declared invalid by the court because of some circumstance that creates a substantial and uncorrectable prejudice to the conduct of a fair trial.

M'Naghten Rule The "right-or-wrong" test of criminal responsibility.

Monroe **v.** *Pape* The Supreme Court ruling that citizens can bring Section 1983 suits against state officials in federal courts without first exhausting state judicial remedies.

Morrissey **v.** *Brewer* The Supreme Court ruling that a parolee facing revocation is entitled to both a preliminary hearing to determine whether he or she actually violated parole and a final hearing to consider not only the facts in question, but also, if there was a violation, what to do about it.

Motion A formal application or request to the court for some action.

Murder The felonious killing of another human being with malice aforethought.

Natural law General principles that determine what is right and wrong according to some higher power.

New Jersey **v.** *T.L.O.* The Supreme Court ruling that school officials, with reasonable grounds to believe that the law or school rules are being violated, may conduct reasonable searches if needed to maintain safety, order, and discipline in a school.

Nolo contendere A plea of "no contest" or "I do not wish to contest," with the same implication as a guilty plea.

Open institutions "Prisons without walls," such as correctional camps, farms, and ranches.

Organized crime Business activities directed toward economic gain through unlawful means.

Palko **v.** *Connecticut* The Supreme Court ruling that the due process clause of the Fourteenth Amendment does not require the states to observe the double jeopardy guarantee of the Fifth Amendment.

Parens patriae A philosophy under which the state takes over the role of parent.

Parole The status of being released from a penal or reformatory institution in which one has served a part of his or her maximum sentence, on the condition of maintaining good behavior and remaining in the custody and under the guidance of the institution or some other agency approved by the state until a final discharge is granted.

Part I offenses Crimes designated by the FBI as the *most serious* and compiled in terms of the number of reports made to law enforcement agencies and the number of arrests made.

Part II offenses Crimes designated by the FBI as *less serious* than the Part I offenses and compiled in terms of the number of arrests made.

Patrol A means of deploying police officers that gives them responsibility for policing activity in a defined area and that usually requires them to make regular circuits of that area.

Peacekeeping role The legitimate right of police to use force in situations in which urgency requires it.

Pear's Case The 1779 legal ruling whereby a person who has legal control of another's property, and converts that property so as to deprive the owner of his possessory rights, is guilty of larceny.

Petition In juvenile proceedings, a document alleging that a youth is a delinquent, a status offender, or a dependent child and asking that the court assume jurisdiction over the juvenile.

Piece-price system A variation of the contract system of prison industry in which the contractor supplies the raw material and receives the finished product, paying the prison a specified amount for each unit produced.

"Plain view" doctrine The rule, from the Supreme Court decision in *Harris* v. *United States,* that anything a police officer sees in plain view, when that officer has a right to be where he or she is, is not the product of a search and is therefore admissible as evidence.

Police brutality The unlawful use of physical force by officers in the performance of their duties.

Police corruption Misconduct by police officers in the forms of illegal activities for economic gain and accepting gratuities, favors, or payment for services that police are sworn to carry out as part of their peacekeeping role.

Police cynicism The notion that all people are motivated by evil and selfishness.

Police discretion The freedom to choose among a variety of alternatives in conducting police operations.

"Police presence" The almost continuous presence of police officers in a place of business for the crime-deterrent effects it affords.

Police professionalism The notion that brutality and corruption are incompetent policing.

Police subculture The values and behavior patterns characteristic of experienced police officers.

Powell v. Alabama The Supreme Court ruling that an indigent charged in a state court with a capital offense has the right to the assistance of counsel at trial under the due process clause of the Fourteenth Amendment.

Premeditation A design or conscious decision to do something before it is actually done.

Presentence investigation An investigation into the background and character of a defendant that assists the court in determining the most appropriate sentence.

Presentment A written notice of accusation issued by a grand jury, based on its own knowledge and observation.

Prisonization The socializing process by which the inmate learns the rules and regulations of the institution and the informal rules, values, customs, and general culture of the penitentiary.

Prisons Correctional institutions maintained by federal and state governments for the confinement of convicted felons.

Privatization of corrections The construction, staffing, and operation of prisons by private industry for profit.

Probable cause Facts or apparent facts that are reliable and generate a reasonable belief that a crime has been committed.

Probation A sentence not involving confinement that imposes conditions and retains authority in the sentencing court to modify the conditions of sentence or to resentence the offender if he or she violates the conditions.

Procedural due process The procedures that are required before the life, liberty, or property of a person may be taken by the government.

Procunier v. Martinez The Supreme Court ruling that prison mail censorship is constitutional only when the practice furthers government interests in security and rehabilitation and when the restrictions are no greater than necessary to satisfy the particular government interest involved.

Protective sweep doctrine The rule that when police officers execute an arrest on or outside private premises, they may conduct a warrantless examination of the entire premises for other persons whose presence would pose a threat, either to their safety or to evidence capable of being removed or destroyed.

Rape Sexual penetration without consent.

Rehabilitation A sentencing philosophy seeking to reintegrate the offender into society.

Release on recognizance (ROR) The release of an accused on his or her own obligation rather than on a monetary bond.

Restitution A condition of probation requiring offenders to compensate their victims for damages or to donate their time in service to the community.

Retribution A sentencing philosophy seeking to create an equal or proportionate relationship between the offense and the punishment.

Rhodes v. Chapman The Supreme Court ruling that cell overcrowding, in and of itself, is neither cruel nor unusual.

Robbery The felonious taking of the money or goods of another, from his person or in his presence and against his will, through the use or threat of force and violence.

Robinson v. California The 1962 Supreme Court ruling that sickness may not be made a crime, nor may sick people by punished for being sick. The Court viewed narcotic addiction to be a "sickness" and held that a state cannot make it a punishable offense.

Ruiz v. Estelle The federal court decision declaring the Texas prison system to be unconstitutional.

Rule of Four The decision of at least four Supreme Court justices that a case merits consideration by the full Court.

Schall v. Martin The Supreme Court ruling that preventive detention is permissible for accused juvenile delinquents when there is evidence that the youth presents a serious risk of committing a crime before adjudication of the case.

Search and seizure The search for and taking of persons and property as evidence of a crime.

Search warrant A written order, issued by a magistrate and directed to a law enforcement office, commanding a search of a specified premises.

Section 1983 The section of the Civil Rights Act of 1871 used by state prisoners as a vehicle for access to the federal courts to litigate inmate rights.

Self-reported crime Crime statistics compiled on the basis of self-reports by offenders.

Separate system A prison system whereby each inmate is kept in solitary confinement in an isolated cell for the purpose of eliminating evil association in congregate quarters.

Separation-of-powers doctrine The principle that power is distributed among three branches of government—the legislative, the executive, and the judicial—for the purpose of ensuring that no one person or group will make the law, interpret the law, and apply the law.

Sequestration The removal of the jurors (and alternates, if any) from all possible outside influences.

Shock incarceration A 3- to 6-month regimen of military drill, drug treatment, physical exercise, hard labor, and academic work in return for having several years removed from an inmate's sentence.

Shock probation Brief incarceration followed by suspension of sentence and probation.

Silent system A prison system whereby inmates experience confinement under a rigid rule of absolute silence at all times.

Sixth Amendment Amendment to the Constitution guaranteeing the right to a speedy and public trial, by an impartial jury, in the district where the offense was committed; notice of charges; confrontation with witnesses; compulsory process for obtaining witnesses; and assistance of counsel.

Speedy trial The Sixth Amendment guarantee that protects an accused from indefinite incarceration prior to coming to trial.

Stack v. *Boyle* The Supreme Court ruling that bail set at a figure higher than an amount reasonably calculated to ensure the presence of the accused at trial and at the time of final submission to sentence is "excessive" under the Eighth Amendment.

Stanford v. *Kentucky* The Supreme Court ruling that the imposition of the death penalty for a crime committed at age 16 or 17 does not constitute cruel and unusual punishment merely because of the accused's age.

State account system A form of prison industry in which inmate production is directed by prison officials, goods are sold on the open market, and inmates receive a share of the profits.

State-use system A form of prison industry in which inmate-produced goods are used in state institutions and bureaus.

Status offenders Youths who, because of their special status as children, can be brought to the attention of the juvenile courts for certain kinds of noncriminal behavior.

Status offense An act declared by statute to be a crime because it violates the standards of behavior expected of children.

Statutory law Law created by statute, handed down by legislatures.

Substantive due process Due process protection against unreasonable, arbitrary, or capricious laws or acts.

Surety A third party who posts a bond for an accused.

Suspended sentence A court disposition of a convicted person, pronouncing a penalty of a fine or commitment to confinement, but unconditionally discharging the defendant or holding execution of the penalty in abeyance upon good behavior.

Tennessee v. *Garner* The Supreme Court decision stating that deadly force against a fleeing felon is proper only when it is necessary to prevent

the escape *and* when there is probable cause to believe that the suspect poses a significant threat to the officers or others.

Terry v. *Ohio* The Supreme Court ruling that when a police officer observes unusual conduct and suspects a crime is about to be committed, he may "frisk" a suspect's outer clothing for dangerous weapons.

Texas Rangers Founded by Stephen Austin in 1823, the first state police agency in the United States.

Theft The unlawful taking, possession, or use of another's property, without the use or threat of force, and with the intent to deprive permanently.

Thornburgh v. *Abbott* The Supreme Court ruling that federal prison regulations restricting prisoners' receipt of publications from outside prison pass First Amendment muster if they are reasonably related to legitimate penological interests.

"Ticket-of-leave" Started by Sir Walter Crofton of Ireland, a system of conditional release from prison that represented an early form of parole.

Total institutions Places that furnish barriers to social interchange with the world at large.

Transactional immunity Immunity against prosecution given to a grand jury witness in return for testifying.

True bill A grand jury's endorsement of the charge or charges specified in the prosecutor's bill.

Truth in sentencing Laws that require offenders to serve a substantial portion of their sentences.

Uniform Crime Reports (**UCR**) The annual publication of the FBI presenting official statistics on the rates and trends in crime in the United States.

United States v. *Calandra* The Supreme Court ruling that refused to extend the exclusionary rule to grand jury questions based on illegally seized evidence.

United States* v. *Leon The Supreme Court ruling that the Fourth Amendment exclusionary rule does not bar the use of evidence obtained by police officers acting in objectively reasonable reliance on a search warrant issued by a magistrate but ultimately found to be unsupported by probable cause.

United States* v. *Wade The Supreme Court ruling that a police lineup identification of a suspect, made without the suspect's attorney present, is inadmissible as evidence at trial.

U.S. courts of appeals The federal courts of appellate jurisdiction.

U.S. district courts The trial courts of the federal judiciary.

U.S. magistrates Federal lower court officials whose powers are limited to trying lesser misdemeanors, setting bail, and assisting district courts in various legal matters.

U.S. Supreme Court The highest court in the nation and the court of last resort.

Use immunity A limited immunity that prohibits the government only from using a grand jury witness's compelled testimony in a subsequent criminal proceeding.

Vengeance A sentencing philosophy seeking satisfaction from knowing or seeing that offenders are punished.

Venire A writ that summons jurors.

Vicarious liability The doctrine under which liability is imposed upon an employer for the acts of employees that are committed in the course and scope of their employment.

Victimization surveys Surveys of the victims of crime based on interviews with representative samples of the household population.

Void-for-vagueness doctrine The rule that criminal laws that are unclear or uncertain as to *what* or to *whom* they apply violate due process.

Voir dire An oath sworn by a juror regarding his or her qualifications.

Waiver of jurisdiction The process by which the juvenile court relinquishes its jurisdiction over a child and transfers the case to a court of criminal jurisdiction for prosecution as an adult.

Walnut Street Jail The first American penitentiary.

Weeks* v. *United States The Supreme Court ruling that a person whose Fourth Amendment rights of security against unreasonable search and seizure are violated by federal agents has the right to require that evidence obtained in the search be excluded from use against him or her in federal courts.

Weems* v. *United States The Supreme Court ruling that a sentence disproportionate to the offense is in violation of the Eighth Amendment ban against cruel and unusual punishment.

Wilson* v. *Seiter The Supreme Court ruling that an inmate alleging that the conditions of his or her confinement violate the Eighth Amendment's prohibition against cruel and unusual punishment must show deliberate indifference on the part of the responsible prison officials.

Witherspoon* v. *Illinois The Supreme Court ruling that states cannot exclude from juries in capital cases *all* persons opposed to the death penalty.

Wolff* v. *McDonnell The Supreme Court ruling that the due process clause of the Fourteenth Amendment protects, in part, state prisoners facing loss of good-time credit or punitive confinement.

Working personality A personality characterized by authoritarianism, cynicism, and suspicion developed in response to danger and the obligation to exercise authority.

LITERARY CREDITS

PHOTO CREDITS

Frontmatter
p. v   © Bob Daemmrich/Stock Boston/PNI
p. v   Crandall/Image Works
p. vi   Barros & Barros/The Image Bank/PNI
p. vi   AP/Wide World
p. vii   Barros & Barros/The Image Bank/PNI
p. x   Everett Collection, Inc.
p. x   © Jack Fields/Photo Researchers, Inc.

Part 1
p. 1   Mitch Kezar/Tony Stone Worldwide

Chapter 1
p. 2   Barros & Barros/The Image Bank/PNI
p. 3   AP/Wide World
p. 5   Steve Ries/Index Stock
p. 6   Liaison Agency
p. 10   AP/Wide World
p. 18   David Woo/Stock Boston/PNI
p. 19   James Aronovsky/Zuma Press
p. 22   AP/Wide World

Chapter 2
p. 26   AP/Wide World
p. 27   AP/Wide World
p. 29   AP/Wide World
p. 35   AP/Wide World
p. 39   AP/Wide World
p. 42   James Prince/Photo Researchers, Inc.
p. 44 (top)   Manny Crisostomo
p. 44 (bottom)   AP/Wide World
p. 48   AP/Wide World
p. 51   Everett Collection, Inc.
p. 52   AP/Wide World

Chapter 3
p. 56   David Young-Wolff/PhotoEdit/PNI
p. 59   National Archives Cities 61/FPG International
p. 61   Bill Gallery/Stock Boston/PNI
p. 62   Mark Reinstein/Image Works
p. 65   AP/Wide World
p. 66   AP/Wide World
p. 69   AP/Wide World
p. 71   Andrew Lichtenstein/Impact Visuals/PNI

Chapter 4
p. 76   Peggy & Ronald Barnett/The Stock Market
p. 77   AP/Wide World
p. 79   Paul Conklin/PhotoEdit

p. 83   AP/Wide World
p. 85   Liaison Agency
p. 91   AP/Wide World
p. 94   Bob Daemmrich/Stock Boston/PNI
p. 99   AP/Wide World
p. 100   AP/Wide World

Part 2
p. 103   © 1999 David Portnoy/Black Star

Chapter 5
p. 104   Everett Collection, Inc.
p. 107   Tom Pettyman/PhotoEdit
p. 108 (top)   *The Detroit News*
p. 108 (bottom)   Bob Daemmrich/Stock Boston/PNI
p. 111   AP/Wide World
p. 113   Everett Collection, Inc.
p. 120   Renai Benali/Liaison Agency
p. 125   AP/Wide World
p. 126   MacPherson/Monkmeyer
p. 127   Corbis/Hulton-Deutsch Collection
p. 128   © Bob Daemmrich/Stock Boston/PNI
p. 130   Susan Farley/*The New York Times*
p. 131   © Jack Fields/Photo Researchers, Inc.
p. 132   Everett Collection, Inc.
p. 135   Brooks Kraft/Sygma

Chapter 6
p. 138   © Allan Clear/Impact Visuals
p. 141   Hans Halbrstadt/Photo Researchers, Inc.
p. 147   © 1997 Jack Kurtz/Impact Visuals
p. 148   Tony Doubeck/*Union Tribune*
p. 150   Ralph Talmont/Aurora/PNI
p. 159   AP/Wide World
p. 161   © 1994 Michael Simpson/FPG International

Chapter 7
p. 166   HO/AP/Wide World
p. 167   Adam Nadel/AP/Wide World
p. 170   AP/Wide World
p. 173   Jeff Share/Black Star
p. 175   Liaison Agency
p. 177   Linda Rosier/*The New York Times*
p. 182   Tony Savino/SIPA
p. 183 (top)   Adam Nadel/AP/Wide World
p. 183 (bottom)   AFP/Corbis
p. 185   Kim Kulish/SABA

Part 3
p. 189   D. Boone/Corbis

Chapter 8
p. 190   © Theo Westenberger/Liaison Agency
p. 197   Western History Collection/University of Oklahoma Library
p. 199   AP/Wide World
p. 206   Harcourt Collection
p. 207   Sygma
p. 209   Liaison Agency
p. 213   AP/Wide World

Chapter 9
p. 218   Corbis
p. 223   Corbis/Christine Osborne
p. 225   Bob Daemmrich/Stock Boston
p. 235   Robert Miller/Library of Congress
p. 238   Topical Press Agency Collection/Liaison Agency
p. 239   David Gifford/Science Photo Library/Photo Researchers, Inc.
p. 241   AP/Wide World
p. 242   AP/Wide World

Chapter 10
p. 258   John Davenport/Liaison Agency
p. 263   P. F. Bentley/Black Star
p. 267   John McCoy/*L.A. Daily News*/Liaison Agency
p. 270   Culver Pictures
p. 274   Crandall/Image Works
p. 282   AP/Wide World
p. 284   AP/Wide World
p. 286   AP/Wide World

Part 4
p. 293   © 1993 Patsy Lynch/Impact Visuals

Chapter 11
p. 294   Corbis
p. 297   Liaison Agency
p. 299   H. Armstrong Roberts
p. 300   American Correctional Association
p. 302   Corbis/Bettmann
p. 308   James Inciardi
p. 311   AP/Wide World

Chapter 12
p. 316   Ferry/Liaison Agency
p. 331   Michael Soluri
p. 333   Woodfin Camp & Associates
p. 339   P. F. Bentley/Black Star
p. 342   1999 Joseph Rodriquez/Black Star

INDEX

abettor, 8

accessory after the fact, 8

accessory before the fact, 8

adjudication, 421–22

adjudication hearing, 422

adjudication inquiry, 421

administrative law, 20–22

Administrative Maximum Facility. *See* ADX

administrative services, of police, 118

adultery, 39

adversary system, 78

ADX (Administrative Maximum Facility), 317, 344

    See also "supermax" prisons

affirmative defense, 231

affirming, by the U.S. Supreme Court, 205

Afghanistan, punishment in, 284

African Americans

    and the criminal justice system, 256

    and the death penalty, 274–75, 276, 285, 291

age of majority, 412

Agnew, Spiro T., 230–31

Aguilar v. *Texas*, 142

AIDS, in prisons, 325, 327

Akayesu, Jean-Paul, 10

Alabama Council on Vocational and Technical Education, 328

Alcatraz Island Penitentiary, 307, 319, 324

Allen, Frederick Lewis, 239

Allen, Harry, 333

allocution, 272

amendments, constitutional. *See individual amendments*; Bill of Rights

American Bar Association, 224

American Civil Liberties Union (ACLU), 180, 238, 239, 276, 288

American Federation of Labor (AFL), 304

American Law Institute, guidelines for parole, 398

American Medical Association, and lethal injection, 282

American Prison Congress, 302

Amnesty International, 288

Amsterdam, Anthony, 275

anomie, 17

appeal, 97, 285–86

    process, 289

    right to, 286–88

appeals courts. *See* appellate courts

appellate courts, 192–93, 198–200

appellate jurisdiction, 198–99

appellate review, 285–89

Argersinger v. *Hamlin*, 212–13, 215

Arkansas prison scandal, 363–64, 365, 369, 376, 377

arms, right to bear, 82–83

    See also Second Amendment

arraignment, 96

arrest, 59, 92

    activity of police, 106

    powers of police, 140

    search incident to, 142–44

arson, 32–33

Ashford, Mary, 80

Ashford v. *Thornton*, 80

asportation, 38

assault, 31–32

assault and battery, 31

Attica Prison, 331, 371, 372, 377

    uprising and revolt (1971), 350–53

Auburn Prison, 295, 300, 304, 313

Augustus, John, 386

automatic reversal rule, 287

automobile search, 145–46, 147

auxiliary services, of police, 118

Bad Boys, 323

bail, 93, 256

    bond business, 222–23

    for juveniles, 420–21

    right to, 220–21

    10 percent cash bond plans, 225–26

    See also Eighth Amendment

Bailey, Walter C., 342

Baldwin, John, 356

Barfield, Velma, 281

Barker, Arthur ("Doc"), 319

Barker, Ma, 319

Barrett, Nicole, 279

Barron v. *Baltimore*, 82–83

Barrow, Clyde, 133, 319

Barry, John V., 375

Bates, Ruby, 208–9

Batson v. *Kentucky*, 245, 246, 256

Bean, Judge Roy, 196–97, 214

Behind the Shield (Niederhoffer), 172

Bell v. *Wolfish*, 373

bench trial, 241

bench warrant, 223

Benton v. *Maryland*, 87, 232

Betts v. *Brady*, 209, 211

bigamy, 39

Big House, The, 323

bilboes, 297

Billington, John, 59

bill of particulars, 234

Bill of Rights, 80–87, 88, 162, 220

    study of, 102

    and the U.S. Supreme Court, 90

    See also individual amendments

bills of attainder, 358

Birdman of Alcatraz, 323

Black, Hugo, 211

blackmail, 37

Blackmun, Harry A., 212–13

Black Muslim movement, 359–60

Blake, Fanchon, 128–29

Blake v. *Los Angeles*, 128–29

Bland Correctional Center, 373–74

blending, 120

"blue wall of silence", 182

Blumstein, Alfred, 72

Bolívar, Simón, 91

Bolivia, government of, 91

Bonaparte, Charles J., 132

bonds. *See* bail

booking, 93

"boosters", 45

boot camps, 431–32

Bostick, Terrance, 149

Boston Prison Society, 295

bounty hunters, 109, 256

Bowers, Michael, 40

Bowers, William J., 285

Bowers v. *Hardwick*, 40

Brady v. *Maryland*, 233

Brady v. *United States*, 232–33

Branch v. *Texas*, 277

Brandeis, Louis, 84

brank, 297

Brave New World (Huxley), 162

Brazil

    jails and prisons in, 310–11

    police wages in, 170

breach of the peace, 44

breaking and entering, 33–34

Breed v. *Jones*, 423, 434

Brennan, William J., Jr., 277, 373

Breyer, Stephen, 207

Brockway, Zebulon, 302–3, 432

Brooks, Charles, Jr., 282

Brown, John, 366

Brown v. *Mississippi*, 155–56, 157, 164, 173–74

Brubaker, 323, 377

brutality, by police, 176, 185

brutalization argument, against the death penalty, 285

Bruton, Jim, 363

Bryan, William Jennings, 239–40

Buenoano, Judy, 281

Bumper v. *North Carolina*, 149

Bureau of Alcohol, Tobacco, and Firearms (ATF), 112

Bureau of Internal Affairs, 181

Bureau of Justice Assistance, 179, 331

Burger, Warren E., 154

burglary, 33–36

    See also robbery

Byrd, James, Jr., 48, 52, 289

Calandra, John, 228
California v. *Stewart*, 158
Cambridge-Somerville Youth Study, 341
Canada
    corrections in, 406
    parole in, 401
capital punishment. *See* death penalty
Capone, Al ("Scarface"), 4, 51, 319
Cardozo, Benjamin, 86
careers, in justice, 21, 53, 73, 99,
    132–33, 163, 214, 253, 288,
    312, 343, 375, 404, 434
Carpenter, John, 366
Carrier's Case, 38
Carroll, George, 145
Carroll, Leo, 335
Carroll doctrine, 145–46
Carroll v. *United States*, 145
case fixing, by police, 169, 171
case law, 11
Cash, David, 3–4, 8, 22, 23
cell block, 318, 320
chain of command, in policing, 116
challenge
    for cause, 244
    peremptory, 244
Chamelin, Neil C., 43
change of venue, 206
Chang Nan-ping, 29
Chapman, Kelly, 373
Chapman v. *California*, 287
charging the jury, 252
Charrière, Henri, 363, 377
Chekhov, Anton, 210
Chevalier, Gabriel, 210
Chicago Boy's Court, 383
Chicago Church Federation, 383
child abuse, 48
child molesting, 40, 48–49
children in need of supervision (CHINS,
    CINS), 425
"child savers", 414
Chile, police wages in, 170
Chimel, Ted Steven, 143–44
Chimel v. *California*, 143–44
China, abduction of women in, 29
Cincinnati police, organization of, 117
circumstantial evidence, 250
citizen dispute settlement, 384
civil commitment, 384
civil death, 359
civil disabilities, of prisoners, 358–63
civilian review boards, 180
civil law, 11
civil rights, of prisoners, 355–57
Civil Rights Act (1871), 180
    Section 1983, 355–57
Civil Rights Act (1964), 128–29, 362
"class cannon", 34–35, 45
classification, of prisoners, 324–26
clearance rate, 119
Cleaver, Eldridge, 323

Clemmer, Donald, 338–39
clinical treatment programs, in prisons,
    329–30
Clinton, William Jefferson, 27, 77, 78,
    100, 332
Clinton Prison, 324
cocaine, 165
    and crime, 71
    in Latin America, 170
    and paper currency, 150
    production of, 41
code law, in Bolivia, 91
coeducational prisons, 336–37
Coffin v. *Reichard*, 355, 376
Coker v. *Georgia*, 279
Coleman, Harold, 263
college students, and attitudes on the
    death penalty, 282
Colombia, crime in, 64–65
colonies, U.S., punishment in, 296–97
Colored Big Brothers, 383
command discretion, 123
common law, 11, 19–20, 91
Commonwealth of Virginia v. *Gilmore*,
    146
community-based correction, 382,
    400–404
community policing, 136
community protection argument, for the
    death penalty, 283
commutation, 97
competent evidence, 250
Comprehensive Drug Abuse and Control
    Act (1970), 41
concurrent sentences, 272
conditional release, 387
confessions, 155, 157–58
    illegal, 206
confidence games, 37
conjugal visitation, in prison, 335–36
Conner, John, 366
consecutive sentences, 272
consent of the victim, 15
consent searches, 148–49
conspiracy, 8
constitution. *See* U.S. Constitution
constitutional amendments. *See individ-*
    ual amendments; Bill of Rights
constitutional law, 20
constitutional rights
    and prison discipline, 363–69
    of prisoners, 358–63
contraband, in prison, 333
contract system, 301
Controlled Substances Act (1970), 41, 43
"convict bogey" syndrome, 333
Cornell, David C., 155
correctional systems, 322–23
correctional treatment, 340–44
correctional treatment specialists, 312
corrections
    in Canada, 406

community-based, 382, 400–404
juvenile, 430–32
officers, 312, 351
privatization of, 374
See also jails; juvenile justice sys-
    tem; prisons
Corrections Connection Network, 343,
    346
corruption, of police, 186
Costello, Frank, 228
Costello v. *United States*, 228
Costello v. *Wainwright*, 369
cottage system, for juveniles, 431
Coulthurst, John Henry ("The Lizard"),
    36
counsel
    right not to have, 212–13
    right to have, 87, 157–58,
    208–13
    See also Sixth Amendment
counterfeiting, 37
court officers, 214
courts
    appellate, 192–93, 198–200
    criminal, 428
    drug, 200
    jurisdiction of, 193
    justice of the peace, 194–95
    lower, 214
    major trial, 198
    municipal, 195–98
    state, 192–201
    U.S. commissioner's, 201–2
    U.S. courts of appeals, 204
    U.S. district, 202–4
    U.S. magistrate's, 201–2
    U.S. Supreme, 204–8
courts of appellate jurisdiction, 192–93,
    198–200
courts of general jurisdiction, 192–93,
    198
courts of last resort, 192–93
    See also appellate courts
courts of limited jurisdiction, 193,
    194–98
    See also lower courts
courts of record, 198
crack-cocaine. *See* cocaine
crime, 4–19
    behavior systems in, 45–53
    categories of, 28–45
    corporate, 46–47
    data on, 71–73
    as drama, 4
    extent of, 62–64
    gender perspectives on, 17, 43, 67,
    124–25, 146, 246, 281, 305, 335,
    432
    historical perspectives on, 6, 50–51,
    59, 80, 109, 174–75, 196–97,
    238–40, 270, 296–97, 319,
    366–67, 386, 416

international perspectives on, 10, 29, 64–65, 91, 131, 170, 199, 242, 284, 310–11, 325, 360, 401
legal definition of, 7
legal perspectives on, 40, 89, 147, 182, 212–13, 228, 278, 327, 365, 393, 426
measurement of, 64
occasional property, 46
organized, 47
parties to, 8
property, 36–38, 46, 120
rates of, 61–62, 64–66, 72
research in, 34–35, 71, 82–83, 110–11, 150, 179, 200, 267, 332, 394, 418–19
self-reported, 70, 74
as sin, 4
as a social construct, 5–7
trends in, 74
unsolved, 23
victimless, 65
victims of, 67, 68, 74, 256
violent, 46, 140, 267, 280
in war, 10
white-collar, 46–47
See also specific types of crime
crime clock, 58, 60
Crime Index, 60
Crime in the United States, 58
crimes known to the police, 59
criminal bankruptcy, 37
criminal behavior, self-reported, 69–71
criminal behavior systems, 46–48
criminal courts, and young offenders, 428
criminal due process, 78–90
criminal homicide, 30–31
criminal intent, 9–11
criminal justice
    careers in. *See* justice, careers in
    diversion, 382–85
    majoring in, 21
    process, 90–97
    programs, 406
Criminal Justice Research and Training Center, 121
criminal justice system, 97–101
    population in, 372, 396
criminal law, 19–22
    violation of, 11–17
    Criminal Law for Policemen (Chamelin and Evans), 43
criminal law revolution, 87, 90
criminal nuisance, 44
crisis intervention counseling, 53
Cristiano, Carmine, 242
Crofton, Sir Walter, 301, 302, 395
cross-examination, 251
cruel and unusual punishment, 87, 275–79, 285, 361, 362, 365, 367, 429
    and the death penalty, 273–74, 275–76, 285

and lethal gas, 280
    See also Eighth Amendment
cruel and unusual punishment argument, against the death penalty, 285
Cruz v. *Beto*, 360
Cummins Prison Farm, 364, 365
custodial interrogation, 155–61
cynanide gas, 281

Dahmer, Jeffrey, 124–25
Darrow, Clarence Seward, 239–40, 245
Darwin, Charles, 238
Day, William R., 152
day fines, 265
deadly force, use of by police, 176–78
"dead time", 273, 400
death penalty, 88, 273–85
    advocates against, 288
    arguments against, 284–85
    attitudes toward, 282, 291
    as cruel and unusual punishment, 275–76
    debate about, 283–85
    and discrimination, 274–75, 283, 285, 291
    since 1976, 279–80
    support for, 274, 283
    and the U.S. Supreme Court, 275–79
    and women, 281, 290
Death Penalty Information Center, 288
"death-qualified" juries, 278
death row, 280, 285
    women on, 281
defendant, 11
defense
    affirmative, 231
    of crime, 11–15
defense's case, presentation of, 251–52
definite sentence, 266
Delaware, corporal punishment in, 366–67
Delaware v. *Prouse*, 146, 147, 287
De Leon, George, 332
deliberation, 30
delinquency, 415
delinquent, 415
    See also juvenile justice system
Derias, Joseph, 366
Dershowitz, Alan M., 13
desecration, 45
detective work, 119–20
detention, juvenile, 420–21, 429–30
detention center, 307–13
detention hearing, 420
determinate sentence, 266, 269
deterrence, as objective of sentencing, 261–62
deterrence argument, for the death penalty, 283
deviance, 5–7
Devil's Island, 363, 377

Dewer, Leroy, 351–52
Diallo, Amadou, 167, 183–84
Dillinger, John, 133, 270, 319
Dilulio, John J., 433
direct evidence, 250
discipline, in prisons, 331–34, 363–69
discipline, of police organizations, 116–18
discrimination
    and the death penalty, 274–75, 283, 285, 291
    in policing, 128–30
    See also racism
discrimination argument, against the death penalty, 284–85
disorderly conduct, 44
disposition, 421–22
disposition hearing, 422
district court judges, 204
disturbing the peace, 44
diversion
    criminal justice, 382–85, 430–32
    impact of, 384–85
    patterns of, 383
DNA, 161
DNA fingerprints, 139, 161, 162, 164
doctrine of implied malice, 31
document examiners, 73
dogs, drug-sniffing, 150
domestic violence, 28, 47, 48–49, 54
double jeopardy, 89, 232
    See also Fifth Amendment
Douglas, William O., 87, 224, 277, 358
Douglas v. *California*, 212
Downum v. *United States*, 232, 236
driving under the influence (DUI), 45
driving while intoxicated (DWI), 45
drug abuse treatment, in prisons, 330–31
drug arrests, 67
drug courts, 200, 201, 216
drug enforcement unit, 121
drug law violations, 41–43
drug offenders, and prison population, 363
drug seizures, 306
drug trafficking, in Latin America, 170
drunk driving, 43
    See also driving under the influence; driving while intoxicated
drunkenness, 44
dual court system, 192
ducking stool, 296–97
due process
    criminal, 78–90
    and medieval torture, 80
    procedural, 89–90
    substantive, 88–89
    in U.S. law, 88
    and the U.S. Supreme Court, 90
due process clause. *See* Fifth Amendment; Fourteenth Amendment

due process of law, 78
Duncan, Elizabeth Ann, 281
Duncan, Gary, 243
Duncan v. *Louisiana*, 240, 243, 256
Dunne, Peter, 285
duress and consent, 14
Durham Rule, 12
Durham v. *United States*, 12
"duty to aid" statute, 22
Dwight, Lewis, 295, 300, 313

Eastern Penitentiary (Pennsylvania),
  298–99, 324
economic argument, for the death
  penalty, 283
education programs, in prisons, 327–28
Edward the Confessor (King), 19
Eighteenth Amendment, 145
Eighth Amendment, 81, 88, 220–21,
  223, 273, 275–77, 280, 285, 355,
  361, 362, 367, 373, 429
Eisenhower, Dwight D., 87
elderly, as crime victims, 74
electric chair, 274
electrocution, 280, 283
Elmira Reformatory, 302–3, 432
embezzlement, 37
Emergency Response Team (ERT), 121
entrapment, 15
Equal Employment Opportunity Act
  (1972), 128
error, prejudicial, 248
Escape from Alcatraz, 323
Escobedo, Danny, 157 58
Escobedo v. *Illinois*, 157–58, 164, 207,
  233
Estelle v. *Gamble*, 362, 374
Evans, Kenneth R., 43
evidence, 250
evolution, theory of, 238–40
examination, direct and redirect, 251
exclusionary rule, 87, 88, 152–54, 206,
  207
excusable homicide, 15–16
execution, methods of, 274, 280–83
  See also death penalty
executive clemency statute, 400
exemplars, nontestimonial, 161
ex parte Hull, 357
ex parte proceedings, 228

Family Reunion Program, 336
Farer, Tom J., 349, 375
Faretta, Anthony, 212–13
Faretta v. *California*, 212–13
Fare v. *Michael C.*, 424
Farrah, Kimberly, 219
Federal Bureau of Investigation (FBI),
  57, 58, 105, 112–13, 134, 136,
  319
  special agents, 132–33

Federal Bureau of Prisons, 306, 309,
  312, 314, 317, 319, 324, 344, 361
federal courts. *See* courts
federal judiciary, 201–8
Federal Kidnapping Act (Lindbergh
  Law), 276
Federal Prison Industries, 329
federal prison system, 305–7
Federal Rules of Criminal Procedure,
  287
Federal Trade Commission (FTC), 113
felony, 18
felony-murder doctrine, 30–31
Field, Stephen J., 275
Fifth Amendment, 80, 81, 86–90,
  155–57, 227, 228, 232, 251, 287,
  362, 368, 373, 424
Fiji, women police in, 131
fines, as sentence, 264–65
fingerprint analysts, 73
fingerprints
  DNA, 164
  on file, 66
First Amendment, 81, 84, 85, 87,
  359–60, 363
first-degree murder, 30
Fiske v. *Kansas*, 84
fixed sentence, 266
flat sentence, 266
flogging, 366–67
Florida v. *Bostick*, 149
Florida v. *Jimeno*, 149
Floyd, Charles ("Pretty Boy"), 319
force, use of by police, 108–11, 136
foreperson, 253
forgery, 37
formal charges, determination of, 95
fornication, 39
Fortas, Abe, 211
Foster v. *California*, 160
Fourteenth Amendment, 80, 84, 86, 87,
  88, 90, 153, 156, 209, 210–12,
  243, 278, 287, 360, 362, 365,
  368, 393
Fourth Amendment, 81, 87, 140, 142,
  143, 145, 147, 148, 152, 153,
  154, 162, 207, 228, 287, 374,
  389, 424, 425, 426
Franks, Robert, 8, 23
Fraternal Order of Police (FOP), 180
fraud, 37, 46
fresh pursuit, 147–48
frisk, 144–45
fruit of the poisonous tree, 145
full enforcement, of the law, 122
Fulwood v. *Clemmer*, 359–60
furlough, 401–4
Furman, William, 277
Furman v. *Georgia*, 277, 283, 284–85,
  290
Furton, Kenneth, 150
Fyfe, James J., 177

Gacy, John Wayne, 4
Gagnon v. *Scarpelli*, 394
gambling, 45
gang theft, 46
gaolbirds, 307
gaols, 307–8
Garcia Meza, Luis, 91
Gardner v. *Florida*, 387–88
gas chamber, 280–81
gender bias, in policing, 128–30
general deterrence, 261
general intent, 9
Genovese, Vito, 53, 228
George III (King), 82
George II (King), 307
Gideon, Clarence Earl, 210–11, 216
Gideon v. *Wainwright*, 87, 210–12, 215
Gilmore, Denise, 146
Gilmore, Gary Mark, 279–80
Ginsburg, Ruth Bader, 207
Girls' Term Court (New York), 425–27
Gitlow, Benjamin, 84
Gitlow v. *New York*, 84–85
Godinez v. *Moran*, 213
Goldberg, Arthur J., 276
"good faith" exception, 154
"good time", 395, 396, 398
Gotti, John, 4, 53
grand jury, 226–29
  accusatory, 227
  complaints against, 227–29
  contempt power of, 229
  investigatory, 227
  and the U.S. Supreme Court, 228
Gravano, Sam ("the Bull"), 53
Gray, Horace, 220 21
Gray, Jimmy Lee, 286, 289
Greenberg, Steven M., 151
Green Haven Prison, 356
Greenholtz v. *Inmates of Nebraska Penal
  and Correctional Complex*, 397
Gregg v. *Georgia*, 277–79
Griggs v. *Duke Power Company*, 128–29
Griswold, Erwin N., 207
Griswold v. *Connecticut*, 87, 88
"guilty" plea, 96, 230
gun control, 82–83
guns, and students, 422, 431

habeas corpus, 355, 356–58
Hale v. *Henkel*, 228
halfway houses, 404
Hampton v. *United States*, 15
hands-off doctrine, 350
harassment, 44
Hardwick, Michael, 40
Harlan, John M., 159
harmless error rule, 287
Harris, James E., 151
Harrison Act (1914), 41, 306
Harris v. *United States*, 151

hate crimes, 27, 28, 47, 49, 52, 54
Hawes-Cooper Act (1929), 304
Hawkins, Gordon J., 283
Hawthorne, Nathaniel, 297
health services, in prisons, 326
hearing
    adjudication, 422
    detention, 420
    disposition, 422
    intake, 417–18
hearsay, 250
Heisley, Webber A., 155
Heston, Charlton, 83
High Court. *See* U.S. Supreme Court
High Street Jail, 296–97
Hinckley, John W., 13, 23
History and Organization of Criminal
    Statistics in the United States
    (Robinson), 71
HIV, in prisons, 325, 327
Hoffman, Walter, 230–31
Holmes, Oliver Wendell, 84
Holt v. *Sarver*, 364, 365, 376
Holtzman, Elizabeth, 17
Holyfield, Evander, 16
Holy Name Society, 383
home furlough, 402
"Homicide: Life in the City", 134
homicides, 30–31
    excusable, 15–16
    justifiable, by police, 178
    number of, 411
    occupational, 62
homosexuality, public opinion of, 28
homosexual rape, 335
Hong Kong prisons, 360, 377
"Honor Roll of Superior Rights", 86, 87
Hoover, J. Edgar, 133, 319, 405
Horn, Robbie, 430
Horton, Willie, 403
"hot" pursuit, 147–48
Howard, John, 297
Howe, Samuel G., 395
Huber, Henry A., 402
Huber Law, 402
Hudson, Ted S., 373–74
Hudson v. *Palmer*, 373–74
Hudson v. *Parker*, 220
Hughes, Charles E., 157
hulks, 307–8
human rights abuse, by police, 182, 186
Human Rights Watch, 182, 315, 360
"hung" jury, 253
Hurtado v. *California*, 227
Hutchinson, Robert, 366–67
Huxley, Aldous, 162

Illinois Juvenile Court Act (1899), 414
Illinois v. *Gates*, 142, 143
Immigration and Naturalization Service
    (INS), 112

imprisonment
    rates of, 324
    as sentence, 265–68
    See also prisons
incapacitation, as objective of sentenc-
    ing, 261
incarceration
    alternatives to, 200
    conditions of, 369–72
    See also prisons
incest, 39
incompetent evidence, 250
indecent exposure (exhibitionism), 39
indeterminate sentence, 265–66, 269
indictment, 95, 226
inducement, 15
industrial prisons, 304–5
industries, prison, 300–301
in forma pauperis, 211
information, 95, 226
initial appearance, 93–94
in loco parentis, 424
inmate code, 339–40
inmate social system, 337–40
inmates. *See* prisoners
inquiry, adjudication, 421
inquiry system, 78
inquisitorial system, 78
In re Gault, 422–23, 430, 434
In re Kemmler, 276
In re Oliver, 237, 240
In re Winship, 423, 430, 434
insanity, 11–13, 231
inside cells, 318
Inside the Walls of Folsom Prison, 323
Institute for Court Management, 195
institutional routines, 323–31
institutions
    correctional, 431–32
    open, 320–21
    women's, 321
    See also jails; prisons
intake hearing, 417–20
intensive probation supervision, 391–92
intermediate appellate courts, 192–93
intermediate courts of appeal, 199–200
intermittent sentence, 268
Internal Revenue Service (IRS), 112
International Association of Chiefs of
    Police (IACP), 129, 180
International Conference of Police Asso-
    ciations (ICPA), 180
international corruption, 171
Interpol, 113
interrogation, custodial, 155–61
Interstate Commerce Commission
    (ICC), 113
investigation
    prearrest, 90–92
    presentence (probation), 387–88
investigative powers, of police, 140
invited error rule, 287

Irish system (indeterminate system), 302
irreversibility argument, against the
    death penalty, 284
Italian courts, 242
Iverson, Sherrice, 3, 8, 22

Jackson, George, 323
Jackson Prison, 324
Jackson v. *Bishop*, 366
Jackson v. *Georgia*, 277
Jagger, Bianca, 281
jailhouse lawyers, 358, 375
jail inmates, and drug use, 309
jails
    conditions in, 309–13
    contemporary, 308–9
    origins of, 307–8
    population of, 308, 309
    See also prisons
"jail time", 273
James, Derrick ("Spiderman"), 36
J.E.B. v. *Alabama ex rel. T.B.*, 246,
    256
Jeleniewski, Eric, 219
Jewish Social Services Bureau, 383
John Paul II (Pope), 281
Johnson, Lyndon B., 211
Johnson v. *Avery*, 357–58
Johnson v. *Zerbst*, 209
joinders, 234
Joliet Penitentiary, 300, 324
Jones v. *North Carolina Prisoners'*
    Labor Union, 362
Jones v. *United States*, 13
jostling, 32
JPs. *See* justices of the peace
"Judge and Jury", 191
"Judge Joe Brown", 191
"Judge Judy", 191
judges
    district court, 204
    sentencing discretion of, 263, 269
judgment, 253–55
judicial circuit, 198
judicial corruption, in Peru, 199
judiciary, federal, 201–8
Judiciary Act (1789), 202, 205, 220
jurisdiction
    of courts, 193
    waiver of, 428
jury, 240–47
    charging of, 252
    deliberation by, 253
    "hung", 253
    petit, 243
    polling of, 255
    selection of, 243–44
    See also grand jury
jury nullification, 254
jury panel, 244
jury tampering, 255

justice
careers in, 21, 53, 73, 99, 132–33,
163, 214, 253, 288, 312, 343,
375, 404, 434
gender perspectives on, 17, 43, 67,
124–25, 146, 246, 281, 305, 335,
432
historical perspectives on, 6, 50–51,
59, 80, 109, 174–75, 196–97,
238–40, 270, 296–97, 319,
366–67, 416
international perspectives on, 10, 29,
64–65, 91, 131, 170, 199, 242,
284, 310–11, 325, 360, 401
juvenile. *See* juvenile justice system
legal perspectives on, 40, 89, 147,
182, 212–13, 228, 278, 327, 365,
393, 426
research in, 34–35, 71, 82–83,
110–11, 150, 179, 200, 267, 332,
394, 418–19
systems of, 78
See also courts; criminal justice
Justice, William Wayne, 370–71
Justice Department, 134, 230, 418
justice of the peace courts, 194–95
justices of the peace (JPs), 194–95, 214
justifiable homicide, 15
by police, 178
justification, of crime, 15–17
Juvenile Justice and Juvenile Delinquency Prevention Act (1974),
427
juvenile justice system
bureaus, 120
corrections, 430–32
courts, 415–17
critical issues in, 425–32
detention, 420–21, 429–30
emergence of, 414
nature of, 412–16
proceedings in, 422–23
juvenile probation officers, 434
juveniles
in adult court, 427–29
arrests of, 417–22, 435
in criminal courts, 428
and the death penalty, 428
and the Fourth Amendment, 424
and *Miranda*, 424
and the U.S. Constitution, 422–25
juveniles in need of supervision (JINS),
425

Kaczynski, Theodore (Ted), 213, 344
Kania, Richard, 177
Kanka, Megan, 89
Karpis, Alvin, 133, 319
Kastigar v. *United States*, 229
Katz, Burton, 191
Kelly, George ("Machine Gun"), 319

Kennedy, Anthony, 207
Kent v. *United States*, 422, 424, 428,
430, 434
Kerner Commission, 174–76
KEY program, 331, 332
kickbacks, 169
kidnapping, 29
King, John William, 289
Klopfer, Peter H., 237
Klopfer v. *North Carolina*, 237
Koch, Ed, 191, 214
Ku Klux Klan, 48, 49, 275

labor unions, in prisons, 362–63
La Cosa Nostra, 51
LaFave, Wayne R., 121–22
Lamb, Charles, 210
Lambert v. *California*, 14
Langtry, Lillie, 196–97
Lansky, Meyer, 53
larceny, 37
lash, 366–67
Latin America, drug trafficking and
police corruption in, 170
law
administrative, 20–22
common, 11, 19–20, 91
constitutional, 20
criminal, 11–17, 19–22
full enforcement of, 122
"good time", 395
natural, 4–5
sanctioned by the state, 17–19
selective enforcement of, 122
statutory, 11, 20
law enforcement agencies, federal,
112–13
Law Enforcement Assistance Administration (LEAA), 68–69, 383
law of the land, 80, 88–89
"Law & Order", 105, 134
lawyers, jailhouse, 358, 375
lease system, 301
Lechter, Hannibal, 344
legal assistants, 253
legislative control, of police conduct,
178–80
Leopold, Nathan F., Jr., 8, 23, 239
lethal gas. *See* gas chamber
lethal injection, 280, 282–83
lettre de cachet, 237
lewdness, 39
Lewinsky, Monica, 77
liability, vicarious, 9
Life and Times of Judge Roy Bean, The,
196
line services, of police, 118
lineups, 159–60
Linkletter v. *Walker*, 153–54
Lippmann, Walter, 240
lockdown, 372

Lockhart v. *McCree*, 278
Loeb, Albert A., 8, 23, 239
loitering, 44
Louima, Abner, 182
lower courts, 214
Luciano, Charles ("Lucky"), 228

Mackey, Wade, 177
Maconochie, (Captain) Alexander,
301–2, 395
Madison, James, 80, 82
Mafia, the, 50–51
Magistrate's Act (1968), 202
magistrate's courts. *See* municipal courts
Magna Carta, 242
mail, in prison, 360–62
Maitland, F. W., 19
major trial courts, 198
See also courts of general jurisdic-
tion
mala in se, 18
mala prohibita, 18
malice aforethought, 30
mandatory release, 398
mandatory sentence, 268, 269
Manhattan Bail Project, 225
Mann, James Robert, 132
Mann Act (1910), 306
manslaughter, 31
Manson, Charles, 4
Mapp, Dollree ("Dolly"), 153
Mapp v. *Ohio*, 87, 152–54, 164, 207,
233
Marijuana Tax Act (1937), 41
mark system, 302
Marshall, John, 83
Marshall, Thurgood, 277, 283, 284–85
Martin, Gregory, 429–30
Martinson, Robert, 342
"Martinson Report", 341–43
Massachusetts v. *Sheppard*, 154
material evidence, 250
maximum expiration date, 400
mayhem, 32
Mazzini, Joseph, 50
McCleskey v. *Zant*, 285
McCrary, Robert L., Jr., 210–11
McKeiver v. *Pennsylvania*, 423
McKinney, Mark, 282
McNabb v. *United States*, 156–57
McVeigh, Timothy, 344
medical rights and services, in prisons,
362
Megan's Law, 89, 101
Mempa v. *Rhay*, 392–93
men, rape of, 43
menacing, 32
Menechino v. *Oswald*, 397
mens rea, 9
mental illness, treatment in prison, 362
mentoring diversion programs, 384

methyl benzoate, 150
Minnesota Gag Law, 84
Minnesota v. *Dickerson*, 145
minorities, and the death penalty, 291
    See also discrimination
minors otherwise in need of supervision
    (MINS), 425
Miranda rights, 158–59, 164, 423
Miranda v. *Arizona*, 88, 158–59, 164,
    207, 233, 423, 424
misdemeanor, 18
misprision of felony, 9
mistake of fact, 14
mistake of law, 14
mistrial, 248
mixed sentence, 390
M'Naghten, Daniel, 12
M'Naghten Rule, 12
Model Penal Code (American Law Insti-
    tute), 398
Monge, Luis Jose, 279, 280
Monroe v. *Pape*, 355–56, 376
Moore v. *Illinois*, 233
Morrisey, John, 393
Morrissey v. *Brewer*, 393, 394, 400
motion, 233
    in arrest of judgment, 255
    for a bill of particulars, 234
    for change of venue, 233
    for continuance, 234–35
    for directed verdict, 251
    for discovery, 233
    for dismissal, 235–36
    for a new trial, 255
    posttrial, 255
    pretrial, 233–36
    for severance of charges, 234
    for severance of defendants, 234
    for suppression, 233–34
multiple-clearance method, 119
municipal courts, 195–98
murder, 30
    rates of, 58, 59
Murphy, Jack ("Murph the Surf"), 36
Murphy, Patrick V., 159
Murton, Thomas O., 363–64
Mussolini, Alessandra, 242

Nash, Frank, 319
Nation, Carry, 6
National Advisory Commission on Civil
    Disorders. *See* Kerner Commis-
    sion
National Advisory Commission on
    Criminal Justice Standards and
    Goals, 72, 194, 200, 264
National Association for the Advance-
    ment of Colored People
    (NAACP), 180, 276
National Center for Women and Polic-
    ing (NCWP), 129–30

National Commission on Law Obser-
    vance and Enforcement, 71
National Conference of Commissioners
    on Uniform State Laws, 423
National Crime Survey (NCS), 68–69,
    74
National Criminal Justice Commission,
    132
National Incident-Based Reporting
    System (NIBRS), 67, 74
National Institute of Justice, 200, 391,
    394, 406
National Lawyers Guild, 375
National Motor Vehicle Theft Act
    (1919), 306
National Opinion Research Center
    (NORC), 67–68
National Parks Service, 112
National Parole Board, 401
natural law, 4–5
Near v. *Minnesota*, 84
negotiated pleas. *See* plea bargaining
Nelson, George ("Baby Face"),
    319
New Jersey v. *T. L. O.*, 425, 426
New Mexico State Penitentiary, 371–72,
    376
New York City Police Department, 167,
    183–84
New York State Governor's Special
    Committee on Criminal Offend-
    ers, 341
New York State Office of Crime Control
    Planning, 341
Niederhoffer, Arthur, 172
Ninth Amendment, 81, 87
Nixon, Richard M., 230–31
"no bill", 95
nolle prosequi, 237, 382, 383
nolo contendere plea, 96, 230–31
nontestimonial exemplars, 161
North Carolina Prisoners' Labor Union
    (PLU), 362
"not guilty by reason of insanity"
    (NGRI) plea, 13, 231
"not guilty" plea, 96, 230
"NYPD Blue", 105, 134

objections, legal, 251
obscenity, 39
occupational homicide, 62
O'Connor, Sandra Day, 207, 246, 369
O'Donnell, Kelly, 281
"Old Red Hannah", 366–67
O'Neil v. *Vermont*, 275
open institutions, 320–21
ordeal by water, 78
organized crime, 28, 49–53
Original Criminal Code of 1676, 20
Oswald, Russell, 352, 353
Owensby, Earle, 323

Palko, Frank, 85–86, 87
Palko v. *Connecticut*, 85–87, 232
Palmer, Russel, 374
paper currency, and cocaine residue, 150
Papillon (Charrière), 363, 377
pardon, 97
parens patriae, 414, 422, 423, 425, 427,
    428, 430
Parker, Bonnie, 133, 319
Parker v. *Gladden*, 87
parole, 97
    administration, 396
    board, 396
    in Canada, 401
    conditions of, 398–99
    control conditions of, 399
    discharge, 400
    eligibility for, 396–99
    elimination of, 405
    guidelines (American Law Institute),
        398
    hearing, 397
    officers, 396, 404
    origins of, 395
    reform conditions of, 399
    revocation of, 399–400
    selection, 397
    services, 399
    supervision, 399
    violation of, 399–400
    vs. probation, 396
paroles, number of, 396
Parole Watch, 406
parties to crime, 8
Part I Offenses, 59–60
Part II Offenses, 60
Pataki, George E., 139, 381, 405
Patel, Marilyn Hall, 280
patrol, by police, 118–19
patronage, by police, 171–72
Payne v. *Tennessee*, 261
Pear's Case, 38
Peel, Sir Robert, 12
penal colonies, 349, 375–76
Penn, William, 296
Pennsylvania State Constabulary, 114
"People's Court, The", 191, 214
People v. *Beardsley*, 8–9
People v. *Lovercamp*, 370
Perez, Leander H., 243
persons in need of supervision (PINS),
    425
Peru
    judicial corruption in, 199, 216
    police wages in, 170
petitions, 356, 417–20
petit jury, 243
Philadelphia Society for Alleviating the
    Miseries of Public Prisons, 297
Phillips, Steven, 220
pickpocketing, 34–35, 37, 54
piece-price system, 301

pillory, 366–67
Pitre, Guiseppe, 51
plagiarism, 37
plain error rule, 287
plaintiff, 11
"plain view" doctrine, 151
plea bargaining, 219, 232–33, 254, 256
pleas
    guilty, 96, 230
    insanity, 13, 231
    nolo contendere, 96, 230–31
    not guilty, 96, 230
    standing mute, 96
    statute of limitations, 231
PMS defense, 17
police
    arrest activity of, 106
    arrest powers of, 140
    assault of, 110
    attitudes toward, 134, 186
    authority of, 176
    brutality of, 176, 185
    as career, 163
    community satisfaction with, 179
    county, 115
    and crime reduction, 140
    and custodial interrogation, 155–61
    cynicism of, 126
    decision-making by, 176
    discretion of, 121–23
    and the drug war, 132
    ethics of, 181
    functions of, 106–11
    and human rights abuse, 186
    investigative powers of, 140
    and judgments of social value, 176
    killed on duty, 116
    misconduct by, 178–85
    municipal, 115
    patrol by, 106, 118–19
    and peacekeeping role, 106, 108
    and public service, 106
    and racism, 178
    and the right to use force, 108–11,
        136
    role of, 106–8
    and search warrants, 140–42
    shootings by, 180
    spot checks by, 146, 147
    violence of, 173–76, 186
    and youths, 417
police corruption, 168–72, 186
    explanations of, 172–73
    international, 171
    in Latin America, 170
    rotten-apple explanation of, 173
    and slippery slope hypothesis, 172
    society-at-large explanation of, 172
    structural explanation of, 172
Police Paramilitary Unit (PPU), 121,
    136
police personality, 123–26

police presence, 168–69
police professionalism, 185
police subculture, 123–26
police work, 106–7
policing
    bureaucracy in, 115–18
    chain of command in, 116
    community, 130–35
    county, 115
    municipal, 115
    organization of, 118
    specialized units of, 120–21
    units of command in, 116
    U.S. systems of, 111–15
    women in, 127–30, 136
Pollock, Sir Frederick, 19
polygamy, 40
pornography, 39
Porter, Anthony, 259
Postal Inspection Service, 112
posttrial motions, 97
Powell v. *Alabama*, 85, 208–9
prearrest investigation, 90–92
preliminary hearing, 94
premeditation, 30
premenstrual syndrome (PMS) defense,
    17
prerelease centers, 404
presentence investigation, 272, 387–88
presentment, 226
President's Commission on Law En-
    forcement and Administration of
    Justice, 67, 71, 98, 194, 195, 202,
    274–75, 285
presumptive fixed sentence, 269
pretrial detention, 223–24
pretrial motions, 96
pretrial release, 220–26
preventive control, of police conduct,
    180
preventive detention, 224
Price, Victoria, 208–9
prima facie case, 251
prison community, 337
prisoners
    civil disabilities of, 358–63
    classification of, 324–26
    drug offenders, 304
    male vs. female, 305
    number of, 304, 322, 363, 369
    petitions filed by, 356
    rights of, 350–78
    social system of, 337–40
    women, 314
prison industries, 300–301, 328–29
prisonization, 337–39
Prison Law Project, 375
prisons
    administration of, 322
    ADX (Administrative Maximum
        Facility), 317, 344
    coeducational, 336–37

contraband in, 333
crowding of, 323
custodial staff in, 323
discipline in, 331–34
facilities in, 324
federal, 305–7
in Hong Kong, 360, 377
industrial, 304–5
labor in, 304, 328–29
labor unions, 362–63
legal services in, 357–58
life in, 346
mail in, 360–62
maximum-security, 318–20
medium-security, 320
minimum-security, 320
personnel in, 322–23
population of, 304, 322, 363, 369
professional staff in, 322–23
racism in, 351
reform of, 373–76
routines in, 323–31
sex in, 334–37
"supermax", 377
types of, 318–22
violence in, 358, 376
women's, 340
See also Arkansas prison scandal;
    Attica Prison; New Mexico State
    Penitentiary; Texas prison suit
privacy, violation of, 45
private security, by police, 171
privatization, of corrections, 374
probable cause, 92, 142, 417
probation
    conditions of, 388–89
    effectiveness of, 394–95
    intensive probation supervision,
        391–92
    juvenile, 430–31
    origins of, 386
    philosophy of, 385–86
    revocation of, 392–94
    services, 389–90
    shock probation, 390–91
    violation of, 392–94
    vs. parole, 396
probation investigation, 387–88
probation officers, 390, 434
procedural due process, 89–90
Procunier v. *Martinez*, 361
procuring, 41
Prohibition, 6
prompt arraignment rule, 156–57
property offenses, 36–38, 46, 120
prostitution, 40, 41
protection, by police, 169
protection of the criminal justice system
    argument, against the death
    penalty, 285
protective sweep doctrine, 151

public inebriate program, 384

Public Interest, 342

public intoxication, 44

public opinion argument, for the death penalty, 283

public order and safety, crimes against, 44–45

public trial, right to, 237–40

    See also Sixth Amendment

punishment

    in the American colonies, 296–97

    corporal, 313

punitive control, of police conduct, 181

Pure Food and Drug Act (1996), 41

pursuit, fresh, 147–48

Quakers, 297

Quinn, William, 353

racism

    of police, 178, 183–84

    in prisons, 351

    See also discrimination

Rand study, of probation effectiveness, 394–95

ransom, 37

rape, 41

    forcible, 39

    of men, 43

    statutory, 39

    as war crime, 10

Reagan, Ronald, 13

real evidence, 250

reasonable certainty, 92

reasonable doubt, 248

rebuttal, 252

recidivists (repeat offenders), 221

reclassification

    of crimes, 120

    of inmates, 326

"Red Hannah", 366–67

reform, of prisons, 373–76

reformatory era, of U.S. prisons, 301–3

refuge movement, 416

regulations, of police organizations, 116–18

rehabilitation, as objective of sentencing, 262

rehabilitative services, prisoners' rights to, 361–62

Rehnquist, William H., 207, 246, 278, 373

Reid, Ed, 50

release, 97

    conditional, 387

    mandatory, 398

    study, 403

    temporary, 401–4

    work, 402–3

release on recognizance (ROR), 94, 225–26

relevant evidence, 250

religious freedom, right to, 359–60

    See also First Amendment

religious programs, in prisons, 327

remanding, by the U.S. Supreme Court, 206

removal of landmarks, 37

reprieve, 97

restitution, 389

retribution, as objective of sentencing, 260–61

retribution argument, for the death penalty, 283

reversing, by the U.S. Supreme Court, 205–6

revocation of probation, 392

Rhodes, James, 373

Rhodes v. *Chapman*, 373

rights, of prisoners, 350–78

right to appeal

    by defendant, 286–87

    by prosecution, 287–88

    and the U.S. Constitution, 286

right to bear arms, 82–83

    See also Second Amendment

right to counsel, 87, 157–58, 208–13

    See also Sixth Amendment

right to public trial, 237–40

    See also Sixth Amendment

right to religious freedom, 359–60

    See also First Amendment

right to speedy trial, 236–37

    See also Sixth Amendment

right to trial by jury, 242–43

    See also Sixth Amendment

Rikers Island Penitentiary, 309–10, 315

Rizzoto, Guiseppe, 51

robbery, 32

    organized, 46

    by police, 169

Robertson, Pat, 28, 281

Robinson, Lewis Newton, 71

Robinson v. *California*, 11, 12

Rockefeller, Nelson, 353, 363

Rockefeller, Winthrop, 363–64

Roosevelt, Theodore, 132, 175

ROR. *See* release on recognizance

rotten-apple explanation, of police corruption, 173

Rubin, H. Ted, 195

Ruffin v. *Commonwealth*, 350

Ruiz v. *Estelle*, 370

Rule of Four, 205

rules, of police organizations, 116–18

rules of evidence, 250

Rwanda, war crimes in, 10

Safir, Howard, 139

same-gender sex, in prison, 334–35

Sanford, Edward T., 84

San Quentin Prison, 280, 324

Santos, Shirley, 17

Scalia, Antonin, 207, 246

scarlet letter, 297

Schall v. *Martin*, 429

Schmerber v. *California*, 146, 161

Schneckloth v. *Bustamonte*, 149

Schwarz, Charles, 182

Schweitzer, Louis, 225

Scopes, John Thomas, 238–40

Scopes "monkey trial", 238–40, 256

"Scottsboro Boys", 85, 208–9, 216

search

    automobile, 145–46

    consent to, 148–49

    incident to arrest, 142–44

    unreasonable, 154

    warrantless, 142–51

search and seizure, 140, 164–65

    illegal, 152, 206

    unreasonable, 87

    See also Fourth Amendment

search warrants, 140–42

Second Amendment, 81, 82–83, 88, 101

second-degree murder, 30

Secret Service, 112

Section 1983, of the Civil Rights Act of 1871, 355–57

secure training and industrial schools, for juveniles, 431

Securities and Exchange Commission (SEC), 113

seduction, 39

selective enforcement, of the law, 122

selective incorporation, 88

self-reported crime studies, 70

sentence

    definite, 266

    determinate, 266

    fixed, 266

    flat, 266

    indeterminate, 265–66

    mixed, 390

    split, 390

    straight, 266

    suspended, 387

sentencing, 97

    alternatives, 264–68

    appellate review of, 288–89

    concurrent vs. consecutive, 272

    disparities in, 268–69

    federal guidelines for, 270–71

    objectives of, 260–62, 263

    process of, 272–73

    reform of, 269–70

    statutory structures for, 262–64

    truth in, 271–72

separate system, for prisons, 298–99

separation-of-powers doctrine, 271

sequestration, 247–48

Serfass v. *United States*, 236

Seventh Amendment, 81, 88

sex, in prison, 334–37

sex offenses, 38–41
sexual assault, 40
  in prisons, 335
shakedown, 169, 320
Shawshank Redemption, The, 323, 346
Sheindlin, Judith, 191
Shepard, Matthew, 27, 28, 30–31, 52,
      54
sheriff officers, 115
sheriff system, 114
shock incarceration, 343, 431
shock probation, 390–91
shootings, by police, 180
"shoot to kill" doctrine, 176
shoplifting, 37, 45
show-ups, 159–60
Siegal, Benjamin ("Bugsy"), 53
Silberman, Matthew, 358
silent system, for prisons, 300, 313
"silver platter" doctrine, 152
Simonsen, Clifford, 333
Simpson, O. J., 162
Sinatra, Frank, 39
Singleton, Edgar, 270
Sing Sing Prison, 300, 301, 304, 324
Sinthasomphone, Konerak, 124–25
Sixth Amendment, 81, 85–87, 157,
      208–13, 236, 242–43, 278, 424
Skolnick, Jerome H., 123–25, 126
Sleepers, 323
slippery slope hypothesis, and police
      corruption, 172
Smith, John, 366
Smith, Samuel W., 280
social system, of inmates, 337–40
society-at-large explanation, of police
      corruption, 172
sodomy, 39, 40
Soledad Brother (Jackson), 323
Soledad Prison, 365
solitary confinement, 364–66
Soul on Ice (Cleaver), 323
*Sourcebook of Criminal Justice
      Statistics,* 72
Souter, David, 207
Special Weapons and Tactics (SWAT),
      120–21
specific deterrence, 261–62
specific intent, 9
speedy trial, right to, 236–37
  See also Sixth Amendment
spending, on corrections, 370
Spinelli v. *United States,* 142
split sentence, 390
spot checks, by police, 146, 147, 287
spousal abuse, 48–49
Stack v. *Boyle,* 221, 224, 255
"standing mute", 96
Stanford, (Reverend) John, 416
Stanford v. *Kentucky,* 429
Starr, Kenneth, 77
Starr Report, 77

state account system, 301
state case, presentation of, 249–51
state courts, 192–201
statement, opening, 248–49
state police agencies, 113–15
state prisons, spending by, 370
states, and speedy trial, 237
state-use system, 301
State v. *Cannon,* 366
State v. *Chile,* 422
status offenders, 425–27, 435
status offense, 412
statute of limitations, plea of, 231
statutory good time, 398
statutory law, 11, 20
statutory structures, for sentencing,
      262–64
Stephen, Sir James Fitzjames, 19
Stevens, John Paul, 207, 273
Stevens v. *United States,* 83
Stewart, A. T., 239
Stewart, Potter, 212, 277
sting operations, 121
stocks and pillory, 297
stolen goods, 37
stop and frisk, 144–45
straight sentence, 266
street time, 400
Strohmeyer, Jeremy, 3–4, 8, 22, 23
structural explanation, of police corrup-
      tion, 172
study release, 403
substantive due process, 88–89
"suicide by cop", 118
summation (closing arguments), 252
Super Bowl, pickpockets at, 34–35, 54
*Superintendent, Massachusetts Correc-
      tional Institute at Walpole* v. *Hill,*
      368
"supermax" prisons, 377
  See also ADX
Supreme Court. *See* U.S. Supreme Court
surety, 220
surrebuttal, 252
suspended sentence, 387
suspension of execution, 387
suspension of imposition, 387
Sutherland, Edwin H., 7
Swain v. *Alabama,* 245

Tactical Neutralization Team (TNT), 121
Tactical Patrol Force (TPF), 120
Taft, William Howard, 145
Takagi, Paul, 177
Talese, Gay, 50
Taliban Islamic rule, punishment under,
      284
Tappan, Paul W., 7, 334
Tate v. *Short,* 264
TC. *See* therapeutic community
temporary release, 401–4

Tennessee v. *Garner,* 177
Tennessee v. *Scopes,* 238–40
10 percent cash bond plans, 225–26
Tenth Amendment, 81
Terry v. *Ohio,* 144–45, 164
testimonial evidence, 250
Texas Prison Suit, 370–71
Texas Rangers, 113–14
theft, 36
  by police, 169
  professional, 47
therapeutic community (TC), 334
  in prisons, 330–31, 332
"thief-takers", 109
Third Amendment, 81, 87, 88
Thomas, Clarence, 207, 246
Thompson v. *Oklahoma,* 429
Thornburgh v. *Abbott,* 361
"three strikes" laws, 266, 267, 290
ticket-of-leave, 302, 395
"time served", 273
Total Crime Index, 60, 61
total institution, 318
Townsend v. *Burke,* 209
Trammel v. *United States,* 250
transactional immunity, 229
treason, 28
Treatment Alternatives to Street Crime
      (TASC), 384
trial
  criminal, 247–55
  by jury, right to, 242–43
  public and speedy, right to, 236–40
  See also Sixth Amendment
trial by ordeal, 78
trial courts. *See* courts of general juris-
      diction; major trial courts
trial *de novo,* 194
trial process, 96–97
Trop v. *Dulles,* 87
true bill, 95, 227
Tucker, Karla Faye, 281
Tucker Prison Farm, 363
Tumey v. *Ohio,* 194, 287
Twining, Albert C., 155
Twining v. *New Jersey,* 155, 156
Tyson, Mike, 16

unfounding, 120
UNICOR, 329
Uniform Crime Reporting Handbook, 66
Uniform Crime Reporting system, 133
Uniform Crime Reports (*UCR*), 58–67,
      69, 72, 74, 415
Uniform Juvenile Court Act (1968),
      423–24
United States ex rel. Gereau v. *Hender-
      son,* 350
United States v. *Ash,* 161
United States v. *Ball,* 68
United States v. *Calandra,* 228

United States v. *Dickerson*, 159
United States v. *Dionisio*, 161
United States v. *Jackson*, 276
United States v. *Leon*, 154
United States v. *Mara*, 161
United States v. *Matlock*, 149
United States v. *Perez*, 232
United States v. *Wade*, 160
United States v. *Warin*, 83
units of command, in policing, 116
U.S. Board of Parole, 397
U.S. Bureau of Justice Statistics, 406,
     430
U.S. Coast Guard, 112
U.S. commissioner's courts, 201–2
U.S. Commission on Civil Rights, 180
U.S. Constitution, 80
     analysis of, 102
     and bills of attainder, 358
     and crime, 28
     and criminal law, 20
     and the exclusionary rule, 152–54
     and probable cause, 142
     and restraints on police powers, 140
     and right to appeal, 286
     and right to bear arms, 82
     and right to speedy and public trial,
          236
     and right to trial by jury, 242
     and the U.S. Supreme Court, 90
     and warrantless search, 142
     See also individual amendments; Bill
          of Rights; constitutional rights
U.S. courts of appeals, 204
U.S. Criminal Code, 112, 203
U.S. Customs Service, 112
U.S. district courts, 202–4
U.S. Federal Sentencing Commission,
     270–71
U.S. Fish and Wildlife Service, 130
U.S. magistrates, 202
U.S. magistrate's courts, 201–2
U.S. Marshals Service, 99, 102, 112
U.S. Supreme Court, 192
     affirming by, 205–6
     and bail, 221
     and the Bill of Rights, 88, 90
     and the death penalty, 275–79
     and due process, 90
     and the exclusionary rule, 152–54
     and grand jury procedure, 228
     impact of, 207
     jurisdictional scope of, 201, 204–5
     and probable cause, 142
     problems of, 206–8

remanding by, 205–6
reversing by, 205–6
and speedy trial, 236–37
and the U.S. Constitution, 90
and the writ of *habeas corpus*, 355
use immunity, 229
usury, 37

vagrancy, 44
Valtierra, Manuel, 157
Van den Haag, Ernest, 273
Varna, Andrew, 50
vengeance, as objective of sentencing,
     261
venire (*venire facias*), 244
venue, 233
Vera Foundation, 225
Vera Institute of Justice, 225
verdict, 253–55
vicarious liability, 9, 11
victim impact statements, 261
victimless crime, 65
victims, of crime, 67, 68, 74, 256
victim survey research, 67–69
Vignera v. *New York*, 158
violation, 18
violation of privacy, 45
violence, by police, 173–76, 186
violent crime, 46, 140, 267, 280
void-for-vagueness doctrine, 89
voir dire, 244–47
Volpe, Justin, 182
Volstead Act (1919), 6, 306
voyeurism (peeping), 40

Wade v. *Hunter*, 232
waiver of jurisdiction, 428
Walnut Street Jail (Philadelphia),
     296–98, 308, 327
war crimes, 10
warrant
     arrest, 92
     search, 140–42
warrantless search, 142–51
Warren, Earl, 87, 173
Wayward Minor Act (1923), 425–27
Webster, Daniel, 88
Weeks v. *United States*, 152, 164
Weems v. *United States*, 276
Wells, Alice Stebbins, 127
Western Penitentiary (Pennsylvania),
     298
Westfield State Farm, 427

Westover v. *United States*, 158
West v. *United States*, 424
whipping, 366–67
White, Byron, 243, 277, 368
White Heat, 323
Wickersham Commission, 71
wife-selling, 29
Wilkerson v. *Utah*, 276
Williams, Alexander S. ("Clubber),
     174–75
Williams v. *Florida*, 243
Williams v. *Illinois*, 264
Wilson, James Q., 72, 133–34,
     337
Wilson, O. W., 172
Wilson, Scott, 366
Wilson, Woodrow, 239
Wilson v. *Seiter*, 374
Winston v. *Lee*, 161
Witherspoon v. *Illinois*, 276, 278
witness, examination of, 251
Wolff v. *Mcdonnell*, 361, 368, 370
Wolfgang, Marvin E., 275
women
     abduction of, 29
     and the death penalty, 281, 290
     on death row, 280, 285
     inmates, 314, 346
     in policing, 127–30, 131, 136
     violence against, 54
women's institutions, 321, 340
working personality, 126
work release, 402–3
Worton, William A., 181
W. P. v. *Verniero*, 89
Wren v. *United States*, 148–49
writ of *certiorari*, 205

"X Files, The", 105, 134, 136

York, Duke of, 307
Yousef, Ramzi, 344
youth bureaus, 120, 384
Youth Counsel Bureau (New York City),
     383, 384
youths, and police, 417
     See also juvenile justice system
youths in need of supervision (YINS),
     425

Zerman, Melvyn, 264
Zimring, Franklin E., 283
Zuazo, Hernan Siles, 91